OpenGL SuperBible, Second Edition

Richard S. Wright, Jr.

Michael Sweet

Waite Group Press
A Division of Macmillan USA, Inc.
201 West 103rd St., Indianapolis, Indiana, 46290 USA

OpenGL SuperBible, Second Edition

International Standard Book Number: 1-57169-164-2

Library of Congress Catalog Card Number: 99-66222

Printed in the United States of America

First Printing: *December 1999*

02   01   00   99   4   3   2   1

Trademarks

Warning and Disclaimer

ASSOCIATE PUBLISHER
Michael Stephens

EXECUTIVE EDITOR
Rosemarie Graham

ACQUISITIONS EDITOR
Shelley Johnston

DEVELOPMENT EDITOR
Heather Goodell

MANAGING EDITOR
Charlotte Clapp

PROJECT EDITOR
Christina Smith

COPY EDITOR
Kris Simmons

INDEXER
Larry Sweazy

PROOFREADERS
Linda Morris
Beth Rago
Tony Reitz

TECHNICAL EDITOR
Brett Hall

TEAM COORDINATOR
Pamalee Nelson

MEDIA DEVELOPER
Andrea Duvall

INTERIOR DESIGNER
Gary Adair

COVER DESIGNER
Alan Clements

COPY WRITER
Eric Borgert

LAYOUT TECHNICIANS
Steve Geiselman
Brad Lenser

CONTENTS AT A GLANCE

PART 4: APPENDIXES

TABLE OF CONTENTS

PART 2: MEAT AND POTATOES—THE STAPLES OF OPENGL RENDERING

CHAPTER 7   RASTER GRAPHICS IN OPENGL   241

PART 4: APPENDIXES

ABOUT THE AUTHORS

Richard S. Wright, Jr. is an OpenGL programmer and consultant for the company he founded, Starstone Software Systems, Inc., just outside Orlando, Florida. Richard also teaches 3D graphics programming at Full Sail in Orlando. Previously with Real 3D/Lockheed Martin, Richard was a regular OpenGL ARB attendee and contributed to the OpenGL 1.2 specification and conformance tests. Richard first learned to program in the eighth grade in 1978 on a paper terminal. At age 16, his parents let him buy a computer instead of a car, and he sold his first computer program less than a year later (and it was a graphics program!). When he graduated from high school, his first job was teaching programming and computer literacy for a local consumer education company. He studied electrical engineering and computer science at the University of Louisville's Speed Scientific School and made it halfway through his senior year before his career got the best of him. A native of Louisville, Kentucky, he now lives with his wife and three children between Orlando and Daytona Beach, Florida. When not programming or dodging hurricanes, Richard is an amateur astronomer, beach bum, and Sunday School teacher.

Michael Sweet is co-owner of Easy Software Products, a small software firm specializing in Internet and printing technologies. He is also a consultant at the Atlantic Test Range and develops mapping software using OpenGL for real-time and post-flight displays. He first started using a computer terminal at the age of 6 and sold his first program at age 12. Michael was hired as a consultant doing computer graphics while finishing his bachelor's degree in computer science at the SUNY Institute of Technology in Utica/Rome, New York. He moved to Maryland shortly after graduating. When he has free time, he enjoys cycling, photography, playing the trumpet, and traveling with his wife, Sandra.

DEDICATION

Dedicated to the memory of Richard S. Wright, Sr.

I Thessalonians 4:16

Thanks, Dad, for just letting me be a nerd.

—Richard S. Wright, Jr.

To my wife, Sandra, for her understanding and support of my work on this book. I couldn't do it without you, hon!

—Michael Sweet

ACKNOWLEDGMENTS

Where do I begin? I thank God for every door of opportunity he has opened for me throughout my life. I thank my wife and family for putting up with me during the most insane period of my life while trying to get this book out the second time in the middle of my company's busiest time of year. LeeAnne, Sara, Stephen, and Alex all were put on hold, promises were broken, weekends lost, voices raised. All I did was work hard; they sacrificed. This book should have their names on it, not mine.

The people at Macmillan have been terrific. I want to thank Shelley Johnston for putting up with my endless excuses for missing deadlines. Of course, I did schedule Hurricane Floyd just so I could milk another week out of the timeline. I'm terribly sorry for the inconvenience this has caused so many other people who were not involved in the book. Heather Goodell was very kind and patient when it came time to deciphering my poor hand-drawn figures. Also, we have Heather to thank for getting the cover art jazzed up for the second edition. Brett Hall was a technical reviewer without peer. His comments and input as well as his thoroughness helped to make this book better than it would have been. There are countless other people at Macmillan whom I can't name. The production and marketing of a book is a huge undertaking, of which I play only a small part.

I also have to thank my many fine past associates from Real 3D, most of whom are now scattered to the wind throughout the industry. They put up with my ranting during the "API Wars," allowed me to participate on their behalf at the OpenGL ARB meetings, and just provided me with the opportunity to work with some of the coolest people and technology on the planet. I owe most of my OpenGL-related experience and knowledge obtained since the first edition of this book to the opportunities afforded me there at Real 3D. I wish things had worked out better for all of us, and I wish them all well in the future. Thanks especially to Dave Bolton who gave us permission to use some of Real 3D's content for the book.

Finally, we should all be grateful for everyone who has fought the good fight to make OpenGL an industry standard on the PC. We owe a great deal to the developers (you know who you are) who stood up and demanded that vendors support them at a time when politics and money threatened to stifle the growth of 3D accelerated graphics on the PC. Thanks also to hardware vendors who listened to their customers instead of following the herd. Now, these vendors rule, and their products simply rock. The wannabes from a couple of years ago, now wish they were....

—Richard S. Wright, Jr.

When I tell people I'm writing a book, the universal response is, "Boy, that must be a lot of work for you." Although this is true, it doesn't acknowledge the contributions of so many people. My wife, Sandra, is my best friend. I couldn't have finished my parts of the first and second editions of this book without her sacrificing our time together. Whenever I became frustrated with a sample program that wasn't working right, or was up until 2 a.m. finishing a chapter, she was there to support me. I can't begin to say how lucky I feel to have her!

The MCP staff have also played an integral part in this process. Our Acquisitions Editor, Shelley Johnston, began this journey right at the time when I thought that we'd never get to update the original SuperBible. Somehow, she managed to get all the paperwork and planning done in a few short weeks. Andrea Duvall, Heather Goodell, Brett Hall, and Christina Smith worked with Richard and me to make the second edition of the *OpenGL SuperBible* the best it could be.

This book includes a lot of sample programs, most of which use Mark Kilgard's OpenGL utility toolkit, GLUT. GLUT has allowed us to concentrate on OpenGL and not the details of Win32 programming in the second edition, which I think has made it a better book as a result. Thank you, Mark, for making GLUT available to the OpenGL community!

Brian Paul's Mesa graphics library provides most of the OpenGL 1.2 functionality. Without the efforts of Brian and many other Mesa contributors, OpenGL support for a lot of platforms wouldn't be available.

Finally, I'd like to thank NIMA for allowing us to include a compressed version of its level 0 Digital Terrain Elevation Database for the world.

—Michael Sweet

TELL US WHAT YOU THINK!

As the reader of this book, you are our most important critic and commentator. We value your opinion and want to know what we're doing right, what we could do better, what areas you'd like to see us publish in, and any other words of wisdom you're willing to pass our way.

As the Executive Editor for the Networking team at Macmillan Computer Publishing, I welcome your comments. You can fax, email, or write me directly to let me know what you did or didn't like about this book—as well as what we can do to make our books stronger.

Please note that I cannot help you with technical problems related to the topic of this book, and that due to the high volume of mail I receive, I might not be able to reply to every message.

When you write, please be sure to include this book's title and author, as well as your name and phone or fax number. I will carefully review your comments and share them with the author and editors who worked on the book.

Fax: 317-581-4770

Email: mstephens@mcp.com

Mail: Michael Stephens
          Associate Publisher
          Waite Group Press
          201 West 103rd Street
          Indianapolis, IN 46290 USA

INTRODUCTION

It's been more than three years since Waite Group Press published the first edition of the *OpenGL SuperBible*. That's 21 years in dog years, and at least 100 in computer years! OpenGL has progressed significantly in this time, both in terms of API additions and functionality and in terms of industry support and popularity.

3D accelerated graphics cards are now a staple for even the most stripped-down PCs. The first edition of the *OpenGL SuperBible* was published on the eve of the "API Wars." This political battle between Microsoft and SGI (who represented the rest of the world) concerned who would control the dominant 3D graphics API in the budding consumer market for 3D accelerated hardware—a market largely driven by consumer games vendors. At the Computer Game Developers Conference in 1997, I could hardly get a graphics card vendor to admit that it offered OpenGL drivers for its hardware. By the following year, if you couldn't demo GLQuake (a popular game that used OpenGL) on your hardware, you didn't show up to the conference. Selling a 3D graphics card today without an OpenGL driver is like trying to sell a printer without Windows printer drivers.

A wounded veteran of the API Wars, I won't discuss all the gory details, but it is clear in the aftermath that OpenGL has an incredible momentum in both the professional and consumer market that won't soon be winding down. In the end, developers control the standards, a lesson that some learn the hard way. By and large, game and simulation developers prefer an open standard such as OpenGL, and no amount of marketing rhetoric can obscure that fact forever.

As well as becoming widely available, OpenGL has grown in its capabilities. The OpenGL specification has seen two revisions since 1.0. (We are currently on 1.2.) Many new features enhance performance, add flexibility, and take advantage of new 3D hardware advancements. In this, the second edition of the *OpenGL SuperBible*, we bring you up to date on these new features, and we take an approach later in the book that is more in tune with the current environment, which is predominately hardware accelerated.

Another interesting side note to the history of OpenGL is the fall to obscurity of the AUX library. We used the AUX library in only one chapter for the first edition, but in this edition, we don't discuss it at all. The AUX library has largely been replaced by a newer and more featured windowing toolkit called GLUT. We use GLUT for all of our examples, at least until the final section of the book.

Finally, I noted in the first edition that I looked forward to the day when color index mode was a thing of the past. No one is using color index mode today, and certainly no one is building new hardware that accelerates this mode. The present mode is at least 16- or 24-bit color with full hardware acceleration, and the future is full 24-bit color with full support for deeper depth, stencil, and alpha buffers as well. (You'll learn about these buffers later; they make graphics cooler and faster!) Color index mode is not discussed in this edition.

What's in This Book

The *OpenGL SuperBible* is divided into three sections. In the first, we introduce the fundamentals of real-time 3D graphics programming with OpenGL. You'll learn to construct a program that uses OpenGL, how to set up your 3D-rendering environment, and how to create basic objects and light and shade them. In Part II, we delve deeper into using OpenGL and some of its advanced features and different special effects. Finally, we wrap up with a section about OpenGL on the Windows platform. You'll learn about the different driver models, hardware and software rendering, pixel formats, rendering contexts, and other Windows-specific features. Our final chapter puts it all together and covers basic real-time rendering techniques for games or simulation.

Part 1: Nuts and Bolts—An Introduction to the OpenGL API

Chapter 1—3D Graphics Fundamentals

This introductory chapter is for newcomers to 3D graphics. It introduces fundamental concepts and some common vocabulary.

Chapter 2—What Is OpenGL?

In this chapter, we provide you with a working knowledge of what OpenGL is, where it came from, and where it is going.

Chapter 3—Using OpenGL

In this chapter, you will write your first program that uses OpenGL. You'll find out what headers and libraries you need to use, how to set up your environment, and how some common conventions can help you remember OpenGL function calls.

Chapter 4—Drawing in Space: Lines, Points, and Polygons

Here, we present the building blocks of 3D graphics programming. You'll find out how to tell a computer to create a three-dimensional object.

Chapter 5—Moving Around in Space: Coordinate Transformations

Now that you're creating three-dimensional shapes in a virtual world, how do you move them around? How do you move yourself around? These are the things you'll learn here.

Chapter 6—Color, Lighting, and Materials

In this chapter, you'll take your three-dimensional "outlines" and give them color. You'll learn how to apply material effects and lights to your graphics to make them look real.

Part 2: Meat and Potatoes—The Staples of OpenGL Rendering

Chapter 7—Raster Graphics in OpenGL

In this chapter, you'll learn how to manipulate bitmap graphics within OpenGL. This includes reading a Windows .BMP file and displaying it in an OpenGL scene.

Chapter 8—Texture Mapping

Texture mapping is one of the most useful features of any 3D graphics toolkit. You'll learn how to wrap bitmaps onto polygons and how to use automatic texture coordinate generation.

Chapter 9—3D Modeling and Object Composition

For this chapter, we show you how to build complex 3D objects out of smaller, less complex 3D objects. We also introduce OpenGL display lists and vertex arrays for improving performance and organizing your models.

Chapter 10—Visual Effects: Blending and Fog

This chapter discusses some other visual special effects, such as alpha blending and fog effects for transparency and depth cues.

Chapter 11—Buffers: Not Just for Animation

This chapter goes into more depth about the various OpenGL buffers. As you'll see, they're not just for screen flipping.

Chapter 12—Beyond Lines and Triangles

The simple triangle is a powerful building block. This chapter gives you some tools for manipulating the mighty triangle. You'll learn about some of OpenGL's built-in quadric surface generation functions and how to use automatic tessellation to break complex shapes into smaller, more digestible pieces.

Chapter 13—Curves and Surfaces: What the #%@!& are NURBS?

This chapter explores the utility functions that evaluate Bézier and NURBS curves and surfaces. You can use these functions to create complex shapes with a small amount of code.

Chapter 14—Interactive Graphics

This chapter explains two OpenGL features: selection and feedback. These groups of functions make it possible for the user to interact with objects in the scene. You can also get rendering details about any single object in the scene.

Chapter 15—Imaging with OpenGL

New to OpenGL 1.2 is the optional imaging subset. This set of functions enables sophisticated image processing within OpenGL.

Chapter 16—Common OpenGL Extensions

Another popular feature of OpenGL is that it can be freely extended by OpenGL vendors. In this chapter, you'll learn about the extension mechanism and how to use some of the popular extensions.

Part 3: OpenGL for Windows: OpenGL + WIN32 = Wiggle

Chapter 17—The OpenGL Pixelformat and Rendering Context

Here, you'll learn how to write real Windows (message-based) programs that use OpenGL. You'll learn about Microsoft's "wiggle" functions that glue OpenGL rendering code to Windows device contexts. Learn how to respond to which Windows messages. Follow an explanation about how OpenGL drivers work with Windows.

Chapter 18—Non-Windowed Rendering

In the real world of application development, you need to be able to send your graphics some place other than the screen. This chapter covers rendering to and saving your graphics as bitmaps and printing your OpenGL renderings.

Chapter 19—Real-Time Programming with OpenGL

Whether you're writing games or real-time simulations, you need to know a few basic techniques. Just as learning a programming language doesn't make you an algorithm expert, learning OpenGL is only the beginning of your real-time 3D-programming journey. In this chapter, we lay down some of the basics and give you a few hints and tips to get you started.

Part 4: Appendixes

Appendix A—A Summary of OpenGL Updates

A summary of the features introduced in OpenGL by version.

Appendix B—Further Reading

A list of additional reading material for more in-depth research on any of the topics covered in this book.

Appendix C—The OpenGL State Machine

An overview of the different OpenGL state variables, and the functions used to set and query them.

Appendix D—Glossary

A glossary of common 3D graphics and OpenGL terms.

Conventions Used in this Book

The following typographic conventions are used in this book:

- Code lines, commands, statements, variables, and any text you type or see on-screen appear in a `computer` typeface.
- Placeholders in syntax description appear in an *`italic computer`* typeface. Replace the placeholder with the actual filename, parameter, or whatever element it represents.
- *Italics* highlight technical terms when they first appear in the text and are being defined.

About the Companion CD

The CD-ROM that comes with the *OpenGL SuperBible* is packed with sample programs, toolkits, source code, and documentation…everything but the kitchen sink! We dig up stuff to put on this CD all the way until press time, so check out the readme.txt file in the root of the CD for a complete list of all the goodies we include.

The CD contains some basic organization. Off the root directory, you'll find

\Book—Beneath this directory, you'll find a directory for each chapter in the book that has programming examples. Each sample has a real name (as opposed to "sample 5.2c") so you can browse the CD with ease and run anything that looks interesting when you first get the book.

\Tools—A collection of third-party tools and libraries appears here. Each has its own subdirectory and documentation from the original vendor. Some of these tools are used by sample programs throughout the book.

Dare to Dream in 3D!

Once-upon-a-time in the early 80s, I was looking at a computer at an electronics store. The salesman approached and began making his pitch. I told him I was learning to program and considering an Amiga over his model. I was briskly informed that I needed to get serious with a computer that the rest of the world was using. An Amiga, he told me, was not good for anything but "making pretty pictures." No one he assured me, could make a living making pretty pictures on his computer....

This was possibly the worst advice I have ever received in the history of bad advice. A few years ago, I forgot about being a "respectable" database/enterprise/yada-yada-yada developer. Now, I write computer games, teach programming, own my own software company, and generally have more fun with my career than should probably be allowed by law!

I hope I can give you some better advice today. Whether you want to write games, military simulations, or scientific visualizations or visualize large corporate databases— OpenGL is the perfect API. It will meet you where you are as a beginner, and it will empower you when you become your own guru of 3D. And yes, my friend, you *can* make a living making pretty pictures with your computer!

—*Richard S. Wright, Jr.*

PART 1

Nuts & Bolts—An Introduction to the OpenGL API

Part 1 of this book introduces you to 3D graphics and programming with OpenGL. We start with a brief discussion and review of real-time 3D graphics principles. Then we delve into the design of OpenGL, its background, purpose, and how it works.

In Chapter 3, you'll start writing your first OpenGL programs. You'll learn about the various libraries and headers needed, and how OpenGL functions and data types are called and named. We'll introduce a portability library called GLUT so you don't have to think about Windows programming, messages, or event handlers while you learn to use OpenGL.

We'll round out Part I with an introduction to actually creating three-dimensional objects and rendering them. You'll learn how to transform (move them around) them, add color and material properties to them, and finally how to shade them with lights so that they actually appear three-dimensional. Part I will provide you with a solid foundation and a good grounding for starting the next section, when you will learn about other special effects and techniques.

3D GRAPHICS FUNDAMENTALS

by Richard S. Wright, Jr.

What's This All About?

This book is about OpenGL, a programming interface for creating real-time 3D graphics. Before we begin talking about what OpenGL is and how it works, you should have at least a high-level understanding of real-time 3D graphics in general. Perhaps you picked up this book because you want to learn to use OpenGL, but you already have a good grasp of real-time 3D principles. If so, great: Skip directly to Chapter 2, "What Is OpenGL?." If you bought this book because the pictures look cool and you want to learn how to do this on your PC…you should start here.

A Brief History of Computer Graphics

The first computer consisted of rows and rows of switches and lights. Technicians and engineers worked for hours, days, or even weeks to program these machines and read the results of their calculations. A pattern of illuminated bulbs conveyed useful information to the computer user or some crude printout was provided. You might say that the first use of computer graphics was a panel of blinking lights. (This idea is supported by stories of early programmers writing programs that served no useful purpose other than creating patterns of blinking and chasing lights!)

Times have changed. From those first "thinking machines," as some called them, sprang fully programmable devices that printed on rolls of paper using something like a teletype machine. Data could be stored efficiently on magnetic tape, on disk, or even on rows of hole-punched paper or stacks of paper-punch cards. The "hobby" of computer graphics was born the day computers first started printing. Because each character in the alphabet had a fixed size and shape, creative programmers in the 70s took delight in creating artistic patterns and images made up of nothing more than asterisks (*).

Enter the CRT

Paper as an output medium for computers is useful and persists today. Laser printers and color ink jet printers have replaced crude ASCII art with crisp presentation quality and near photographic reproductions of artwork. Paper, however, can get expensive to replace on a regular basis, and using it consistently is wasteful of our natural resources, especially because most of the time we don't really need hard copy output of calculations or database queries.

The *CRT* (cathode ray tube) was a tremendously useful addition to the computer. The original computer monitors, CRTs were initially just video terminals that displayed ASCII text just like the first paper terminals–but CRTs were perfectly capable of drawing points and lines as well as alphabetic characters. Soon, other symbols and graphics began to supplement the character terminal. Programmers used computers and their monitors to create graphics that supplemented textual or tabular output. The first algorithms for creating lines and curves were developed and published; computer graphics became a science rather than a pastime.

The first computer graphics displayed on these terminals were *two-dimensional*, or 2D. These flat lines, circles, and polygons were used to create graphics for a variety of purposes. Graphs and plots could display scientific or statistical data as tables and figures could not. More adventurous programmers even created simple arcade games such as *Lunar Lander* and *Pong* using simple graphics consisting of little more than line drawings that were refreshed (redrawn) several times a second.

The term *real time* was first applied to computer graphics that were animated. A broader use of the word in computer science simply means that the computer can process input as fast or faster than the input is being supplied. For example, talking on the phone is a real-time activity of humans. You speak and the listener hears it immediately and responds–allowing you to hear immediately and respond again, and so on. In contrast, writing a letter is not a real-time activity.

Applying the term real-time to computer graphics means that the computer is producing an animation or sequence of images directly in response to some input, such as a joystick, keyboard strokes, and so on. Real-time computer graphics can display a wave form being measured by electronic equipment, numerical readouts, or interactive games.

Going 3D

The term *three-dimensional*, or *3D*, means that an object being described or displayed has three dimensions of measurement: width, height, and depth. An example of a two-dimensional object is a piece of paper on your desk with a drawing or writing on it. A three-dimensional object is the can of soda next to it. The soft drink can is round (width and height) and tall (depth). Depending on your perspective, you can alter which side of the can is the width or height, but the fact remains that there are three dimensions to the can. Figure 1.1 shows how we might measure the dimensions of the can and piece of paper.

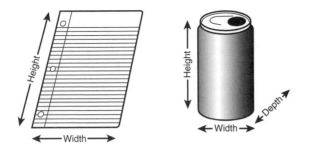

Figure 1.1   Measuring two- and three-dimensional objects.

For centuries, artists have known how to make a painting appear to have real depth. A painting is inherently a two-dimensional object because it is nothing more than canvas with paints applied. Similarly, 3D computer graphics are actually two-dimensional images on a flat computer screen that provide an illusion of depth, or a third dimension.

2D + Perspective = 3D

The first computer graphics no doubt appeared similar to Figure 1.2, where you can see a simple three-dimensional cube drawn with nine line segments. What makes the cube look three-dimensional is perspective, or the angle between the lines that lend the illusion of depth.

Figure 1.2   A simple wireframe 3D cube.

To truly see in 3D, you need to actually view the object with both eyes or supply each eye with separate and unique images of the object. Take a look at Figure 1.3. Each eye receives a two-dimensional image that is much like a temporary photograph on the retina (the back part of your eye). These two images are slightly different because they are received at two different angles. (Your eyes are spaced apart on purpose.) The brain then combines these slightly different images to produce a single, composite 3D picture in your head.

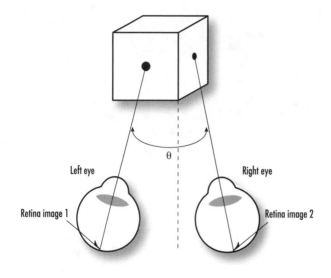

Figure 1.3   How you see three dimensions.

In Figure 1.3, the angle θ between the images gets smaller as the object goes farther away. You can amplify this 3D effect by increasing the angle between the two images. *Viewmasters* (those hand-held stereoscopic viewers you probably had as a kid) and 3D movies capitalize on this effect by placing each of your eyes on a separate lens or by providing color-filtered glasses that separate two superimposed images. These images are usually over-enhanced for dramatic or cinematic purposes.

A computer screen is one flat image on a flat surface, not two images from different perspectives falling on each eye. As it turns out, most of what is considered to be 3D computer graphics is actually an approximation of true 3D. This approximation is achieved in the same way that artists have rendered drawings with apparent depth for years, using the same tricks that nature provides for people with one eye.

You might have noticed at sometime in your life that if you cover one eye, the world does not suddenly fall flat! What happens when you cover one eye? You might think you are still seeing in 3D, but try this experiment: Place a glass or some other object just out of arm's reach, off to your left side. (If it is close, this trick won't work.) Cover your right eye with your right hand and reach for the glass. (Maybe you should use an empty plastic one!) Notice that you have a more difficult time estimating how much farther you need to reach (if at all) before you touch the glass. Now, uncover your right eye and reach for the glass, and you can easily discern how far you need to lean to reach the glass. You now know why people with one eye often have difficulty with distance perception.

Perspective alone is enough to lend the appearance of three dimensions. Note the cube shown previously in Figure 1.2. Even without coloring or shading, the cube still has the appearance of a three-dimensional object. Stare at the cube for long enough, however, and the front and back of the cube switch places. Your brain is confused by the lack of any surface coloration in the drawing. Figure 1.4 has an exaggerated perspective but still can produce the "popping" effect when you stare at it.

3D Artifacts

The reason the world doesn't become suddenly flat when you cover one eye is that many of a 3D world's effects are still present when viewed two-dimensionally. The effects are just enough to trigger your brain's ability to discern depth. The most obvious cue is that nearby objects appear larger than distant objects. This perspective effect is called *foreshortening*. This effect and color changes, textures, lighting, shading, and variations of color intensities (due to lighting) together add up to our perception of a three-dimensional image. In the next section, we take a survey of these tricks.

A Survey of 3D Effects

Now you have some idea that the illusion of 3D is created on a flat computer screen by means of a bag full of perspective and artistic tricks. Let's review some of these effects so we can refer to them later in the book, and you'll know what we are talking about.

The first term you should know is *render*. Rendering is the act of taking a geometric description of a three-dimensional object and turning it into an image of that object onscreen. All of the following 3D effects are applied when rendering the objects or scene.

Perspective

Perspective refers to the angles between lines that lend the illusion of three dimensions. Figure 1.4 shows a three-dimensional cube drawn with lines. This is a powerful illusion, but it can still cause perception problems as we mentioned earlier. (Just stare at it for a while, and it starts popping in and out.) In Figure 1.5, on the other hand, the brain is given more clues as to the true orientation of the cube because of *hidden line removal*. You expect the front of an object to obscure the back of the object from view. For solid surfaces, we call this *hidden surface removal*.

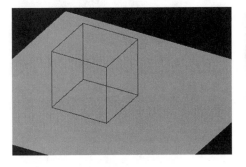

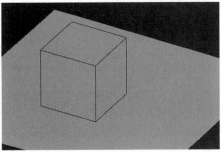

Figure 1.4   A line-drawn three-dimensional cube.

Figure 1.5   A more convincing solid cube.

Color and Shading

Moving beyond line drawing, we want to add color to create solid objects. Figure 1.6 shows what happens when we naively add red to the color of the cube. It doesn't look like a cube anymore. By applying different colors to each side, as shown in Figure 1.7, we regain our perception of a solid object.

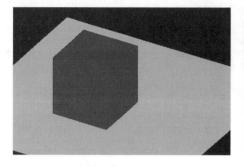

Figure 1.6 Adding color alone can create further confusion.

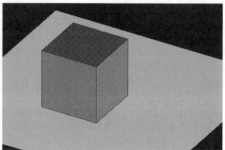

Figure 1.7 Adding different colors increases the illusion of three dimensions.

Light and Shadows

Making each side of the cube a different color helps your eye pick out the different sides of the object. By shading each side appropriately, we can give the cube the appearance of being one solid color (or material) but also show it is illuminated by a light at an angle, as shown in Figure 1.8. Figure 1.9 goes a step further by adding a shadow behind the cube.

Figure 1.8 Proper shading creates the illusion of illumination.

Figure 1.9 Adding a shadow to further increase realism.

Texture Mapping

Achieving a high level of realism with nothing but thousands or millions of tiny lit and shaded polygons is a matter of brute force. Unfortunately, the more geometry you throw at graphics hardware, the longer it is going to take to render. A clever technique allows you to use simpler geometry but achieve a higher degree of realism. This technique takes an image, such as a photograph of a real surface or detail, and then applies that image to the surface of a polygon.

Instead of plain materials, you can have wood grains, cloth, bricks, and so on. This technique of applying an image to a polygon to supply additional detail is called *texture mapping*. The image you supply is called a *texture*, and the individual elements of the texture are called *texels*. Figure 1.10 shows the familiar cube example with textures applied to each polygon.

Figure 1.10   Texture mapping adds detail without adding additional geometry.

Fog

Most of us know what fog is. Fog is an atmospheric effect that adds haziness to objects in a scene, which is usually a relation of how far away the objects in the scene are from the viewer. Objects very far away (or nearby if the fog is thick) might even be totally obscured.

Figure 1.11 shows the skyfly GLUT demo with fog enabled. Note how the fog lends substantially to the believability of the terrain.

Blending and Transparency

Blending is the combination of colors or objects on the screen. This is similar to the effect you get with double-exposure photography, where two images are superimposed. You can use the blending effect for a variety of purposes. By varying the amount each object is blended with the scene, you can make objects look transparent such that you see the object and what is behind it (such as glass).

Figure 1.11   Fog effects are a convincing illusion for wide open spaces.

You can also use blending to achieve an illusion of reflection, as shown in Figure 1.12. You see a textured cube rendered twice–once above a marble floor and once blended with the marble floor, lending the appearance of a reflection in a shiny marble surface.

Figure 1.12   Blending used to achieve a reflection effect.

Anti-Aliasing

Aliasing is an effect that is visible onscreen due to the fact that an image consists of discrete pixels. In Figure 1.13, you can see that the lines that make up the cube have jagged edges (sometimes called *jaggies*). By carefully blending the lines with the background color, you can eliminate the jagged edges and give the lines a smooth appearance, as shown in Figure 1.14. This blending technique is called *anti-aliasing*. You can also apply anti-aliasing to polygon edges, making an object or scene look more realistic than computer generated.

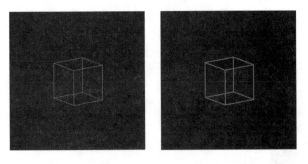

Figure 1.13 Cube with jagged lines drawn.

Figure 1.14 Cube with smoother anti-aliased lines.

Common Uses for 3D Graphics

3D graphics have many uses in modern computer applications. Applications for real-time 3D graphics range from interactive games and simulations to data visualization for scientific, medical, or business uses. Higher-end 3D graphics find their way into movies and technical and educational publications as well.

Real-Time 3D

As defined earlier, real-time 3D graphics are animated and interactive with the user. One of the earliest uses for real-time 3D graphics was in military flight simulators. Even today, flight simulators are a popular diversion for the home enthusiast. Figure 1.15 shows a screen shot from a popular flight simulator that uses OpenGL for 3D rendering (www.flightgear.org).

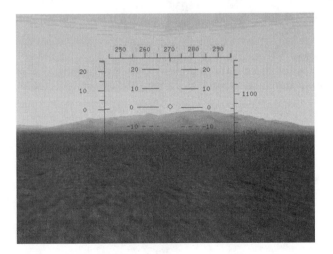

Figure 1.15 A popular OpenGL-based flight simulator from Flight Gear.

Figures 1.16 through 1.20 show some additional applications of real-time 3D graphics on the modern PC. All of these images were rendered using OpenGL on a PC.

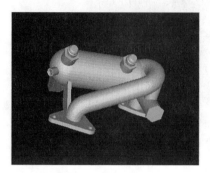

Figure 1.16   3D graphics used for computer-aided design (CAD).

Figure 1.17   3D graphics used for architectural or civil planning (image courtesy of Real 3D, Inc.).

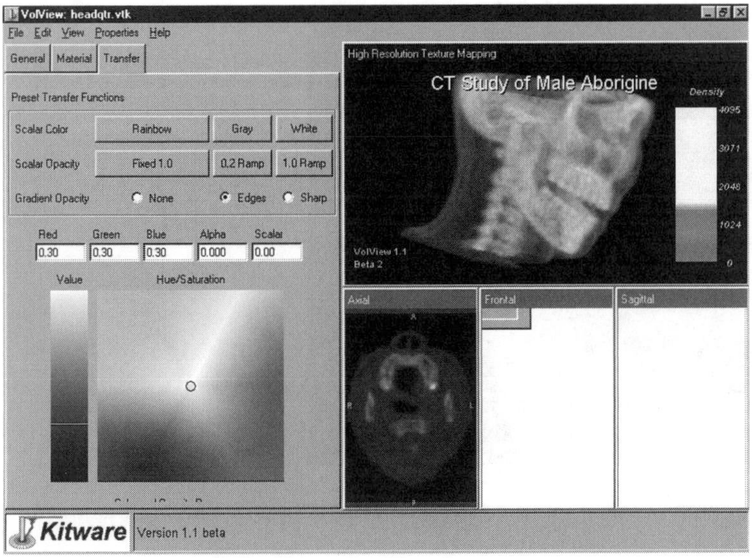

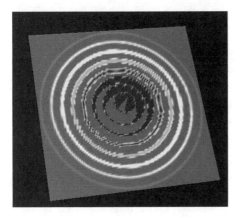

Figure 1.18   3D graphics used for medical imaging applications (VolView by Kitware).

Figure 1.19   3D graphics used for scientific visualization.

Figure 1.20   3D graphics used for entertainment (Descent 3 from Outrage Entertainment, Inc.).

Non–Real-Time 3D

Some compromise is required for real-time 3D applications. Given more processing time, you can generate higher quality 3D graphics. Typically, you design models and scenes, and a *ray tracer* processes the definition to produce a high-quality 3D image. The typical process is that some modeling application uses real-time 3D graphics to interact with the artist to create the content. Then, the frames are sent to another application (the ray tracer), which renders the image. Rendering a single frame for a movie such as *Toy Story* could take hours on a very fast computer, for example. Rendering and saving many thousands of frames generates an animated sequence for playback. Although the playback might appear real-time, the content is not interactive, so it is not considered real-time, but rather pre-rendered.

Figure 1.21 shows an example from the CD-ROM. This spinning image shows crystal letters that spell OpenGL. The letters are transparent and fully anti-aliased and show a myriad of reflections and shadow effects. The file to play this animation on your computer is opengl.avi in the root directory of your CD-ROM. This huge file (more than 35MB!) took three days to render on a 400Mhz PC.

Figure 1.21   High-quality pre-rendered animation.

Basic 3D Programming Principles

Now, you have a pretty good idea of the basics of real-time 3D. We've covered some terminology and some sample applications on the PC. How do you actually create these images on your PC? Well, that's what the rest of this book is about! You still need a little more introduction to the basics, which we present here.

Immediate Mode and Retained Mode (Scene Graphs)

There are two different approaches to programming APIs for real-time 3D graphics. The first approach is called *retained mode*. In retained mode, you provide the API or toolkit with a description of your objects and the scene. The graphics package then creates the image onscreen. The only additional manipulation you might make is to give commands to change the location and viewing orientation of the user (also called the *camera*) or other objects in the scene.

This type of approach is typical of ray tracers and many commercial flight simulators and image generators. Programmatically, the structure that is built is called a *scene graph*. The scene graph is a data structure (a DAG, or directed acyclic graph, for you computer science majors) that contains all the objects in your scene and their relationships to one another. The Fahrenheit Scene Graph is an example of a retained-mode API being developed by Microsoft and Silicon Graphics that uses OpenGL (a lower level API) for rendering.

The second approach to 3D rendering is called *immediate mode*. Most retained mode APIs or scene graphs are using an immediate mode API internally to actually perform the rendering. In immediate mode, you don't describe your models and environment from as high a level. Instead, you issue commands directly to the graphics processor that has an immediate effect on its state and the state of all subsequent commands.

For example, you can render a series of textured polygons to represent the sky. Then, issue a command to turn off texturing, followed by a command to turn on lighting. Thereafter, all geometry that you render is affected by the lighting parameters you specified earlier.

Coordinate Systems

Let's consider now how we describe objects in three dimensions. Before you can specify an object's location and size, you need a frame of reference to measure and locate against. When you draw lines or plot points on a simple flat computer screen, you specify a position in terms of a row and column. For example, a standard VGA screen has 640 pixels from the left to right and 480 pixels from top to bottom. To specify a point in the middle of the screen, you specify that a point should be plotted at (320,240)–that is, 320 pixels from the left of the screen and 240 pixels down from the top of the screen.

In OpenGL, or almost any 3D API, when you create a window to draw in, you must also specify the *coordinate system* you want to use and how to map the specified coordinates into physical screen pixels. Let's first see how this applies to two-dimensional drawing and then extend the principle to three dimensions.

2D Cartesian Coordinates

The most common coordinate system for two-dimensional plotting is the *Cartesian* coordinate system. Cartesian coordinates are specified by an x coordinate and a y coordinate. The x coordinate is a measure of position in the horizontal direction, and y is a measure of position in the vertical direction.

The *origin* of the Cartesian system is at x=0, y=0. Cartesian coordinates are written as coordinate pairs in parentheses, with the x coordinate first and the y coordinate second, separated by a comma. For example, the origin is written as (0,0). Figure 1.22 depicts the Cartesian coordinate system in two dimensions. The x and y lines with tick marks are called the *axes* and can extend from negative to positive infinity. Note that this figure represents the true Cartesian coordinate system pretty much as you used it in grade school. Today, differing window mapping modes can cause the coordinates you specify when drawing to be interpreted differently. Later in the book, you'll see how to map this true coordinate space to window coordinates in different ways.

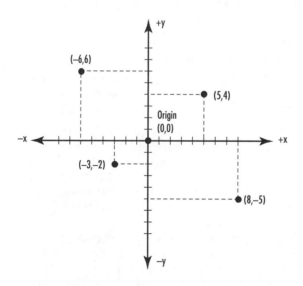

Figure 1.22   The Cartesian plane.

The x-axis and y-axis are *perpendicular* (intersecting at a right angle) and together define the *xy plane*. A plane is, most simply put, a flat surface. In any coordinate system, two axes that intersect at right angles define a plane. In a system with only two axes, there is naturally only one plane to draw on.

Coordinate Clipping

A window is measured physically in terms of pixels. Before you can start plotting points, lines, and shapes in a window, you must tell OpenGL how to translate specified coordinate pairs into screen coordinates. You do this by specifying the region of Cartesian space that occupies the window; this region is known as the *clipping area*. In two-dimensional space, the clipping area is the minimum and maximum x and y values that are inside the window. Another way of looking at this is specifying the origin's location in relation to the window. Figure 1.23 shows two common clipping areas.

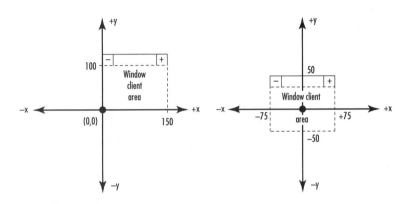

Figure 1.23   Two clipping areas.

In the first example, on the left of Figure 1.23, x coordinates in the window range left to right from 0 to +150, and the y coordinates range bottom to top from 0 to +100. A point in the middle of the screen would be represented as (75,50). The second example shows a clipping area with x coordinates ranging left to right from –75 to + 75 and y coordinates ranging bottom to top from –50 to +50. In this example, a point in the middle of the screen would be at the origin (0,0). It is also possible using OpenGL functions (or ordinary Windows functions for GDI drawing) to turn the coordinate system upside down or flip it right to left. In fact, the default mapping for Windows windows is for positive y to move down from the top to bottom of the window. Although useful when drawing text from top to bottom, this default mapping is not as convenient for drawing graphics.

Viewports: Mapping Drawing Coordinates to Window Coordinates

Rarely will your clipping area width and height exactly match the width and height of the window in pixels. The coordinate system must therefore be mapped from logical Cartesian coordinates to physical screen pixel coordinates. This mapping is specified by a setting known as the *viewport*. The viewport is the region within the window's client area that is used for drawing the clipping area. The viewport simply maps the clipping area to a region of the window. Usually, the viewport is defined as the entire window, but this is not strictly necessary; for instance, you might only want to draw in the lower half of the window.

Figure 1.24 shows a large window measuring 300×200 pixels with the viewport defined as the entire client area. If the clipping area for this window were set to 0 to 150 along the x-axis and 0 to 100 along the y-axis, the logical coordinates would be mapped to a larger screen coordinate system in the viewing window. Each increment in the logical coordinate system would be matched by two increments in the physical coordinate system (pixels) of the window.

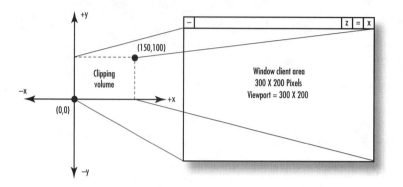

Figure 1.24   A viewport defined as twice the size of the clipping area.

In contrast, Figure 1.25 shows a viewport that matches the clipping area. The viewing window is still 300×200 pixels, however, and this causes the viewing area to occupy the lower-left side of the window.

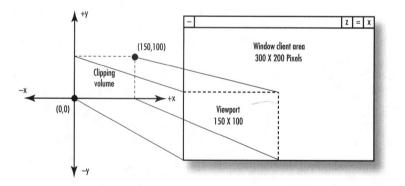

Figure 1.25   A viewport defined as the same dimensions as the clipping area.

You can use viewports to shrink or enlarge the image inside the window and to display only a portion of the clipping area by setting the viewport to be larger than the window's client area.

The Vertex–A Position in Space

In both 2D and 3D, when you draw an object, you actually compose it with several smaller shapes called *primitives*. Primitives are one- or two-dimensional entities or surfaces such as points, lines, and polygons (a flat, multisided shape) that are assembled in 3D space to create 3D objects. For example, a three-dimensional cube consists of six two-dimensional squares, each placed on a separate face. Each corner of the square (or of any primitive) is called a *vertex*. These *vertices* are then specified to occupy a particular coordinate in 2D or 3D space. A vertex is nothing more than a coordinate in 2D or 3D space. You'll learn about all the OpenGL primitives and how to use them in Chapter 4, "Drawing in Space: Lines, Points, and Polygons."

3D Cartesian Coordinates

Now, we extend our two-dimensional coordinate system into the third dimension and add a depth component. Figure 1.26 shows the Cartesian coordinate system with a new axis, z. The z-axis is perpendicular to both the x- and y-axes. It represents a line drawn perpendicularly from the center of the screen heading toward the viewer. (We have rotated our view of the coordinate system from Figure 1.22 to the left with respect to the y-axis and down and back with respect to the x-axis. If we hadn't, the z-axis would come straight out at you and you wouldn't see it.) Now, we specify a position in three-dimensional space with three coordinates–x, y, and z. Figure 1.26 shows the point (4,4,4) for clarification.

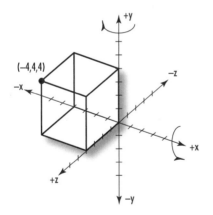

Figure 1.26   Cartesian coordinates in three dimensions.

Projections: Getting 3D to 2D

You've seen how to specify a position in 3D space using Cartesian coordinates. No matter how we might convince your eye, however, pixels on a screen have only two dimensions. How does OpenGL translate these Cartesian coordinates into two-dimensional coordinates that can be plotted on a screen? The short answer is "Trigonometry and simple matrix manipulation." Simple? Well, not really; we could actually go on for many pages and lose most of our readers who didn't take or don't remember their linear algebra from college explaining this "simple" technique. You'll learn more about it in Chapter 5, "Moving Around in Space: Coordinate Transformations," and for a deeper discussion, you can check out the references in Appendix B, "Further Reading." Fortunately, you don't need to understand the math in order to use OpenGL to create graphics.

All you really need to understand to get the most from this book is a concept called *projection*. The 3D coordinates are projected onto a 2D surface (the window background). It's like tracing the outlines of some object behind a piece of glass with a black marker. When the object is gone or you move the glass, you can still see the outline of the object with its angular edges. In Figure 1.27, a house in the background is traced onto a flat piece of glass. By specifying the projection, you specify the *clipping volume* (remember clipping areas?) that you want displayed in your window and how it should be translated.

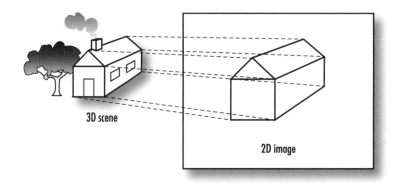

Figure 1.27 A 3D image projected onto a 2D surface.

Orthographic Projections

You are mostly concerned with two main types of projections in OpenGL. The first is called an *orthographic* or parallel projection. You use this projection by specifying a square or rectangular clipping volume. Anything outside this clipping area is not drawn. Furthermore, all objects that have the same dimensions appear the same size, regardless of whether they are far away or nearby. This type of projection (shown in Figure 1.28) is most often used in architectural design, CAD (computer aided design), or 2D graphs.

You specify the clipping volume in an orthographic projection by specifying the far, near, left, right, top, and bottom clipping planes. Objects and figures that you place within this viewing volume are then projected (taking into account their orientation) to a 2D image that appears on your screen.

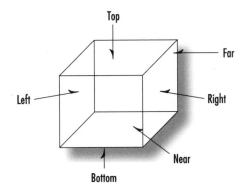
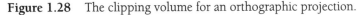

Figure 1.28   The clipping volume for an orthographic projection.

Perspective Projections

The second and more common projection is the perspective projection. This projection adds the effect that distant objects appear smaller than nearby objects.
The viewing volume (see Figure 1.29) is something like a pyramid with the top shaved off. This shaved-off part is called the *frustum*. Objects nearer to the front of the viewing volume appear close to their original size, but objects near the back of the volume shrink as they are projected to the front of the volume. This type of projection gives the most realism for simulation and 3D animation.

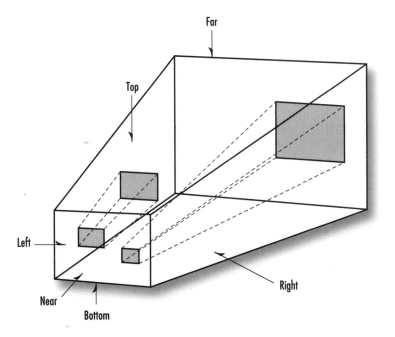

Figure 1.29   The clipping volume (frustum) for a perspective projection.

Summary

In this chapter, we have introduced the basics of 3D graphics. You've seen why you actually need two images of an object from different angles in order to perceive true three-dimensional space. You've also seen the illusion of depth created in a 2D drawing by means of perspective, hidden line removal, and coloring, shading, and other techniques. The Cartesian coordinate system was introduced for 2D and 3D drawing, and you learned about two methods used by OpenGL to project three-dimensional drawings onto a two-dimensional screen.

We purposely left out the details of how these effects are actually created by OpenGL. In the chapters that follow, you will find out how to employ these techniques and take maximum advantage of OpenGL's power. On the companion CD, you'll find one program for this chapter that demonstrates the 3D effects covered in this chapter. In block, pressing the spacebar advances you from a wireframe cube to a fully lit and textured block complete with shadow. You won't understand the code at this point, but it makes a powerful demonstration of what is to come. By the time you finish this book, you will be able to revisit this example and even be able to write it from scratch yourself.

2

WHAT IS OPENGL?

by Richard S. Wright, Jr.

OpenGL is strictly defined as "a software interface to graphics hardware." In essence, it is a 3D graphics and modeling library that is extremely portable and very fast. Using OpenGL, you can create elegant and beautiful 3D graphics with nearly the visual quality of a ray tracer. The greatest advantage to using OpenGL is that it is orders of magnitude faster than a ray tracer. It uses algorithms carefully developed and optimized by Silicon Graphics, Inc. (SGI), an acknowledged world leader in computer graphics and animation.

OpenGL is not a programming language like C or C++. It is more like the C runtime library, which provides some prepackaged functionality. There really is no such thing as an "OpenGL program," but rather a program the developer wrote that "happens" to use OpenGL as one of its APIs. You might use the Windows API to access a file or the Internet, and you might use OpenGL to create real-time 3D graphics.

OpenGL is intended for use with computer hardware that is designed and optimized for the display and manipulation of 3D graphics. Software-only, "generic" implementations of OpenGL are also possible, and the Microsoft implementations fall into this category.

OpenGL is used for a variety of purposes, from CAD engineering and architectural applications to modeling programs used to create computer-generated dinosaurs in blockbuster movies. The introduction of an industry-standard 3D API to a mass-market operating system such as Microsoft Windows has some exciting repercussions. With hardware acceleration and fast PC microprocessors becoming commonplace, 3D graphics will soon be typical components of consumer and business applications, not only of games and scientific applications.

Who remembers when spreadsheets had only 2D graphics and charting capabilities? If you think adding 3D to ordinary applications is extravagant, take a look at the bottom line of the companies that first exploited this idea. Quattro Pro, one of the first to simplify 3D charting, nearly captured the entire spreadsheet market. Today, it takes far more than flat, two-dimensional pie charts to guarantee long-term success for spreadsheet applications.

This isn't to say that everyone will be using OpenGL to make pie and bar charts for business applications. Nevertheless, appearances count for a lot. The success or failure of products with otherwise roughly equivalent features often depends on "sex appeal." And you can add a lot of sex appeal with good 3D graphics!

Evolution of a Standard

OpenGL is a relatively new industry standard that in only a few years has gained an enormous following. The forerunner of OpenGL was IRIS GL from Silicon Graphics. This was the 3D programming API for that company's high-end IRIS graphics workstations. These computers were more than just general-purpose computers; they had specialized hardware optimized for the display of sophisticated graphics. The hardware provided ultrafast matrix transformations (a prerequisite for 3D graphics), hardware support for depth buffering, and other features. When SGI tried porting IRIS GL to other hardware platforms, however, problems occurred.

OpenGL is the result of SGI's efforts to improve IRIS GL's portability. The new graphics API would offer the power of GL but would be "open," allowing for easier adaptability to other hardware platforms and operating systems.

The OpenGL ARB

An open standard is not really open if only one vendor controls it. SGI's business at the time was high-end computer graphics. Once you're at the top, you find that the opportunities for growth are somewhat limited. SGI realized that it would also be good for them to do something good for the industry to help grow the market for high-end computer graphics hardware. A truly open standard embraced by a number of vendors would make it easier for programmers to create applications and content that is available for a wider variety of platforms. Software is what sells computers, and if SGI wanted to sell more computers, it needed more software that would run on its computers. Other vendors realized this, too, and the OpenGL Architecture Review Board (ARB) was born.

Although SGI controlled licensing of the OpenGL API, the founding members of the OpenGL ARB were SGI, Digital Equipment Corporation, IBM, Intel, and Microsoft. On July 1, 1992, Version 1.0 of the OpenGL specification was introduced. More recently, as of version 1.2, the ARB consists of more than 10 members and meets four times a year to maintain and enhance the specification and to make plans to promote the OpenGL standard.

These meetings are open to the public, and nonmember companies can participate in discussions and even vote in straw polls. Permission to attend must be requested in advance, and meetings are kept small to improve productivity. Nonmember companies actually contribute significantly to the specification and do meaningful work on the conformance tests and other subcommittees.

Licensing and Conformance

An *implementation* of OpenGL is either a software library that creates three-dimensional images in response to the OpenGL function calls or a driver for a hardware device (usually a display card) that does the same. Hardware implementations are typically many times faster than software implementations and are now quite common even on inexpensive PCs.

A vendor who wants to create and market an OpenGL implementation must first license OpenGL from SGI. SGI provides the licensee with a sample implementation (entirely in software) and a device driver kit if the licensee is a PC hardware vendor. The vendor then uses this to create its own optimized implementation and can add value with its own extensions. Competition among vendors typically is based on performance, image quality, and driver stability.

In addition, the vendor's implementation must pass the *OpenGL conformance tests*. These tests are designed to ensure that an implementation is complete (it contains all the necessary function calls) and produces 3D rendered output that is reasonably acceptable for a given set of functions.

The Future of OpenGL

OpenGL today is widely recognized and accepted as an industry standard API for real-time 3D graphics. Despite the efforts of one of the ARB's own founding members (Microsoft), it has even become quite popular as an API for developing real-time 3D games in the consumer market space.

In late 1997, Microsoft and SGI jointly announced a new graphics API called Fahrenheit. Many saw this announcement as the beginning of the end for OpenGL and for open standards. A split API, the Fahrenheit low-level API was to be the "best" of OpenGL and Direct 3D (a Microsoft proprietary API that competes with OpenGL), and the Fahrenheit scene graph was to be a retained-mode API that initially ran on OpenGL or Direct 3D. Later versions of the Fahrenheit scene graph would run on OpenGL or the new Fahrenheit low-level API. This arrangement implies on the surface that OpenGL would survive the Fahrenheit low-level introduction, but not Direct 3D. Direct 3D would then have become the union of two competing APIs (OpenGL and Direct 3D). Many predicted that with this new evolution, the need for OpenGL would greatly diminish.

However, as Fahrenheit has developed, SGI has backed off plans for supporting the Fahrenheit low-level API on anything other than the Windows platform. This means that although Direct 3D will be improved (because it will become more like OpenGL), OpenGL will remain the open standard of choice for those requiring a portable and open standard. The Fahrenheit low-level API will most likely end up just another proprietary Microsoft Windows API.

Developers have continued to be attracted to OpenGL, and despite any political pressures, hardware vendors must satisfy the developers who make software that runs on their hardware. Ultimately, consumer dollars determine what standard survives, and developers who use OpenGL are turning out better applications in less time than their competitors. Only a few years ago, game developers were creating games with Microsoft's Direct 3D first because that was the only available API with a hardware driver model under Windows—and then porting to OpenGL occasionally so that the same games ran under Windows NT. Today, many game companies are doing OpenGL versions first and then porting to Direct 3D because it enables them to finish and demonstrate their games faster. It turns out that competitive advantage is more profitable than political alliances.

How Does OpenGL Work?

OpenGL is a procedural rather than a descriptive graphics API. Instead of describing the scene and how it should appear, the programmer actually prescribes the steps necessary to achieve a certain appearance or effect. These "steps" involve calls to this highly portable API, which includes more than 200 commands and functions. These commands are used to draw graphics primitives such as points, lines, and polygons in three dimensions. In addition, OpenGL supports lighting and shading, texture mapping, blending, transparency, animation, and many other special effects and capabilities.

OpenGL does not include any functions for window management, user interaction, or file I/O. Each host environment (such as Microsoft Windows) has its own functions for this purpose and is responsible for implementing some means of handing over to OpenGL the drawing control of a window or bitmap.

There is no "OpenGL file format" for models or virtual environments. These environments are constructed by the programmer to suit their own high-level needs and then carefully programmed using the lower-level OpenGL commands.

Generic Implementations

As mentioned previously, a generic implementation is a software implementation. Hardware implementations are created for a specific hardware device, such as a graphics card or image generator. A generic implementation can technically run just about anywhere as long as the system has the ability to display the generated graphics image.

Figure 2.1 shows the typical place that OpenGL and a generic implementation occupy when an application is running. The typical program calls many functions, some of which the programmer creates, some of which are provided by the operating system or the programming language's runtime library. Windows applications wanting to create output onscreen usually call a Windows API called the GDI (Graphics Device Interface). The GDI contains methods that allow you to write text in a window, draw simple 2D lines, and so on.

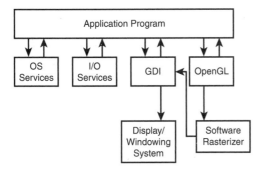

Figure 2.1   OpenGL's place in a typical application program.

Usually, graphics card vendors supply a hardware driver that GDI interfaces with to create output on your monitor. A software implementation of OpenGL takes graphics requests from an application and constructs (*rasterizes*) a color image of the 3D graphics. It then supplies this image to the GDI for display on the monitor. On other operating systems, the process is pretty much equivalent, but you replace the GDI with that operating system's native display services.

There are a couple of common generic implementations of OpenGL. Microsoft has shipped its software implementation with every version of Windows NT since version 3.5 and Windows 95 (Service Release 2 and later). Windows 2000 will also contain support for OpenGL.

SGI released a software implementation of OpenGL for Windows that greatly outper-formed Microsoft's implementation on MMX-enhanced CPUs. This implementation is not officially supported but is still in wide use. Mesa 3D is another "unofficial" OpenGL software implementation that is widely supported in the open source com-munity. Mesa 3D is not an OpenGL license, so it is an "OpenGL work-alike" rather than an official implementation. In any respect other than legal, you can essentially consider it to be an OpenGL implementation none-the-less. The Mesa contributors even make an attempt to pass the OpenGL conformance tests.

Hardware Implementations

A hardware implementation of OpenGL usually takes the form of a graphics card driver. Figure 2.2 shows its relationship to the application similarly to the way Figure 2.1 did for software implementations. Note that the OpenGL API calls are passed to a hardware driver. This driver does not pass its output to the Windows GDI for display; the driver interfaces directly with the graphics display hardware.

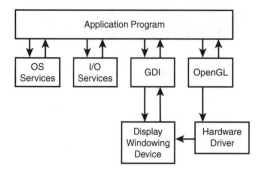

Figure 2.2   Hardware-accelerated OpenGL's place in a typical application program.

A hardware implementation is often referred to as an accelerated implementation because hardware-assisted 3D graphics usually far outperform software-only implementations. What isn't shown in Figure 2.2 is that sometimes part of the OpenGL functionality is still implemented in software as part of the driver, and other features and functionality can be passed directly to the hardware. This idea brings us to our next topic—the OpenGL *pipeline*.

The Pipeline

The word pipeline is used to describe a process that can take two or more distinct stages or steps. Figure 2.3 shows a simplified version of the OpenGL pipeline. As an application makes OpenGL API function calls, the commands are placed in a command buffer. This buffer eventually fills with commands, vertex data, texture data, and so on. When the buffer is flushed, either programmatically or by the driver's design, the commands and data are passed to the next stage in the pipeline.

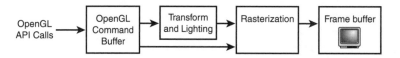

Figure 2.3   A simplified version of the OpenGL pipeline.

Vertex data is usually transformed and lit initially. In subsequent chapters, you'll find out more about what this means. For now, you can consider "Transform and Lighting" to be a mathematically intensive stage where points used to describe an object's geometry are recalculated for the given object's location and orientation. Lighting calculations are performed as well to indicate how brightly the colors should be at each vertex.

Once this stage is complete, the data is fed to the rasterization portion of the pipeline. The rasterizer actually creates the color image from the geometric, color, and texture data.

The image is then placed in the *frame buffer*. The frame buffer is the memory of the graphics display device, which means the image is displayed on your screen.

This diagram is a simplistic view of the OpenGL pipeline, but it is sufficient for your current understanding of 3D graphics rendering. At a high level, this is an accurate view, so we aren't compromising your understanding, but at a low level, there are many more boxes inside each of the boxes shown here. There are also some exceptions, such as the arrow in the figure where some commands skip the Transform and Lighting (T&L) stage altogether (such as displaying raw image data on the screen). A more detailed look at the OpenGL pipeline is outside the scope of this book, and we refer you to Appendix B, "Further Reading."

Early OpenGL hardware accelerators were nothing more than fast rasterizers. They only accelerated the rasterization portion of the pipeline. The host system's CPU did transform and lighting in a software implementation of that portion of the pipeline. Higher end accelerators (more expensive) had T&L on the graphics accelerator. This arrangement put more of the OpenGL pipeline in hardware and thus provided for higher performance.

The current trend, even for low-end consumer hardware, is to put the T&L stage in hardware as well. The net effect of this arrangement is that higher detailed models and more complex graphics are possible at real-time rendering rates on inexpensive consumer hardware. Games and applications developers can capitalize on this effect, yielding far more detailed and visually rich environments in the years to come.

The State Machine

We said before that OpenGL is an immediate-mode API. Each command has an immediate effect based on the current rendering state. Rendering states are flags that specify which features are on and off and how they should be applied. Some examples are such questions as, "Is lighting enabled? Is texturing turned on? Is fog enabled, and what is its density?" Each state variable is either on or off or contains some numeric value. States can be set and read by the OpenGL functions described in Appendix C, "The OpenGL State Machine."

Summary

In this chapter, you've learned about the beginnings and evolution of the OpenGL API and standard. You've found out that OpenGL is an open standard not controlled by one company, but influenced by many for the good of the industry as well as SGI. We've discussed how OpenGL has grown in popularity and will likely continue to do so.

You've also learned a little about how OpenGL works on your computer, with either a software implementation or a specific hardware device. We introduced the OpenGL pipeline and state machine at a very high level to give you a flavor of the basic operation of the API.

3

USING OPENGL

by Richard S. Wright, Jr.

What you'll learn in this chapter:

- Which headers and libraries are used with OpenGL
- How the GLUT library provides basic windowing functions on just about any platform
- How to use GLUT with OpenGL to create a window and draw in it
- How to use the OpenGL default coordinate system
- How to create composite colors using the RGB (red, green, blue) components
- How viewports affect image dimensions
- How to scale your drawing to fit any size window
- How to perform simple animation using double buffering
- How to draw some predefined objects

Now that you've been introduced to OpenGL and the principles of real-time 3D graphics, it's time to set our hands to writing some OpenGL code. This chapter starts with an overview of how OpenGL works with your compiler, and you'll learn some conventions for naming variables and functions. If you have already written some OpenGL programs, you may have "discovered" many of these details for yourself. If that is the case, you might just want to skim through the first section and jump right into using the GLUT library.

OpenGL: An API, Not a Language

OpenGL is not a programming language; it is an API (Application Programming Interface). Whenever we say that a program is OpenGL-based or an OpenGL application, we mean that it was written in some programming language (such as C or C++) that makes calls to one or more of the OpenGL libraries. We are not saying that the program uses OpenGL exclusively to do drawing. It might combine the best features of two different graphics packages. Or it might use OpenGL for only a few specific tasks and environment-specific graphics (such as the Windows GDI) for others.

As an API, the OpenGL library follows the C calling convention. This means programs in C can easily call functions in the API either because the functions are themselves written in C or because a set of intermediate C functions is provided that calls functions written in assembler or some other language. In this book, the sample programs are written in C. C++ programs can easily access C functions and APIs in the same manner as C, with only some minor considerations. Most C++ programmers can still program in C, and we don't want to exclude anyone or place any additional burden on the reader (such as having to get used to C++ syntax). Other programming languages—such as so-called 4GLs (fourth-generation languages) like Visual Basic—that can call functions in C libraries can also make use of OpenGL. These languages are often a moving target in terms of trying to write sample programs, so we are going to stick to good, old-fashioned C.

Libraries and Headers

Although OpenGL is a "standard" programming library, there are many implementations of this library. (See Chapter 17, "The OpenGL Pixel Format and Rendering Context," for more details.) Microsoft Windows ships with support for OpenGL as a software renderer. This means that when a program written to use OpenGL makes OpenGL function calls, the Microsoft implementation performs the 3D rendering functions and you see the results in your application window. The actual Microsoft software implementation is in the *opengl32.dll* dynamic link library, located in the Windows system directory. On most platforms, the OpenGL library is accompanied by the OpenGL utility library (GLU), which on Windows is in *glu32.dll*, also located in the system directory. The utility library is a set of utility functions that do common (but sometimes complex) tasks, such as special matrix calculations, or provide support for common types of curves and surfaces.

To make a call to a function in a DLL, you need to link your program to an import library. Details on how to compile and link programs with your compiler are beyond the scope of this book, and we couldn't cover all the different compilers available anyway. If you want detailed information on how DLLs work on Windows, consult one of the Windows programming books in Appendix B, "Further Reading." The import library provided by Microsoft with its programming tools is opengl32.lib for OpenGL and glu32.lib for the OpenGL utility library. To create programs that use OpenGL with Microsoft's tools, you need to add these two libraries to your list of import libraries.

Prototypes for all OpenGL functions, types, and macros are contained (by convention) in the header file gl.h. Microsoft programming tools ship with this file, and so do most other programming environments for the Windows or other platforms (at least those that natively support OpenGL). The utility library functions are prototyped in a different file, glu.h. These files are usually located in a special directory in your `include` path. The following code shows the typical initial header inclusions for a typical Windows program that uses OpenGL:

```
#include<windows.h>
#include<gl/gl.h>
#include<gl/glu.h>
```

Hardware Acceleration

Creating interactive 3D graphics is an exceptionally time-consuming task, even on the fastest CPUs available today. For this reason, many graphics card vendors are including 3D hardware acceleration as a feature of their graphics cards. These graphics cards have specialized graphics processors that are designed specifically for the task of 3D graphics generation. Unlike a general-purpose CPU, these dedicated processors are capable of tremendously speeding up 3D graphics rendering tasks. OpenGL was originally intended to give programmers a standardized interface for 3D graphics that could work seamlessly with 3D hardware when present.

If you link to the Microsoft OpenGL import libraries mentioned previously, your programs are automatically able to take advantage of any 3D graphics board that has an OpenGL driver for Windows available for it. (Most do.) Some caveats apply, but we discuss the various driver models in more detail later in Chapter 17.

Other Implementations

There are still good reasons why you might not want to link your programs to Microsoft's OpenGL implementation. Some hardware vendors might supply their own versions with significant enhancements to OpenGL that aren't available via Microsoft's libraries. (Microsoft's slowness in incorporating the latest OpenGL features into its implementation is one good reason for doing this!) You might get better performance or visual quality with a different implementation.

SGI's OpenGL for Windows is a good example. SGI's implementation uses MMX instructions (those Intel Multimedia instructions in MMX-enabled processors), which dramatically improves the performance of texture mapping in software without a 3D graphics accelerator. SGI was clever, however, because it too can detect the presence of a valid Windows OpenGL hardware driver. If it's present, the SGI software implementation backs out gracefully and allows the hardware implementation to do the rendering. Although now unsupported by SGI, this implementation is very good and still very popular. You should install the SGI OpenGL SDK and set up the GLUT library (coming up soon). The SGI implementation uses opengl.dll and glu.dll (along with opengl.lib and glu.lib) to avoid potential confusion with Microsoft's DLLs. It also comes with its own versions of gl.h and glu.h that contain prototypes and definitions for some SGI-specific extensions and features. (See Chapter 16, "Common OpenGL Extensions.") You can still use the Microsoft headers if you do not want to take advantage of these.

Another popular software implementation is the Mesa library. This library is actually a "work-alike" and not an official OpenGL implementation. It is an open source project, and although it doesn't quite achieve the quality of SGI's official implementation, it is still popular—perhaps mostly so because it is the basis of many "unofficial" OpenGL "mini-drivers" both for Windows and for Linux platforms. (Mini-drivers are discussed in Chapter 17.) You can use Mesa as a replacement for Microsoft's opengl32.dll (without the hardware support), or you can link directly to it as a static library. The Mesa distribution (included on the CD-ROM) includes make files and instructions for use.

At the time this book was written, Mesa had full support for the OpenGL 1.2 function set. This is another strong endorsement for this implementation because most hardware vendors (and Microsoft) still do not have support for OpenGL 1.2 features. Some of the samples later in the book use Mesa to demonstrate OpenGL 1.2 functionality.

API Specifics

OpenGL was designed by some clever people who had a lot of experience designing graphics programming APIs. They applied some standard rules to the way functions were named and variables were declared. The API is simple and clean and very easy to extend by vendors. OpenGL tries to avoid as much *policy* as possible. Policy refers to assumptions that the designers make about how the API will be used by programmers. Examples of policies are assuming that you always specify vertex data as floating-point values, assuming that fog is always enabled before any rendering occurs, or assuming that all objects in a scene are affected by the same lighting parameters. To do so eliminates many of the popular rendering techniques that have developed over time.

Data Types

To make it easier to port OpenGL code from one platform to another, OpenGL defines its own data types. These data types map to normal C data types that you can use instead, if you want. The various compilers and environments, however, have their own rules for the size and memory layout of various C variables. By using the OpenGL defined variable types, you can insulate your code from these types of changes.

Table 3.1 lists the OpenGL data types, their corresponding C data types under the 32-bit Windows environments (Win32), and the appropriate suffix for literals. In this book, we use the suffixes for all literal values. You will see later that these suffixes are also used in many OpenGL function names.

Table 3.1 *OpenGL Variable Types and Corresponding C Data Types*

OpenGL Data Type	Internal Representation	Defined as C Type	C Literal Suffix
GLbyte	8-bit integer	signed char	b
GLshort	16-bit integer	short	s
GLint, GLsizei	32-bit integer	song	l
GLfloat, GLclampf	32-bit floating point	float	f
GLdouble, GLclampd	64-bit floating point	double	d
GLubyte, GLboolean	8-bit unsigned integer	unsigned char	ub
GLushort	16-bit unsigned integer	unsigned short	us
GLuint, GLenum, GLbitfield	32-bit unsigned integer	unsigned long	ui

All data types start with a GL to denote OpenGL. Most are followed by their corresponding C data types (byte, short, int, float, and so on). Some have a u first to denote an unsigned data type, such as ubyte to denote an unsigned byte. For some uses, a more descriptive name is given, such as size to denote a value of length or depth. For example, GLsizei is an OpenGL variable denoting a size parameter that is represented by an integer. The clamp is used for color composition and stands for color amplitude. This data type appears with both f and d suffixes to denote float and double data types. The GLboolean variables are used to indicate true and False conditions, GLenum for enumerated variables, and GLbitfield for variables that contain binary bit fields.

Pointers and arrays are not given any special consideration. An array of 10 GLshort variables is simply declared as

```
GLshort shorts[10];
```

and an array of 10 pointers to GLdouble variables is declared with

```
GLdouble *doubles[10];
```

Some other pointer object types are used for NURBS and quadrics. They require more explanation and are covered in later chapters.

Function Naming Conventions

OpenGL functions all follow a naming convention that tells you which library the function is from and often how many and what type of arguments the function takes. All functions have a root that represents the function's corresponding OpenGL command. For example, the glColor3f function has the root Color. The gl prefix represents the gl library, and the 3f suffix means the function takes three floating-point arguments. All OpenGL functions take the following format:

`<Library prefix><Root command><Optional argument count><Optional argument type>`

Figure 3.1 illustrates the parts of an OpenGL function. This sample function with the suffix 3f takes three floating-point arguments. Other variations take three integers (glColor3i), three doubles (glColor3d), and so forth. This convention of adding the number and type of arguments (see Table 3.1) to the end of OpenGL functions makes it easy to remember the argument list without having to look it up. Some versions of glColor take four arguments to specify an alpha component (transparency), as well.

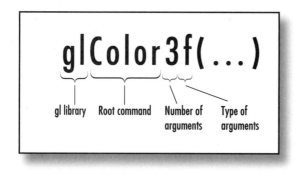

Figure 3.1 A dissected OpenGL function.

In the reference sections of this book, these "families" of functions are listed by their library prefix and root. All the variations of glColor (glColor3f, glColor4f, glColor3i, and so on) are listed under a single entry—glColor.

Many C/C++ compilers for Windows assume that any floating-point literal value is of type double unless explicitly told otherwise via the suffix mechanism. When using literals for floating-point arguments, if you don't specify that these arguments are of type float instead of double, the compiler issues a warning while compiling because it detects that you are passing a double to a function defined to accept only floats, resulting in a possible loss of precision. As OpenGL programs grow, these warnings quickly number in the hundreds and make it difficult to find any real syntax errors. You can turn off these warnings using the appropriate compiler options—but we advise against this. It's better to write clean, portable code the first time. So clean up those warning messages by cleaning up the code (in this case, by explicitly using the `float` type)—not by disabling potentially useful warnings.

Additionally, you might be tempted to use the functions that accept double-precision floating-point arguments, rather than go to all the bother of specifying your literals as floats. However, OpenGL uses floats internally, and using anything other than the single-precision floating-point functions adds a performance bottleneck because the values are converted to floats anyway before being processed by OpenGL—not to mention that every `double` takes up twice as much memory as a `float`. For a program with a lot of numbers floating around, these performance hits can add up pretty fast.

Platform Independence

OpenGL is a powerful and sophisticated API for creating 3D graphics, with more than 300 commands that cover everything from setting material colors and reflective properties to doing rotations and complex coordinate transformations. You might be s urprised that OpenGL has not a single function or command relating to window or screen management. In addition, there are no functions for keyboard input or mouse interaction. Consider, however, that one of the primary goals of the OpenGL designers was platform independence. Creating and opening a window is done differently under the various platforms. Even if OpenGL did have a command for opening a window, would you use it or would you use the operating system's own built-in API call?

Another platform issue is the handling of keyboard and mouse input events under the different operating systems and environments. If every environment handled these events the same, we would have only one environment to worry about and no need for an "open" API. This is not the case, however, and it probably won't happen within our brief lifetimes! So OpenGL's platform independence comes at the cost of OS and GUI functions.

Using GLUT

In the beginning, there was AUX, the OpenGL auxiliary library. The AUX library was created to facilitate the learning and writing of OpenGL programs without being distracted by the minutiae of any particular environment, be it UNIX, Windows, or whatever. You wouldn't write "final" code when using AUX; it was more of a preliminary staging ground for testing your ideas. A lack of basic GUI features limited the library's use for building useful applications.

Only a couple of years ago, most OpenGL samples circulating the Web (and OpenGL book samples!) were written using the AUX library. The Windows implementation of the AUX library was very buggy and prone to cause frequent crashes. The lack of any GUI features whatsoever was another drawback in the modern GUI-oriented world.

AUX has largely been replaced by the GLUT library for cross-platform programming examples and demonstrations. GLUT stands for *OpenGL utility toolkit* (not to be confused with the more standard GLU—*OpenGL utility library*). GLUT was written by Mark Kilgard while at SGI as a more capable replacement for the AUX library and included some GUI features to at least make sample programs more usable under X Window. This replacement includes using pop-up menus, managing other windows, and even providing joystick support! GLUT is not public domain, but it is free and free to redistribute. The latest GLUT distribution available at the time of printing is on the CD with this book. To get later distributions, visit the GLUT Web site at `http://reality.sgi.com/opengl/glut3/glut3.html`.

For most of this book, we use GLUT as our program framework. This decision serves two purposes. The first is that it makes most of the book accessible to a wider audience than only Windows programmers. With a little effort, the experienced Linux or Mac programmers should be able to set up GLUT for their programming environments and follow along most of the examples in this book.

The second point is that using GLUT eliminates the need to know and understand basic Windows programming. The last three chapters of this book delve more deeply into topics that are closely tied to standard Windows programming techniques. Although we explain the general concepts, we do not claim to write a book about Windows programming, but about OpenGL. Using GLUT for the basic coverage of the API, we make life a bit easier for the Windows novice as well.

It's unlikely that all of the functionality of a commercial application will be embodied entirely in the code used to draw in 3D, so you can't rely entirely on the GLUT library for everything. Nevertheless, the GLUT library excels in its role for learning and demonstration exercises. Even for an experienced Windows programmer, it is still easier to employ the GLUT library to iron out 3D graphics code before integrating it into a complete application.

Setting Up Your Programming Environment

There is no "correct" programming environment for this book. We could not possibly cover all the different ways you can configure your compiler and programming environment. As we've stated before, the purpose of this book is to teach you OpenGL, not C programming or how to use Visual C++/C++ Builder/and so on. What we can do, however, is tell you the recommended environment and configuration.

Afterward, you can install the GLUT libraries and samples. Makefiles for several platforms are included. The CD-ROM contains glut32.dll (located in the \tools\glut-3.7\lib\glut subdirectory). This DLL is precompiled and linked to the SGI OpenGL implementation. Copy this file into your Windows system directory. The link library, glut32.lib, is located in the same directory. You should copy this file to your programming environments library directory.

Finally, you need the header file glut.h. It is located in the \tools\glut-3.7\include\GL directory. A good place to put this header is in the same directory where your development environment keeps gl.h and glu.h.

All of the examples in this book were compiled with Microsoft's Visual C++ 6.0. In each sample directory, you will find a Visual C++ project workspace file (in addition to the C source code for the sample program). If you install the preceding libraries as recommended, and you are using Visual C++, you can just open the project files to access the sample programs. You can also open the project files to see how we included the import libraries in the Project/Settings dialog (Link tab).

Your First Program

To understand the GLUT library better, take a look at possibly the world's shortest OpenGL program, which was written using the GLUT library. Listing 3.1 presents the SIMPLE program. Its output is shown in Figure 3.2. You'll also learn just a few things about OpenGL along the way!

Listing 3.1 *Source Code for SIMPLE—A Very Simple OpenGL Program*

```c
// Simple.c
// The Simplest OpenGL program with GLUT
// OpenGL SuperBible, 2nd Edition
// Richard S. Wright Jr.

#include <windows.h>
#include <gl\glut.h>

// Called to draw scene
void RenderScene(void)
    {
    // Clear the window with current clearing color
    glClear(GL_COLOR_BUFFER_BIT);


    // Flush drawing commands
    glFlush();
    }

// Set up the rendering state
void SetupRC(void)
    {
    glClearColor(0.0f, 0.0f, 1.0f, 1.0f);
    }
```

continued on next page

continued from previous page

```
// Main program entry point
void main(void)
    {
    glutInitDisplayMode(GLUT_SINGLE | GLUT_RGB);
    glutCreateWindow("Simple");
    glutDisplayFunc(RenderScene);

    SetupRC();

    glutMainLoop();
    }
```

Figure 3.2 Output from the SIMPLE program.

To build this program, you need to set your compiler and link options to build a Win32 console (or text-based) application. You need to link to the GLUT library glut32.lib. If you use GLUT under the recommended configuration, you do not have to link specifically to the OpenGL import libraries because GLUT is already linked to the SGI implementation.

The SIMPLE program doesn't do much. When run from the command line (or development environment), it creates a standard GUI window with the caption "Simple" and a clear blue background. If you are running Visual C++, then when you terminate the program, you see the message "Press any key to continue" in the console window. You need to press a key to terminate the program. This standard feature of the Microsoft IDE for running a console application ensures that you can see whatever output your program places onscreen (the console window) before the window vanishes. If you run the program from the command line, you don't get this behavior. If you double-click on the program file from Explorer, you see the console window, but it vanishes when the program terminates.

This simple program contains four GLUT library functions (prefixed with glut) and three "real" OpenGL functions (prefixed with gl). Let's examine the program line by line, after which we introduce some more functions and substantially improve on our first example.

The Headers

There are only two include files:

```
#include <windows.h>
#include <gl/glut.h>
```

These includes define the function prototypes used by the program. The windows.h header file is required by all Windows applications and contains most of the WIN32 function prototypes. This file is actually optional because the WIN32 version of GLUT has windows.h included in glut.h. Unless you are shooting for complete portability, it is a good habit to always include this file first. The header file glut.h also includes the gl.h and glu.h headers that define the OpenGL and GLU library functions. If we weren't using GLUT (see Chapters 17 and beyond), we would also need to include these files.

The Body

Next, we skip down to the entry point of all C programs:

```
void main(void)
    {
```

Console-mode C and C++ programs always start execution with the function main. If you are an experienced Windows nerd, you might wonder where WinMain is in this example. It's not there because we start with a console-mode application, so we don't have to start with window creation and a message loop. It is possible with Win32 to create graphical windows from console applications, just as it is possible to create console windows from GUI applications. These details are buried within the GLUT library. (Remember, the GLUT library is designed to hide just these kinds of platform details.)

Display Mode: Single Buffered

The first line of code

```
glutInitDisplayMode(GLUT_SINGLE | GLUT_RGB);
```

tells the GLUT library what type of display mode to use when creating the window. The flags here tell it to use a single-buffered window (GLUT_SINGLE) and to use RGBA color mode (GLUT_RGBA). A single-buffered window means that all drawing commands are performed on the window displayed. An alternative is a double-buffered window, where the drawing commands are actually executed to create a scene offscreen and then quickly swapped into view on the window. This method is often used to produce animation effects and is demonstrated later in this chapter. In fact, we use double-buffered mode for most of the rest of the book. RGBA color mode means that you specify colors by supplying separate intensities of red, green, and blue components.

Creating the OpenGL Window

The next call to the GLUT library actually creates the window on the screen. The code

```
glutCreateWindow("Simple");
```

creates the window and sets the caption to "Simple." The single argument to glutCreateWindow is the caption for the window title bar.

Displaying Callback

The next line of GLUT specific code is

```
glutDisplayFunc(RenderScene);
```

This establishes the previously defined function RenderScene as the display callback function. What this means is that GLUT calls the function pointed to here whenever the window needs to be drawn. This call occurs when the window is first displayed or when the window is resized or uncovered, for example. This is where we put our OpenGL rendering function calls.

Set Up the Context and Go!

The next line is neither GLUT nor OpenGL specific but is a convention that we follow throughout the book:

```
SetupRC();
```

This function is where we do any OpenGL initialization that should be performed before rendering. Many of the OpenGL states need to be set only once and do not need to be reset every time you render a frame (a screen full of graphics).

The last GLUT function call comes at the end of the program:

```
glutMainLoop();
}
```

This function starts the GLUT framework running. After you define callbacks for screen display and other functions (coming up!), you turn GLUT loose. This function processes all the operating system specific messages, keystrokes, and so on until you terminate the program.

OpenGL Graphics Calls

The SetupRC function contains a single OpenGL function call:

```
glClearColor(0.0f, 0.0f, 1.0f, 1.0f);
```

This function sets the color used for clearing the window. The prototype for this function is

```
void glClearColor(GLclampf red, GLclampf green, GLclampf blue, GLclampf alpha);
```

GLclampf is defined as a float under most implementations of OpenGL. In OpenGL, a single color is represented as a mixture of red, green, and blue components. The range for each component can vary from 0.0 to 1.0. This is similar to the Windows specification of colors using the RGB macro to create a COLORREF value. The difference is that in Windows, each color component in a COLORREF can range from 0 to 255, giving a total of 256×256×256—or more than 16 million colors. With OpenGL, the values for each component can be any valid floating-point value between 0 and 1, thus yielding a theoretically infinite number of potential colors. Practically speaking, color output is limited on most devices to 24 bits (16 million colors).

Naturally, both Windows and OpenGL take this color value and convert it internally to the nearest possible exact match with the available video hardware and palette. We explore this concept more closely in Chapter 17.

Table 3.2 lists some common colors and their component values. You can use these values with any of the OpenGL color-related functions.

Table 3.2   *Some Common Composite Colors*

Composite Color	Red Component	Green Component	Blue Component
Black	0.0	0.0	0.0
Red	1.0	0.0	0.0
Green	0.0	1.0	0.0
Yellow	1.0	1.0	0.0
Blue	0.0	0.0	1.0
Magenta	1.0	0.0	1.0
Cyan	0.0	1.0	1.0
Dark gray	0.25	0.25	0.25
Light gray	0.75	0.75	0.75
Brown	0.60	0.40	0.12
Pumpkin orange	0.98	0.625	0.12
Pastel pink	0.98	0.04	0.7
Barney purple	0.60	0.40	0.70
White	1.0	1.0	1.0

The last argument to `glClearColor` is the alpha component. The alpha component is used for blending and special effects such as translucence. Translucence refers to an object's ability to allow light to pass through it. Suppose you are representing a piece of red stained glass, but a blue light is shining behind it. The blue light affects the appearance of the red in the glass (blue + red = purple). You can use the alpha component value to make a blue color that is semitransparent so it works like a sheet of glass; an object behind it shows through. There is more to this type of effect than just using the alpha value, and in Chapter 10, "Visual Effects: Blending and Fog," you'll learn more about this; until then, you should leave the alpha value as 1.

Actually Clear

All we have done at this point is set OpenGL to use blue for the clearing color. In our `RenderScene` function, we need an instruction to do the actual clearing:

```
glClear(GL_COLOR_BUFFER_BIT);
```

The `glClear` function clears a particular buffer or combination of buffers. A buffer is a storage area for image information. The red, green, and blue components of a drawing are usually collectively referred to as the *color buffer* or *pixel buffer*.

There is more than one kind of buffer in OpenGL, and they are covered in more detail in Chapter 11, "Buffers: Not Just for Animation." For the next several chapters, all you really need to understand is that the color buffer is where the displayed image is stored internally and that clearing the buffer with `glClear` removes the drawing from the window.

Flushing That Queue

Our final OpenGL function call comes last:

```
glFlush();
```

This line causes any unexecuted OpenGL commands to be executed; we have one at this point—`glClear`.

Internally, OpenGL uses a rendering pipeline that processes commands sequentially. OpenGL commands and statements often are queued up until the OpenGL driver processes several "requests" at once. This setup improves performance, especially when constructing complex objects. Drawing is accelerated because the slower graphics hardware is accessed less often for a given set of drawing instructions. (When Win32 was first introduced, this same concept was added to the Windows GDI to improve graphics performance under Windows NT.) In our short program, the `glFlush` function simply tells OpenGL that it should proceed with the drawing instructions supplied thus far before waiting for any more drawing commands.

It might not be the most interesting OpenGL program in existence, but simple.c demonstrates the basics of getting a window up using the GLUT library, and it shows you how to specify a color and clear the window. Next, we want to spruce up our program by adding some more GLUT library and OpenGL functions.

Drawing Shapes with OpenGL

The simple.c program made an empty window with a blue background. Now, let's do some drawing in the window. In addition, we want to be able to move and resize the window and have our rendering code respond appropriately. In Listing 3.2, you can see the modifications. Figure 3.3 shows the output of this program (GLRect).

Listing 3.2 *Drawing a Centered Rectangle with OpenGL*

```c
// GLRect.c
// Drawing a simple 3D rectangle program with GLUT
// OpenGL SuperBible, 2nd Edition
// Richard S. Wright Jr.

#include <windows.h>
#include <gl/glut.h>

// Called to draw scene
void RenderScene(void)
    {
    // Clear the window with current clearing color
    glClear(GL_COLOR_BUFFER_BIT);

    // Set current drawing color to red
    //           R    G    B
    glColor3f(1.0f, 0.0f, 0.0f);

    // Draw a filled rectangle with current color
    glRectf(100.0f, 150.0f, 150.0f, 100.0f);

    // Flush drawing commands
    glFlush();
    }


// Set up the rendering state
void SetupRC(void)
    {
    // Set clear color to blue
    glClearColor(0.0f, 0.0f, 1.0f, 1.0f);
```

continued on next page

continued from previous page

```
    }


// Called by GLUT library when the window has changed size
void ChangeSize(GLsizei w, GLsizei h)
    {
    // Prevent a divide by zero
    if(h == 0)
        h = 1;

    // Set viewport to window dimensions
        glViewport(0, 0, w, h);

    // Reset coordinate system
    glMatrixMode(GL_PROJECTION);
    glLoadIdentity();

    // Establish clipping volume (left, right, bottom, top, near, far)
    if (w <= h)
        glOrtho (0.0f, 250.0f, 0.0f, 250.0f*h/w, 1.0, -1.0);
    else
        glOrtho (0.0f, 250.0f*w/h, 0.0f, 250.0f, 1.0, -1.0);

    glMatrixMode(GL_MODELVIEW);
    glLoadIdentity();
    }

// Main program entry point
void main(void)
    {
    glutInitDisplayMode(GLUT_SINGLE | GLUT_RGB);
    glutCreateWindow("GLRect");
    glutDisplayFunc(RenderScene);
        glutReshapeFunc(ChangeSize);

    SetupRC();

    glutMainLoop();
    }
```

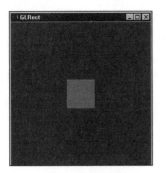

Figure 3.3 Output from the GLRect program.

Drawing a Rectangle

Previously, all our program did was clear the screen. We've now added the following lines of drawing code:

```
// Set current drawing color to red
//              R    G  B
glColor3f(1.0f, 0.0f, 0.0f);

// Draw a filled rectangle with current color
glRectf(100.0f, 150.0f, 150.0f, 100.0f);
```

These lines set the color used for future drawing operations (lines and filling) with the call to glColor3f. Then, glRectf draws a filled rectangle.

The glColor3f function selects a color in the same manner as glClearColor, but no alpha translucency component needs to be specified (the default value for alpha is 1.0 for completely opaque):

```
void glColor3f(GLfloat red, GLfloat green, GLfloat blue);
```

The glRectf function takes floating-point arguments, as denoted by the trailing f. The number of arguments is not used in the function name because all glRect variations take four arguments. The four arguments of glRectf,

```
void glRectf(GLfloat x1, GLfloat y1, GLfloat x2, GLfloat y2);
```

represent two coordinate pairs—(x1, y1) and (x2, y2). The first pair represents the upper-left corner of the rectangle, and the second pair represents the lower-right corner.

How does OpenGL map these coordinates to actual Window positions? This is done in the callback function ChangeSize. This function is set as the callback function for whenever the window changes size (when it is stretched, maximized, and so on). This is set by the `glutReshapeFunc`, in the same way that the display callback function is set:

```
glutReshapeFunc(ChangeSize);
```

Anytime the Window size or dimensions change, you need to reset the coordinate system.

Scaling to the Window

In nearly all windowing environments, the user can at any time change the size and dimensions of the window. When this happens, the window usually responds by redrawing its contents, taking into consideration the window's new dimensions. Sometimes, you might want to simply clip the drawing for smaller windows or display the entire drawing at its original size in a larger window. For our purposes, we usually want to scale the drawing to fit within the window, regardless of the size of the drawing or window. Thus, a very small window would have a complete but very small drawing, and a larger window would have a similar but larger drawing. You see this effect in most drawing programs when you stretch a window as opposed to enlarging the drawing. Stretching a window usually doesn't change the drawing size, but magnifying the image makes it grow.

Setting the Viewport and Clipping Volume

In Chapter 2, "What Is OpenGL?" we discussed how the viewport and clipping volume affect the coordinate range and scaling of 2D and 3D drawings in a 2D window on the computer screen. Now, we examine the setting of viewport and clipping volume coordinates in OpenGL.

Although our drawing is a 2D flat rectangle, we are actually drawing in a 3D coordinate space. The `glRectf` function draws the rectangle in the xy plane at z = 0. Your perspective is along the positive z-axis to see the square rectangle at z = 0. (If you're feeling lost here, review this material in Chapter 1, "3D Graphics Fundamentals.")

Whenever the window size changes, the viewport and clipping volume must be re-defined for the new window dimensions. Otherwise, you see an effect like the one shown in Figure 3.4, where the mapping of the coordinate system to screen coordinates stays the same regardless of the window size.

Because window size changes are detected and handled differently under various environments, the GLUT library provides the function `glutReshapeFunc`, which registers a callback that the GLUT library will call whenever the window dimensions change. The function you pass to `glutReshapeFunc` is prototyped like this:

```
void ChangeSize(GLsizei w, GLsizei h);
```

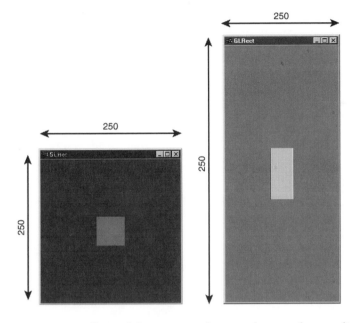

Figure 3.4 Effects of changing window size, but not the coordinate system.

We have chosen `ChangeSize` as a descriptive name for this function, and we use that name for our future examples.

The `ChangeSize` function receives the new width and height whenever the window size changes. We can use this information to modify the mapping of our desired coordinate system to real screen coordinates, with the help of two OpenGL functions: `glViewport` and `glOrtho`.

Defining the Viewport

To understand how the viewport definition is achieved, let's look more carefully at the `ChangeSize` function. It first calls `glViewport` with the new width and height of the window. The `glViewport` function is defined as

```
void glViewport(GLint x, GLint y, GLsizei width, GLsizei height);
```

The x and y parameters specify the lower-left corner of the viewport within the window, and the `width` and `height` parameters specify these dimensions in pixels. Usually, x and y are both zero, but you can use viewports to render more than one drawing in different areas of a window. The viewport defines the area within the window in actual screen coordinates that OpenGL can use to draw in (see Figure 3.5). The current clipping volume is then mapped to the new viewport. If you specify a viewport that is smaller than the window coordinates, the rendering is scaled smaller, as you see in Figure 3.5.

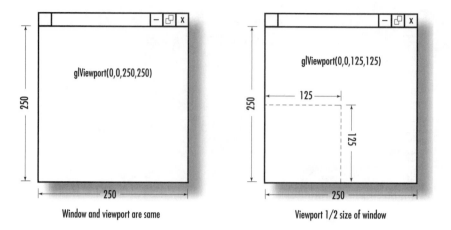

Figure 3.5 Viewport-to-window mapping.

Defining the Clipping Volume

The last requirement of our ChangeSize function is to redefine the clipping volume so that the aspect ratio remains square. The aspect ratio is the ratio of the number of pixels along a unit of length in the vertical direction to the number of pixels along the same unit of length in the horizontal direction. An aspect ratio of 1.0 defines a square aspect ratio. An aspect ratio of 0.5 specifies that for every two pixels in the horizontal direction for a unit of length, there is one pixel in the vertical direction for the same unit of length.

If a viewport is specified that is not square and it is mapped to a square clipping volume, then the image will be distorted. For example, a viewport matching the window size and dimensions but mapped to a square clipping volume would cause images to appear tall and thin in tall and thin windows and wide and short in wide and short windows. In this case, our square would only appear square when the window was sized to be a square.

In our example, an orthographic projection is used for the clipping volume (see Chapter 1). The OpenGL command to create this projection is glOrtho:

```
void glOrtho(GLdouble left, GLdouble right, GLdouble bottom,
             GLdouble top, GLdouble near, GLdouble far );
```

In 3D Cartesian space, the left and right values specify the minimum and maximum coordinate value displayed along the x-axis; bottom and top are for the y-axis. The near and far parameters are for the z-axis, generally with negative values extending away from the viewer (see Figure 3.6).

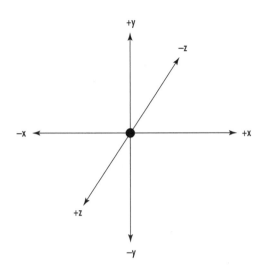

Figure 3.6 Cartesian space.

Just before the code using `glOrtho`, you'll notice these two function calls:

```
// Reset coordinate system
glMatrixMode(GL_PROJECTION);
glLoadIdentity();
```

The subject of matrices comes up in Chapter 5, "Moving Around in Space: Coordinate Transformations," and we discuss this in more detail. The projection matrix is where you actually define your viewing volume. The single call to `glLoadIdentity` is needed because `glOrtho` doesn't really establish the clipping volume, but rather modifies the existing clipping volume. It multiplies the matrix that describes the current clipping volume by the matrix that describes the clipping volume described in its arguments. For now, you just need to know that `glLoadIdentity` serves to "reset" the coordinate system before any matrix manipulations are performed. Without this "reset" every time `glOrtho` is called, each successive call to `glOrtho` could result in a further corruption of our intended clipping volume, which might not even display our rectangle.

The last two lines of code

```
glMatrixMode(GL_MODELVIEW);
glLoadIdentity();
```

tell OpenGL that all future transformations will affect our models (what we draw). We purposely do not cover model transformation until Chapter 5. You do need to know now, however, how to set up these things with their default values. Otherwise, if you get adventurous and start experimenting, your output might not match what you expect.

Keeping a Square Square

The following code does the actual work of keeping our "square" square.

```
if (w <= h)
glOrtho (0, 250, 0, 250*h/w, 1.0, -1.0);
else
glOrtho (0, 250*w/h, 0, 250, 1.0, -1.0);
```

Our clipping volume (visible coordinate space) is modified so that the left-hand side is always at x = 0. The right-hand side extends to 250 unless the window is wider than it is tall. In that case, the right-hand side is extended by the aspect ratio of the window. The bottom is always at y = 0 and extends upward to 250 unless the window is taller than it is wide. In that case, the upper coordinate is extended by the aspect ratio. This serves to keep a square coordinate region 250×250 available regardless of the shape of the window. Figure 3.7 shows how this works.

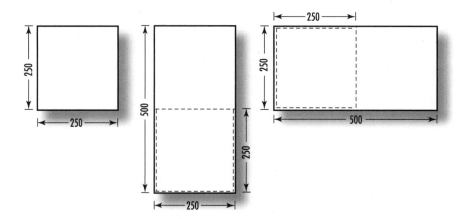

Figure 3.7 Clipping region for three different windows.

Animation with OpenGL and GLUT

So far, we've discussed the basics of using the GLUT library for creating a window and using OpenGL commands for the actual drawing. You will often want to move or rotate your images and scenes, creating an animated effect. Let's take the previous example, which draws a square, and make the square bounce off the sides of the window. You could create a loop that continually changes your object's coordinates before calling the RenderScene function. This would cause the square to appear to move around within the window.

The GLUT library provides the ability to register a callback function that makes it easier to set up a simple animated sequence. This function, glutTimerFunc, takes the name of a function to call and the amount of time to wait before calling the function:

```
void glutTimerFunc(unsigned int msecs, void (*func)(int value), int value);
```

This code sets up GLUT to wait msecs milliseconds before calling the function func. You can pass a user-defined value in the value parameter. The function called by the timer has the following prototype:

```
void TimerFunction(int value);
```

Unlike the Windows timer, this function is only fired once. To effect a continuous animation, you must reset the timer again in the timer function.

In our GLRECT program, we can change the hard-coded values for the location of our rectangle to variables and then constantly modify those variables in the timer function. This will cause the rectangle to appear to move across the window. Let's look at an example of this kind of animation. In Listing 3.3, we modify Listing 3.2 to bounce the square around off the inside borders of the window. We need to keep track of the position and size of the rectangle as we go along and account for any changes in window size.

Listing 3.3   *Animated Bouncing Square*

```
// Bounce.c
// Demonstrates a simple animated rectangle program with GLUT
// OpenGL SuperBible, 2nd Edition
// Richard S. Wright Jr.

#include <windows.h>
#include <gl/glut.h>

// Initial square position and size
GLfloat x1 = 100.0f;
GLfloat y1 = 150.0f;
GLsizei rsize = 50;

// Step size in x and y directions
// (number of pixels to move each time)
GLfloat xstep = 1.0f;
GLfloat ystep = 1.0f;

// Keep track of windows changing width and height
GLfloat windowWidth;
GLfloat windowHeight;
```

continued on next page

continued from previous page

```
// Called to draw scene
void RenderScene(void)
    {
    // Clear the window with current clearing color
    glClear(GL_COLOR_BUFFER_BIT);

        // Set current drawing color to red
    //            R     G      B
    glColor3f(1.0f, 0.0f, 0.0f);

    // Draw a filled rectangle with current color
    glRectf(x1, y1, x1+rsize, y1+rsize);

    // Flush drawing commands and swap
        glutSwapBuffers();
    }

// Called by GLUT library when idle (window not being
// resized or moved)
void TimerFunction(int value)
    {
    // Reverse direction when you reach left or right edge
    if(x1 > windowWidth-rsize ¦¦ x1 < 0)
        xstep = -xstep;

    // Reverse direction when you reach top or bottom edge
    if(y1 > windowHeight-rsize ¦¦ y1 < 0)
        ystep = -ystep;


    // Check bounds. This is in case the window is made
    // smaller and the rectangle is outside the new
    // clipping volume
    if(x1 > windowWidth-rsize)
        x1 = windowWidth-rsize-1;

    if(y1 > windowHeight-rsize)
        y1 = windowHeight-rsize-1;

    // Actually move the square
    x1 += xstep;
    y1 += ystep;

    // Redraw the scene with new coordinates
        glutPostRedisplay();
    glutTimerFunc(33,TimerFunction, 1);
```

```
    }

// Set up the rendering state
void SetupRC(void)
    {
    // Set clear color to blue
    glClearColor(0.0f, 0.0f, 1.0f, 1.0f);
    }



// Called by GLUT library when the window has changed size
void ChangeSize(GLsizei w, GLsizei h)
    {
    // Prevent a divide by zero
    if(h == 0)
        h = 1;

    // Set viewport to window dimensions
        glViewport(0, 0, w, h);

    // Reset coordinate system
    glMatrixMode(GL_PROJECTION);
    glLoadIdentity();

    // Keep the square square; this time, save calculated
    // width and height for later use
    if (w <= h)
        {
        windowHeight = 250.0f*h/w;
        windowWidth = 250.0f;
        }
else
        {
        windowWidth = 250.0f*w/h;
        windowHeight = 250.0f;
        }

    // Set the clipping volume
    glOrtho(0.0f, windowWidth, 0.0f, windowHeight, 1.0f, -1.0f);

    glMatrixMode(GL_MODELVIEW);
    glLoadIdentity();
    }
```

continued on next page

continued from previous page

```
// Main program entry point
void main(void)
    {
glutInitDisplayMode(GLUT_DOUBLE | GLUT_RGB);
    glutCreateWindow("Bounce");
    glutDisplayFunc(RenderScene);
glutReshapeFunc(ChangeSize);
glutTimerFunc(33, TimerFunction, 1);

    SetupRC();

    glutMainLoop();
    }
```

Double-Buffering

One of the most important features of any graphics packages is support for double buffering. This feature allows you to execute your drawing code while rendering to an offscreen buffer. Then, a swap command places your drawing onscreen instantly.

Double buffering can serve two purposes. The first is that some complex drawings might take a long time to draw and you might not want each step of the image composition to be visible. Using double buffering, you can compose an image and display it only after it is complete. The user never sees a partial image; only after the entire image is ready is it blasted to the screen.

A second use for double buffering is for animation. Each frame is drawn in the offscreen buffer and then swapped quickly to the screen when ready. The GLUT library supports double-buffered windows. Note in Listing 3.3 the line

```
glutInitDisplayMode(GLUT_DOUBLE | GLUT_RGB);
```

We have changed `GLUT_SINGLE` to `GLUT_DOUBLE`. This causes all the drawing code to render in an offscreen buffer.

Next, we also changed the end of our `RenderScene` function:

```
. . .
    // Flush drawing commands and swap
glutSwapBuffers();
    }
```

No longer are we calling `glFlush`. That's because when we perform a buffer swap, we are implicitly performing a flush operation.

These changes cause a smoothly animated bouncing rectangle, shown in Figure 3.8. The function `glutSwapBuffers` still performs the flush, even if you are running in single-buffered mode. Simply change `GLUT_DOUBLE` back to `GLUT_SINGLE` in the bounce sample to see the animation without double buffering. As you'll see, the rectangle is constantly blinking and stuttering, a very unpleasant and poor animation with single buffering.

Figure 3.8 Follow the bouncing square.

Finally Some 3D!

So far, all our samples have been simple rectangles in the middle of the window; they either scaled to the new window size or bounced around off the walls. By now, you might be bouncing off some walls of your own, waiting anxiously to see something in 3D. Wait no more!

As mentioned earlier, we have been drawing in 3D all along, but our view of the rectangle has been perpendicular to the clipping volume. If we could just rotate the clipping volume with respect to the viewer, we might actually see something with a little depth. However, we aren't going to get into coordinate transformations and rotations until Chapter 5. And even if we started that work now, a flat rectangle isn't very interesting, even when viewed from an angle.

To see some depth, we need to draw an object that is not flat. The GLUT library contains nearly a dozen 3D objects—from a sphere to a teapot—that can be created with a single function call. These functions are of the form `glutSolidxxxx` or `glutWirexxxx`, where `xxxx` names the solid or wireframe object that is created. For example, the following command draws a wireframe teapot of approximately 1.0 units in diameter:

```
glutWireTeapot(1.0f);
```

If we define a clipping volume that extends from -100 to 100 along all three axes, we get the wireframe teapot shown in Figure 3.9. The teapot is probably the best example at this point because the other objects still look two-dimensional when viewed from a parallel projection. The program that produced this image is found in this chapter's subdirectory on the CD-ROM in shapes.c.

Figure 3.9 A wireframe teapot.

In this sample program, we cheated big time! There are a lot of things in this program we haven't covered yet. A GLUT-based pop-up menu (right-click in the window) lets you select between a wireframe or solid version of all the GLUT predefined objects. We added lighting effects (Chapter 6, "Color, Lighting, and Materials") so you can see the surface of the solid 3D objects, and we've added modelview transformations (Chapter 7, "Raster Graphics in OpenGL") so you can rotate the object around (use the arrow keys) to see the 3D effect. Figure 3.10 shows these effects taken together.

Figure 3.10 A fully lit and transformed solid teapot.

Hey, we have to whet your appetite for what comes later in the book!

Summary

In this chapter, we introduced GLUT, the OpenGL utility toolkit, and presented the fundamentals of writing a program that uses OpenGL. We used this library to show the easiest possible way to create a window and draw in it using OpenGL commands. You learned to use the GLUT library to create windows that can be resized, as well as create a simple animation. You were also introduced to the process of using OpenGL to do drawing—composing and selecting colors, clearing the screen, drawing a rectangle, and setting the viewport and clipping volume to scale images to match the window size. We discussed the various OpenGL data types and the headers and libraries required to build programs that use OpenGL.

The GLUT library contains many other functions to handle keyboard and mouse input as well. You are encouraged to explore the upcoming reference section of this chapter to discover some of the other uses and features of the GLUT library. The GLUT library distribution on the CD is fully documented and contains a plethora of other functions and features. There are even some additional toolkits built on GLUT included with sample programs.

With this foundation, we move forward in the chapters ahead. You'll learn more about creating viewing volumes, drawing points and lines, and moving objects without having to manually change (*transform*) the position of your models (or rectangles!).

Reference Section

glClearColor

Purpose	Sets the color and alpha values to use for clearing the color buffers.
Include File	<gl.h>
Syntax	void glClearColor(GLclampf red, GLclampf green, GLclampf blue, GLclampf alpha);
Description	Sets the fill values to be used when clearing the red, green, blue, and alpha buffers (jointly called the color buffer). The values specified are clamped to the range [0.0f, 1.0f].
Parameters	
red	GLclampf: The red component of the fill value.
green	GLclampf: The green component of the fill value.
blue	GLclampf: The blue component of the fill value.
alpha	GLclampf: The alpha component of the fill value.
Returns	None.
Example	See the GLRECT example from this chapter.

glFlush

Purpose	Flushes OpenGL command queues and buffers.
Include File	<gl.h>
Syntax	void glFlush(void);

Description	OpenGL commands are often queued and executed in batches to optimize performance. This can vary among hardware, drivers, and OpenGL implementations. The `glFlush` command causes any waiting commands to be executed.
Returns	None.
Example	See the SIMPLE example from this chapter.

glOrtho

Purpose	Sets or modifies the clipping volume extents.
Include File	<gl.h>
Syntax	void glOrtho(GLdouble *left*, GLdouble *right*, GLdouble *bottom*, GLdouble *top*, GLdouble *near*, GLdouble *far*);
Description	This function describes a parallel clipping volume. This projection means that objects far from the viewer do not appear smaller (in contrast to a perspective projection). Think of the clipping volume in terms of 3D Cartesian coordinates, in which case left and right are the minimum and maximum x values, top and bottom the minimum and maximum y values, and near and far the minimum and maximum z values.
Parameters	
left	GLdouble: The leftmost coordinate of the clipping volume.
right	GLdouble: The rightmost coordinate of the clipping volume.
bottom	GLdouble: The bottommost coordinate of the clipping volume.
top	GLdouble: The topmost coordinate of the clipping volume.
near	GLdouble: The maximum distance from the origin to the viewer.
far	GLdouble: The maximum distance from the origin away from the viewer.
Returns	None.
Example	See any sample program from this chapter.
See Also	glViewport

glViewport

Purpose	Sets the portion of a window that can be drawn in by OpenGL.
Include File	<gl.h>
Syntax	void glViewport(GLint *x*, GLint *y*, GLsizei *width*, GLsizei *height*);
Description	Sets the region within a window that is used for mapping the clipping volume coordinates to physical window coordinates.

Parameters

x	GLint: The number of pixels from the left side of the window to start the viewport.
y	GLint: The number of pixels from the bottom of the window to start the viewport.
width	GLsizei: The width in pixels of the viewport.
height	GLsizei: The height in pixels of the viewport.
Returns	None.
Example	See any sample program from this chapter.
See Also	glOrtho

glRect

Purpose	Draws a flat rectangle.
Include File	<gl.h>
Variations	void glRectd(GLdouble *x1*, GLdouble *y1*, GLdouble *x2*, GLdouble *y2*); void glRectf(GLfloat *x1*, GLfloat *y1*, GLfloat *x2*, GLfloat *y2*); void glRecti(GLint *x1*, GLint *y1*, GLint *x2*, GLint *y2*); void glRects(GLshort *x1*, GLshort *y1*, GLshort *x1*, GLshort *y2*); void glRectdv(const GLdouble **v1*, const GLdouble **v2*); void glRectfv(const GLfloat **v1*, const GLfloat **v2*); void glRectiv(const GLint **v1*, const GLint **v2*); void glRectsv(const GLshort **v1*, const GLshort **v2*);
Description	This function is an efficient method of specifying a rectangle as two corner points. The rectangle is drawn in the xy plane at z = 0.
Parameters	
x1, y1	Specifies the upper-left corner of the rectangle.
x2, y2	Specifies the lower-right corner of the rectangle.
*v1	An array of two values specifying the upper-left corner of the rectangle. Could also be described as v1[2].
*v2	An array of two values specifying the lower-right corner of the rectangle. Could also be described as v2[2].
Returns	None.
Example	See the GLRECT sample from this chapter.

glutCreateWindow

Purpose	Creates an OpenGL enabled window.
Include File	<glut.h>
Syntax	`void glutCreateWindow(char *name);`
Description	This function creates a top-level window in GLUT. This is considered the *current* window.
Parameters	
name	`char *`: The caption the window is to bear.
Returns	None.
Example	See any sample program from this chapter.
See Also	`glutInitDisplayMode`

glutDisplayFunc

Purpose	Sets the display callback function for the current window.
Include File	<glut.h>
Syntax	`void glutDisplayFunc(void (*func)(void);`
Description	This function tells GLUT which function to call whenever the windows contents must be drawn. This can occur when the window is resized or uncovered or when GLUT is specifically asked to refresh with a call to the `glutPostRedisplay` function. Note that GLUT does not explicitly call a `glFlush` or a `glutSwapBuffers` for you after this function is called.
Parameters	
func	`(*func)(void)`: The name of the function that does the rendering.
Returns	None.
Example	See any sample program from this chapter.
See Also	`glFlush, glutSwapBuffers, glutReshapeFunc`

glutInitDisplayMode

Purpose	Initializes the display mode of the GLUT library OpenGL window.
Include File	<glut.h>
Syntax	`void glutInitDisplayMode(unsigned int mode);`
Description	This is the first function that must be called by a GLUT-based program to set up the OpenGL window. This function sets the characteristics of the window that OpenGL will use for drawing operations.

Parameters

mode   `unsigned int`: A mask or bitwise combination of masks from Table 3.3. These mask values may be combined with a bitwise `OR`.

Returns   None.

Example   To create a window that uses double buffering and RGBA color mode, call

```
glutInitDisplayMode(GLUT_DOUBLE | GLUT_RGBA);
```

See Also   `glutCreateWindow`

Table 3.3   *Mask Values for Window Characteristics*

Mask Value	Meaning
`GLUT_SINGLE`	Specifies a single-buffered window
`GLUT_DOUBLE`	Specifies a double-buffered window
`GLUT_RGBA`	Specifies an RGBA-mode window
`GLUT_DEPTH`	Specifies a 32-bit depth buffer
`GLUT_STENCIL`	Specifies a stencil buffer
`GLUT_ACCUM`	Specifies an accumulation buffer
`GLUT_ALPHA`	Specifies a destination alpha buffer

glutKeyboardFunc

Purpose   Sets the keyboard callback function for the current window.

Include File   <glut.h>

Syntax   `void glutKeyboardFunc(void (*func)(unsigned char key, int x, int y);`

Description   This function establishes a call back function called by GLUT whenever one of the ASCII generating keys is pressed. Non-ASCII generating keys such as the Shift key are handled by the `glutSpecialFunc` callback. In addition to the ASCII value of the keystroke, the current x and y position of the mouse are returned.

Parameters

func   `(*func)(unsigned char key, int x, int y)`: The name of the function to be called by GLUT when a keystroke occurs.

Returns   None.

Example   The following code shows a keystroke handler being defined and registered with GLUT:

```
void KeyboardHandler(unsigned char key, int x, int y)
    {
    . . .
    }

glutKeyboardFunc(KeyboardHandler);
```

See Also   glutSpecialFunc, glutMouseFunc

glutMainLoop

Purpose	Starts the main GLUT processing loop.
Include File	<glut.h>
Syntax	void glutMainLoop(void);
Description	This function begins the main GLUT event-handling loop. The event loop is where all keyboard, mouse, timer, redraw, and other window messages are handled. This function does not return until program termination.
Parameters	None.
Returns	None.
Example	See any sample program from this chapter.

glutMouseFunc

Purpose	Sets the mouse callback function for the current window.
Include File	<glut.h>
Syntax	void glutMouseFunc(void (*func)(int *button*, int *state*, int *x*, int y);
Description	This function establishes a callback function called by GLUT whenever a mouse event occurs. Three values are valid for the button parameter: GLUT_LEFT_BUTTON, GLUT_MIDDLE_BUTTON, and GLUT_RIGHT_BUTTON. The state parameter is either GLUT_UP or GLUT_DOWN.
Parameters	
func	(*func)(int *button*, int *state*, int *x*, int y): The name of the function to be called by GLUT when a mouse event occurs.
Returns	None.
Example	The following code shows a mouse event handler being defined and registered with GLUT. The mouse handler tests for the left mouse button being pressed. If so, the program sounds a beep (MessageBeep is a Windows API call):

```
void MouseHandler(int button, int state, int x, int y)
    {
    if(button == GLUT_LEFT_BUTTON && state == GLUT_DOWN)
        MessageBeep(-1);
    . . .
    }

glutMouseFunc(MouseHandler);
```

See Also   `glutSpecialFunc, glutKeyboardFunc`

glutReshapeFunc

Purpose	Sets the window reshape callback function for the current window.
Include File	<glut.h>
Syntax	`void glutReshapeFunc(void (*func)(int width, int height);`
Description	This function establishes a callback function called by GLUT whenever the window changes size or shape (including at least once when the window is created). The callback function receives the new width and height of the window.
Parameters	
func	`(*func)(int x, int y)`: The name of the function to be called by GLUT when the window size changes.
Returns	None.
Example	See any sample program from this chapter.
See Also	`glutDisplayFunc`

glutPostRedisplay

Purpose	Tells GLUT to refresh the current window.
Include File	<glut.h>
Syntax	`void glutPostRedisplay(void);`
Description	This function informs the GLUT library that the current window needs to be refreshed. Multiple calls to this function before the next refresh result in only one repainting of the window.
Parameters	None.
Returns	None.
Example	See the bounce sample from this chapter.
See Also	`glutDisplayFunc`

glutSolidCone, glutWireCone

Purpose	Draws a solid or wireframe cone.
Include File	<glut.h>
Syntax	void glutSolidCone(GLdouble *base*, GLdouble *height*, GLint *slices*, GLint *stacks*); void glutWireCone(GLdouble *base*, GLdouble *height*, GLint *slices*, GLint *stacks*);
Description	Draws a solid or wire cone. The base of the cone is at the origin (0,0,0); the top of the cone is measured along the z axis.
Parameters	
base	GLdouble: The radius of the bottom of the cone.
height	GLdouble: The height of the cone.
slices	GLint: Number of subdivisions around the z axis.
stacks	GLint: Number of subdivisions along the z axis.
Returns	None.
Example	See the shapes sample. This program exercises all of the GLUT library's solid and wireframe objects.

glutSolidCube, glutWireCube

Purpose	Draws a solid or wireframe cube.
Include File	<glut.h>
Syntax	void glutSolidCube(GLdouble *size*); void glutWireCube(GLdouble *size*);
Description	Draws a solid or wire cube at the origin (0,0,0). The cube extends from the origin to +/- size/2.0 along the x, y, and z axis.
Parameters	
size	GLdouble: The length of the sides of the cube.
Returns	None.
Example	See the shapes sample. This program exercises all of the GLUT library's solid and wireframe objects.

glutSolidDodecahedron, glutWireDodecahedron

Purpose	Draws a solid or wireframe dodecahedron.
Include File	<glut.h>

Syntax	`void glutSolidDodecahedron(void);`
	`void glutWireDodecahedron(void);`
Description	Draws a solid or wire dodecahedron. A dodecahedron is a 12-sided closed solid. The center of the dodecahedron is at the origin (0,0,0), and the radius is the square root of 3.
Parameters	None.
Returns	None.
Example	See the shapes sample. This program exercises all of the GLUT library's solid and wireframe objects.

glutSolidIcosahedron, glutWireIcosahedron

Purpose	Draws a solid or wireframe icosahedron.
Include File	<glut.h>
Syntax	`void glutSolidIcosahedron(void);`
	`void glutWireIcosahedron(void);`
Description	Draws a solid or wire icosahedron. An icosahedron is a 20-sided closed solid. The center of the icosahedron is at the origin (0,0,0) and has a radius of 1.0.
Parameters	None.
Returns	None.
Example	See the shapes sample. This program exercises all of the GLUT library's solid and wireframe objects.

glutSolidOctahedron, glutWireOctahedron

Purpose	Draws a solid or wireframe octahedron.
Include File	<glut.h>
Syntax	`void glutSolidOctahedron(void);`
	`void glutWireOctahedron(void);`
Description	Draws a solid or wire octahedron. An octahedron is an eight-sided closed solid. The center of the octahedron is at the origin (0,0,0) and has a radius of 1.0.
Parameters	None.
Returns	None.
Example	See the shapes sample. This program exercises all of the GLUT library's solid and wireframe objects.

glutSolidSphere, glutWireSphere

Purpose	Draws a wireframe sphere.
Include File	<glut32.h>
Syntax	void glutWireSphere(GLdouble *radius*, GLint *slices*, GLint *stacks*); void glutSolidSphere(GLdouble *radius*, GLint *slices*, GLint *stacks*);
Description	Draws a solid or wireframe sphere centered at (0,0,0) with a radius of 1.0. The smoothness of the sphere is determined by the number of subdivisions around and along the z axis.
Parameters	
radius	GLdouble: The radius of the sphere.
slices	GLdouble: The number of subdivisions around the z axis of the sphere. These are like lines of longitude on a globe.
stacks	GLdouble: The number of subdivisions along the z axis. These are like lines of latitude on a globe.
Returns	None.
Example	See the shapes sample. This program exercises all of the GLUT library's solid and wireframe objects.

glutSolidTetrahedron, glutWireTetrahedron

Purpose	Draws a solid or wireframe tetrahedron.
Include File	<glut.h>
Syntax	void glutSolidTetrahedron(void); void glutWireTetrahedron(void);
Description	Draws a solid or wire tetrahedron. A tetrahedron is a four-sided closed solid. The center of the tetrahedron is at the origin (0,0,0), and the radius is the square root of 3.
Parameters	None.
Returns	None.
Example	See the shapes sample. This program exercises all of the GLUT library's solid and wireframe objects.

glutSolidTorus, glutWireTorus

Purpose	Draws a solid or wireframe torus.
Include File	<glut.h>

Syntax	`void glutSolidTorus(GLdouble innerRadius, GLdouble outerRadius, GLint nSides, GLint nRings);` `void glutWireTorus(GLdouble innerRadius, GLdouble outerRadius, GLint nSides, GLint nRings);`
Description	Draws a solid or wireframe torus. A torus is shaped like a doughnut or an automobile tire inner tube. The smoothness of the torus surface is determined by the number of sides for each radial section and the number of radial divisions.
Parameters	
innerRadius	`GLdouble`: The radius of the inner rings.
outerRadius	`GLdouble`: The outer radius of the torus.
nSides	`GLint`: The number of subdivisions for each radial section.
nRings	`GLint`: The number of radial sections.
Returns	None.
Example	See the shapes sample. This program exercises all of the GLUT library's solid and wireframe objects.

glutSolidTeapot, glutWireTeapot

Purpose	Draws a solid or wireframe teapot.
Include File	<glut.h>
Syntax	`void glutSolidTeapot(GLdouble size);` `void glutWireTeapot(GLdouble size);`
Description	Draws a solid or wireframe teapot. This is the famous teapot seen so widely in computer graphics samples. In addition to surface normals for lighting, texture coordinates are also generated.
Parameters	
size	`GLdouble`: The approximate radius of the teapot. A sphere of this radius would totally enclose the model.
Returns	None.
Example	See the shapes sample. This program exercises all of the GLUT library's solid and wireframe objects.

glutSpecialFunc

Purpose	Sets a special keyboard callback function for the current window for non-ASCII keystrokes.
Include File	<glut.h>

Syntax	void glutSpecialFunc(void (*func)(int *key*, int *x*, int *y*);
Description	This function establishes a callback function called by GLUT whenever one of the non-ASCII generating keys is pressed. Non-ASCII generating keys are keystrokes such as the Shift key, which can't be identified by an ASCII value. In addition, the current x and y position of the mouse are returned. Valid values for the key parameter are listed in Table 3.4.
Parameters	
func	(*func)(int *key*, int *x*, int *y*): The name of the function to be called by GLUT when a non-ASCII keystroke occurs.
Returns	None.
Example	The following code shows a special keystroke handler being defined and registered with GLUT. The function sounds a beep when the F1 key is pressed (MessageBeep is a Windows API function call):

```
void SpecialKeyHandler(int key, int x, int y)
    {
    if(key == GLUT_KEY_F1)
    MessageBeep(-1);
    . . .
    }

glutSpecialFunc(SpedialKeyHandler);
```

See Also	glutKeyboardFunc, glutMouseFunc

Table 3.4 *Non-ASCII Key Values Passed to the* glutSpecialFunc *Callback*

Key Value	Keystroke
GLUT_KEY_F1	F1 key
GLUT_KEY_F2	F2 key
GLUT_KEY_F3	F3 key
GLUT_KEY_F4	F4 key
GLUT_KEY_F5	F5 key
GLUT_KEY_F6	F6 key
GLUT_KEY_F7	F7 key
GLUT_KEY_F8	F8 key
GLUT_KEY_F9	F9 key
GLUT_KEY_F10	F10 key
GLUT_KEY_F11	F11 key
GLUT_KEY_F12	F12 key
GLUT_KEY_LEFT	Left arrow key

Key Value	Keystroke
GLUT_KEY_RIGHT	Right arrow key
GLUT_KEY_UP	Up arrow key
GLUT_KEY_DOWN	Down arrow key
GLUT_KEY_PAGE_UP	Page Up key
GLUT_KEY_PAGE_DOWN	Page Down key
GLUT_KEY_HOME	Home key
GLUT_KEY_END	End key
GLUT_KEY_INSERT	Insert key

glutSwapBuffers

Purpose	Performs a buffer swap in double-buffered mode.
Include File	<glut.h>
Syntax	`void glutSwapBuffers(void);`
Description	When the current GLUT window is operating in double-buffered mode, this function performs a flush of the OpenGL pipeline and does a buffer swap (places the hidden rendered image onscreen). If the current window is not in double-buffered mode, a flush of the pipeline is still performed.
Parameters	None.
Returns	None.
Example	See the bounce sample from this chapter.
See Also	`glutDisplayFunc`

glutTimerFunc

Purpose	Registers a callback function to be called by GLUT after the timeout value expires.
Include File	<glut.h>
Syntax	`void glutTimerFunc(unsigned int msecs, (*func)(int value),int value);`
Description	This function registers a callback function that should be called after *msecs* milliseconds have elapsed. The callback function is passed the user-specified value in the *value* parameter.
Parameters	
msecs	`unsigned int`: The number of milliseconds to wait before calling the specified function.

func	`void (*func)(int value)`: The name of the function to be called when the timeout value expires.
value	`int`: User-specified value passed to the callback function when it is executed.
Returns	None.
Example	See the bounce sample from this chapter.

4

DRAWING IN SPACE: LINES, POINTS, AND POLYGONS

by Richard S. Wright, Jr.

What you'll learn in this chapter:

How To...	Functions You'll Use
Draw points, lines, and shapes	`glBegin/glEnd/glVertex`
Set shape outlines to wireframe or solid objects	`glPolygonMode`
Set point sizes for drawing	`glPointSize`
Set line drawing width	`glLineWidth`
Perform hidden surface removal	`glCullFace`
Set patterns for broken lines	`glLineStipple`
Set polygon fill patterns	`glPolygonStipple`

If you've ever had a chemistry class (and probably even if you haven't), you know that all matter consists of atoms and that all atoms consist of only three things: protons, neutrons, and electrons. All the materials and substances you have ever come into contact with—from the petals of a rose to the sand on the beach—are just different arrangements of these three fundamental building blocks. Although this explanation is a little oversimplified for almost anyone beyond the third or fourth grade, it demonstrates a powerful principle: With just a few simple building blocks, you can create highly complex and beautiful structures.

The connection is fairly obvious. Objects and scenes that you create with OpenGL also consist of smaller, simpler shapes, arranged and combined in various and unique ways. This chapter explores these building blocks of 3D objects, called *primitives*. All primitives in OpenGL are one- or two-dimensional objects, ranging from single points to lines and complex polygons. In this chapter, you will learn everything you need to know to draw objects in three dimensions from these simpler shapes.

Drawing Points in 3D

When you first learned to draw any kind of graphics on any computer system, you probably started with pixels. A pixel is the smallest element on your computer monitor, and on color systems, that pixel can be any one of many available colors. This is computer graphics at its simplest: Draw a point somewhere on the screen, and make it a specific color. Then, build on this simple concept, using your favorite computer language to produce lines, polygons, circles, and other shapes and graphics. Perhaps even a GUI....

With OpenGL, however, drawing on the computer screen is fundamentally different. You're not concerned with physical screen coordinates and pixels, but rather positional coordinates in your viewing volume. You let OpenGL worry about how to get your points, lines, and everything else translated from your established 3D space to the 2D image made by your computer screen.

This chapter and the next cover the most fundamental concepts of OpenGL or any 3D graphics toolkit. In the upcoming chapter, we provide substantial detail about how this transformation from 3D space to the 2D landscape of your computer monitor takes place, as well as how to transform (rotate, translate, and scale) your objects. For now, we take this ability for granted in order to focus on plotting and drawing in a 3D coordinate system. This approach might seem backwards, but if you first know how to draw something and then worry about all the ways to manipulate your drawings, the material in Chapter 5, "Moving Around in Space: Coordinate Transformations," is more interesting and easier to learn. Once you have a solid understanding of graphics primitives and coordinate transformations, you will be able to quickly master any 3D graphics language or API.

Setting Up a 3D Canvas

Figure 4.1 shows a simple viewing volume that we use for the examples in this chapter. The area enclosed by this volume is a Cartesian coordinate space that ranges from −100 to +100 on all three axes, x, y, and z. (For a review of Cartesian coordinates, see Chapter 1, "3D Graphics Fundamentals.") Think of this viewing volume as your three-dimensional canvas on which you draw with OpenGL commands and functions.

We established this volume with a call to glOrtho, much as we did for others in the previous chapters. Listing 4.1 shows the code for the ChangeSize function that gets called when the window is sized (including when it is first created). This code looks a little different from that in previous chapters, and you'll notice some unfamiliar functions (glMatrixMode, glLoadIdentity). We spend more time on these in Chapter 5, exploring their operation in more detail.

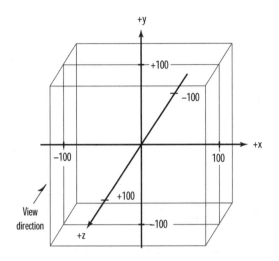

Figure 4.1 Cartesian viewing volume measuring 100×100×100.

Listing 4.1 *Code to Establish the Viewing Volume in Figure 4.1*

```
// Change viewing volume and viewport.  Called when window is resized
void ChangeSize(GLsizei w, GLsizei h)
    {
    GLfloat nRange = 100.0f;

    // Prevent a divide by zero
    if(h == 0)
        h = 1;

    // Set Viewport to window dimensions
        glViewport(0, 0, w, h);

    // Reset projection matrix stack
    glMatrixMode(GL_PROJECTION);
    glLoadIdentity();

    // Establish clipping volume (left, right, bottom, top, near, far)
        if (w <= h)
        glOrtho (-nRange, nRange, -nRange*h/w, nRange*h/w, -nRange, nRange);
else
```

continued on next page

continued from previous page

```
        glOrtho (-nRange*w/h, nRange*w/h, -nRange, nRange, -nRange, nRange);

// Reset Model view matrix stack
glMatrixMode(GL_MODELVIEW);
glLoadIdentity();
}
```

> ## WHY THE CART BEFORE THE HORSE?
>
> Look at any of the source code in this chapter, and you'll notice some new functions in the RenderScene functions: glRotate, glPushMatrix, and glPopMatrix. Although they're covered in more detail in Chapter 5, we're introducing them now. They implement some important features that we want you to have as soon as possible. These functions let you plot and draw in 3D and help you easily visualize your drawing from different angles. All of this chapter's sample programs employ the arrow keys for rotating the drawing around the x- and y-axes. Look at any 3D drawing dead-on (straight down the z-axis), and it might still look two-dimensional. But when you can spin the drawings around in space, it's much easier to see the 3D effects of what you're drawing.
>
> There is a lot to learn about drawing in 3D, and in this chapter, we want you to focus on that. By changing only the drawing code for any of the examples that follow, you can start experimenting right away with 3D drawing and still get interesting results. Later, you'll learn how to manipulate drawings using the other functions.

A 3D Point: the Vertex

To specify a drawing point in this 3D "palette," we use the OpenGL function glVertex—without a doubt the most used function in all of the OpenGL API. This is the "lowest common denominator" of all the OpenGL primitives: a single point in space. The glVertex function can take from two to four parameters of any numerical type, from bytes to doubles, subject to the naming conventions discussed in Chapter 3, "Using OpenGL."

The following single line of code specifies a point in our coordinate system located 50 units along the x-axis, 50 units along the y-axis, and 0 units out the z-axis:

```
glVertex3f(50.0f, 50.0f, 0.0f);
```

Figure 4.2 illustrates this point. Here, we chose to represent the coordinates as floating-point values, as we do for the remainder of the book. Also, the form of glVertex that we use takes three arguments for the x, y, and z coordinate values, respectively.

Two other forms of glVertex take two and four arguments, respectively. We can represent the same point in Figure 4.2 with this code:

```
glVertex2f(50.0f, 50.0f);
```

This form of glVertex takes only two arguments that specify the x and y values and assumes the z coordinate to be 0.0 always. The form of glVertex taking four arguments, glVertex4, uses a fourth coordinate value w (set to 1.0 by default when not specified) for scaling purposes. You will learn more about this in Chapter 5 when we spend more time exploring coordinate transformations.

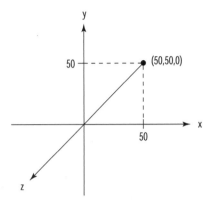

Figure 4.2   The point (50,50,0) as specified by glVertex3f(50.0f, 50.0f, 0.0f).

Draw Something!

Now, we have a way of specifying a point in space to OpenGL. What can we make of it, and how do we tell OpenGL what to do with it? Is this vertex a point that should just be plotted? Is it the endpoint of a line or the corner of a cube? The geometric definition of a vertex is not just a point in space, but rather the point at which an intersection of two lines or curves occurs. This is the essence of primitives.

A primitive is simply the interpretation of a set or list of vertices into some shape drawn on the screen. There are ten primitives in OpenGL, from a simple point drawn in space to a closed polygon of any number of sides. You use the glBegin command to tell OpenGL to begin interpreting a list of vertices as a particular primitive. You then end the list of vertices for that primitive with the glEnd command. Kind of intuitive, don't you think?

Drawing Points

Let's begin with the first and simplest of primitives: points. Look at the following code:

```
glBegin(GL_POINTS);                 // Select points as the primitive
    glVertex3f(0.0f, 0.0f, 0.0f);       // Specify a point
    glVertex3f(50.0f, 50.0f, 50.0f);    // Specify another point
glEnd();                        // Done drawing points
```

The argument to glBegin, GL_POINTS, tells OpenGL that the following vertices are to be interpreted and drawn as points. Two vertices are listed here, which translates to two specific points, both of which would be drawn.

This brings up an important point about glBegin and glEnd: You can list multiple primitives between calls as long as they are for the same primitive type. In this way, with a single glBegin/glEnd sequence, you can include as many primitives as you like. This next code segment is wasteful and will execute more slowly than the preceding code:

```
glBegin(GL_POINTS);          // Specify point drawing
    glVertex3f(0.0f, 0.0f, 0.0f);
glEnd();

glBegin(GL_POINTS);          // Specify another point
    glVertex3f(50.0f, 50.0f, 50.0f);
glEnd()
```

INDENTING YOUR CODE

In the foregoing examples, did you notice the indenting style used for the calls to glVertex? This convention is used by most OpenGL programmers to make the code easier to read. It is not required, but it does make it easier to find where primitives start and stop.

Our First Example

The code in Listing 4.2 draws some points in our 3D environment. It uses some simple trigonometry to draw a series of points that form a corkscrew path up the z-axis. This code is from the POINTS program, which is on the CD in the subdirectory for this chapter. All of the sample programs use the framework we established in Chapter 3. Notice that in the SetupRC function, we are setting the current drawing color to green.

Listing 4.2   *Rendering Code to Produce a Spring-Shaped Path of Points*

```
// Define a constant for the value of PI
#define GL_PI 3.1415f

// This function does any needed initialization on the rendering
// context.
void SetupRC()
    {
    // Black background
    glClearColor(0.0f, 0.0f, 0.0f, 1.0f );

    // Set drawing color to green
    glColor3f(0.0f, 1.0f, 0.0f);
```

```
}


// Called to draw scene
void RenderScene(void)
    {
    GLfloat x,y,z,angle; // Storage for coordinates and angles

    // Clear the window with current clearing color
    glClear(GL_COLOR_BUFFER_BIT);

    // Save matrix state and do the rotation
    glPushMatrix();
    glRotatef(xRot, 1.0f, 0.0f, 0.0f);
    glRotatef(yRot, 0.0f, 1.0f, 0.0f);

    // Call only once for all remaining points
    glBegin(GL_POINTS);

    z = -50.0f;
    for(angle = 0.0f; angle <= (2.0f*GL_PI)*3.0f; angle += 0.1f)
        {
        x = 50.0f*sin(angle);
        y = 50.0f*cos(angle);

        // Specify the point and move the Z value up a little
        glVertex3f(x, y, z);
        z += 0.5f;
        }

    // Done drawing points
    glEnd();

    // Restore transformations
    glPopMatrix();

    // Flush drawing commands
    glFlush();
    }
```

Only the code between calls to glBegin and glEnd is important for our purpose in this and the other examples for this chapter. This code calculates the x and y coordinates for an angle that spins between 0° and 360° three times. We express this programmatically in radians rather than degrees; if you don't know trigonometry, you can take our word for it. If you're interested, see the box, "The Trigonometry of Radians/Degrees." Each time a point is drawn, the z value is increased slightly. When this program is run, all you see is a circle of points because you are initially looking directly down the z-axis. To see the effect, use the arrow keys to spin the drawing around the x- and y-axes. The effect is illustrated in Figure 4.3.

Figure 4.3 Output from the POINTS sample program.

ONE THING AT A TIME

Again, don't get too distracted by the functions in this sample that we haven't covered yet (glPushMatrix, glPopMatrix, and glRotate). These functions are used to rotate the image around so you can better see the positioning of the points as they are drawn in 3D space. We cover these functions in some detail in Chapter 5. If we hadn't used these features now, you wouldn't be able to see the effects of your 3D drawings, and this and the following sample programs wouldn't be very interesting to look at. For the rest of the sample code in this chapter, we only show the code that includes the glBegin and glEnd statements.

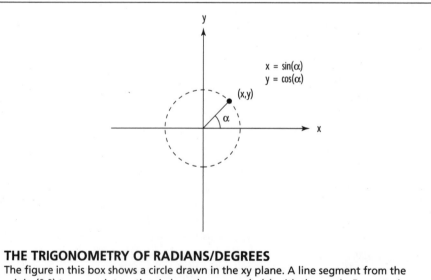

$$x = \sin(\alpha)$$
$$y = \cos(\alpha)$$

THE TRIGONOMETRY OF RADIANS/DEGREES

The figure in this box shows a circle drawn in the xy plane. A line segment from the origin (0,0) to any point on the circle makes an angle (a) with the x-axis. For any given angle, the trigonometric functions sine and cosine return the x and y values of the point on the circle. By stepping a variable that represents the angle all the way around the origin, we can calculate all the points on the circle. Note that the C runtime functions sin() and cos() accept angle values measured in radians instead of degrees. There are 2*PI radians in a circle, where PI is a nonrational number that is approximately 3.1415. (Nonrational means there are an infinite number of values past the decimal point.)

Setting the Point Size

When you draw a single point, the size of the point is one pixel by default. You can change this with the function `glPointSize`:

```
void glPointSize(GLfloat size);
```

The `glPointSize` function takes a single parameter that specifies the approximate diameter in pixels of the point drawn. Not all point sizes are supported, however, and you should make sure the point size you specify is available. Use the following code to get the range of point sizes and the smallest interval between them:

```
GLfloat sizes[2];      // Store supported point size range
GLfloat step;          // Store supported point size increments

// Get supported point size range and step size
glGetFloatv(GL_POINT_SIZE_RANGE,sizes);
glGetFloatv(GL_POINT_SIZE_GRANULARITY,&step);
```

Here, the sizes array will contain two elements that contain the smallest and the largest valid value for `glPointsize`. In addition, the variable step will hold the smallest step size allowable between the point sizes. The OpenGL specification only requires that one point size, 1.0, be supported. The Microsoft software implementation of OpenGL, for example, allows for point sizes from 0.5 to 10.0, with 0.125 the smallest step size. Specifying a size out of range is not interpreted as an error. Instead, the largest or smallest supported size is used, whichever is closest to the value specified.

OPENGL STATE VARIABLES

As we discussed in Chapter 2, "What Is OpenGL?" OpenGL maintains the state of many of its internal variables and settings. This collection of settings is called the OpenGL State Machine. You can query the State Machine to determine the state of any of its variables and settings. Any feature or capability you enable or disable with `glEnable`/`glDisable`, as well as numeric settings set with `glSet`, can be queried with the many variations of `glGet`.

Let's look at a sample that uses these new functions. The code in Listing 4.3 produces the same spiral shape as our first example, but this time, the point sizes are gradually increased from the smallest valid size to the largest valid size. This example is from the program POINTSZ in the CD subdirectory for this chapter. The output from POINTSZ shown in Figure 4.4 was run on Microsoft's software implementation of OpenGL. Figure 4.5 shows the same program run on a hardware accelerator that supports much larger point sizes.

Figure 4.4   Output from the POINTSZ program.

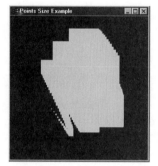

Figure 4.5   Output from POINTSZ on hardware supporting much larger point sizes.

Listing 4.3   *Code from POINTSZ That Produces a Spiral with Gradually Increasing Point Sizes*

```
// Define a constant for the value of PI
#define GL_PI 3.1415f

// Called to draw scene
void RenderScene(void)
    {
    GLfloat x,y,z,angle;    // Storage for coordinates and angles
    GLfloat sizes[2];     // Store supported point size range
    GLfloat step;         // Store supported point size increments
    GLfloat curSize;      // Store current point size
    ...
    ...

    // Get supported point size range and step size
    glGetFloatv(GL_POINT_SIZE_RANGE,sizes);
    glGetFloatv(GL_POINT_SIZE_GRANULARITY,&step);

    // Set the initial point size
```

```
curSize = sizes[0];

// Set beginning z coordinate
z = -50.0f;

// Loop around in a circle three times
for(angle = 0.0f; angle <= (2.0f*GL_PI)*3.0f; angle += 0.1f)
    {
    // Calculate x and y values on the circle
    x = 50.0f*sin(angle);
    y = 50.0f*cos(angle);

    // Specify the point size before the primitive is specified
    glPointSize(curSize);

    // Draw the point
    glBegin(GL_POINTS);
        glVertex3f(x, y, z);
    glEnd();

    // Bump up the z value and the point size
    z += 0.5f;
    curSize += step;
    }
...
...
}
```

This example demonstrates a couple of important things. For starters, notice that
`glPointSize` must be called outside the `glBegin/glEnd` statements. Not all OpenGL
functions are valid between these function calls. Although `glPointSize` affects all
points drawn after it, you don't begin drawing points until you call
`glBegin(GL_POINTS)`. For a complete list of valid functions that you can call within a
`glBegin/glEnd` sequence, see the "Reference Section" at the end of the chapter.

Another thing you may notice (depending on your hardware) is that if you specify a
point size larger than what is returned in the `size` variable, OpenGL will use the
largest available point size, but will not keep growing. This is a general observation
about OpenGL function parameters that have a valid range. Values outside the range
will be *clamped* to the range. Values too low will be made the lowest valid value, and
values too high will be made the highest valid value.

The most obvious thing you probably noticed about the POINTSZ excerpt is that the
larger point sizes are represented simply by larger squares. This is the default behavior,
but it typically is undesirable for many applications. Also, you might wonder why you
can increase the point size by a value less than one. If a value of 1.0 represents one
pixel, how do you draw less than a pixel or, say, 2.5 pixels?

The answer is that the point size specified in `glPointSize` isn't the exact point size in pixels, but the approximate diameter of a circle containing all the pixels that are used to draw the point. You can get OpenGL to draw the points as better points (that is, small filled circles) by enabling point smoothing. Together with line smoothing, point smoothing falls under the topic of *anti-aliasing*. *Anti-aliasing* is a technique used to smooth out jagged edges and round out corners; it is covered in more detail in Chapter 10, "Visual Effects: Blending and Fog."

Drawing Lines in 3D

The `GL_POINTS` primitive we have been using thus far is pretty straightforward; for each vertex specified, it draws a point. The next logical step is to specify two vertices and draw a line between them. This is exactly what the next primitive, `GL_LINES`, does. The following short section of code draws a single line between two points (0,0,0) and (50,50,50):

```
glBegin(GL_LINES);
    glVertex3f(0.0f, 0.0f, 0.0f);
    glVertex3f(50.0f, 50.0f, 50.0f);
glEnd();
```

Note here that two vertices specify a single primitive. For every two vertices specified, a single line is drawn. If you specify an odd number of vertices for `GL_LINES`, the last vertex is just ignored. Listing 4.4, from the LINES sample program on the CD, shows a more complex sample that draws a series of lines fanned around in a circle. Each point specified in this sample is paired with a point on the opposite side of a circle. The output from this program is shown in Figure 4.6.

Figure 4.6　Output from the LINES sample program.

Listing 4.4 *Code from the Sample Program LINES That Displays a Series of Lines Fanned in a Circle*

```
// Call only once for all remaining points
glBegin(GL_LINES);

// All lines lie in the xy plane.
z = 0.0f;
for(angle = 0.0f; angle <= GL_PI*3.0f; angle += 0.5f)
    {
    // Top half of the circle
    x = 50.0f*sin(angle);
    y = 50.0f*cos(angle);
    glVertex3f(x, y, z);        // First endpoint of line

    // Bottom half of the circle
    x = 50.0f*sin(angle+3.1415f);
    y = 50.0f*cos(angle+3.1415f);
    glVertex3f(x, y, z);        // Second endpoint of line
    }

// Done drawing points
glEnd();
```

Line Strips and Loops

The next two OpenGL primitives build on GL_LINES by allowing you to specify a list of vertices through which a line is drawn. When you specify GL_LINE_STRIP, a line is drawn from one vertex to the next in a continuous segment. The following code draws two lines in the xy plane that are specified by three vertices. Figure 4.7 shows an example.

```
glBegin(GL_LINE_STRIP);
    glVertex3f(0.0f, 0.0f, 0.0f);      // V0
    glVertex3f(50.0f, 50.0f, 0.0f);    // V1
    glVertex3f(50.0f, 100.0f, 0.0f);   // V2
glEnd();
```

The last line-based primitive is the GL_LINE_LOOP. This primitive behaves just like a GL_LINE_STRIP, but one final line is drawn between the last vertex specified and the first one specified. This is an easy way to draw a closed-line figure. Figure 4.8 shows a GL_LINE_LOOP drawn using the same vertices as for the GL_LINE_STRIP in Figure 4.7.

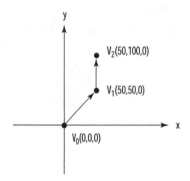

Figure 4.7 An example of a GL_LINE_STRIP specified by three vertices.

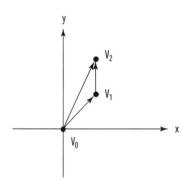

Figure 4.8 The same vertices from Figure 4.7 used by a GL_LINE_LOOP primitive.

Approximating Curves with Straight Lines

The POINTS sample program, shown earlier in Figure 4.3, showed you how to plot points along a spring-shaped path. You might have been tempted to push the points closer and closer together (by setting smaller values for the angle increment) to create a smooth spring-shaped curve instead of the broken points that only approximated the shape. This perfectly valid operation can move quite slowly for larger and more complex curves with thousands of points.

A better way of approximating a curve is to use a GL_LINE_STRIP to play connect-the-dots. As the dots move closer together, a smoother curve materializes without your having to specify all those points. Listing 4.5 shows the code from Listing 4.2, with GL_POINTS replaced by GL_LINE_STRIP. The output from this new program, LSTRIPS, is shown in Figure 4.9. As you can see, the approximation of the curve is quite good. You will find this handy technique almost ubiquitous among OpenGL programs.

Figure 4.9 Output from the LSTRIPS program approximating a smooth curve.

Listing 4.5 *Code from the Sample Program LSTRIPS, Demonstrating Line Strips*

```
// Call only once for all remaining points
glBegin(GL_LINE_STRIP);

z = -50.0f;
for(angle = 0.0f; angle <= (2.0f*GL_PI)*3.0f; angle += 0.1f)
    {
    x = 50.0f*sin(angle);
    y = 50.0f*cos(angle);

    // Specify the point and move the z value up a little
    glVertex3f(x, y, z);
    z += 0.5f;
    }

// Done drawing points
glEnd();
```

Setting the Line Width

Just as you can set different point sizes, you can also specify various line widths when drawing lines by using the `glLineWidth` function:

```
void glLineWidth(GLfloat width);
```

The `glLineWidth` function takes a single parameter that specifies the approximate width, in pixels, of the line drawn. Just like point sizes, not all line widths are supported, and you should make sure the line width you want to specify is available. Use the following code to get the range of line widths and the smallest interval between them:

```
GLfloat sizes[2];    // Store supported line width range
GLfloat step;        // Store supported line width increments
```

```
// Get supported line width range and step size
glGetFloatv(GL_LINE_WIDTH_RANGE,sizes);
glGetFloatv(GL_LINE_WIDTH_GRANULARITY,&step);
```

Here, the sizes array will contain two elements that contain the smallest and the largest valid value for glLineWidth. In addition, the variable step will hold the smallest step size allowable between the line widths. The OpenGL specification only requires that one line width, 1.0, be supported. The Microsoft implementation of OpenGL allows for line widths from 0.5 to 10.0, with 0.125 the smallest step size.

Listing 4.6 shows code for a more substantial example of glLineWidth. It's from the program LINESW and draws 10 lines of varying widths. It starts at the bottom of the window at –90 on the y-axis and climbs the y-axis 20 units for each new line. Every time it draws a new line, it increases the line width by 1. Figure 4.10 shows the output for this program.

Figure 4.10 Demonstration of glLineWidth from the LINESW program.

Listing 4.6 *Drawing Lines of Various Widths*

```
// Called to draw scene
void RenderScene(void)
    {
    GLfloat y;                   // Storage for varying Y coordinate
    GLfloat fSizes[2];           // Line width range metrics
    GLfloat fCurrSize;           // Save current size

    ...
    ...
    ...

    // Get line size metrics and save the smallest value
    glGetFloatv(GL_LINE_WIDTH_RANGE,fSizes);
    fCurrSize = fSizes[0];

    // Step up y axis 20 units at a time
```

```
for(y = -90.0f; y < 90.0f; y += 20.0f)
    {
    // Set the line width
    glLineWidth(fCurrSize);

    // Draw the line
    glBegin(GL_LINES);
        glVertex2f(-80.0f, y);
        glVertex2f(80.0f, y);
    glEnd();

    // Increase the line width
    fCurrSize += 1.0f;
    }

...
...
}
```

Notice that we used `glVertex2f` this time instead of `glVertex3f` to specify the coordinates for the lines. As mentioned, this is only a convenience because we are drawing in the xy plane, with a z value of zero. To see that you are still drawing lines in three dimensions, simply use the arrow keys to spin your lines around. You easily see that all the lines lie on a single plane.

Line Stippling

In addition to changing line widths, you can create lines with a dotted or dashed pattern, called *stippling*. To use line stippling, you must first enable stippling with a call to

```
glEnable(GL_LINE_STIPPLE);
```

Then, the function `glLineStipple` establishes the pattern that the lines uses for drawing:

```
void glLineStipple(GLint factor, GLushort pattern);
```

> **REMINDER**
> Any feature or ability that is enabled by a call to glEnable can be disabled by a call to glDisable.

The pattern parameter is a 16-bit value that specifies a pattern to use when drawing the lines. Each bit represents a section of the line segment that is either on or off. By default, each bit corresponds to a single pixel, but the `factor` parameter serves as a multiplier to increase the width of the pattern. For example, setting `factor` to `5` causes each bit in the pattern to represent five pixels in a row that are either on or off. Furthermore, bit 0 (the least significant bit) of the pattern is used first to specify the line. Figure 4.11 illustrates a sample bit pattern applied to a line segment.

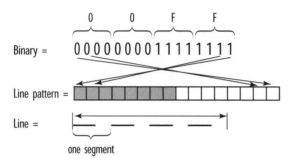

Figure 4.11 Stipple pattern is used to construct a line segment.

WHY ARE THESE PATTERNS BACKWARD?
You might wonder why the bit pattern for stippling is used in reverse when drawing the line. Internally, it's much faster for OpenGL to shift this pattern to the left one place each time it needs to get the next mask value. OpenGL was designed for high performance graphics and frequently employs similar tricks elsewhere.

Listing 4.7 shows a sample of using a stippling pattern that is just a series of alternating on and off bits (0101010101010101). This code is taken from the LSTIPPLE program, which draws 10 lines from the bottom of the window up the y-axis to the top. Each line is stippled with the pattern 0x5555, but for each new line, the pattern multiplier is increased by 1. You can clearly see the effects of the widened stipple pattern in Figure 4.12.

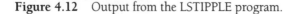

Figure 4.12 Output from the LSTIPPLE program.

Listing 4.7 *Code from LSTIPPLE That Demonstrates the Effect of* `factor` *on the Bit Pattern*

```
// Called to draw scene
void RenderScene(void)
    {
    GLfloat y;                  // Storage for varying y coordinate
    GLint factor = 1;           // Stippling factor
    GLushort pattern = 0x5555;  // Stipple pattern

...
...

    // Enable Stippling
    glEnable(GL_LINE_STIPPLE);

    // Step up Y axis 20 units at a time
    for(y = -90.0f; y < 90.0f; y += 20.0f)
        {
        // Reset the repeat factor and pattern
        glLineStipple(factor,pattern);

        // Draw the line
        glBegin(GL_LINES);
            glVertex2f(-80.0f, y);
            glVertex2f(80.0f, y);
        glEnd();

        factor++;
        }
    ...
    ...
    }
```

Just the ability to draw points and lines in 3D gives you a significant set of tools for creating your own 3D masterpiece. The commercial application shown in Figure 4.13 was written by the author. Note that the OpenGL rendered map is rendered entirely of solid and stippled line strips.

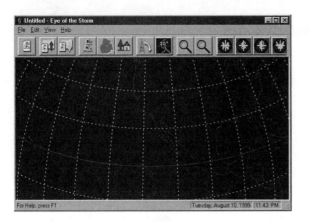

Figure 4.13 A 3D map rendered with solid and stippled lines.

Drawing Triangles in 3D

You've seen how to draw points and lines and even how to draw some enclosed polygons with GL_LINE_LOOP. With just these primitives, you could easily draw any shape possible in three dimensions. You could, for example, draw six squares and arrange them so they form the sides of a cube.

You might have noticed, however, that any shapes you create with these primitives are not filled with any color; after all, you are only drawing lines. In fact, all that arranging six squares produces is a wireframe cube, not a solid cube. To draw a solid surface, you need more than just points and lines; you need polygons. A polygon is a closed shape that may or may not be filled with the currently selected color, and it is the basis of all solid-object composition in OpenGL.

Triangles: Your First Polygon

The simplest polygon possible is the triangle, with only three sides. The GL_TRIANGLES primitive draws triangles by connecting three vertices together. The following code draws two triangles using three vertices each, as shown in Figure 4.14:

```
glBegin(GL_TRIANGLES);
    glVertex2f(0.0f, 0.0f);          // V0
    glVertex2f(25.0f, 25.0f);        // V1
    glVertex2f(50.0f, 0.0f);         // V2

    glVertex2f(-50.0f, 0.0f);        // V3
    glVertex2f(-75.0f, 50.0f);       // V4
    glVertex2f(-25.0f, 0.0f);        // V5
glEnd();
```

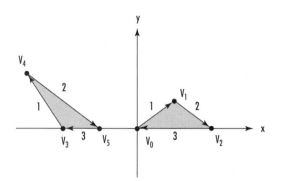

Figure 4.14   Two triangles drawn using `GL_TRIANGLES`.

Note that the triangles will be filled with the currently selected drawing color. If you don't specify a drawing color at some point, you can't be certain of the result. (There is no default drawing color.)

CHOOSE THE FASTEST PRIMITIVES FOR PERFORMANCE

The triangle is the primitive of choice for the OpenGL programmer. You will find that, with a little work, any polygonal shape can be composed of one or more triangles placed carefully together. Most 3D accelerated hardware is highly optimized for drawing triangles. In fact, you will see many 3D benchmarks measured in triangles per second.

Winding

An important characteristic of any polygonal primitive is illustrated in Figure 4.14. Notice the arrows on the lines that connect the vertices. When the first triangle is drawn, the lines are drawn from V0 to V1, then to V2, and finally back to V0 to close the triangle. This path is in the order that the vertices are specified, and for this example, that order is clockwise from your point of view. The same directional characteristic is present for the second triangle as well.

The combination of order and direction in which the vertices are specified is called *winding*. The triangles in Figure 4.14 are said to have clockwise winding because they are literally wound in the clockwise direction. If we reverse the positions of V4 and V5 on the triangle on the left, we get counterclockwise winding. Figure 4.15 shows two triangles, each with opposite windings.

OpenGL by default considers polygons that have counterclockwise winding to be front facing. This means that the triangle on the left in Figure 4.15 is showing us the front of the triangle, and the one on the right is showing the back side of the triangle.

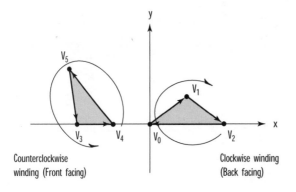

Figure 4.15   Two triangles with different windings.

Why is this important? As you will soon see, you will often want to give the front and back of a polygon different physical characteristics. You can hide the back of a polygon altogether or give it a different color and reflective property (see Chapter 6, "Color, Lighting, and Materials"). It's important to keep the winding of all polygons in a scene consistent, using front-facing polygons to draw the outside surface of any solid objects. In the upcoming section on solid objects, we demonstrate this principle using some models that are more complex.

If you need to reverse the default behavior of OpenGL, you can do so by calling the function

```
glFrontFace(GL_CW);
```

The `GL_CW` parameter tells OpenGL that clockwise-wound polygons are to be considered front facing. To change back to counterclockwise winding for the front face, use `GL_CCW`.

Triangle Strips

For many surfaces and shapes, you need to draw several connected triangles. You can save a lot of time by drawing a strip of connected triangles with the `GL_TRIANGLE_STRIP` primitive. Figure 4.16 shows the progression of a strip of three triangles specified by a set of five vertices numbered V0 through V4. Here, you see the vertices are not necessarily traversed in the same order they were specified. The reason for this is to preserve the winding (counterclockwise) of each triangle.

(By the way, for the rest of our discussion of polygonal primitives, we won't be showing you any more code fragments to demonstrate the vertices and the glBegin statements. You should have the swing of things by now. Later, when we have a real sample program to work with, we resume the examples.)

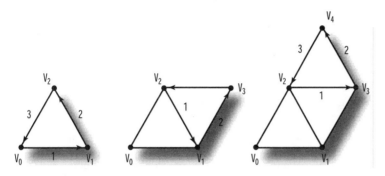

Figure 4.16 The progression of a GL_TRIANGLE_STRIP.

There are two advantages to using a strip of triangles instead of specifying each triangle separately. First, after specifying the first three vertices for the initial triangle, you only need to specify a single point for each additional triangle. This saves a lot of program or data storage space when you have many triangles to draw. The second advantage is performance. Fewer vertices mean a faster transfer from your computer's memory to your graphics card and fewer vertex transformations (see Chapters 2 and 5).

MODELING TIP

Another advantage to composing large flat surfaces out of several smaller triangles is that when lighting effects are applied to the scene, OpenGL can better reproduce the simulated effects. You'll learn to apply this technique, called tesselation, in Chapter 12, "Beyond Lines and Triangles."

Triangle Fans

In addition to triangle strips, you can use GL_TRIANGLE_FAN to produce a group of connected triangles that fan around a central point. Figure 4.17 shows a fan of three triangles produced by specifying four vertices. The first vertex, V0, forms the origin of the fan. After the first three vertices are used to draw the initial triangle, all subsequent vertices are used with the origin (V0) and the vertex immediately preceding it (Vn–1) to form the next triangle. Notice that the vertices are traversed in a clockwise direction, rather than counterclockwise.

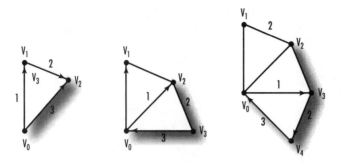

Figure 4.17 The progression of `GL_TRIANGLE_FAN`. >

Building Solid Objects

Composing a solid object out of triangles (or any other polygon) involves more than assembling a series of vertices in a 3D coordinate space. Let's examine the sample program TRIANGLE, which uses two triangle fans to create a cone in our viewing volume. The first fan produces the cone shape, using the first vertex as the point of the cone and the remaining vertices as points along a circle further down the z-axis. The second fan forms a circle and lies entirely in the xy plane, making up the bottom surface of the cone.

The output from TRIANGLE is shown in Figure 4.18. Here, you are looking directly down the z-axis and can only see a circle composed of a fan of triangles. The individual triangles are emphasized by coloring them alternately green and red.

The code for the `SetupRC` and `RenderScene` functions is shown in Listing 4.8. (You will see some unfamiliar variables and specifiers that are explained shortly.) This program demonstrates several aspects of composing 3D objects. Right-click in the window and you will notice an Effects menu; this will be used to enable and disable some 3D drawing features so we can explore some of the characteristics of 3D object creation. We'll be describing these as we progress.

Figure 4.18 Initial output from the TRIANGLE sample program.

Listing 4.8   *SetupRC and RenderScene Code for the TRIANGLE Sample Program*

```
// This function does any needed initialization on the rendering
// context.
void SetupRC()
    {
    // Black background
    glClearColor(0.0f, 0.0f, 0.0f, 1.0f );

    // Set drawing color to green
    glColor3f(0.0f, 1.0f, 0.0f);

    // Set color shading model to flat
    glShadeModel(GL_FLAT);

    // Clockwise-wound polygons are front facing; this is reversed
    // because we are using triangle fans
    glFrontFace(GL_CW);
    }



// Called to draw scene
void RenderScene(void)
    {
    GLfloat x,y,angle;        // Storage for coordinates and angles
    int iPivot = 1;           // Used to flag alternating colors

    // Clear the window and the depth buffer
    glClear(GL_COLOR_BUFFER_BIT | GL_DEPTH_BUFFER_BIT);

    // Turn culling on if flag is set
    if(bCull)
        glEnable(GL_CULL_FACE);
    else
        glDisable(GL_CULL_FACE);

    // Enable depth testing if flag is set
    if(bDepth)
        glEnable(GL_DEPTH_TEST);
    else
        glDisable(GL_DEPTH_TEST);

    // Draw the back side as a polygon only, if flag is set
    if(bOutline)
        glPolygonMode(GL_BACK,GL_LINE);
    else
```

continued on next page

continued from previous page

```
        glPolygonMode(GL_BACK,GL_FILL);


    // Save matrix state and do the rotation
    glPushMatrix();
    glRotatef(xRot, 1.0f, 0.0f, 0.0f);
    glRotatef(yRot, 0.0f, 1.0f, 0.0f);


    // Begin a triangle fan
    glBegin(GL_TRIANGLE_FAN);

    // Pinnacle of cone is shared vertex for fan, moved up z-axis
    // to produce a cone instead of a circle
    glVertex3f(0.0f, 0.0f, 75.0f);

    // Loop around in a circle and specify even points along the circle
    // as the vertices of the triangle fan
    for(angle = 0.0f; angle < (2.0f*GL_PI); angle += (GL_PI/8.0f))
        {
        // Calculate x and y position of the next vertex
        x = 50.0f*sin(angle);
        y = 50.0f*cos(angle);

        // Alternate color between red and green
        if((iPivot %2) == 0)
            glColor3f(0.0f, 1.0f, 0.0f);
        else
            glColor3f(1.0f, 0.0f, 0.0f);

        // Increment pivot to change color next time
        iPivot++;

        // Specify the next vertex for the triangle fan
        glVertex2f(x, y);
        }

    // Done drawing fan for cone
    glEnd();


    // Begin a new triangle fan to cover the bottom
    glBegin(GL_TRIANGLE_FAN);

    // Center of fan is at the origin
    glVertex2f(0.0f, 0.0f);
    for(angle = 0.0f; angle < (2.0f*GL_PI); angle += (GL_PI/8.0f))
```

```
    {
    // Calculate x and y position of the next vertex
    x = 50.0f*sin(angle);
    y = 50.0f*cos(angle);

    // Alternate color between red and green
    if((iPivot %2) == 0)
        glColor3f(0.0f, 1.0f, 0.0f);
    else
        glColor3f(1.0f, 0.0f, 0.0f);

    // Increment pivot to change color next time
    iPivot++;

    // Specify the next vertex for the triangle fan
    glVertex2f(x, y);
    }

// Done drawing the fan that covers the bottom
glEnd();

// Restore transformations
glPopMatrix();

// Flush drawing commands
glFlush();
}
```

Setting Polygon Colors

Until now, we have set the current color only once and drawn only a single shape. Now, with multiple polygons, things get slightly more interesting. We want to use different colors so we can see our work more easily. Colors are actually specified per vertex, not per polygon. The shading model affects whether the polygon is solidly colored (using the current color selected when the last vertex was specified) or smoothly shaded between the colors specified for each vertex.

The line glShadeModel(GL_FLAT); tells OpenGL to fill the polygons with the solid color that was current when the polygon's last vertex was specified. This is why we can simply change the current color to red or green before specifying the next vertex in our triangle fan. On the other hand, the line glShadeModel(GL_SMOOTH); would tell OpenGL to shade the triangles smoothly from each vertex, attempting to interpolate the colors between those specified for each vertex. You'll learn much more about color and shading in Chapter 6.

Hidden Surface Removal

Hold down one of the arrow keys to spin the cone around, and don't select anything from the Effects menu yet. You'll notice something unsettling: The cone appears to be swinging back and forth plus and minus 180°, with the bottom of the cone always facing you, but not rotating a full 360°. Figure 4.19 shows this more clearly.

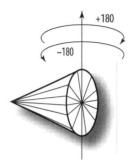

Figure 4.19   The rotating cone appears to be wobbling back and forth.

This wobbling happens because the bottom of the cone is drawn after the sides of the cone are drawn. No matter how the cone is oriented, the bottom is drawn on top of it, producing the "wobbling" illusion. This effect is not limited to the various sides and parts of an object. If more than one object is drawn and one is in front of the other (from the viewer's perspective), the last object drawn still appears over the previously drawn object.

You can correct this peculiarity with a simple feature called depth testing (introduced briefly in Chapters 1 and 2). Depth testing is an effective technique for hidden surface removal, and OpenGL has functions that do this for you behind the scenes. The concept is simple: When a pixel is drawn, it is assigned a value (called the z value) that denotes its distance from the viewer's perspective. Later, when another pixel needs to be drawn to that screen location, the new pixel's z value is compared to that of the pixel that is already stored there. If the new pixel's z value is higher, it is closer to the viewer and thus in front of the previous pixel, so the previous pixel is obscured by the new pixel. If the new pixel's z value is lower, it must be behind the existing pixel and thus is not obscured. This maneuver is accomplished internally by a depth buffer, which is discussed in greater detail in Chapter 11, "Buffers: Not Just for Animation." Most all of the samples in this book use depth testing.

To enable depth testing, simply call

```
glEnable(GL_DEPTH_TEST);
```

Depth testing is enabled in Listing 4.8 when the **bDepth** variable is set to **True**, and it is disabled if **bDepth** is **False**:

```
// Enable depth testing if flag is set
if(bDepth)
    glEnable(GL_DEPTH_TEST);
else
    glDisable(GL_DEPTH_TEST);
```

The bDepth variable is set when you select Depth Test from the Effects menu. In addition, the depth buffer must be cleared each time the scene is rendered. The depth buffer is analogous to the color buffer in that it contains information about the distance of the pixels from the observer. This information is used to determine whether any pixels are hidden by pixels closer to the observer:

```
// Clear the window and the depth buffer
glClear(GL_COLOR_BUFFER_BIT | GL_DEPTH_BUFFER_BIT);
```

A right click with the mouse opens a pop-up menu that allows you to toggle depth testing on and off. Figure 4.20 shows the TRIANGLE program with depth testing enabled. It also shows the cone with the bottom correctly hidden behind the sides. You can see that depth testing is practically a prerequisite for creating 3D objects out of solid polygons.

Figure 4.20   The bottom of the cone is now correctly placed behind the sides for this orientation.

Culling: Hiding Surfaces for Performance

You can see that there are obvious visual advantages to not drawing a surface that is obstructed by another. Even so, you pay some performance overhead because every pixel drawn must be compared with the previous pixel's z value. Sometimes, however, you know that a surface will never be drawn anyway, so why specify it? *Culling* is the term used to describe the technique of eliminating geometry that we know will never be seen. By not sending this geometry to your OpenGL driver and hardware, you can make significant performance improvements. One culling technique is backface culling, which eliminates the backsides of a surface.

In our working example, the cone is a closed surface and we never see the inside. OpenGL is actually (internally) drawing the back sides of the far side of the cone and then the front sides of the polygons facing us. Then, by a comparison of z buffer values, the far side of the cone is eliminated. Figures 4.21a and 4.21b show our cone at a particular orientation with depth testing turned on (a) and off (b). Notice that the green and red triangles that make up the cone sides change when depth testing is enabled. Without depth testing, the sides of the triangles at the far side of the cone show through.

Figure 4.21a   With depth testing.

Figure 4.21b   Without depth testing.

Earlier in the chapter, we explained how OpenGL uses winding to determine the front and back sides of polygons and that it is important to keep the polygons that define the outside of your objects wound in a consistent direction. This consistency is what allows us to tell OpenGL to render only the front, only the back, or both sides of polygons. By eliminating the back sides of the polygons, we can drastically reduce the amount of necessary processing to render the image. Even though depth testing will eliminate the appearance of the inside of objects, internally OpenGL must take them into account unless we explicitly tell it not to.

Backface culling is enabled or disabled for our program by the following code from Listing 4.8:

```
// Clockwise-wound polygons are front facing; this is reversed
// because we are using triangle fans
glFrontFace(GL_CW);
...
...


// Turn culling on if flag is set
if(bCull)
    glEnable(GL_CULL_FACE);
else
    glDisable(GL_CULL_FACE);
```

Note that we first changed the definition of front-facing polygons to assume clockwise winding (because our triangle fans are all wound clockwise).

Figure 4.22 demonstrates that the bottom of the cone is gone when culling is enabled. This is because we didn't follow our own rule about all the surface polygons having the same winding. The triangle fan that makes up the bottom of the cone is wound clockwise, like the fan that makes up the sides of the cone, but the front side of the cone's bottom section is facing the inside. See Figure 4.23.

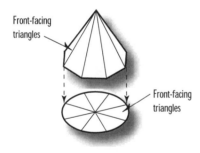

Figure 4.22   The bottom of the cone is culled because the front-facing triangles are inside.

Figure 4.23   How the cone was assembled from two triangle fans.

We could have corrected this by changing the winding rule, by calling

```
glFrontFace(GL_CCW);
```

just before we drew the second triangle fan. But in this example, we wanted to make it easy for you to see culling in action, as well as get set up for our next demonstration of polygon tweaking.

WHY DO WE NEED BACKFACE CULLING?
You might wonder, "If backface culling is so desirable, why do we need the ability to turn it on and off?" Backface culling is useful when drawing closed objects or solids, but you won't always be rendering these types of geometry. Some flat objects (such as paper) can still be seen from both sides. If the cone we are drawing here were made of glass or plastic, you would actually be able to see the front and the back sides of the geometry. (See Chapter 10 for a discussion of drawing transparent objects.)

Polygon Modes

Polygons don't have to be filled with the current color. By default, polygons are drawn solid, but you can change this behavior by specifying that polygons are to be drawn as outlines or just points (only the vertices are plotted). The function `glPolygonMode` allows polygons to be rendered as filled solids, as outlines, or as points only. In addition, you can apply this rendering mode to both sides of the polygons or only to the front or back. The following code from Listing 4.8 shows the polygon mode being set to outlines or solid, depending on the state of the Boolean variable `bOutline`:

```
// Draw back side as a polygon only, if flag is set
if(bOutline)
    glPolygonMode(GL_BACK,GL_LINE);
else
    glPolygonMode(GL_BACK,GL_FILL);
```

Figure 4.24 shows the back sides of all polygons rendered as outlines. (We had to disable culling to produce this image; otherwise, the inside would be eliminated and you'd get no outlines.) Notice that the bottom of the cone is now wireframe instead of solid, and you can see up inside the cone where the inside walls are also drawn as wireframe triangles.

Figure 4.24 Using `glPolygonMode` to render one side of the triangles as outlines.

Other Primitives

Triangles are the preferred primitive for object composition because most OpenGL hardware specifically accelerates triangles, but they are not the only primitives available. Some hardware provides for acceleration of other shapes as well, and programmatically, it might be simpler to use a general-purpose graphics primitive. The remaining OpenGL primitives provide for rapid specification of a quadrilateral or quadrilateral strip, as well as a general-purpose polygon. If you know your code is going to be run in an environment that accelerates general-purpose polygons, these primitives might be your best bet in terms of performance.

Four-Sided Polygons: Quads

If you add one more side to a triangle, you get a quadrilateral, or a four-sided figure. OpenGL's GL_QUADS primitive draws a four-sided polygon. In Figure 4.25, a quad is drawn from four vertices. Note also that quads have clockwise winding.

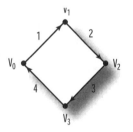

Figure 4.25 An example of GL_QUADS.

Quad Strips

As you can for triangles, you can specify a strip of connected quadrilaterals with the GL_QUAD_STRIP primitive. Figure 4.26 shows the progression of a quad strip specified by six vertices. Quad strips, like single GL_QUADS, maintain a clockwise winding.

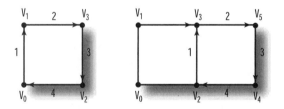

Figure 4.26 Progression of GL_QUAD_STRIP.

General Polygons

The final OpenGL primitive is the GL_POLYGON, which you can use to draw a polygon having any number of sides. Figure 4.27 shows a polygon consisting of five vertices. Polygons created with GL_POLYGON have clockwise winding.

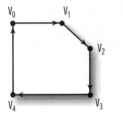

Figure 4.27   Progression of GL_POLYGON.

WHAT ABOUT RECTANGLES?
All 10 of the OpenGL primitives are used with glBegin/glEnd to draw general-purpose polygonal shapes. One shape is so common, it has a special function instead of being a primitive; that shape is the rectangle. It was actually the first shape you learned to draw back in Chapter 3. The function glRect provides an easy and convenient mechanism for specifying rectangles without having to resort to GL_QUADS.

Filling Polygons, or Stippling Revisited

There are two methods for applying a pattern to solid polygons. The customary method is texture mapping, where a bitmap is mapped to the surface of a polygon, and this is covered in Chapter 8, "Texture Mapping." Another way is to specify a stippling pattern, as we did for lines. A polygon stipple pattern is nothing more than a 32×32 monochrome bitmap that is used for the fill pattern.

To enable polygon stippling, call

```
glEnable(GL_POLYGON_STIPPLE);
```

and then call

```
glPolygonStipple(pBitmap);
```

pBitmap is a pointer to a data area containing the stipple pattern. Hereafter, all polygons are filled using the pattern specified by pBitmap (GLubyte *). This pattern is similar to that used by line stippling, except the buffer is large enough to hold a 32-by-32-bit pattern. Also, the bits are read with the MSB (most significant bit) first, which is just the opposite of line stipple patterns. Figure 4.28 shows a bit pattern for a campfire that we use for a stipple pattern.

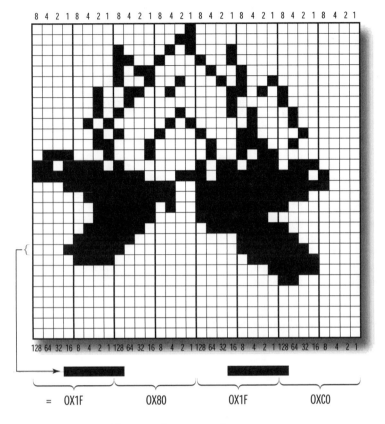

Figure 4.28   Building a polygon stipple pattern.

PIXEL STORAGE
As you will learn in Chapter 7, "Raster Graphics in OpenGL," you can modify the way pixels for stipple patterns are interpreted by using the glPixelStore function. For now, however, we stick to the simple default polygon stippling.

To construct a mask to represent this pattern, we store one row at a time from the bottom up. Fortunately, unlike line stipple patterns, the data is by default interpreted just as it is stored, with the most significant bit read first. Each byte can then be read from left to right and stored in an array of GLubyte large enough to hold 32 rows of 4 bytes apiece.

Listing 4.9 shows the code used to store this pattern. Each row of the array represents a row from Figure 4.28. The first row in the array is the last row of the figure, and so on, up to the last row of the array and the first row of the figure.

Listing 4.9 *The Mask Definition for the Campfire in Figure 4.28*

```
// Bitmap of campfire
GLubyte fire[] = { 0x00, 0x00, 0x00, 0x00,
                   0x00, 0x00, 0x00, 0x00,
                   0x00, 0x00, 0x00, 0x00,
                   0x00, 0x00, 0x00, 0x00,
                   0x00, 0x00, 0x00, 0x00,
                   0x00, 0x00, 0x00, 0x00,
                   0x00, 0x00, 0x00, 0xc0,
                   0x00, 0x00, 0x01, 0xf0,
                   0x00, 0x00, 0x07, 0xf0,
                   0x0f, 0x00, 0x1f, 0xe0,
                   0x1f, 0x80, 0x1f, 0xc0,
                   0x0f, 0xc0, 0x3f, 0x80,
                   0x07, 0xe0, 0x7e, 0x00,
                   0x03, 0xf0, 0xff, 0x80,
                   0x03, 0xf5, 0xff, 0xe0,
                   0x07, 0xfd, 0xff, 0xf8,
                   0x1f, 0xfc, 0xff, 0xe8,
                   0xff, 0xe3, 0xbf, 0x70,
                   0xde, 0x80, 0xb7, 0x00,
                   0x71, 0x10, 0x4a, 0x80,
                   0x03, 0x10, 0x4e, 0x40,
                   0x02, 0x88, 0x8c, 0x20,
                   0x05, 0x05, 0x04, 0x40,
                   0x02, 0x82, 0x14, 0x40,
                   0x02, 0x40, 0x10, 0x80,
                   0x02, 0x64, 0x1a, 0x80,
                   0x00, 0x92, 0x29, 0x00,
                   0x00, 0xb0, 0x48, 0x00,
                   0x00, 0xc8, 0x90, 0x00,
                   0x00, 0x85, 0x10, 0x00,
                   0x00, 0x03, 0x00, 0x00,
                   0x00, 0x00, 0x10, 0x00 };
```

To make use of this stipple pattern, we must first enable polygon stippling and then specify this pattern as the stipple pattern. The PSTIPPLE sample program does this and then draws an octagon using the stipple pattern. Listing 4.10 shows the pertinent code, and Figure 4.29 shows the output from PSTIPPLE.

Figure 4.29   Output from the PSTIPPLE program.

Listing 4.10   *Code from PSTIPPLE That Draws a Stippled Octagon*

```
// This function does any needed initialization on the rendering
// context.
void SetupRC()
    {
    // Black background
    glClearColor(0.0f, 0.0f, 0.0f, 1.0f );

    // Set drawing color to red
    glColor3f(1.0f, 0.0f, 0.0f);

    // Enable polygon stippling
    glEnable(GL_POLYGON_STIPPLE);

    // Specify a specific stipple pattern
    glPolygonStipple(fire);
    }


// Called to draw scene
void RenderScene(void)
    {
    // Clear the window
    glClear(GL_COLOR_BUFFER_BIT);

    ...
    ...

    // Begin the stop sign shape,
    // use a standard polygon for simplicity
    glBegin(GL_POLYGON);
        glVertex2f(-20.0f, 50.0f);
```

continued on next page

continued from previous page

```
        glVertex2f(20.0f, 50.0f);
        glVertex2f(50.0f, 20.0f);
        glVertex2f(50.0f, -20.0f);
        glVertex2f(20.0f, -50.0f);
        glVertex2f(-20.0f, -50.0f);
        glVertex2f(-50.0f, -20.0f);
        glVertex2f(-50.0f, 20.0f);
    glEnd();

    ...
    ...

    // Flush drawing commands
    glFlush();
    }
```

Figure 4.30 shows the octagon rotated somewhat. You'll notice that the stipple pattern is still used, but the pattern is not rotated with the polygon. The stipple pattern is only used for simple polygon filling onscreen. If you need to map a bitmap to a polygon so that it mimics the polygon's surface, you must use texture mapping (Chapter 8).

Figure 4.30   PSTIPPLE output with the polygon rotated, showing that the stipple pattern is not rotated.

Polygon Construction Rules

When you are using many polygons to construct a complex surface, you need to remember two important rules.

The first rule is that all polygons must be planar. That is, all the vertices of the polygon must lie in a single plane, as illustrated in Figure 4.31. The polygon cannot twist or bend in space.

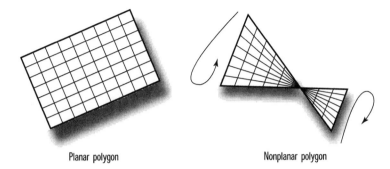

Planar polygon   Nonplanar polygon

Figure 4.31   Planar versus nonplanar polygons.

Here is yet another good reason to use triangles. No triangle can ever be twisted so that all three points do not line up in a plane because mathematically it only takes three points to define a plane. (If you can plot an invalid triangle, aside from winding it in the wrong direction, the Nobel Prize committee might be looking for you!)

The second rule of polygon construction is that the polygon's edges must not intersect, and the polygon must be convex. A polygon intersects itself if any two of its lines cross. "Convex" means that the polygon cannot have any indentions. A more rigorous test of a convex polygon is to draw some lines through it. If any given line enters and leaves the polygon more than once, the polygon is not convex. Figure 4.32 gives examples of good and bad polygons.

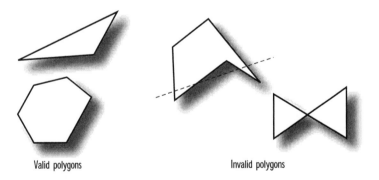

Valid polygons   Invalid polygons

Figure 4.32   Some valid and invalid primitive polygons.

WHY THE LIMITATIONS ON POLYGONS?
You might wonder why OpenGL places the restrictions on polygon construction. Handling polygons can become quite complex, and OpenGL's restrictions allow it to use very fast algorithms for rendering these polygons. We predict that you'll not find these restrictions burdensome and that you'll be able to build any shapes or objects you need using the existing primitives. (And you can use GL_LINES to draw an otherwise illegal shape, too.) Chapter 12 discusses some techniques for breaking a complex shape into smaller triangles.

Subdivision and Edges

Even though OpenGL can only draw convex polygons, there's still a way to create a nonconvex polygon—by arranging two or more convex polygons together. For example, let's take a four-point star as shown in Figure 4.33. This shape is obviously not convex and thus violates OpenGL's rules for simple polygon construction. However, the star on the right is composed of six separate triangles, which are legal polygons.

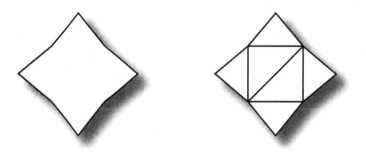

Figure 4.33   A nonconvex four-point star made up of six triangles.

When the polygons are filled, you won't be able to see any edges and the figure will seem to be a single shape onscreen. However, if you use glPolygonMode to switch to an outline drawing, it is distracting to see all those little triangles making up some larger surface area.

OpenGL provides a special flag called an *edge flag* to address those distracting edges. By setting and clearing the edge flag as you specify a list of vertices, you inform OpenGL which line segments are considered border lines (lines that go around the border of your shape) and which ones are not (internal lines that shouldn't be visible). The glEdgeFlag function takes a single parameter that sets the edge flag to True or False. When the function is set to True, any vertices that follow mark the beginning of a boundary line segment. Listing 4.11 shows an example of this from the STAR sample program on the CD.

Listing 4.11 *Sample Usage of `glEdgeFlag` from the STAR Program*

```
// Begin the triangles
glBegin(GL_TRIANGLES);

    glEdgeFlag(bEdgeFlag);
    glVertex2f(-20.0f, 0.0f);
    glEdgeFlag(TRUE);
    glVertex2f(20.0f, 0.0f);
    glVertex2f(0.0f, 40.0f);

    glVertex2f(-20.0f,0.0f);
    glVertex2f(-60.0f,-20.0f);
    glEdgeFlag(bEdgeFlag);
    glVertex2f(-20.0f,-40.0f);
    glEdgeFlag(TRUE);

    glVertex2f(-20.0f,-40.0f);
    glVertex2f(0.0f, -80.0f);
    glEdgeFlag(bEdgeFlag);
    glVertex2f(20.0f, -40.0f);
    glEdgeFlag(TRUE);

    glVertex2f(20.0f, -40.0f);
    glVertex2f(60.0f, -20.0f);
    glEdgeFlag(bEdgeFlag);
    glVertex2f(20.0f, 0.0f);
    glEdgeFlag(TRUE);

    // Center square as two triangles
    glEdgeFlag(bEdgeFlag);
    glVertex2f(-20.0f, 0.0f);
    glVertex2f(-20.0f,-40.0f);
    glVertex2f(20.0f, 0.0f);

    glVertex2f(-20.0f,-40.0f);
    glVertex2f(20.0f, -40.0f);
    glVertex2f(20.0f, 0.0f);
    glEdgeFlag(TRUE);

// Done drawing Triangles
glEnd();
```

The Boolean variable **bEdgeFlag** is toggled on and off by a menu option to make the edges appear and disappear. If this flag is **True**, all edges are considered boundary edges and appear when the polygon mode is set to **GL_LINES**. In Figures 4.34a and 4.34b, you can see the output from STAR, showing the wireframe star with and without edges.

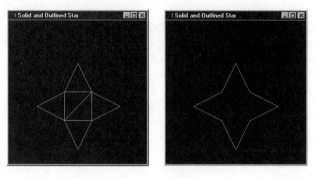

Figure 4.34a STAR program with edges enabled.

Figure 4.34b STAR program without edges enabled.

Summary

We've covered a lot of ground in this chapter. At this point, you can create your 3D space for rendering, and you know how to draw everything from points and lines to complex polygons. We've also shown you how to assemble these two-dimensional primitives as the surface of three-dimensional objects.

We encourage you to experiment with what you have learned in this chapter. Use your imagination and create some of your own 3D objects before moving on to the rest of the book. You'll then have some personal samples to work with and enhance as you learn and explore new techniques throughout the book.

Reference Section

glBegin

Purpose	Used to denote the beginning of a group of vertices that define one or more primitives.
Include File	<gl.h>
Syntax	void glBegin(GLenum *mode*);
Description	This function is used in conjunction with glEnd to delimit the vertices of an OpenGL primitive. You can include multiple vertices sets within a single glBegin/glEnd pair, as long as they are for the same primitive type. You can also make other settings with additional OpenGL commands that affect the vertices following them. You may call only these OpenGL functions within a glBegin/glEnd sequence: glVertex, glColor, glIndex, glNormal, glEvalCoord, glCallList, glCallLists, glTexCoord, glEdgeFlag, and glMaterial.

Parameters

mode GLenum: This value specifies the primitive to be constructed. It can be any of the values in Table 4.1.

Returns None.

Example You can find this ubiquitous function in literally every example and supplementary sample in this chapter. The following code shows a single point being drawn at the origin of the x,y,z coordinate system:

```
glBegin(GL_POINTS)
    glVertex3f(0.0f, 0.0f, 0.0f); //plots point at origin
glEnd();
```

See Also glEnd, glVertex

Table 4.1 *OpenGL Primitives Supported by* glBegin

Mode	Primitive Type
GL_POINTS	The specified vertices are used to create a single point each.
GL_LINES	The specified vertices are used to create line segments. Every two vertices specify a single and separate line segment. If the number of vertices is odd, the last one is ignored.
GL_LINE_STRIP	The specified vertices are used to create a line strip. After the first vertex, each subsequent vertex specifies the next point to which the line is extended.
GL_LINE_LOOP	Behaves as GL_LINE_STRIP, except a final line segment is drawn between the last and the first vertex specified. This is typically used to draw closed regions that might violate the rules regarding GL_POLYGON usage.
GL_TRIANGLES	The specified vertices are used to construct triangles. Every three vertices specify a new triangle. If the number of vertices is not evenly divisible by three, the extra vertices are ignored.
GL_TRIANGLE_STRIP	The specified vertices are used to create a strip of triangles. After the first three vertices are specified, each of any subsequent vertices is used with the two preceding ones to construct the next triangle. Each triplet of vertices (after the initial set) is automatically rearranged to ensure consistent winding of the triangles.
GL_TRIANGLE_FAN	The specified vertices are used to construct a triangle fan. The first vertex serves as an origin, and each vertex after the third is combined with the foregoing one and the origin. Any number of triangles may be fanned in this manner.
GL_QUADS	Each set of four vertices is used to construct a quadrilateral (a four-sided polygon). If the number of vertices is not evenly divisible by four, the remaining ones are ignored.

continued on next page

continued from previous page

Mode	Primitive Type
GL_QUAD_STRIP	The specified vertices are used to construct a strip of quadrilaterals. One quadrilateral is defined for each pair of vertices after the first pair. Unlike the vertex ordering for GL_QUADS, each pair of vertices is used in the reverse order specified to ensure consistent winding.
GL_POLYGON	The specified vertices are used to construct a convex polygon. The polygon edges must not intersect. The last vertex is automatically connected to the first vertex to ensure the polygon is closed.

glCullFace

Purpose	Specifies whether the front or back of polygons should be eliminated from drawing.
Include File	<gl.h>
Syntax	void glCullFace(GLenum *mode*);
Description	This function disables lighting, shading, and color calculations and operations on either the front or back of a polygon. Eliminates unnecessary rendering computations because the back side of polygons are never visible regardless of rotation or translation of the objects. Culling is enabled or disabled by calling glEnable and glDisable with the GL_CULL_FACE parameter. The front and back of the polygon are defined by use of glFrontFace and by the order in which the vertices are specified (clockwise or counterclockwise winding).
Parameters	
mode	GLenum: Specifies which face of polygons should be culled. May be either GL_FRONT or GL_BACK.
Returns	None.
Example	The following code (from the TRIANGLE example in this chapter) shows how the color and drawing operations are disabled for the inside of the cone when the Boolean variable bCull is set to True:

```
// Clockwise-wound polygons are front facing; this is reversed
// because we are using triangle fans
glFrontFace(GL_CW);

...
...
...

// Turn culling on if flag is set
if(bCull)
```

```
        glEnable(GL_CULL_FACE);
    else
        glDisable(GL_CULL_FACE);
```

See Also   glFrontFace, glLightModel

glEdgeFlag

Purpose	Flags polygon edges as either boundary or nonboundary edges. You can use this d to determine whether interior surface lines are visible.
Include File	<gl.h>
Variations	void glEdgeFlag(GLboolean *flag*); void glEdgeFlagv(const GLboolean **flag*);
Description	When two or more polygons are joined to form a larger region, the edges on the outside define the boundary of the newly formed region. This function flags inside edges as nonboundary. This is used only when the polygon mode is set to either GL_LINE or GL_POINT.
Parameters	
flag	GLboolean: Sets the edge flag to this value, True or False.
**flag*	const GLboolean *: A pointer to a value that is used for the edge flag.
Returns	None.
Example	The following code from the STAR program in this chapter sets the edge flag to FALSE for triangle borders inside the region of the star. It draws the star either as a solid, an outline, or only the vertices:

```
// Draw back side as a polygon only, if flag is set
if(iMode == MODE_LINE)
    glPolygonMode(GL_FRONT_AND_BACK,GL_LINE);

if(iMode == MODE_POINT)
    glPolygonMode(GL_FRONT_AND_BACK,GL_POINT);

if(iMode == MODE_SOLID)
    glPolygonMode(GL_FRONT_AND_BACK,GL_FILL);


// Begin the triangles
glBegin(GL_TRIANGLES);

    glEdgeFlag(bEdgeFlag);
    glVertex2f(-20.0f, 0.0f);
    glEdgeFlag(TRUE);
    glVertex2f(20.0f, 0.0f);
    glVertex2f(0.0f, 40.0f);
```

```
glVertex2f(-20.0f,0.0f);
glVertex2f(-60.0f,-20.0f);
glEdgeFlag(bEdgeFlag);
glVertex2f(-20.0f,-40.0f);
glEdgeFlag(TRUE);

glVertex2f(-20.0f,-40.0f);
glVertex2f(0.0f, -80.0f);
glEdgeFlag(bEdgeFlag);
glVertex2f(20.0f, -40.0f);
glEdgeFlag(TRUE);

glVertex2f(20.0f, -40.0f);
glVertex2f(60.0f, -20.0f);
glEdgeFlag(bEdgeFlag);
glVertex2f(20.0f, 0.0f);
glEdgeFlag(TRUE);

// Center square as two triangles
glEdgeFlag(bEdgeFlag);
glVertex2f(-20.0f, 0.0f);
glVertex2f(-20.0f,-40.0f);
glVertex2f(20.0f, 0.0f);

glVertex2f(-20.0f,-40.0f);
glVertex2f(20.0f, -40.0f);
glVertex2f(20.0f, 0.0f);
glEdgeFlag(TRUE);

// Done drawing Triangles
glEnd();
```

See Also   glBegin, glPolygonMode

glEnd

Purpose	Terminates a list of vertices that specify a primitive initiated by glBegin.
Include File	<gl.h>
Syntax	void glEnd();
Description	This function is used in conjunction with glBegin to delimit the vertices of an OpenGL primitive. You can include multiple vertices sets within a single glBegin/glEnd pair, as long as they are for the same primitive type. You can also make other settings with additional OpenGL commands that affect the vertices following them. You may call only these OpenGL functions within a glBegin/glEnd sequence: glVertex, glColor, glIndex, glNormal, glEvalCoord, glCallList, glCallLists, glTexCoord, glEdgeFlag, and glMaterial.

Returns	None.
Example	You can find this ubiquitous function in literally every example and supplementary sample in this chapter. The following code shows a single point being drawn at the origin of the x,y,z coordinate system:

```
glBegin(GL_POINTS)
    glVertex3f(0.0f, 0.0f, 0.0f);
glEnd();
```

See Also	glBegin, glVertex

glFrontFace

Purpose	Defines which side of a polygon is the front or back.
Include File	<gl.h>
Syntax	void glFrontFace(GLenum *mode*);
Description	When a scene comprises objects that are closed (you cannot see the inside), color or lighting calculations on the inside of the object are unnecessary. The glCullFace function turns off such calculations for either the front or back of polygons. The glFrontFace function determines which side of the polygons is considered the front. If the vertices of a polygon as viewed from the front are specified so that they travel clockwise around the polygon, the polygon is said to have clockwise winding. If the vertices travel counterclockwise, the polygon is said to have counterclockwise winding. This function allows you to specify either the clockwise or counterclockwise wound face to be the front of the polygon.
Parameters	
mode	GLenum: Specifies the orientation of front-facing polygons: clockwise (GL_CW) or counterclockwise (GL_CCW).
Returns	None.
Example	The following code from the TRIANGLE example in this chapter shows how the color and drawing operations are disabled for the inside of the cone. It is also necessary to indicate which side of the triangles are the outside by specifying clockwise winding:

```
// Clockwise wound polygons are front facing, this is reversed
// because we are using triangle fans
glFrontFace(GL_CW);

    ...
    ...
    ...

// Turn culling on if flag is set
```

```
      if(bCull)
          glEnable(GL_CULL_FACE);
      else
          glDisable(GL_CULL_FACE);
```

See Also   glCullFace, glLightModel

glGetPolygonStipple

Purpose   Returns the current polygon stipple pattern.

Include File   <gl.h>

Syntax   void glGetPolygonStipple(GLubyte *mask);

Description   This function copies a 32×32-bit pattern that represents the polygon stipple
                    pattern into a user specified buffer. The pattern is copied to the memory loca-
                    tion pointed to by *mask*. The packing of the pixels is affected by the last call
                    to glPixelStore.

Parameters

*mask   GLubyte: A pointer to where the polygon stipple pattern is to be copied.

Returns   None.

Example   The following code segment retrieves the current stipple pattern:

```
GLubyte mask[32*4];     // 4 bytes = 32bits per row X 32 rows
...
...
glGetPolygonStipple(mask);
```

See Also   glPolygonStipple, glLineStipple, glPixelStore

glLineStipple

Purpose   Specifies a line stipple pattern for line-based primitives GL_LINES,
                    GL_LINE_STRIP, and GL_LINE_LOOP.

Include File   <gl.h>

Syntax   void glLineStipple(GLint *factor*, GLushort *pattern*);

Description   This function uses the bit pattern to draw stippled (dotted and dashed) lines.
                    The bit pattern begins with bit 0 (the rightmost bit), so the actual drawing
                    pattern is the reverse of what is actually specified. The factor parameter is
                    used to widen the number of pixels drawn or not drawn along the line speci-
                    fied by each bit in pattern. By default, each bit in the pattern specifies one
                    pixel. To use line stippling, you must first enable stippling by calling

```
glEnable(GL_LINE_STIPPLE);
```

Line stippling is disabled by default. If you are drawing multiple line segments, the pattern is reset for each new segment. That is, if a line segment is drawn such that it terminates halfway through the pattern, the next line segment specified is unaffected.

Parameters

factor   GLint: Specifies a multiplier that determines how many pixels will be affected by each bit in the pattern parameter. Thus, the pattern width is multiplied by this value. The default value is 1 and the maximum value is clamped to 255.

pattern   GLushort: Sets the 16-bit stippling pattern. The least significant bit (bit 0) is used first for the stippling pattern. The default pattern is all 1s.

Returns   None.

Example   The following code from the LSTIPPLE sample program shows a series of lines drawn using a stipple pattern of 0x5555 (01010101), which draws a dotted line. The repeat factor is increased for each line drawn to demonstrate the widening of the dot pattern:

```
// Called to draw scene
void RenderScene(void)
    {
    GLfloat y;              // Storage for varying Y coordinate
    GLint factor = 1;         // Stippling factor
    GLushort pattern = 0x5555;    // Stipple pattern


    . . .
    . . .

    // Enable Stippling
glEnable(GL_LINE_STIPPLE);

    // Step up Y axis 20 units at a time
    for(y = -90.0f; y < 90.0f; y += 20.0f)
        {
        // Reset the repeat factor and pattern
        glLineStipple(factor,pattern);

        // Draw the line
        glBegin(GL_LINES);
            glVertex2f(-80.0f, y);
            glVertex2f(80.0f, y);
        glEnd();

        factor++;
        }
    . . .
    . . .
    }
```

See Also   `glPolygonStipple`

glLineWidth

Purpose   Sets the width of lines drawn with `GL_LINES`, `GL_LINE_STRIP`, or `GL_LINE_LOOP`.

Include File   <gl.h>

Syntax   `void glLineWidth(GLfloat width );`

Description   This function sets the width in pixels of lines drawn with any of the line-based primitives.

You can get the current line width setting by calling

```
GLfloat fSize;
...
glGetFloatv(GL_LINE_WIDTH, &fSize);
```

The current line-width setting will be returned in `fSize`. In addition, you can find the minimum and maximum supported line widths by calling

```
GLfloat fSizes[2];
...
glGetFloatv(GL_LINE_WIDTH_RANGE,fSizes);
```

In this instance, the minimum supported line width will be returned in `fSizes[0]`, and the maximum supported width will be stored in `fSizes[1]`. Finally, you can find the smallest supported increment between line widths by calling

```
GLfloat fStepSize;
...
glGetFloatv(GL_LINE_WIDTH_GRANULARITY,&fStepSize);
```

For any implementation of OpenGL, the only line width guaranteed to be supported is 1.0. For the Microsoft Windows generic implementation, the supported line widths range from 0.5 to 10.0, with a granularity of 0.125.

Parameters

width   `GLfloat`: Sets the width of lines that are drawn with the line primitives. The default value is 1.0.

Returns   None.

Example   The following code from the LINESW sample program demonstrates drawing lines of various widths:

```
void RenderScene(void)
    {
    GLfloat y;          // Storage for varying Y coordinate
    GLfloat fSizes[2];     // Line width range metrics
```

```
GLfloat fCurrSize;      // Save current size

...
...
...

// Get line size metrics and save the smallest value
glGetFloatv(GL_LINE_WIDTH_RANGE,fSizes);
fCurrSize = fSizes[0];

// Step up Y axis 20 units at a time
for(y = -90.0f; y < 90.0f; y += 20.0f)
    {
    // Set the line width
    glLineWidth(fCurrSize);

    // Draw the line
    glBegin(GL_LINES);
        glVertex2f(-80.0f, y);
        glVertex2f(80.0f, y);
    glEnd();

    // Increase the line width
    fCurrSize += 1.0f;
    }

...
...
}
```

See Also   glPointSize

glPointSize

Purpose   Sets the point size of points drawn with GL_POINTS.

Include File <gl.h>

Syntax   void glPointSize(GLfloat *size*);

Description This function sets the diameter in pixels of points drawn with the GL_POINTS primitive. You can get the current pixel size setting by calling

```
GLfloat fSize;
...
glGetFloatv(GL_POINT_SIZE, &fSize);
```

The current pixel size setting will be returned in fSize. In addition, you can find the minimum and maximum supported pixel sizes by calling

```
GLfloat fSizes[2];
```

```
   ...
   glGetFloatv(GL_POINT_SIZE_RANGE,fSizes);
```

In this instance, the minimum supported point size will be returned in
`fSizes[0]`, and the maximum supported size will be stored in `fSizes[1]`.
Finally, you can find the smallest supported increment between pixel sizes by
calling

```
GLfloat fStepSize;
   ...
   glGetFloatv(GL_POINT_SIZE_GRANULARITY,&fStepSize);
```

For any implementation of OpenGL, the only point size guaranteed to be
supported is 1.0. For the Microsoft Windows generic implementation, the
point sizes range from 0.5 to 10.0, with a granularity of 0.125.

Parameters

size GLfloat: Sets the diameter of drawn points. The default value is 1.0.

Returns None.

Example The following code from the POINTSZ sample program from this chapter
gets the point size range and granularity and uses them to gradually increase
the size of points used to plot a spiral pattern.

```
GLfloat x,y,z,angle;    // Storage for coordinates and angles
GLfloat sizes[2];       // Store supported point size range
GLfloat step;           // Store supported point size increments
GLfloat curSize;        // Store current size

   ...
   ...

// Get supported point size range and step size
   glGetFloatv(GL_POINT_SIZE_RANGE,sizes);
   glGetFloatv(GL_POINT_SIZE_GRANULARITY,&step);

// Set the initial point size
curSize = sizes[0];

// Set beginning z coordinate
z = -50.0f;

// Loop around in a circle three times
for(angle = 0.0f; angle <= (2.0f*3.1415f)*3.0f; angle += 0.1f)
    {
    // Calculate x and y values on the circle
    x = 50.0f*sin(angle);
    y = 50.0f*cos(angle);

    // Specify the point size before the primitive
```

```
glPointSize(curSize);

// Draw the point
glBegin(GL_POINTS);
    glVertex3f(x, y, z);
glEnd();

// Bump up the z value and the point size
z += 0.5f;
curSize += step;
}
```

See Also   glLineWidth

glPolygonMode

Purpose	Sets the rasterization mode used to draw polygons.
Include File	<gl.h>
Syntax	void glPolygonMode(GLenum *face*, GLenum *mode*);
Description	This function allows you to change how polygons are rendered. By default, polygons are filled or shaded with the current color or material properties. However, you may also specify that only the outlines or only the vertices are drawn. Furthermore, you may apply this specification to the front, back, or both sides of polygons.
Parameters	
face	GLenum: Specifies which face of polygons is affected by the mode change: GL_FRONT, GL_BACK, or GL_FRONT_AND_BACK.
mode	GLenum: Specifies the new drawing mode. GL_FILL is the default, producing filled polygons. GL_LINE produces polygon outlines, and GL_POINT only plots the points of the vertices. The lines and points drawn by GL_LINE and GL_POINT are affected by the edge flag set by glEdgeFlag.
Returns	None.
Example	The following code from the TRIANGLE example of this chapter sets the back side of polygons to be drawn as outlines or filled regions, depending on the value of the Boolean variable bOutline:

```
// Draw back side as a polygon only, if flag is set
if(bOutline)
    glPolygonMode(GL_BACK,GL_LINE);
else
    glPolygonMode(GL_BACK,GL_FILL);
```

See Also   glEdgeFlag, glLineStipple, glLineWidth, glPointSize, glPolygonStipple

glPolygonStipple

Purpose	Sets the pattern used for polygon stippling.
Include File	<gl.h>
Syntax	`void glPolygonStipple(const GLubyte *mask );`
Description	You can use a 32×32-bit stipple pattern for filled polygons by using this function and enabling polygon stippling by calling `glEnable(GL_POLYGON_STIPPLE)`. The 1s in the stipple pattern are filled with the current color, and 0s are not drawn.

Parameters

*mask	`const GLubyte`: Points to a 32×32-bit storage area that contains the stipple pattern. The packing of bits within this storage area is affected by `glPixelStore`. By default, the MSB (most significant bit) is read first when determining the pattern.
Returns	None.
Example	The following code from the PSTIPPLE program on the CD in this chapter's subdirectory enables polygon stippling, establishes a stipple pattern, and then draws a polygon in the shape of an octagon (a stop sign):

```
// Bitmap of camp fire
GLubyte fire[] = { 0x00, 0x00, 0x00, 0x00,
                   0x00, 0x00, 0x00, 0x00,
                   0x00, 0x00, 0x00, 0x00,
                   0x00, 0x00, 0x00, 0x00,
                   . . .

                   . . .
                   0x00, 0x85, 0x10, 0x00,
                   0x00, 0x03, 0x00, 0x00,
                   0x00, 0x00, 0x10, 0x00 };
// Enable polygon stippling
glEnable(GL_POLYGON_STIPPLE);

// Specify a specific stipple pattern
glPolygonStipple(fire);
}
```

See Also	`glLineStipple, glGetPolygonStipple, glPixelStore`

glVertex

Purpose	Specifies the 3D coordinates of a vertex.
Include File	<gl.h>
Variations	`void glVertex2d(GLdouble x, GLdouble y);`
	`void glVertex2f(GLfloat x, GLfloat y);`

```
void glVertex2i(GLint x, GLint y);
void glVertex2s(GLshort x, GLshort y);
void glVertex3d(GLdouble x, GLdouble y, GLdouble z);
void glVertex3f(GLfloat x, GLfloat y, GLfloat z);
void glVertex3i(GLint x, GLint y, GLint z);
void glVertex3s(GLshort x, GLshort y, GLshort z);
void glVertex4d(GLdouble x, GLdouble y, GLdouble z, GLdouble w);
void glVertex4f(GLfloat x, GLfloat y, GLfloat z, GLfloat w);
void glVertex4i(GLint x, GLint y, GLint z, GLint w);
void glVertex4s(GLshort x, GLshort y, GLshort z, GLshort w);
void glVertex2dv(const GLdouble *v);
void glVertex2fv(const GLfloat *v);
void glVertex2iv(const GLint *v);
void glVertex2sv(const GLshort *v);
void glVertex3dv(const GLdouble *v);
void glVertex3fv(const GLfloat *v);
void glVertex3iv(const GLint *v);
void glVertex3sv(const GLshort *v);
void glVertex4dv(const GLdouble *v);
void glVertex4fv(const GLfloat *v);
void glVertex4iv(const GLint *v);
void glVertex4sv(const GLshort *v);
```

Description   This function is used to specify the vertex coordinates of the points, lines, and polygons specified by a previous call to glBegin. You cannot call this function outside the scope of a glBegin/glEnd pair.

Parameters

x, y, z   The x, y, and z coordinates of the vertex. When z is not specified, the default value is 0.0.

w   The w coordinate of the vertex. This coordinate is used for scaling purposes and by default is set to 1.0. Scaling occurs by dividing the other three coordinates by this value.

*v   An array of values that contain the two, three, or four values needed to specify the vertex.

Returns   None.

Example   You can find this ubiquitous function in literally every example and supplementary sample in this chapter. The following code shows a single point being drawn at the origin of the x,y,z coordinate system:

```
glBegin(GL_POINTS)
    glVertex3f(0.0f, 0.0f, 0.0f);
glEnd();
```

See Also   glBegin, glEnd

5

MOVING AROUND IN SPACE: COORDINATE TRANSFORMATIONS

by Richard S. Wright, Jr.

What you'll learn in this chapter:

How to...	Functions You'll Use
Establish your position in the scene	gluLookAt/glTranslate/glRotate
Position objects within the scene	glTranslate/glRotate
Scale objects	glScale
Establish a perspective transformation	gluPerspective
Perform your own matrix transformations	glLoadMatrix/glMultMatrix

In Chapter 4, "Drawing in Space: Lines, Points, and Polygons," you learned how to draw points, lines, and various primitives in 3D. To turn a collection of shapes into a coherent scene, you must arrange them in relation to one another and to the viewer. In this chapter, you'll start moving shapes and objects around in your coordinate system. (Actually, you don't move the objects, but rather shift the coordinate system to create the view you want.) The ability to place and orient your objects in a scene is a crucial tool for any 3D graphics programmer. As you will see, it is actually convenient to describe your objects' dimensions around the origin and then translate and rotate the objects into the desired position.

Is This the Dreaded Math Chapter?

In most books on 3D graphics programming, yes, this would be the dreaded math chapter. However, you can relax; we take a more moderate approach to these principles than some texts.

The keys to object and coordinate transformations are two modeling matrices maintained by OpenGL. To familiarize you with these matrices, this chapter strikes a compromise between two extremes in computer graphics philosophy. On one hand, we could warn you, "Please review a textbook on linear algebra before reading this chapter." On the other hand, we could perpetuate the deceptive reassurance that you can "learn to do 3D graphics without all those complex mathematical formulas." But we don't agree with either camp.

In reality, you can get along just fine without understanding the finer mathematics of 3D graphics, just as you can drive your car every day without having to know anything at all about automotive mechanics and the internal combustion engine. But you'd better know enough about your car to realize that you need an oil change every so often, that you have to fill the tank with gas regularly, and that you must change the tires when they get bald. This knowledge makes you a responsible (and safe!) automobile owner. If you want to be a responsible and capable OpenGL programmer, the same standards apply. You want to understand at least the basics so you know what can be done and what tools best suit the job.

Even if you don't have the ability to multiply two matrices in your head, you need to know what matrices are and that they are the means to OpenGL's 3D magic. But before you go dusting off that old linear algebra textbook (doesn't everyone have one?), have no fear: OpenGL does all the math for you. Think of it as using a calculator to do long division when you don't know how to do it on paper. Although you don't have to do it yourself, you still know what it is and how to apply it. See—you can have your cake and eat it too!

That said, a basic understanding of 3D math and transformations can be a powerful and essential tool for real-time programming. If you think we are going to treat this subject superficially, fear not! In Chapter 19, "Real-Time Programming with OpenGL," we go a little deeper into understanding the mechanics of geometry transformation. This understanding is a requirement for high-performance 3D graphics, but not necessarily a requirement to start doing useful work. In most of this book, we cover walking; in Chapter 19, we take all this knowledge and show you how to run with it.

Understanding Transformations

Transformations make possible the projection of 3D coordinates onto a 2D screen. Transformations also allow you to rotate objects around, move them about, and even stretch, shrink, and warp them. Rather than modify your object directly, a transformation modifies the coordinate system. Once a transformation rotates the coordinate system, the object appears rotated when it is drawn. Three types of transformations occur between the time you specify your vertices and the time they appear on the screen: viewing, modeling, and projection. In this section, we examine the principles of each type of transformation, which you will find summarized in Table 5.1.

Table 5.1   *Summary of the OpenGL Transformations*

Transformation	Use
Viewing	Specifies the location of the viewer or camera
Modeling	Moves objects around the scene
Modelview	Describes the duality of viewing and modeling transformations
Projection	Clips and sizes the viewing volume
Viewport	Scales the final output to the window

Eye Coordinates

An important concept throughout this chapter is that of eye coordinates. *Eye coordinates* are from the viewpoint of the observer, regardless of any transformations that may occur; think of them as "absolute" screen coordinates. Thus, eye coordinates are not real coordinates, but rather represent a virtual fixed coordinate system that is used as a common frame of reference. All of the transformations discussed in this chapter are described in terms of their effects relative to the eye coordinate system.

Figure 5.1 shows the eye coordinate system from two viewpoints. On the left (a), the eye coordinates are represented as seen by the observer of the scene (that is, perpendicular to the monitor). On the right (b), the eye coordinate system is rotated slightly so you can better see the relation of the z-axis. Positive x and y are pointed right and up, respectively, from the viewer's perspective. Positive z travels away from the origin toward the user, and negative z values travel farther away from the viewpoint into the screen.

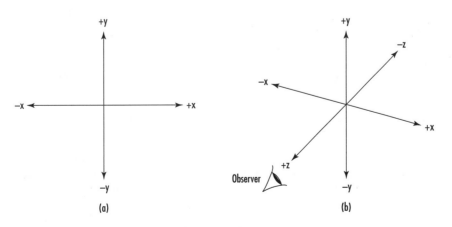

(a)   (b)

Figure 5.1   Two perspectives of eye coordinates.

When you draw in 3D with OpenGL, you use the Cartesian coordinate system. In the absence of any transformations, the system in use is identical to the eye coordinate system. All of the various transformations change the current coordinate system with respect to the eye coordinates. This, in essence, is how you move and rotate objects in your scene—by moving and rotating the coordinate system with respect to eye coordinates. Figure 5.2 gives a two-dimensional example of the coordinate system rotated 45° clockwise by eye coordinates. A square plotted on this rotated coordinate system would also appear rotated.

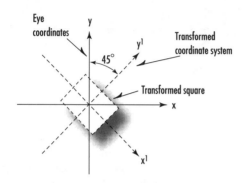

Figure 5.2   A coordinate system rotated with respect to eye coordinates.

In this chapter, you'll study the methods by which you modify the current coordinate system before drawing your objects. You can even save the state of the current system, do some transformations and drawing, and then restore the state and start over again. By chaining these events together, you will be able to place objects all about the scene and in various orientations.

Viewing Transformations

The viewing transformation is the first to be applied to your scene. It is used to determine the vantage point of the scene. By default, the point of observation is at the origin (0,0,0) looking down the negative z-axis ("into" the monitor screen). This point of observation is moved relative to the eye coordinate system to provide a specific vantage point. When the point of observation is located at the origin, objects drawn with positive z values are behind the observer.

The viewing transformation allows you to place the point of observation anywhere you want and looking in any direction. Determining the viewing transformation is like placing and pointing a camera at the scene.

In the scheme of things, you must specify the viewing transformation before any other transformations. This is because it moves the currently working coordinate system in respect to the eye coordinate system. All subsequent transformations then occur based on the newly modified coordinate system. Later, you'll see more easily how this works, when we actually start looking at how to make these transformations.

Modeling Transformations

Modeling transformations are used to manipulate your model and the particular objects within it. These transformations move objects into place, rotate them, and scale them. Figure 5.3 illustrates three modeling transformations that you will apply to your objects. Figure 5.3a shows translation, where an object is moved along a given axis. Figure 5.3b shows a rotation, where an object is rotated about one of the axes. Finally, Figure 5.3c shows the effects of scaling, where the dimensions of the object are increased or decreased by a specified amount. Scaling can occur nonuniformly (the various dimensions can be scaled by different amounts), so you can use scaling to stretch and shrink objects.

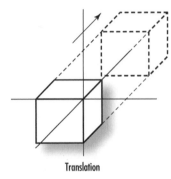

Translation

(a)

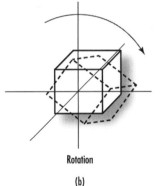

Rotation

(b)

Scaling

(c)

Figure 5.3 The modeling transformations.

The final appearance of your scene or object can depend greatly on the order in which the modeling transformations are applied. This is particularly true of translation and rotation. Figure 5.4a shows the progression of a square rotated first about the z-axis and then translated down the newly transformed x-axis. In Figure 5.4b, the same square is first translated down the x-axis and then rotated around the z-axis. The difference in the final dispositions of the square occurs because each transformation is performed with respect to the last transformation performed. In Figure 5.4a, the square is rotated with respect to the origin first. In 5.4b, after the square is translated, the rotation is performed around the newly translated origin.

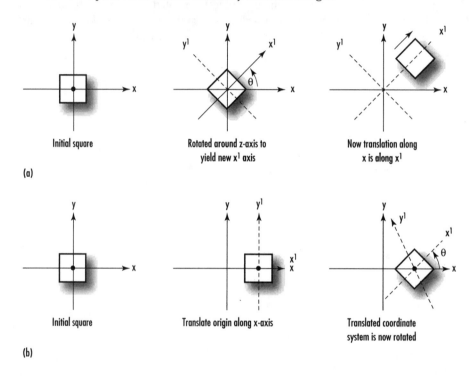

Figure 5.4 Modeling transformations: rotation/translation and translation/rotation.

The Modelview Duality

The viewing and the modeling transformations are, in fact, the same in terms of their internal effects as well as their effects on the final appearance of the scene. The distinction between the two is made purely as a convenience for the programmer. There is no real difference between moving an object backward and moving the reference system forward; as shown in Figure 5.5, the net effect is the same. (You experience this first-hand when you're sitting in your car at an intersection and you see the car next to you roll forward; it might seem to you that your own car is rolling backwards.) The term *modelview* indicates that you can think of this transformation either as the modeling transformation or the viewing transformation, but in fact there is no distinction; thus, it is the modelview transformation.

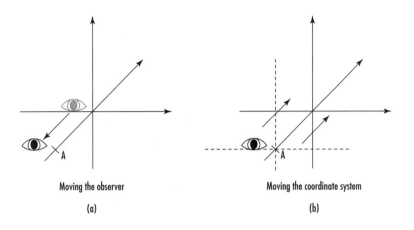

Moving the observer

(a)

Moving the coordinate system

(b)

Figure 5.5 Two ways of looking at the viewing transformation.

The viewing transformation, therefore, is essentially nothing but a modeling transformation that you apply to a virtual object (the viewer) before drawing objects. As you will soon see, new transformations are repeatedly specified as you place more objects in the scene. By convention, the initial transformation provides a reference from which all other transformations are based.

Projection Transformations

The projection transformation is applied to your final modelview orientation. This projection actually defines the viewing volume and establishes clipping planes (see the review in Chapter 1, "3D Graphics Fundamentals"). More specifically, the projection transformation specifies how a finished scene (after all the modeling is done) is translated to the final image on the screen. You will learn about two types of projections in this chapter: orthographic and perspective.

In an *orthographic* projection, all the polygons are drawn onscreen with exactly the relative dimensions specified. This is typically used for CAD or rendering two-dimensional images such as blueprints or two-dimensional graphs.

A *perspective* projection shows objects and scenes more as they appear in real life than in a blueprint. The trademark of perspective projections is foreshortening, which makes distant objects appear smaller than nearby objects of the same size. Lines in 3D space that might be parallel do not always appear parallel to the viewer. In a railroad track, for instance, the rails are parallel, but with perspective projection, they appear to converge at some distant point. We call this point the vanishing point.

The benefit of perspective projection is that you don't have to figure out where lines converge or how much smaller distant objects are. All you need to do is specify the scene using the modelview transformations and then apply the perspective projection. OpenGL works all the magic for you. Figure 5.6 compares orthographic and perspective projections on two different scenes.

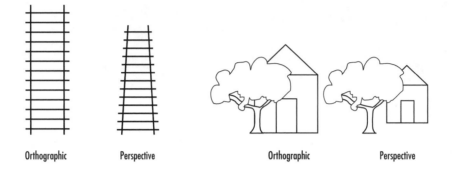

Figure 5.6 Two examples of orthographic versus perspective projections.

Orthographic projections are used most often for 2D drawing purposes where you want an exact correspondence between pixels and drawing units. This might be for a schematic layout, or perhaps a 2D graphing application. You also can use an orthographic projection for 3D renderings when the depth of the rendering has a very small depth in comparison to the distance from the viewpoint. Perspective projections are used for rendering scenes that contain wide open spaces, or objects that need to have the foreshortening effect applied. For the most part, perspective projections are typical.

Viewport Transformations

When all is said and done, you end up with a two-dimensional projection of your scene that will be mapped to a window somewhere on your screen. This mapping to physical window coordinates is the last transformation that is done, and it is called the *viewport* transformation. The viewport was discussed briefly in Chapter 3, "Using OpenGL," where you used it to stretch an image or keep a scene squarely placed in a rectangular window.

Matrix Munching

Now that you're armed with some basic vocabulary and definitions of transformations, you're ready for some simple matrix mathematics. Let's examine how OpenGL performs these transformations and get to know the functions you call to achieve your desired effects.

The mathematics behind these transformations are greatly simplified by the mathematical notation of the matrix. You can achieve each of the transformations we have discussed by multiplying a matrix that contains the vertices by a matrix that describes the transformation. Thus, all the transformations achievable with OpenGL can be described as a multiplication of two or more matrices.

What Is a Matrix?

A matrix is nothing more than a set of numbers arranged in uniform rows and columns—in programming terms, a two-dimensional array. A matrix doesn't have to be square, but each row or column must have the same number of elements as every other row or column in the matrix. Figure 5.7 presents some examples of matrices. (These don't represent anything in particular but only serve to demonstrate matrix structure.) Note that it is valid for a matrix to have a single column.

$$
\begin{bmatrix} 1 & 4 & 7 \\ 2 & 5 & 8 \\ 3 & 6 & 9 \end{bmatrix}
\begin{bmatrix} 0 & 42 \\ 1.5 & 0.877 \\ 2 & 14 \end{bmatrix}
\begin{bmatrix} 1 \\ 2 \\ 3 \\ 4 \end{bmatrix}
$$

Figure 5.7   Three examples of matrices.

Matrix transformations are actually not difficult to understand but can be intimidating. Because an understanding of matrix transformations is fundamental to many 3D tasks, you should still make an attempt to become familiar with them later. However, because you don't need to understand this topic to use OpenGL, we won't devote the space required here. Appendix B, "Further Reading," lists some good texts on this subject.

The Transformation Pipeline

To effect the types of transformations described in this chapter, you will modify two matrices in particular: the modelview matrix and the projection matrix. Don't worry, OpenGL gives you some high-level functions that you can call for these transformations. After you've mastered the basics of the OpenGL API, you will undoubtedly start trying some of the more advanced 3D rendering techniques. Only then will you need to call the lower-level functions that actually set the values contained in the matrices.

The road from raw vertex data to screen coordinates is a long one. Figure 5.8 is a flowchart of this process. First, your vertex is converted to a 1-by-4 matrix in which the first three values are the x, y, and z coordinates. The fourth number is a scaling factor that you can apply manually by using the vertex functions that take four values. This is the w coordinate, usually 1.0 by default. You will seldom modify this value directly.

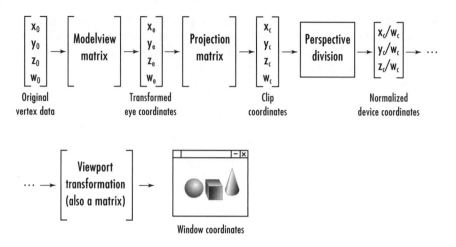

Figure 5.8 The vertex transformation pipeline.

The vertex is then multiplied by the modelview matrix, which yields the transformed eye coordinates. The eye coordinates are then multiplied by the projection matrix to yield clip coordinates. This effectively eliminates all data outside the viewing volume. The clip coordinates are then divided by the w coordinate to yield normalized device coordinates. The w value may have been modified by the projection matrix or the modelview matrix, depending on the transformations that may have occurred. Again, OpenGL and the high-level matrix functions hide all this from you.

Finally, your coordinate triplet is mapped to a 2D plane by the viewport transformation. This is also represented by a matrix, but not one that you will specify or modify directly. OpenGL sets it up internally depending on the values you specified to `glViewport`.

The Modelview Matrix

The modelview matrix is a 4×4 matrix that represents the transformed coordinate system you are using to place and orient your objects. The vertices you provide for your primitives are used as a single-column matrix and multiplied by the modelview matrix to yield new transformed coordinates in relation to the eye coordinate system.

In Figure 5.9, a matrix containing data for a single vertex is multiplied by the modelview matrix to yield new eye coordinates. The vertex data is actually four elements with an extra value w that represents a scaling factor. This value is set by default to 1.0, and rarely will you change this yourself.

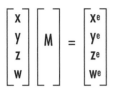

Figure 5.9 Matrix equation that applies the modelview transformation to a single vertex.

Translation

Let's take an example that modifies the modelview matrix. Say you want to draw a cube using the GLUT library's `glutWireCube` function. You simply call

```
glutWireCube(10.0f);
```

and you have a cube centered at the origin that measures 10 units on a side. To move the cube up the y-axis by 10 units before drawing it, you multiply the modelview matrix by a matrix that describes a translation of 10 units up the y-axis and then do your drawing. In skeleton form, the code looks like this:

```
// Construct a translation matrix for positive 10 Y
...

// Multiply it by the modelview matrix
...

// Draw the cube
glutWireCube(10.0f);
```

Actually, such a matrix is fairly easy to construct, but it requires quite a few lines of code. Fortunately, a high-level function is provided that does this for you:

```
void glTranslatef(GLfloat x, GLfloat y, GLfloat z);
```

This function takes as parameters the amount to translate along the x, y, and z directions. It then constructs an appropriate matrix and does the multiplication. Now, the pseudo code looks like the following, and the effect is illustrated in Figure 5.10.

```
// Translate up the y-axis 10 units
glTranslatef(0.0f, 10.0f, 0.0f);

// Draw the cube
glutWireCube(10.0f);
```

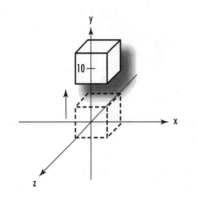

Figure 5.10   A cube translated 10 units in the positive y direction.

Rotation

To rotate an object about one of the three axes, you have to devise a rotation matrix to be multiplied by the modelview matrix. Again, a high-level function comes to the rescue:

```
glRotatef((GLfloat angle, GLfloat x, GLfloat y, GLfloat z);
```

Here, we perform a rotation around the vector specified by the x, y, and z arguments. The angle of rotation is in the counterclockwise direction measured in degrees and specified by the argument angle. In the simplest of cases, the rotation is around one of the axes, so you need to specify only that value.

You can also perform a rotation around an arbitrary axis by specifying x, y, and z values for that vector. To see the axis of rotation, you can just draw a line from the origin to the point represented by (x,y,z). The following code rotates the cube by 45° around an arbitrary axis specified by (1,1,1), as illustrated in Figure 5.11:

```
// Perform the transformation
glRotatef(90.0f, 1.0f, 1.0f, 1.0f);

// Draw the cube
glutWireCube(10.0f);
```

Scaling

A scaling transformation increases the size of your object by expanding all the vertices along the three axes by the factors specified. The function

```
glScalef(GLfloat x, GLfloat y, GLfloat z);
```

multiplies the x, y, and z values by the scaling factors specified.

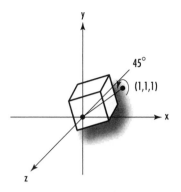

Figure 5.11 A cube rotated about an arbitrary axis.

Scaling does not have to be uniform. You can use it to stretch or squeeze objects as well. For example, the following code produces a cube that is twice as large along the x- and z-axes as the cubes discussed in the previous examples, but still the same along the y-axis. The result is shown in Figure 5.12.

```
// Perform the scaling transformation
glScalef(2.0f, 1.0f, 2.0f);

// Draw the cube
glutWireCube(10.0f);
```

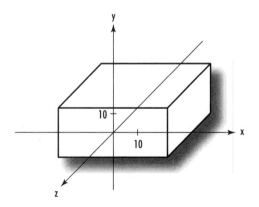

Figure 5.12 A nonuniform scaling of a cube.

The Identity Matrix

You might be wondering about now why we had to bother with all this matrix stuff in the first place. Can't we just call these transformation functions to move our objects around and be done with it? Do we really need to know that it is the modelview matrix that is modified?

The answer is yes and no, (but it's no only if you are drawing a single object in your scene). This is because the effects of these functions are cumulative. Each time you call one, the appropriate matrix is constructed and multiplied by the current modelview matrix. The new matrix then becomes the current modelview matrix, which is then multiplied by the next transformation, and so on.

Suppose you want to draw two spheres—one 10 units up the positive y-axis and one 10 units out the positive x-axis, as shown in Figure 5.13. You might be tempted to write code that looks something like this:

```
// Go 10 units up the y-axis
glTranslatef(0.0f, 10.0f, 0.0f);

// Draw the first sphere
glutSolidSphere(1.0f,15,15);

// Go 10 units out the x-axis
glTranslatef(10.0f, 0.0f, 0.0f);

// Draw the second sphere
glutSolidSphere(1.0f);
```

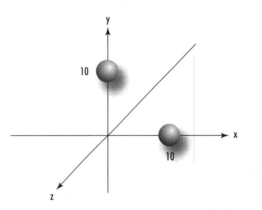
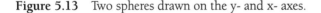

Figure 5.13 Two spheres drawn on the y- and x- axes.

Consider, however, that each call to `glTranslate` is cumulative on the modelview matrix, so the second call translates 10 units in the positive x direction from the previous translation in the y direction. This yields the results shown in Figure 5.14.

You can make an extra call to `glTranslate` to back down the y-axis 10 units in the negative direction, but this makes some complex scenes difficult to code and debug not to mention you throw extra transformation math at the CPU. A simpler method is to reset the modelview matrix to a known state—in this case, centered at the origin of our eye coordinate system.

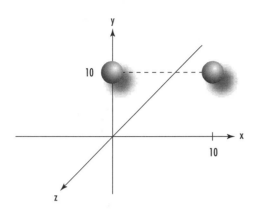

Figure 5.14 The result of two consecutive translations.

You reset the origin by loading the modelview matrix with the identity matrix. The *identity matrix* specifies that no transformation is to occur, in effect saying that all the coordinates you specify when drawing are in eye coordinates. An identity matrix contains all 0s with the exception of a diagonal row of 1s. When this matrix is multiplied by any vertex matrix, the result is that the vertex matrix is unchanged. Figure 5.15 shows this equation.

$$
\begin{bmatrix} 8.0 \\ 4.5 \\ -2.0 \\ 1.0 \end{bmatrix}
\begin{bmatrix} 1.0 & 0 & 0 & 0 \\ 0 & 1.0 & 0 & 0 \\ 0 & 0 & 1.0 & 0 \\ 0 & 0 & 0 & 1.0 \end{bmatrix}
=
\begin{bmatrix} 8.0 \\ 4.5 \\ -2.0 \\ 1.0 \end{bmatrix}
$$

Figure 5.15 Multiplying a vertex by the identity matrix yields the same vertex matrix.

As we've already stated, the details of performing matrix multiplication are outside the scope of this book. For now, just remember this: Loading the identity matrix means that no transformations are performed on the vertices. In essence, you are resetting the modelview matrix back to the origin.

The following two lines load the identity matrix into the modelview matrix:

```
glMatrixMode(GL_MODELVIEW);
glLoadIdentity();
```

The first line specifies that the current operating matrix is the modelview matrix. Once you set the current operating matrix (the matrix that your matrix functions are affecting), it remains the active matrix until you change it. The second line loads the current matrix (in this case, the modelview matrix) with the identity matrix.

Now, the following code produces results as shown earlier in Figure 5.13:

```
// Set current matrix to modelview and reset
glMatrixMode(GL_MODELVIEW);
glLoadIdentity();

// Go 10 units up the y-axis
glTranslatef(0.0f, 10.0f, 0.0f);

// Draw the first sphere
glutSolidSphere(1.0f, 15, 15);

// Reset modelview matrix again
glLoadIdentity();

// Go 10 units out the x-axis
glTranslatef(10.0f, 0.0f, 0.0f);

// Draw the second sphere
glutSolidSphere(1.0f, 15, 15);
```

The Matrix Stacks

It is not always desirable to reset the modelview matrix to identity before placing every object. Often, you want to save the current transformation state and then restore it after some objects have been placed. This approach is most convenient when you have initially transformed the modelview matrix as your viewing transformation (and thus are no longer located at the origin).

To facilitate this, OpenGL maintains a *matrix stack* for both the modelview and projection matrices. A matrix stack works just like an ordinary program stack. You can push the current matrix onto the stack to save it and then make your changes to the current matrix. Popping the matrix off the stack restores it. Figure 5.16 shows the stack principle in action.

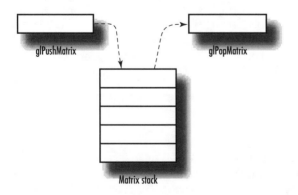

Figure 5.16 The matrix stack in action.

> **TEXTURE MATRIX STACK**
> The texture stack is another matrix stack available to the programmer. It is used for the transformation of texture coordinates. Chapter 8, "Texture Mapping," examines texture mapping and texture coordinates and contains a discussion of the texture matrix stack.

The stack depth can reach a maximum value that can be retrieved with a call to either

```
glGet(GL_MAX_MODELVIEW_STACK_DEPTH);
```

or

```
glGet(GL_MAX_PROJECTION_STACK_DEPTH);
```

If you exceed the stack depth, you get a `GL_STACK_OVERFLOW` error; if you try to pop a matrix value off the stack when there is none, you generate a `GL_STACK_UNDERFLOW` error. The stack depth is implementation dependent. For the Microsoft software implementation, the values are 32 for the modelview and 2 for the projection stack.

A Nuclear Example

Let's put to use what we have learned. In the next example, we build a crude, animated model of an atom. This atom has a single sphere at the center to represent the nucleus and three electrons in orbit about the atom. We use an orthographic projection, as we have previously in this book. (Some other interesting projections are covered in the upcoming section, "Using Projections.")

Our ATOM program uses the GLUT timer callback mechanism (discussed in Chapter 3) to redraw the scene about 10 times per second. Each time the `Render` function is called, the angle of revolution about the nucleus is incremented. Also, each electron lies in a different plane. Listing 5.1 shows the `Render` function for this example, and the output from the ATOM program is shown in Figure 5.17.

Listing 5.1   *Render Function from ATOM Sample Program*

```
// Called to draw scene
void RenderScene(void)
    {
    // Angle of revolution around the nucleus
    static float fElect1 = 0.0f;

    // Clear the window with current clearing color
    glClear(GL_COLOR_BUFFER_BIT | GL_DEPTH_BUFFER_BIT);
```

continued on next page

continued from previous page

```
// Reset the modelview matrix
glMatrixMode(GL_MODELVIEW);
glLoadIdentity();


// Translate the whole scene out and into view
// This is the initial viewing transformation
glTranslatef(0.0f, 0.0f, -100.0f);

// Red Nucleus

glColor3ub(255, 0, 0);
glutSolidSphere(10.0f, 15, 15);

// Yellow Electrons

glColor3ub(255,255,0);

// First Electron Orbit
// Save viewing transformation
glPushMatrix();

// Rotate by angle of revolution
glRotatef(fElect1, 0.0f, 1.0f, 0.0f);

// Translate out from origin to orbit distance
glTranslatef(90.0f, 0.0f, 0.0f);

// Draw the electron
glutSolidSphere(6.0f, 15, 15);

// Restore the viewing transformation
glPopMatrix();

// Second Electron Orbit
glPushMatrix();
glRotatef(45.0f, 0.0f, 0.0f, 1.0f);
glRotatef(fElect1, 0.0f, 1.0f, 0.0f);
glTranslatef(-70.0f, 0.0f, 0.0f);
glutSolidSphere(6.0f, 15, 15);
glPopMatrix();


// Third Electron Orbit
```

```
glPushMatrix();
glRotatef(360.0f, -45.0f, 0.0f, 0.0f, 1.0f);
glRotatef(fElect1, 0.0f, 1.0f, 0.0f);
glTranslatef(0.0f, 0.0f, 60.0f);
glutSolidSphere(6.0f, 15, 15);
glPopMatrix();


// Increment the angle of revolution
fElect1 += 10.0f;
if(fElect1 > 360.0f)
    fElect1 = 0.0f;

// Show the image
glutSwapBuffers();
}
```

Let's examine the code for placing one of the electrons, a couple of lines at a time. The first line saves the current modelview matrix by pushing the current transformation on the stack:

```
// First Electron Orbit
// Save viewing transformation
glPushMatrix();
```

Now, the coordinate system is rotated around the y-axis by an angle fElect1:

```
// Rotate by angle of revolution
glRotatef(fElect1, 0.0f, 1.0f, 0.0f);
```

The electron is drawn by translating down the newly rotated coordinate system:

```
// Translate out from origin to orbit distance
    glTranslatef(90.0f, 0.0f, 0.0f);
```

Then, the electron is drawn (as a solid sphere), and we restore the modelview matrix by popping it off the matrix stack:

```
// Draw the electron
    glutSolidSphere(6.0f, 15, 15);

    // Restore the viewing transformation
    glPopMatrix();
```

The other electrons are placed similarly.

Figure 5.17 Output from the ATOM sample program.

Using Projections

In our examples so far, we have used the modelview matrix to position our vantage point of the viewing volume and to place our objects therein. The projection matrix actually specifies the size and shape of our viewing volume.

Thus far in this book, we have created a simple parallel viewing volume using the function glOrtho, setting the near and far, left and right, and top and bottom clipping coordinates. When the projection matrix is loaded with the identity matrix, the diagonal line of 1s specifies that the clipping planes extend from the origin to positive or negative 1 in all directions. The projection matrix does no scaling or perspective adjustments. To see these effects, you must use a perspective projection. The next two sample programs, ORTHO and PERSPECT, are not covered in detail from the standpoint of their source code. These examples use lighting and shading that you haven't covered yet to help highlight the differences between an orthographic and a perspective projection. These interactive samples make it much easier for you to see firsthand how the projection can distort the appearance of an object. If possible, you should run these examples while reading the next two sections.

Orthographic Projections

An orthographic projection, used for most of this book so far, is square on all sides. The logical width is equal at the front, back, top, bottom, left, and right sides. This produces a parallel projection, which is useful for drawings of specific objects that do not have any foreshortening when viewed from a distance. This is good for CAD, 2D graphs, or architectural drawings, for which you want to represent the exact dimensions and measurements onscreen.

Figure 5.18 shows the output from the sample program ORTHO on the CD in this chapter's subdirectory. To produce this hollow, tube-like box, we used an orthographic projection just as we did for all our previous examples. Figure 5.19 shows the same box rotated more to the side so you can see how long it actually is.

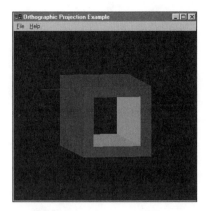

Figure 5.18   A hollow square tube shown with an orthographic projection.

Figure 5.19   A side view showing the length of the square tube.

In Figure 5.20, you're looking directly down the barrel of the tube. Because the tube does not converge in the distance, this is not an entirely accurate view of how such a tube appears in real life. To add some perspective, we must use a perspective projection.

Perspective Projections

A perspective projection performs perspective division to shorten and shrink objects that are farther away from the viewer. The width of the back of the viewing volume does not have the same measurements as the front of the viewing volume. Thus, an object of the same logical dimensions appears larger at the front of the viewing volume than if it were drawn at the back of the viewing volume.

The picture in our next example is of a geometric shape called a frustum. A frustum is a section of a pyramid viewed from the narrow end to the broad end. Figure 5.21 shows the frustum, with the observer in place.

Figure 5.20   Looking down the barrel of the tube.

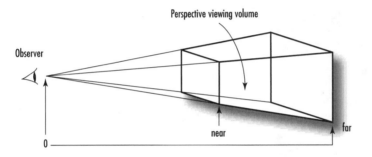

Figure 5.21   A perspective projection defined by a frustum.

You can define a frustum with the function `glFrustum`. Its parameters are the coordinates and distances between the front and back clipping planes. However, `glFrustum` is not intuitive about setting up your projection to get the desired effects. The utility function `gluPerspective` is easier to use and somewhat more intuitive for most purposes:

```
void gluPerspective(GLdouble fovy, GLdouble aspect,
                GLdouble zNear, GLdouble zFar);
```

Parameters for the `gluPerspective` function are a field-of-view angle in the vertical direction; the aspect ratio of the height to width; and the distances to the near and far clipping planes. (See Figure 5.22.) You find the aspect ratio by dividing the width (w) by the height (h) of the front clipping plane.

Listing 5.2 shows how we change our orthographic projection from the previous examples to use a perspective projection. Foreshortening adds realism to our earlier orthographic projections of the square tube (Figures 5.23, 5.24, and 5.25). The only substantial change we made for our typical projection code in Listing 5.2 is the added call to `gluPerspective`.

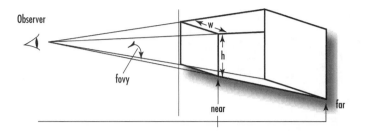

Figure 5.22   The frustum as defined by `gluPerspective`.

Figure 5.23   The square tube with a perspective projection.

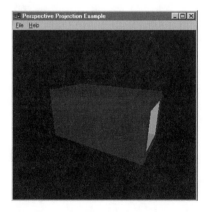

Figure 5.24   Side view with foreshortening.

Figure 5.25   Looking down the barrel of the tube with perspective added.

Listing 5.2   *Setting Up the Perspective Projection for the PERSPECT Sample Program*

```
// Change viewing volume and viewport.  Called when window is resized
void ChangeSize(GLsizei w, GLsizei h)
    {
    GLfloat fAspect;

    // Prevent a divide by zero
    if(h == 0)
        h = 1;

    // Set viewport to window dimensions
glViewport(0, 0, w, h);

    fAspect = (GLfloat)w/(GLfloat)h;

    // Reset coordinate system
    glMatrixMode(GL_PROJECTION);
    glLoadIdentity();

    // Produce the perspective projection
    gluPerspective(60.0f, fAspect, 1.0, 400.0);

    glMatrixMode(GL_MODELVIEW);
    glLoadIdentity();
    }
```

We made the same changes to the ATOM example in ATOM2 to add perspective. Run the two side-by-side and you see how the electrons appear to be smaller as they swing far away behind the nucleus.

A Far-Out Example

For a complete example showing modelview manipulation and perspective projections, we have modeled the Sun and the Earth/Moon system in revolution. This is a classic example of nested transformations with objects being transformed relative to one another using the matrix stack. We have enabled some lighting and shading for drama so you can more easily see the effects of our operations. You'll be learning about shading and lighting in the next two chapters.

In our model, we have the Earth moving around the Sun and the Moon revolving around the Earth. A light source is placed behind the observer to illuminate the Sun sphere (which also produces the illusion that the Sun is the light source). The light is then moved to the center of the Sun in order to light the Earth and Moon from the direction of the Sun, thus producing phases. This is a dramatic example of how easy it is to produce realistic effects with OpenGL.

Listing 5.3 shows the code that sets up our projection and the rendering code that keeps the system in motion. A timer elsewhere in the program invalidates the window 10 times a second to keep the **Render** function in action. Notice in Figures 5.26 and 5.27 that when the Earth appears larger, it's on the near side of the Sun; on the far side, it appears smaller.

Listing 5.3   *Code That Produces the Sun/Earth/Moon System*

```
// Change viewing volume and viewport.  Called when window is resized
void ChangeSize(GLsizei w, GLsizei h)
    {
    GLfloat fAspect;

    // Prevent a divide by zero
    if(h == 0)
        h = 1;

    // Set viewport to window dimensions
    glViewport(0, 0, w, h);

    // Calculate aspect ratio of the window
    fAspect = (GLfloat)w/(GLfloat)h;

    // Set the perspective coordinate system
    glMatrixMode(GL_PROJECTION);
    glLoadIdentity();

    // Field of view of 45 degrees, near and far planes 1.0 and 425
    gluPerspective(45.0f, fAspect, 1.0, 425.0);
```

continued on next page

continued from previous page

```
    // Modelview matrix reset
    glMatrixMode(GL_MODELVIEW);
    glLoadIdentity();
    }
// Called to draw scene
void RenderScene(void)
    {
    // Earth and Moon angle of revolution
    static float fMoonRot = 0.0f;
    static float fEarthRot = 0.0f;

    // Clear the window with current clearing color
    glClear(GL_COLOR_BUFFER_BIT | GL_DEPTH_BUFFER_BIT);

    // Save the matrix state and do the rotations
    glMatrixMode(GL_MODELVIEW);
    glPushMatrix();

    // Set light position before viewing transformation
    glLightfv(GL_LIGHT0,GL_POSITION,lightPos);

    // Translate the whole scene out and into view
    glTranslatef(0.0f, 0.0f, -300.0f);

    // Set material color, Red
    // Sun
    glColor3ub(255, 255, 0);
    glutSolidSphere(15.0f, 15, 15);

    // Move the light after we draw the sun!
    glLightfv(GL_LIGHT0,GL_POSITION,lightPos);

    // Rotate coordinate system
    glRotatef(fEarthRot, 0.0f, 1.0f, 0.0f);

    // Draw the Earth
    glColor3ub(0,0,255);
    glTranslatef(105.0f,0.0f,0.0f);
    glutSolidSphere(15.0f, 15, 15);


    // Rotate from Earth-based coordinates and draw Moon
    glRGB(200,200,200);
    glRotatef(fMoonRot,0.0f, 1.0f, 0.0f);
    glTranslatef(30.0f, 0.0f, 0.0f);
    fMoonRot+= 15.0f;
    if(fMoonRot > 360.0f)
        fMoonRot = 0.0f;
```

```
glutSolidSphere(6.0f, 15, 15);


// Restore the matrix state
glPopMatrix();    // Modelview matrix


// Step earth orbit 5 degrees
fEarthRot += 5.0f;
if(fEarthRot > 360.0f)
    fEarthRot = 0.0f;

// Show the image    glutSwapBuffers();
}
```

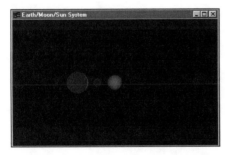

Figure 5.26   The Sun/Earth/Moon system with the Earth on the near side.

Figure 5.27   The Sun/Earth/Moon system with the Earth on the far side.

Advanced Matrix Manipulation

You don't have to use the high-level functions to produce your transformations. We recommend that you do, however, because those functions often are highly optimized for their particular purpose, whereas the low-level functions are designed for general use. For example, you can actually translate a vertex much faster than using a

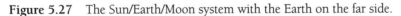

matrix multiply, and many drivers employ such optimizations. Two of these low-level functions make it possible for you to load your own matrix and multiply it into either the modelview or projection matrix stacks.

Loading a Matrix

You can load an arbitrary matrix into the projection, modelview, or texture matrix stacks. First, declare an array to hold the 16 values of a 4×4 matrix. Make the desired matrix stack the current one, and call `glLoadMatrix`.

The matrix is stored in column-major order, which simply means that each column is traversed first from top to bottom. Figure 5.28 shows the matrix elements in numbered order. The following code shows an array being loaded with the identity matrix and then being loaded into the modelview matrix stack. This is equivalent to calling `glLoadIdentity` using the higher-level functions.

```
// Equivalent, but more flexible
glFloat m[] = { 1.0f, 0.0f, 0.0f, 0.0f,
0.0f, 1.0f, 0.0f, 0.0f,
                0.0f, 0.0f, 1.0f, 0.0f,
                0.0f, 0.0f, 0.0f, 1.0f };

glMatrixMode(GL_MODELVIEW);
glLoadMatrixf(m);
```

$$\begin{bmatrix} a_0 & a_4 & a_8 & a_{12} \\ a_1 & a_5 & a_9 & a_{13} \\ a_2 & a_6 & a_{10} & a_{14} \\ a_3 & a_7 & a_{11} & a_{15} \end{bmatrix}$$

Figure 5.28 Column-major matrix ordering.

Performing Your Own Transformations

You can load an array with an arbitrary matrix if you want and multiply it, too, into one of the three matrix stacks. The following code shows a transformation matrix that translates 10 units along the x-axis. This matrix is then multiplied into the modelview matrix. You can also achieve this affect (and probably more efficiently) by calling `glTranslatef`:

```
// Define the Translation matrix
glFloat m[] = { 1.0f, 0.0f, 0.0f, 10.0f,
0.0f, 1.0f, 0.0f, 0.0f,
                0.0f, 0.0f, 1.0f, 0.0f,
```

```
        0.0f, 0.0f, 0.0f, 1.0f };

// Multiply the translation matrix by the current modelview
// matrix. The new matrix becomes the modelview matrix
glMatrixMode(GL_MODELVIEW);
glMultMatrixf(m);
```

Other Transformations

There's no particular advantage in duplicating the functionality of `gLoadIdentity` or `glTranslatef` by specifying a matrix. The real reason for allowing manipulation of arbitrary matrices is to allow for complex matrix transformations. One such use is for drawing shadows, and you'll see that in action toward the end of the next chapter. You can also use these matrix functions to do your own transformations. Why would you want to do this after I told you to let OpenGL do it for you? You'll see in Chapter 19 how we can employ a new type of culling called *frustum culling* to eliminate geometry before sending primitives to the OpenGL driver. As you'll learn then, this approach can have a dramatic performance impact. You'll also learn about another real-time technique for angular transformations using *quaternions*, and the problem they solve: *gimbal lock*.

Summary

In this chapter, you've learned concepts crucial to using OpenGL for creation of 3D scenes. Even if you can't juggle matrices in your head, you now know what matrices are and how they are used to perform the various transformations. You've also learned how to manipulate the modelview and projection matrix stacks to place your objects in the scene and to determine how they are viewed onscreen.

Finally, we also showed you the functions needed to perform your own matrix magic if you are so inclined. These functions allow you to create your own matrices and load them into the matrix stack or multiply them by the current matrix first.

Reference Section

glFrustum

Purpose	Multiplies the current matrix by a perspective matrix.
Include File	<gl.h>
Syntax	void glFrustum(GLdouble *left*, GLdouble *right*, GLdouble *bottom*, GLdouble *top*, GLdouble *near*, GLdouble *far*);

Description	This function creates a perspective matrix that produces a perspective projection. The eye is assumed to be located at (0,0,0), with *far* being the distance of the far clipping plane and *near* specifying the distance to the near clipping plane. Both values must be positive. This function can adversely affect the precision of the depth buffer if the ratio of far to near (*far/near*) is large.
Parameters	
left, right	GLdouble: Coordinates for the left and right clipping planes.
bottom, top	GLdouble: Coordinates for the bottom and top clipping planes.
near, far	GLdouble: Distance to the near and far clipping planes. Both of these values must be positive.
Returns	None.
Example	The following code sets up a perspective matrix that defines a viewing volume from 0 to −100 on the z-axis. The x and y extents are 100 units in the positive and negative directions:

```
glLoadMatrix(GL_PROJECTION);
glLoadIdentify();
glFrustum(-100.0f, 100.0f, -100.0f, 100.0f, 0.0f, 100.0f);
```

See Also	glOrtho, glMatrixMode, glMultMatrix, glViewport

glLoadIdentity

Purpose	Sets the current matrix to identity.
Include File	<gl.h>
Syntax	void glLoadIdentity(void);
Description	This function replaces the current transformation matrix with the identity matrix. This essentially resets the coordinate system to eye coordinates.
Returns	None.
Example	The following code shows the modelview matrix being set to identity:

```
glMatrixMode(GL_MODELVIEW);
glLoadIdentity();
```

See Also	glLoadMatrix, glMatrixMode, glMultMatrix, glPushMatrix

glLoadMatrix

Purpose	Sets the current matrix to the one specified.
Include File	<gl.h>
Variations	`void glLoadMatrixd(const GLdouble *m);` `void glLoadMatrixf(const GLfloat *m);`
Description	Replaces the current transformation matrix with an arbitrary matrix supplied. It might be more efficient to use some of the other matrix manipulation functions, such as `glLoadIdentity`, `glRotate`, `glTranslate`, and `glScale`.
Parameters	
*m	`GLdouble` or `GLfloat`: This array represents a 4×4 matrix that will be used for the current transformation matrix. The array is stored in column-major order as 16 consecutive values.
Returns	None.
Example	The following two segments of code are equivalent. They both load the modelview matrix with the identity matrix:

```
// Efficient way
glMatrixMode(GL_MODELVIEW);
glLoadIdentity();

// Equivalent, but more flexible
glFloat m[] = { 1.0f, 0.0f, 0.0f, 0.0f,
    0.0f, 1.0f, 0.0f, 0.0f,
        0.0f, 0.0f, 1.0f, 0.0f,
        0.0f, 0.0f, 0.0f, 1.0f };

glMatrixMode(GL_MODELVIEW);
glLoadMatrixf(m);
```

See Also	`glLoadIdentity`, `glMatrixMode`, `glMultMatrix`, `glPushMatrix`

glMatrixMode

Purpose	Specifies the current matrix (`GL_PROJECTION`, `GL_MODELVIEW`, or `GL_TEXTURE`).
Include File	<gl.h>
Syntax	`void glMatrixMode(GLenum mode );`
Description	This function is used to determine which matrix stack (`GL_MODELVIEW`, `GL_PROJECTION`, or `GL_TEXTURE`) is used for matrix operations.

Parameters

mode   GLenum: Identifies which matrix stack is used for subsequent matrix operations. Any of the values in Table 5.2 are accepted.

Returns   None.

Example   The following common two lines of code select the modelview matrix stack for matrix operations, and then load the identity matrix:

```
glMatrixMode(GL_MODELVIEW);
glLoadMatrixf(m);
```

See Also   glLoadMatrix, glPushMatrix

Table 5.2 *Valid Matrix Mode Identifiers for* glMatrixMode

Mode	Matrix Stack
GL_MODELVIEW	Matrix operations affect the modelview matrix stack. (Used to move objects around the scene.)
GL_PROJECTION	Matrix operations affect the projection matrix stack. (Used to define clipping volume.)
GL_TEXTURE	Matrix operations affect the texture matrix stack. (Manipulates texture coordinates.)

glMultMatrix

Purpose   Multiplies the current matrix by the one specified.

Include File   <gl.h>

Variations   void glMultMatrixd(const GLdouble *m);
                          void glMultMatrixf(const GLfloat *m);

Description   This function multiplies the currently selected matrix stack with the one specified. The resulting matrix is then stored as the current matrix at the top of the matrix stack.

Parameters

*m   GLdouble or GLfloat: This array represents a 4×4 matrix that will be multiplied by the current matrix. The array is stored in column-major order as 16 consecutive values.

Returns   None.

Example
The following code creates a translation matrix and multiplies it by the current modelview matrix. The newly created matrix replaces the values in the modelview matrix. The multiplication shown here could also have been accomplished by calling `glTranslate(10.0f, 0.0f, 0.0f);`:

```
// Define the translation matrix
glFloat m[] = { 1.0f, 0.0f, 0.0f, 10.0f,
     0.0f, 1.0f, 0.0f, 0.0f,
          0.0f, 0.0f, 1.0f, 0.0f,
          0.0f, 0.0f, 0.0f, 1.0f };

// Multiply the translation matrix by the current modelview
// matrix. The new matrix becomes the modelview matrix
glMatrixMode(GL_MODELVIEW);
glMultMatrixf(m);
```

See Also
glMatrixMode, glLoadIdentity, glLoadMatrix, glPushMatrix

glPopMatrix

Purpose
Pops the current matrix off the matrix stack.

Include File
<gl.h>

Syntax
`void glPopMatrix(void);`

Description
This function is used to pop the last (topmost) matrix off the current matrix stack. This is most often used to restore the previous condition of the current transformation matrix if it was saved with a call to `glPushMatrix`.

Returns
None.

Example
The following code is from the ATOM example program for this chapter. This section saves the modelview matrix state with a call to `glPushMatrix` (which is centered in the atom). Then, the coordinate system is rotated and translated appropriately to place the electron, which is represented by a small sphere. The coordinate system is then restored by a call to `glPopMatrix` before the next electron is drawn:

```
// First Electron Orbit
glPushMatrix();
glRotatef(fElect1, 0.0f, 1.0f, 0.0f);
glTranslatef(90.0f, 0.0f, 0.0f);
auxSolidSphere(6.0f);
glPopMatrix();
```

See Also
glPushMatrix

glPushMatrix

Purpose	Pushes the current matrix onto the matrix stack.
Include File	<gl.h>
Syntax	`void glPushMatrix(void);`
Description	This function is used to push the current matrix onto the current matrix stack. This is most often used to save the current transformation matrix so that it can be restored later with a call to `glPopMatrix`.
Returns	None.
Example	See `glPopMatrix`.
See Also	`glPopMatrix`

glRotate

Purpose	Rotates the current matrix by a rotation matrix.
Include File	<gl.h>
Variations	`void glRotated(GLdouble angle, GLdouble x, GLdouble y, GLdouble z);` `void glRotatef(GLfloat angle, GLfloat x, GLfloat y, GLfloat z);`
Description	This function multiplies the current matrix by a rotation matrix that performs a counterclockwise rotation around a directional vector that passes from the origin through the point (x,y,z). The newly rotated matrix becomes the current transformation matrix.
Parameters	
angle	`GLdouble` or `GLfloat`: The angle of rotation in degrees. The angle produces a counterclockwise rotation.
x, y, z	`GLdouble` or `GLfloat`: A direction vector from the origin that is used as the axis of rotation.
Returns	None.
Example	The following code from the SOLAR sample program places the Moon in orbit around the earth. The current modelview matrix stack is centered at the Earth's position when it is rotated by the current revolution of the Moon and then translated out to its position away from the Earth.

```
// Moon
glRGB(200,200,200);
glRotatef(fMoonRot,0.0f, 1.0f, 0.0f);
glTranslatef(30.0f, 0.0f, 0.0f);
```

```
        fMoonRot+= 15.0f;
        if(fMoonRot > 360.0)
            fMoonRot = 15.0f;

        auxSolidSphere(6.0f);
```

See Also   glScale, glTranslate

glScale

Purpose	Multiplies the current matrix by a scaling matrix.
Include File	<gl.h>
Variations	void glScaled(GLdouble *x*, GLdouble *y*, GLdouble *z*); void glScalef(GLfloat *x*, GLfloat *y*, GLfloat *z*);
Description	This function multiplies the current matrix by a scaling matrix. The newly scaled matrix becomes the current transformation matrix.
Parameters	
x, y, z	GLdouble or GLfloat: Scale factors along the x-, y-, and z-axes.
Returns	None.
Example	The following code modifies the modelview matrix to produce flattened-out objects. The vertices of all subsequent primitives are reduced by half in the y direction:

```
    glMatrixMode(GL_MODELVIEW);
    glLoadIdentity();

    glScalef(1.0f, 0.5f, 1.0f);
```

See Also   glRotate, glTranslate

glTranslate

Purpose	Multiplies the current matrix by a translation matrix.
Include File	<gl.h>
Variations	void glTranslated(GLdouble *x*, GLdouble *y*, GLdouble *z*); void glTranslatef(GLfloat *x*, GLfloat *y*, GLfloat *z*);
Description	This function multiplies the current matrix by a translation matrix. The newly translated matrix becomes the current transformation matrix.
Parameters	
x, y, z	GLdouble or GLfloat: The x, y, and z coordinates of a translation vector.

Returns	None.
Example	The following code is from the sample program SOLAR. It places a blue sphere 105 units along the positive x-axis away from the origin:

```
// Earth
glColor3f(0.0f,0.0f,1.0f);
glTranslatef(105.0f,0.0f,0.0f);
auxSolidSphere(15.0f);
```

See Also	glRotate, glScale

gluLookAt

Purpose	Defines a viewing transformation.
Include File	<glu.h>
Syntax	void gluLookAt(GLdouble *eyex*, GLdouble *eyey*, GLdouble *eyez*, GLdouble *centerx*, GLdouble *centery*, GLdouble *centerz*, GLdouble *upx*, GLdouble *upy*, GLdouble *upz*);
Description	Defines a viewing transformation based on the position of the eye, the position of the center of the scene, and a vector pointing up from the viewer's perspective.
Parameters	
eyex, eyey, eyez	GLdouble: x, y, and z coordinates of the eye point.
centerx, centery, centerz	GLdouble: x, y, and z coordinates of the center of the scene being looked at.
upx, upy, upz	GLdouble: x, y, and z coordinates that specify the up vector.
Returns	None.
Example	The following code resets the viewing transformation based on a given location and viewing direction:

```
// Reset the modelview matrix
glMatrixMode(GL_MODELVIEW);
glLoadIdentity();

// Set viewing transformation based on position and direction.
gluLookAt(locX, locY, locZ, dirX, dirY, dirZ, 0.0f, 1.0f, 0.0f);
```

Here, locX through locY specify the location of the eye point (the observer's point of view), and dirX through dirZ represent the direction in which the viewer is pointed. The last three values specify the direction vector that should be considered up.

See Also	glFrustum, gluPerspective

gluOrtho2D

Purpose	Defines a two-dimensional orthographic projection.
Include File	<glu.h>
Syntax	`void gluOrtho2D(GLdouble left, GLdouble right, GLdouble bottom, GLdouble top);`
Description	This function defines a 2D orthographic projection matrix. This projection matrix is equivalent to calling `glOrtho` with *near* and *far* set to 0 and 1, respectively.
Parameters	
left, right	`GLdouble`: Specifies the far-left and far-right clipping planes.
bottom, top	`GLdouble`: Specifies the top and bottom clipping planes.
Returns	None.
Example	The following line of code sets up a 2D viewing volume that allows drawing in the xy plane from −100 to +100 along the x- and y-axes. Positive y is up, and positive x is to the right:

```
gluOrtho2D(-100.0, 100.0, -100.0, 100.0);
```

See Also	glOrtho, gluPerspective

gluPerspective

Purpose	Defines a viewing perspective projection matrix.
Include File	<glu.h>
Syntax	`void gluPerspective(GLdouble fovy, GLdouble aspect, GLdouble zNear, GLdouble zFar);`
Description	This function creates a matrix that describes a viewing frustum in world coordinates. The aspect ratio should match the aspect ratio of the viewport (specified with `glViewport`). The perspective division is based on the field-of-view angle and the distance to the near and far clipping planes.
Parameters	
fovy	`GLdouble`: The field of view in degrees, in the y direction.
aspect	`GLdouble`: The aspect ratio. This is used to determine the field of view in the x direction. The aspect ratio is x/y.
zNear, zFar	`GLdouble`: The distance from the viewer to the near and far clipping plane. These values are always positive.
Returns	None.

Example

The following code is from the sample program SOLAR. It creates a perspective projection that makes planets on the far side of the Sun appear smaller than when on the near side:

```
// Change viewing volume and viewport.
// Called when window is resized
void ChangeSize(GLsizei w, GLsizei h)
    {
    GLfloat fAspect;

    // Prevent a divide by zero
    if(h == 0)
        h = 1;

    // Set viewport to window dimensions
glViewport(0, 0, w, h);

    // Calculate aspect ratio of the window
    fAspect = (GLfloat)w/(GLfloat)h;

    // Reset coordinate system
    glMatrixMode(GL_PROJECTION);
    glLoadIdentity();

    gluPerspective(45.0f, fAspect, 1.0, 425.0);

    // Modelview matrix reset
    glMatrixMode(GL_MODELVIEW);
    glLoadIdentity();
    }
```

See Also

glFrustum, gluOrtho2D

6

COLOR, LIGHTING, AND MATERIALS

by Richard S. Wright, Jr.

What you'll learn in this chapter:

How to...	Functions You'll Use
Specify a color in terms of RGB components	`glColor`
Set the shading model	`glShadeModel`
Set the lighting model	`glLightModel`
Set lighting parameters	`glLight`
Set material reflective properties	`glColorMaterial/glMaterial`
Use surface normals	`glNormal`

This chapter discusses color and lighting: in our opinion, the honey spot of OpenGL. This is the chapter where 3D graphics really start to look interesting, and it only gets better from here. You've been learning OpenGL from the ground up—how to put programs together and then how to assemble objects from primitives and manipulate them in 3D space. Until now, we've been laying the foundation, and you still can't tell what the house is going to look like! To recoin a phrase, "Where's the beef?"

To put it succinctly, the beef starts here. For most of the rest of this book, science takes a back seat and magic rules. According to Arthur C. Clarke, "Any sufficiently advanced technology is indistinguishable from magic." Of course, there is no real magic involved in color and lighting, but it sure can seem that way at times. (If you want to dig into the mathematics, see Appendix B, "Further Reading.")

Another name for this chapter might be "Adding Realism to Your Scenes." You see, there is more to an object's color in the real world than just what color we might tell OpenGL to make it. In addition to having a color, objects can appear shiny or dull or can even glow with their own light. An object's apparent color varies with bright or dim lighting, and even the color of the light hitting an object makes a difference. An illuminated object can even be shaded across its surface when lit or viewed from an angle.

What Is Color?

First, let's talk a little bit about color itself. How is a color made in nature, and how do we see colors? Understanding color theory and how the human eye sees a color scene will lend some insight into how you create a color programmatically. (If color theory is old hat to you, you can probably skip this section.)

Light as a Wave

Color is simply a wavelength of light that is visible to the human eye. If you had any physics classes in school, you might remember something about light being both a wave and a particle. It is modeled as a wave that travels through space much as a ripple through a pond, and it is modeled as a particle, such as a raindrop falling to the ground. If this seems confusing, you know why most people don't study quantum mechanics!

The light you see from nearly any given source is actually a mixture of many different kinds of light. These kinds of light are identified by their wavelengths. The wavelength of light is measured as the distance between the peaks of the light wave, as illustrated in Figure 6.1.

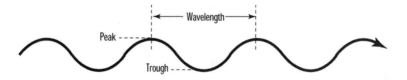

Figure 6.1   How a wavelength of light is measured.

Wavelengths of visible light range from 390 nanometers (one billionth of a meter) for violet light to 720 nanometers for red light; this range is commonly called the spectrum. You've undoubtedly heard the terms ultraviolet and infrared; these represent light not visible to the naked eye, lying beyond the ends of the spectrum. You will recognize the spectrum as containing all the colors of the rainbow. See Figure 6.2.

Light as a Particle

"Okay, Mr. Smart Brain," you might ask. "If color is a wavelength of light and the only visible light is in this 'rainbow' thing, where is the brown for my Fig Newtons or the black for my coffee or even the white of this page?" We begin answering that question by telling you that black is not a color, nor is white. Actually, black is the absence of

COLOR, LIGHTING, AND MATERIALS

color, and white is an even combination of all the colors at once. That is, a white object reflects all wavelengths of colors evenly, and a black object absorbs all wavelengths evenly.

Figure 6.2   The spectrum of visible light.

As for the brown of those fig bars and the many other colors that you see, they are indeed colors. Actually, at the physical level, they are composite colors. They are made of varying amounts of the "pure" colors found in the spectrum. To understand how this works, think of light as a particle. Any given object when illuminated by a light source is struck by "billions and billions" (my apologies to Carl Sagan) of photons, or tiny light particles. Remembering our physics mumbo jumbo, each of these photons is also a wave, which has a wavelength and thus a specific color in the spectrum.

All physical objects consist of atoms. The reflection of photons from an object depends on the kinds of atoms, the amount of each kind, and the arrangement of atoms in the object. Some photons are reflected and some are absorbed (the absorbed photons are usually converted to heat), and any given material or mixture of materials (such as your fig bar) reflects more of some wavelengths than others. Figure 6.3 illustrates this principle.

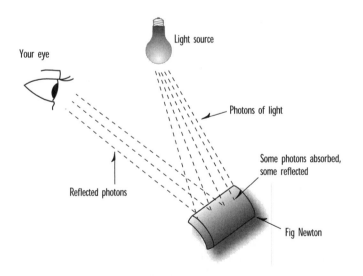

Figure 6.3   An object reflects some photons and absorbs others.

Your Personal Photon Detector

The reflected light from your fig bar, when seen by your eye, is interpreted as color. The billions of photons enter your eye and are focused onto the back of your eye, where your retina acts as sort of a photographic plate. The retina's millions of cone cells are excited when struck by the photons, and this causes neural energy to travel to your brain, which interprets the information as light and color. The more photons that strike the cone cells, the more excited they get. This level of excitation is interpreted by your brain as the brightness of the light, which makes sense; the brighter the light, the more photons there are to strike the cone cells.

The eye has three kinds of cone cells. All of them respond to photons, but each kind responds most to a particular wavelength. One is more excited by photons that have reddish wavelengths, one by green wavelengths, and one by blue wavelengths. Thus, light that is composed mostly of red wavelengths excites red-sensitive cone cells more than the other cells, and your brain receives the signal that the light you are seeing is mostly reddish. You do the math: A combination of different wavelengths of various intensities will, of course, yield a mix of colors. All wavelengths equally represented thus is perceived as white, and no light of any wavelength is black.

You can see that any "color" that your eye perceives actually consists of light all over the visible spectrum. The "hardware" in your eye detects what it sees in terms of the relative concentrations and strengths of red, green, and blue light. Figure 6.4 shows how brown comprises a photon mix of 60 percent red photons, 40 percent green photons, and 10 percent blue photons.

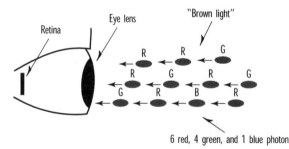

Figure 6.4 How the "color" brown is perceived by the eye.

The Computer as a Photon Generator

Now that you understand how the human eye discerns colors, it makes sense that when we want to generate a color with a computer, we do so by specifying separate intensities for the red, green, and blue components of the light. It so happens that color computer monitors are designed to produce three kinds of light (can you guess which three?), each with varying degrees of intensity. In the back of your computer monitor is an electron gun that shoots electrons at the back of the screen you view. This screen contains phosphors that emit red, green, and blue light when struck by the electrons. The intensity of the light emitted varies with the intensity of the electron beam. (Okay, how then do color LCDs work? We leave this as an exercise for the reader!) These three color phosphors are packed closely together to make up a single physical dot on the screen. See Figure 6.5.

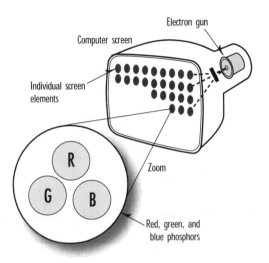

Figure 6.5   How a computer monitor generates colors.

You might recall that in Chapter 3, "Using OpenGL," we explained how OpenGL defines a color exactly as intensities of red, green, and blue, with the `glColor` command.

PC Color Hardware

There once was a time when state-of-the-art PC graphics hardware meant the Hercules graphics card. This card could produce bitmapped images with a resolution of 720×348. The drawback was that each pixel had only two states: on and off. At that time, bitmapped graphics of any kind on a PC was a big deal, and you could produce some great monochrome graphics—even 3D!

Actually predating the Hercules card was the CGA card, the Color Graphics Adapter. Introduced with the first IBM PC, this card could support resolutions of 320×200 pixels and could place any four of 16 colors on the screen at once. A higher resolution (640×200) with two colors was also possible but wasn't as effective or cost conscious as the Hercules card. (Color monitors = $$$.) CGA was puny by today's standards; it was even outmatched then by the graphics capabilities of a $200 Commodore 64 or Atari home computer at the time. Lacking adequate resolution for business graphics or even modest modeling, CGA was used primarily for simple PC games or business applications that could benefit from colored text. Generally, it was hard to make a good business justification for this more expensive hardware.

The next big breakthrough for PC graphics came when IBM introduced the Enhanced Graphics Adapter (EGA) card. This one could do more than 25 lines of colored text in new text modes, and for graphics, it could support 640×350 pixel bitmapped graphics in 16 colors! Other technical improvements eliminated some flickering problems of the CGA ancestor and provided for better and smoother animation. Now arcade-style games, real business graphics, and even simple 3D graphics became not only possible but even reasonable on the PC. This advance was a giant move beyond CGA, but still PC graphics were in their infancy.

The last mainstream PC graphics standard set by IBM was the VGA card (which stood for Vector Graphics Array rather than the commonly held Video Graphics Adapter). This card was significantly faster than the EGA; it could support 16 colors at a higher resolution (640×480) and 256 colors at a lower resolution of 320×200. These 256 colors were selected from a palette of more than 16 million possible colors. That's when the floodgates opened for PC graphics. Near photo-realistic graphics become possible on PCs. Ray tracers, 3D games, and photo-editing software began to pop up in the PC market.

IBM, as well, had a high-end graphics card—the 8514—for its "workstations." This card could do 1,024×768 graphics at 256 colors. IBM thought this card would only be used by CAD and scientific applications! But one thing is certain about the consumer market: They always want more. It was this short-sightedness that cost IBM its role as standard setter in the PC graphics market. Other vendors began to ship "Super-VGA" cards that could display higher and higher resolutions, with more and more colors. First, we saw 800×600, then 1024×768 and even higher, with first 256 colors, and then 32,000, and 65,000. Today, 24-bit color cards can display 16 million colors at resolutions far above 1,024×768. Even entry-level Windows PCs sold today can support at least 65,000 colors at resolutions of 1,024×768.

All this power makes for some really cool possibilities—photo-realistic 3D graphics, to name just one. When Microsoft ported OpenGL to the Windows platform, that enabled creation of high-end graphics applications for PCs. Combine today's fast processors with 3D-graphics accelerated graphics cards, and you can get the kind of performance possible only a few years ago on $100,000 graphics workstations—for the cost of a Wal-Mart Christmas special! Today's typical home machines are capable of sophisticated simulations, games, and more. Our children will laugh at the term "virtual reality" in the same way we smile at those old Buck Rogers rocket ships.

PC Display Modes

Microsoft Windows revolutionized the world of PC graphics in two respects. First, it created a mainstream graphical operating environment that was adopted by the business world at large and, soon thereafter, the consumer market. Second, it made PC graphics significantly easier for programmers to do. With Windows, the hardware was "virtualized" by Windows display device drivers. Instead of having to write instructions directly to the video hardware, programmers today can write to a single API, and

Windows handles the specifics of talking to the hardware. Typically, Microsoft provides in the Windows base package (usually with vendor assistance) drivers for the more popular graphics cards. Hardware vendors with later hardware and software revisions ship their cards with Windows drivers and often provide updates to these drivers on their Web sites.

Screen Resolution

Screen resolution for today's PCs can vary from 640×80 pixels up to 1,600×1,200 or more. Screen resolution, however, is not usually a prime limiting factor in writing graphics applications. The lower resolution of 640×480 is considered adequate for some graphics display tasks. More important is the size of the window, and this is taken into account easily with clipping volume and viewport settings (see Chapter 3). By scaling the size of the drawing to the size of the window, you can easily account for the various resolutions and window size combinations that can occur. Well-written graphics applications display the same approximate image regardless of screen resolution. The user should automatically be able to see more and sharper details as the resolution increases.

Color Depth

If an increase in screen resolution or in the number of available drawing pixels in turn increases the detail and sharpness of the image, so too should an increase in available colors improve the clarity of the resulting image. An image displayed on a computer that can display millions of colors should look remarkably better than the same image displayed with only 16 colors. In programming, there are really only three color depths that you need to worry about: 4-bit, 8-bit, and 24-bit.

4-Bit Color

On the low end, your program might run in a video mode that only supports 16 colors—called 4-bit mode because there are 4 bits devoted to color information for each pixel. These 4 bits represent a value from 0 to 15 that provides an index into a set of 16 predefined colors. (When you have a limited number of colors that are accessed by index, this is called a *palette*.) With only 16 colors at your disposal, there is little you can do to improve the clarity and sharpness of your image. It is generally accepted that most serious graphics applications can safely ignore the 16-color mode.

8-Bit Color

The 8-bit color mode supports up to 256 colors on the screen. This is a substantial improvement over 4-bit color, but still limiting. Most PC OpenGL hardware accelerators do not accelerate 8-bit color, but for software rendering, it is possible to get satisfactory results under Windows with certain considerations. The most important consideration is the construction of the correct color palette. This topic is covered briefly in Chapter 17, "The OpenGL Pixel Format and Rendering Context."

24-Bit Color

The best quality image production available today on PCs is 24-bit color mode. In this mode, a full 24 bits are devoted to each pixel to hold 8 bits of color data for each of the red, green, and blue color components (8 + 8 + 8 = 24). You have the capability to put any of more than 16 million possible colors in every pixel on the screen. The most obvious drawback to this mode is the amount of memory required for high-resolution screens (more than 2MB for a 1,024×768 screen). Indirectly, it is also much slower to move larger chunks of memory around when doing animation or just drawing on the screen. Fortunately, today's accelerated graphics adapters are optimized for these types of operations and are shipping with larger amounts of onboard memory to accommodate the extra memory usage.

Other Color Depths

For saving memory or improving performance, many display cards also support various other color modes.

In the area of performance improvement, some cards support a 32-bit color mode sometimes called true color mode. Actually, the 32-bit color mode cannot display any more colors than the 24-bit mode, but it improves performance by aligning the data for each pixel on a 32-bit address boundary. Unfortunately, this results in a wasted 8-bits (1 byte) per pixel. On today's 32-bit Intel PCs, a memory address evenly divisible by 32 results in much faster memory access. Modern OpenGL accelerators also support 32-bit mode, with 24 bits being reserved for the RGB colors and 8 bits being used for destination alpha storage (see Chapter 10, "Visual Effects: Blending and Fog," and Chapter 17).

Another popular display mode, 16-bit color, is sometimes supported to use memory more efficiently. This allows one of 65,536 possible colors for each pixel. This is practically as effective as 24-bit color for photographic image reproduction, as it can be difficult to tell the difference between 16-bit and 24-bit color modes for most photographic images. The savings in memory and the increase in display speed have made this popular for the first generation of consumer "game" 3D accelerators. The added color fidelity of 24-bit mode really adds to an image's quality, especially with blending operations. (See Chapter 10 for details on blending with OpenGL.)

Using Color in OpenGL

You now know that OpenGL specifies an exact color as separate intensities of red, green, and blue components. You also know that modern PC hardware might be able to display nearly all of these combinations or only a very few. How, then, do we specify a desired color in terms of these red, green, and blue components?

The Color Cube

Because a color is specified by three positive color values, we can model the available colors as a volume that we shall call the RGB colorspace. Figure 6.6 shows what this colorspace looks like at the origin with red, green, and blue as the axes. The red, green, and blue coordinates are specified just like x, y, and z coordinates. At the origin (0,0,0), the relative intensities of all the components is zero, and the resulting color is black. The maximum available on the PC for storage information is 24 bits, so with 8 bits for each component, let's say that a value of 255 along the axis represents full saturation of that component. We then end up with a cube measuring 255 on each side. The corner directly opposite black, where the concentrations are (0,0,0), is white, with relative concentrations of (255,255,255). At full saturation (255) from the origin along each axis lies the pure colors of red, green, and blue.

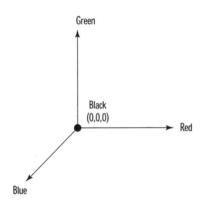

Figure 6.6   The origin of RGB colorspace.

This "color cube" (see Figure 6.7) contains all the possible colors, either on the surface of the cube or within the interior of the cube. For example, all possible shades of gray between black and white lie internally on the diagonal line between the corner at (0,0,0) and (255,255,255).

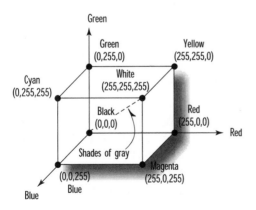

Figure 6.7   The RGB colorspace.

Figure 6.8 is a screen shot of the smoothly shaded color cube produced by a sample program from this chapter, ccube. The surface of this cube shows the color variations from black on one corner to white on the opposite corner. Red, green, and blue are present on their corners 255 units from black. Additionally, the colors yellow, cyan, and magenta have corners showing the combination of the other three primary colors. You can also spin the color cube around to examine all of its sides by pressing the arrow keys.

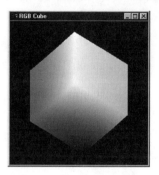

Figure 6.8   Output from ccube is this color cube.

Setting the Drawing Color

Let's briefly review the glColor function. It is prototyped as follows:

```
void glColor<x><t>(red, green, blue, alpha);
```

In the function name, the *<x>* represents the number of arguments; it might be **3** for three arguments of red, green, and blue or **4** for four arguments to include the alpha component. (The alpha component specifies the translucency of the color and is covered in more detail in Chapter 10.) For the time being, just use a three-argument version of the function.

The *<t>* in the function name specifies the argument's data type and can be b, d, f, i, s, ub, ui, or us, for byte, double, float, integer, short, unsigned byte, unsigned integer, and unsigned short data types. Another version of the function has a v appended to the end; this version takes an array that contains the arguments (the v stands for vectored). In the "Reference Section" you will find an entry with more details on the glColor function.

Most OpenGL programs that you'll see use glColor3f and specify the intensity of each component as 0.0 for none or 1.0 for full intensity. However, it might be easier, if you have Windows programming experience, to use the glColor3ub version of the function. This version takes three unsigned bytes, from 0 to 255, to specify the intensities of red, green, and blue. Using this version of the function is like using the Windows RGB macro to specify a color:

```
glColor3ub(0,255,128) = RGB(0,255,128)
```

In fact, this might make it easier for you to match your OpenGL colors to existing RGB colors used by your program for other non-OpenGL drawing tasks.

Shading

Our previous working definition for `glColor` was that this function sets the current drawing color, and all objects drawn after this command have the last color specified. Now that we have discussed the OpenGL drawing primitives (Chapter 4, "Drawing in Space: Lines, Points, and Polygons"), we can expand this definition to this: The `glColor` function sets the current color that is used for all vertices drawn after the command. So far, all of our examples have drawn wireframe objects or solid objects with each face a different but solid color. If we specify a different color for each vertex of a primitive (either point, line, or polygon), what color is the interior?

Let's answer this question first regarding points. A point has only one vertex, and whatever color you specify for that vertex is the resulting color for that point.

A line, however, has two vertices and each can be set to a different color. The color of the line depends on the shading model. Shading is simply defined as the smooth transition from one color to the next. Any two points in our RGB colorspace (refer to Figure 6.7) can be connected by a straight line.

Smooth shading causes the colors along the line to vary as they do through the color cube from one color point to the other. In Figure 6.9, the color cube is shown with the black and white corners pointed out. Below it is a line with two vertices, one black and one white. The colors selected along the length of the line match the colors along the straight line in the color cube, from the black to the white corners. This results in a line that progresses from black through lighter shades of gray and eventually to white.

You can do shading mathematically by finding the equation of the line connecting two points in the three-dimensional RGB colorspace. Then, simply loop through from one end of the line to the other, retrieving coordinates along the way to provide the color of each pixel on the screen. Many good books on computer graphics explain the algorithm to accomplish this, scale your color line to the physical line on the screen, and so on. Fortunately, OpenGL does all this work for you!

The shading exercise becomes slightly more complex for polygons. A triangle, for instance, can also be represented as a plane within the color cube. Figure 6.10 shows a triangle with each vertex at full saturation for the red, green, and blue color components. The code to display this triangle is in Listing 6.1 and in the sample program triangle on the CD.

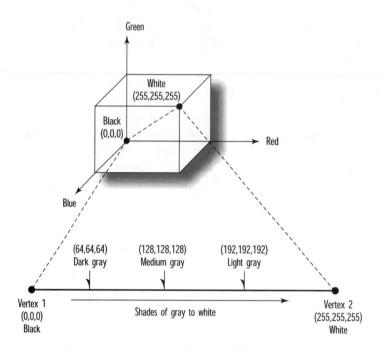

Figure 6.9 How a line is shaded from black to white.

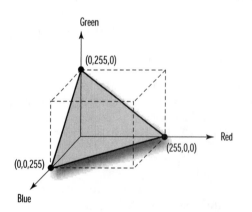

Figure 6.10 A triangle in RGB colorspace.

Listing 6.1 *Drawing a Smooth-Shaded Triangle with Red, Green, and Blue Corners*

```
// Enable smooth shading
glShadeModel(GL_SMOOTH);

// Draw the triangle
```

```
glBegin(GL_TRIANGLES);
    // Red Apex
    glColor3ub((GLubyte)255,(GLubyte)0,(GLubyte)0);
    glVertex3f(0.0f,200.0f,0.0f);

    // Green on the right bottom corner
    glColor3ub((GLubyte)0,(GLubyte)255,(GLubyte)0);
    glVertex3f(200.0f,-70.0f,0.0f);

    // Blue on the left bottom corner
    glColor3ub((GLubyte)0,(GLubyte)0,(GLubyte)255);
    glVertex3f(-200.0f, -70.0f, 0.0f);
glEnd();
```

Setting the Shading Model

The first line of Listing 6.1 actually sets the shading model OpenGL uses to do smooth shading—the model we have been discussing. This is the default shading model, but it's a good idea to call this function anyway to ensure that your program is operating the way you intended.

(The other shading model that can be specified with `glShadeModel` is `GL_FLAT` for flat shading. Flat shading means that no shading calculations are performed on the interior of primitives. Generally, with flat shading, the color of the primitive's interior is the color that was specified for the last vertex. The only exception is for a `GL_POLYGON` primitive, in which case the color is that of the first vertex.)

Then, the code in Listing 6.1 sets the top of the triangle to be pure red, the lower-right corner to be green, and the remaining bottom-left corner to be blue. Because smooth shading is specified, the interior of the triangle is shaded to provide a smooth transition between each corner.

The output from the triangle program is shown in Figure 6.11. This represents the plane shown graphically in Figure 6.10.

Figure 6.11   Output from the triangle program.

Polygons, more complex than triangles, can also have different colors specified for each vertex. In these instances, the underlying logic for shading can become more intricate. Fortunately, you never have to worry about it with OpenGL. No matter how complex your polygon, OpenGL successfully shades the interior points between each vertex.

Color in the Real World

Real objects don't appear in a solid or shaded color based solely on their RGB values. Figure 6.12 shows the output from the program jet from the CD. It's a simple jet airplane, hand plotted with triangles using only the methods covered so far in this book. As usual, jet and the other programs in this chapter allow you to spin the object around by using the arrow keys to better see the effects.

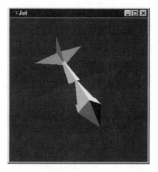

Figure 6.12   A simple jet built by setting a different color for each triangle.

The selection of colors is meant to highlight the three-dimensional structure of the jet. Aside from the crude assemblage of triangles, however, you can see that it looks hardly anything like a real object. Suppose you constructed a model of this airplane and painted each flat surface the colors represented. The model would still appear glossy or flat depending on the kind of paint used, and the color of each flat surface would vary with the angle of your view and any sources of light.

OpenGL does a reasonably good job of approximating the real world in terms of lighting conditions. Unless an object emits its own light, it is illuminated by three different kinds of light: ambient, diffuse, and specular.

Ambient Light

Ambient light is light that doesn't come from any particular direction. It has a source, but the rays of light have bounced around the room or scene and become directionless. Objects illuminated by ambient light are evenly lit on all surfaces in all directions. You can think of all previous examples in this book as being lit by a bright ambient light because the objects were always visible and evenly colored (or shaded) regardless of their rotation or viewing angle. Figure 6.13 shows an object illuminated by ambient light.

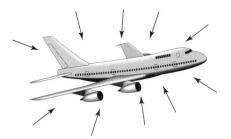

Figure 6.13   An object illuminated purely by ambient light.

Diffuse Light

Diffuse light comes from a particular direction but is reflected evenly off a surface. Even though the light is reflected evenly, the object surface is brighter if the light is pointed directly at the surface than if the light grazes the surface from an angle. A good example of a diffuse light source is fluorescent lighting or sunlight streaming in a side window at noon. In Figure 6.14, the object is illuminated by a diffuse light source.

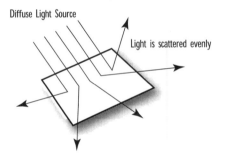

Figure 6.14   An object illuminated by a purely diffuse light source.

Specular Light

Like diffuse light, specular light is directional, but it is reflected sharply and in a particular direction. A highly specular light tends to cause a bright spot on the surface it shines upon, which is called the specular highlight. A spotlight and the Sun are examples of specular light. Figure 6.15 shows an object illuminated by a purely specular light source.

Put It All Together

No single light source is composed entirely of any of the three types of light just described. Rather, it is made up of varying intensities of each. For example, a red laser beam in a lab is composed of almost a pure-red specular component. However, smoke or dust particles scatter the beam, so it can be seen traveling across the room. This scattering represents the diffuse component of the light. If the beam is bright and no other light sources are present, you notice objects in the room taking on a red hue. This is a very small ambient component of that light.

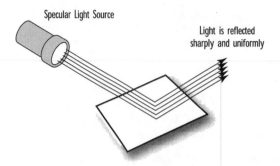

Specular Light Source

Light is reflected
sharply and uniformly

Figure 6.15 An object illuminated by a purely specular light source.

Thus, a light source in a scene is said to be composed of three lighting components: ambient, diffuse, and specular. Just like the components of a color, each lighting component is defined with an RGBA value that describes the relative intensities of red, green, and blue light that make up that component. (We ignore the alpha component until Chapter 10—when you learn how the specular color is blended with textures.) For example, our red laser light might be described by the component values in Table 6.1.

Table 6.1	Color and Light Distribution for a Red Laser Light Source			
	Red	**Green**	**Blue**	**Alpha**
Specular	0.99	0.0	0.0	1.0
Diffuse	0.10	0.0	0.0	1.0
Ambient	0.05	0.0	0.0	1.0

Note that the red laser beam has no green or blue light. Also, note that specular, diffuse, and ambient light can each range in intensity from 0.0 to 1.0. You could interpret this table as saying that the red laser light in some scenes has a very high specular component, a small diffuse component, and a very small ambient component. Wherever it shines, you are probably going to see a reddish spot. Also, because of conditions (smoke, dust, and so on) in the room, the diffuse component allows the beam to be seen traveling through the air. Finally, the ambient component—likely due to smoke or dust particles, as well—scatters a tiny bit of light all about the room. Ambient and diffuse components of light are frequently combined because they are so similar in nature.

Materials in the Real World

Light is only part of the equation. In the real world, objects do have a color of their own. Earlier in this chapter, we described the color of an object as defined by its reflected wavelengths of light. A blue ball reflects mostly blue photons and absorbs most others. This assumes that the light shining on the ball has blue photons in it to be reflected and detected by the observer. Generally, most scenes in the real world are illuminated by a white light containing an even mixture of all the colors. Under white light, therefore, most objects appear in their proper or "natural" colors. However, this is not always so; put the blue ball in a dark room with only a yellow light, and the ball appears black to the viewer because all the yellow light is absorbed and there is no blue to be reflected.

Material Properties

When we use lighting, we do not describe polygons as having a particular color, but rather as consisting of materials that have certain reflective properties. Instead of saying that a polygon is red, we say that the polygon is made of a material that reflects mostly red light. We are still saying that the surface is red, but now we must also specify the material's reflective properties for ambient, diffuse, and specular light sources. A material might be shiny and reflect specular light very well, while absorbing most of the ambient or diffuse light. Conversely, a flat colored object might absorb all specular light and not look shiny under any circumstances. Another property to be specified is the emission property for objects that emit their own light, such as taillights or glow-in-the-dark watches.

Adding Light to Materials

Setting lighting and material properties to achieve the desired effect takes some practice. There are no color cubes or rules of thumb to give you quick and easy answers. This is where analysis gives way to art, and science yields to magic. The CD subdirectory for this chapter contains a supplementary sample program called matlight (for Materials and Lighting Studio). This program allows you to change material and lighting properties on-the-fly for a scene composed of some simple objects. You can use matlight to get a feel for the various lighting and material property settings. In addition, because the source is included, you can also substitute your own objects in matlight and work out the lighting and material details before committing your scene to code. (Note that the source uses MFC and Visual C++. This isn't an "official" sample program, and it involves other aspects of Windows programming besides OpenGL that are outside the scope of this book.)

When drawing an object, OpenGL decides which color to use for each pixel in the object. That object has reflective "colors," and the light source has "colors" of its own. How does OpenGL determine which colors to use? Understanding this is not difficult, but it does take some simple grade-school multiplication. (See, that teacher told you you'd need it one day!)

Each vertex of your primitives is assigned an RGB color value based on the net effect of the ambient, diffuse, and specular illumination multiplied by the ambient, diffuse, and specular reflectance of the material properties. By making use of smooth shading between the vertices, the illusion of illumination is achieved.

Calculating Ambient Light Effects

First, you need to put away the notion of color and instead think only in terms of red, green, and blue intensities. For an ambient light source of half-intensity red, green, and blue components, you have an RGB value for that source of (0.5, 0.5, 0.5). If this ambient light illuminates an object with ambient reflective properties specified in RGB terms of (.50, 1.0, .50), then the net "color" component from the ambient light is

(0.50 * .50, 0.5 * 1.0, 0.50 * .50) = (0.25, 0.5, 0.25)

which is the result of multiplying each of the ambient light source terms by each of the ambient material property terms. See Figure 6.16.

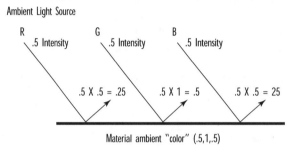

Ambient Light Source

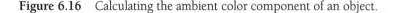

Figure 6.16   Calculating the ambient color component of an object.

Thus, the material color components actually determine the percentage of incident light that is reflected. In our example, the ambient light had a red component that was at one-half intensity, and the material ambient property of .5 specified that one-half of that half-intensity light was reflected. Half of a half is a fourth, or 0.25.

Diffuse and Specular Effects

Ambient light is as simple as it gets. Diffuse light also has RGB intensities that interact in the same way with material properties. However, diffuse light is directional, and the intensity at the surface of the object varies depending on the angle between the surface and the light source, the distance to the light source is, any attenuation factors (is it foggy between the light and the surface?), and so on. The same goes for specular light sources and intensities. The net effect in terms of RGB values is figured the same way as for ambient light, with the intensity of the light source (adjusted for the angle of incidence) being multiplied by the material reflectance. Finally, all three RGB terms are added to yield a final color for the object. If any single color component is above 1.0, it is clamped to that value. (You can't get more intense than full intensity!)

Generally, the ambient and diffuse components of light sources and materials are the same and have the greatest effect in determining the color of the object. Specular light and material properties tend to be light gray or white. The specular component depends significantly on the angle of incidence, and specular highlights on an object are usually white.

Adding Light to a Scene

This text might seem like a lot of theory to digest all of a sudden. Let's slow down and start exploring some examples of the OpenGL code needed for lighting; this exploration will also help reinforce what you've just learned. We demonstrate some additional features and requirements of lighting in OpenGL. The next few examples build on our jet program. The initial version contains no lighting code and just draws triangles with hidden surface elimination (depth testing) enabled. When we're done, the jet's metallic surface glistens in the sunlight as you rotate it with the arrow keys.

Enable the Lighting

To tell OpenGL to use lighting calculations, call glEnable with the GL_LIGHTING parameter:

```
glEnable(GL_LIGHTING);
```

This alone tells OpenGL to use material properties and lighting parameters in determining the color for each vertex in your scene. However, without any specified material properties or lighting parameters, your object remains dark and unlit as shown in Figure 6.17. Look at the code for any of the jet-based sample programs, and you see that we have called a function SetupRC right after creating the rendering context. This is where we do any initialization of lighting parameters.

Figure 6.17   An unlit jet reflects no light.

Set Up the Lighting Model

After enabling lighting calculations, the first thing you need to do is set up the lighting model. The three parameters that affect the lighting model are set with the glLightModel function.

The first lighting parameter used in our next example is GL_LIGHT_MODEL_AMBIENT. This lets you specify a global ambient light that illuminates all objects evenly from all sides. The following code specifies a bright white light:

```
// Bright white light - full intensity RGB values
   GLfloat ambientLight[] = { 1.0f, 1.0f, 1.0f, 1.0f };
```

```
// Enable lighting
glEnable(GL_LIGHTING);

// Set light model to use ambient light specified by ambientLight[]
glLightModelfv(GL_LIGHT_MODEL_AMBIENT,ambientLight);
```

The variation of glLightModel shown here, glLightModelfv, takes as its first parameter the lighting model parameter being modified or set and then an array of the
RGBA values that make up the light. The default RGBA values of this global ambient
light are (0.2, 0.2, 0.2, 1.0), which is fairly dim. Other lighting model parameters allow
you to determine whether the front, back, or both sides of polygons are illuminated
and how the calculation of specular lighting angles is performed. See the "Reference
Section" at the end of the chapter for more information on these parameters.

Set Material Properties

Now that we have an ambient light source, we need to set some material properties so
that our polygons reflect light and we can see our jet. There are two ways to set material
properties. The first is to use the function glMaterial before specifying each polygon
or set of polygons. Examine the following code fragment:

```
Glfloat gray[] = { 0.75f, 0.75f, 0.75f, 1.0f };
...
...
glMaterialfv(GL_FRONT, GL_AMBIENT_AND_DIFFUSE, gray);

glBegin(GL_TRIANGLES);
    glVertex3f(-15.0f,0.0f,30.0f);
    glVertex3f(0.0f, 15.0f, 30.0f);
    glVertex3f(0.0f, 0.0f, -56.0f);
glEnd();
```

The first parameter to glMaterialfv specifies whether the front, back, or both
(GL_FRONT, GL_BACK, or GL_FRONT_AND_BACK) take on the material properties specified. The second parameter tells which properties are being set; in this instance, both
the ambient and diffuse reflectances are set to the same values. The final parameter is
an array containing the RGBA values that make up these properties. All primitives
specified after the glMaterial call are affected by the last values set, until another call
to glMaterial is made.

Under most circumstances, the ambient and diffuse components are the same, and
unless you want specular highlights (sparkling, shiny spots), you don't need to define
specular reflective properties. Even so, it would still be quite tedious if we had to
define an array for every color in our object and call glMaterial before each polygon
or group of polygons.

This leads us to the second and preferred way of setting material properties, called
color tracking. With color tracking, you can tell OpenGL to set material properties by

only calling glColor. To enable color tracking, call glEnable with the GL_COLOR_MATERIAL parameter:

```
glEnable(GL_COLOR_MATERIAL);
```

Then, the function glColorMaterial specifies the material parameters that follow the values set by glColor.

For example, to set the ambient and diffuse properties of the fronts of polygons to track the colors set by glColor, call

```
glColorMaterial(GL_FRONT,GL_AMBIENT_AND_DIFFUSE);
```

The earlier code fragment setting material properties would then be as follows. This looks like more code, but it actually saves many lines of code and executes faster as the number of polygons grows:

```
// Enable color tracking
glEnable(GL_COLOR_MATERIAL);

// Front material ambient and diffuse colors track glColor
glColorMaterial(GL_FRONT,GL_AMBIENT_AND_DIFFUSE);

...
...
glcolor3f(0.75f, 0.75f, 0.75f);
glBegin(GL_TRIANGLES);
    glVertex3f(-15.0f,0.0f,30.0f);
    glVertex3f(0.0f, 15.0f, 30.0f);
    glVertex3f(0.0f, 0.0f, -56.0f);
glEnd();
```

Listing 6.2 contains the code we add with the SetupRC function to our jet example to set up a bright ambient light source and to set the material properties that allow the object to reflect light and be seen. We have also changed the colors of the jet so that each section is a different color rather than each polygon. Notice in the final output (see Figure 6.18) that it's not much different from the image before we had lighting. However, if we reduce the ambient light by half, we get the image shown in Figure 6.19. To reduce it by half, we set the ambient light RGBA values to the following:

```
GLfloat ambientLight[] = { 0.5f, 0.5f, 0.5f, 1.0f };
```

You can see how we might reduce the ambient light in a scene to produce a dimmer image. This is useful for simulations in which dusk approaches gradually or when a more direct light source is blocked, as when an object is in the shadow of another, larger object.

Figure 6.18 Output from completed ambient sample program.

Figure 6.19 Output from the ambient program when the light source is cut in half.

Listing 6.2 *Setup for Ambient Lighting Conditions*

```
// This function does any needed initialization on the rendering
// context.  Here it sets up and initializes the lighting for
// the scene.
void SetupRC()
    {
    // Light values
    // Bright white light
    GLfloat ambientLight[] = { 1.0f, 1.0f, 1.0f, 1.0f };

    glEnable(GL_DEPTH_TEST);    // Hidden surface removal
    glEnable(GL_CULL_FACE);      // Do not calculate inside of jet
    glFrontFace(GL_CCW);        // Counterclockwise polygons face out

    // Lighting stuff
    glEnable(GL_LIGHTING);     // Enable lighting

    // Set light model to use ambient light specified by ambientLight[]
```

```
glLightModelfv(GL_LIGHT_MODEL_AMBIENT,ambientLight);


glEnable(GL_COLOR_MATERIAL);     // Enable material color tracking

// Front material ambient and diffuse colors track glColor
glColorMaterial(GL_FRONT,GL_AMBIENT_AND_DIFFUSE);

// Nice light blue background
glClearColor(0.0f, 0.0f, 05.f,1.0f);
}
```

Using a Light Source

Manipulating the ambient light has its uses, but for most applications attempting to model the real world, you must specify one or more specific sources of light. In addition to their intensities and colors, these sources have a location and a direction. The placement of these lights can dramatically affect the appearance of your scene.

OpenGL supports at least eight independent light sources located anywhere in your scene or out of the viewing volume. You can locate a light source an infinite distance away and make its light rays parallel or make it a nearby light source radiating outward. You can also specify a spotlight with a specific cone of light radiating from it, as well as manipulate its characteristics.

Which Way Is Up?

When you specify a light source, you tell OpenGL where it is and in which direction it's shining. Often, the light source shines in all directions, or it can be directional. Either way, for any object you draw, the rays of light from any source (other than a pure ambient source) strike the surface of the polygons that make up the object at an angle. Of course, in the case of a directional light, the surfaces of all polygons might not necessarily be illuminated. To calculate the shading effects across the surface of the polygons, OpenGL must be able to calculate the angle.

In Figure 6.20, a polygon (a square) is being struck by a ray of light from some source. The ray makes an angle (A) with the plane as it strikes the surface. The light is then reflected at an angle (B) toward the viewer (or you wouldn't see it). These angles are used in conjunction with the lighting and material properties we have discussed thus far to calculate the apparent color of that location. It happens by design that the locations used by OpenGL are the vertices of the polygon. By calculating the apparent colors for each vertex and then doing smooth shading between them, the illusion of lighting is created. Magic!

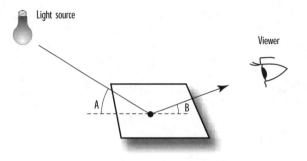

Figure 6.20   Light is reflected off objects at specific angles.

From a programming standpoint, this presents a slight conceptual difficulty. Each polygon is created as a set of vertices, which are nothing more than points. Each vertex is then struck by a ray of light at some angle. How then do you (or OpenGL) calculate the angle between a point and a line (the ray of light)? Of course, you can't geometrically find the angle between a single point and a line in 3D space because there are an infinite number of possibilities. Therefore, you must associate with each vertex some piece of information that denotes a direction upward from the vertex and away from the surface of the primitive.

Surface Normals

A line from the vertex in the upward direction starts in some imaginary plane (or your polygon) at a right angle. This line is called a *normal vector*. That phrase normal vector might sound like something the *Star Trek* crew members toss around, but it just means a line perpendicular to a real or imaginary surface. A vector is a line pointed in some direction, and the word normal is just another way for eggheads to say perpendicular (intersecting at a 90° angle). As if the word perpendicular weren't bad enough! Therefore, a normal vector is a line pointed in a direction that is at a 90° angle to the surface of your polygon. Figure 6.21 presents examples of 2D and 3D normal vectors.

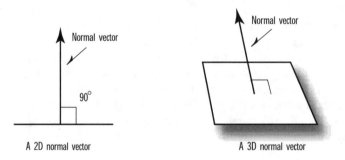

Figure 6.21   A 2D and a 3D normal vector.

You might already be asking why we must specify a normal vector for each vertex. Why can't we just specify a single normal for a polygon and use it for each vertex? We can—and for our first few examples, we do. However, there are times when you don't want each normal to be exactly perpendicular to the surface of the polygon. You may have noticed that many surfaces are not flat! You can approximate these surfaces with flat, polygonal sections, but you end up with a jagged or multifaceted surface. Later, we discuss a technique to produce the illusion of smooth curves with flat polygons by "tweaking" your surface normals (more magic!). But first things first.

Specifying a Normal

To see how we specify a normal for a vertex, let's take a look at Figure 6.22—a plane floating above the xz plane in 3D space. We've made this simple to demonstrate the concept. Notice the line through the vertex (1,1,0) that is perpendicular to the plane. If we select any point on this line, say (1,10,0), then the line from the first point (1,1,0) to the second point (1,10,0) is our normal vector. The second point specified actually indicates that the direction from the vertex is up in the y direction. This is also used to indicate the front and back sides of polygons, as the vector travels up and away from the front surface.

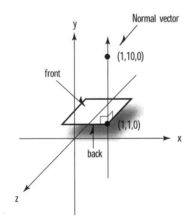

Figure 6.22 A normal vector traveling perpendicular from the surface.

You can see that this second point is the number of units in the x, y, and z directions for some point on the normal vector away from the vertex. Rather than specify two points for each normal vector, we can subtract the vertex from the second point on the normal, yielding a single coordinate triplet that indicates the x, y, and z steps away from the vertex. For our example, this is

(1,10,0)–(1,1,0) = (1–1, 10–1, 0) = (0, 9, 0)

Another way of looking at this is if the vertex were translated to the origin, the point specified by subtracting the two original points would still specify the direction pointing away and at a 90° angle from the surface. Figure 6.23 shows the newly translated normal vector.

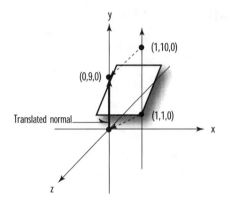

Figure 6.23   The newly translated normal vector.

The vector is a directional quantity that tells OpenGL which direction the vertices (or polygon) face. This next code segment shows a normal vector being specified for one of the triangles in the jet sample program:

```
glBegin(GL_TRIANGLES);
    glNormal3f(0.0f, -1.0f, 0.0f);
    glVertex3f(0.0f, 0.0f, 60.0f);
    glVertex3f(-15.0f, 0.0f, 30.0f);
    glVertex3f(15.0f,0.0f,30.0f);
glEnd();
```

The function **glNormal3f** takes the coordinate triplet that specifies a normal vector pointing in the direction perpendicular to the surface of this triangle. In this example, the normals for all three vertices have the same direction, which is down the negative y axis. This is a simple example because the triangle is lying flat in the xz plane, and it actually represents a bottom section of the jet.

The prospect of specifying a normal for every vertex or polygon in your drawing might seem daunting, especially because few surfaces lie cleanly in one of the major planes. Never fear, we shortly present a reusable function that you can call again and again to calculate your normals for you.

POLYGON WINDING

Take special note of the order of the vertices in the jet's triangle. If you view this triangle being drawn from the direction in which the normal vector points, the corners appear counterclockwise around the triangle. This is called *polygon winding*. By default, the front of a polygon is defined as the side from which the vertices appear to be wound in a counterclockwise fashion.

Unit Normals

As OpenGL does its magic, all surface normals must eventually be converted to unit normals. A unit normal is just a normal vector that has a length of 1. The normal in Figure 6.23 has a length of 9. You can find the length of any normal by squaring each component, adding them together, and taking the square root. Divide each component of the normal by the length, and you get a vector pointed in exactly the same direction, but only 1 unit long. In this case, our new normal vector is specified as (0,1,0). This is called normalization. Thus, for lighting calculations, all normal vectors must be normalized. Talk about jargon!

You can tell OpenGL to convert your normals to unit normals automatically, by enabling normalization with `glEnable` and a parameter of `GL_NORMALIZE`:

```
glEnable(GL_NORMALIZE);
```

This does, however, have performance penalties. It's far better to calculate your normals ahead of time as unit normals instead of relying on OpenGL to do this for you.

You should note that calls to the `glScale` transformation function also scale the length of your normals. If you use `glScale` and lighting, you can get undesired results from your OpenGL lighting. If you have specified unit normals for all your geometry and used a constant scaling factor with `glScale` (all geometry is scaled by the same amount), then a new alternative to `GL_NORMALIZE` (new to OpenGL 1.2) is `GL_RESCALE_NORMALS`. Enable this parameter with a call such as

```
glEnable(GL_RESCALE_NORMALS);
```

This tells OpenGL that your normals are not unit length, but they can all be scaled by the same amount to make them unit length. OpenGL figures this out by examining the modelview matrix. This results in fewer mathematical operations per vertex than are otherwise required.

Because it is better to give OpenGL unit normals, a simple method that scales (normalizes) vectors to unit length is a handy piece of code to have lying around. Given any normal vector specified by a coordinate triplet that indicates the direction from the origin, you can easily find the equivalent unit normal vector with the function in Listing 6.3.

Listing 6.3 *A function That Reduces Any Normal Vector to a Unit Normal Vector*

```
// Reduces a normal vector specified as a set of three coordinates
// to a unit normal vector of length 1.
void ReduceToUnit(float vector[3])
    {
    float length;

    // Calculate the length of the vector
    length = (float)sqrt((vector[0]*vector[0]) +
                  (vector[1]*vector[1]) +
                (vector[2]*vector[2]));

    // Keep the program from blowing up by providing an acceptable
    // value for vectors whose length may be calculated too close to zero.
    if(length == 0.0f)
        length = 1.0f;

    // Dividing each element by the length will result in a
    // unit normal vector.
    vector[0] /= length;
    vector[1] /= length;
    vector[2] /= length;
    }
```

Finding a Normal

Figure 6.24 presents another polygon that is not simply lying in one of the axis planes. The normal vector pointing away from this surface is more difficult to guess, so we need an easy way to calculate the normal for any arbitrary polygon in 3D coordinates.

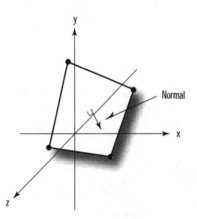

Figure 6.24 A nontrivial normal problem.

You can easily calculate the normal vector for any polygon consisting of at least three points that lie in a single plane (a flat polygon). Figure 6.25 shows three points, P1, P2, and P3, that you can use to define two vectors: vector V1 from P1 to P2, and vector V2 from P1 to P2. Mathematically, two vectors in three-dimensional space define a plane. (Your original polygon lies in this plane.) If you take the cross product of those two vectors (written mathematically as V1×V2), the resulting vector is perpendicular to that plane (or normal). Figure 6.26 shows the vector V3 derived by taking the cross product of V1 and V2.

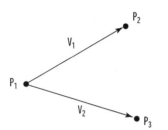

Figure 6.25 Two vectors defined by three points on a plane.

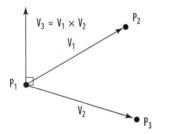

Figure 6.26 A normal vector as the cross product of two vectors.

Don't worry if you don't know how to take the cross product of two vectors; all you need is the function in Listing 6.4. To use this function, pass it an array containing any three vertices from your polygon (specified in counterclockwise winding order), and an array that will contain the normal vector on return. The constant values x, y, and z are provided for your benefit if you want to see how the function works.

Listing 6.4 *Function to Calculate a Normal Vector with Any Three Vertices from a Polygon*

```
// Points p1, p2, & p3 specified in counterclockwise order
void calcNormal(float v[3][3], float out[3])
    {
    float v1[3],v2[3];
```

continued on next page

continued from previous page

```
    static const int x = 0;
    static const int y = 1;
    static const int z = 2;

    // Calculate two vectors from the three points
    v1[x] = v[0][x] - v[1][x];
    v1[y] = v[0][y] - v[1][y];
    v1[z] = v[0][z] - v[1][z];

    v2[x] = v[1][x] - v[2][x];
    v2[y] = v[1][y] - v[2][y];
    v2[z] = v[1][z] - v[2][z];

    // Take the cross product of the two vectors to get
    // the normal vector, which will be stored in out[]
    out[x] = v1[y]*v2[z] - v1[z]*v2[y];
    out[y] = v1[z]*v2[x] - v1[x]*v2[z];
    out[z] = v1[x]*v2[y] - v1[y]*v2[x];

    // Normalize the vector (shorten length to one)
    ReduceToUnit(out);
    }
```

Setting Up a Source

Now that you understand the requirements of setting up your polygons to receive and interact with a light source, it's time to turn on the lights! Listing 6.5 shows the SetupRC function from the sample program litjet. Part of the setup process for this sample program creates a light source and places it to the upper left, slightly behind the viewer. The light source GL_LIGHT0 has its ambient and diffuse components set to the intensities specified by the arrays ambientLight[] and diffuseLight[]. This results in a moderate white light source:

```
GLfloat  ambientLight[] = { 0.3f, 0.3f, 0.3f, 1.0f };
GLfloat  diffuseLight[] = { 0.7f, 0.7f, 0.7f, 1.0f };
...
...
// Set up and enable light 0
glLightfv(GL_LIGHT0,GL_AMBIENT,ambientLight);
glLightfv(GL_LIGHT0,GL_DIFFUSE,diffuseLight);
```

Finally, the light source GL_LIGHT0 is enabled:

```
glEnable(GL_LIGHT0);
```

The light is positioned by this code, located in the ChangeSize function:

```
GLfloat lightPos[] = { -50.f, 50.0f, 100.0f, 1.0f };
```

```
...
...
glLightfv(GL_LIGHT0,GL_POSITION,lightPos);
```

Here, `lightPos[]` contains the position of the light. The last value in this array is 1.0, which specifies that the designated coordinates are the position of the light source. If the last value in the array is 0.0, it indicates that the light is an infinite distance away along the vector specified by this array. We touch more on this later. Lights are like geometric objects in that they can be moved around by the modelview matrix. By placing the light's position when the viewing transformation is performed, we ensure the light is in the proper location.

Listing 6.5   *Light and Rendering Context Setup for litjet*

```
// This function does any needed initialization on the rendering
// context.  Here it sets up and initializes the lighting for
// the scene.
void SetupRC()
    {
    // Light values and coordinates
    GLfloat  ambientLight[] = { 0.3f, 0.3f, 0.3f, 1.0f };
    GLfloat  diffuseLight[] = { 0.7f, 0.7f, 0.7f, 1.0f };

    glEnable(GL_DEPTH_TEST);    // Hidden surface removal
    glFrontFace(GL_CCW);        // Counterclockwise polygons face out
    glEnable(GL_CULL_FACE);        // Do not calculate inside of jet

    // Enable lighting
    glEnable(GL_LIGHTING);

    // Set up and enable light 0
    glLightfv(GL_LIGHT0,GL_AMBIENT,ambientLight);
    glLightfv(GL_LIGHT0,GL_DIFFUSE,diffuseLight);
    glEnable(GL_LIGHT0);

    // Enable color tracking
    glEnable(GL_COLOR_MATERIAL);

    // Set material properties to follow glColor values
    glColorMaterial(GL_FRONT, GL_AMBIENT_AND_DIFFUSE);

    // Light blue background
    glClearColor(0.0f, 0.0f, 1.0f, 1.0f );
    }
```

Setting the Material Properties

Notice in Listing 6.5 that color tracking is enabled, and the properties to be tracked are the ambient and diffuse reflective properties for the front surface of the polygons. This is just as it was defined in the ambient sample program:

```
// Enable color tracking
glEnable(GL_COLOR_MATERIAL);

// Set material properties to follow glColor values
glColorMaterial(GL_FRONT, GL_AMBIENT_AND_DIFFUSE);
```

Specifying the Polygons

The rendering code from the first two jet samples changes considerably now to support the new lighting model. Listing 6.6 is an excerpt taken from the RenderScene function from litjet.

Listing 6.6 *Code Sample That Sets Color and Calculates and Specifies Normals and Polygons*

```
float normal[3];    // Storage for calculated surface normal
...
...
// Set material color
glColor3ub(0, 255, 0);
glBegin(GL_TRIANGLES);
    glNormal3f(0.0f, -1.0f, 0.0f);
    glVertex3f(0.0f, 0.0f, 60.0f);
    glVertex3f(-15.0f, 0.0f, 30.0f);
    glVertex3f(15.0f,0.0f,30.0f);
// glEnd();


{
// Vertices for this triangle
float v[3][3] =    {{ 15.0f, 0.0f, 30.0f},
            { 0.0f, 15.0f, 30.0f},
            { 0.0f, 0.0f, 60.0f}};

// Calculate the normal for the plane
calcNormal(v,normal);

// Draw the triangle using the plane normal
// for all the vertices
// glBegin(GL_TRIANGLES);
    glNormal3fv(normal);
```

```
    glVertex3fv(v[0]);
    glVertex3fv(v[1]);
    glVertex3fv(v[2]);
// glEnd();

}
```

You notice that we are calculating the normal vector using our code in Listing 6.4. Also, the material properties are now following the colors set by `glColor`. One other thing you notice is that not every triangle is blocked by `glBegin`/`glEnd` functions. (They have been commented out.) You can specify once that you are drawing triangles, and every three vertices are used for a new triangle until you specify otherwise with `glEnd`. For very large numbers of polygons, this can considerably boost performance by eliminating many unnecessary function calls.

Figure 6.27 shows the output from the completed litjet sample program. The jet is now a single shade of gray instead of multiple colors. We did this to make it easier to see the lighting effects on the surface. Even though the plane is one solid "color," you can still see the shape due to the lighting. By rotating the jet around with the arrow keys, you can see the dramatic shading effects as the surface of the jet moves in the light.

Figure 6.27   Output from the litjet program.

PERFORMANCE TIP

The most obvious way to improve the performance of this code is to calculate all the normal vectors ahead of time and store them for use in the Render function. Before you pursue this, read Chapter 9, "3D Modeling and Object Composition," for the material on display lists and vertex arrays. Display lists and vertex arrays provide a means of storing calculated values not only for the normal vectors, but for the polygon data as well. Remember, these examples are meant to demonstrate the concepts. They are not necessarily the most efficient code possible.

Lighting Effects

The ambient and diffuse light from the litjet example are sufficient to provide the illusion of lighting. The surface of the jet appears shaded according to the angle of the incident light. As the jet rotates, these angles change and you can see the lighting effects changing in such a way that you can easily guess where the light is coming from.

We ignored the specular component of the light source, however, as well as the specular reflectivity of the material properties on the jet. Although the lighting effects are pronounced, the surface of the jet is rather flatly colored. Ambient and diffuse lighting and material properties are all you need if you are modeling clay, wood, cardboard, cloth, or some other flatly colored object. But for metallic surfaces such as the skin of an airplane, some shine is often desirable.

Specular Highlights

Specular lighting and material properties add needed gloss to the surface of your objects. This shininess has a whitening effect on an object's color and can produce specular highlights when the angle of incident light is sharp in relation to the viewer. A specular highlight is what occurs when nearly all the light striking the surface of an object is reflected away. The white sparkle on a shiny red ball in the sunlight is good example of a specular highlight.

Specular Light

You can easily add a specular component to a light source. The following code shows the light source setup for the litjet program, modified to add a specular component to the light:

```
// Light values and coordinates
GLfloat  ambientLight[] = { 0.3f, 0.3f, 0.3f, 1.0f };
GLfloat  diffuseLight[] = { 0.7f, 0.7f, 0.7f, 1.0f };
GLfloat  specular[] = { 1.0f, 1.0f, 1.0f, 1.0f};

...
...


// Enable lighting
glEnable(GL_LIGHTING);

// Set up and enable light 0
glLightfv(GL_LIGHT0,GL_AMBIENT,ambientLight);
glLightfv(GL_LIGHT0,GL_DIFFUSE,diffuseLight);
glLightfv(GL_LIGHT0,GL_SPECULAR,specular);
glEnable(GL_LIGHT0);
```

The `specular[]` array specifies a very bright white light source for the specular component of the light. Our purpose here is to model bright sunlight. The line

```
glLightfv(GL_LIGHT0,GL_SPECULAR,specular);
```

simply adds this specular component to the light source `GL_LIGHT0`.

If this were the only change you made to litjet, you wouldn't see any difference in the jet's appearance. We haven't yet defined any specular reflectance properties for the material properties.

Specular Reflectance

Adding specular reflectance to material properties is just as easy as adding the specular component to the light source. This next code segment shows the code from litjet, again modified to add specular reflectance to the material properties:

```
// Light values and coordinates
GLfloat  specref[] =  { 1.0f, 1.0f, 1.0f, 1.0f };

...
...


// Enable color tracking
glEnable(GL_COLOR_MATERIAL);

// Set material properties to follow glColor values
glColorMaterial(GL_FRONT, GL_AMBIENT_AND_DIFFUSE);

// All materials hereafter have full specular reflectivity
// with a high shine
glMaterialfv(GL_FRONT, GL_SPECULAR,specref);
glMateriali(GL_FRONT,GL_SHININESS,128);
```

As before, we enable color tracking so that the ambient and diffuse reflectance of the materials follow the current color set by the `glColor` functions. (Of course, we don't want the specular reflectance to track `glColor` because we are specifying it separately and it doesn't change.)

Now, we've added an array `specref[]` that contains the RGBA values for our specular reflectance. This array of all 1s produces a surface that reflects nearly all incident specular light. The line

```
glMaterialfv(GL_FRONT, GL_SPECULAR,specref);
```

sets the material properties for all subsequent polygons to have this reflectance. Because we do not call `glMaterial` again with the `GL_SPECULAR` property, all materials have this property. We did this on purpose because we want the entire jet to appear made of metal or very shiny composites.

What we have done here in our setup routine is important: We have specified that the ambient and diffuse reflective material properties of all future polygons (until we say otherwise with another call to glMaterial or glColorMaterial) change as the current color changes, but that the specular reflective properties remain the same.

Specular Exponent

As stated earlier, high specular light and reflectivity brighten the colors of the object. For this example, the present extremely high specular light (full intensity) and specular reflectivity (full reflectivity) result in a jet that appears almost totally white or gray except where the surface points away from the light source (in which case, it is black and unlit). To temper this effect, we use the next line of code after the specular component is specified, as follows:

```
glMateriali(GL_FRONT,GL_SHININESS,128);
```

The GL_SHININESS property sets the specular exponent of the material, which specifies how small and focused the specular highlight is. A value of 0 specifies an unfocused specular highlight, which is actually what is producing the brightening of the colors evenly across the entire polygon. If you set this value, you reduce the size and increase the focus of the specular highlight, causing a shiny spot to appear. The larger the value, the more shiny and pronounced the surface. The range of this parameter is 1–128 for all implementations of OpenGL.

Listing 6.7 shows the new SetupRC code in the sample program shinyjet. This is the only code that changed from litjet (other than the title of the window) to produce a very shiny and glistening jet. Figure 6.28 shows the output from this program, but to fully appreciate the effect, you should run the program and hold down one of the arrow keys to spin the jet about in the sunlight.

Figure 6.28 Output from the shinyjet program.

Listing 6.7 *Setup from shinyjet to Produce Specular Highlights on the Jet*

```
// This function does any needed initialization on the rendering
// context.  Here it sets up and initializes the lighting for
// the scene.
void SetupRC()
    {
    // Light values and coordinates
    GLfloat  ambientLight[] = { 0.3f, 0.3f, 0.3f, 1.0f };
    GLfloat  diffuseLight[] = { 0.7f, 0.7f, 0.7f, 1.0f };
    GLfloat  specular[] = { 1.0f, 1.0f, 1.0f, 1.0f};
    GLfloat  specref[] =  { 1.0f, 1.0f, 1.0f, 1.0f };


    glEnable(GL_DEPTH_TEST);     // Hidden surface removal
    glFrontFace(GL_CCW);         // Counterclockwise polygons face out
    glEnable(GL_CULL_FACE);       // Do not calculate inside of jet

    // Enable lighting
    glEnable(GL_LIGHTING);

    // Set up and enable light 0
    glLightfv(GL_LIGHT0,GL_AMBIENT,ambientLight);
    glLightfv(GL_LIGHT0,GL_DIFFUSE,diffuseLight);
    glLightfv(GL_LIGHT0,GL_SPECULAR,specular);
    glEnable(GL_LIGHT0);

    // Enable color tracking
    glEnable(GL_COLOR_MATERIAL);

    // Set material properties to follow glColor values
    glColorMaterial(GL_FRONT, GL_AMBIENT_AND_DIFFUSE);

    // All materials hereafter have full specular reflectivity
    // with a high shine
    glMaterialfv(GL_FRONT, GL_SPECULAR,specref);
    glMateriali(GL_FRONT,GL_SHININESS,128);


    // Light blue background
    glClearColor(0.0f, 0.0f, 1.0f, 1.0f );
    }
```

Normal Averaging

Earlier, we mentioned that by "tweaking" your normals, you can produce apparently smooth surfaces with flat polygons. This technique, known as normal averaging, produces some interesting optical illusions. Say you have a sphere made up of quads and triangles like the one shown in Figure 6.29.

If each face of the sphere had a single normal specified, the sphere would look like a large faceted jewel. By specifying the "true" normal for each vertex, however, the lighting calculations at each vertex produce values that are smoothly interpolated by OpenGL across the face of the polygon. Thus, the flat polygons are shaded as if they were a smooth surface.

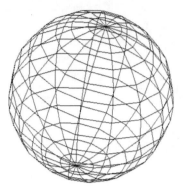

Figure 6.29   A typical sphere made up of quads and triangles.

What do we mean by "true" normal? The polygonal representation is only an approximation of the true surface. Theoretically, if we used enough polygons, the surface would appear smooth. This is similar to the idea we used in Chapter 4 to draw a smooth curve with a series of short line segments. If we consider each vertex to be a point on the true surface, then the actual normal value for that surface is the true normal for the surface.

For our case of the sphere, the normal would point directly out from the center of the sphere through each vertex. We show this graphically for a simple 2D case in Figures 6.30 and 6.31. In Figure 6.30, each flat segment has a normal pointing perpendicular to its surface. This is done just like we did for our litjet example previously. Figure 6.31, however, shows how each normal is not perpendicular to the line segment but is perpendicular to the surface of the sphere, or the *tangent* line to the surface.

The tangent line is a line that touches the curve in one place and does not penetrate it. The 3D equivalent is a tangent plane. In Figure 6.31, you can see the outline of the actual surface and that the normal is actually perpendicular to the line tangent to the surface.

For a sphere, calculation of the normal is pretty simple. (The normal actually has the same values as the vertex!) For other nontrivial surfaces, it might not be so easy. In such cases, you calculate the normals for each polygon that shared a vertex. The actual normal you assign to that vertex is the average of these normals. The visual effect is a nice smooth regular surface, even though it is actually composed of a myriad small flat segments.

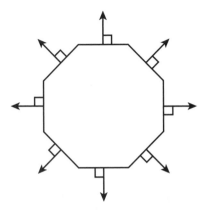

Figure 6.30 An approximation with normals perpendicular to each face.

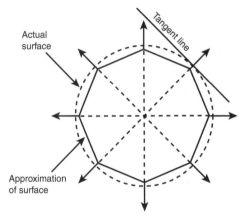

Figure 6.31 Each normal is perpendicular to the surface itself.

Putting It All Together

Now, it's time for a more complex sample program. We demonstrate how to use normals to create a smooth appearance of a surface, how to move a light around in a scene, how to create a spot light, and finally, one of the drawbacks of OpenGL lighting.

Our next sample program spot does all of this. We create a solid sphere in the center of our viewing volume with `glutSolidSphere`. We shine a spotlight on this sphere that we can move around, and we can change the "smoothness" of the normals and demonstrate some of the limitations of OpenGL lighting.

So far, we have been specifying a light's position with `glLight` as follows:

```
// Array to specify position
GLfloat  lightPos[] = { 0.0f, 150.0f, 150.0f, 1.0f };



...
...



// Set the light position
glLightfv(GL_LIGHT0,GL_POSITION,lightPos);
```

The array `lightPos[]` contains the x, y, and z values that specify either the light's actual position in the scene or the direction from which the light is coming. The last value, a 1.0 in this case, indicates that the light is actually present at this location. By default, the light radiates equally in all directions from this location—but you can change this default to make a spotlight effect.

To make a light source an infinite distance away and coming from the direction specified by this vector, you place a 0.0 in this last `lightPos[]` array element. A directional light source, as this is called, strikes the surface of your objects evenly. That is, all the light rays are parallel. In a positional light source, on the other hand, the light rays diverge from the light source. The specular highlights achieved in the shinyjet example are not possible with a directional light source. Rather than the glistening spot, the entire face of the triangles that make up the jet would be white when they faced the light source dead on. (The light rays strike the surface at a 90° angle.)

Creating a Spotlight

Creating a spotlight is no different from creating any other directional light source. The code in Listing 6.8 shows the `SetupRC` function from the spot sample program. This program places a blue sphere in the center of the window. A spotlight is created that can be moved vertically with the up and down arrow keys and horizontally with the left and right arrow keys. As the spotlight moves over the surface of the sphere, a specular highlight follows it on the surface.

Listing 6.8   *Lighting Setup for the spot Sample Program*

```
// Light values and coordinates
GLfloat  lightPos[] = { 0.0f, 0.0f, 75.0f, 1.0f };
GLfloat  specular[] = { 1.0f, 1.0f, 1.0f, 1.0f};
GLfloat  specref[] =  { 1.0f, 1.0f, 1.0f, 1.0f };
GLfloat  ambientLight[] = { 0.5f, 0.5f, 0.5f, 1.0f};
GLfloat  spotDir[] = { 0.0f, 0.0f, -1.0f };


// This function does any needed initialization on the rendering
// context.  Here it sets up and initializes the lighting for
```

```
// the scene.
void SetupRC()
    {
    glEnable(GL_DEPTH_TEST);    // Hidden surface removal
    glFrontFace(GL_CCW);        // Counterclockwise polygons face out
    glEnable(GL_CULL_FACE);        // Do not try to display the back sides

    // Enable lighting
    glEnable(GL_LIGHTING);

    // Set up and enable light 0
    // Supply a slight ambient light so the objects can be seen
    glLightModelfv(GL_LIGHT_MODEL_AMBIENT, ambientLight);

    // The light is composed of just diffuse and specular components
    glLightfv(GL_LIGHT0,GL_DIFFUSE,ambientLight);
    glLightfv(GL_LIGHT0,GL_SPECULAR,specular);
    glLightfv(GL_LIGHT0,GL_POSITION,lightPos);

    // Specific spot effects
    // Cut off angle is 60 degrees
    glLightf(GL_LIGHT0,GL_SPOT_CUTOFF,60.0f);

    // Fairly shiny spot
    glLightf(GL_LIGHT0,GL_SPOT_EXPONENT,100.0f);

    // Enable this light in particular
    glEnable(GL_LIGHT0);

    // Enable color tracking
    glEnable(GL_COLOR_MATERIAL);

    // Set material properties to follow glColor values
    glColorMaterial(GL_FRONT, GL_AMBIENT_AND_DIFFUSE);

    // All materials hereafter have full specular reflectivity
    // with a high shine
    glMaterialfv(GL_FRONT, GL_SPECULAR,specref);
    glMateriali(GL_FRONT, GL_SHININESS,128);


    // Black background
    glClearColor(0.0f, 0.0f, 0.0f, 1.0f );
    }
```

The following lines from the listing are actually what make a positional light source into a spotlight:

```
// Specific spot effects
// Cut off angle is 60 degrees
glLightf(GL_LIGHT0,GL_SPOT_CUTOFF,60.0f);

// Fairly shiny spot
glLightf(GL_LIGHT0,GL_SPOT_EXPONENT,100.0f);
```

The GL_SPOT_CUTOFF value specifies the radial angle of the cone of light emanating from the spotlight. For a normal positional light, this value is 180° so that the light is not confined to a cone. Spotlights emit a cone of light, and objects outside this cone are not illuminated. Figure 6.32 shows how this angle translates to the cone width.

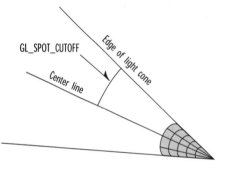

Figure 6.32 The angle of the spotlight cone.

Drawing a Spotlight

When you place a spotlight in a scene, the light must come from somewhere. Just because you have a source of light at some location doesn't mean that you see a bright spot there. For our spot sample program, we placed a red cone at the spotlight source to show where the light was coming from. Inside the end of this cone, we placed a bright yellow sphere to simulate a light bulb.

This sample has a pop-up menu that we use to demonstrate several things. The pop-up menu contains items to set flat and smooth shading and to produce a sphere for low, medium, and high *tessellation*. Tessellation means to break a mesh of polygons into a finer mesh of polygons. It n also be used to turn concave polygons and shapes into a collection of convex polygons (see Chapter 12, "Beyond Lines and Triangles"). Figure 6.33 shows a wireframe representation of a highly tessellated sphere next to one that has few polygons.

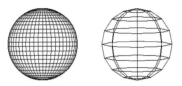

Figure 6.33 On the left is a highly tessellated sphere; on the right, a sphere made up of few polygons.

Figure 6.34 shows our sample in its initial state with the spotlight moved off slightly to one side. (Use the arrow keys to move the spotlight.) The sphere consists of few polygons, which are flat shaded. Using the pop-up menu (right mouse click), you can switch between smooth and flat shading and between very low, medium, and very high tessellation for the sphere. Listing 6.9 shows the complete code to render the scene.

Figure 6.34 The spot sample—low tessellation, flat shading.

Listing 6.9 *The Rendering Function for spot, Showing How the Spotlight is Moved*

```
// Called to draw scene
void RenderScene(void)
    {
    if(iShade == MODE_FLAT)
        glShadeModel(GL_FLAT);
    else //      iShade = MODE_SMOOTH;
        glShadeModel(GL_SMOOTH);

    // Clear the window with current clearing color
    glClear(GL_COLOR_BUFFER_BIT | GL_DEPTH_BUFFER_BIT);

    // First place the light
    // Save the coordinate transformation
    glPushMatrix();
```

continued on next page

continued from previous page

```
        // Rotate coordinate system
        glRotatef(yRot, 0.0f, 1.0f, 0.0f);
        glRotatef(xRot, 1.0f, 0.0f, 0.0f);

        // Specify new position and direction in rotated coords.
        glLightfv(GL_LIGHT0,GL_POSITION,lightPos);
        glLightfv(GL_LIGHT0,GL_SPOT_DIRECTION,spotDir);

        // Draw a red cone to enclose the light source
        glColor3ub(255,0,0);

        // Translate origin to move the cone out to where the light
        // is positioned.
        glTranslatef(lightPos[0],lightPos[1],lightPos[2]);
        glutSolidCone(4.0f,6.0f,15,15);

        // Draw a smaller displaced sphere to denote the light bulb
        // Save the lighting state variables
        glPushAttrib(GL_LIGHTING_BIT);

            // Turn off lighting and specify a bright yellow sphere
            glDisable(GL_LIGHTING);
                glColor3ub(255,255,0);
            glutSolidSphere(3.0f, 15, 15);

        // Restore lighting state variables
        glPopAttrib();

    // Restore coordinate transformations
    glPopMatrix();


    // Set material color and draw a sphere in the middle
    glColor3ub(0, 0, 255);

    if(iTess == MODE_VERYLOW)
        glutSolidSphere(30.0f, 7, 7);
    else
        if(iTess == MODE_MEDIUM)
            glutSolidSphere(30.0f, 15, 15);
        else //  iTess = MODE_MEDIUM;
            glutSolidSphere(30.0f, 50, 50);

    // Display the results
    glutSwapBuffers();
    }
```

The variables `iTess` and `iMode` are set by the GLUT menu handler and control how many sections the sphere is broken into and whether flat or smooth shading is employed. Note that the light is positioned before any geometry is rendered. As pointed out in Chapter 2, "What Is OpenGL?" OpenGL is an immediate-mode API; if you want an object to be illuminated, you have to put the light where you want it before drawing the object.

You can see in Figure 6.34 that the sphere is coarsely lit and each flat face is clearly evident. Switching to smooth shading helps little as shown in Figure 6.35.

Increasing the tessellation helps as shown in Figure 6.36, but you still see disturbing artifacts as you move the spotlight around the sphere. These lighting artifacts are one of the drawbacks of OpenGL lighting. A better way to characterize this is that this is a drawback of vertex lighting (not necessarily OpenGL!). By lighting the vertices and then interpolating between them, we get a crude approximation of lighting. This is sufficient for many cases, but as you can see in our spot example, it is not in others. If you switch to very high tessellation and move the spotlight, you see the lighting blemishes have all but vanished.

Figure 6.35 Smoothly shaded but inadequate tessellation.

As OpenGL hardware accelerators begin to accelerate transformations and lighting effects, and as CPUs become more powerful, you will be able to more finely tessellate your geometry for better OpenGL-based lighting effects.

The final observation you need to make about the spot sample appears when you set the sphere for medium tessellation and flat shading. As shown in Figure 6.37, each face of the sphere is flatly lit. Each vertex is the same color but is modulated by the value of the normal and the light. With flat shading, each polygon is made the color of the first vertex color specified and not smoothly interpolated between each one.

Figure 6.36 Choosing a finer mesh of polygons yields better vertex lighting.

Figure 6.37 A multi-facetted sphere.

Shadows

A chapter on color and lighting naturally begs the topic of shadows. Adding shadows to your scenes can greatly improve their realism and visual effectiveness. In Figures 6.38 and 6.39, you see two views of a lighted cube. Although both are lit, the one with a shadow is more convincing than the one without the shadow.

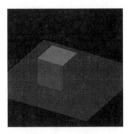

Figure 6.38   Lighted cube without a shadow.

Figure 6.39   Lighted cube with a shadow.

What Is a Shadow?

Conceptually, drawing a shadow is quite simple. A shadow is produced when an object keeps light from a light source from striking some object or surface behind the object casting the shadow. The area on the shadowed object's surface, outlined by the object casting the shadow, appears dark. We can produce a shadow programmatically by flattening the original object into the plane of the surface in which the object lies. The object is then drawn in black or some dark color, perhaps with some translucence. There are various methods for drawing shadows, some quite complex. Some of the references in Appendix B contain details on these techniques. For our purposes, we demonstrate one of the simpler methods, which works quite well when casting shadows on a flat surface (such as the ground). Figure 6.40 illustrates this flattening.

The process of squishing an object against another surface is accomplished using some of those advanced matrix manipulations we touched on in Chapter 5, "Moving Around in Space: Coordinate Transformations." Here, we boil it down to make it as simple as possible.

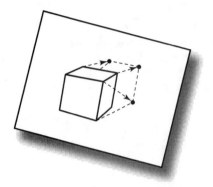

Figure 6.40   Flattening an object to create a shadow.

Squish Code

We need to flatten the modelview projection matrix so that any and all objects drawn into it are now in this flattened two-dimensional world. No matter how the object is oriented, it is squished into the plane in which the shadow lies. The second consideration is the distance and direction of the light source. The direction of the light source determines the shape of the shadow and influences the size. If you've ever seen your shadow in the late or early morning hours, you know how long and warped your shadow can appear depending on the position of the Sun.

The function in Listing 6.10 takes three points that lie in the plane in which you want the shadow to appear (these three points cannot be along the same straight line!), the position of the light source, and finally a pointer to a transformation matrix that this function constructs. Without delving too much into linear algebra, what this function does is deduce the coefficients of the equation of the plane in which the shadow appears and use it along with the lighting position to build a transformation matrix. If you multiply this matrix by the current modelview matrix, all further drawing is flattened into this plane.

Listing 6.10   *Function to Make a Shadow Transformation Matrix*

```
// Creates a shadow projection matrix out of the plane equation
// coefficients and the position of the light. The return value is stored
// in destMat[][]
void MakeShadowMatrix(GLfloat points[3][3], GLfloat lightPos[4],
                                            GLfloat destMat[4][4])
    {
    GLfloat planeCoeff[4];
    GLfloat dot;
```

```
// Find the plane equation coefficients
// Find the first three coefficients the same way we
// find a normal.
calcNormal(points,planeCoeff);

// Find the last coefficient by back substitutions
planeCoeff[3] = - (
    (planeCoeff[0]*points[2][0]) + (planeCoeff[1]*points[2][1]) +
    (planeCoeff[2]*points[2][2]));


// Dot product of plane and light position
dot = planeCoeff[0] * lightPos[0] +
      planeCoeff[1] * lightPos[1] +
      planeCoeff[2] * lightPos[2] +
      planeCoeff[3] * lightPos[3];

// Now do the projection
// First column
destMat[0][0] = dot - lightPos[0] * planeCoeff[0];
destMat[1][0] = 0.0f - lightPos[0] * planeCoeff[1];
destMat[2][0] = 0.0f - lightPos[0] * planeCoeff[2];
destMat[3][0] = 0.0f - lightPos[0] * planeCoeff[3];

// Second column
destMat[0][1] = 0.0f - lightPos[1] * planeCoeff[0];
destMat[1][1] = dot - lightPos[1] * planeCoeff[1];
destMat[2][1] = 0.0f - lightPos[1] * planeCoeff[2];
destMat[3][1] = 0.0f - lightPos[1] * planeCoeff[3];

// Third Column
destMat[0][2] = 0.0f - lightPos[2] * planeCoeff[0];
destMat[1][2] = 0.0f - lightPos[2] * planeCoeff[1];
destMat[2][2] = dot - lightPos[2] * planeCoeff[2];
destMat[3][2] = 0.0f - lightPos[2] * planeCoeff[3];

// Fourth Column
destMat[0][3] = 0.0f - lightPos[3] * planeCoeff[0];
destMat[1][3] = 0.0f - lightPos[3] * planeCoeff[1];
destMat[2][3] = 0.0f - lightPos[3] * planeCoeff[2];
destMat[3][3] = dot - lightPos[3] * planeCoeff[3];
}
```

A Shadow Example

To demonstrate the use of the function in Listing 6.10, we suspend our jet in air high above the ground. We place the light source directly above and a bit to the left of the jet. As you use the arrow keys to spin the jet around, the shadow cast by the jet appears flattened on the ground below. The output from this shadow sample program is shown in Figure 6.41.

Figure 6.41   Output from the shadow sample program.

The code in Listing 6.11 shows how the shadow projection matrix was created for this example. Note that we create the matrix once in `SetupRC` and save it in a global variable.

Listing 6.11   *Setting Up the Shadow Projection Matrix*

```
GLfloat lightPos[] = { -75.0f, 150.0f, -50.0f, 0.0f };
...
...

// Transformation matrix to project shadow
GLfloat shadowMat[4][4];
...
...

// This function does any needed initialization on the rendering
// context.  Here it sets up and initializes the lighting for
// the scene.
void SetupRC()
    {
    // Any three points on the ground (counterclockwise order)
    GLfloat points[3][3] = {{ -30.0f, -149.0f, -20.0f }, { -30.0f,
                                                -149.0f, 20.0f },
                        { 40.0f, -149.0f, 20.0f }};

    glEnable(GL_DEPTH_TEST);    // Hidden surface removal
    glFrontFace(GL_CCW);        // Counterclockwise polygons face out
    glEnable(GL_CULL_FACE);         // Do not calculate inside of jet
```

```
    // Enable lighting
    glEnable(GL_LIGHTING);

    ...
// Code to set up lighting, etc.
    ...


    // Light blue background
    glClearColor(0.0f, 0.0f, 1.0f, 1.0f );

    // Calculate projection matrix to draw shadow on the ground
    MakeShadowMatrix(points, lightPos, shadowMat);
    }
```

Listing 6.12 shows the rendering code for the shadow example. We first draw ground. Then, we draw the jet as we normally do, restore the modelview matrix, and multiply it by the shadow matrix. This creates our squish projection matrix. Then, we draw the jet again. (We've modified our code to accept a flag telling the DrawJet function to render in color or black.) After restoring the modelview matrix once again, we draw a small yellow sphere to approximate the position of the light. Note that we disable depth testing before we draw a plane below the jet to indicate the ground.

This rectangle lies in the same plane in which our shadow is drawn, and we want to make sure the shadow is drawn. We have never before discussed what happens if you draw two objects or planes in the same location. We have discussed depth testing as a means to determine what is drawn in front of what, however. If two objects occupy the same location, usually the last one drawn is shown. Sometimes, however, an effect called z-fighting causes fragments from both objects to be intermingled, resulting in a mess! See Chapter 11, "Buffers: Not Just for Animation," for a detailed discussion of the depth buffer.

Listing 6.12 *Render the Jet and its Shadow*

```
// Called to draw scene
void RenderScene(void)
    {
    // Clear the window with current clearing color
    glClear(GL_COLOR_BUFFER_BIT | GL_DEPTH_BUFFER_BIT);

    // Draw the ground; we do manual shading to a darker green
    // in the background to give the illusion of depth
    glBegin(GL_QUADS);
        glColor3ub(0,32,0);
        glVertex3f(400.0f, -150.0f, -200.0f);
        glVertex3f(-400.0f, -150.0f, -200.0f);
        glColor3ub(0,255,0);
```

continued on next page

continued from previous page

```
        glVertex3f(-400.0f, -150.0f, 200.0f);
        glVertex3f(400.0f, -150.0f, 200.0f);
    glEnd();

    // Save the matrix state and do the rotations
    glPushMatrix();

    // Draw jet at new orientation; put light in correct position
    // before rotating the jet
    glEnable(GL_LIGHTING);
    glLightfv(GL_LIGHT0,GL_POSITION,lightPos);
    glRotatef(xRot, 1.0f, 0.0f, 0.0f);
    glRotatef(yRot, 0.0f, 1.0f, 0.0f);

    DrawJet(FALSE);

    // Restore original matrix state
    glPopMatrix();


    // Get ready to draw the shadow and the ground
    // First disable lighting and save the projection state
    glDisable(GL_DEPTH_TEST);
    glDisable(GL_LIGHTING);
    glPushMatrix();

    // Multiply by shadow projection matrix
    glMultMatrixf((GLfloat *)shadowMat);

    // Now rotate the jet around in the new flattened space
    glRotatef(xRot, 1.0f, 0.0f, 0.0f);
    glRotatef(yRot, 0.0f, 1.0f, 0.0f);

    // Pass true to indicate drawing shadow
    DrawJet(TRUE);

    // Restore the projection to normal
    glPopMatrix();

    // Draw the light source
    glPushMatrix();
    glTranslatef(lightPos[0],lightPos[1], lightPos[2]);
    glColor3ub(255,255,0);
    glutSolidSphere(5.0f,10,10);
    glPopMatrix();
```

```
// Restore lighting state variables
glEnable(GL_DEPTH_TEST);

// Display the results
glutSwapBuffers();
}
```

Summary

In this chapter, you have been introduced to some of the magical and powerful capabilities of OpenGL. We started with adding color to your 3D scenes and smooth shading. You then saw how to specify one or more light sources and define their lighting characteristics in terms of ambient, diffuse, and specular components. We explained how the corresponding material properties interact with these light sources and demonstrated some special effects, such as adding specular highlights and softening sharp edges.

Also covered were lighting positions and the creation and manipulation of spotlights. The high-level matrix munching function presented here makes shadow generation as easy as it gets.

Reference Section

glColor

Purpose	Sets the current color when in RGBA color mode.
Include File	`<gl.h>`
Variations	

```
void glColor3b(GLbyte red, GLbyte green, GLbyte blue);
void glColor3b(GLbyte red, GLbyte green, GLbyte blue);
void glColor3d(GLdouble red, GLdouble green, GLdouble blue);
void glColor3f(GLfloat red, GLfloat green, GLfloat blue);
void glColor3i(GLint red, GLint green, GLint blue);
void glColor3s(GLshort red, GLshort green, GLshort blue);
void glColor3ub(GLubyte red, GLubyte green, GLubyte blue);
void glColor3ui(GLuint red, GLuint green, GLuint blue);
void glColor3us(GLushort red, GLushort green, GLushort blue);
void glColor4b(GLbyte red, GLbyte green, GLbyte blue, GLbyte alpha);
void glColor4d(GLdouble red, GLdouble green, GLdouble blue,
➥GLdouble alpha);
void glColor4f(GLfloat red, GLfloat green, GLfloat blue, GLfloat
➥alpha);
void glColor4i(GLint red, GLint green, GLint blue, GLint alpha);
```

continued on next page

```
void glColor4s(GLshort red, GLshort green, GLshort blue, GLshort
➥alpha);
void glColor4ub(GLubyte red, GLubyte green, GLubyte blue, GLubyte
➥alpha);
void glColor4ui(GLuint red, GLuint green, GLuint blue, GLuint
➥alpha);
void glColor4us(GLushort red, GLushort green, GLushort blue,
➥GLushort alpha);
void glColor3bv(const GLbyte *v);
void glColor3dv(const GLdouble *v);
void glColor3fv(const GLfloat *v);
void glColor3iv(const GLint *v);
void glColor3sv(const GLshort *v);
void glColor3ubv(const GLubyte *v);
void glColor3uiv(const GLuint *v);
void glColor3usv(const GLushort *v);
void glColor4bv(const GLbyte *v);
void glColor4dv(const GLdouble *v);
void glColor4fv(const GLfloat *v);
void glColor4iv(const GLint *v);
void glColor4sv(const GLshort *v);
void glColor4ubv(const GLubyte *v);
void glColor4uiv(const GLuint *v);
void glColor4usv(const GLushort *v);
```

Description   This function sets the current color by specifying separate red, green, and blue components of the color. Some functions also accept an alpha component. Each component represents the range of intensity from zero (0.0) to full intensity (1.0). Functions with the v suffix take a pointer to an array that specifies the components. Each element in the array must be the same type. When the alpha component is not specified, it is implicitly set to 1.0. When non–floating-point types are specified, the range from zero to the largest value represented by that type is mapped to the floating-point range 0.0 to 1.0.

Parameters

red   Specifies the red component of the color.

green   Specifies the green component of the color.

blue   Specifies the blue component of the color.

alpha   Specifies the alpha component of the color. Used only in variations that take four arguments.

*v   A pointer to an array of red, green, blue, and possibly alpha values.

Returns   None.

Example   The following code from the ccube example sets one of the corners of the color cube to white:

```
// Front face
glBegin(GL_POLYGON);

// White
glColor3ub((GLubyte) 255, (GLubyte)255, (GLubyte)255);
glVertex3f(50.0f,50.0f,50.0f);
...
```

See Also   glColorMaterial, glMaterial

glColorMask

Purpose	Enables or disables modification of color components in the color buffers.
Include File	<gl.h>
Syntax	void glColorMask(GLboolean bRed, GLboolean bGreen, GLboolean bBlue, GLboolean bAlpha);
Description	This function allows changes to individual color components in the color buffer to be disabled or enabled. (All are enabled by default.) For example, setting the bAlpha argument to GL_FALSE disallows changes to the alpha color components.

Parameters

bRed	GLboolean: Specifies whether the red component can be modified.
bGreen	GLboolean: Specifies whether the green component can be modified.
bBlue	GLboolean: Specifies whether the blue component can be modified.
bAlpha	GLboolean: Specifies whether the alpha component can be modified.
Returns	None.
Example	The following code masks all colors except red from being written to the color buffer. This results in turning all rendered objects to shades of red. (This is similar to black and white grayscale, but you might call this redscale!)

```
glColorMask(GL_TRUE, GL_FALSE, GL_FALSE, GL_FALSE);
```

See Also   glColor

glColorMaterial

Purpose	Allows material colors to track the current color as set by glColor.
Include File	<gl.h>
Syntax	void glColorMaterial(GLenum face, GLenum mode);
Description	This function allows material properties to be set without having to call glMaterial directly. By using this function, you can set certain material properties to follow the current color as specified by glColor. By default, color

tracking is disabled; to enable it, you must also call
`glEnable(GL_COLOR_MATERIAL)`. To disable color tracking again, call
`glDisable(GL_COLOR_MATERIAL)`.

Parameters

face   GLenum: Specifies whether the front (GL_FRONT), back (GL_BACK), or both
(GL_FRONT_AND_BACK) should follow the current color.

mode   GLenum: Specifies which material property should be following the current
color. This can be GL_EMISSION, GL_AMBIENT, GL_DIFFUSE, GL_SPECULAR, or
GL_AMBIENT_AND_DIFFUSE.

Returns   None.

Example   The following code from the ambient sample program enables color tracking
and then sets the front material parameters for ambient and diffuse reflectivity
to follow the colors specified by `glColor`:

```
glEnable(GL_COLOR_MATERIAL);   // Enable material color tracking

// Front material ambient and diffuse colors track glColor
glColorMaterial(GL_FRONT,GL_AMBIENT_AND_DIFFUSE);
```

See Also   glColor, glMaterial, glLight, glLightModel

glCullFace

Purpose   Specifies whether the front or back of polygons should be eliminated from
drawing.

Include File   <gl.h>

Syntax   `void glCullFace(GLenum mode);`

Description   This function disables lighting, shading, and color calculations and operations on either the front or back of a polygon. If, for instance, an object is
closed in so that the back side of the polygons is never visible regardless of
rotation or translation, this eliminates unnecessary computations in the display of the scene. Culling is enabled or disabled by calling `glEnable` and
`glDisable` with the GL_CULL_FACE parameter. The front and back of the
polygon are defined by use of the `glFrontFace` function and the order in
which the vertices are specified (clockwise or counterclockwise winding).

Parameters

mode   GLenum: Specifies which face of polygons should be culled. Can be either
GL_FRONT or GL_BACK.

Returns   None.

Example   The following code from the ambient example from this chapter shows how
the color and drawing operations are disabled for the inside of the jet. It is

also necessary to indicate which side of the polygon is the outside by specifying clockwise or counterclockwise winding:

```
glEnable(GL_CULL_FACE);     // Do not calculate inside of jet
    glFrontFace(GL_CCW);     // Counterclockwise polygons face out
```

See Also   glFrontFace, glLightModel

glFrontFace

Purpose	Defines which side of a polygon is the front or back.
Include File	<gl.h>
Syntax	void glFrontFace(GLenum mode);
Description	When a scene consists of objects that are closed (you cannot see the inside), there is no need to do color or lighting calculations on the inside of the object. The glCullFace function turns off such calculations for either the front or back of polygons. The glFrontFace function determines which side of the polygons is considered the front. If the vertices of a polygon are specified such that they travel around the polygon in a clockwise fashion, the polygon is said to have clockwise winding. If the vertices travel counterclockwise, the polygon is said to have counterclockwise winding. This function allows either the clockwise or counterclockwise wound face to be considered the front of the polygon.
Parameters	
mode	GLenum: Specifies the orientation of front-facing polygons, clockwise (GL_CW) or counterclockwise (GL_CCW).
Returns	None.
Example	The following code from the ambient example from this chapter shows how the color and drawing operations are disabled for the inside of the jet. It is also necessary to indicate which side of the polygon is the outside by specifying clockwise or counterclockwise winding:

```
glEnable(GL_CULL_FACE);     // Do not calculate inside of jet
    glFrontFace(GL_CCW);     // Counterclockwise polygons face out
```

See Also   glCullFace, glLightModel

glGetMaterial

Purpose	Returns the current material property settings.
Include File	<gl.h>
Variations	void glGetMaterialfv(GLenum face, GLenum pname, GLfloat *params); void glGetMaterialiv(GLenum face, GLenum pname, GLint *params);

Description   Use this function to query the current front or back material properties. The return values are stored at the address pointed to by `params`. For most properties, this is an array of four values containing the RGBA components of the property specified.

Parameters

face   GLenum: Specifies whether the front (`GL_FRONT`) or back (`GL_BACK`) material properties are being sought.

pname   GLenum: Specifies which material property is being queried. Valid values are `GL_AMBIENT`, `GL_DIFFUSE`, `GL_SPECULAR`, `GL_EMISSION`, `GL_SHININESS`, and `GL_COLOR_INDEXES`.

params   GLint* or GLfloat*: An array of integer or floating-point values representing the return values. For `GL_AMBIENT`, `GL_DIFFUSE`, `GL_SPECULAR`, and `GL_EMISSION`, this is a four-element array containing the RGBA values of the property specified. For `GL_SHININESS`, a single value representing the specular exponent of the material is returned. `GL_COLOR_INDEXES` returns an array of three elements containing the ambient, diffuse, and specular components in the form of color indexes. `GL_COLOR_INDEXES` is only used for color index lighting.

Returns   None.

Example   The following code shows how all the current material properties are read and stored:

```
// Storage for all the material properties
GLfloat ambientMat[4],diffuseMat[4],specularMat[4],emissionMat[4];
GLfloat shine;
...
...
// Read all the material properties
glGetMaterialfv(GL_FRONT,GL_AMBIENT,ambientMat);
glGetMaterialfv(GL_FRONT,GL_DIFFUSE,diffuseMat);
glGetMaterialfv(GL_FRONT,GL_SPECULAR,specularMat);
glGetMaterialfv(GL_FRONT,GL_EMISSION,emissionMat);
glGetMaterialfv(GL_FRONT,GL_SHININESS,&shine);
```

See Also   glMaterial

glGetLight

Purpose   Returns information about the current light source settings.

Include File   <gl.h>

Variations   void glGetLightfv(GLenum light, GLenum pname, GLfloat *params);
void glGetLightiv(GLenum light, GLenum pname, GLint *params);

Description   Use this function to query the current settings for one of the eight supported light sources. The return values are stored at the address pointed to by `params`. For most properties, this is an array of four values containing the RGBA components of the properties specified.

Parameters

light   GLenum: The light source for which information is being requested. This ranges from 0 to `GL_MAX_LIGHTS` (8 for Windows NT and Windows 95). Constant light values are enumerated from `GL_LIGHT0` to `GL_LIGHT7`.

pname   GLenum: Specifies which property of the light source is being queried. Any of the following values are valid: `GL_AMBIENT`, `GL_DIFFUSE`, `GL_SPECULAR`, `GL_POSITION`, `GL_SPOT_DIRECTION`, `GL_SPOT_EXPONENT`, `GL_SPOT_CUTOFF`, `GL_CONSTANT_ATTENUATION`, `GL_LINEAR_ATTENUATION`, and `GL_QUADRATIC_ATTENUATION`.

params   GLfloat* or GLint*: An array of integer or floating-point values representing the return values. These return values are in the form of an array of four or three or a single value. Table 6.2 shows the return value meanings for each property.

Returns   None.

Example   The following code shows how all the lighting properties for the light source `GL_LIGHT0` are retrieved and stored:

```
// Storage for the light properties
GLfloat ambientComp[4],diffuseComp[4],specularComp[4]
...
...
// Read the light components
glGetLightfv(GL_LIGHT0,GL_AMBIENT,ambientComp);
glGetLightfv(GL_FRONT,GL_DIFFUSE,diffuseComp);
glGetLightfv(GL_FRONT,GL_SPECULAR,specularComp);
```

See Also   `glLight`

Table 6.2   *Valid Lighting Parameters for* `glGetLight`

Property	Meaning of Return Values
GL_AMBIENT	Four RGBA components.
GL_DIFFUSE	Four RGBA components.
GL_SPECULAR	Four RGBA components.
GL_POSITION	Four elements that specify the position of the light source. The first three elements specify the position of the light. The fourth, if 1.0, specifies that the light is at this position. Otherwise, the light source is directional and all rays are parallel.
GL_SPOT_DIRECTION	Three elements specifying the direction of the spotlight. This vector is not normalized and is in eye coordinates.
GL_SPOT_EXPONENT	A single value representing the spot exponent.
GL_SPOT_CUTOFF	A single value representing the cutoff angle of the spot source.

`GL_CONSTANT_ATTENUATION`	A single value representing the constant attenuation of the light.
`GL_LINEAR_ATTENUATION`	A single value representing the linear attenuation of the light.
`GL_QUADRATIC_ATTENUATION`	A single value representing the quadratic attenuation of the light.

glLight

Purpose   Sets light source parameters for one of the eight available light sources.

Include File   <gl.h>

Variations
```
void glLightf(GLenum light, GLenum pname, GLfloat param);
void glLighti(GLenum light, GLenum pname, GLint param);
void glLightfv(GLenum light, GLenum pname, const GLfloat*params);
void glLightiv(GLenum light, GLenum pname, const GLint *params);
```

Description   Use this function to set the lighting parameters for one of the eight supported light sources. The first two variations of this function require only a single parameter value to set one of the following properties: `GL_SPOT_EXPONENT`, `GL_SPOT_CUTOFF`,`GL_CONSTANT_ATTENUATION`, `GL_LINEAR_ATTENUATION`, and `GL_QUADRATIC_ATTENUATION`. The second two variations are used for lighting parameters that require an array of multiple values. These include `GL_AMBIENT`, `GL_DIFFUSE`, `GL_SPECULAR`, `GL_POSITION`, and `GL_SPOT_DIREC-TION`. You can also use these variations with single valued parameters by specifying a single element array for `*params`.

Parameters

light   GLenum: Specifies which light source is being modified. This ranges from 0 to `GL_MAX_LIGHTS` (8 for Windows NT and Windows 95). Constant light values are enumerated from `GL_LIGHT0` to `GL_LIGHT7`.

pname   GLenum: Specifies which lighting parameter is being set by this function call. See Table 6.2 for a complete list and the meaning of these parameters.

param   GLfloat or GLint: For parameters that are specified by a single value, this specifies that value. These parameters are `GL_SPOT_EXPONENT`, `GL_SPOT_CUTOFF`, `GL_CONSTANT_ATTENUATION`, `GL_LINEAR_ATTENUATION`, and `GL_QUADRATIC_ATTENUATION`. These parameters only have meaning for spotlights.

params   GLfloat* or GLint*: An array of values that fully describe the parameters being set. See Table 6.2 for a list and the meaning of these parameters.

Returns   None.

Example   The following code from the litjet sample program sets up a single light source to the upper left behind the viewer. The light source is composed only of moderate ambient and diffuse components:
```
// Light values and coordinates
  GLfloat  whiteLight[] = { 0.5f, 0.5f, 0.5f, 1.0f };
GLfloat lightPos[] = { -50.f, 50.0f, -100.0f, 0.0f };
```

```
    . . .
    . . .

// Enable lighting
glEnable(GL_LIGHTING);

        // Set up and enable light 0
    glLightfv(GL_LIGHT0,GL_AMBIENT_AND_DIFFUSE,whiteLight);
    glLightfv(GL_LIGHT0,GL_POSITION,lightPos);
        glEnable(GL_LIGHT0);
```

See Also   glGetLight

glLightModel

Purpose	Sets the lighting model parameters used by OpenGL.
Include File	<gl.h>
Variations	`void glLightModelf(GLenum pname, GLfloat param)`
	`void glLightModeli(GLenum pname, GLint param);`
	`void glLightModelfv(GLenum pname, const GLfloat *params);`
	`void glLightModeliv(GLenum pname, const GLint *params);`

Description   You use this function to set the lighting model parameters used by
OpenGL. You can set any or all of three lighting model parameters.
GL_LIGHT_MODEL_AMBIENT is used to set a default ambient illumination
for a scene. By default, this light has an RGBA value of (0.2, 0.2, 0.2, 1.0).
Only the last two variations can be used to set this lighting model because
they take pointers to an array that can contain the RGBA values.
The GL_LIGHT_MODEL_TWO_SIDE parameter is specified to indicate whether
both sides of polygons are illuminated. By default, only the front (defined by
winding) of polygons is illuminated, using the front material properties as
specified by glMaterial. Finally, specifying a lighting model parameter of
GL_LIGHT_MODEL_LOCAL_ VIEWER modifies the calculation of specular reflection angles, whether the view is down along the –z-axis or from the origin of
the eye coordinate system.

Parameters

pname   GLenum: Specifies a lighting model parameter. GL_LIGHT_MODEL_AMBIENT,
GL_LIGHT_MODEL_LOCAL_VIEWER, and GL_LIGHT_MODEL_TWO_SIDE are accepted.

param   GLfloat or GLint: For GL_LIGHT_MODEL_LOCAL_VIEWER, a value of 0.0 indicates that specular lighting angles take the view direction to be parallel to and
in the direction of the –z-axis. Any other value indicates that the view is from
the origin of eye coordinate system. For GL_LIGHT_MODEL_TWO_SIDE, a value
of 0.0 indicates that only the fronts of polygons are to be included in illumination calculations. Any other value indicates that both the front and back are
included. This parameter has no effect on points, lines, or bitmaps.

params	GLfloat* or GLint*: For `GL_LIGHT_MODEL_AMBIENT` or `GL_LIGHT_MODEL_` `LOCAL_VIEWER`, this points to an array of integers or floating-point values, only the first element of which is used to set the parameter value. For `GL_LIGHT_` `MODEL_AMBIENT`, this array points to four values that indicate the RGBA components of the ambient light.
Returns	None.
Example	The following code from this chapter's ambient example sets up a global ambient light source consisting of a full-intensity white light:

```
// Bright white light
GLfloat ambientLight[] = { 1.0f, 1.0f, 1.0f, 1.0f };

glEnable(GL_DEPTH_TEST);      // Hidden surface removal
glEnable(GL_CULL_FACE);        // Do not calculate inside of jet
glFrontFace(GL_CCW);          // Counterclockwise polygons face out

// Enable lighting
glEnable(GL_LIGHTING);

// Set light model to use ambient light specified by ambientLight
glLightModelfv(GL_LIGHT_MODEL_AMBIENT,ambientLight);
```

See Also	`glLight`, `glMaterial`

glMaterial

Purpose	Sets material parameters for use by the lighting model.
Include File	<gl.h>
Variations	`void glMaterialf(GLenum face, GLenum pname, GLfloat param);` `void glMateriali(GLenum face, GLenum pname, GLint param);` `void glMaterialfv(GLenum face, GLenum pname, const GLfloat` ➥`*params)` `void glMaterialiv(GLenum face, GLenum pname, const GLint` ➥`*params);`
Description	Use this function to set the material reflectance properties of polygons. The `GL_AMBIENT`, `GL_DIFFUSE`, and `GL_SPECULAR` properties affect how these components of incident light are reflected. `GL_EMISSION` is used for materials that appear to give off their own light. `GL_SHININESS` can vary from 0 to 128, with the higher values producing a larger specular highlight on the material surface. You use `GL_COLOR_INDEXES` for material reflectance properties in color index mode.
Parameters	
face	GLenum: Specifies whether the front, back, or both material properties of the polygons are being set by this function. May be either `GL_FRONT`, `GL_BACK`, or `GL_FRONT_AND_BACK`.

pname	GLenum: For the first two variations, this specifies the single-valued material parameter being set. Currently, the only single-valued material parameter is GL_SHININESS. The second two variations, which take arrays for their parameters, can set the following material properties: GL_AMBIENT, GL_DIFFUSE, GL_SPECULAR, GL_EMISSION, GL_SHININESS, GL_AMBIENT_AND_DIFFUSE, or GL_COLOR_INDEXES.
param	GLfloat or GLint: Specifies the value to which the parameter specified by pname (GL_SHININESS) is set.
params	GLfloat* or GLint*: An array of floats or integers that contain the components of the property being set.
Returns	None.
Example	See the litjet sample program from this chapter.
See Also	glGetMaterial, glColorMaterial, glLight, glLightModel

glNormal

Purpose	Defines a surface normal for the next vertex or set of vertices specified.
Include File	<gl.h>

Variations	void glNormal3b(GLbyte nx, GLbyte ny, GLbyte nz);
	void glNormal3d(GLdouble nx, GLdouble ny, GLdouble nz);
	void glNormal3f(GLfloat nx, GLfloat ny, GLfloat nz);
	void glNormal3i(GLint nx, GLint ny, GLint nz);
	void glNormal3s(GLshort nx, GLshort ny, GLshort nz);
	void glNormal3bv(const GLbyte *v);
	void glNormal3dv(const GLdouble *v);
	void glNormal3fv(const GLfloat *v);
	void glNormal3iv(const GLint *v);
	void glNormal3sv(const GLshort *v);

Description	The normal vector specifies which direction is up and perpendicular to the surface of the polygon. This is used for lighting and shading calculations. Specifying a unit vector of length 1 improves rendering speed. OpenGL automatically converts your normals to unit normals if you enable this with glEnable(GL_NORMALIZE);.
Parameters	
nx	Specifies the x magnitude of the normal vector.
ny	Specifies the y magnitude of the normal vector.
nz	Specifies the z magnitude of the normal vector.
v	Specifies an array of three elements containing the x, y, and z magnitudes of the normal vector.
Returns	None.

Example   The following code from the litjet sample program from this chapter demonstrates setting a normal vector for each polygon before it is rendered:

```
// Vertices for this panel
float normal[3];
float v[3][3] =    {{ 15.0f, 0.0f, 30.0f},
            { 0.0f, 15.0f, 30.0f},
            { 0.0f, 0.0f,   60.0f}};

// Calculate the normal for the plane
calcNormal(v,normal);

// Draw the triangle using the plane normal
// for all the vertices
glBegin(GL_TRIANGLES);
    glNormal3fv(normal);
    glVertex3fv(v[0]);
    glVertex3fv(v[1]);
    glVertex3fv(v[2]);
glEnd();
```

See Also   glTexCoord, glVertex

glShadeModel

Purpose   Sets the default shading to flat or smooth.

Include File <gl.h>

Syntax   void glShadeModel(GLenum mode);

Description   OpenGL primitives are always shaded, but the shading model can be flat
(GL_FLAT) or smooth (GL_SMOOTH). In the simplest of scenarios, one color is
set with glColor before a primitive is drawn. This primitive is solid and flat
(does not vary) throughout, regardless of the shading. If a different color is
specified for each vertex, then the resulting image varies with the shading
model. With smooth shading, the color of the polygon's interior points are
interpolated from the colors specified at the vertices. This means the color
varies from one color to the next between two vertices. The color variation
follows a line through the color cube between the two colors. If lighting is
enabled, OpenGL does other calculations to determine the correct value for
each vertex. In flat shading, the color specified for the last vertex is used
throughout the region of the primitive. The only exception is for GL_POLYGON,
in which case, the color used throughout the region is the one specified for
the first vertex.

Parameters

mode   GLenum: Specifies the shading model to use, either GL_FLAT or GL_SMOOTH. The default is GL_SMOOTH.

Returns   None.

Example   The following line of code sets the shading from smooth to flat:

```
glShadeModel(GL_FLAT);
```

See Also   glColor, glLight, glLightModel

PART 2

Meat & Potatoes—The Staples of OpenGL Rendering

If you've been reading this book from front to back as a tutorial, you are now quite well grounded in the use of OpenGL for basic 3D rendering. Now that you know how to work the stove, it's time to cook! In Part 2, the sample programs are going to start getting a lot more interesting and involved. Each example may spark some creative ember in you to further expand it into a game or simulation of your own.

We'll start with bitmapped graphics and texture mapping. Then we'll talk about how OpenGL supports the construction and storage of 3D models, and how to achieve special effects with fog and blending. Finally, we'll discuss the generation of smooth curves and surfaces and how the user can interact with objects onscreen.

Since this book is about the OpenGL API, we need to focus on that, and thus we can't cover every 3D technique to which OpenGL can be applied (see Appendix B however for whole books on nothing but technique!). We do hope however that in the coming chapters as we cover the various functions, that we give you enough of a sampling to get you started on an exciting new programming discipline.

7

RASTER GRAPHICS IN OPENGL

by Michael Sweet

What you'll learn in this chapter:

How to...	Functions You'll Use
Draw bitmap images	glBitmap
Use bitmap fonts	glCallLists/glGenLists/ glListBase/wglUseFontBitmaps
Draw color images	glDrawPixels
Read and copy color images onscreen	glReadPixels/glCopyPixels
Read and write Windows bitmap files	LoadDIBitmap/SaveDIBitmap

You've probably heard a lot of sales hype about how much better it is to work with 3D graphics than with those 2D graphics from years ago. Although this is true for the most part, ultimately those 3D graphics are drawn in two dimensions on your screen. *Raster graphics* are these two-dimensional arrays of colors and are used not only for displaying 3D graphics on the screen, but also for printing images on raster printers or motion-picture film.

In addition to the vector and polygon functions we've examined so far, OpenGL provides several functions that directly manage 2D bitmaps and images. Those functions are the subject of this chapter.

Drawing Bitmaps

Bitmaps in OpenGL are two-color images that are used to quickly draw characters or symbols (such as icons) onscreen. This diverges from the (incorrect) Microsoft Windows definition that includes multicolored images as well. OpenGL provides a single function to draw bitmaps, glBitmap. When you draw a bitmap with glBitmap, the first color (0) is transparent. The second color (1) is drawn using the current color and lighting material attributes.

Figure 7.1 shows an OpenGL bitmap image of a smiley face. The code to draw this window (Listing 7.1) consists of the bitmap data followed by a call to glBitmap.

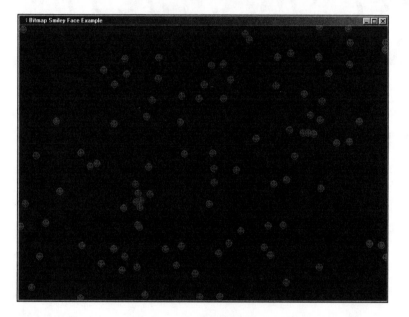

Figure 7.1   Output from smiley face glBitmap example.

Listing 7.1   glBitmap *Example*

```
void
Redraw()
    {
    int             i;          /* Looping var */
    static GLubyte smiley[] = /* 16x16 smiley face */
        {
        0x03, 0xc0, 0, 0, /*       ****          */
        0x0f, 0xf0, 0, 0, /*      ********        */
        0x1e, 0x78, 0, 0, /*     ****  ****       */
        0x39, 0x9c, 0, 0, /*    ***  **  ***      */
```

```
    0x77, 0xee, 0, 0, /*  *** ****** ***  */
    0x6f, 0xf6, 0, 0, /*  ** ******** **  */
    0xff, 0xff, 0, 0, /* ****************  */
    0xff, 0xff, 0, 0, /* ****************  */
    0xff, 0xff, 0, 0, /* ****************  */
    0xff, 0xff, 0, 0, /* ****************  */
    0x73, 0xce, 0, 0, /*  ***  ****  ***  */
    0x73, 0xce, 0, 0, /*  ***  ****  ***  */
    0x3f, 0xfc, 0, 0, /*   ************   */
    0x1f, 0xf8, 0, 0, /*    **********    */
    0x0f, 0xf0, 0, 0, /*     ********     */
    0x03, 0xc0, 0, 0  /*       ****       */
    };

glClearColor(0.0, 0.0, 0.0, 1.0);
glClear(GL_COLOR_BUFFER_BIT);

/*This bitmap is aligned to 4-byte boundaries...*/
glPixelTransferi(GL_UNPACK_ALIGNMENT, 4);

glColor3f(1.0, 0.0, 0.0);
for (i = 0; i < 100; i ++)
    {
    glRasterPos2i(rand() % rect->right, rand() % rect->bottom);
    glBitmap(16, 16, 8.0, 8.0, 0.0, 0.0, smiley);
    }

glFinish();
}
```

In this example, we have defined a 16×16 pixel bitmap image of a smiley face. The bitmap is an array of 64 GLubytes (unsigned bytes) with 4 bytes per line in the image. (The last two bytes in each line are unused.) Bit 7 of the first byte corresponds to the bottom-left corner.

SOME THINGS TO NOTE ABOUT OPENGL BITMAPS

OpenGL bitmaps are usually defined "upside down." That is, they are stored from bottom to top. To define them from top to bottom, you must specify a negative height. Also, because of bugs in the Microsoft OpenGL libraries, you must align each scanline (row) of bitmap data to a 32-bit boundary. With a properly functioning OpenGL library, you can use the glPixelStore function described later in this chapter to change the bitmap alignment.

After we have defined a bitmap image to draw, we must specify the current raster position by calling the glRasterPos function:

```
glRasterPos2i(rand() % rect->right, rand() % rect->bottom);
```

In this example, we randomly position our smiley face within the client area of our window. The raster position is specified in world/model coordinates just like a `glVertex` position. Besides `glRasterPos2i`, a `glRasterPos2f` function positions the bitmap using floating-point coordinates.

To draw the bitmap, call the `glBitmap` function. In this case, we draw a 16×16 bitmap whose center lies at (8.0, 8.0) in the bitmap. After the bitmap is drawn, the raster position is moved (0.0, 0.0) pixels:

```
glBitmap(GLsizei width, GLsizei height,
    GLfloat xorig, GLfloat yorig,
    GLfloat xmove, GLfloat ymove,
    const GLubyte *bits)
```

The `width` and `height` parameters specify the width and height of the bitmap. The `bits` argument contains the bitmap you want to draw and is 32-bit aligned. `xorig` and `yorig` contain the center location of the bitmap. After the bitmap is drawn, the current raster position is moved by (`xmove`,`ymove`) pixels. The `xmove` and `ymove` parameters are normally used for bitmap fonts (described later) to advance to the next character "cell."

Raster Graphics Clipping

When you draw polygons and other vector drawing primitives, OpenGL automatically clips the appropriate parts of the primitives to the current window. Clipping for bitmaps works a little differently, however.

When you set the current raster position with `glRasterPos`, OpenGL also sets a raster position valid flag that is used for clipping. This flag is true if the raster position lies inside the current viewport and false otherwise. If the raster position you specify lies outside of the current viewport, the bitmap or image is not drawn, even if part of the bitmap or image is visible. Any additional bitmaps or images are also not drawn until you use a valid raster position. This is particularly important when drawing strings of characters with bitmap fonts.

That said, there are ways to "trick" OpenGL into drawing bitmaps partially off the screen. Start by setting the raster position to a location that is inside the current viewport. Then, use the `xorig` and `yorig` arguments to `glBitmap` to offset the bitmap:

```
glBitmap(width, height, xorig, yorig, 0.0, 0.0, bits);
```

By using an empty bitmap (width and height equal to 0), you can also use the `xmove` and `ymove` arguments to offset the raster position prior to drawing any bitmaps:

```
glBitmap(0, 0, 0.0, 0.0, xmove, ymove, NULL);
```

We use this technique later to justify text and offset color images.

Bitmap Fonts

One important application of bitmaps is displaying character strings. Under ordinary circumstances, you have to define a bitmap array for each character and then draw the bitmaps as necessary to display the string. Fortunately, the Microsoft Windows WIN32 libraries provide a function called `wglUseFontBitmaps` to generate these bitmaps from font files loaded on your system.

To use these font bitmaps, OpenGL provides three functions, `glGenLists`, `glListBase`, and `glCallLists`. The `glGenLists` function generates a contiguous series of OpenGL display list IDs that hold the character bitmaps created by `wglUseFontBitmaps`:

```
Gluint  base;
HDC     hdc;

base = glGenLists(96);
wglUseFontBitmaps(hdc, 32, 96, base);
```

This creates 96 character bitmaps from the current font starting at character 32, the ASCII code for the space character. To display a string of characters using these bitmaps, you use a combination of `glListBase` and `glCallLists`:

```
char *s;

glListBase(base - 32);
glCallLists(strlen(s), GL_UNSIGNED_BYTE, s);
```

The `glListBase` function sets the base display list ID. `glCallList` and `glCallLists` add this number to the display list IDs passed to them. Among other things, you can use `glListBase` to select character fonts built with `wglUseFontBitmaps`. The `glCallLists` function calls a series of display lists based upon the array of characters (unsigned bytes) you pass in, which draws the character string.

Building a Simple Font Library

Although the `wglCreateFontBitmaps` function simplifies font creation, you still have to do a lot just to output a character string. You can build a usable font library fairly easily, however. To start, we need to define a data structure to hold the list base and the widths of all characters in the font:

```
typedef struct
    {
    GLuint base;         /* Display list number of first character */
    int    widths[256]; /* Width of each character in pixels */
    int    height;       /* Height of characters */
    } GLFONT;
```

Now that we have the a data structure to hold the font information, let's make a font creation function:

```
GLFONT *                        /* O - Font data */
FontCreate(HDC        hdc,      /* I - Device Context */
        const char *typeface,   /* I - Font specification */
        int        height,      /* I - Font height/size in pixels */
        int        weight,      /* I - Weight of font (bold, etc) */
        DWORD      italic)      /* I - Text is italic */
    {
    GLFONT *font;               /* Font data pointer */
    HFONT  fontid;              /* Windows font ID */
    int    charset;             /* Character set code */
```

The `typeface` argument is simply the name of the font, such as Courier or Helvetica, and specifies the style of character that you want. The `height`, `weight`, and `italic` arguments are passed directly to `wglUseFontBitmaps` and set the size and appearance of the characters.

The first thing `FontCreate` does is allocate memory for the font data and display lists for the bitmaps:

```
if ((font = calloc(1, sizeof(GLFONT))) == (GLFONT *)0)
    return ((GLFONT *)0);

if ((font->base = glGenLists(256)) == 0)
    {
    free(font);
    return (0);
    }
```

Before you create the font bitmaps, you need to decide on a character set. Normally, you use the ANSI character set (`ANSI_CHARSET`), which provides the ISO-8859-1 character set with additional accented characters between codes 128 and 159. For the Symbol font, we need to use the symbol character set (`SYMBOL_CHARSET`) so that we can display those special Greek letters and mathematical symbols:

```
if (stricmp(typeface, "symbol") == 0)
    charset = SYMBOL_CHARSET;
else
    charset = ANSI_CHARSET;
```

Next, we use the `CreateFont` function to load a bitmap font for our use:

```
fontid = CreateFont(height, 0, 0, 0, weight, italic, FALSE, FALSE,
                charset, OUT_TT_PRECIS, CLIP_DEFAULT_PRECIS,
                DRAFT_QUALITY, DEFAULT_PITCH, typeface);

SelectObject(hdc, fontid);
```

Then, we create the `glBitmaps` from this font:

```
wglUseFontBitmaps(hdc, 0, 256, font->base);
```

Finally, we collect the width information for the font and store it in the `widths` array:

```
GetCharWidth(hdc, 0, 255, font->widths);
font->height = height;

return (font);
}
```

Destroying Bitmap Fonts

To complement `FontCreate`, you need a font destruction function:

```
void
FontDestroy(GLFONT *font) /* I - Font to destroy */
    {
    if (font == (GLFONT *)0)
        return;
```

When we destroy the font, we need to delete all of the display lists we created and then free the memory:

```
glDeleteLists(font->base, 256);
free(font);
}
```

Drawing Using Bitmap Fonts

Now that we have functions to create and destroy fonts, it would be nice to be able to draw some character strings. For starters, we need a "puts" function:

```
void
FontPuts(GLFONT     *font, /* I - Font to use */
         const char *s)    /* I - String to display */
    {
    if (font == (GLFONT *)0 ¦¦ s == (char *)0)
        return;
```

As noted before, we can use the `glListBase` function to select a font. However, calling `glListBase` by itself can have unwanted side effects; namely, it might cause your program to display the wrong display list in some other part of your program.

To avoid this problem, we save the current list base by pushing the list attributes with `glPushAttrib` and restoring it with `glPopAttrib`:

```
glPushAttrib(GL_LIST_BIT);
glListBase(font->base);
```

```
glCallLists(strlen(s), GL_UNSIGNED_BYTE, s);
glPopAttrib();
}
```

That's all there is to it!

Displaying Formatted Text

Most programs need to display more than static text. Using sprintf before every call to FontPuts isn't much fun, so instead, we make our own printf-style function to do the job:

```
#include <stdarg.h>

void
FontPrintf(GLFONT    *font,    /* I - Font to use */
           int       align,    /* I - Alignment to use */
           const char *format, /* I - printf() style format string */
           ...)                /* I - Other arguments as necessary */
    {
    va_list       ap;          /* Argument pointer */
    unsigned char s[1024],     /* Output string */
                  *ptr;        /* Pointer into string */
    int           width;       /* Width of string in pixels */

    if (font == (GLFONT *)0 || format == (char *)0)
        return;
```

The FontPrintf function uses the <stdarg.h> header file to manage the variable number of arguments needed for vsprintf. The vsprintf function formats the string to be drawn:

```
va_start(ap, format);
vsprintf((char *)s, format, ap);
va_end(ap);
```

Next, we'd like to be able to justify the text. The align argument specifies the alignment: Numbers less than 0 specify right justification, numbers greater than 0 specify left justification, and a value equal to 0 specifies center justification.

To justify the text, we need to compute the string width in pixels from the font data:

```
for (ptr = s, width = 0; *ptr; ptr ++)
    width += font->widths[*ptr];
```

Then, we use the glBitmap empty bitmap trick to offset the text:

```
if (align < 0)
    glBitmap(0, 0, 0, 0, -width, 0, NULL);
else if (align == 0)
    glBitmap(0, 0, 0, 0, -width / 2, 0, NULL);
```

Finally, we call `FontPuts` to draw the string:

```
FontPuts(font, s);
}
```

The complete code for the font functions appears in the BOOK\CHAP07\FONTTEST\font.c file. Prototypes are in the BOOK\CHAP07\FONTTEST\font.h file.

A Simple Text Drawing Program

A library isn't much without sample code to show you how to use it. Now that we have all of these functions to draw text, let's write a small program that uses them.

The `Resize` function needs to set up the viewport and projection matrix:

```
glViewport(0, 0, width, height);
glMatrixMode(GL_PROJECTION);
glLoadIdentity();
glOrtho(0.0, (float)width, 0.0, (float)height, -1.0, 1.0);
glMatrixMode(GL_MODELVIEW);
```

Later in the `Redraw` function, we clear the window to black and display the text:

```
void
Redraw(void)
    {
    /* Clear the window to black */
    glClearColor(0.0, 0.0, 0.0, 1.0);
    glClear(GL_COLOR_BUFFER_BIT);

    /* Draw a vertical line down the center of the window */
    glColor3f(1.0, 1.0, 1.0);
    glBegin(GL_LINES);
    glVertex2i(Width / 2, 0);
    glVertex2i(Width / 2, Height);
    glEnd();

    /* Draw text left justified... */
    glColor3f(1.0, 0.0, 0.0);
    glRasterPos2i(Width / 2, 3 * Height / 4);
    FontPrintf(Font, 1, "Left Justified Text");

    /* Draw text centered... */
    glColor3f(0.0, 1.0, 0.0);
    glRasterPos2i(Width / 2, 2 * Height / 4);
    FontPrintf(Font, 0, "Centered Text");

    /* Draw right-justified text... */
    glColor3f(0.0, 0.1, 0.0);
```

```
glRasterPos2i(Width / 2, 1 * Height / 4);
FontPrintf(Font, -1, "Right Justified Text");

glFinish();
}
```

The final code appears in BOOK\CHAP07\FONTTEST\fonttest.c and Figure 7.2.

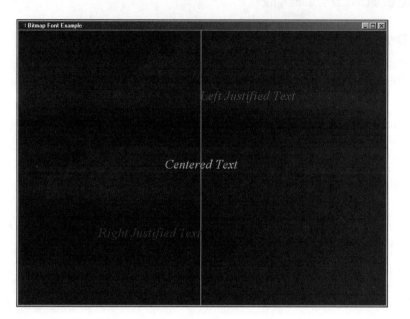

Figure 7.2   Bitmap text drawn using OpenGL.

Bitmaps with Color—Pixmaps

Bitmaps with more than two colors are usually called *pixmaps* (short for pixel maps) and are used as background images or textures (covered in the next chapter). In OpenGL, pixmaps are generally either 8-bit color index images or 24-bit RGB images. Pixmaps can also contain transparency information, commonly called the *alpha* channel.

Drawing Pixmaps

OpenGL provides a single function for drawing pixmaps called `glDrawPixels`. Like `glBitmap`, `glDrawPixels` uses the current raster position to define the lower-left corner of the image. Unlike `glBitmap`, you cannot specify a raster origin or movement:

```
BITMAPINFO *BitmapInfo;
GLubyte    *BitmapBits;
```

```
glPixelStorei(GL_UNPACK_ALIGNMENT, 4);
glPixelZoom(xscale, yscale);
glRasterPos2i(x, y);
glDrawPixels(BitmapInfo->bmiHeader.biWidth,
             BitmapInfo->bmiHeader.biHeight,
             GL_RGB, GL_UNSIGNED_BYTE, BitmapBits);
```

The glDrawPixels function accepts five arguments:

```
glDrawPixels(GLsizei width, GLsizei height,
             GLenum format, GLenum type,
             Glvoid *pixels)
```

The format parameter specifies the colorspace of the pixmap, as described in Table 7.1.

Table 7.1 *Common OpenGL Pixel Formats*

Format	Description
GL_COLOR_INDEX	Color index pixels
GL_LUMINANCE	Grayscale pixels
GL_BGR_EXT	BGR pixels
GL_BGR	BGR pixels (OpenGL 1.2)
GL_RGB	RGB pixels
GL_RGBA	RGB + alpha pixels

The type parameter specifies the type of each color component, as outlined in Table 7.2.

Table 7.2 *Common OpenGL Pixel Types*

Type	Description
GL_BYTE	Signed 8-bit values (–128 to 127)
GL_UNSIGNED_BYTE	Unsigned 8-bit values (0 to 255)
GL_BITMAP	Bitmap image (0 to 1)

The width and height arguments specify the width and height of the image. As in glBitmap, pixmaps are defined upside-down. You can specify a negative height to invert the image.

The pixels argument points to the image data. As in glBitmap, the image data must provide each scanline at a 32-bit boundary.

A Windows .BMP File Viewer

Now that we've covered the basics of using `glDrawPixels`, let's write a Windows .BMP file viewing program using OpenGL. Our goals with this program are fairly straightforward:

- Load any Windows .BMP file.
- Scale the image to fit inside the window.

The final code for this program appears in BOOK\CHAP07\BMPVIEW\bmpview.c and is discussed in the following sections.

About Windows Bitmap Files

Despite their limitations, Windows .BMP files are probably the most common and widely supported files used by PCs containing from 2 to 16.7 million colors. With only a few exceptions, .BMP files do not utilize data compression, making it easy to read and write these files in your OpenGL programs.

A .BMP file is organized into three or four sections depending on the types of colors used (see Figure 7.3). All .BMP files start with a `BITMAPFILEHEADER` structure containing an identification string (`"BM"`), the total size of the file, and an offset to the actual image data:

```
typedef struct
    {
    WORD  bfType;      /* "BM" */
    DWORD bfSize;      /* Size of file in bytes */
    WORD  bfReserved1; /* Reserved, always 0 */
    WORD  bfReserved2; /* Reserved, always 0 */
    DWORD bfOffBits;   /* Offset to image in bytes */
    } BITMAPFILEHEADER;
```

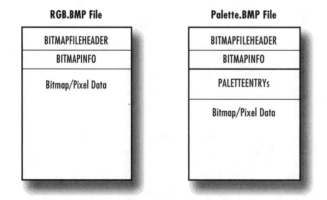

Figure 7.3   BMP file organization.

Following the file header is a `BITMAPINFO` structure that describes the contents of the image:

```
typedef struct
    {
    DWORD biSize;            /* Size of BITMAPINFOHEADER in bytes */
    LONG  biWidth;           /* Width of image in pixels */
    LONG  biHeight;          /* Height of image in pixels */
    WORD  biPlanes;          /* # of color planes (always 1) */
    WORD  biBitCount;        /* # of color bits */
    DWORD biCompression;     /* Type of compression used */
    DWORD biSizeImage;       /* Size of the image in bytes */
    LONG  biXPelsPerMeter;   /* Horizontal pixels per meter */
    LONG  biYPelsPerMeter;   /* Vertical pixels per meter */
    DWORD biClrUsed;         /* Number of color used */
    DWORD biClrImportant;    /* Number of 'important' colors */
    } BITMAPINFO;
```

For our sample program, the important fields in this header are the `biWidth`, `biHeight`, and `biBitCount` fields. The `biSize` field is also sometimes used, but when reading .BMP files, you need to check whether `biSize` is 0. If it is, you need to compute the size yourself.

Following the header is the color palette (for indexed images) and the image data.

Reading .BMP Files

Because the .BMP file format is so simple, reading a .BMP file is almost trivial. You start by opening the file in binary mode and reading a `BITMAPFILEHEADER` structure:

```
if ((fp = fopen(filename, "rb")) == NULL)
    return (NULL);

fread(&header, sizeof(BITMAPFILEHEADER), 1, fp);

if (header.bfType != 'MB') /* Check for BM reversed... */
    {
    /* Not a bitmap file - return NULL... */

    fclose(fp);
    return (NULL);
    }
```

If the header looks good, you then read the `BITMAPINFO` structure along with any color palette information:

```
infosize = header.bfOffBits - sizeof(BITMAPFILEHEADER);
fread(*info, 1, infosize, fp);
```

Next, you figure out how large the image data is:

```
if ((bitsize = (*info)->bmiHeader.biSizeImage) == 0)
    bitsize = ((*info)->bmiHeader.biWidth *
               (*info)->bmiHeader.biBitCount + 7) / 8 *
               abs((*info)->bmiHeader.biHeight);
```

Finally, you read the bitmap data and close the file:

```
fread(bits, 1, bitsize, fp);
fclose(fp);
```

The files BOOK\CHAP07\BMPVIEW\bitmap.h and BOOK\CHAP07\BMPVIEW\bitmap.c contain the final code for LoadDIBitmap with error-checking code.

Displaying the Bitmap

To display the bitmap, we use the glDrawPixels function. As with most OpenGL programs, you start by setting the current viewport and viewing transformations:

```
glViewport(0, 0, Width, Height);

glMatrixMode(GL_PROJECTION);
glLoadIdentity();
glOrtho(0.0, (GLfloat)Width, 0.0, (GLfloat)Height, -1.0, 1.0);
glMatrixMode(GL_MODELVIEW);
```

After this, you set the raster position and draw the image:

```
glRasterPos2i(0, 0);
glDrawPixels(BitmapInfo->bmiHeader.biWidth,
             BitmapInfo->bmiHeader.biHeight,
             GL_BGR_EXT, GL_UNSIGNED_BYTE, BitmapBits);
```

The format parameter is set to GL_BGR_EXT, which specifies that the image data is provided in blue-green-red order instead of red-green-blue. The first reason we do this is that a 24-bit .BMP file stores the color information in this order. The second, more important reason is that it is considerably faster than GL_RGB, at least under Windows.

The GL_BGR_EXT colorspace is supported under Windows but not generally on other operating systems. Beginning with OpenGL 1.2, the GL_BGR_EXT colorspace is a standard feature and is called GL_BGR instead.

Scaling the Image

Using `glDrawPixels` alone won't accomplish one of our bitmap viewer program's goals: to scale the image to fit inside the window.

To do this, we use the `glPixelZoom` function, which takes two arguments:

```
glPixelZoom(GLfloat xscale, GLfloat yscale);
```

The `xscale` and `yscale` arguments specify the horizontal and vertical scaling of the image:

```
glPixelZoom(1.0, 1.0);    /* Don't scale the image */
glPixelZoom(-1.0, 1.0);   /* Flip the image horizontally */
glPixelZoom(1.0, -2.0);   /* Flip the image and double the height */
glPixelZoom(0.33, 0.33);  /* Draw the image 1/3 size */
```

As you can see, `glPixelZoom` allows you to scale and flip an image just about any way you like. For other non-linear effects such as rippling water, you need to use texture mapping, which is discussed in the next chapter.

To scale the image to fit the current window while maintaining a 1:1 aspect ratio, we need to compute the minimum scaling ratio horizontally and vertically:

```
xsize = Width;
ysize = BitmapInfo->bmiHeader.biHeight * xsize /
        BitmapInfo->bmiHeader.biWidth;
if (ysize > Height)
    {
    ysize = Height;
    xsize = BitmapInfo->bmiHeader.biWidth * ysize /
            BitmapInfo->bmiHeader.biHeight;
    }

xscale  = (float)xsize / (float)BitmapInfo->bmiHeader.biWidth;
yscale  = (float)ysize / (float)BitmapInfo->bmiHeader.biHeight;
```

Finally, instead of drawing the image in the lower-left corner of the window, we want to center the image:

```
xoffset = (Width - xsize) * 0.5;
yoffset = (Height - ysize) * 0.5;
```

The final code for the `Redraw` function is in BOOK\CHAP07\BMPVIEW\bmpview.c. Figure 7.4 shows the output of the bmpview example.

Figure 7.4 Bitmap file sample window.

Drawing Images with Transparency

You can also draw images with transparency using the alpha channel (the A in RGBA) and OpenGL blending. You can learn more about blending in Chapter 10, "Visual Effects: Blending and Fog."

Because .BMP files cannot contain an alpha channel, you can simulate it by loading the bitmap data and replacing a particular color in the image with transparency.

To do this, we first load the image with `LoadBitmap`. Then, we copy the BGR data from the bitmap into an array to hold RGBA data:

```
GLubyte *                      /* O - RGBA bitmap data */
LoadRGBA(const char *filename, /* I - Filename */
        BITMAPINFO *info)      /* O - Bitmap information */
    {
    GLubyte    *bgr;           /* BGR bitmap data */
    GLubyte    *rgba;          /* RGBA bitmap data */
    int        x, y;           /* Looping vars */
    int        length;         /* Length of scanline */
    GLubyte    *bgr_ptr;       /* Pointer into BGR data */
```

```
GLubyte     *rgba_ptr;        /* Pointer into RGBA data */

bgr    = LoadBitmap(filename, &info);
rgba   = malloc(info->biWidth * info->biHeight * 4);
length = (info->biWidth * 3 + 3) & ~3;
```

Once we have the bitmap data in memory, we loop through each pixel in the image. For this example, we replace black pixels (BGR = 0, 0, 0) with RGBA pixels with an alpha value of 0. Other colors get an alpha value proportionate to the brightness of the pixel. Finally, we want to swap the blue and red channels so the order of the colors is correct:

```
for (y = 0; y < info->biHeight; y ++)
    {
    bgr_ptr  = bgr + y * length;
    rgba_ptr = rgba + y * info->biWidth * 4;

    for (x = 0; x < info->biWidth; x ++, bgr_ptr += 3, rgba_ptr += 4)
        {
        rgba_ptr[0] = bgr_ptr[2];
        rgba_ptr[1] = bgr_ptr[1];
        rgba_ptr[2] = bgr_ptr[0];
        rgba_ptr[3] = (bgr_ptr[0] + bgr_ptr[1] + bgr_ptr[2]) / 3;
        }
    }
free(bgr);
return (rgba);
}
```

Now that we have an RGBA image, we need to draw it. As before, we start by positioning the image with glRasterPos. We also enable blending with the existing screen contents and the RGBA image, using the alpha channel to mix the colors:

```
glRasterPos2i(x, y);
glBlendFunc(GL_SRC_ALPHA, GL_ONE_MINUS_SRC_ALPHA);
glEnable(GL_BLENDING);
glDrawPixels(info->biWidth, info->biHeight, GL_RGBA, GL_UNSIGNED_BYTE,
             rgba);
```

The glEnable(GL_BLENDING) and glBlendFunc calls are explained in Chapter 10.

Figure 7.5 shows the output of the BOOK\CHAP07\GALAXY\galaxy.c sample program that draws images with transparency using these coding techniques.

Figure 7.5   Galaxy sample program showing transparency.

Drawing Indexed Images

When using GL_COLOR_INDEX colors, you can remap the colors in your pixmap or bitmap using the glPixelMap or glPixelTransfer functions. The glPixelTransfer function lets you specify scaling and offsets for color index and RGB values. For example, to brighten an RGB image by 10 percent, you can use

```
glPixelTransferf(GL_RED_SCALE, 1.1);
glPixelTransferf(GL_GREEN_SCALE, 1.1);
glPixelTransferf(GL_BLUE_SCALE, 1.1);
```

Similarly, to offset the color indices of a bitmap to the palette entries you have defined for it, use

```
glPixelTransferi(GL_INDEX_OFFSET, bitmap_entry);
```

Sometimes, it is necessary to apply more complicated color corrections than simple linear scale and offset. One application is gamma correction; the intensity of each color value is adjusted to a power curve that compensates for irregularities on your monitor or printer (see Figure 7.6). The glPixelMap function allows you to do this by specifying a lookup table:

```
GLfloat     lut[256];
GLfloat     gamma_value;
int         i;
```

```
gamma_value = 1.7; /* For NTSC video monitors */
for (i = 0; i < 256; i ++)
  lut[i] = pow(i / 255.0, 1.0 / gamma_value);

glPixelTransferi(GL_MAP_COLOR, GL_TRUE);
glPixelMap(GL_PIXEL_MAP_R_TO_R, 256, lut);
glPixelMap(GL_PIXEL_MAP_G_TO_G, 256, lut);
glPixelMap(GL_PIXEL_MAP_B_TO_B, 256, lut);
```

Figure 7.6 Image without gamma correction (left) and with a gamma correction of 1.7 (right) .

Panning an Image

You can use the `glPixelStore` function to pan inside an image. For example, to display the center 300×300 pixel area of a 640×480 pixel image, you use

```
glPixelStorei(GL_UNPACK_ROW_LENGTH, 640);
glPixelStorei(GL_UNPACK_SKIP_PIXELS, (640 - 300) / 2);
glPixelStorei(GL_UNPACK_SKIP_ROWS, (480 - 300) / 2);
glDrawPixels(300, 300, GL_RGB, GL_UNSIGNED_BYTE, BitmapBits);
```

Note that the `GL_UNPACK_ROW_LENGTH`, `GL_UNPACK_SKIP_PIXELS`, and `GL_UNPACK_SKIP_ROWS` attributes refer to the original pixmap size in pixels and not the size after zooming.

Reading Images

OpenGL provides a function called `glReadPixels` that can read an image from the screen. Beyond the obvious application of saving an image of your creation to disk, you can also use it for cool effects with texturing (covered in the next chapter).

Unlike glDrawPixels, glReadPixels ignores the current raster position and requires you to specify an (x,y) viewport coordinate for the lower-left corner of the image to read. Listing 7.2 shows how to read the current viewport into a Windows bitmap structure suitable for saving to a file or using as a texture.

Listing 7.2   ReadDIBitmap *Function*

```
/*
 * 'ReadDIBitmap()' - Read the current OpenGL viewport into a
 *                    24-bit RGB bitmap.
 *
 * Returns the bitmap pixels if successful and NULL otherwise.
 */

GLubyte *                       /* O - Bitmap data */
ReadDIBitmap(BITMAPINFO **info) /* O - Bitmap information */
    {
    long    i, j,               /* Looping var */
            bitsize,            /* Total size of bitmap */
            width;              /* Aligned width of a scanline */
    GLint   viewport[4];        /* Current viewport */
    GLubyte *bits;              /* RGB bits */
    GLubyte *rgb,               /* RGB looping var */
            temp;               /* Temporary var for swapping */

    /* Grab the current viewport... */
    glGetIntegerv(GL_VIEWPORT, viewport);

    /* Allocate memory for the header and bitmap... */
    if ((*info = (BITMAPINFO *)malloc(sizeof(BITMAPINFOHEADER))) == NULL)
        {
        /* Couldn't allocate memory for bitmap info - return NULL... */
        return (NULL);
        }

    width   = viewport[2] * 3;      /* Real width of scanline */
    width   = (width + 3) & ~3;     /* Aligned to 4 bytes */
    bitsize = width * viewport[3];  /* Size of bitmap, aligned */

    if ((bits = calloc(bitsize, 1)) == NULL)
        {
        /* Couldn't allocate memory for bitmap pixels - return NULL... */
        free(*info);
```

```
        return (NULL);
        }

    /* Read pixels from the frame buffer... */
    glFinish();                            /* Finish all OpenGL commands */
    glPixelStorei(GL_PACK_ALIGNMENT, 4);   /* Force 4-byte alignment */
    glPixelStorei(GL_PACK_ROW_LENGTH, 0);
    glPixelStorei(GL_PACK_SKIP_ROWS, 0);
    glPixelStorei(GL_PACK_SKIP_PIXELS, 0);

    glReadPixels(0, 0, viewport[2], viewport[3], GL_BGR_EXT, GL_UNSIGNED_BYTE,
                 bits);

/* Finally, initialize the bitmap header information... */
    (*info)->bmiHeader.biSize        = sizeof(BITMAPINFOHEADER);
    (*info)->bmiHeader.biWidth        = viewport[2];
    (*info)->bmiHeader.biHeight       = viewport[3];
    (*info)->bmiHeader.biPlanes       = 1;
    (*info)->bmiHeader.biBitCount     = 24;
    (*info)->bmiHeader.biCompression  = BI_RGB;
    (*info)->bmiHeader.biSizeImage    = bitsize;
    (*info)->bmiHeader.biXPelsPerMeter = 2952; /* 75 DPI */
    (*info)->bmiHeader.biYPelsPerMeter = 2952; /* 75 DPI */
    (*info)->bmiHeader.biClrUsed      = 0;
    (*info)->bmiHeader.biClrImportant = 0;

    return (bits);
    }
```

One important thing to note is that Windows bitmaps (and OpenGL pixmaps by default) must have the beginning of each line at a 32-bit boundary. The glPixelStorei calls will make sure that your code and the OpenGL library agree on this. (Note that some platforms don't 32-bit align pixel data.) To calculate the aligned size do the following:

```
width = viewport[2] * 3;  /* Real width of scanline */
width = (width + 3) & ~3; /* Aligned to 4 bytes */
```

Once you have computed the actual byte width of the viewport (in this case, three bytes for every pixel wide), you have to round that width up to the nearest 32-bit (or 4-byte) boundary. The total size of the pixmap then becomes

```
bitsize = width * viewport[3]; /* Size of bitmap, aligned */
```

After allocating memory for the pixmap, we call glReadPixels and fill in the Windows BITMAPHEADER structure.

Copying Images

OpenGL also provides a function to copy an area on the screen to another location, such as what's needed for scrolling or "magnifying glass" views:

```
int mousex, mousey;

glReadBuffer(GL_FRONT);
glDrawBuffer(GL_FRONT);
glPixelZoom(2.0, 2.0);
glRasterPos2i(0, 0);
glCopyPixels(mousex - 8, mousey - 8, 16, 16, GL_COLOR);
```

The `glCopyPixels` function copies pixels from the given location to the current raster position. Pixel zoom is applied to the output pixels but not to the input pixels. In the preceding example, a 16×16 pixel image is copied to the lower-left corner of the window and scaled to 32×32 pixels. Offsets and sizes specified with calls to `glPixelStore` do not affect `glCopyPixels`. Changes made with `glPixelTransfer` and `glPixelMap` do affect it, however.

Writing .BMP Files

As they say in car repair manuals, installation is the reverse of removal. To write a .BMP file, we simply add a `BITMAPFILEHEADER` structure to the bitmap in memory and write it to disk, as shown in Listing 7.3.

Listing 7.3   SaveDIBitmap *Function*

```
int                                 /* O - 0 on success, -1 on error */
SaveDIBitmap(const char *filename,  /* I - File to save to */
             BITMAPINFO *info,      /* I - Bitmap information */
             GLubyte    *bits)      /* I - Bitmap pixel bits */
    {
    FILE            *fp;            /* Open file pointer */
    int             size,          /* Size of file */
                    infosize,      /* Size of bitmap info */
                    bitsize;       /* Size of bitmap pixels */
    BITMAPFILEHEADER header;        /* File header */

    /* Try opening the file; use "wb" mode to write this *binary* file. */
    if ((fp = fopen(filename, "wb")) == NULL)
        return (-1);

    if (info->bmiHeader.biSizeImage == 0)    /* Figure out the bitmap size */
        bitsize = (info->bmiHeader.biWidth *
                   info->bmiHeader.biBitCount + 7) / 8 *
                   abs(info->bmiHeader.biHeight);
```

```
else
  bitsize = info->bmiHeader.biSizeImage;

infosize = sizeof(BITMAPINFOHEADER);
size     = sizeof(BITMAPFILEHEADER) + infosize + bitsize;

/* Write the file header, bitmap information, and bitmap pixel data... */
header.bfType      = 'MB'; /* Non-portable... sigh */
header.bfSize      = size;
header.bfReserved1 = 0;
header.bfReserved2 = 0;
header.bfOffBits   = sizeof(BITMAPFILEHEADER) + infosize;

if (fwrite(&header, 1, sizeof(BITMAPFILEHEADER), fp) <
        sizeof(BITMAPFILEHEADER))
    {
    /* Couldn't write the file header - return... */
    fclose(fp);
    return (-1);
    }

if (fwrite(info, 1, infosize, fp) < infosize)
    {
    /* Couldn't write the bitmap header - return... */
    fclose(fp);
    return (-1);
    }

if (fwrite(bits, 1, bitsize, fp) < bitsize)
    {
    /* Couldn't write the bitmap - return... */
    fclose(fp);
    return (-1);
    }

/* OK, everything went fine - return... */
fclose(fp);
return (0);
}
```

Summary

In this chapter, you have learned about most of the OpenGL bitmap functions. Beyond the simple application of character fonts, bitmaps can be full-color images for window backgrounds or texture images (covered in the next chapter). You can use OpenGL functions such as `glPixelMap`, `glPixelTransfer`, `glPixelZoom`, and `glBlendFunc` for special effects, as well.

Reference Section

glCopyPixels

Purpose	To copy a block of pixels in the frame buffer.
Include File	<GL/gl.h>
Syntax	void glCopyPixels(GLint *x*, GLint *y*, GLsizei *width*, GLsizei *height*, GLenum *type*);
Description	This function copies pixel data from the indicated area in the frame buffer to the current raster position. Use glRasterPos to set the current raster position. If the current raster position is not valid, then no pixel data is copied.
	Calls to glDrawBuffer, glPixelMap, glPixelTransfer, glPixelZoom, and glReadBuffer affect the operation of glCopyPixels.
Parameters	
x	GLint: The lower-left corner window horizontal coordinate.
y	GLint: The lower-left corner window vertical coordinate.
width	GLsizei: The width of the image in pixels.
height	GLsizei: The height of the image in pixels. If negative, the image is drawn from top to bottom. By default, images are drawn bottom to top.
type	GLenum: The type of pixel values to be copied.

Table 7.3 *Pixel Value Types*

Type	Description
GL_COLOR	Color buffer values
GL_STENCIL	Stencil buffer values
GL_DEPTH	Depth buffer values

Returns	None.
Example	See the example in BOOK\CHAP07\BMPVIEW\bmpview.c.
See Also	glDrawBuffer, glPixelMap, glPixelStore, glPixelTransfer, glPixelZoom, glReadBuffer

glDrawPixels

Purpose	To draw a block of pixels into the frame buffer.
Include File	<GL/gl.h>
Syntax	void glDrawPixels(GLsizei *width*, GLsizei *height*, GLenum *format*, GLenum *type*, const Glvoid **pixels*);
Description	This function copies pixel data from memory to the current raster position. Use glRasterPos to set the current raster position. If the current raster position is not valid, then no pixel data is copied.
	Besides the *format* and *type* arguments, several other parameters define the encoding of pixel data in memory and control the processing of the pixel data before it is placed in the frame buffer. See the references for glDrawBuffer, glPixelMap, glPixelStore, glPixelTransfer, and glPixelZoom.
Parameters	
width	GLsizei: The width of the image in pixels.
height	GLsizei: The height of the image in pixels. If negative, the image is drawn from top to bottom. By default, images are drawn bottom to top.
format	GLenum: The colorspace of the pixels to be drawn.

Table 7.4 *Color Formats*

Format	Description
GL_COLOR_INDEX	Color index pixels
GL_LUMINANCE	Grayscale pixels
GL_LUMINANCE_ALPHA	Grayscale and alpha pixels (2 components)
GL_RGB	RGB pixels (three components)
GL_RGBA	RGBA pixels (four components)
GL_RED	Red pixels
GL_GREEN	Green pixels
GL_BLUE	Blue pixels
GL_ALPHA	Alpha pixels
GL_STENCIL_INDEX	Stencil buffer values
GL_DEPTH_COMPONENT	Depth buffer values
GL_BGR_EXT	BGR pixels (three components)

type	GLenum: The data type of the pixels to be drawn.

Table 7.5 *Color Value Types*

Type	Description
GL_BYTE	Signed 8-bit values (–128 to 127)
GL_UNSIGNED_BYTE	Unsigned 8-bit values (0 to 255)
GL_BITMAP	Bitmap image (0 to 1)
GL_SHORT	Signed 16-bit values (–32,768 to 32,767)
GL_UNSIGNED_SHORT	Unsigned 16-bit values (0 to 65,535)
GL_INT	Signed 32-bit values (–2,147,483,648 to 2,147,483,647)
GL_UNSIGNED_INT	Unsigned 32-bit values (0 to 4,294,967,295)
GL_FLOAT	32-bit floating-point values (GLfloat)

pixels	Glvoid *: A pointer to the pixel data for the image.
Returns	None.
Known Bugs	The GL_UNPACK_ALIGNMENT parameter for glPixelStore is presently ignored by the Microsoft version of glDrawPixels.
Example	See the example in BOOK\CHAP07\BMPVIEW\bmpview.c.
See Also	glDrawBuffer, glPixelMap, glPixelStore, glPixelTransfer, glPixelZoom

glPixelMap

Purpose	To define a lookup table for pixel transfers.
Include File	<GL/gl.h>
Syntax	void glPixelMapfv(GLenum *map*, GLint *mapsize*, const ➡GLfloat *values*); void glPixelMapuiv(GLenum *map*, GLint *mapsize*, const ➡GLuint *values*); void glPixelMapusv(GLenum *map*, GLint *mapsize*, const ➡GLushort *values*);
Description	glPixelMap sets lookup tables for glCopyPixels, glDrawPixel, glReadPixels, glTexImage1D, and glTexImage2D. These lookup tables, or maps, are only used if the corresponding GL_MAP_COLOR or GL_MAP_STENCIL option is enabled with glPixelTransfer. Maps are applied prior to drawing and after reading values from the frame buffer.
Parameters	
map	GLenum: The type of map being defined

Table 7.6 *Pixel Mapping Types*

Type	Description
GL_PIXEL_MAP_I_TO_I	Define a map for color indices.
GL_PIXEL_MAP_S_TO_S	Define a map for stencil values.
GL_PIXEL_MAP_I_TO_R	Define a map from color indices to red values.
GL_PIXEL_MAP_I_TO_G	Define a map from color indices to green values.
GL_PIXEL_MAP_I_TO_B	Define a map from color indices to blue values.
GL_PIXEL_MAP_I_TO_A	Define a map from color indices to alpha values.
GL_PIXEL_MAP_R_TO_R	Define a map for red values.
GL_PIXEL_MAP_G_TO_G	Define a map for green values.
GL_PIXEL_MAP_B_TO_B	Define a map for blue values.
GL_PIXEL_MAP_A_TO_A	Define a map for alpha values.

mapsize	GLint: The size of the lookup table.
values	GLfloat *, GLuint *, GLushort *: The lookup table.
Returns	None.
Example	See the example in BOOK\CHAP07\BMPVIEW\bmpview.c.
See Also	glCopyPixels, glDrawPixels, glPixelStore, glPixelTransfer, glReadPixels, glTexImage1D, glTexImage2D

glPixelStore

Purpose	To control how pixels are stored or read from memory.
Include File	<GL/gl.h>
Syntax	void glPixelStorei(GLenum *pname*, GLint *param*)void ➥glPixelStoref(GLenum *pname*, GLfloat *param*);
Description	This function controls how pixels are stored with glReadPixels and read for glDrawPixels, glTexImage1D, and glTexImage2D. It does not affect the operation of glCopyPixels.
Parameters	
pname	GLenum: The parameter to set.

Table 7.7 *Pixel Storage Types*

Name	Default	Description
GL_PACK_SWAP_BYTES*	GL_TRUE	If true, all multibyte values have their bytes swapped when stored in memory.
GL_PACK_LSB_FIRST	GL_FALSE	If true, bitmaps have their leftmost pixel stored in bit 0 instead of bit 7.
GL_PACK_ROW_LENGTH	0	Set the pixel width of the image. If 0, the *width* argument is used instead.
GL_PACK_SKIP_PIXELS	0	Set the number of pixels to skip horizontally in the image.
GL_PACK_SKIP_ROWS	0	Set the number of pixels to skip vertically in the image.
GL_PACK_ALIGNMENT	4	Set the alignment of each scanline in the image. See the Known Bugs section.
GL_UNPACK_SWAP_BYTES*	GL_TRUE	If true, all multibyte values have their bytes swapped when read from memory.
GL_UNPACK_LSB_FIRST	GL_FALSE	If true, bitmaps have their leftmost pixel read from bit 0 instead of bit 7.
GL_UNPACK_ROW_LENGTH	0	Set the pixel width of the image. If 0, the *width* argument is used instead.
GL_UNPACK_SKIP_PIXELS	0	Set the number of pixels to skip horizontally in the image.
GL_UNPACK_SKIP_ROWS	0	Set the number of pixels to skip vertically in the image.
GL_UNPACK_ALIGNMENT	4	Set the alignment of each scanline in the image. See the Known Bugs section.

* **GL_TRUE** *for little-endian,* **GL_FALSE** *for big-endian.*

param	GLint, GLfloat: The parameter value.
Returns	None.
Known Bugs	The GL_PACK_ALIGNMENT and GL_UNPACK_ALIGNMENT parameters for glPixelStore are presently ignored by Microsoft OpenGL.
Example	See the example in BOOK\CHAP07\BITS\bits.c.
See Also	glDrawPixels, glReadPixels, glTexImage1D, glTexImage2D

glPixelTransfer

Purpose	To set pixel transfer modes.
Include File	<GL/gl.h>
Syntax	void glPixelTransferi(GLenum *pname*, GLint *param*); void glPixelTransferf(GLenum *pname*, GLfloat *param*);
Description	This function sets pixel transfer modes for glCopyPixels, glDrawPixels, glReadPixels, glTexImage1D, and glTexImage2D.
Parameters	
pname	GLenum: The transfer parameter to set.

Table 7.8   *Pixel Transfer Types*

Parameter	Description
GL_MAP_COLOR	When set to GL_TRUE, enables pixel maps defined with glPixelMap for color indices and RGBA values.
GL_MAP_STENCIL	When set to GL_TRUE, enables pixel maps defined with glPixelMap for stencil values.
GL_INDEX_SHIFT	Specifies the amount to bitshift color indices. Positive values shift indices to the left. Negative values shift indices to the right.
GL_INDEX_OFFSET	Specifies an offset to be added to every color index.
GL_RED_SCALE	Specifies a floating-point scaling factor for red color values.
GL_RED_BIAS	Specifies a bias that is added to every red color value.
GL_GREEN_SCALE	Specifies a floating-point scaling factor for green color values.
GL_GREEN_BIAS	Specifies a bias that is added to every green color value.
GL_BLUE_SCALE	Specifies a floating-point scaling factor for blue color values.
GL_BLUE_BIAS	Specifies a bias that is added to every blue color value.
GL_ALPHA_SCALE	Specifies a floating-point scaling factor for alpha color values.
GL_ALPHA_BIAS	Specifies a bias that is added to every alpha color value.
GL_DEPTH_SCALE	Specifies a floating-point scaling factor for depth values.
GL_DEPTH_BIAS	Specifies a bias that is added to every depth value.

param	GLint, GLfloat: The parameter value.
Returns	None.
Example	See the example in BOOK\CHAP07\BMPVIEW\bmpview.c.
See Also	glCopyPixels, glDrawPixels, glPixelMap, glReadPixels, glTexImage1D, glTexImage2D

glPixelZoom

Purpose	To set the scaling for pixel transfers.
Include File	<GL/gl.h>
Syntax	void glPixelZoom(GLfloat *xfactor*, GLfloat *yfactor*)
Description	This function sets pixel scaling for glCopyPixels, glDrawPixels, glReadPixels, glTexImage1D, and glTexImage2D.

Pixels are scaled using the "nearest neighbor" algorithm when they are read from memory or the frame buffer. In the case of glCopyPixels and glDrawPixels, the scaled pixels are drawn in the frame buffer at the current raster position.

For glReadPixels, pixels are written to the supplied memory buffer. When reading a zoomed image, you should compute the image size as follows:

```
int new_width, new_height;
int width, height;

new_width = xfactor * width + 0.5;
    new_height = yfactor * height + 0.5;
```

Parameters	
xfactor	GLfloat: The horizontal scaling factor (1.0 is no scaling).
yfactor	GLfloat: The vertical scaling factor (1.0 is no scaling).
Returns	None.
Example	See the example in BOOK\CHAP07\BMPVIEW\bmpview.c.
See Also	glCopyPixels, glDrawPixels, glReadPixels, glTexImage1D, glTexImage2D

glReadPixels

Purpose	To read a block of pixels from the frame buffer.
Include File	<GL/gl.h>
Syntax	void glReadPixels(GLint *x*, GLint *y*, GLsizei *width*, GLsizei *height*, GLenum *format*, GLenum *type*, const GLvoid *pixels*);
Description	This function copies pixel data from the frame buffer to memory.

Besides the *format* and *type* arguments, several other parameters define the encoding of pixel data in memory and control the processing of the pixel data before it is placed in the memory buffer. See the references for glPixelMap, glPixelStore, glPixelTransfer, and glReadBuffer.

Parameters

x	GLint: The lower-left corner window horizontal coordinate.
y	GLint: The lower-left corner window vertical coordinate.
width	GLsizei: The width of the image in pixels.
height	GLsizei: The height of the image in pixels.
format	GLenum: The colorspace of the pixels to be read.

Table 7.9 *Color Formats*

Format	Description
GL_COLOR_INDEX	Color index pixels
GL_LUMINANCE	Grayscale pixels
GL_LUMINANCE_ALPHA	Grayscale and alpha pixels (two components)
GL_RGB	RGB pixels (three components)
GL_RGBA	RGBA pixels (four components)
GL_RED	Red pixels
GL_GREEN	Green pixels
GL_BLUE	Blue pixels
GL_ALPHA	Alpha pixels
GL_STENCIL_INDEX	Stencil buffer values
GL_DEPTH_COMPONENT	Depth buffer values

type	GLenum: The data type of the pixels to be drawn.

Table 7.10 *Pixel Types*

Type	Description
GL_BYTE	Signed 8-bit values (–128 to 127)
GL_UNSIGNED_BYTE	Unsigned 8-bit values (0 to 255)
GL_BITMAP	Bitmap image (0 to 1)
GL_SHORT	Signed 16-bit values (–32,768 to 32,767)
GL_UNSIGNED_SHORT	Unsigned 16-bit values (0 to 65,535)
GL_INT	Signed 32-bit values (–2,147,483,648 to 2,147,483,647)
GL_UNSIGNED_INT	Unsigned 32-bit values (0 to 4,294,967,295)
GL_FLOAT	32-bit floating-point values (GLfloat)

pixels	GLvoid *: A pointer to the pixel data for the image.
Returns	None.
Known Bugs	The GL_PACK_ALIGNMENT parameter for glPixelStore is presently ignored by the Microsoft version of glReadPixels.
Example	See the example in BOOK\CHAP07\BITS\bits.c.
See Also	glPixelMap, glPixelStore, glPixelTransfer, glReadBuffer

8

TEXTURE MAPPING

by Michael Sweet

What you'll learn in this chapter:

How to...	Functions You'll Use
Drape images onto polygons	glTexImage1D/glTexImage2D
Use .BMP files as textures	TextureLoad
Automatically generate texture coordinates	glTexGen
Use mipmapping	gluBuild1DMipmaps/ gluBuild2DMipmaps
Use texture objects	glBindTexture/glGenTextures/ glTexturePriorities
Use 3D textures	glTexImage3D

Texture mapping is probably the most significant advance in computer graphics in the last 10 years. OpenGL provides texture image mapping functions that fit images onto polygons in your scene. How those images are put onto the polygons is up to you.

Games, including Quake, use texture mapping for realistic images of rooms and monsters. Texture mapping is also used for anti-aliased text, reflection mapping, and a whole host of other applications that take images and add them to polygons.

Texture mapping requires intensive calculations, so it can be slow on a 2D graphics card because your processor has to do all the work. The good news is that affordable 3D graphics cards that support OpenGL texturing in hardware are now available, some providing performance found on million-dollar graphics supercomputers only a few years ago.

The examples in this chapter will run on any Windows-compatible graphics card. If your graphics card supports 16- to 32-bit "true color" displays, you want to use them. Besides better-looking scenes, you'll find that the true color modes are actually faster.

The Basics of Texture Mapping

Texture mapping in OpenGL is fairly straightforward. To begin with, every texture is an image of some sort.

A 1D texture is an image with width but no height, or vice versa; 1D textures are a single pixel wide or high. You might think that 1D textures aren't very useful, but in fact, they can take the place of more conventional color-shading techniques and accelerate rendering in the process. Figure 8.1 shows a 1D "ROY-G-BIV" (Red, Orange, Yellow, Green, Blue, Indigo, Violet) texture that is used to display a rainbow. The texture image is a line of pixels (color values) covering the color spectrum seen in a rainbow. The equivalent nontextured scene would contain seven times the polygons of the textured one and require much more rendering time.

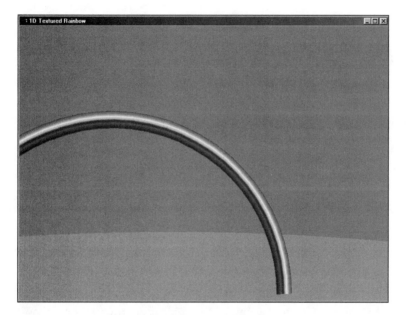

Figure 8.1   1D textured rainbow.

A 2D texture is an image that is more than 1 pixel wide and high and is generally loaded from a Windows .BMP file. Two-dimensional textures are commonly used to replace complex surface geometry (a lot of polygons) on buildings, trees, and so forth. You can also use these 2D textures to add realistic background details like clouds in the sky.

The 1D and 2D textures you've seen so far are composed of RGB color values. Textures can also consist of color indices or luminance (gray) levels and can include alpha (transparency) values. The latter is useful for defining natural objects such as trees because the alpha value can be used to make the tree visible but let the background show through. You'll learn more about alpha transparency in Chapter 10, "Visual Effects: Blending and Fog."

Some hardware also supports 3D (volume) textures with OpenGL. Volume textures are used for viewing CAT, MRI, and other 3D "scans." Unfortunately, even a small 256×256×256 grayscale-alpha texture image needs a whopping 32MB of memory. 3D texturing is a standard feature in OpenGL 1.2 and is available as an extension to OpenGL 1.1.

Defining Texture Images

Naturally, you must define a texture image before you can draw textured polygons in OpenGL. Texture images follow the same storage rules as bitmaps (discussed in Chapter 7, "Raster Graphics in OpenGL").

TEXTURE IMAGE DIMENSIONS
The OpenGL standard requires that texture images' dimensions must be a power of two. Texture images can also have one or two border pixels around their edges to define the color of polygons that fall outside the texture image.

Defining 1D Textures

OpenGL provides a single function for defining 1D textures: `glTexImage1D`. The `glTexImage1D` function accepts eight arguments:

```
void glTexImage1D(GLenum target, GLint level, GLint components,
                  GLsizei width, GLint border, GLenum format,
                  GLenum type, const GLvoid *pixels)
```

The *target* argument specifies which texture should be defined; this argument must be `GL_TEXTURE_1D`. The *level* argument indicates the texture image's level of detail and is usually `0`. Other values are used for mipmapped textures (described later in this chapter). The *components* argument specifies the number of color values used for each pixel. For color index textures, components must be `1`. Values of `3` and `4` are used for RGB and RGBA texture images, respectively.

width and *border* specify the size of the texture image. The `border` value controls the number of border pixels OpenGL should expect (and use) and can have a value of `0`, `1`, or `2` (see the section titled "Texture Wrapping" for more information). The *width* parameter specifies the width of the main texture image (without the border pixels) and must be a power of 2.

The *format* argument indicates the type of color values to expect—`GL_COLOR_INDEX`, `GL_LUMINANCE`, `GL_RED`, `GL_GREEN`, `GL_BLUE`, `GL_ALPHA`, `GL_LUMINANCE_ALPHA`, `GL_RGB`, or `GL_RGBA`. The Windows and Silicon Graphics OpenGL implementations also define image formats with the blue and red components swapped, GL_BGR_EXT and GL_BGRA_EXT. These formats are available as standard formats in OpenGL 1.2 (GL_BGR and GL_BGRA).

You'll find an example of defining a 1D texture in the sample code BOOK\CHAP8\tex1d\tex1d.c on the source code CD-ROM:

```
static GLubyte roygbiv_image[8][3] =
    {
    { 0x3f, 0x00, 0x3f }, /* Dark Violet (for 8 colors...) */
    { 0x7f, 0x00, 0x7f }, /* Violet */
    { 0xbf, 0x00, 0xbf }, /* Indigo */
    { 0x00, 0x00, 0xff }, /* Blue */
    { 0x00, 0xff, 0x00 }, /* Green */
    { 0xff, 0xff, 0x00 }, /* Yellow */
    { 0xff, 0x7f, 0x00 }, /* Orange */
    { 0xff, 0x00, 0x00 }  /* Red */
    };

glTexImage1D(GL_TEXTURE_1D, 0, 3, 8, 0, GL_RGB, GL_UNSIGNED_BYTE,
            roygbiv_image);
```

Defining 2D Textures

To define a 2D texture image in OpenGL, you call glTexImage2D. The glTexImage2D function takes a *height* argument in addition to the ones that glTexImage1D uses, as follows:

```
void glTexImage2D(GLenum target, GLint level, GLint components,
                GLsizei width, GLsizei height, GLint border,
                GLenum format, GLenum type, const GLvoid *pixels)
```

As in glTexImage1D, the *width* and *height* arguments must be a power of 2.

Texture Modes

OpenGL defines three texturing modes for different types of rendering. The first (and default) mode is GL_MODULATE, which modulates the current lighting and color information with the texture image (see Figure 8.2). It is the mode you will use most often.

The second mode is GL_DECAL, which only uses the texture image; color and lighting information won't change the texture's appearance. This mode is often used with reflection mapping but can also be used to produce special effects with multi-pass rendering.

Figure 8.2 2D textured teapot.

The last mode is GL_BLEND, which you can use with one and two component textures. The texture image is blended with the current texture color and the current lighting and color information. You can use GL_BLEND to store a land mask, for example, where the current color is blue, the texture color is green, and the texture image defines the amount of each color to use.

You set the texture mode using the glTexEnvi function:

```
glTexEnvi(GL_TEXTURE_ENV, GL_TEXTURE_MODE, mode);
```

For the GL_BLEND mode, the texture color is set using the glTexEnvfv function:

```
GLfloat rgba[4];
glTexEnvfv(GL_TEXTURE_ENV, GL_TEXTURE_COLOR, rgba);
```

Texture Filters

OpenGL uses texture filters to interpolate between texture pixels. OpenGL provides two types of texture filters: the minification filter (GL_TEXTURE_MIN_FILTER) for polygons that are smaller than the texture image and the magnification filter (GL_TEXTURE_MAG_FILTER) for polygons that are larger than the texture image.

You use the `glTexParameteri` function to set the filters:

```
glTexParameteri(GL_TEXTURE_2D, GL_TEXTURE_MAG_FILTER, filter);
glTexParameteri(GL_TEXTURE_2D, GL_TEXTURE_MIN_FILTER, filter);
```

Table 8.1 lists the filters you can use.

Table 8.1 *Texture Image Filters*

Filter	Description
GL_NEAREST	Nearest-neighbor filtering.
GL_LINEAR	Linear interpolation.
GL_NEAREST_MIPMAP_NEAREST	Nearest-neighbor mipmapped filtering (GL_TEXTURE_MIN_FILTER only).
GL_NEAREST_MIPMAP_LINEAR	Linear interpolated mipmaps (GL_TEXTURE_MIN_FILTER only).
GL_LINEAR_MIPMAP_NEAREST	Linear interpolation of mipmaps (GL_TEXTURE_MIN_FILTER only).
GL_LINEAR_MIPMAP_LINEAR	Linear interpolation of interpolated mipmaps (GL_TEXTURE_MIN_FILTER only).

GL_NEAREST filtering takes the closest pixel in the texture image rather than interpolate between pixels. It is by far the fastest texture filter, but the quality can leave much to be desired.

The MIPMAP filters are covered later in this chapter.

Texture Coordinates

Texture coordinates associate a particular location in the texture image with vertices in a polygon. For 1D texture images, the `glTexCoord1` functions set the position within the texture image:

```
glTexCoord1d(GLdouble s);
glTexCoord1f(GLfloat s);
glTexCoord1i(GLint s);
```

The s coordinate is 0.0 for the leftmost pixel in the texture image and 1.0 for the rightmost pixel (0 and 1 for integer coordinates). Values outside this range are handled differently based on the wrap parameter for the texture, described later.

2D texture images add a t coordinate for the vertical axis of the image. The `glTexCoord2` functions set the position within 2D textures:

```
glTexCoord2d(GLdouble s, GLdouble t);
glTexCoord2dv(GLdouble *st);
glTexCoord2f(GLfloat s, GLfloat t);
```

```
glTexCoord2fv(GLfloat *st);
glTexCoord2i(GLint s, GLint t);
glTexCoord2iv(GLint *st);
```

For the *t* coordinate, 0.0 represents the bottom of the texture image and 1.0 the top (0 and 1 for integer coordinates).

Texture Wrapping

As noted previously, texture coordinates normally lie between 0.0 and 1.0, inclusive. When the coordinates go outside this range, they are either clamped (*wrap* = GL_CLAMP, the default) or repeated (*wrap* = GL_REPEAT).

Figure 8.3 shows how the GL_CLAMP mode works. When the texture coordinates hit the edges of the image, they are stopped at the edge instead of wrapping around to the other side. If you define additional border pixels, they will be used instead of the edge pixels.

For GL_REPEAT, the texture image is repeated as necessary, wrapping around to the other side of the image so that a repeated pattern is visible.

The glTexParameteri function sets the wrap mode:

```
glTexParameteri(GL_TEXTURE_1D, GL_TEXTURE_WRAP_S, wrap);
glTexParameteri(GL_TEXTURE_2D, GL_TEXTURE_WRAP_S, wrap);
glTexParameteri(GL_TEXTURE_2D, GL_TEXTURE_WRAP_T, wrap);
```

Figure 8.3 GL_CLAMP texture mode.

Putting It All Together—A 1D Texture Example

Now that we've covered all the basics, let's put them together to make a program that draws a textured rainbow.

First, we need to define the texture image:

```
static GLubyte roygbiv_image[8][3] =
    {
    { 0x3f, 0x00, 0x3f }, /* Dark Violet (for 8 colors...) */
    { 0x7f, 0x00, 0x7f }, /* Violet */
    { 0xbf, 0x00, 0xbf }, /* Indigo */
    { 0x00, 0x00, 0xff }, /* Blue */
    { 0x00, 0xff, 0x00 }, /* Green */
    { 0xff, 0xff, 0x00 }, /* Yellow */
    { 0xff, 0x7f, 0x00 }, /* Orange */
    { 0xff, 0x00, 0x00 }  /* Red */
    };
```

```
glTexImage1D(GL_TEXTURE_1D, 0, 3, 8, 0, GL_RGB, GL_UNSIGNED_BYTE,
             roygbiv_image);
```

Then, we need to enable texture mapping for the display. As with most drawing features in OpenGL, you use the glEnable function to turn it on:

```
glEnable(GL_TEXTURE_1D);
```

Finally, we draw an arc across the "sky" using a quadrilateral strip. The lower part of the rainbow uses a texture coordinate of 0.0, and the upper part uses 1.0:

```
glBegin(GL_QUAD_STRIP);
glColor3f(1.0, 1.0, 1.0);
for (th = 0.0; th <= M_PI; th += (0.03125 * M_PI))
    {
    /* Bottom edge of rainbow... */
    x = cos(th) * 50.0;
    y = sin(th) * 50.0;
    z = -50.0;
    glTexCoord1f(0.0);
    glVertex3f(x, y, z);

    /* Top edge of rainbow... */
    x = cos(th) * 55.0;
    y = sin(th) * 55.0;
    z = -50.0;
    glTexCoord1f(1.0);
    glVertex3f(x, y, z);
    }
glEnd();
```

The results appear in Figure 8.1. You can find the code for this program in CHAP8\tex1d\tex1d.c on the source CD.

A 2D Texturing Example

For our first 2D texturing program, we draw a teapot using `glutSolidTeapot`. As before, the first thing we do is define the texture image:

```
GLubyte   *bits;
BITMAPINFO *info;

bits = LoadDIBitmap("pot.bmp", &info);
glTexImage2D(GL_TEXTURE_2D, 0, 3, info->bmiHeader.biWidth,
            info->bmiHeader.biHeight, 0,
            GL_BGR_EXT, GL_UNSIGNED_BYTE, bits);
```

For this display, we need to repeat the texture image over the pot, so we set the wrap modes to `GL_REPEAT`:

```
glTexParameteri(GL_TEXTURE_2D, GL_TEXTURE_WRAP_S, GL_REPEAT);
glTexParameteri(GL_TEXTURE_2D, GL_TEXTURE_WRAP_T, GL_REPEAT);
```

Next, we enable 2D texturing with `glEnable`:

```
glEnable(GL_TEXTURE_2D);
```

Finally, we draw the pot with `glutSolidTeapot`:

```
glColor3f(1.0, 1.0, 1.0);
glutSolidTeapot(10.0);
```

The final display is shown in Figure 8.2; the code is available in BOOK\CHAP8\tex2d\tex2d.c on the source CD.

Using More Than One Texture Image

Scenes can contain multiple textures; you just have to define each texture before you draw each part of the scene. However, loading textures can slow down your program, especially if the texture images are large.

OpenGL solves this problem with *texture objects*. Like display lists, texture objects are identified by a single number. However, texture objects only contain texture information, and display lists can contain any OpenGL drawing calls. This allows OpenGL hardware to keep multiple textures in memory instead of loading them every time.

Managing Texture Objects

To manage texture objects, you use the `glGenTextures`, `glBindTexture`, and `glDeleteTextures` functions. `glGenTextures` reserves one or more texture object numbers for your program:

```
GLuint texture_objects[5];
glGenTextures(5, texture_objects);

GLuint texture_object;
glGenTextures(1, &texture_object);
```

Once you have the texture object numbers, you use `glBindTexture` to select the texture object:

```
glBindTexture(GL_TEXTURE_1D, texture_object);
glBindTexture(GL_TEXTURE_2D, texture_object);
```

After you bind the texture object, any texture functions you call (`glTexImage2D` and so on) are stored in the texture object and restored the next time you call `glBindTexture`.

To delete one or more texture objects, use the `glDeleteTextures` function:

```
GLuint texture_objects[5];
glDeleteTextures(5, texture_objects);

GLuint texture_object;
glDeleteTextures(1, &texture_object);
```

Keeping Texture Objects in Memory

OpenGL automatically keeps the most recently used texture objects in memory. However, if your graphics card provides only 8MB of texture memory and you have 30MB of textures, this method of texture shuffling doesn't work too well.

To improve the performance of programs using large textures, OpenGL provides a `glPrioritizeTextures` function to specify which textures are most important:

```
GLuint texture_objects[5];
GLclampf texture_priorities[5];

glPrioritizeTextures(5, texture_objects, texture_priorities);
```

The `texture_priorities` array provides a numeric priority for each texture object listed from 0.0 (lowest priority) to 1.0 (highest priority). Giving a texture image a priority of 1.0 doesn't guarantee that the texture is kept in memory, but if there *is* enough memory available, it *will* be resident when you need it.

A Simple Texture Object Loader

We need a function to load texture images from .BMP files for the rest of the examples in this chapter. Listing 8.1 contains the `TextureLoad` function, which accepts a .BMP filename, an alpha mask flag, the texture filters, and a wrap mode. You can find this code in BOOK\CHAP8\terrain1\texture.c.

After loading the .BMP file, the TextureLoad function generates and binds a texture object using the glGenTextures and glBindTexture functions:

```
glGenTextures(1, &texture);
glBindTexture(type, texture);
```

Then, the texture parameters are set:

```
glTexParameteri(type, GL_TEXTURE_MAG_FILTER, magfilter);
glTexParameteri(type, GL_TEXTURE_MIN_FILTER, minfilter);
glTexParameteri(type, GL_TEXTURE_WRAP_S, wrap);
glTexParameteri(type, GL_TEXTURE_WRAP_T, wrap);
glTexEnvi(type, GL_TEXTURE_ENV_MODE, GL_MODULATE);
```

If we want a texture image with an alpha component, we generate it from the dark areas of the image, just as we did in Chapter 7 for the galaxy example.

Finally, we use glTexImage1D or glTexImage2D to define the texture image.

Listing 8.1 TextureLoad *Function*

```
/*
 * 'TextureLoad()' - Load a bitmap file and define it as a 1D or 2D texture.
 *
 * Returns 0 on success or -1 on error.
 */

GLuint                          /* O - Texture object or 0 on error */
TextureLoad(char      *filename, /* I - Bitmap file to load */
            GLboolean alpha,     /* I - Generate alpha for bitmap */
            GLenum    minfilter, /* I - Minification filter */
            GLenum    magfilter, /* I - Magnification filter */
            GLenum    wrap)      /* I - Repeat or clamp */
    {
    int        i;               /* Looping var */
    BITMAPINFO    *info;        /* Bitmap information */
    GLubyte    *bits;           /* Bitmap RGB pixels */
    GLubyte    *ptr;            /* Pointer into bit buffer */
    GLubyte    *rgba;           /* RGBA pixel buffer */
    GLubyte    *rgbaptr;        /* Pointer into RGBA buffer */
    GLubyte    temp;            /* Swapping variable */
    GLenum     type;            /* Texture type */
    GLuint     texture;         /* Texture object */

    /* Try loading the bitmap file... */
    bits = LoadDIBitmap(filename, &info);
    if (bits == (GLubyte *)0)
```

continued on next page

continued from previous page

```
            return (0);

#ifdef WIN32 /* This already done by non-WIN32 LoadDIBitmap */
    /*
     * Convert the bitmap data from BGR to RGB. Since texture images
     * must be a power of two, and since we can figure that we won't
     * have a texture image as small as 2x2 pixels, we ignore any
     * alignment concerns...
     */

    for (i = info->bmiHeader.biWidth * info->bmiHeader.biHeight, ptr = bits;
         i > 0;
      i --, ptr += 3)
        {
    /* Swap red and blue */
    temp    = ptr[0];
    ptr[0] = ptr[2];
    ptr[2] = temp;
    }
#endif /* WIN32 */

    /* Figure out the type of texture... */
    if (info->bmiHeader.biHeight == 1)
        type = GL_TEXTURE_1D;
    else
        type = GL_TEXTURE_2D;

    /* Create and bind a texture object */
    glGenTextures(1, &texture);
    glBindTexture(type, texture);

    /* Set texture parameters */
    glTexParameteri(type, GL_TEXTURE_MAG_FILTER, magfilter);
    glTexParameteri(type, GL_TEXTURE_MIN_FILTER, minfilter);
    glTexParameteri(type, GL_TEXTURE_WRAP_S, wrap);
    glTexParameteri(type, GL_TEXTURE_WRAP_T, wrap);
    glTexEnvi(type, GL_TEXTURE_ENV_MODE, GL_MODULATE);

    if (alpha)
        {
    /* Create and use an RGBA image... */
        rgba = malloc(info->bmiHeader.biWidth * info->bmiHeader.biHeight * 4);

        for (i = info->bmiHeader.biWidth * info->bmiHeader.biHeight,
             rgbaptr = rgba, ptr = bits;
             i > 0;
          i --, rgbaptr += 4, ptr += 3)
            {
```

```
            rgbaptr[0] = ptr[0];
            rgbaptr[1] = ptr[1];
            rgbaptr[2] = ptr[2];
            rgbaptr[3] = (ptr[0] + ptr[1] + ptr[2]) / 3;
        }

    /*
     * Set texture image; if the minification filter uses mipmapping
     * then use gluBuild2D/1DMipmaps() to load the texture...
     */

    if (type == GL_TEXTURE_2D)
        glTexImage2D(type, 0, 4, info->bmiHeader.biWidth,
                      info->bmiHeader.biHeight, 0, GL_RGBA,
                      GL_UNSIGNED_BYTE, rgba);
    else
        glTexImage1D(type, 0, 4, info->bmiHeader.biWidth,
                      0, GL_RGBA, GL_UNSIGNED_BYTE, rgba);

    /* Free the RGBA buffer */
    free(rgba);
    }
else
    {
    /*
     * Set texture image; if the minification filter uses mipmapping
     * then use gluBuild2D/1DMipmaps() to load the texture...
     */

    if (type == GL_TEXTURE_2D)
        glTexImage2D(type, 0, 3, info->bmiHeader.biWidth,
                      info->bmiHeader.biHeight, 0, GL_RGB,
                      GL_UNSIGNED_BYTE, bits);
    else
        glTexImage1D(type, 0, 3, info->bmiHeader.biWidth,
                      0, GL_RGB, GL_UNSIGNED_BYTE, bits);
    }

/* Free the bitmap and return... */
free(info);
free(bits);

return (texture);
}
```

A Terrain Viewing Program

Our first program using texture objects draws a textured sky and flat ground (see Figure 8.4). For the sky, we draw a 32-sided dome that covers our scene. The texture coordinates are positioned in a circle around the sky texture image, providing a realistic sky:

```
glEnable(GL_TEXTURE_2D);
glBindTexture(GL_TEXTURE_2D, SkyTexture);

glColor3f(1.0, 1.0, 1.0);
glBegin(GL_TRIANGLE_FAN);
glTexCoord2f(0.5, 0.5);
glVertex3f(0.0, TERRAIN_VIEW, 0.0);
for (theta = 0.0; theta < (2.1 * M_PI); theta += M_PI / 8)
    {
    ct = cos(theta);
    st = sin(theta);
    glTexCoord2f(0.5 + 0.3 * ct, 0.5 + 0.3 * st);
    glVertex3f(ct * TERRAIN_VIEW * 0.7071,
               TERRAIN_VIEW * 0.7071,
               st * TERRAIN_VIEW * 0.7071);
    }
glEnd();

glBegin(GL_TRIANGLE_STRIP);
for (theta = 0.0; theta < (2.1 * M_PI); theta += M_PI / 8)
    {
    ct = cos(theta);
    st = sin(theta);
    glTexCoord2f(0.5 + 0.3 * ct, 0.5 + 0.3 * st);
    glVertex3f(ct * TERRAIN_VIEW * 0.7071,
               TERRAIN_VIEW * 0.7071,
               st * TERRAIN_VIEW * 0.7071);
    glTexCoord2f(0.5 + 0.5 * ct, 0.5 + 0.5 * st);
    glVertex3f(ct * TERRAIN_VIEW, -100.0,
               st * TERRAIN_VIEW);
    }
glEnd();
```

The ground for our program is a simple flat plane with y = 0:

```
glEnable(GL_TEXTURE_2D);
```

```
glBindTexture(GL_TEXTURE_2D, LandTexture);

glColor3f(0.3, 0.8, 0.2);

glBegin(GL_QUADS);
glTexCoord2f(0.0, 0.0);
glVertex3f(-0.5 * TERRAIN_SIZE, 0.0, -0.5 * TERRAIN_SIZE);
glTexCoord2f(50.0, 0.0);
glVertex3f( 0.5 * TERRAIN_SIZE, 0.0, -0.5 * TERRAIN_SIZE);
glTexCoord2f(50.0, 50.0);
glVertex3f( 0.5 * TERRAIN_SIZE, 0.0,  0.5 * TERRAIN_SIZE);
glTexCoord2f(0.0, 50.0);
glVertex3f(-0.5 * TERRAIN_SIZE, 0.0,  0.5 * TERRAIN_SIZE);
glEnd();
```

The final program produces the output in Figure 8.4. To fly through the terrain, hold a mouse button down in the window and drag the mouse to roll, pitch, and turn. If you have a joystick attached to your system, it will work as well.

The source appears in BOOK\CHAP8\terrain1\terrain1.c on the source CD.

Figure 8.4 Textured land and sky.

Making the Terrain More Interesting

In the first program, we drew a flat plane for the terrain. For the second program, we generate a fractal terrain.

The fractal algorithm subdivides square areas of the terrain and raises or lowers the middle and edge points (see Figure 8.5). This continues until all of the terrain array has been subdivided.

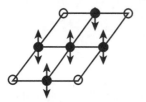

Figure 8.5   Subdividing the fractal terrain.

To draw the terrain, we use a sequence of triangle strips that share adjacent columns:

```
glEnable(GL_CULL_FACE);
glEnable(GL_DEPTH_TEST);
glDepthFunc(GL_LEQUAL);

for (i = 0, tp = Terrain[0]; i < (TERRAIN_COUNT - 1); i ++)
    {
    glBegin(GL_TRIANGLE_STRIP);
    for (j = 0; j < TERRAIN_COUNT; j ++, tp ++)
        {
        glTexCoord2f(50.0 * i / (TERRAIN_COUNT - 1),
                    50.0 * j / (TERRAIN_COUNT - 1));
        glVertex3fv(tp[0].v);

        glTexCoord2f(50.0 * (i + 1) / (TERRAIN_COUNT - 1),
                    50.0 * j / (TERRAIN_COUNT - 1));
        glVertex3fv(tp[TERRAIN_COUNT].v);
        }
    glEnd();
    }
glDisable(GL_CULL_FACE);
glDisable(GL_DEPTH_TEST);
```

The final code is in BOOK\CHAP8\terrain2\terrain2.c. The display produced is in Figure 8.6.

Figure 8.6   Fractal terrain program.

Automatically Generating Texture Coordinates

Generating all those texture coordinates can be tedious. Fortunately, OpenGL has an answer that we can use! In the current drawing code, we issue `glTexCoord2f` calls

```
glTexCoord2f(50.0 * i / (TERRAIN_COUNT - 1), 50.0 * j / (TERRAIN_COUNT - 1));
```

for each and every point in the terrain. But instead of doing this for each point, we can use the `glTexGen` functions to define the s and t coordinates in terms of the x and z position in the scene. (y is used for the height.) To generate coordinates for our terrain, then, we can use the following:

```
static GLfloat s_vector[4] = { 50.0 / TERRAIN_SIZE, 0, 0, 0 };
static GLfloat t_vector[4] = { 0, 0, 50.0 / TERRAIN_SIZE, 0 };

glTexGeni(GL_S, GL_TEXTURE_GEN_MODE, GL_OBJECT_LINEAR);
glTexGenfv(GL_S, GL_OBJECT_PLANE, s_vector);

glTexGeni(GL_T, GL_TEXTURE_GEN_MODE, GL_OBJECT_LINEAR);
glTexGenfv(GL_T, GL_OBJECT_PLANE, t_vector);
```

Here, the `GL_OBJECT_LINEAR` mapping mode maps the texture coordinates from object coordinates:

```
coordinate = X * vector[0] + Y * vector[1] +
             Z * vector[2] + W * vector[3]
```

The vector array is specified with the glTexGen function:

```
void glTexGenfv(GLenum coord, GLenum pname, GLint *params)
```

where the *coord* parameter specifies which texture image coordinate to generate, GL_S or GL_T, and the *pname* parameter specifies the vector to define—in this case, GL_OBJECT_PLANE. Finally, the *params* array specifies the object plane vector that is used to compute the texture coordinate.

To make OpenGL use these generated coordinates, you must enable texture coordinate generation, as follows:

```
glEnable(GL_TEXTURE_GEN_S);
glEnable(GL_TEXTURE_GEN_T);
```

The file BOOK\CHAP8\terrain3\terrain3.c contains a version of our terrain viewing program that uses generated texture coordinates. You can use the same techniques with a 1D texture image. For the 1D image, you'd probably generate the s coordinate from the height (y) to color the terrain based upon the height of the terrain. Generating texture coordinates is usually faster than specifying them manually in immediate mode but is slower when using display lists.

Other Generation Modes

OpenGL provides two other generation modes, GL_EYE_LINEAR and GL_SPHERE_MAP. GL_EYE_LINEAR defines the texture coordinates in terms of the eye (projected) coordinates. For the terrain viewing program, the texture on the terrain would stay relatively constant instead of varying based on the terrain.

GL_SPHERE_MAP is typically used for reflection mapping. The texture coordinates are computed by measuring the azimuth and elevation of the transformed object coordinates from the origin, so you can define a texture image of a room (or scene or whatever) with a polar projection. The "reflection" of the rest of the room is then mapped based upon the direction of the vertices from the center. You can also use GL_SPHERE_MAP for our sky dome and texture.

Mipmapped Textures

So far, we've dealt exclusively with single-texture images. That is, whenever we draw a textured polygon, the polygon is painted with a single 1D or 2D image. This is fine for some scenes, but animated displays often need various levels of detail, depending on the distance from the viewer. For example, when walking through a virtual room, you might want a high-resolution image of a picture close up, but only the outline at a distance.

OpenGL supports textures with multiple images, called mipmapped textures. Mipmapping selects the texture image closest to the screen resolution for a polygon. Loading mipmapped textures takes slightly longer than loading standard textures, but the visual results are impressive. In addition, mipmapped textures can improve display performance by reducing the need for GL_LINEAR image filters—smaller mipmap textures can be used instead of scaling the one texture image.

Another reason to use mipmapped textures is to reduce *texture swim*. You can see this pretty easily in the distance with the terrain programs in this chapter.

WHAT DOES THE MIP IN MIPMAPPED MEAN?
Mip is Latin for "many." Mipmapping means "many images."

Defining Mipmapped Textures

You define mipmapped textures by providing a specific level parameter for each image. For the ROY-G-BIV texture in the previous example, you use the following:

```
static unsigned char roygbiv_image0[16][3];
static unsigned char roygbiv_image1[8][3];
static unsigned char roygbiv_image2[4][3];
static unsigned char roygbiv_image3[2][3];
static unsigned char roygbiv_image4[1][3];

glTexParameteri(GL_TEXTURE_1D, GL_TEXTURE_MAG_FILTER, GL_LINEAR);
glTexParameteri(GL_TEXTURE_1D, GL_TEXTURE_MIN_FILTER,
                GL_NEAREST_MIPMAP_LINEAR);

glTexImage1D(GL_TEXTURE_1D, 0, 3, 16, 0, GL_RGB, GL_UNSIGNED_BYTE,
                roygbiv_image0);
glTexImage1D(GL_TEXTURE_1D, 1, 3, 8, 0, GL_RGB, GL_UNSIGNED_BYTE,
                roygbiv_image1);
glTexImage1D(GL_TEXTURE_1D, 2, 3, 4, 0, GL_RGB, GL_UNSIGNED_BYTE,
                roygbiv_image2);
glTexImage1D(GL_TEXTURE_1D, 3, 3, 2, 0, GL_RGB, GL_UNSIGNED_BYTE,
                roygbiv_image3);
glTexImage1D(GL_TEXTURE_1D, 4, 3, 1, 0, GL_RGB, GL_UNSIGNED_BYTE,
                roygbiv_image4);
```

The image levels are specified in the first parameter to glTexImage1D. The level 0 image is your primary, highest-resolution image for the texture. The level 1 image is one quarter the size of the primary image, and so forth until you end up with a 1×1 texture image.

When drawing polygons with a mipmapped texture, you need to use one of the minification filters (GL_TEXTURE_MIN_FILTER) in Table 8.2.

Table 8.2   *Minification Filters*

Filter	Description
GL_NEAREST_MIPMAP_NEAREST	Use the image nearest to the screen (polygon) resolution. Use the GL_NEAREST filter when texturing with this image.
GL_NEAREST_MIPMAP_LINEAR	Use the image nearest to the screen (polygon) resolution. Use the GL_LINEAR filter when texturing with this image.
GL_LINEAR_MIPMAP_NEAREST	Linearly interpolate between the two images nearest to the screen (polygon) resolution. Use the GL_NEAREST filter when texturing with this image.
GL_LINEAR_MIPMAP_LINEAR	Linearly interpolate between the two images nearest to the screen (polygon) resolution. Use the GL_LINEAR filter when texturing with this image.

The GL_LINEAR_MIPMAP_NEAREST and GL_LINEAR_MIPMAP_LINEAR filters can be expensive in terms of display performance. GL_NEAREST_MIPMAP_NEAREST is roughly equivalent to GL_NEAREST in performance but generally produces much better results. Mipmap images are normally chosen by comparing the size of the polygon as it will be drawn on the screen to the sizes of the mipmap images.

Generating Mipmaps Automatically

To make your life a bit easier, the OpenGL utility library (GLU32.LIB) provides two functions that automatically generate mipmapped images based on a single, high-resolution texture. In the following code, the gluBuild1DMipmaps and gluBuild2DMipmaps functions take the place of glTexImage1D and glTexImage2D:

```
/* 1D texture */
glTexParameteri(GL_TEXTURE_1D, GL_TEXTURE_MAG_FILTER, GL_LINEAR);
glTexParameteri(GL_TEXTURE_1D, GL_TEXTURE_MIN_FILTER,
             GL_NEAREST_MIPMAP_LINEAR);
gluBuild1DMipmaps(GL_TEXTURE_1D, 3, 8, 0, GL_RGB, GL_UNSIGNED_BYTE,
                roygbiv_image);

/* 2D texture */
glTexParameteri(GL_TEXTURE_2D, GL_TEXTURE_MAG_FILTER, GL_LINEAR);
glTexParameteri(GL_TEXTURE_2D, GL_TEXTURE_MIN_FILTER,
             GL_NEAREST_MIPMAP_NEAREST);
gluBuild2DMipmaps(GL_TEXTURE_2D, 3, info->bmiHeader.biWidth,
                info->bmiHeader.biHeight, 0, GL_RGB,
                GL_UNSIGNED_BYTE, rgb);
```

Because the gluBuild1DMipmaps and gluBuild2DMipmaps functions create images from one image, the appearance of some textured images might not be accurate. It's like drawing text characters at different sizes; scaling the bitmaps doesn't always generate good-looking results! When you run into this sort of problem, generate your mipmap images manually.

Controlling the Level of Detail

As noted before, mipmaps are usually chosen based on the size of the polygon being drawn. OpenGL 1.2 adds some control over this, allowing you to specify the minimum and maximum levels of detail that are used. Aside from controlling the display quality, you can also set the minimum and maximum levels of detail or reduce texture memory usage.

You use the `glTexParameterf` function to set the level of detail limits:

```
glTexParameterf(GL_TEXTURE_ENV, GL_TEXTURE_MIN_LOD, min_lod);
glTexParameterf(GL_TEXTURE_ENV, GL_TEXTURE_MAX_LOD, max_lod);
```

The `lod` values are numbers representing the level of detail passed in with the `glTexImage1D` and `glTexImage2D` functions.

Adding Mipmaps to the Terrain Viewer

You might have noticed that the polygons in the distance "shimmer" as you fly over the terrain. This is due to aliasing effects produced by the texture image. To get rid of most of those effects, we change the terrain viewer to use a mipmapped texture image for the terrain.

To keep things simple, we use the `gluBuild2DMipmaps` function. This involves a small modification to the `TextureLoad` function:

```
/*
 * Set texture image; if the minification filter uses mipmapping,
 * then use gluBuild2D/1DMipmaps() to load the texture...
 */

if (minfilter == GL_LINEAR || minfilter == GL_NEAREST)
    glTexImage2D(type, 0, 3, info->bmiHeader.biWidth,
                 info->bmiHeader.biHeight, 0, GL_RGB,
                 GL_UNSIGNED_BYTE, bits);
else
    gluBuild2DMipmaps(type, 3, info->bmiHeader.biWidth,
                      info->bmiHeader.biHeight, GL_RGB,
                      GL_UNSIGNED_BYTE, bits);
```

If the minification filter is `GL_LINEAR` or `GL_NEAREST`, we continue using `glTexImage2D`. Otherwise, we use `gluBuild2DMipmaps`.

In BOOK\CHAP8\terrain4\terrain4.c, we load the textures using the `GL_LINEAR_MIPMAP_LINEAR` filter, which provides the best quality output possible. The completed code produces the improved display in Figure 8.7.

Figure 8.7 Mipmapped terrain viewer.

Lighting with Textures

Like all OpenGL drawing primitives, textured polygons can be lit by a variety of sources to produce more realistic displays. However, you can only use lighting with textures in GL_MODULATE or GL_BLEND mode; lighting effects are not applied in GL_DECAL mode.

To add lighting to our terrain viewing program, we need to generate lighting normals for our terrain. The usual way to generate normals is to compute the cross product of two vectors defining the plane of the polygon (see Figure 8.8).

Figure 8.8 Finding the lighting normal on a grid.

Fortunately, computing lighting normals for a grid of elevations is fairly easy as the cross product is simplified to

```
/*
 * Compute the cross product of the vectors above and to
 * the right (simplified for this special case).
 */
```

```
nx = tp[0].v[1] - tp[1].v[1];
ny = -1.0;
nz = tp[0].v[1] - tp[TERRAIN_COUNT].v[1];
nw = -1.0 / sqrt(nx * nx + ny * ny + nz * nz);

/* Normalize the normal vector and store it... */
tp->n[0] = nx * nw;
tp->n[1] = ny * nw;
tp->n[2] = nz * nw;
```

Then, we just send the lighting normals when we draw the grid:

```
for (i = 0, tp = Terrain[0]; i < (TERRAIN_COUNT - 1); i ++)
    {
    glBegin(GL_TRIANGLE_STRIP);
    for (j = 0; j < TERRAIN_COUNT; j ++, tp ++)
        {
        glNormal3fv(tp[0].n);
        glVertex3fv(tp[0].v);

        glNormal3fv(tp[TERRAIN_COUNT].n);
        glVertex3fv(tp[TERRAIN_COUNT].v);
        }
    glEnd();
    }
```

The final code is in BOOK\CHAP8\terrain5\terrain5.c and the display in Figure 8.9.

Figure 8.9   Terrain with lighting effects.

Rendering Specular Highlights

When lighting is enabled, the material color (which might not necessarily be the current drawing color) is modulated (multiplied) by the texture image color. This works great for diffuse lighting, but you lose all specular highlights; they get multiplied by the texture color, so you just get a bright pixel, but not a white pixel.

To work around this limitation, you need to draw the scene twice—once without texturing to get the specular highlights and once with the textures to get the final scene. You merge the two "frames" using OpenGL blending, which is described in more detail in Chapter 10.

CONSTANT COLOR

OpenGL 1.2 and some versions of OpenGL 1.1 include support for rendering specular highlights using a constant color. See the OpenGL Web site for more information.

To add specular highlights to our teapot example from earlier in this chapter, we start by turning off all lighting except for the specular component and drawing a teapot without texturing:

```
glLightModelfv(GL_LIGHT_MODEL_AMBIENT, dark);

glLightfv(GL_LIGHT0, GL_DIFFUSE, dark);
glLightfv(GL_LIGHT0, GL_SPECULAR, bright);
glLightfv(GL_LIGHT0, GL_POSITION, pos);

glMaterialfv(GL_FRONT, GL_AMBIENT, dark);
glMaterialfv(GL_FRONT, GL_DIFFUSE, dark);
glMaterialfv(GL_FRONT, GL_SPECULAR, bright);
glMateriali(GL_FRONT, GL_SHININESS, 128);

glColor3f(1.0, 1.0, 1.0);
glutSolidTeapot(10.0);
```

That step generates an image of the teapot with just the specular highlight. Next, we use blending to add the textured teapot with normal lighting:

```
glBlendFunc(GL_ONE, GL_ONE);
glEnable(GL_BLEND);
glEnable(GL_TEXTURE_2D);

glLightModelfv(GL_LIGHT_MODEL_AMBIENT, normal);

glLightfv(GL_LIGHT0, GL_AMBIENT, normal);
glLightfv(GL_LIGHT0, GL_DIFFUSE, normal);
```

```
glLightfv(GL_LIGHT0, GL_SPECULAR, dark);

glMaterialfv(GL_FRONT, GL_AMBIENT, normal);
glMaterialfv(GL_FRONT, GL_DIFFUSE, normal);
glMaterialfv(GL_FRONT, GL_SPECULAR, dark);
glMateriali(GL_FRONT, GL_SHININESS, 0);

glutSolidTeapot(10.0);
```

The results in Figure 8.10 are obvious: You get the full lighting effect without much effort. You can find the complete source code for the specular teapot in BOOK\CHAP8\specular\specular.c.

Figure 8.10   Textured teapot with specular highlights.

Replacing Texture Image Data

A few applications require you to modify the textures you have defined. The `glTexSubImage1D` and `glTexSubImage2D` functions allow you to do this:

```
glTexSubImage1D(GL_TEXTURE_1D, level, xoffset, width, format, type, pixels);
glTexSubImage2D(GL_TEXTURE_2D, level, xoffset, yoffset, width, height, format,
          type, pixels);
```

The *pixels* you pass in replace those currently loaded for that texture image. You could use this to update a texture image of a television with a current video frame, for example.

Using `glTexSubImage1D` and `glTexSubImage2D` can be more efficient than redefining the entire texture image, but they should never be used to replace texture objects, which are more efficient.

3D Texturing

OpenGL 1.2 and some versions of OpenGL 1.1 include 3D texture support. 3D textures are three-dimensional images usually used for solid modeling and other types of visualization that utilize layers of images to produce a solid 3D display.

3D texturing is still in its infancy, and many OpenGL vendors do not yet support it. The free Mesa library provides a software implementation of 3D texturing that you can use for simple displays, but the performance is not exciting.

Another issue with 3D texturing is the size of the texture images. As noted before, a simple 256×256×256 luminance-alpha texture image requires 32MB of memory, more than is typically found on PC OpenGL cards.

Limitations aside, 3D texturing provides a unique solution to the 3D visualization problem that is not available in other 3D toolkits.

A Simple 3D Texture Program

BOOK\CHAP8\tex3d\tex3d.c contains a simple 3D texturing program that generates a 16×16×16 RGBA texture image (a rainbow core with a white shell). A cube with a quadrant cut out of it is then drawn to reveal the inside of the cube.

The drawing function starts simply by defining the 3D texture using the `glTexImage3D` function:

```
/* Define the 3D texture image. */
glTexParameteri(GL_TEXTURE_3D, GL_TEXTURE_MAG_FILTER, GL_LINEAR);
glTexParameteri(GL_TEXTURE_3D, GL_TEXTURE_MIN_FILTER, GL_LINEAR);

glTexImage3D(GL_TEXTURE_3D, 0, 3, 16, 16, 16, 0, GL_RGB, GL_UNSIGNED_BYTE,
            Texture);
glEnable(GL_TEXTURE_3D);
```

Next, we draw the faces of a cube with the front-right corner taken out of it:

```
/* Draw a 3D cube with a quadrant cut away... */
glBegin(GL_TRIANGLE_STRIP);

glTexCoord3f(0.0, 0.0, 0.0);
glVertex3f(-10.0, -10.0, 10.0);
glTexCoord3f(0.0, 1.0, 0.0);
glVertex3f(-10.0, 10.0, 10.0);

glTexCoord3f(0.5, 0.0, 0.0);
glVertex3f(0.0, -10.0, 10.0);
```

```
glTexCoord3f(0.5, 1.0, 0.0);
glVertex3f(0.0, 10.0, 10.0);

glTexCoord3f(0.5, 0.0, 0.5);
glVertex3f(0.0, -10.0, 0.0);
glTexCoord3f(0.5, 1.0, 0.5);
glVertex3f(0.0, 10.0, 0.0);

glTexCoord3f(1.0, 0.0, 0.5);
glVertex3f(10.0, -10.0, 0.0);
glTexCoord3f(1.0, 1.0, 0.5);
glVertex3f(10.0, 10.0, 0.0);

glTexCoord3f(1.0, 0.0, 1.0);
glVertex3f(10.0, -10.0, -10.0);
glTexCoord3f(1.0, 1.0, 1.0);
glVertex3f(10.0, 10.0, -10.0);

glEnd();
```

The key for 3D texturing in this code is the call to glTexCoord3f, which specifies the s, t, and r coordinates within the texture image.

Summary

In this chapter, you've learned how to texture map images onto polygons and other primitives using OpenGL. Texturing can provide that extra measure of realism that makes computer graphics so exciting to work with.

The OpenGL glTexParameter functions provide many ways to improve the quality of texture images when they are drawn. Mipmapped texture images provide multiple levels of detail that improve rendering quality and speed. Linear interpolation of texture images can improve certain types of textures, such as the sky texture used in the sample project.

Texture objects allow you to use multiple textures efficiently. You can control which texture objects are more likely to be resident in memory using the glPrioritizeTextures function.

The glTexGen functions can simplify the generation of texture coordinates by removing unnecessary or tedious calculations. By removing large amounts of conditional glTexCoord calls, automatic coordinate generation also simplifies programs that must display both textured and nontextured scenes.

Texture lighting eliminates specular highlights due to the color modulation. These highlights can be restored using a two-pass rendering technique.

3D texturing provides a unique solution to visualizing solids, but its availability is limited at this time. Limitations in available texture memory are also a consideration.

Reference Section

glTexCoord

Purpose	Specifies the current texture image coordinate for textured polygon rendering.
Include File	<GL/gl.h>
Syntax	`void glTexCoord1{dfis}(type s);`
	`void glTexCoord1{dfis}v(type *s);`
	`void glTexCoord2{dfis}(type s, type t);`
	`void glTexCoord2{dfis}v(type *st);`
	`void glTexCoord3{dfis}(type s, type t, type r);`
	`void glTexCoord3{dfis}v(type *str);`
	`void glTexCoord4{dfis}(type s, type t, type r, type q);`
	`void glTexCoord4{dfis}v(type *strq);`
Description	These functions set the current texture image coordinate in one to four dimensions. For example, the s and t parameters correspond to the horizontal and vertical image coordinates of a 2D texture image.
Parameters	
s	The horizontal texture image coordinate.
t	The vertical texture image coordinate.
r	The texture image depth coordinate.
q	The texture image "time" coordinate.
Returns	None.
Example	See the example in BOOK\CHAP8\TEX1D\tex1d.c on the source code CD-ROM.
See Also	`glTexEnv, glTexGen, glTexImage1D, glTexImage2D, glTexParameter`

glTexEnv

Purpose	Sets texturing parameters.
Include File	<GL/gl.h>
Syntax	`void glTexEnvf(GLenum target, GLenum pname, GLfloat param);`
	`void glTexEnvfv(GLenum target, GLenum pname, GLfloat *param);`
	`void glTexEnvi(GLenum target, GLenum pname, GLint param);`
	`void glTexEnviv(GLenum target, GLenum pname, GLint *param);`

Description	The glTexEnv functions set texture mapping parameters that control how texture images are mapped to polygons. The GL_DECAL texturing mode uses a texture image directly to draw polygons. GL_BLEND and GL_MODULATE texture modes use the GL_TEXTURE_ENV_COLOR color and the current frame buffer to determine what pixels are textured.

Parameters

target GLenum: The texture environment to define; must be GL_TEXTURE_ENV.

pname GLenum: The parameter name to define. Valid names are as follows:

GL_TEXTURE_ENV_MODE Specifies the type of texturing to do.

GL_TEXTURE_ENV_COLOR Specifies the color to use for blending.

param The parameter value. For GL_TEXTURE_ENV_COLOR, param is a pointer to an RGBA color value. For GL_TEXTURE_ENV_MODE, it can be one of the following constants:

GL_DECAL Texture images are directly mapped to the frame buffer.

GL_BLEND Texture images are blended with a constant color (GL_TEXTURE_ENV_COLOR) before being mapped to the frame buffer.

GL_MODULATE Texture images are multiplied with the frame buffer before being mapped to it.

Returns None.

Example See the example in BOOK\CHAP8\TEX1D\tex1d.c on the source code CD-ROM.

See Also glTexCoord, glTexGen, glTexImage1D, glTexImage2D, glTexParameter

glTexGen

Purpose Defines parameters for texture coordinate generation.

Include File <GL/gl.h>

Syntax
```
void glTexGend(GLenum coord, GLenum pname, GLdouble
param);
void glTexGenf(GLenum coord, GLenum pname, GLfloat
param);
void glTexGeni(GLenum coord, GLenum pname, GLint param);
void glTexGendv(GLenum coord, GLenum pname, GLdouble
*param);
```

```
void glTexGenfv(GLenum coord, GLenum pname, GLfloat
*param);
void glTexGeniv(GLenum coord, GLenum pname, GLint
*param);
```

Description

This function sets parameters for texture coordinate generation when one or more of GL_TEXTURE_GEN_S, GL_TEXTURE_GEN_T, GL_TEXTURE_GEN_R, or GL_TEXTURE_GEN_Q is enabled with glEnable.

When GL_TEXTURE_GEN_MODE is set to GL_OBJECT_LINEAR, texture coordinates are generated by multiplying the current object (vertex) coordinates by the constant vector specified by GL_OBJECT_PLANE:

```
coordinate = v[0] * p[0] + v[1] * p[1] + v[2] * p[2] + v[3] * p[3]
```

For GL_EYE_LINEAR, the eye coordinates (object coordinate multiplied through the GL_MODELVIEW matrix) are used.

When GL_TEXTURE_GEN_MODE is set to GL_SPHERE_MAP, coordinates are generated in a sphere about the current viewing position or origin.

Parameters

coord

GLenum: The texture coordinate to map. Must be one of GL_S, GL_T, GL_R, or GL_Q.

pname

GLenum: The parameter to set. Must be one of GL_TEXTURE_GEN_MODE, GL_OBJECT_PLANE, or GL_EYE_PLANE.

param

The parameter value. For GL_TEXTURE_GEN_MODE, param is one of the following:

GL_OBJECT_LINEAR	Texture coordinates are calculated from object (vertex) coordinates.
GL_EYE_LINEAR	Texture coordinates are calculated by eye coordinates (object coordinates multiplied through the GL_MODELVIEW matrix).
GL_SPHERE_MAP	Texture coordinates are generated in a sphere around the viewing position.

For GL_OBJECT_PLANE and GL_EYE_PLANE, param is a four-element array that is used as a multiplier for object or eye coordinates.

Returns

None.

Example

See the example in BOOK\CHAP8\TERRAIN3\terrain3.c on the source code CD-ROM.

See Also

glTexCoord, glTexEnv, glTexImage1D, glTexImage2D, glTexParameter

glTexImage1D

Purpose	Defines a one-dimensional texture image.
Include File	<GL/gl.h>
Syntax	void glTexImage1D(GLenum *target*, GLint *level*, GLint *components*, GLsizei *width*, GLint *border*, GLenum *format*, GLenum *type*, const GLvoid **pixels*);
Description	This function defines a one-dimensional texture image. The image data is subject to modes defined with glPixelMap, glPixelStore, and glPixelTransfer.

Parameters

target	GLenum: Must be GL_TEXTURE_1D.
level	GLint: The level of detail. Usually 0 unless mipmapping is used.
components	GLint: The number of color components, from 1 to 4.
width	GLsizei: The width of the texture image. This must be a power of 2 or follow the formula $2^n + 2 *$ border.
border	GLint: The width of the border. Must be 0, 1, or 2.
format	GLenum: The format of the pixel data. Valid formats are as follows:

GL_COLOR_INDEX	Pixel values are color indices.
GL_RED	Pixel values are red intensities.
GL_GREEN	Pixel values are green intensities.
GL_BLUE	Pixel values are blue intensities.
GL_ALPHA	Pixel values are alpha intensities.
GL_RGB	Pixel values are RGB colors.
GL_RGBA	Pixel values are RGBA colors.
GL_LUMINANCE	Pixel values are grayscale colors.
GL_LUMINANCE_ALPHA	Pixel values are alpha and grayscale colors.

type	GLenum: The data type of each pixel value (see glDrawPixels).
pixels	GLvoid *: The pixel data.
Returns	None.
Known Bugs	The GL_PACK_ALIGNMENT and GL_UNPACK_ALIGNMENT parameters for glPixelStore are presently ignored.
Example	See the example in BOOK\CHAP8\TEX1D\tex1d.c on the source code CD-ROM.
See Also	glPixelMap, glPixelStore, glPixelTransfer, glTexImage2D

glTexImage2D

Purpose	Defines a two-dimensional texture image.
Include File	<GL/gl.h>
Syntax	void glTexImage2D(GLenum *target*, GLint *level*, GLint *components*, GLsizei *width*, GLsizei *height*, GLint *border*, GLenum *format*, GLenum *type*, const GLvoid **pixels*);
Description	This function defines a two-dimensional texture image. The image data is subject to modes defined with glPixelMap, glPixelStore, and glPixelTransfer.

Parameters

target	GLenum: Must be GL_TEXTURE_2D.
level	GLint: The level of detail. Usually 0 unless mipmapping is used.
components	GLint: The number of color components, from 1 to 4.
width	GLsizei: The width of the texture image. This must be a power of 2 or follow the formula $2^n + 2 *$ border.
height	GLsizei: The height of the texture image. This must be a power of 2 or follow the formula $2^m + 2 *$ border.
border	GLint: The width of the border. Must be 0, 1, or 2.
format	GLenum: The format of the pixel data. Valid formats are as follows:

GL_COLOR_INDEX	Pixel values are color indices.
GL_RED	Pixel values are red intensities.
GL_GREEN	Pixel values are green intensities.
GL_BLUE	Pixel values are blue intensities.
GL_ALPHA	Pixel values are alpha intensities.
GL_RGB	Pixel values are RGB colors.
GL_RGBA	Pixel values are RGBA colors.
GL_LUMINANCE	Pixel values are grayscale colors.
GL_LUMINANCE_ALPHA	Pixel values are alpha and grayscale colors.

type	GLenum: The data type of each pixel value (see glDrawPixels).
pixels	GLvoid *: The pixel data.
Returns	None.
Known Bugs	The GL_PACK_ALIGNMENT and GL_UNPACK_ALIGNMENT parameters for glPixelStore are presently ignored.
Example	See the example in BOOK\CHAP8\TEX2D\tex2d.c on the source code CD-ROM.
See Also	glPixelMap, glPixelStore, glPixelTransfer, glTexImage1D

glTexImage3D

Purpose	Defines a three-dimensional texture image.
Include File	<GL/gl.h>
Syntax	void glTexImage3D(GLenum *target*, GLint *level*, GLint *components*, GLsizei *width*, GLsizei *height*, GLsizei *depth*, GLint *border*, GLenum *format*, GLenum *type*, const GLvoid **pixels*);
Description	This function defines a three-dimensional texture image. The image data is subject to modes defined with **glPixelMap**, **glPixelStore**, and **glPixelTransfer**.
	This function is only available with OpenGL 1.2.

Parameters

target	GLenum: Must be GL_TEXTURE_3D.
level	GLint: The level of detail. Usually **0** unless mipmapping is used.
components	GLint: The number of color components, from 1 to 4.
width	GLsizei: The width of the texture image. This must be a power of 2 or follow the formula $2^n + 2$ * **border**.
height	GLsizei: The height of the texture image. This must be a power of 2 or follow the formula $2^m + 2$ * border.
depth	GLsizei: The depth of the texture image. This must be a power of 2 or follow the formula $2^l + 2$ * border.
border	GLint: The width of the border. Must be **0**, **1**, or **2**.
format	GLenum: The format of the pixel data. Valid formats are as follows:

GL_COLOR_INDEX	Pixel values are color indices.
GL_RED	Pixel values are red intensities.
GL_GREEN	Pixel values are green intensities.
GL_BLUE	Pixel values are blue intensities.
GL_ALPHA	Pixel values are alpha intensities.
GL_RGB	Pixel values are RGB colors.
GL_RGBA	Pixel values are RGBA colors.
GL_LUMINANCE	Pixel values are grayscale colors.
GL_LUMINANCE_ALPHA	Pixel values are alpha and grayscale colors.

type	GLenum: The data type of each pixel value (see **glDrawPixels**).
pixels	GLvoid *: The pixel data.
Returns	None.

Known Bugs	The GL_PACK_ALIGNMENT and GL_UNPACK_ALIGNMENT parameters for glPixelStore are presently ignored.
Example	See the example in BOOK\CHAP8\TEX3D\tex3d.c on the source code CD-ROM.
See Also	glPixelMap, glPixelStore, glPixelTransfer, glTexImage1D, glTexImage3d

glTexParameter

Purpose	Sets texture image parameters.
Include File	<GL/gl.h>

Syntax	void glTexParameterf(GLenum *target*, GLenum *pname*, GLfloat *param*);
	void glTexParameterfv(GLenum *target*, GLenum *pname*, GLfloat **param*);
	void glTexParameteri(GLenum *target*, GLenum *pname*, GLint *param*);
	void glTexParameteriv(GLenum *target*, GLenum *pname*, GLint **param*);

Description	This function sets filter and repetition parameters for texture images.
Parameters	
target	GLenum: Must be one of GL_TEXTURE_1D or GL_TEXTURE_2D.
pname	GLenum: The texturing parameter to set. Valid names are as follows:

GL_TEXTURE_MIN_FILTER	Specifies the texture image minification (reduction) method or filter.
GL_TEXTURE_MAX_FILTER	Specifies the texture image magnification (enlargement) method or filter.
GL_TEXTURE_WRAP_S	Specifies handling of texture s coordinates outside the range of 0.0 to 1.0.
GL_TEXTURE_WRAP_T	Specifies handling of texture t coordinates outside the range of 0.0 to 1.0.
GL_BORDER_COLOR	Specifies a border color for textures without borders.

param	For GL_TEXTURE_MIN_FILTER, param is one of the following:
	For GL_TEXTURE_MAX_FILTER, param is either GL_NEAREST or GL_LINEAR. You can set GL_TEXTURE_WRAP_S and GL_TEXTURE_WRAP_T to GL_REPEAT or GL_CLAMP. GL_REPEAT causes the texture image to be repeated over the polygon. GL_CLAMP uses the specified border pixels or a constant border color on areas that fall outside of the 0.0–1.0 texture coordinate range.
	For GL_BORDER_COLOR, param is an RGBA color array that is used as a constant border color when a texture image has no border pixels defined.
Returns	None.
Example	See the example in BOOK\CHAP8\TEX2D\tex2d.c on the source code CD-ROM.
See Also	glTexCoord, glTexEnv, glTexGen, glTexImage1D, glTexImage2D

9

3D MODELING AND OBJECT COMPOSITION

by Richard S. Wright, Jr.

What you'll learn in this chapter:

How to...	Functions You'll Use
Assemble polygons to create 3D objects	glBegin/glEnd/glVertex
Optimize object display with display lists	glNewList/glEndList/glCallList
Store and render geometry more efficiently	glEnableClientState/ glDisableClientState/ glVertexPointer/glNormalPointer/ glTexCoordPointer/glColorPointer/ glEdgeFlagPointer/glArrayElement/ glDrawElements/glDrawArrays/ glInterleavedArrays

Your quiver is full of OpenGL arrows by now and it's time to go hunting. Unlike previous chapters, this is going to be a project chapter, where you can put some of this stuff to practical use. We are going to define a problem or goal and pursue it to its logical end: a finished program. Along the way, you'll gain some insight in how to break your objects and scenes into smaller, more manageable pieces. We compose a complex object out of smaller, simpler objects, which in turn are composed of just the OpenGL primitives. Finally, we discuss some compact data structures that you can use to store your models called vertex arrays.

Defining the Task

To demonstrate building a figure out of smaller simpler figures, we use an interesting, yet simple example that creates a model of a metallic bolt (such as those holding your disk drive together). Although this particular bolt might not exist in any hardware store, it will have the essential features. We make the bolt as simple as possible while still retaining the flavor of our task.

The bolt will have a six-sided head and a threaded shaft, as do many typical steel bolts. Because this is a learning exercise, we simplify the threads by making them raised on the surface of the bolt shaft rather than carved out of the shaft.

Figure 9.1 is a rough sketch of what we're aiming for. We build the three major components of this bolt—the head, the shaft, and the threads—individually and then put them together to form the final object.

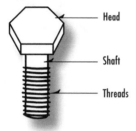
— Head

— Shaft

— Threads

Figure 9.1　The hex bolt to be modeled in this chapter.

Choosing a Projection

Before we start constructing, we need a projection, a frame of reference for placing the objects. For an example like this, an orthogonal projection is the best choice. This projection is a typical choice for applications such as CAD, in which an object is being modeled and measured exactly. This bolt has a specific width, height, and number of threads and is comparatively small. Using a perspective projection would make sense if we were modeling something larger such as a landscape, where the effect would be more apparent.

Listing 9.1 is the code that creates the viewing volume. It creates an orthogonal projection and represents a coordinate system that reaches 100 units along the x- and y-axes. An extra 100 units is supplied along the z-axis, where the viewer will be located.

Listing 9.1　*Setting Up the Orthogonal Projection for This Chapter's Examples*

```
// Change viewing volume and viewport. Called when window is resized
void ChangeSize(GLsizei w, GLsizei h)
    {
    GLfloat nRange = 100.0f;
```

```
    // Prevent a divide by zero
    if(h == 0)
        h = 1;

    // Set viewport to window dimensions
glViewport(0, 0, w, h);

    // Reset coordinate system
    glMatrixMode(GL_PROJECTION);
    glLoadIdentity();

    // Establish clipping volume (left, right, bottom, top, near, far)
if (w <= h)
        glOrtho (-nRange, nRange, -nRange*h/w, nRange*h/w,
                                  -nRange*2.0f, nRange*2.0f);
    else
        glOrtho (-nRange*w/h, nRange*w/h, -nRange, nRange,
                                  -nRange*2.0f, nRange*2.0f);
    glMatrixMode(GL_MODELVIEW);
    glLoadIdentity();
    }
```

Choosing the Lighting and Material Properties

With the projection chosen, the next step is to select a lighting model for our view of the bolt. Listing 9.2 is the code to set up the rendering context, including the lighting and material properties. We make sure the ambient light is bright enough to see all the features and include a specular component to make it glisten just as a real metal bolt would. The single light source is positioned to the upper left of the viewer.

Listing 9.2   *Setting Up the Rendering Context and Lighting Conditions*

```
// This function does any needed initialization on the rendering
// context. Here it sets up and initializes the lighting for
// the scene.
void SetupRC()
    {
    // Light values and coordinates
    GLfloat   ambientLight[] = {0.4f, 0.4f, 0.4f, 1.0f };
    GLfloat   diffuseLight[] = {0.7f, 0.7f, 0.7f, 1.0f };
    GLfloat   specular[] = { 0.9f, 0.9f, 0.9f, 1.0f};
    Glfloat   lightPos[] = { -50.0f, 200.0f, 200.0f, 1.0f };
    GLfloat   specref[] = { 0.6f, 0.6f, 0.6f, 1.0f };


    glEnable(GL_DEPTH_TEST);    // Hidden surface removal
    glEnable(GL_CULL_FACE);     // Do not calculate inside of solid object

    // Enable lighting
```

continued on next page   311

continued from previous page

```
    glEnable(GL_LIGHTING);

    // Set up light 0
    glLightModelfv(GL_LIGHT_MODEL_AMBIENT,ambientLight);
    glLightfv(GL_LIGHT0,GL_AMBIENT,ambientLight);
    glLightfv(GL_LIGHT0,GL_DIFFUSE,diffuseLight);
    glLightfv(GL_LIGHT0,GL_SPECULAR,specular);

    // Position and turn on the light
    glLightfv(GL_LIGHT0,GL_POSITION,lightPos);
    glEnable(GL_LIGHT0);

    // Enable color tracking
    glEnable(GL_COLOR_MATERIAL);

    // Set material properties to follow glColor values
    glColorMaterial(GL_FRONT, GL_AMBIENT_AND_DIFFUSE);

    // All materials hereafter have full specular reflectivity
    // with a moderate shine
    glMaterialfv(GL_FRONT, GL_SPECULAR,specref);
    glMateriali(GL_FRONT,GL_SHININESS,64);

    // Black background
    glClearColor(0.0f, 0.0f, 0.0f, 1.0f );
    }
```

Displaying the Results

Once we have determined the viewing, lighting, and material parameters, all that remains is to render the scene. Listing 9.3 shows the code outline used to display our bolt and bolt pieces. The SomeFunc function call is just a placeholder for function calls to render the head, shaft, and threads individually. We save the matrix state, perform any rotations (defined by the keyboard activity, as in all this book's previous examples), and call a function that renders some specific object or part of an object.

Listing 9.3   *Rendering the Object, Allowing for Rotated Views*

```
// Called to draw scene
void RenderScene(void)
    {
    // Clear the window with current clearing color
    glClear(GL_COLOR_BUFFER_BIT | GL_DEPTH_BUFFER_BIT);

    // Save the matrix state
    glMatrixMode(GL_MODELVIEW);
```

```
glPushMatrix();

// Rotate about x- and y-axes
glRotatef(xRot, 1.0f, 0.0f, 0.0f);
glRotatef(yRot, 0.0f, 1.0f, 0.0f);

// Specific code to draw the object...
 ...
 ... SomeFunc();     // Placeholder


glPopMatrix();

// Flush drawing commands and swap buffers
glutSwapBuffers();
}
```

This covers all the basic elements of creating a viewing volume, setting up your rendering environment, and rendering a simple geometric object. Now we need to start thinking of a real scene or model that may consist of several individual elements all brought together for the final effect.

Constructing a Model, One Piece at a Time

Any given programming task can be separated into smaller, more manageable tasks. This makes the smaller pieces easier to handle and code and introduces some reusability into our code base, as well. Three-dimensional modeling is no exception; you will create large complex systems out of many smaller and more manageable pieces.

We have decided to break the bolt down into three pieces: head, shaft, and thread. Certainly, this makes it much simpler for us to consider each section graphically, but it also gives us three objects that we can reuse. In more complex modeling applications, this reusability is of crucial importance. In a CAD-type application, for example, you would probably have many different bolts to model with various lengths, thickness, and thread density. Instead of the RenderHead function that draws the head of the bolt in this example, you might want to write a function that takes parameters specifying the number of sides, thickness, and diameter of the bolt head.

Another thing we do is model each piece of our bolt in coordinates that are most convenient for describing the object. Most often, objects are modeled around the origin and then translated and rotated into place. Later, when composing the final object, we can translate the components, rotate them, and even scale them if necessary to assemble our composite object.

The Head

The head of our bolt has six smooth sides and is smooth on top and bottom. We can construct this solid object with two hexagons that represent the top and bottom of the head and a series of quadrilaterals around the edges to represent the sides. We could use a GL_QUAD_STRIP to draw this with a minimum number of vertices; however, as we discussed previously in Chapter 6, "Color, Lighting, and Materials," this would require that each edge share a surface normal. By using quads (GL_QUADS), we can at least cut down on sending one additional vertex to OpenGL per side. For a small model such as this, the difference is negligible. For larger models, this step could mean a significant savings.

Figure 9.2 illustrates how the bolt head is constructed with the triangle fan and quads. We use a triangle fan with six triangles for the top and bottom sections of the head. Then, each face of the side of the bolt is composed of a single quad.

Figure 9.2   Primitive outline of bolt head.

A total of 18 primitives are used to draw the head of the bolt: 6 triangles (or one fan) each on the top and bottom and 6 quads to compose the sides of the bolt head. Listing 9.4 is the function that renders the head of the bolt. Figure 9.3 shows the output of this program, head, in this chapter's subdirectory on the CD. Notice that this code contains no functions that we haven't yet covered, but it's more substantial than any of the simpler chapter examples. Also, make note of the fact that the origin of the coordinate system is in the dead center of the bolt head.

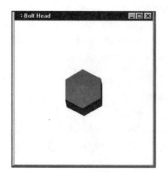

Figure 9.3   Output from the head program.

Listing 9.4 *Rendering the Head of the Bolt*

```
// Creates the head of the bolt
void RenderHead(void)
    {
    float x,y,angle;              // Calculated positions
    float height = 25.0f;          // Thickness of the head
    float diameter = 30.0f;         // Diameter of the head
    float normal[3],corners[4][3];   // Storage of vertices and normals
    float step = (3.1415f/3.0f);    // step = 1/6th of a circle = hexagon


    // Set material color for head of bolt
    glColor3f(0.0f, 0.0f, 0.7f);

    // Begin a new triangle fan to cover the top
    glBegin(GL_TRIANGLE_FAN);

        // All the normals for the top of the bolt point straight up
        // the z-axis.
        glNormal3f(0.0f, 0.0f, 1.0f);

        // Center of fan is at the origin
        glVertex3f(0.0f, 0.0f, height/2.0f);

        // Divide the circle up into 6 sections and start dropping
        // points to specify the fan. We appear to be winding this
        // fan backwards. This has the effect of reversing the winding
        // of what would have been a CW wound primitive. Avoiding a state
        // change with glFrontFace().
        for(angle = (2.0f*3.1415f); angle >= 0; angle -= step)
            {
            // Calculate x and y position of the next vertex
            x = diameter*(float)sin(angle);
            y = diameter*(float)cos(angle);

            // Specify the next vertex for the triangle fan
            glVertex3f(x, y, height/2.0f);
            }

        // Last vertex closes the fan
        glVertex3f(0.0f, diameter, height/2.0f);

    // Done drawing the fan that covers the bottom
    glEnd();
```

continued on next page

continued from previous page

```
// Begin a new triangle fan to cover the bottom
glBegin(GL_TRIANGLE_FAN);

    // Normal for bottom points straight down the negative z-axis
    glNormal3f(0.0f, 0.0f, -1.0f);

    // Center of fan is at the origin
    glVertex3f(0.0f, 0.0f, -height/2.0f);

    // Divide the circle up into 6 sections and start dropping
    // points to specify the fan
    for(angle = 0.0f; angle < (2.0f*3.1415f); angle += step)
        {
        // Calculate x and y position of the next vertex
        x = diameter*(float)sin(angle);
        y = diameter*(float)cos(angle);

        // Specify the next vertex for the triangle fan
        glVertex3f(x, y, -height/2.0f);
        }

    // Last vertex, used to close the fan
    glVertex3f(0.0f, diameter, -height/2.0f);

// Done drawing the fan that covers the bottom
glEnd();


// Build the sides out of triangles (two each). Each face
// will consist of two triangles arranged to form a
// quadrilateral
glBegin(GL_QUADS);

    // Go around and draw the sides
    for(angle = 0.0f; angle < (2.0f*3.1415f); angle += step)
        {
        // Calculate x and y position of the next hex point
        x = diameter*(float)sin(angle);
        y = diameter*(float)cos(angle);

        // Start at bottom of head
        corners[0][0] = x;
        corners[0][1] = y;
        corners[0][2] = -height/2.0f;

        // Extrude to top of head
        corners[1][0] = x;
        corners[1][1] = y;
```

```
            corners[1][2] = height/2.0f;

            // Calculate the next hex point
            x = diameter*(float)sin(angle+step);
            y = diameter*(float)cos(angle+step);

            // Make sure we aren't done before proceeding
            if(angle+step < 3.1415*2.0)
                {
                // If we are done, just close the fan at a
                // known coordinate.
                corners[2][0] = x;
                corners[2][1] = y;
                corners[2][2] = height/2.0f;

                corners[3][0] = x;
                corners[3][1] = y;
                corners[3][2] = -height/2.0f;
                }
            else
                {
                // We aren't done, the points at the top and bottom
                // of the head.
                corners[2][0] = 0.0f;
                corners[2][1] = diameter;
                corners[2][2] = height/2.0f;

                corners[3][0] = 0.0f;
                corners[3][1] = diameter;
                corners[3][2] = -height/2.0f;
                }

            // The normal vectors for the entire face will
            // all point the same direction
            calcNormal(corners, normal);
            glNormal3fv(normal);

            // Specify each triangle separately to lie next
            // to each other.
            glVertex3fv(corners[0]);
            glVertex3fv(corners[1]);
            glVertex3fv(corners[2]);
            glVertex3fv(corners[3]);
            }

    glEnd();
    }
```

The Shaft

The shaft of the bolt is nothing more than a cylinder with a bottom on it. We compose a cylinder by plotting xz values around in a circle and then take two y values at these points and get polygons that approximate the wall of a cylinder. This time, however, we compose this wall entirely out of a quad strip because each adjacent quad can share a normal for smooth shading (see Chapter 6). Figure 9.4 shows the outline of the cylinder.

Figure 9.4   The progression of quads around the shaft body.

We also create the bottom of the shaft with a triangle fan as we did for the bottom of the bolt head previously. Notice now however, that the smaller step size around the circle yields smaller flat facets, which make the cylinder wall more closely approximate a smooth curve. The step size also just happens to match that used for the shaft wall so that they match evenly.

Listing 9.5 is the code to produce this cylinder. Notice that the normals are not calculated for the quads using the vertices of the quads. We usually set the normal to be the same for all vertices, but here, we break with this tradition to specify a new normal for each vertex. Because we are simulating a curved surface, the normal specified for each vertex is normal to the actual curve. (If this sounds confusing, review Chapter 6 on normals and lighting effects.)

Listing 9.5   *Rendering the Shaft of the Bolt*

```
// Creates the shaft of the bolt as a cylinder with one end
// closed.
void RenderShaft(void)
    {
    float x,z,angle;            // Used to calculate cylinder wall
    float height = 75.0f;        // Height of the cylinder
    float diameter = 20.0f;       // Diameter of the cylinder
    float normal[3],corners[2][3];   // Storage for vertex calculations
    float step = (3.1415f/50.0f);   // Approximate the cylinder wall with
                                // 100 flat segments.

    // Set material color for head of screw
    glColor3f(0.0f, 0.0f, 0.7f);
```

```
// First assemble the wall as 100 quadrilaterals formed by
// placing adjoining quads together
glBegin(GL_QUAD_STRIP);

// Go around and draw the sides
for(angle = (2.0f*3.1415f); angle > 0.0f; angle -= step)
    {
    // Calculate x and y position of the first vertex
    x = diameter*(float)sin(angle);
    z = diameter*(float)cos(angle);

    // Get the coordinate for this point and extrude the
    // length of the cylinder.
    corners[0][0] = x;
    corners[0][1] = -height/2.0f;
    corners[0][2] = z;

    corners[1][0] = x;
    corners[1][1] = height/2.0f;
    corners[1][2] = z;

    // Instead of using real normal to actual flat section,
    // use what the normal would be if the surface was really
    // curved. Since the cylinder goes up the y-axis, the normal
    // points from the y-axis out directly through each vertex.
    // Therefore we can use the vertex as the normal, as long as
    // we reduce it to unit length first and assume the y component
    // to be zero
    normal[0] = corners[1][0];
    normal[1] = 0.0f;
    normal[2] = corners[1][2];

    // Reduce to length of one and specify for this point
    ReduceToUnit(normal);
    glNormal3fv(normal);
    glVertex3fv(corners[0]);
    glVertex3fv(corners[1]);
    }

    // Make sure there are no gaps by extending last quad to
    // the original location
    glVertex3f(diameter*(float)sin(2.0f*3.1415f),
               -height/2.0f,
               diameter*(float)cos(2.0f*3.1415f));

    glVertex3f(diameter*(float)sin(2.0f*3.1415f),
               height/2.0f,
```

continued on next page

continued from previous page

```
                    diameter*(float)cos(2.0f*3.1415f));

glEnd();    // Done with cylinder sides

// Begin a new triangle fan to cover the bottom
glBegin(GL_TRIANGLE_FAN);
    // Normal points down the y-axis
    glNormal3f(0.0f, -1.0f, 0.0f);

    // Center of fan is at the origin
    glVertex3f(0.0f, -height/2.0f, 0.0f);

    // Spin around matching step size of cylinder wall
    for(angle = (2.0f*3.1415f); angle > 0.0f; angle -= step)
        {
        // Calculate x and y position of the next vertex
        x = diameter*(float)sin(angle);
        z = diameter*(float)cos(angle);

        // Specify the next vertex for the triangle fan
        glVertex3f(x, -height/2.0f, z);
        }

    // Be sure loop is closed by specifying initial vertex
    // on arc as the last one
    glVertex3f(diameter*(float)sin(2.0f*3.1415f),
               -height/2.0f,
               diameter*(float)cos(2.0f*3.1415f));
glEnd();
}
```

Fortunately, the cylinder is wrapped symmetrically around the y-axis. Thus, you can find the normal for each vertex by normalizing (reducing to length 1) the vertex itself. Figure 9.5 shows the output from the shaft program. You need to use the arrow keys to move the shaft around a bit to achieve this perspective.

Figure 9.5 Output from the shaft program.

The Thread

The thread is the most complex part of the bolt. It's composed of two planes arranged in a V shape that follows a corkscrew pattern up the length of the shaft. It is created as two flat segments arranged in a V pattern. Figure 9.6 illustrates the triangle outline of this shape, and Listing 9.6 is the OpenGL code used to produce this shape.

Figure 9.6   Progression of triangle outline of thread.

Listing 9.6   *Rendering the Thread of the Bolt*

```
// Creates the thread
void RenderThread(void)
    {
    float x,y,z,angle;              // Calculate coordinates and step angle
    float height = 75.0f;          // Height of the threading
    float diameter = 20.0f;         // Diameter of the threading
    float normal[3],corners[4][3];   // Calculated normal and corners
    float step = (3.1415f/32.0f);   // One revolution
    float revolutions = 7.0f;       // How many times around the shaft?
    float threadWidth = 2.0f;       // How wide is the thread?
    float threadThick = 3.0f;       // How thick is the thread?
    float zstep = .125f;            // How much does the thread move up
                                    // the z-axis each time a new segment
                                    // is drawn?

    // 360 degrees in radians
    #define PI2 (2.0f*3.1415f)

    // Set material color for head of screw
    glColor3f(0.0f, 0.0f, 0.4f);


    z = -height/2.0f+2;    // Starting spot almost to the end
```

continued on next page

continued from previous page

```
// Go around and draw the sides until finished spinning up
for(angle = 0.0f; angle < PI2*revolutions; angle += step)
    {
    // Calculate x and y position of the next vertex
    x = diameter*(float)sin(angle);
    y = diameter*(float)cos(angle);

    // Store the next vertex next to the shaft
    corners[0][0] = x;
    corners[0][1] = y;
    corners[0][2] = z;

    // Calculate the position away from the shaft
    x = (diameter+threadWidth)*(float)sin(angle);
    y = (diameter+threadWidth)*(float)cos(angle);

    corners[1][0] = x;
    corners[1][1] = y;
    corners[1][2] = z;

    // Calculate the next position away from the shaft
    x = (diameter+threadWidth)*(float)sin(angle+step);
    y = (diameter+threadWidth)*(float)cos(angle+step);

    corners[2][0] = x;
    corners[2][1] = y;
    corners[2][2] = z + zstep;

    // Calculate the next position along the shaft
    x = (diameter)*(float)sin(angle+step);
    y = (diameter)*(float)cos(angle+step);

    corners[3][0] = x;
    corners[3][1] = y;
    corners[3][2] = z+ zstep;


    // We'll be using triangles, so make
    // counterclockwise polygons face out
    glFrontFace(GL_CCW);
    glBegin(GL_TRIANGLES);    // Start the top section of thread

        // Calculate the normal for this segment
        calcNormal(corners, normal);
        glNormal3fv(normal);

        // Draw two triangles to cover area
```

```
        glVertex3fv(corners[0]);
        glVertex3fv(corners[1]);
        glVertex3fv(corners[2]);

        glVertex3fv(corners[2]);
        glVertex3fv(corners[3]);
        glVertex3fv(corners[0]);

    glEnd();


    // Move the edge along the shaft slightly up the z-axis
    // to represent the bottom of the thread
    corners[0][2] += threadThick;
    corners[3][2] += threadThick;

    // Recalculate the normal since points have changed; this
    // time it points in the opposite direction, so reverse it
    calcNormal(corners, normal);
    normal[0] = -normal[0];
    normal[1] = -normal[1];
    normal[2] = -normal[2];

    // Switch to clockwise facing out for underside of the
    // thread.
    glFrontFace(GL_CW);

    // Draw the two triangles
    glBegin(GL_TRIANGLES);
        glNormal3fv(normal);

        glVertex3fv(corners[0]);
        glVertex3fv(corners[1]);
        glVertex3fv(corners[2]);

        glVertex3fv(corners[2]);
        glVertex3fv(corners[3]);
        glVertex3fv(corners[0]);

    glEnd();

    // Creep up the z-axis
    z += zstep;
    }
}
```

Figure 9.7 shows the output of the thread program.

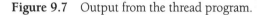

Figure 9.7 Output from the thread program.

Putting the Model Together

The bolt is assembled by drawing all three sections in their appropriate location. All sections are translated and rotated appropriately into place. The shaft is not modified at all and the threads must be rotated to match the shaft. The head of the bolt must be rotated and translated to put it in its proper place.

Listing 9.7 is the rendering code that manipulates and renders the three bolt components. Figure 9.8 shows the final output of the bolt program.

Figure 9.8 Output from the bolt program.

Listing 9.7 *Rendering Code to Draw the Completed Bolt*

```
// Called to draw the entire bolt
void RenderScene(void)
    {
    // Clear the window with current clearing color
    glClear(GL_COLOR_BUFFER_BIT | GL_DEPTH_BUFFER_BIT);

    // Save the matrix state and do the rotations
```

```
glMatrixMode(GL_MODELVIEW);

// Rotate and translate, and then render the bolt head
glPushMatrix();
    glRotatef(xRot, 1.0f, 0.0f, 0.0f);
    glRotatef(yRot, 0.0f, 1.0f, 0.0f);
    glTranslatef(0.0f, 0.0f, 55.0f);
    RenderHead();
glPopMatrix();


// Save matrix state, rotate, translate, and draw the
// shaft and thread together
glPushMatrix();
glRotatef(xRot, 1.0f, 0.0f, 0.0f);
glRotatef(yRot, 0.0f, 1.0f, 0.0f);
glTranslatef(0.0f, 0.0f, 40.0f);

// Render just the hexagonal head of the nut
RenderShaft();
RenderThread();

glPopMatrix();

// Flush drawing commands
glFlush();
```

So why all the gymnastics to place all these pieces together? We easily could have adjusted our geometry so that all the pieces would be drawn in their correct location. The point shown here is that many pieces modeled about their own local origins can be arranged together in a scene quite easily to create a more sophisticated model or environment. This basic principle and technique is the foundation of creating your own scene graph (see Chapter 1, "3D Graphics Fundamentals") or virtual environment. We put this into real practice later in Chapter 19, "Real-Time Programming with OpenGL."

Preprocessing Your Models

Our last program produces a fairly good representation of the metal bolt we set out to model. Consisting of more than 1,700 triangles, this is the most complex example in this book so far in terms of geometry. Comparatively speaking, however, this number of triangles isn't anywhere close to the largest number of polygons you'll encounter when composing larger scenes and more complex objects. In fact, the latest 3D accelerated graphics cards are rated at millions of triangles per second, and that's for the cheap ones! One of the goals of this chapter is to introduce you to some more efficient ways to store and render your geometry.

> **OPTIMIZING MODEL CREATION**
> In our bolt example, we constructed the model by applying mathematics to represent the curves and surfaces as equations. Using points along these equations, we constructed a series of triangles to create the representative shape. Although the bolt head and shaft were simple, the code to create the thread geometry can be a bit more intimidating. In general, creating models or geometry can be quite time-consuming due to many factors. Perhaps you have to compute all of the vertices and normals such as we have here. Perhaps you need to read these values from disk or retrieve them over a network. With these considerations in mind, it is possible that rendering performance could be hampered more by other tasks related to creating the geometry than by the actual rendering itself. OpenGL provides two solutions to overcoming these issues, each of which has its own merits. These solutions, Display Lists, and Vertex Arrays, are the main focus of the remainder of this chapter.

Display Lists

OpenGL provides a facility to create a preprocessed set of OpenGL commands, called a *display list*. Creating a display list is a straightforward process. Just as you delimit an OpenGL primitive with `glBegin/glEnd`, you delimit a display list with `glNewList/glEndList`. A display list, however, is named with an integer value that you supply. The following code represents a typical example of display list creation:

```
GLuint nName;
...
nName = glGenLists(1);

glNewList(nName,GL_COMPILE);
...
...
// Some OpenGL Code
...
...
glEndList();
...
glDeleteLists(nName, 1);
```

You can't just use any name for a display list. First, you must generate an empty display list for use. The function `glGenLists` does this for you. It takes a single parameter that tells OpenGL how many display list names you want. The display lists created are named sequentially, with the first name returned by the function. In our example here, we are just generating a single list. We generate a range of display lists for our next sample program.

Now that we have a valid display list name, we tell OpenGL to begin compiling a list of OpenGL commands with the `glNewList` function. As the second parameter to `glNewList`, you can specify `GL_COMPILE` or `GL_COMPILE_AND_EXECUTE`. This tells OpenGL whether to compile and store the OpenGL commands or to compile, store, and execute the commands as they occur.

To terminate the creation of the display list, you call `glEndList`. Then, later, when you need to execute the display list, simply call

```
glCallList(nName);
```

The value of `nName` identifies the display list you want to invoke. Finally, you need to remember to release the memory occupied by the display list or lists with a call to `glDeleteLists`. This function takes the first name to delete and the range of values following that to delete. You do not need to delete all the lists at once, even if you created them all together.

Display List Caveats

A few important points about display lists are worth mentioning at this point. Although on most implementations, a display list should improve performance, your mileage may vary depending on the amount of effort the vendor puts into optimizing display list creation and execution. Most implementations, for example, store calls to `glTexImage2D` very poorly, and you are better off using texture objects instead (see Chapter 8, "Texture Mapping").

Display lists are typically very good at creating precompiled lists of OpenGL commands, especially if the list contains state changes (turning lighting on and off, for example). If you do not create a display list name with `glGenLists` first, you might get a working display list on some implementations, but not on others. Finally, display lists cannot contain calls that create display lists. You can have one display list call another, but you cannot put calls to `glNewLists/glEndList` inside a display list.

A Display List Sample

Listing 9.8 contains the pertinent code for our new example, dlbolt, which makes use of display lists to produce the bolt. In this code, we create a display list for each part of the bolt and then play each list back to create the completed bolt.

Listing 9.8 *New Spinning Bolt Code Using Display Lists*

```
// Storage for display list name base
GLuint nPartsList;
GLuint HEAD_LIST, SHAFT_LIST, THREAD_LIST;
. . .


// Called to draw the entire bolt
void RenderScene(void)
    {
    // Clear the window with current clearing color
    glClear(GL_COLOR_BUFFER_BIT | GL_DEPTH_BUFFER_BIT);
```

continued on next page

continued from previous page

```
    // Save the matrix state
    glMatrixMode(GL_MODELVIEW);
    glPushMatrix();

    // Rotate about x- and y-axes
    glRotatef(xRot, 1.0f, 0.0f, 0.0f);
    glRotatef(yRot, 0.0f, 0.0f, 1.0f);

    // Render, starting with the shaft
    glCallList(SHAFT_LIST);

    glPushMatrix();
    glRotatef(-90.0f, 1.0f, 0.0f, 0.0f);
    glCallList(THREAD_LIST);

    glTranslatef(0.0f,0.0f,45.0f);
    glCallList(HEAD_LIST);
    glPopMatrix();

    glPopMatrix();

    // Swap buffers
    glutSwapBuffers();
    }


// This function does any needed initialization on the rendering
// context.
void SetupRC()
    {
. . .


    // Set three display list names
    HEAD_LIST = nPartsList;
    SHAFT_LIST = nPartsList+1;
    THREAD_LIST = nPartsList+2;

    glNewList(HEAD_LIST,GL_COMPILE);
        RenderHead();
    glEndList();

    glNewList(SHAFT_LIST,GL_COMPILE);
        RenderShaft();
    glEndList();

    glNewList(THREAD_LIST,GL_COMPILE);          RenderThread();
    glEndList();
```

```
}

int main(int argc, char* argv[])
    {
    glutInit(&argc, argv);
    glutInitDisplayMode(GLUT_DOUBLE | GLUT_RGB | GLUT_DEPTH);
    glutCreateWindow("Display List Bolt");
    glutReshapeFunc(ChangeSize);
    glutSpecialFunc(SpecialKeys);
    glutDisplayFunc(RenderScene);

    // Create three display list names
    nPartsList = glGenLists(3);

    SetupRC();
    glutMainLoop();

    // Delete the display lists
    glDeleteLists(nPartsList, 3);
    return 0;
    }
```

A QUICK NOTE ABOUT THE DLBOLT CODE

You'll see that we defined some variables to identify the display lists more easily. These variables simply map to the numeric value that identifies the display list. Take note also that we allocated the display lists before calling SetupRC to build them. These lists are also destroyed just before the program terminates.

Vertex Arrays

Display lists are useful for precompiling a set of OpenGL commands. In our previous example, display lists were perhaps a bit underused because all we really encapsulated was the creation of the geometry. You might consider that we could just as easily have created some arrays to store the vertex data for the models and thus saved all the computation time just as easily as the display lists.

You *might* be right about this. Some implementations store display lists more efficiently than others, and if *all* you're really compiling is the vertex data, why bother? This is a valid observation, and unless you are precompiling other OpenGL commands that contain state information, or matrix calculations (for example, a series of matrix operations would be stored in the display list as a single resulting matrix), you probably would be just as well off using arrays to store your vertex data. In OpenGL, we refer to this array of vertices as a *vertex array*. As you'll soon see, OpenGL even has some special support for vertex arrays as of version 1.1.

Creating an Array

Let's look at our previous bolt model and use that as a basis for our discussion of vertex arrays. The head of the bolt contains very few vertices, so there is little point in putting any extra work into this. The shaft contains quite a few vertices to create a smooth cylinder and the triangle fan at the bottom. We still leave this as a display list because we would probably expect little benefit from using arrays.

The bolt thread is a different story altogether. Although instructional to the reader for previous examples, the function `BuildThread` is a model of OpenGL inefficiency. As the points for each triangle along the thread are calculated, they are used to specify both the top and bottom triangles of the thread. Between each triangle, we change the polygon winding from clockwise to counterclockwise. This happens many hundreds of times. State changes slow OpenGL down considerably (see Chapter 17, "The OpenGL Pixel Format and Rendering Context"). Changing the thread into two arrays, one for the top and one for the bottom, and then rendering each section separately will save enough state changes that you will likely see a performance boost on almost any OpenGL implementation.

Let's look at the changes we need to make to `BuildThread` to create arrays containing the vertex data. Listing 9.9 shows the new function that instead of rendering the thread fills arrays with the vertex data. We have two arrays for both the top and bottom triangle vertices, as well as two arrays, one each for the top and bottom normals (that's four arrays altogether).

Listing 9.9   *Changes to Store the Thread Data in Arrays*

```
// Pointers for the vertex arrays
GLfloat *pThreadTopData = NULL;
GLfloat *pThreadTopNormals = NULL;
GLfloat *pThreadBottomData = NULL;
GLfloat *pThreadBottomNormals = NULL;
GLuint uiVertCount = 2694;        // How many vertices?
. . .
. . .
// Creates the thread
void BuildThread(void)
    {
    float x,y,z,angle;              // Calculate coordinates and step angle
    float height = 75.0f;           // Height of the threading
    float diameter = 20.0f;         // Diameter of the threading
    float normal[3],corners[4][3];  // Storage for calculate normal and corners
    float step = (3.1415f/32.0f);   // one revolution
    float revolutions = 7.0f;       // How many times around the shaft?
    float threadWidth = 2.0f;       // How wide is the thread?
    float threadThick = 3.0f;       // How thick is the thread?
    float zstep = .125f;            // How much does the thread move up
```

```
                              // the z-axis each time a new segment
                              // is drawn?
int nTopVerts = 0;
int nBottomVerts = 0;

// 360 degrees in radians
#define PI2 (2.0f*3.1415f)


z = -height/2.0f+2; // Starting spot almost to the end

// Go around and draw the sides until finished spinning up
for(angle = 0.0f; angle < PI2*revolutions; angle += step)
    {
    // Calculate x and y position of the next vertex
    x = diameter*(float)sin(angle);
    y = diameter*(float)cos(angle);

    // Store the next vertex next to the shaft
    corners[0][0] = x;
    corners[0][1] = y;
    corners[0][2] = z;

    // Calculate the position away from the shaft
    x = (diameter+threadWidth)*(float)sin(angle);
    y = (diameter+threadWidth)*(float)cos(angle);

    corners[1][0] = x;
    corners[1][1] = y;
    corners[1][2] = z;

    // Calculate the next position away from the shaft
    x = (diameter+threadWidth)*(float)sin(angle+step);
    y = (diameter+threadWidth)*(float)cos(angle+step);

    corners[2][0] = x;
    corners[2][1] = y;
    corners[2][2] = z + zstep;

    // Calculate the next position along the shaft
    x = (diameter)*(float)sin(angle+step);
    y = (diameter)*(float)cos(angle+step);

    corners[3][0] = x;
    corners[3][1] = y;
    corners[3][2] = z+ zstep;
```

continued on next page

continued from previous page

```
// Add these to the list of vertices
memcpy((pThreadTopData+nTopVerts), &corners[0], sizeof(GLfloat)*3);
memcpy((pThreadTopData+nTopVerts+(3)), &corners[1], sizeof(GLfloat)*3);
memcpy((pThreadTopData+nTopVerts+(6)), &corners[2], sizeof(GLfloat)*3);

memcpy((pThreadTopData+nTopVerts+(9)), &corners[2], sizeof(GLfloat)*3);
memcpy((pThreadTopData+nTopVerts+(12)), &corners[3], sizeof(GLfloat)*3);
memcpy((pThreadTopData+nTopVerts+(15)), &corners[0], sizeof(GLfloat)*3);

// Calculate the normal for this segment
calcNormal(corners, normal);

// Copy it for every face
memcpy((pThreadTopNormals+nTopVerts), normal, sizeof(GLfloat)*3);
memcpy((pThreadTopNormals+nTopVerts+(3)), normal, sizeof(GLfloat)*3);
memcpy((pThreadTopNormals+nTopVerts+(6)), normal, sizeof(GLfloat)*3);
memcpy((pThreadTopNormals+nTopVerts+(9)), normal, sizeof(GLfloat)*3);
memcpy((pThreadTopNormals+nTopVerts+(12)), normal, sizeof(GLfloat)*3);
memcpy((pThreadTopNormals+nTopVerts+(15)), normal, sizeof(GLfloat)*3);
nTopVerts += 18;


// Move the edge along the shaft slightly up the z-axis
// to represent the bottom of the thread
corners[0][2] += threadThick;
corners[3][2] += threadThick;

// Recalculate the normal since points have changed; this
// time it points in the opposite direction, so reverse it
calcNormal(corners, normal);
normal[0] = -normal[0];
normal[1] = -normal[1];
normal[2] = -normal[2];

memcpy((pThreadBottomData+nBottomVerts), &corners[0],
                              sizeof(GLfloat)*3);
memcpy((pThreadBottomData+nBottomVerts+3), &corners[1],
                              sizeof(GLfloat)*3);
memcpy((pThreadBottomData+nBottomVerts+6), &corners[2],
                              sizeof(GLfloat)*3);

memcpy((pThreadBottomData+nBottomVerts+9), &corners[2],
                              sizeof(GLfloat)*3);
memcpy((pThreadBottomData+nBottomVerts+12), &corners[3],
                              sizeof(GLfloat)*3);
memcpy((pThreadBottomData+nBottomVerts+15), &corners[0],
                              sizeof(GLfloat)*3);
```

```
        memcpy((pThreadBottomNormals+nBottomVerts), normal,
                                    sizeof(GLfloat)*3);
        memcpy((pThreadBottomNormals+nBottomVerts+3), normal,
                                    sizeof(GLfloat)*3);
        memcpy((pThreadBottomNormals+nBottomVerts+6), normal,
                                    sizeof(GLfloat)*3);
        memcpy((pThreadBottomNormals+nBottomVerts+9), normal,
                                    sizeof(GLfloat)*3);
        memcpy((pThreadBottomNormals+nBottomVerts+12), normal,
                                    sizeof(GLfloat)*3);
        memcpy((pThreadBottomNormals+nBottomVerts+15), normal,
                                    sizeof(GLfloat)*3);

        nBottomVerts += 18;

        // Creep up the z-axis
        z += zstep;
        }
    }
. . .
. . .
int main(int argc, char* argv[])
    {
    glutInit(&argc, argv);

    // Allocate space for the geometry
    pThreadTopData = malloc(sizeof(GLfloat) * uiVertCount * 3);
    pThreadTopNormals = malloc(sizeof(GLfloat) * uiVertCount * 3);
    pThreadBottomData = malloc(sizeof(GLfloat) * uiVertCount * 3);
    pThreadBottomNormals = malloc(sizeof(GLfloat) * uiVertCount * 3);

    glutInitDisplayMode(GLUT_DOUBLE | GLUT_RGB | GLUT_DEPTH);
    glutCreateWindow("Vertex Array Bolt");
    glutReshapeFunc(ChangeSize);
    glutSpecialFunc(SpecialKeys);
    glutDisplayFunc(RenderScene);
    SetupRC();
    glutMainLoop();

    // Free previously allocated space
    free(pThreadTopData);
    free(pThreadTopNormals);
    free(pThreadBottomData);
    free(pThreadBottomNormals);

    return 0;
    }
```

First, you'll notice at the beginning of the program that we created pointers for the vertex arrays. These pointers are declared outside the scope of any function so that they are accessible everywhere in the program:

```
// Pointers for the vertex arrays
GLfloat *pThreadTopData = NULL;
GLfloat *pThreadTopNormals = NULL;
GLfloat *pThreadBottomData = NULL;
GLfloat *pThreadBottomNormals = NULL;
GLuint uiVertCount = 2694;        // How many vertices?
```

Memory for these arrays is allocated and released in the main program function:

```
// Allocate space for the geometry
    pThreadTopData = malloc(sizeof(GLfloat) * uiVertCount * 3);
    pThreadTopNormals = malloc(sizeof(GLfloat) * uiVertCount * 3);
    pThreadBottomData = malloc(sizeof(GLfloat) * uiVertCount * 3);
    pThreadBottomNormals = malloc(sizeof(GLfloat) * uiVertCount * 3);
. . .


. . .
    // Free previously allocated space
    free(pThreadTopData);
    free(pThreadTopNormals);
    free(pThreadBottomData);
    free(pThreadBottomNormals);
```

Accessing an Array

In the RenderScene function, the call to the thread display list would be replaced by the following code:

```
// Draw the top of the thread
    glBegin(GL_TRIANGLES);
        for(i = 0; i < uiVertCount; i++)
            {
            glNormal3fv(pThreadTopNormals + (i*3));
            glVertex3fv(pThreadTopData + (i * 3));
            }
    glEnd();

    // Draw the bottom of the thread
    glFrontFace(GL_CW);
    glBegin(GL_TRIANGLES);
        for(i = 0; i < uiVertCount; i++)
            {
            glNormal3fv(pThreadBottomNormals + (i*3));
            glVertex3fv(pThreadBottomData + (i * 3));
            }
    glEnd();
    glFrontFace(GL_CCW);
```

This is more code than simply calling a display list, and we have consumed significantly more memory because many of the vertices and normals were previously shared. However, as pointed out earlier, the fewer number of state changes more than makes up for any performance penalty. This also gives you a compact format in which you can save and read models from disk. With some clever programming, you could save more memory and enhance performance by keeping repeated normals and vertices in the array only once. As you'll soon see, OpenGL will even help you out with this.

OpenGL Support for Vertex Arrays

We've shown now that we can take it upon ourselves to store vertex data in an array. We can then use this array to feed vertices and normals (and colors and texture coordinates and so on) to OpenGL very quickly. OpenGL 1.1 added native support for vertex arrays to make it even easier to use vertex arrays than shown in our modifications to the RenderScene function.

Creating OpenGL vertex arrays is exactly the same as creating the vertex arrays for the last example. If you examine the source to vabolt on the CD, you'll find that in the RenderScene function, we used several variations on vertex arrays. The vertex arrays are created just as they are for Listing 9.9 and are rendered in a variety of ways. (Each is bracketed by comments so you can select various ones.)

To use OpenGL's native vertex array functionality, you must first enable vertex array support with the glEnableClientState and glDisableClientState functions. Each function takes as an argument the type of array to enable or disable. Valid values are GL_VERTEX_ARRAY, GL_NORMAL_ARRAY, GL_COLOR_ARRAY, GL_INDEX_ARRAY, GL_EDGE_FLAG_ARRAY, and GL_TEXTURE_COORD_ARRAY.

For our vabolt example, the following lines of code tell OpenGL that we will be using vertex arrays for vertices and normals:

```
// Do the vertex array thing
    glEnableClientState(GL_NORMAL_ARRAY);
    glEnableClientState(GL_VERTEX_ARRAY);
```

Telling OpenGL to use vertex arrays is only the beginning. You must also tell OpenGL where the data is located. You must first have allocated the array space as shown in Listing 9.8. Then, a set of functions allows you to specify a pointer for each array type. For our example, we use the following code:

```
glVertexPointer(3, GL_FLOAT, 0, pThreadTopData);
glNormalPointer(GL_FLOAT, 0, pThreadTopNormals);
```

The first parameter to glVertexPointer tells how many coordinates are in the array per vertex (2, 3, or 4). The second parameter tells what kind of data is being used (floats, in this case). The third parameter specifies a byte offset between each vertex. A zero value here means the array is tightly packed, as we have done. (There is no space or other information between each vertex in the array.) The final parameter is a pointer to the actual array of data.

The `glNormalPointer` function is similar. However, normals always consist of three coordinates, so the first parameter is unnecessary. Similar functions exist for the other array types, and you can read about them in the reference section (`glColorPointer`, `glTexCoordPointer`, and `glEdgeFlagPointer`).

Using Array Elements

Now that we have told OpenGL that we want to use vertex arrays, and we have informed OpenGL where the data is, how do we use them? After all, until this point, we still could use the code presented earlier to access the array data:

```
// Draw the top of the thread
   glBegin(GL_TRIANGLES);
       for(i = 0; i < uiVertCount; i++)
           {
           glNormal3fv(pThreadTopNormals + (i*3));
           glVertex3fv(pThreadTopData + (i * 3));
           }
   glEnd();
```

The first function to help make the preceding code a bit shorter and more efficient is `glArrayElement`. This function takes one parameter, which specifies which element in the enabled arrays to access. The following code shows how the preceding code is changed using `glArrayElement`:

```
// Draw the top of the thread
   glBegin(GL_TRIANGLES);
           for(i = 0; i < uiVertCount; i++)
               glArrayElement(i);
       glEnd();
```

Because we have enabled the arrays for vertex and normal data, the single `glArrayElement` call is equivalent to both a `glNormal` and a `glVertex` call. You can see immediately that we appear to have saved one function call and two multiplies in our code to calculate where the appropriate vertex data is located. We can also pass colors, texture coordinates, and edge flags this way, further increasing the advantage of using this method.

Although on the surface, this might appear to be a minor performance enhancement from the application's side, you can also enable important optimizations within the OpenGL driver or implementation. By using vertex arrays, it becomes possible for an implementation to perform block copies of the data and to optimize data transfer. This might not always be the case, but at the very least, you have still made your code more efficient, and there are further opportunities for optimization.

Specifying a Block of Primitives

The previous example of using `glArrayElement` would be a fairly typical use of vertex arrays if this were as far as vertex arrays went. As it turns out, this use is so prevalent that it too is encapsulated into a single OpenGL function called `glDrawArrays`. The entire `glBegin`/`loop`/`glEnd` sequence shown previously can now be replaced by a single line of code:

```
glDrawArrays(GL_TRIANGLES,0, uiVertCount);
```

This function simply takes as arguments the type of primitive to construct from the array data, the first array element to access, and how many array elements to use. Not only does this function further reduce your own code and function call count, but also it provides the OpenGL implementation an even greater opportunity to exploit larger block copies of data internally.

Indexed Vertex Arrays

Although we have shown you how to reduce the function call overhead of your code, and perhaps give the OpenGL implementation some opportunity for optimization, we can still go farther. In high-performance, real-time graphics, reducing memory usage is an important means of performance tuning. The less data that must be read from memory, moved over a bus, or sent to a graphics card, the faster these operations can happen.

In the thread example, many normals and vertices were repeated. We can save a considerable amount of memory if we can reuse a normal or vertex in a vertex array without having to store it more than once. Not only is memory saved, but also a good OpenGL implementation is optimized to only transform these vertices once, saving valuable transformation time.

Instead of creating a vertex array containing all the vertices for a given geometric object, you can create an array containing only the *unique* vertices for the object. Then, you can use another array of index values to specify the geometry. These indexes reference the vertex values in the first array. Figure 9.9 shows this relationship.

Each vertex consists of three floating-point values, but each index is only an integer value. A float and an integer are four bytes on most machines, which means you save eight bytes for each reused vertex for the cost of four extra bytes for every vertex. For a small number of vertices, the savings might not be great; in fact, you might even use more memory using an indexed array than you would have by just repeating vertex information. For larger models, however, the savings can be substantial.

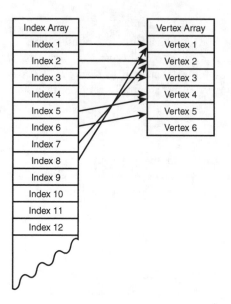

Figure 9.9 An index array referencing an array of unique vertices.

Figure 9.10 shows a cube with each vertex numbered. For our next sample program, cubedx, we create a cube using indexed vertex arrays.

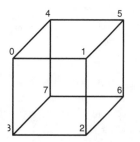

Figure 9.10 A cube containing six unique numbered vertices.

Listing 9.10 shows the code from the cubedx program to render the cube using indexed vertex arrays. The six unique vertices are in the `corners` array, and the indexes are in the `indexes` array. Note, in `RenderScene`, we set the polygon mode to `GL_LINE` so that the cube is wireframed.

Listing 9.10 *Code from the cubedx Program to Use Indexed Vertex Arrays*

```
// Array containing the six vertices of the cube
static GLfloat corners[] = { -25.0f, 25.0f, 25.0f, // 0 // Front of cube
```

```
                    25.0f,  25.0f,  25.0f, // 1
                    25.0f, -25.0f,  25.0f,// 2
                   -25.0f, -25.0f,  25.0f,// 3
                   -25.0f,  25.0f, -25.0f,// 4  // Back of cube
                    25.0f,  25.0f, -25.0f,// 5
                    25.0f, -25.0f, -25.0f,// 6
                   -25.0f, -25.0f, -25.0f };// 7

// Array of indexes to create the cube
static GLubyte indexes[] = { 0, 1, 2, 3,     // Front face
               4, 5, 1, 0,    // Top face
               3, 2, 6, 7,    // Bottom face
               5, 4, 7, 6,    // Back face
               1, 5, 6, 2,    // Right face
               4, 0, 3, 7 };   // Left face

void RenderScene(void)
    {
    // Clear the window with current clearing color
    glClear(GL_COLOR_BUFFER_BIT | GL_DEPTH_BUFFER_BIT);

    // Make the cube a wireframe
    glPolygonMode(GL_FRONT_AND_BACK, GL_LINE);


    // Save the matrix state
    glMatrixMode(GL_MODELVIEW);
    glPushMatrix();

    // Rotate about x- and y-axes
    glRotatef(xRot, 1.0f, 0.0f, 0.0f);
    glRotatef(yRot, 0.0f, 0.0f, 1.0f);

    // Enable and specify the vertex array
    glEnableClientState(GL_VERTEX_ARRAY);
    glVertexPointer(3, GL_FLOAT, 0, corners);

    // Using DrawArrays
    glDrawElements(GL_QUADS, 24, GL_UNSIGNED_BYTE, indexes);


    glPopMatrix();

    // Swap buffers
    glutSwapBuffers();
    }
```

OpenGL has native support for indexed vertex arrays, as shown in the function
glDrawElements. The key line in Listing 9.10 is

glDrawElements(GL_QUADS, 24, GL_UNSIGNED_BYTE, indexes);

This is much like the function glDrawArrays mentioned earlier, but now we are specifying an index array that determines the order in which the enabled vertex arrays are
traversed. Figure 9.11 shows the output from the program cubedx.

Figure 9.11   A wireframe cube drawn with an indexed vertex array.

A variation on glDrawElement added to OpenGL in version 1.2 is the function
glDrawRangeElements. This function is documented in the reference section and simply adds two parameters to specify the range of indexes that will be valid. This hint
can enable some OpenGL implementations to prefetch the vertex data, a potentially
worthwhile performance optimization.

One last vertex array function you'll find in the reference section is
glInterleavedArrays. This allows you to combine several arrays into one aggregate
array. There is no change to your access or traversal of the arrays, but the organization
in memory can significantly enhance performance on some hardware implementations.

Vertex Arrays and Display Lists

Finally, we want to talk about combining our two techniques for geometry storage. It
is perfectly valid to create a vertex array inside a display list and to call the Vertex
Array evaluation functions to render your geometry. Be warned that although calls to
set the vertex array pointers are valid, the calls themselves are not stored as part of the
display list. There are reasons you would or would not want to do this.

A good reason to do this is that some implementations may do a better job of optimizing your geometry as a display list than as a vertex array. This is especially true if you
are using lit geometry (specifying normals) and are running in an environment that
has hardware-accelerated transform and lighting.

A good reason not to do this is if your geometry is not static. Perhaps you are modeling some flexible surface or a morphing solid. You can change the vertex data pointed to by your Vertex Arrays between calls that evaluate your geometry. If these calls are made inside the creation of a display list, the display list creates a "snap shot" of the vertex data at that time. The real trade-off here is a potential performance optimization against some added flexibility in handling your vertex data.

Summary

First, we used this chapter to slow down somewhat and just talk about how to build a three-dimensional object, starting with using the OpenGL primitives to create simple 3D pieces and then assembling them into a larger and more complex object. Learning the API is the easy part, but your level of experience in assembling 3D objects and scenes will be what differentiates you from your peers. Once an object or scene is broken down into small and potentially reusable components, you can save building time by using display lists. You'll find many more functions for utilizing and managing display lists in the reference section.

The last half of the chapter was concerned not with how to organize your objects, but with how to organize the geometry data used to construct these objects. By packing all the vertex data together in a single data structure (an array), you enable the OpenGL implementation to make potentially valuable performance optimizations. In addition, you can stream the data to disk and back—thus storing the geometry in a format that is literally ready to use by OpenGL. Although OpenGL does not have a "model format" as some higher level APIs do, the vertex array construct is certainly a good place to start if you want to build your own.

Reference Section

glArrayElement

Purpose	Specifies an array element used to render a vertex.
Include File	<gl.h>
Syntax	`void glArrayElement(GLint index);`
Description	This function is used with a `glBegin/glEnd` pair to specify vertex data. The indexed element from any enabled vertex arrays are passed to OpenGL as part of the primitive definition.
Parameters	
array	`GLint`: The index of the array element to use.
Returns	None.

Example   The following example shows normals and vertex data contained in arrays being used to render a series of triangles:

```
glBegin(GL_TRIANGLES);
        for(i = 0; i < uiVertCount; i++)
            glArrayElement(i);
    glEnd();
```

See Also   glDrawArrays, glDrawElements, glDrawRangeElements, glInterleavedArrays

glDrawArrays

Purpose   Creates a sequence of primitives from any enabled vertex arrays.

Include File   <gl.h>

Syntax   void glDrawArrays(GLenum *mode*, GLint *first*, GLsizei *count*);

Description   This function is used to render a series of primitives using the data in the currently enabled vertex arrays. The function takes the primitive type and processes all the vertices within the specified range.

Parameters

mode   GLenum: The kind of primitive to render. This can be any of the valid OpenGL primitive types: GL_POINTS, GL_LINES, GL_LINE_LOOP, GL_LINE_STRIP, GL_TRIANGLES, GL_TRIANGLE_STIP, GL_TRIAN-GLE_FAN, GL_QUADS, GL_QUAD_STRIP, and GL_POLYGON.

first   GLint: The first index of the enabled arrays to use.

count   GLsizei: The number of indexes to use.

Returns   None.

Example   The following example shows a simple one-line command to render a strip of triangles from the enabled vertex arrays:

```
glDrawArrays(GL_TRIANGLE_STRIP,0, uiVertCount);
```

See Also   glDrawElements, glDrawRangeElements, glInterleavedArrays

glEnableClientState/glDisableClientState

Purpose   Specifies the array type to enable or disable for use with OpenGL vertex arrays.

Include File   <gl.h>

Syntax	void glEnableClientState(GLenum *array*); void glDisableClientState(GLenum *array*);
Description	These functions tell OpenGL that you will or will not be specifying vertex arrays for geometry definitions. Each array type can be enabled or disabled individually. The use of vertex arrays does not preclude use of the normal glVertex family of functions. The specification of vertex arrays cannot be stored in a display list.
Parameters	
array	GLenum: The name of the array to enable or disable. Valid values are GL_VERTEX_ARRAY, GL_COLOR_ARRAY, GL_INDEX_ARRAY, GL_NORMAL_ARRAY, GL_TEXTURE_COORD_ARRAY, and GL_EDGE_FLAG_ARRAY.
Returns	None.
Example	The following example tells OpenGL that you will be specifying vertices, normals, and texture coordinates as vertex arrays:

```
glEnableClientState(GL_TEXTURE_COORD_ARRAY);
glEnableClientState(GL_VERTEX_ARRAY);
glEnableClientState(GL_NORMAL_ARRAY);
```

See Also	glVertexPointer, glNormalPointer, glTexCoordPointer, glColorPointer, glEdgeFlagPointer

glCallList

Purpose	Executes a display list.
Include File	<gl.h>
Syntax	void glCallList(GLuint *list*);
Description	Executes the display list identified by list. The OpenGL state machine is not restored after this function is called, so it is a good idea to call glPushMatrix beforehand and glPopMatrix afterwards. Calls to glCallList can be nested. The function glGet with the argument GL_MAX_LIST_NESTING returns the maximum number of allowable nests. For Microsoft Windows, this value is 64.
Parameters	
list	GLuint: Identifies the display list to be executed.
Returns	None.
Example	The following code saves the matrix state before calling a display list. It then restores the state afterwards. This code is from the dlbolt sample program from this chapter's subdirectory on the CD:

```
// Save the current transform state
glPushMatrix();

// Draw the bolt including nested display lists
glCallList(BOLT_HEAD);

// Restore state
glPopMatrix();
```

See Also   glCallLists, glDeleteLists, glGenLists, glNewList

glCallLists

Purpose   Executes a list of display lists.

Include File   <gl.h>

Syntax   `void glCallLists(GLsizei n, GLenum type, const GLvoid *lists);`

Description   This function calls the display lists listed in the `*lists` array sequentially. This array can be of nearly any data type. The result is converted or clamped to the nearest integer value to determine the actual index of the display list. Optionally, the list values can be off-set by a value specified by the function `glListBase`.

Parameters

n   `GLsizei`: Number of elements in the array of display lists.

type   `GLenum`: Specifies the data type of the array stored at `*lists`. This can be any one of the following values: GL_BYTE, GL_UNSIGNED_BYTE, GL_SHORT, GL_UNSIGNED_SHORT, GL_INT, GL_UNSIGNED_INT, GL_FLOAT, GL_2_BYTES, GL_3_BYTES, and GL_4_BYTES.

*lists   `GLvoid`: An array of elements of the type specified in `type`. The data type is `void` to allow any of the preceding data types to be used.

Returns   None.

Example   The following code shows how to call a list of display lists with a single call:

```
// Storage for the display list identifiers
int lists;
...
...
// Create list names
lists = glGenLists(50);

// Build some fifty display lists //////////
// First list
```

```
glNewList(lists,GL_COMPILE);
    ...
    ...
glEndList();

// Second list
glNewList(lists+1,GL_COMPILE);
    ...
    ...
glEndList();

// And so on ...
  ...
  ...

// Call all fifty lists with a single call
glCallLists(50, GL_INT, lists);
```

See Also   glCallList, glDeleteLists, glGenLists, glListBase, glNewList

glColorPointer

Purpose	Defines an array of color data for OpenGL vertex array functionality.
Include File	<gl.h>
Syntax	void glColorPointer(GLint *size*, GLenum *type*, GLsizei *stride*, const GLvoid **pointer*);
Description	This function defines the location, organization, and type of data to be used for vertex color data when OpenGL is using the vertex array functions. The buffer pointed to by this function can contain dynamic data but must remain valid data. The data is read afresh from the vertex array buffer supplied here whenever OpenGL evaluates vertex arrays.

Parameters

size	GLint: Specifies the number of components per color. Valid values are 3 and 4.
type	GLenum: Specifies the data type of the array. This can be any of the valid OpenGL data types for color component data: GL_BYTE, GL_UNSIGNED_BYTE, GL_SHORT, GL_UNSIGNED_SHORT, GL_INT, GL_UNSIGNED_INT, GL_FLOAT, and GL_DOUBLE.
stride	GLsizei: Specifies the byte offset between colors in the array. A value of 0 indicates that the data is tightly packed.
pointer	GLvoid*: A pointer that specifies the location of the beginning of the vertex array data.

Returns	None.
Example	The following example shows the vertex, color, and normal arrays being enabled, and then pointers to vertex and normal data are given to OpenGL for future use:

```
glEnableClientState(GL_NORMAL_ARRAY);
glEnableClientState(GL_VERTEX_ARRAY);
glEnableClientState(GL_COLOR_ARRAY);

glVertexPointer(3, GL_FLOAT, 0, pVertexData);
glColorPointer(3, GL_FLOAT, 0, pColorData);
glNormalPointer(GL_FLOAT, 0, pNormalData);
```

See Also	glVertexPointer, glNormalPointer, glTexCoordPointer, glEdgeFlagPointer, glInterleavedArrays

glDeleteLists

Purpose	Deletes a continuous range of display lists.
Include File	<gl.h>
Syntax	void glDeleteLists(GLuint *list*, GLsizei range);
Description	This function deletes a range of display lists. The range goes from an initial value and proceeds until the number of lists deleted as specified by range is completed. Deleting unused display lists can save considerable memory. Unused display lists in the range of those specified are ignored and do not cause an error.
Parameters	
list	GLuint: The integer name of the first display list to delete.
range	GLsizei: The number of display lists to be deleted following the initially specified list.
Returns	None.
Example	The following single line of code shows any and all display lists with identifiers between 1 and 50 being deleted:

```
glDeleteLists(1, 50);
```

See Also	glCallList, glCallLists, glGenLists, glIsList, glNewList

glDrawElements

Purpose	Renders primitives from array data, using an index into the array.
Include File	<gl.h>

Syntax	void glDrawElements(GLenum *mode*, GLsizei *count*, GLenum *type*, GLvoid *pointer);
Description	Rather than traverse the array data sequentially, this function traverses an index array sequentially. This index array typically accesses the vertex data in a nonsequential and often repetitious way, allowing for shared vertex data.
Parameters	
mode	GLenum: Specifies the primitive type to be rendered: GL_POINTS, GL_LINES, GL_LINE_LOOP, GL_LINE_STRIP, GL_TRIANGLES, GL_TRIANGLE_FAN, GL_TRIANGLE_STRIP, GL_QUAD, GL_QUAD_STRIP, or GL_POLYGON.
count	GLsizei: Specifies the byte offset between coordinates in the array. A value of 0 indicates that the data is tightly packed.
type	GLenum: Specifies the type of data used in the index array. This can be any one of GL_UNSIGNED_BYTE, GL_UNSIGNED_SHORT, or GL_UNSIGNED_INT.
pointer	GLvoid*: A pointer that specifies the location of the index array.
Returns	None.
Example	The following example shows the typical sequence to use an indexed vertex array:

```
// Enable and specify the vertex array
glEnableClientState(GL_VERTEX_ARRAY);
glVertexPointer(3, GL_FLOAT, 0, corners);

// Using DrawArrays
glDrawElements(GL_QUADS, 24, GL_UNSIGNED_BYTE, indexes);
```

See Also	glArrayElement, glDrawArrays, glDrawRangeElements

glDrawRangeElements

Purpose	Renders primitives from array data, using an index into the array and a specified range of valid index values.
Include File	<gl.h>
Syntax	void glDrawElements(GLenum *mode*, GLuint *start*, GLuint *end*, GLsizei *count*, GLenum *type*, GLvoid *pointer);
Description	Rather than traverse the array data sequentially, this function traverses an index array sequentially. This index array typically accesses the vertex data in a nonsequential and often repetitious way, allowing for shared vertex data. In addition to this shared functionality with glDrawElements, this function takes a range of valid

index values. Some OpenGL implementations can use this information to prefetch the vertex data for higher performance.

Parameters

mode   `GLenum`: Specifies the primitive type to be rendered: `GL_POINTS`, `GL_LINES`, `GL_LINE_LOOP`, `GL_LINE_STRIP`, `GL_TRIANGLES`, `GL_TRI-ANGLE_FAN`, `GL_TRIANGLE_STRIP`, `GL_QUAD`, `GL_QUAD_STRIP`, or `GL_POLYGON`.

start   `GLint`: The first index of the index range that will be used.

end   `GLint`: The last index of the index range that will be used.

count   `GLsizei`: Specifies the byte offset between coordinates in the array. A value of `0` indicates that the data is tightly packed.

type   `GLenum`: Specifies the type of data used in the index array. This can be any one of `GL_UNSIGNED_BYTE`, `GL_UNSIGNED_SHORT`, or `GL_UNSIGNED_INT`.

pointer   `GLvoid*`: A pointer that specifies the location of the index array.

Returns   None.

Example   The following example shows the typical sequence to use an indexed vertex array:

```
// Enable and specify the vertex array
glEnableClientState(GL_VERTEX_ARRAY);
glVertexPointer(3, GL_FLOAT, 0, corners);

// Using DrawArrays
glDrawElements(GL_QUADS, 24, GL_UNSIGNED_BYTE, indexes);
```

See Also   `glArrayElement`, `glDrawArrays`, `glDrawElements`

glEdgeFlagPointer

Purpose   Defines an array of edge flags for OpenGL vertex array functionality.

Include File   <gl.h>

Syntax   `void glEdgeFlagPointer(GLsizei stride, const GLvoid *pointer);`

Description This function defines the location of data to be used for the edge flag array when OpenGL is using the vertex array functions. The buffer pointed to by this function can contain dynamic data but must remain valid data. The data is read afresh from the vertex array buffer supplied here whenever OpenGL evaluates vertex arrays. Note that there is no `type` argument as in the other vertex array pointer functions. The data type for edge flags must be `GLboolean`.

Parameters

stride   `GLsizei`: Specifies the byte offset between edge flags in the array. A value of `0` indicates that the data is tightly packed.

pointer   `GLvoid*`: A pointer that specifies the location of the beginning of the vertex array data.

Returns   None.

Example   The following example shows vertex, edge, and normal arrays being enabled, and then pointers to vertex and normal data are given to OpenGL for future use.

```
glEnableClientState(GL_NORMAL_ARRAY);
glEnableClientState(GL_VERTEX_ARRAY);
glEnableClientState(GL_EDGE_FLAG_ARRAY);

glVertexPointer(3, GL_FLOAT, 0, pVertexData);
glNormalPointer(GL_FLOAT, 0, pNormalData);
glEdgeFlagPointer(0, pEdgeData);
```

See Also   `glColorPointer`, `glNormalPointer`, `glTexCoordPointer`, `glVertexPointer`

glEndList

Purpose   Delimits the end of a display list.

Include File   <gl.h>

Syntax   `void glEndList( void);`

Description   Display lists are created by first calling `glNewList`. Thereafter, all OpenGL commands are compiled and placed in the display list. The `glEndList` function terminates the creation of this display list.

Returns   None.

Example   The following sample code shows an example of a display list being delimited by `glNewList` and `glEndList`. This particular display list is composed by nesting two other display lists within it:

```
// Begin delimit of list
glNewList(BOLT_LIST,GL_COMPILE);

    // Display list calls two previously defined display lists
    glCallList(SHAFT_LIST);
    glCallList(THREAD_LIST);

// End this display list
glEndList();
```

See Also   `glCallList`, `glCallLists`, `glDeleteLists`, `glGenLists`, `glIsList`

glGenLists

Purpose	Generates a continuous range of empty display lists.
Include File	<gl.h>
Syntax	GLuint glGenLists(GLsizei *range*);
Description	This function creates a range of empty display lists. The number of lists generated depends on the value specified in **range**. The return value is then the first display list in this range of empty display lists. The purpose of this function is to reserve a range of display list values for future use.

Parameters

range	GLsizei: The number of empty display lists requested.
Returns	The first display list of the range requested. The display list values following the return value up to range −1 are created empty.
Example	The following code allocates an array of 25 integers that will be used to store 25 display lists. Each element in the array must be assigned a valid display list name that can be used later. Because display list names are always sequential, this isn't strictly necessary. Managing your lists in this manner enables you to manage them as you would manage texture objects (see Chapter 8), which are not guaranteed to be sequential.

```
int lists[25];  // Space for 25 display lists
int first;      // Index of the first display list name available
int x;          // Looping variable
 ...
 ...

// Get the first display list identifier
first = glGenLists(25);

// Loop and assign each element in the array
// with a valid display list
for(x = 0; x < 25; x++)
   lists[x] = first + x ;
```

See Also	glCallList, glCallLists, glDeleteLists, glNewList

glInterleavedArrays

Purpose	Enables and disables multiple vertex arrays simultaneously and specifies an address that points to all of the vertex data contained in one aggregate array.
Include File	<gl.h>

Syntax	`void glInterleavedArrays(GLenum format, GLsizei stride, GLvoid *pointer);`
Description	Similar to the `glXXXPointer` functions, this function enables and disables several vertex arrays simultaneously. All of the enabled arrays are interleaved together in one aggregate array. This functionality could be achieved by careful use of the `stride` parameter in the other vertex array functions, but this function saves several steps and can be highly optimized by the OpenGL implementation.
Parameters	
format	`GLenum`: Specifies the packing format of the vertex data in the interleaved array. This can be any one of the values shown in Table 9.1.
stride	`GLsizei`: Specifies the byte offset between coordinates in the array. A value of 0 indicates that the data is tightly packed.
pointer	`GLvoid*`: A pointer that specifies the location of the interleaved array.
Returns	None.
Example	The following example shows the typical use of vertex arrays to specify vertex and texture data. Then, the same task is accomplished with a single call to `glInterleavedArrays`:

```
float [] pVertexData = { ...};

    // Enable and specify the vertex array
    glEnableClientState(GL_VERTEX_ARRAY);
    glEnableClientState(GL_TEXTURE_COORD_ARRAY);
    glVertexPointer(3, GL_FLOAT, sizeof(float)*2, pVertexData);
    glTexCoordPointer(2, GL_FLOAT, sizeof(float)*3, pVertexData);

    // Using glInterleavedArrays
    glInterleavedArrays(GL_T2F_V3F, 0, pVertexData);
```

Table 9.1 *Supported Interleaved Vertex Array Formats*

Format	Details
GL_V2F	Two GL_FLOAT values for the vertex data.
GL_V3F	Three GL_FLOAT values for the vertex data.
GL_C4UB_V2F	Four GL_UNSIGNED_BYTE values for color data and two GL_FLOAT values for the vertex data.
GL_C4UB_V3F	Four GL_UNSIGNED_BYTE values for color data and three GL_FLOAT values for vertex data.

Table 9.1 *Continued*

Format	Details
GL_C3F_V3F	Three GL_FLOAT values for color data and three GL_FLOAT values for vertex data.
GL_N3F_V3F	Three GL_FLOAT values for normal data and three GL_FLOAT values for vertex data.
GL_C4F_N3F_V3F	Four GL_FLOAT values for color data, three GL_FLOAT values for normal data, and three GL_FLOAT values for vertex data.
GL_T2F_V3F	Two GL_FLOAT values for texture coordinates, three GL_FLOAT values for vertex data.
GL_T4F_V4F	Four GL_FLOAT values for texture coordinates and four GL_FLOAT values for vertex data.
GL_T2F_C4UB_V3F	Two GL_FLOAT values for texture coordinates, four GL_UNSIGNED_BYTE values for color data, and three GL_FLOAT values for vertex data.
GL_T2F_C3F_V3F	Two GL_FLOAT values for texture data, three GL_FLOAT values for color data, and three GL_FLOAT values for vertex data.
GL_T2F_N3F_V3F	Two GL_FLOAT values for texture coordinates, three GL_FLOAT values for normals, and three GL_FLOAT values for vertex data.
GL_T2F_C4F_N3F_V3F	Two GL_FLOAT values for texture coordinates, four GL_FLOAT values for color data, three GL_FLOAT values for normals, and three GL_FLOAT values for vertex data.
GL_T4F_C4F_N3F_V4F	Four GL_FLOAT values for texture coordinates, four GL_FLOAT values for colors, three GL_FLOAT values for normals, and four GL_FLOAT for vertex data.

See Also   glColorPointer, glEdgeFlagPointer, glNormalPointer, glTexCoordPointer, glVertexPointer

glIsList

Purpose	Tests for the existence of a display list.
Include File	<gl.h>
Syntax	GLboolean glIsList(GLuint *list*);
Description	This function is used to find out whether a display list exists for a given identifier. You can use this function to test display list values before using them.

Parameters

list   GLuint: The value of a potential display list. This function tests this value to see whether a display list is defined for it.

Returns   GL_TRUE if the display list exists; otherwise, GL_FALSE.

Example   The following code loops through an array that should contain valid display lists. The display list identifier is tested for validity, and if valid, it is called:

```
int lists[25];    // Array of display lists
int x;            // Looping variable
 ...
 ...

for(x = 0; x < 25; x++)
    if(glIsList(lists[x])
        glCallList(lists[x]);
```

See Also   glCallList, glCallLists, glDeleteLists, glGenLists, glNewList

glListBase

Purpose   Specifies an offset to be added to the list values specified in a call to glCallLists.

Include File   <gl.h>

Syntax   void glListBase(GLuint *base*);

Description   The function glCallLists calls a series of display lists listed in an array. This function sets an offset value that can be added to each display list name for this function. By default, this is zero. You can retrieve the current value by calling glGet(GL_LIST_BASE).

Parameters

base   GLuint: Sets an integer offset value that will be added to display list names specified in calls to glCallLists. This value is 0 by default.

Returns   None.

Example   The following code creates an array of display lists using the wglFontBitmaps function (see Chapter 17). A call to glListBase sets the offset to be the beginning of the display list names for the character set. Then, the ASCII value of each character in the string becomes an offset into this list. When glCallLists is called using a string of characters, the appropriate display list for that character is invoked. Chapter 17 provides a more complete example of wglFontBitmaps:

```
char *szMsg = "Hello from OpenGL";
int nListBase;
nListBase = glGenLists(255);
...
...
wglUseFontBitmaps(hDC, 0, 255, nListBase);
...
// Display a string onscreen
glListBase(nListBase)
glCallLists(strlen(szMsg), GL_UNSIGNED_BYTE, szMsg);
```

See Also   glCallLists

glNewList

Purpose	Begins the creation or replacement of a display list.
Include File	<gl.h>
Syntax	void glNewList(GLuint *list*, GLenum *mode*);
Description	A display list is a group of OpenGL commands that are stored for execution on command. You can use display lists to speed up drawings that are computationally intensive or that require data to be read from a disk. The glNewList function begins a display list with an identifier specified by the integer list parameter. The display list identifier is used by glCallList and glCallLists to refer to the display list. If it's not unique, a previous display list may be overwritten. You can use glGenLists to reserve a range of display list names and glIsList to test a display list identifier before using it. Display lists can be compiled only or compiled and executed. After glNewList is called, all OpenGL commands are stored in the display list in the order they were issued until glEndList is called. The following commands are executed when called and are never stored in the display list itself: glIsList, glGenLists, glDeleteLists, glFeedbackBuffer, glSelectBuffer, glRenderMode, glReadPixels, glPixelStore, glFlush, glFinish, glIsEnabled, and glGet.

Parameters

list	GLuint: The numerical name of the display list. If the display list already exists, it is replaced by the new display list.
mode	GLenum: Display lists may be compiled and executed later or compiled and executed simultaneously. Specify GL_COMPILE to only compile the display list or GL_COMPILE_AND_EXECUTE to execute the display list as it is being compiled.
Returns	None.

Example   The following is an example of a display list being delimited by
glNewList and glEndList. This particular display list is composed
by nesting two other display lists within it:

```
// Begin delimit of list
glNewList(BOLT_LIST,GL_COMPILE);

    // Display list calls two previously defined display lists
    glCallList(SHAFT_LIST);
    glCallList(THREAD_LIST);

// End this display list
glEndList();
```

See Also   glCallList, glCallLists,
                                        glDeleteLists, glGenLists, glIsList

glNormalPointer

Purpose   Defines an array of normals for OpenGL vertex array functionality.

Include File   <gl.h>

Syntax   void glNormalPointer(GLenum *type*, GLsizei *stride*, const
                    GLvoid **pointer*);

Description   This function defines the location, organization, and type of data to
                    be used for vertex normals when OpenGL is using the vertex array
                    functions. The buffer pointed to by this function can contain
                    dynamic data but must remain valid data. The data is read afresh
                    from the vertex array buffer supplied here whenever OpenGL evalu-
                    ates vertex arrays.

Parameters

type   GLenum: Specifies the data type of the array. This can be any of the
                    valid OpenGL data types for vertex normals: GL_BYTE, GL_SHORT,
                    GL_INT, GL_FLOAT, and GL_DOUBLE.

stride   GLsizei: Specifies the byte offset between normals in the array. A
                    value of 0 indicates that the data is tightly packed.

pointer   GLvoid*: A pointer that specifies the location of the beginning of the
                    vertex normal array data.

Returns   None.

Example   The following example shows both the vertex and normal arrays
                    being enabled, and then pointers to vertex and normal data are
                    given to OpenGL for future use:

```
glEnableClientState(GL_NORMAL_ARRAY);
glEnableClientState(GL_VERTEX_ARRAY);
```

```
glVertexPointer(3, GL_FLOAT, 0, pThreadTopData);
glNormalPointer(GL_FLOAT, 0, pThreadTopNormals);
```

See Also   glColorPointer, glVertexPointer, glTexCoordPointer, glEdgeFlagPointer, glInterleavedArrays

glTexCoordPointer

Purpose   Defines an array of texture coordinates for OpenGL vertex array functionality.

Include File   <gl.h>

Syntax   void glTexCoordPointer(GLint *size*, GLenum *type*, GLsizei *stride*, const GLvoid *pointer*);

Description   This function defines the location, organization, and type of data to be used for texture coordinates when OpenGL is using the vertex array functions. The buffer pointed to by this function can contain dynamic data but must remain valid data. The data is read afresh from the vertex array buffer supplied here whenever OpenGL evaluates vertex arrays.

Parameters

size   GLint: Specifies the number of coordinates per array element. Valid values are 1, 2, 3, and 4.

type   GLenum: Specifies the data type of the array. This can be any of the valid OpenGL data types for texture coordinates: GL_SHORT, GL_INT, GL_FLOAT, and GL_DOUBLE.

stride   GLsizei: Specifies the byte offset between coordinates in the array. A value of 0 indicates that the data is tightly packed.

pointer   GLvoid*: A pointer that specifies the location of the beginning of the vertex array data.

Returns   None.

Example   The following example shows both the vertex and texture arrays being enabled, and then pointers to vertex and texture data are given to OpenGL for future use:

```
glEnableClientState(GL_TEXTURE_COORD_ARRAY);
glEnableClientState(GL_VERTEX_ARRAY);

glVertexPointer(3, GL_FLOAT, 0, pVertexData);
glTexCoordPointer(2, GL_FLOAT, 0, pTextureData);
```

See Also   glColorPointer, glNormalPointer, glVertexPointer, glEdgeFlagPointer, glInterleavedArrays

glVertexPointer

Purpose	Defines an array of vertex data for OpenGL vertex array functionality.
Include File	<gl.h>
Syntax	void glVertexPointer(GLint *size*, GLenum *type*, GLsizei *stride*, const GLvoid **pointer*);
Description	This function defines the location, organization, and type of data to be used for vertex data when OpenGL is using the vertex array functions. The buffer pointed to by this function can contain dynamic data but must remain valid data. The data is read afresh from the vertex array buffer supplied here whenever OpenGL evaluates vertex arrays.

Parameters

size	GLint: Specifies the number of vertices per coordinate. Valid values are 2, 3, and 4.
type	GLenum: Specifies the data type of the array. This can be any of the valid OpenGL data types for vertex data: GL_SHORT, GL_INT, GL_FLOAT, and GL_DOUBLE.
stride	GLsizei: Specifies the byte offset between vertices in the array. A value of 0 indicates that the data is tightly packed.
pointer	GLvoid*: A pointer that specifies the location of the beginning of the vertex array data.
Returns	None.
Example	The following example shows both the vertex and normal arrays being enabled, and then pointers to vertex and normal data are given to OpenGL for future use:

```
glEnableClientState(GL_NORMAL_ARRAY);
glEnableClientState(GL_VERTEX_ARRAY);

glVertexPointer(3, GL_FLOAT, 0, pThreadTopData);
glNormalPointer(GL_FLOAT, 0, pThreadTopNormals);
```

See Also	glColorPointer, glNormalPointer, glTexCoordPointer, glEdgeFlagPointer, glInterleavedArrays

10

VISUAL EFFECTS: BLENDING AND FOG

by Michael Sweet

What you'll learn in this chapter:

How to...	Functions You'll Use
Display transparent or translucent lines and polygons	`glBlendFunc`
Add weather haze and fog effects	`glFog`

This chapter introduces the color blending and fog functions provided by OpenGL, both of which you can use to add that last bit of realism you need.

The color blending functions support effects such as transparency that can simulate windows, drinking glasses, and other transparent objects. The fog functions add a variable amount of color to the polygons you draw, producing a scene that looks "hazy" or just downright dreary!

Something to remember when using these special effects is that they don't look good on an 8-bit display. Make sure your programs contain the option of disabling these effects when running on 8-bit displays.

Blending

Blending in OpenGL provides pixel-level control of RGBA color storage in the color buffer. Blending operations cannot be used in color index mode and are disabled in color index windows.

To enable blending in RGBA windows, you must first call `glEnable(GL_BLEND)`. After this, you call `glBlendFunc` with two arguments: the source and the destination colors' blending functions (see Tables 10.1 and 10.2). By default, these arguments are GL_ONE and GL_ZERO, respectively, which is equivalent to glDisable(GL_BLEND).

The blend functions are applied to the source color set by glColor and the destination color in the color buffer. The results of the blending functions are added together to generate the new color value, which is put onscreen.

Table 10.1 *Blending Functions for Source Color*

Function	Blend Factor
GL_ZERO	Source color = 0,0,0,0.
GL_ONE	Source color is used as is.
GL_DST_COLOR	Source color is multiplied by the destination pixel color.
GL_ONE_MINUS_DST_COLOR	Source color is multiplied by (1,1,1,1 – destination color).
GL_SRC_ALPHA	Source color is multiplied by source alpha.
GL_ONE_MINUS_SRC_ALPHA	Source color is multiplied by (1 – source alpha).
GL_DST_ALPHA	Source color is multiplied by destination alpha; not supported by Microsoft OpenGL generic implementation.
GL_ONE_MINUS_DST_ALPHA	Source color is multiplied by (1 – destination alpha); not supported by Microsoft OpenGL generic implementation.
GL_SRC_ALPHA_SATURATE	Source color is multiplied by the minimum of the source and (1 – destination) alpha value; not supported by Microsoft OpenGL generic implementation.

Table 10.2 *Blending Functions for Destination Color*

Function	Blend Factor
GL_ZERO	Destination color = 0,0,0,0.
GL_ONE	Destination color is used as is.
GL_SRC_COLOR	Destination color is multiplied by the source pixel color.
GL_ONE_MINUS_SRC_COLOR	Destination color is multiplied by (1,1,1,1 – source color).
GL_SRC_ALPHA	Destination color is multiplied by source alpha.
GL_ONE_MINUS_SRC_ALPHA	Destination color is multiplied by (1 – source alpha).
GL_DST_ALPHA	Destination color is multiplied by destination alpha; not supported by Microsoft OpenGL generic implementation.

Function	Blend Factor
GL_ONE_MINUS_DST_ALPHA	Destination color is multiplied by (1 – destination alpha); not supported by Microsoft OpenGL generic implementation.
GL_SRC_ALPHA_SATURATE	Destination color is multiplied by the minimum of the source and (1 – destination alpha); not supported by Microsoft OpenGL generic implementation.

Using Blending for Transparency

Transparency is perhaps the most typical use of blending, often used for windows, bottles, water, and other 3D objects that you can see through. You can also use transparency to combine multiple images or for "soft" brushes in a paint program.

Following are the blending functions for all of these applications:

```
glEnable(GL_BLEND);
glBlendFunc(GL_SRC_ALPHA, GL_ONE_MINUS_SRC_ALPHA);
```

This combination takes the source color, scales it based on the alpha component, and then adds the destination pixel color scaled by 1 minus the alpha value. Stated more simply, this blending function takes a fraction of the current drawing color and overlays it on the pixel on the screen. The alpha component of the color can be from 0 (completely transparent) to 1 (completely opaque), as follows:

```
Rd = Rs * As + Rd * (1 - As)
Gd = Gs * As + Gd * (1 - As)
Bd = Bs * As + Bd * (1 - As)
```

Because only the source alpha component is used, you do not need a graphics board that supports alpha color planes in the color buffer. This is important because the standard Microsoft OpenGL generic (software) implementation does not support alpha color planes.

Something to remember with alpha-blended transparency is that the normal depth buffer test can interfere with the effect you're trying to achieve. To make sure that your transparent polygons and lines are drawn properly, always draw them from back to front and draw them after any solid (nontransparent) objects.

BOOK\CHAP10\BLENDPOT\blendpot.c on the CD is the code used to draw the transparent teapot in Figure 10.1. In the Redraw function, we draw the two teapots from back to front to ensure that the rear teapot shows through the front one. You'll notice that some artifacts remain visible in the front teapot where the surface polygons intersect. You can't eliminate these completely, but you can reduce them by sorting the polygons by depth first and enabling backface culling with glEnable(GL_CULL_FACE).

Figure 10.1 Transparent teapots.

The first thing `Redraw` does is set the blending function to do transparency based on the drawing (source) color's alpha component:

```
glBlendFunc(GL_SRC_ALPHA, GL_ONE_MINUS_SRC_ALPHA);
```

Next, the opaque teapot is drawn with blending disabled so that we can always see the teapot through the transparent one:

```
glDisable(GL_BLEND);
glColor3f(1.0, 1.0, 0.0);
glutSolidTeapot(1.0);
```

Finally, blending is enabled, and the transparent teapot is drawn with an alpha (transparency) value of 0.25:

```
glEnable(GL_BLEND);
glColor4f(1.0, 1.0, 1.0, 0.25);
glutSolidTeapot(1.0);
```

Using Blending with Anti-Aliasing

You can use the same blending functions to enhance the appearance of anti-aliased points, lines, and polygons. On systems with hardware-assisted anti-aliasing and blending, blending produces results similar to full-screen anti-aliased scenes made using the accumulation buffer (described in Chapter 11, "Buffers: Not Just for Animation"). At the same time, blending is several times faster than accumulation because the scene needs to be drawn only once.

To draw a scene using blending and anti-aliased primitives, call the following functions:

```
glEnable(GL_BLEND);
glBlendFunc(GL_SRC_ALPHA, GL_ONE_MINUS_SRC_ALPHA);
glEnable(GL_LINE_SMOOTH);
glEnable(GL_POINT_SMOOTH);
glEnable(GL_POLYGON_SMOOTH);
```

Note, however, that this type of blending works well only if you have 24 bits or more of color precision. Lesser color depths produce visible artifacts at the seams of polygons.

Using Blending for a Paint Program

The same techniques used for 3D graphics can be applied to 2D graphics. In the case of paint programs, we can use blending to create soft-edged "brushes." To start, we define *luminance-alpha* images of each brush. A *luminance-alpha image* contains luminance (grayscale) and alpha values. The alpha portion of the image defines how much color actually is drawn on the page (see Figure 10.2).

Figure 10.2   Painting using luminance-alpha images.

To "paint" using this brush image, we use the same blending functions as before:

```
glBlendFunc(GL_SRC_ALPHA, GL_ONE_MINUS_SRC_ALPHA);
```

To get different colors, we use the `glPixelTransfer` function to set the `GL_RED_SCALE`, `GL_GREEN_SCALE`, and `GL_BLUE_SCALE` values:

```
glPixelTransferf(GL_RED_SCALE, red);
glPixelTransferf(GL_GREEN_ SCALE, green);
glPixelTransferf(GL_BLUE_ SCALE, blue);
```

BOOK\CHAP10\PAINT\paint.c is a simple paint program that uses a 7×7 pixelbrush image for painting. The Motion callback handles drawing in the window. When you hold down the left mouse button, the callback paints at the current mouse position using `glDrawPixels`:

```
glRasterPos2i(x, y);
glBitmap(0, 0, 0, 0, -3, -3, NULL);
glDrawPixels(7, 7, GL_LUMINANCE_ALPHA, GL_UNSIGNED_BYTE, Brush[0]);
```

Revisiting the Terrain Viewing Program

The terrain viewing program in Chapter 8, "Texture Mapping," shows a barren landscape. To add some water to the scene, we can draw a flat plane at altitude 0 after the terrain is drawn, effectively "flooding" the landscape with water.

To keep things simple, we use the same texture image as the landscape, but when we draw the water in the Redraw function, we'll use a partially transparent blue color and blending:

```
glBlendFunc(GL_SRC_ALPHA, GL_ONE_MINUS_SRC_ALPHA);
glEnable(GL_BLEND);

glColor4f(0.0, 0.0, 0.25, 0.75);
for (i = 0; i < (TERRAIN_COUNT - 1); i ++)
    {
    glBegin(GL_TRIANGLE_STRIP);
    glNormal3f(0.0, 1.0, 0.0);
    for (j = 0; j < TERRAIN_COUNT; j ++)
        {
        glTexCoord2i(i, j);
        glVertex3f(i * TERRAIN_SPACING - 0.5 * TERRAIN_SIZE, 0.0,
                   0.5 * TERRAIN_SIZE - j * TERRAIN_SPACING);

        glTexCoord2i(i + 1, j);
        glVertex3f((i + 1) * TERRAIN_SPACING - 0.5 * TERRAIN_SIZE, 0.0,
                   0.5 * TERRAIN_SIZE - j * TERRAIN_SPACING);
        }
    glEnd();
    }
```

The final program appears in BOOK\CHAP10\TERRAIN6\terrain6.c on the CD and in Figure 10.3.

Figure 10.3 Terrain program with water.

Fog

OpenGL provides depth *cueing* (shading based upon distance) and atmospheric effects through the `glFog` function. Essentially, fog provides a way of adding (mixing) a pre-defined color with each vertex or texture image based upon the distance from the user. Fog is often used in flight simulators and animation packages to provide the final real-world look to computer graphics.

OpenGL supports three kinds of fog: `GL_LINEAR` for depth cueing, `GL_EXP` for heavy fog or clouds, and `GL_EXP2` for smoke and weather haze. Figure 10.4 shows `GL_LINEAR` fog; later, in Figure 10.6, you can see the effect of `GL_EXP` fog.

You choose the type of fog (or fog mode) using `glFogi`:

```
glFogi(GL_FOG_MODE, GL_LINEAR);

glFogi(GL_FOG_MODE, GL_EXP);

glFogi(GL_FOG_MODE, GL_EXP2);
```

Once you have chosen the fog type, you must choose a fog color that will be mixed with your scene using the `glFogfv` or `glFogiv` functions:

```
GLfloat fog_color[4] = { r, g, b, a };
glFogfv(GL_FOG_COLOR, fog_color);

GLint fog_color[4] = { r, g, b, a };
glFogiv(GL_FOG_COLOR, fog_color);
```

For depth cueing, you generally want to make the fog color the same as the background (black in Figure 10.4). This choice makes the depth cueing look "correct" to the eye; that is, objects farther away appear to fade into the background. For some applications, you might want to give the fog a bright color such as yellow, instead, so that objects stand out more against the background.

Drawing Depth-Cued Teapots

BOOK\CHAP10\DEPTHPOT\depthpot.c draws two teapots using depth cueing. The Redraw function handles all graphics drawing and starts by setting the fog color to black and the fog mode to GL_LINEAR:

```
static float    fog_color[4] = { 0.0, 0.0, 0.0, 0.0 };

glEnable(GL_FOG);
glFogf(GL_FOG_MODE, GL_LINEAR);
glFogfv(GL_FOG_COLOR, fog_color);
glFogf(GL_FOG_START, 10.0);
glFogf(GL_FOG_END, 20.0);
```

The GL_FOG_START and GL_FOG_END parameters specify the start and end distances in world coordinates for the fog. Objects closer than the GL_FOG_START distance are rendered without fog effects. Objects farther than the GL_FOG_END distance are rendered with maximum fog effects.

Finally, it draws both teapots at different distances from the viewer. The results are visibly obvious.

Figure 10.4   Teapots drawn using GL_LINEAR fog.

Other Types of Fog

For the other fog types, you'll probably make the fog color white or some other light color. In addition to the fog color, GL_EXP and GL_EXP2 fog types have an additional density parameter:

```
glFogf(GL_FOG_DENSITY, density);
```

The *density* parameter can be any number greater than 0.0, but typically you keep it less than 0.1. Figure 10.5 shows how the density of fog affects how much of the fog color is used.

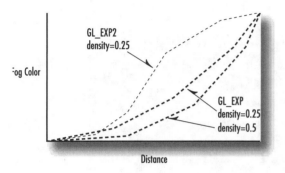

Figure 10.5 Fog color intensity versus distance.

Fog Distance

The fog distance is the transformed z component of all glVertex calls. This z coordinate lies in the range 0.0 to 1.0 and is the same number that is stored in the depth buffer. The fog distance and density determine how much fog color is mixed in.

By default, fog is applied at all depths from 0.0 to 1.0. The GL_FOG_START and GL_FOG_END parameters restrict the range of depth values used for fog calculations. This range is typically used to more accurately model fog density when the immediate area in front of the viewer is not covered (for example, when flying through clouds, the breaks between clouds are not as dense) or for prematurely "fogging out" the scene before the far plane is reached.

Back to the Terrain Viewing Program

Weather haze effects are the perfect addition to the terrain viewing program of Chapter 8. In Figure 10.6, you can see the fantastic improvement in image quality, which was achieved by adding the following three lines of code to the Redraw function:

```
GLfloat fogcolor[4] = { 1.0, 1.0, 1.0, 1.0 };

glFogf(GL_FOG_DENSITY, 0.0025);
```

```
glFogi(GL_FOG_MODE, GL_EXP);
glFogfv(GL_FOG_COLOR, fogcolor);
```

The fog color in this case was defined as a solid white RGBA color (1.0,1.0,1.0,1.0). To improve the output even more at the expense of speed, we can also call

```
glHint(GL_FOG_HINT, GL_NICEST);
```

This forces fog to be evaluated at every pixel rather than every vertex. For most scenes, this means OpenGL must perform 100 times as many calculations, so make sure you have hardware acceleration!

BOOK\CHAP10\TERRAIN7\terrain7.c contains the updated terrain viewer using fog.

Figure 10.6   Terrain viewing program with GL_EXP.

Summary

Blending and fog complete the OpenGL library and are yet another source for making the images you generate more realistic. Blending provides transparency effects and improves anti-aliasing of points, lines, and polygons. Fog supports a variety of depth cueing and weather effects that make images look less exact and, ironically, more like the real world.

Reference Section

glBlendFunc

Purpose	Sets color blending functions.
Include File	<GL/gl.h>
Syntax	void glBlendFunc(GLenum *sfactor*, GLenum *dfactor*);
Description	This function sets the source and destination blending factors for color blending. You must call glEnable(GL_BLEND) to enable color blending. Blending is available only in RGBA drawing contexts. The default settings for blending are glBlendFunc(GL_ONE, GL_ZERO).
Parameters	
sfactor	GLenum: The source color's blending function.
dfactor	GLenum: The destination pixelcolor's blending function.
Returns	None.
Example	See the examples in BOOK\CHAP07\GALAXY\galaxy.c, BOOK\CHAP10\BLENDPOT\blendpot.c, BOOK\CHAP10\PAINT\paint.c, and BOOK\CHAP10\TERRAIN6\terrain6.c on the CD.

glFog

Purpose	Specifies fog parameters.
Include File	<GL/gl.h>
Syntax	void glFogf(GLenum *pname*, GLfloat *param*);
	void glFogfv(GLenum *pname*, GLfloat **params*);
	void glFogi(GLenum *pname*, GLint *param*);
	void glFogiv(GLenum *pname*, GLint **params*);
Description	The glFog functions set fog parameters. To draw using fog, you must call glEnable(GL_FOG).
Parameters	
pname	GLenum: The parameter to set. Valid names are as follows:

GL_FOG_COLOR	The color of the fog; must be an array of four numbers representing the RGBA color.
GL_FOG_DENSITY	The fog density; a number greater than 0.0. The density is used only for the GL_EXP and GL_EXP2 fog modes.
GL_FOG_END	The farthest distance to which the fog is applied. This is an untransformed z (depth) value.

	GL_FOG_INDEX	The color index to use for fog if the OpenGL drawing context is in color index mode.
	GL_FOG_MODE	The fog type; specifies the formula used to render fog effects (GL_LINEAR, GL_EXP, or GL_EXP2).
	GL_FOG_START	The closest distance to which fog is applied. This is an untransformed z (depth) value.
param	GLfloat, GLint: The parameter value.	
params	GLfloat *, GLint *: A pointer to the parameter array.	
Returns	None.	
Example	See the examples in BOOK\CHAP10\TERRAIN7\terrain7.c and BOOK\CHAP10\DEPTHPOT\depthpot.c on the CD.	

11

BUFFERS: NOT JUST FOR ANIMATION

by Michael Sweet

What you'll learn in this chapter:

How to...	Functions You'll Use

Set up buffers	`ChoosePixelFormat/DescribePixelFormat/GetDC/`
	`SetPixelFormat/glutInitDisplayMode/`
	`wglCreateContext/wglMakeCurrent`

Use the depth buffer	`glEnable/glDepthFunc/glDepthRange`
Use the stencil buffer	`glEnable/glStencilFunc`
Use the accumulation buffer	`glEnable/glAccum`

In the previous chapters, we've used buffers for color and depth information. OpenGL provides several kinds of buffers that are linked by the OpenGL graphics context:

- Color buffer
- Depth buffer
- Stencil buffer
- Accumulation buffer

Each buffer has specific capabilities beyond simple double buffering for animation and depth buffering for hidden surface removal.

What Are Buffers?

A buffer in OpenGL is essentially a two-dimensional array of values that correspond to pixels in a window or offscreen image. Each buffer has the same number of columns and rows (width and height) as the current client area of a window but holds a different range and type of values. See Figure 11.1.

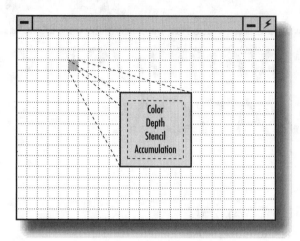

Figure 11.1   OpenGL buffer organization.

Buffers in the WIN32 Environment

Up to now, we've been using the GLUT functions to select the buffers to use in our programs. These GLUT functions simplify the selection process, but with most WIN32 toolkits, you need to set things up "by hand."

The WIN32 API defines several constructs for OpenGL:

- Pixel format
- Device context
- Rendering context

Pixel Formats

Pixel formats describe the number and type of buffers available in your window. Pixel formats are numbered starting at 1 and are described with the PIXELFORMATDESCRIPTOR structure in Table 11.1.

Table 11.1 PIXELFORMATDESCRIPTOR *Structure Members*

Member	Description
nSize	The size of the structure.
nVersion	The version of the structure; it must be 1.
dwFlags	Pixel format option flags (see Table 11.2).
iPixelType	PFD_RGBA (for RGB windows) or PFD_INDEX (for color index windows).
cColorBits	The number of color index bits available/needed.
cRedBits	The number of red color bits available/needed.
cRedShift	The number of bits to shift for red values; used with color palettes.
cGreenBits	The number of green color bits available/needed.
cGreenShift	The number of bits to shift for green values; used with color palettes.
cBlueBits	The number of blue color bits available/needed.
cBlueShift	The number of bits to shift for blue values; used with color palettes.
cAlphaBits	The number of alpha color bits available/needed; this is always 0 for the generic (software) OpenGL implementation.
cAlphaShift	The number of bits to shift for alpha values; this is always 0 for the generic (software) OpenGL implementation.
cAccumBits	The number of color index bits available/needed for accumulation.
cAccumRedBits	The number of red color bits available/needed for accumulation.
cAccumGreenBits	The number of green color bits available/needed for accumulation.
cAccumBlueBits	The number of blue color bits available/needed for accumulation.
cAccumAlphaBits	The number of alpha color bits available/needed for accumulation.
cDepthBits	The number of depth buffer bits available/needed.
cStencilBits	The number of stencil buffer bits available/needed.
cAuxBuffers	The number of auxiliary buffer bits available/needed; this is always 0 for the generic (software) OpenGL implementation.
iLayerType	This member is no longer used or supported by the WIN32 API.
bReserved	This member is reserved for future use.
dwLayerMask	This member is no longer used or supported by the WIN32 API.
dwVisibleMask	Specifies the RGBA or indexed color that is transparent; this value is used for overlay pixel formats.
dwDamageMask	This member is no longer used or supported by the WIN32 API.

The dwFlags member defines what capabilities are needed and consists of the bitwise OR of the constants in Table 11.2.

Table 11.2 dwFlags *Constants*

Constant	Description
PFD_DRAW_TO_WINDOW	This pixel format will be used or is used to draw to a window.
PFD_DRAW_TO_BITMAP	This pixel format will be used or is used to draw to an offscreen buffer.
PFD_SUPPORT_GDI	This pixel format needs to support or supports GDI drawing functions.
PFD_SUPPORT_OPENGL	This pixel format needs to support or supports OpenGL drawing functions.
PFD_GENERIC_ACCELERATED	This pixel format is hardware accelerated; if PFD_GENERIC_FORMAT is also set, the OpenGL driver uses the Microsoft generic implementation and accelerates some specific drawing operations.
PFD_GENERIC_FORMAT	This pixel format uses the Microsoft generic (software) implementation of OpenGL.
PFD_NEED_PALETTE	This pixel format requires a logical color palette to produce the correct colors.
PFD_NEED_SYSTEM_PALETTE	The graphics hardware only supports a fixed 256-color display palette (typically 3 bits of red and green and 2 bits of blue); you must use SetSystemPaletteUse to use the hardware palette.
PFD_DOUBLEBUFFER	This pixel format needs/has double-buffering capabilities.
PFD_STEREO	This pixel format needs/has stereo display capabilities.
PFD_SWAP_LAYER_BUFFERS	This pixel format can swap individual layers.
PFD_DEPTH_DONTCARE	When choosing a pixel format, it doesn't matter whether a depth buffer is available.
PFD_DOUBLEBUFFER_DONTCARE	When choosing a pixel format, it doesn't matter whether double buffering is available.
PFD_STEREO_DONTCARE	When choosing a pixel format, it doesn't matter whether stereo display capabilities are available.
PFD_SWAP_COPY	Specifies that the back buffer is copied to the front buffer when swapping.
PFD_SWAP_EXCHANGE	Specifies that the back buffer and front buffer are exchanged when swapping.

Device Contexts

Device contexts are integers of type HDC that associate drawing attributes with a specific display or printer device and pixel format. Most OpenGL programs use a single device context that is associated with the pixel format and rendering context.

Rendering Contexts

Rendering contexts are integersof type `HGLRC` that associate OpenGL state information, display lists, and texture objects with a device context and pixel format. Only one rendering context can be active in each thread of your program at any given time.

Configuring Buffers Using WIN32 Functions

Setting up OpenGL buffers using the WIN32 API requires the following tasks:

1. Get a device context.
2. Set the pixel format.
3. Create a color palette as needed.
4. Create a rendering context.

Getting a Device Context

The `GetDC` function returns a device context for the specified window:

```
HDC   dc;
HWND window;

dc = GetDC(window);
```

The *window* parameter can be any valid window.

Setting the Pixel Format

Before you set the pixel format with the `SetPixelFormat` function, you need to select a pixel format for the window. The WIN32 API provides two functions to do this. The first is `ChoosePixelFormat`, which accepts a `PIXELFORMATDESCRIPTOR` structure that describes the minimum buffer requirements:

```
int                    format;
PIXELFORMATDESCRIPTOR pfd;

memset(&pfd, 0, sizeof(pfd));
pfd.nSize       = sizeof(pfd);
pfd.nVersion    = 1;
pfd.dwFlags     = PFD_DRAW_TO_WINDOW | PFD_SUPPORT_OPENGL;
pfd.iPixelType  = PFD_TYPE_RGBA;
pfd.cDepthBits  = 16;

format = ChoosePixelFormat(dc, &pfd);
DescribePixelFormat(dc, format, sizeof(pfd), &pfd);
SetPixelFormat(dc, format, &pfd);
```

This code chooses an RGB pixel format that has a depth buffer of at least 16 bits. However, if a graphics card supports both accelerated and nonaccelerated OpenGL pixel formats, you can get the nonaccelerated pixel format.

To choose an accelerated pixel format, you need to instead use the `DescribePixelFormat` function to get a list of available formats and pick one yourself:

```
int                     max_format;
int                     format;
HDC                     dc;
PIXELFORMATDESCRIPTOR   pfd;

for (i = 1, max_formats = 1; i <= max_formats; i ++)
    {
    max_formats = DescribePixelFormat(dc, format, sizeof(pfd), &pfd);
    if ((pfd.dwFlags & PFD_GENERIC_FORMAT) == 0 && /* Accelerated OpenGL */
        pfd.iPixelType == PFD_TYPE_RGBA &&         /* RGB color */
        pfd.cDepthBits >= 16)          /* Depth buffer at least 16 bits deep */
        break;
    }

SetPixelFormat(dc, format, &pfd);
```

Ideally, you also look for the best pixel format as well, with the most acceleration or depth bits (or whatever you need most). This and other WIN32-specific issues are covered in detail in Chapter 17, "The OpenGL Pixelformat and Rendering Context."

Creating a Color Palette as Needed

Some pixel formats might require a color palette to operate properly. We can check for this by looking at the `dwFlags` member of the `PIXELFORMATDESCRIPTOR` structure:

```
if (pfd.dwFlags & PFD_NEED_PALETTE)
    {
    /* Need to create a color palette */
    }
```

The palette requirements are described in the `PIXELFORMATDESCRIPTOR` structure in the `cRedBits`, `cRedShift`, `cGreenBits`, `cGreenShift`, `cBlueBits`, and `cBlueShift` members. Once we have the pixel format information, we have to create a 256-color palette (see Listing 11.1).

Listing 11.1 *Creating a 256-Color Palette*

```
HDC                     hdc;
PIXELFORMATDESCRIPTOR   pfd;
HPALETTE                palette;
LOGPALETTE              *pal;
int                     ind,
                        num_colors,
                        red, num_reds,
                        blue, num_blues,
                        green, num_greens;
```

```
/* First allocate logical color palette entries... */
num_colors = 1 << pfd.cColorBits;
pal        = (PLOGPALETTE)LocalAlloc(LMEM_FIXED, sizeof(LOGPALETTE) +

pal->palVersion    = 0x300;
pal->palNumEntries = num_colors;

num_reds   = (1 << pfd.cRedBits) - 1;
num_greens = (1 << pfd.cGreenBits) - 1;
num_blues  = (1 << pfd.cBlueBits) - 1;

for (blue = 0; blue <= num_blues; blue ++)
    for (green = 0; green <= num_greens; green ++)
        for (red = 0; red <= num_reds; red ++)
        {
        ind = (red << pfd.cRedShift) |
              (green << pfd.cGreenShift) |
              (blue << pfd.cBlueShift);

        pal->palPalEntry[ind].peRed   = 255 * red / num_reds;
        pal->palPalEntry[ind].peGreen = 255 * green / num_greens;
        pal->palPalEntry[ind].peBlue  = 255 * blue / num_blues;
        pal->palPalEntry[ind].peFlags = 0;
        }

palette = CreatePalette(pal);
SelectPalette(hdc, palette, FALSE);
RealizePalette(hdc);

LocalFree(pal);
```

The loop uses the cRedShift, cGreenShift, and cBlueShift members to correctly align the red, green, and blue indices for the color palette. The result is a 256-color palette of evenly spaced red, green, and blue values.

Creating a Rendering Context

Once we have selected a pixel format and retrieved a device context, we can create the rendering context using the wglCreateContext function:

```
HDC   dc;
HGLRC rc;

rc = wglCreateContext(dc);
```

Finally, to use the rendering context and draw using OpenGL functions, we use the wglMakeCurrent function:

```
HDC dc;
HGLRC rc;
```

```
wglMakeCurrent(dc, rc);
```

A sample program that uses the WIN32 API to draw two cylinders appears in BOOK\CHAP11\WIN32\win32.c.

Configuring Buffers Using GLUT Functions

GLUT provides a single function to select the buffers you need:

```
void glutInitDisplayMode(int modes);
```

The *modes* argument can be the bitwise OR of any of the constants in Table 11.3.

Table 11.3   `glutInitDisplayMode` *Constants*

Constant	Description
GLUT_RGB, GLUT_RGBA	Select an RGB pixel format
GLUT_INDEX	Select a color index pixel format
GLUT_SINGLE	Select a single-buffered pixel format
GLUT_DOUBLE	Select a double-buffered pixel format
GLUT_ACCUM	Need an accumulation buffer
GLUT_ALPHA	Need an alpha buffer
GLUT_DEPTH	Need a depth buffer
GLUT_STENCIL	Need a stencil buffer
GLUT_MULTISAMPLE	Need a multisample buffer
GLUT_STEREO	Select a stereo pixel format
GLUT_LUMINANCE	Select a luminance (grayscale) pixel format

All of these constants correspond directly to fields in the WIN32 PIXELFORMATDESCRIPTOR structure described in the previous section. GLUT automatically selects the best pixel format available that meets the mode requirements you specify and chooses an accelerated pixel format over a nonaccelerated format.

Obviously, the GLUT method of setting up OpenGL buffers is much easier than using the WIN32 API.

Picking Only the Buffers You Need

Most systems have a limited amount of memory to hold buffers for OpenGL. Under Windows, if you pick a combination of buffers that cannot be supported by the graphics card, the Microsoft generic (software) OpenGL implementation takes over, eliminating hardware acceleration. To help prevent this from happening, you should only select the buffers that you actually need. The WIN32 functions also allow you to pick and choose combinations of buffers and features that are accelerated. See Chapter 17 for examples of this.

The Color Buffer

The color buffer holds pixel color information. Each pixel can contain a color index or red/green/blue/alpha (RGBA) values that describe the appearance of that pixel. RGBA pixels are displayed directly using the closest available colors onscreen. The generic OpenGL implementation from Microsoft does not support alpha color values at this time.

The appearance of color index pixels is determined by looking up the index in an RGB color table. Under Windows, these color tables are implemented using a logical color palette. Color index mode is useful for displaying tabular data graphically (for example, stress or force meters), as shown in the second depth buffer example in "Another Application of the Depth Buffer."

Double Buffering

Double buffering provides an additional offscreen color buffer that is often used for animation. With double buffering, you can draw a scene offscreen and quickly "swap" it onto the screen, eliminating the annoying flicker that would otherwise be present.

Double buffering affects only the color buffer and does not provide a second depth, accumulation, or stencil buffer. If you choose a pixel format with double buffering, OpenGL selects the "back" buffer for drawing. You can change this using the `glDrawBuffer` function to specify one of the values in Table 11.4.

Table 11.4   `glDrawBuffer` *Values*

Buffer	Description
GL_FRONT	Draw only to the front (visible) color buffer.
GL_BACK	Draw only to the back (hidden) color buffer.
GL_FRONT_AND_BACK	Draw to both the front and back color buffers.

Stereo Buffering

Stereo buffering provides an additional color buffer in single-buffered mode and two additional color buffers in double-buffered mode to generate a left- and right-eye screen image. (See Table 11.5.) You can generate true three-dimensional images by choosing the correct viewing positions for each eye, usually offset by a few "inches" to simulate the distance between our eyes. Stereo buffering is not available on most PC graphics cards.

In addition to specifying the front or back buffer for drawing, the `glDrawBuffer` function can select the left- or right-eye buffers.

Table 11.5   *Stereo Buffer Values*

Buffer	Description
GL_LEFT_FRONT	Draw only to the left-front buffer.
GL_LEFT_BACK	Draw only to the left-back buffer.
GL_RIGHT_FRONT	Draw only to the right-front buffer.
GL_RIGHT_BACK	Draw only to the right-back buffer.
GL_FRONT	Draw to both the left- and right-front buffers.
GL_BACK	Draw to both the left- and right-back buffers.
GL_FRONT_AND_BACK	Draw to both the front and back color buffers.

Swapping Buffers

OpenGL does support double buffering, but there is no OpenGL function to actually swap the front and back buffers. Fortunately, every windowing system with OpenGL support has a function call to accomplish this. Under Windows, this call is `SwapBuffers`:

```
HDC dc;

SwapBuffers(dc);
```

The *dc* argument is the device context for the window in which you are drawing. If you have chosen a stereo-buffered pixel format, both the left and right eyes are swapped by the one call.

GLUT provides a window-system independent function of its own that does the same thing:

```
glutSwapBuffers();
```

The Depth Buffer

The depth buffer holds distance values for each pixel. Each value represents the pixel's distance from the viewer and is scaled to fill the current near/far clipping volume. The software implementation of OpenGL under Windows supports both 16- and 32-bit depth values.

You usually use the depth buffer to perform hidden surface removal. Hidden surface removal is a process that occurs naturally in the real world; when one solid (opaque) object is placed in front of another, the nearer object hides some or all of the one behind it.

In OpenGL, you can also use the depth buffer for some interesting effects, such as cutting away the front of objects to show the inner surfaces (see Figures 11.2 and 11.3.)

Enabling Depth Comparisons

Like most features in OpenGL, you must first enable depth testing using `glEnable` to do any hidden surface removal or other applications of the depth buffer:

```
glEnable(GL_DEPTH_TEST);
```

Similarly, don't forget to disable depth testing once you have finished drawing the parts of the scene that need it using `glDisable`:

```
glDisable(GL_DEPTH_TEST);
```

Depth Comparisons

When you draw in a window using OpenGL, the z position of each pixel is compared with the value in the depth buffer. If the result of the comparison is `True`, the pixel is stored in the color buffer along with its depth. OpenGL defines eight depth-compa-rison functions that you can use for depth buffering (see Table 11.6).

The default comparison function is `GL_LESS`. To change it, call `glDepthFunc`:

```
GLenum function;
```

```
glDepthFunc(function);
```

Using the `GL_LESS` function, pixels in a polygon are drawn if the depth value of the pixel is less than the depth value in the depth buffer.

Table 11.6 *Depth Comparison Functions*

Name	Function
GL_NEVER	Always false.
GL_LESS	True if source z is less than depth z.
GL_EQUAL	True if source z is equal to depth z.
GL_LEQUAL	True if source z is less than or equal to depth z.
GL_GREATER	True if source z is greater than depth z.
GL_NOTEQUAL	True if source z not equal to depth z.
GL_GEQUAL	True if source z is greater than or equal to depth z.
GL_ALWAYS	Always true.

Figures 11.2 and 11.3 show the difference between the `GL_LESS` and `GL_GREATER` functions.

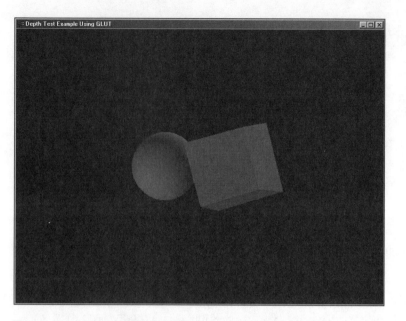

Figure 11.2   Typical depth buffering with GL_LESS.

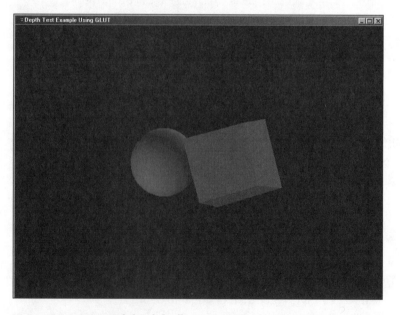

Figure 11.3   Typical depth buffering with GL_GREATER.

Depth Values

Depth values are the projected Z coordinates that go from 0.0 at the front of the viewing frustum to 1.0 at the back. When you use the GL_EQUAL and GL_NOTEQUAL depth comparisons, it is sometimes necessary to alter the range of depth values to reduce the number of available values (keeping the number of values to a minimum).
Use glDepthRange, as follows:

```
GLfloat near, far;

glDepthRange(near, far);
```

The *near* and *far* parameters are floating-point numbers between 0.0 and 1.0, inclusive. The defaults are 0.0 for *near* and 1.0 for *far*. Normally, *near* is less than *far*, but you can also reverse the order to achieve special effects or use the GL_GREATER and GL_GEQUAL functions. Reducing the range of values stored in the depth buffer does not affect clipping, but it does affect the depth buffer accuracy and can lead to errors in hidden surface removal in the display because objects closer than the *near* value or further than the *far* value are clamped. The effect would be like flattening the front or back of an object, but not quite as pretty.

Some depth comparisons need a different initial depth value. By default, the depth buffer is cleared to 1.0 with the glClear function. To specify a different value, use the glClearDepth function:

```
GLfloat depth;

glClearDepth(depth);
```

The *depth* parameter is a floating-point number between 0.0 and 1.0, inclusive, unless you have defined a smaller range with glDepthRange. In general, use a value of 0.0 for GL_GREATER and GL_GEQUAL comparisons and 1.0 for GL_LESS and GL_LEQUAL comparisons.

Applications of the Depth Buffer

The usual application of the depth buffer is to remove hidden surfaces. As noted earlier, you can also use the depth buffer to cut away the front parts of a scene. The WIN32 and GLUT examples (BOOK\CHAP11\WIN32\win32.c and BOOK\CHAP11\GLUT\glut.c) demonstrate this type of application. The key to this program is the use of glDepthFunc and glClearDepth:

```
glDepthFunc(depth_function);
```

Here, we use a global variable to hold the current depth function.
The depth_function variable is initialized to GL_LESS when the program starts. When the user presses the D key, the toggle_depth callback function switches this between GL_GREATER and GL_LESS:

```
if (depth_function == GL_LESS)
    glClearDepth(1.0);
else
    glClearDepth(0.0);
```

The `glClearDepth` call is needed to provide the correct initial depth value for the window because the depth value is 1.0 by default. Nothing is drawn when the depth function is set to `GL_GREATER` because no pixel could possibly have a depth value greater than 1.0.

Another Application of the Depth Buffer

You can also use the depth buffer to generate a contour mapping of a scene, which shows different colors for each depth. You can generate contour maps using the `glReadPixels` function and by specifying the depth component as the value of interest, as follows:

```
glReadPixels(x, y, width, height, GL_DEPTH_COMPONENT, type, pixels);
```

The returned depth values can then be scaled and assigned to color values that can be displayed as a contour image, especially in color index mode, like this:

```
#define WIDTH 320
#define HEIGHT 200
GLfloat pixels[WIDTH * HEIGHT];
int     i;

/* Draw the scene... */
glEnable(GL_DEPTH_TEST);
...
/* Grab the depth buffer */
glReadPixels(0, 0, WIDTH, HEIGHT, GL_DEPTH_COMPONENT, GL_FLOAT, pixels);
/* Convert depth values to color indices */
for (i = 0; i < (WIDTH * HEIGHT); i ++)
  pixels[i] = pixels[i] * 255.0; /* Assume 256 color palette */
/* Display the new pixels on the screen */
glDisable(GL_DEPTH_TEST);
glDrawPixels(0, 0, WIDTH, HEIGHT, GL_COLOR_INDEX, GL_FLOAT, pixels);
```

In a real application, you probably want to provide some user control over the color palette and range of values. You can also use RGBA color values to enhance a scene, using `glBlendFunc` to mix the "normal" image with the "depth" image. Finally, using the `glPixelMap` and `glPixelStore` functions, you can display a contour image in an RGB window. (See Chapter 7, "Raster Graphics in OpenGL," for details.)

Cutting Away Parts of a Scene

Let's see how to cut away parts of a scene—an engine block, for instance—to show some internal operation that is not normally visible. BOOK\CHAP11\CUTAWAY\ cutaway.c is an example of using the depth buffer for this purpose (see Figure 11.4).

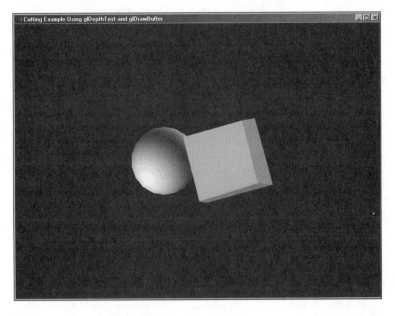

Figure 11.4 Depth buffer cutout window.

The heart of this program is the Redraw function, which draws a picture of a cube and sphere being cut by a moving plane. To cut away parts of the scene, we first draw the cutting plane. Instead of drawing to the color buffer, we begin by disabling drawing to the color buffer with glDrawBuffer:

```
glDrawBuffer(GL_NONE);
```

Then, we draw the cutting plane in the window to initialize the depth buffer to the cutting plane depth:

```
GLfloat cutting_plane;

glBegin(GL_POLYGON);
glVertex3f(-100.0, 100.0, cutting_plane);
glVertex3f(100.0, 100.0, cutting_plane);
glVertex3f(100.0, -100.0, cutting_plane);
glVertex3f(-100.0, -100.0, cutting_plane);
glEnd();
```

You can also use the `glClearDepth` function if you know the normalized depth value (the z value scaled to the 0.0 to 1.0 range). Once the cutting plane is drawn, we re-enable color buffer drawing with

```
glDrawBuffer(GL_BACK);
```

and proceed with drawing the cube and sphere. The invisible plane we drew restricts what is drawn onscreen to polygons that lie behind it, effectively cutting away parts of the scene.

The Stencil Buffer

The stencil buffer provides many options to restrict drawing on the screen and has many applications that the depth buffer just can't do. At its simplest level, the stencil buffer can block out certain areas on the screen. For example, a flight simulation program might use the stencil buffer to restrict drawing operations to the inside of the aircraft's round controls such as the artificial horizon and airspeed indicators.

Perhaps the most exciting application of the stencil buffer is for shadows. Depending on your graphics hardware, you can generate hard and soft shadows from multiple light sources, making your scenes more realistic and exciting (see the references in Appendix B, "Further Reading").

Using the Stencil Buffer

To use the stencil buffer, you have to first request one. For Windows, this means setting the `cStencilBits` field in the Pixel Format Descriptor (PFD) for your window, as in

```
pfd.cStencilBits = 1;
```

For GLUT, you just need to add the **GLUT_STENCIL** constant to the `glutInitDisplayMode` call:

```
glutInitDisplayMode(GLUT_RGB ¦ GLUT_DEPTH ¦ GLUT_STENCIL);
```

Once you have requested a stencil buffer, you must enable stenciling by calling `glEnable(GL_STENCIL_TEST)`. Without this call, all stencil buffer operations are disabled.

Stencil Buffer Functions

There are four stenciling functions in OpenGL:

```
void glClearStencil(GLint s)
void glStencilFunc(GLenum func, GLint ref, GLuint mask)
void glStencilMask(GLuint mask)
void glStencilOp(GLenum fail, GLenum zfail, GLzpass)
```

The `glClearStencil` function is similar to `glClearColor`, `glClearDepth`, and `glClearIndex`; it provides the initial value that is stored in the stencil buffer when `glClear(GL_STENCIL_BIT)` is called. By default, a 0 stencil value is stored in the stencil buffer.

Unlike with the depth and color buffers, you don't always clear the stencil buffer every time you redisplay your scene. In the flight simulator example mentioned earlier, the aircraft control area might never change position or size, so redrawing into the stencil buffer would be unnecessary.

Drawing into the Stencil Buffer

Once you have enabled the `GL_STENCIL_TEST` attribute with `glEnable`, you still need to set up how the stencil buffer operates. By default, it does nothing, allowing drawing to occur anywhere on the screen without updating the stencil buffer. To make stenciling work effectively, however, we need to put values into the stencil buffer. The `glStencilFunc` and `glStencilOp` functions handle this interaction.

The `glStencilFunc` function defines a comparison function, reference value, and mask for all stencil buffer operations. The valid functions are in Table 11.7.

Table 11.7 *Stenciling Functions*

Function	Description
GL_NEVER	The stencil test always fails (no drawing occurs).
GL_LESS	Passes if the reference value is less than the stencil value.
GL_LEQUAL	Passes if the reference value is less than or equal to the stencil value.
GL_GREATER	Passes if the reference value is greater than the stencil value.
GL_GEQUAL	Passes if the reference value is greater than or equal to the stencil value.
GL_EQUAL	Passes if the reference value is equal to the stencil value.
GL_NOTEQUAL	Passes if the reference value is not equal to the stencil value.
GL_ALWAYS	The default; stencil test always passes (drawing always occurs).

Coupled with the stencil function is the stencil operation, defined with `glStencilOp`. Valid operations are in Table 11.8.

Table 11.8 *Stenciling Operations*

Operation	Description
GL_KEEP	Keep the current stencil buffer contents.
GL_ZERO	Set the stencil buffer value to 0.

continued on next page

continued from previous page

Operation	Description
GL_REPLACE	Set the stencil buffer value to the function reference value.
GL_INCR	Increment the current stencil buffer value.
GL_DECR	Decrement the current stencil buffer value.
GL_INVERT	Bitwise invert the current stencil buffer value.

Normally, you use a mask image to outline the area in which drawing is to take place. Here is an example of the calls needed to draw a mask image into the stencil buffer:

```
glStencilFunc(GL_ALWAYS, 1, 1);
glStencilOp(GL_REPLACE, GL_REPLACE, GL_REPLACE);
```

Then, you issue drawing commands that store a value of 1 in the stencil buffer. To draw using the stencil buffer mask, do the following prior to drawing the scene:

```
glStencilFunc(GL_EQUAL, 1, 1);
glStencilOp(GL_KEEP, GL_KEEP, GL_KEEP);
```

Because this operates with all OpenGL drawing functions, including **glBitmap**, you can use the stencil buffer to create many special "hole" effects for animations. BOOK\CHAP11\STENCIL\stencil.c contains a version of the cut-away example that uses the stencil buffer instead of the depth buffer to cut away the middle of the cube (see Figure 11.5).

Figure 11.5 Stencil cutout window.

The following is the heart of this program, which uses the functions just described:

```
glStencilFunc(GL_ALWAYS, 1, 1);
glStencilOp(GL_REPLACE, GL_REPLACE, GL_REPLACE);

glPushMatrix();
glTranslatef(-1.0, 0.0, -20.0);
glutSolidSphere(1.0);
glPopMatrix();
```

Once the stencil image is drawn, we draw the cube wherever the sphere was not drawn:

```
glStencilFunc(GL_NOTEQUAL, 1, 1);
glStencilOp(GL_KEEP, GL_KEEP, GL_KEEP);

glPushMatrix();
glTranslatef(1.0, 0.0, -20.0);
glRotatef(15.0, 0.0, 1.0, 0.0);
glRotatef(15.0, 0.0, 0.0, 1.0);
glutSolidCube(2.0);
glPopMatrix();
```

The Accumulation Buffer

The accumulation buffer provides support for many special effects such as motion blur and depth-of-field. It also supports full-screen anti-aliasing, although other methods (such as multisampling and blending with primitive anti-aliasing) are better suited to this task.

The accumulation buffer is considerably less complex than the other buffers discussed so far. It has a single function, glAccum, that manages all accumulation buffer actions. The actions that can be performed are in Table 11.9.

Table 11.9 *Accumulation Operations*

Operation	Description
GL_ACCUM	Add scaled color-buffer values to the accumulation buffer.
GL_LOAD	Load scaled color-buffer values into the accumulation buffer, replacing whatever had been there before.
GL_ADD	Add a constant color to the accumulation buffer's values.
GL_MULT	Multiply color values in the accumulation buffer by a constant color (filtering effects).
GL_RETURN	Copy the accumulation buffer into the main color buffer.

The normal way you use the accumulation buffer is to render multiple views into it and display the final composite scene with glAccum(GL_RETURN, 1.0).

Using the Accumulation Buffer for Motion Blur

As a co-worker once said, "It's easy to make any application of the accumulation buffer look like motion blur." The problem is akin to what happens if your hands shake (or if you stop panning) as you take a picture with a camera; too much jitter blurs the image.

You'll find that rendering motion blur is a little more complicated than just drawing a sequence of frames with the camera moving between each frame. We perceive motion blur when an object moves faster than our eyes can track it. In essence, the picture changes as the brain is "processing" the image, but the focus on the moving target is never lost. In a camera, light entering the lens exposes the film for a finite amount of time. Depending on the camera and photographer, the amount of blur might be small around the edges, or it could streak across the image.

When you simulate motion blur with computer graphics, it is important to remember that the current (or final) position of the object you are blurring must look more solid (or focused) than the rest of the frames. The easiest way to accomplish this is to use a larger color scaling factor when accumulating the current frame so that more of the color values from the final frame stand out from the rest. A typical implementation looks something like this:

```
/* Draw the current frame */
draw_frame(0);
/* Load the accumulation buffer with 50% of the current frame */
glAccum(GL_LOAD, 0.5);

/* Draw the last 10 frames and accumulate 5% for each */
for (i = 1; i <= 10; i ++)
    {
    draw_frame(-i);
    glAccum(GL_ACCUM, 0.05);
    }

/* Display the final scene */
glAccum(GL_RETURN, 1.0);
```

Notice that you don't have to use glClear to initialize the accumulation buffer contents, as you do with the color, depth, and stencil buffers. Instead, most often you use glAccum(GL_LOAD, s) on the first frame of the scene. The program in BOOK\CHAP11\MOTION\motion.c demonstrates motion blur on the cube and sphere (see Figure 11.6).

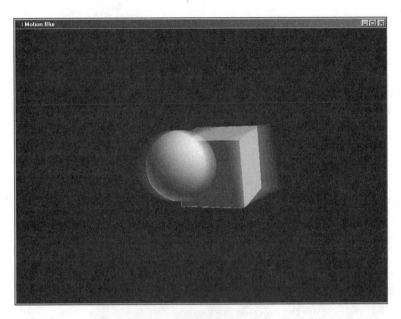

Figure 11.6   Motion blur window.

Using the Accumulation Buffer for Anti-Aliasing

Another application of the accumulation buffer is full-scene anti-aliasing.
The basic strategy is to jitter the image one-half a pixel in several directions, to blur
the edges of an image but not the solid areas. Accumulating as little
as four of these "jittered" scenes produces remarkably smoother images.
The sample program in BOOK\CHAP11\ANTIALIAS\antialias.c uses this technique to
draw the cube and sphere with full-scene anti-aliasing (see Figure 11.7).

The heart of the Redraw function is the accumulation loop:

```
int     i;
GLfloat right, left, range;
GLfloat jitter[4][2] =
    {
        { -0.20,  0.35 },
        {  0.20, -0.35 },
        { -0.30, -0.15 },
        {  0.30,  0.15 }
    };

range = right - left;

for (i = 0; i < 4; i ++)
    {
```

```
/* Translate the image slightly */
glPushMatrix();
glTranslate(jitter[i][0] * range / width,
            jitter[i][1] * range / height, 0.0);

/* Draw the scene */
...

/* Accumulate... */
if (i == 0)
    glAccum(GL_LOAD, 0.25);
else
    glAccum(GL_ACCUM, 0.25);
}

glAccum(GL_RETURN, 1.0);
```

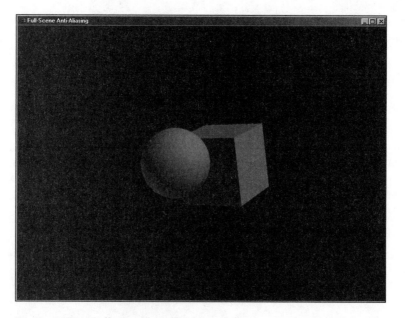

Figure 11.7   Full-scene anti-aliasing window.

Just about any values for the jitter array work as long as the coordinates lie within a unit square—that is, a square that is one pixel on a side.

The left and right variables define the world coordinates on the sides of the viewing frustum. If you are using the gluPerspective function, the left and right sides of the window can be computed with

```
GLfloat left, right;
GLfloat width, height;
GLfloat fov;
GLfloat nearz, farz;

gluPerspective(fov, width / height, nearz, farz);

right = tan(fov * M_PI / 180.0 / 2.0) * width / height * nearz;
left = -right;
```

Costs of Full-Scene Anti-Aliasing

Anti-aliasing with the accumulation buffer does carry a price in speed, however. If you want to do any real-time anti-aliased animation, you have to look at graphics hardware that supports multisampling to do your anti-aliasing for you or use blending and primitive smoothing. The accumulation buffer is just too slow for interactive work.

If you are generating stills or stop-motion animations, the accumulation buffer gives you anti-aliasing and simulated depth-of-field that simply are not possible with multi-sampling.

Summary

In this chapter, we have learned about all of the different types of buffers that are available in OpenGL. Besides hidden surface removal, the depth buffer can cut away parts of a scene. The stencil buffer can mask off areas of the screen or produce shadow effects. You can use the accumulation buffer to do full-scene anti-aliasing, motion blur, depth-of-field, and other complex special effects.

Reference Section

glAccum

Purpose	Operates on the accumulation buffer to establish pixel values.
Include File	<GL/gl.h>
Syntax	`void glAccum(GLenum func, GLfloat value);`
Description	This function operates on the accumulation buffer. Except for `GL_RETURN`, color values are scaled by the *value* parameter and added or stored into the accumulation buffer. For `GL_RETURN`, the accumulation buffer's color values are scaled by the *value* parameter and stored in the current color buffer.

Parameters

func	GLenum: The accumulation function to apply.
value	GLfloat: The fractional amount of accumulation to perform.
Returns	None.
Example	See the BOOK\CHAP11\MOTION\motion.c and BOOK\CHAP11\ANTIALIAS\antialias.c examples on the source code CD-ROM.
See Also	ChoosePixelFormat, SetPixelFormat

glClearColor

Purpose	Specifies a color value for the color buffer.
Include File	<GL/gl.h>
Syntax	void glClearColor(GLfloat *red*, GLfloat *green*, GLfloat *blue*, GLfloat *alpha*);
Description	This function sets the color value that is used when clearing the color buffer with glClear(GL_COLOR_BUFFER_BIT).

Parameters

red	GLfloat: The red color value for the color buffer.
green	GLfloat: The green color value for the color buffer.
blue	GLfloat: The blue color value for the color buffer.
alpha	GLfloat: The alpha color value for the color buffer.
Returns	None.
See Also	ChoosePixelFormat, SetPixelFormat

glClearDepth

Purpose	Specifies a depth value for the depth buffer.
Include File	<GL/gl.h>
Syntax	void glClearDepth(GLclampd *depth*);
Description	This function sets the depth value that is used when clearing the depth buffer with glClear(GL_DEPTH_BUFFER_BIT).

Parameters

depth	GLclampd: The clear value for the depth buffer.
Returns	None.
See Also	ChoosePixelFormat, SetPixelFormat

glClearIndex

Purpose	Specifies a color index value for the color buffer.
Include File	<GL/gl.h>
Syntax	void glClearIndex(GLfloat *index*);
Description	This function sets the color index value that is used when clearing the color buffer with glClear(GL_COLOR_BUFFER_BIT).
Parameters	
index	GLfloat: The color index value for the color buffer.
Returns	None.
See Also	ChoosePixelFormat, SetPixelFormat

glClearStencil

Purpose	Specifies a stencil value for the stencil buffer.
Include File	<GL/gl.h>
Syntax	void glClearStencil(GLint *value*);
Description	This function sets the stencil value that is used when clearing the stencil buffer with glClear(GL_STENCIL_BUFFER_BIT).
Parameters	
value	GLint: The clear value for the stencil buffer.
Returns	None.
See Also	ChoosePixelFormat, SetPixelFormat

glDepthFunc

Purpose	Sets the depth test function.
Include File	<GL/gl.h>
Syntax	void glDepthFunc(GLenum *func*);
Description	This function sets the depth buffer test function for hidden surface removal.
Parameters	
func	GLenum: The depth buffer comparison function to use.
Returns	None.
Example	See the BOOK\CHAP11\WIN32\win32.c and BOOK\CHAP11\GLUT\glut.c examples on the source code CD-ROM.
See Also	ChoosePixelFormat, SetPixelFormat

glDepthRange

Purpose	Sets the range of depth values in the depth buffer.
Include File	<GL/gl.h>
Syntax	void glDepthRange(GLclampd *near*, GLclampd *far*);
Description	This function sets the range of depth buffer values that are used for depth comparisons for hidden surface removal. It is legal for *near* to be greater than *far*.
Parameters	
near	GLclampd: The near depth value.
far	GLclampd: The far depth value.
Returns	None.
Example	See the BOOK\CHAP11\WIN32\win32.c and BOOK\CHAP11\GLUT\glut.c examples on the source code CD-ROM.
See Also	ChoosePixelFormat, SetPixelFormat

glDrawBuffer

Purpose	Selects a color buffer for drawing.
Include File	<GL/gl.h>
Syntax	void glDrawBuffer(GLenum *mode*);
Description	This function selects a color buffer for subsequent drawing operations. You typically call it to select the front or back color buffer in a double-buffered drawing context.
Parameters	
mode	GLenum: A constant (see Tables 11.4 and 11.5) selecting the color buffer to draw into. For example, to select the back color buffer for drawing, you use
	glDrawBuffer(GL_BACK)
Returns	None.
Known Bugs	The generic Microsoft implementation does not support stereo drawing buffers or the mode value GL_NONE.
Example	See the BOOK\CHAP11\CUTAWAY\cutaway.c example on the source code CD-ROM.
See Also	ChoosePixelFormat, SetPixelFormat

12

BEYOND LINES AND TRIANGLES

by Michael Sweet

What you'll learn in this chapter:

How to...	Functions You'll Use
Create quadrics to draw simple geometric shapes	`gluNewQuadric`
dDraw common geometric shapes	`gluCylinder/gluDisk/gluSphere`
Draw the shapes using different OpenGL primitives	`gluQuadricDrawStyle`
Use lighting and texturing with quadrics	`gluQuadricNormals/gluQuadricTexture`
Draw complex polygons	`gluTessBeginPolygon/gluTessEndPolygon`
Draw height fields	`glBegin/glVertex/glEnd`

Although OpenGL provides a complete set of drawing primitives, most interesting graphics displays would be too difficult to design if there were no way to represent common geometric objects or complex shapes.

The OpenGL utility library (glu32.lib) provides this functionality, including a robust polygon tessellation interface that can handle rendering of complex polygons and functions that render cones, cylinders, disks, and spheres.

What is tessellation, you ask? According to the American Heritage Dictionary

tes·sel·late—verb, transitive (**tes·sel·lat·ed, tes·sel·lat·ing, tes·sel·lates**) To form into a mosaic pattern, as by using small squares of stone or glass.

tessellation—noun

A computer graphics tessellator takes one or more connected sets of points and forms a series of polygons that fill to form the described shape. In place of stone and glass, it uses triangles and pixels. A polygon tessellator is specially designed to manage the drawing of polygons that have unusual attributes such as holes.

The OpenGL utility library also provides tessellators that form cones, cylinders, disks, and spheres. These shape functions use a special tessellator called a *quadric*.

Quadrics

Every quadric you draw on the screen has a state (or collection of settings) associated with it. The `gluNewQuadric` function creates an opaque state variable that describes the current drawing style, orientation, lighting mode, texturing mode, and callback functions, as follows:

```
GLUquadricObj *obj;

obj = gluNewQuadric();
```

Note that a quadric state does not include the geometric shape to be drawn. Instead, it describes how to draw geometric shapes. This allows you to reuse quadrics for many different kinds of shapes.

Changing the Way Quadrics Are Drawn

Once you create a quadric, you can customize the drawing of shapes by changing the quadric state. The GLU functions for this are `gluQuadricDrawStyle`, `gluQuadricNormals`, `gluQuadricOrientation`, and `gluQuadricTexture`:

```
void gluQuadricDrawStyle(GLUquadricObj *obj, GLenum drawStyle)
void gluQuadricNormals(GLUquadricObj *obj, GLenum normals)
void gluQuadricOrientation(GLUquadricObj *obj, GLenum orientation)
void gluQuadricTexture(GLUquadricObj *obj, GLboolean textureCoords)
```

The `gluQuadricDrawStyle` function selects the type of OpenGL drawing primitives that are used to draw the shape. The default style is to fill shapes using polygon and triangle strip primitives (`GLU_FILL`). Table 12.1 shows the possible styles.

Table 12.1   *Quadric Drawing Styles*

Style	Description
GLU_FILL	Quadrics are drawn filled in, using polygon and triangle strip primitives.
GLU_LINE	Quadrics are drawn "wireframe," using line primitives.
GLU_SILHOUETTE	Quadrics are drawn using line primitives; only the outside edges are drawn.
GLU_POINT	Quadrics are drawn using point primitives.

Lighting normals are usually generated automatically for quadrics.
The `gluQuadricNormals` function controls calculation of normals. Table 12.2 lists the possible lighting calculations.

Table 12.2   *Quadric Lighting Normal Modes*

Normal Mode	Description
GLU_NONE	No lighting normals are generated.
GLU_FLAT	Lighting normals are generated for each polygon to create a faceted appearance.
GLU_SMOOTH	Lighting normals are generated for each vertex to create a smooth appearance.

To control the direction of lighting normals, the `gluQuadricOrientation` function is provided to make normals point outwards (`GLU_OUTSIDE`) or inwards (`GLU_INSIDE`). This has particular application with spheres (that is, if you are inside or outside the sphere).

Finally, texture coordinates can be generated automatically for your quadrics. The `gluQuadricTexture` function enables (`GL_TRUE`) or disables (`GL_FALSE`) texture coordinate generation. We cover exactly how texture coordinates are chosen as we start drawing quadrics on the screen.

As you may remember, texture coordinates are used for mapping texture images onto polygons (see Chapter 8, "Texture Mapping").

Drawing Cylinders

Cylinders are drawn using `gluCylinder`. A cylinder drawn with this function is essentially a tube that runs along the z-axis (see Figure 12.1). The ends of the cylinder are never filled in:

```
void gluCylinder(GLUquadricObj *obj,
                 GLdouble baseRadius,
                 GLdouble topRadius,
                 GLdouble height,
                 GLint slices,
                 GLint stacks)
```

The *baseRadius* and *topRadius* arguments specify the radius of the cylinder at the bottom and top of the cylinder. The *height* argument specifies the actual height (or length) of the tube.

The *slices* argument controls how many subdivisions are used around the cylinder (the sides), and the *stacks* argument controls how many subdivisions are generated along the cylinder. Generally, you make *slices* a number around 20 to give the cylinder a smooth appearance. Values below this yield a faceted appearance. When you utilize spotlighting or a lot of specular highlights, you also want the *stacks* argument set high, usually the same as the height argument. Otherwise, set *stacks* to 2 to account for the top and bottom of the cylinder.

You can also use cylinders to generate faceted surfaces such as a pencil or a tool socket.

As Figure 12.1 shows, the ends of cylinders are not filled in; if you want to cap the ends of yourcylinders, use a disk, which is described later.

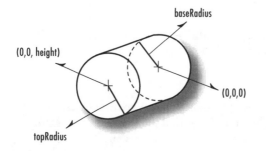

Figure 12.1   Quadric cylinders.

Texturing and Cylinders

When texturing a gluCylinder shape, textures are wrapped from the forward edge (0,*radius*,0) of the cylinder. This means your texture images should be upside down to display properly on the cylinder. We use textures with cylinders in the pencil project in this chapter.

Drawing Cones

Although the OpenGL utility library does not include a special cone-drawing function, you can use the gluCylinder function to make cones simply by specifying a *topRadius* or *bottomRadius* of 0.0.

Drawing Disks

Disks are round, flat shapes that can contain holes. Examples of disks include coins and washers:

```
void gluDisk(GLUquadricObj *obj,
             GLdouble innerRadius,
             GLdouble outerRadius,
```

```
        GLint slices,
        GLint loops)
```

The *innerRadius* and *outerRadius* arguments control the size of the hole and disk, respectively. If the *innerRadius* argument is 0.0, the disk is drawn as a solid circle (see Figure 12.2).

The *slices* argument sets the number of sides the disk has and generally should be a number around 20 to make the disk look round. The *loops* argument controls the number of concentric rings that are drawn for the disk (between the inner and outer radii); you should usually set it to 1 for circles and 2 for washers. As is true for cylinders, using larger values for loops improves specular lighting and spotlight effects.

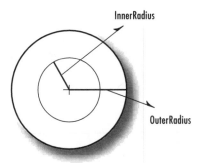

Figure 12.2   Quadric disks.

Disks and Textures

Texture images for disks are mapped so that the texture image just touches the disk at the edges. The top of the texture image is mapped to the top of the disk, the left side at degrees in the disk, and so forth.

Drawing Partial Disks

The OpenGL utility library also provides a function to display partial disks. When drawing a partial disk, you specify a start angle and sweep angle for the disk. The *startAngle* argument specifies a clockwise angle in degrees from the top of the disk. The *sweepAngle* argument specifies the number of degrees of arc to draw. For instance, 90° is a quarter disk, and so forth:

```
void gluPartialDisk(GLUquadricObj *obj,
                    GLdouble innerRadius,
                    GLdouble outerRadius,
                    GLint slices,
```

```
        GLint loops,
        GLdouble startAngle,
        GLdouble sweepAngle)
```

You can also use partial disks to draw pie charts or special polar graphs.

Drawing Spheres

Spheres are hollow balls or globes. When you draw a sphere, you specify the radius of the sphere:

```
void gluSphere(GLUquadricObj *obj,
        GLdouble radius,
        GLint slices,
        GLint stacks)
```

If you think of the sphere as a globe, the *slices* argument represents the number of lines of longitude, and the *stacks* argument represents the number of lines of latitude (see Figure 12.3).

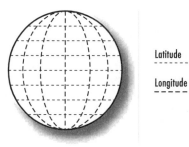

Latitude
- - - - - - - - - -

Longitude
- - - - - - - -

Figure 12.3   Quadric spheres.

Spheres and Textures

Texture images are mapped to spheres using longitude and latitude coordinates. A world map image would wrap perfectly around the sphere.

Drawing a Pencil

To close this section we write a little program that rotates an image of a pencil (see Figure 12.4). The pencil consists of three cylinders and two texture images (see Figure 12.5). The first texture image has the typical symbol for a #2 pencil, and the words "OpenGL Country Club" wrapped around the pencil. For the end and the sharpened point of the pencil, we use a second image of wood with exposed lead (well, carbon).

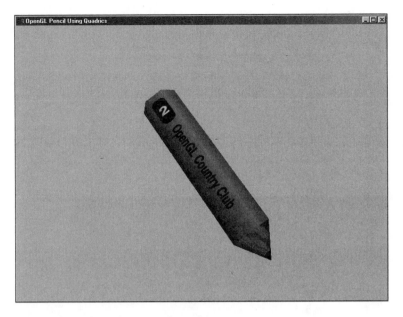

Figure 12.4 Quadric pencil window.

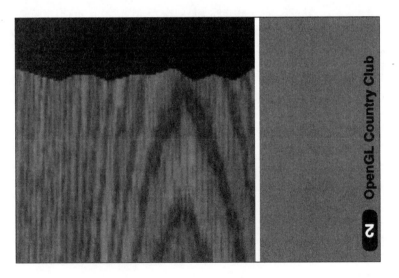

Figure 12.5 Pencil and lead texture images.

The point of the pencil, obviously, is a cone. The end of the pencil isn't quite as obvious. Because it's flat, you might expect to use a disk for the end. Unfortunately, the result of the way texture images are applied to disks doesn't look right with our texture image; the lead would be displayed around the outside of the disk instead of the inside. Instead, we make the end using a cylinder with a *height* and *topRadius* of 0.0.

Because quadrics are drawn from (0, 0, 0), you have to translate the coordinates of the pieces prior to drawing them. For example, to draw the body of the pencil, you do this:

```
glPushMatrix();
    glTranslatef(0.0, 0.0, -20.0);
    gluCylinder(PencilObj, 5.0, 5.0, 40.0, 6, 2);
glPopMatrix();
```

In the pencil drawing program, the Redraw function handles drawing everything. The first thing we display is the body of the pencil, which is a six-sided cylinder:

```
gluQuadricNormals(PencilObj, GLU_FLAT);
glBindTexture(GL_TEXTURE_2D, PencilTexture);

glPushMatrix();
    glTranslatef(0.0, 0.0, -20.0);
    gluCylinder(PencilObj, 5.0, 5.0, 40.0, 6, 2);
glPopMatrix();
```

Next, we display the point and end of the pencil using the "lead" texture image. We use six-sided cylinders to do the work we need:

```
gluQuadricNormals(PencilObj, GLU_SMOOTH);
glBindTexture(GL_TEXTURE_2D, LeadTexture);

glPushMatrix();
    glTranslatef(0.0, 0.0, 20.0);
    gluCylinder(PencilObj, 5.0, 0.0, 7.5, 6, 2);
glPopMatrix();

glPushMatrix();
    glTranslatef(0.0, 0.0, -20.0);
    gluCylinder(PencilObj, 5.0, 0.0, 0.0, 6, 2);
glPopMatrix();
```

The complete code appears in BOOK\CHAP12\PENCIL\pencil.c.

Complex Polygons

What makes polygons complex? Well, in OpenGL a complex polygon is one that is either concave (the polygon contains a "dent") or has holes in it. Figure 12.6 shows some simple and complex polygons that you might need to render at some time.

OpenGL's GL_POLYGON primitive can only render simple, convex polygons. A polygon is convex if no point lies inside a line between any two vertices. That is, if you can draw a line between two vertices of a polygon and the line goes into empty space outside the polygon edge, the polygon is not convex; it is concave or complex.

Concave polygons are nonconvex polygons that have no unfilled holes in their interiors. The top-right polygon in Figure 12.6 is concave, but the one below it is not because it contains a hole in the middle of the filled area.

Complex polygons have holes or twists in them. The lower-right polygon in Figure 12.6 is complex.

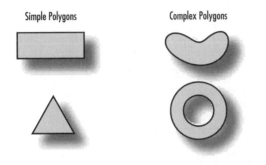

Figure 12.6 Simple and complex polygons.

GLU 1.1 and GLU 1.2

Unfortunately, you are likely to find two different versions of the OpenGL utility library. Although the quadric interface is identical in both GLU 1.1 and GLU 1.2, the polygon tessellator interface is not.

Most OpenGL 1.1 and 1.2 implementations, including the Microsoft and Silicon Graphics OpenGL libraries, have GLU 1.2. One notable exception is the Mesa graphics library, which supports the OpenGL 1.2 function set but only includes a GLU library compatible with GLU 1.1.

Because the GLU 1.1 and 1.2 interfaces are not that different, we demonstrate both. Also, the GLU 1.1 interface is still available in GLU 1.2.

To detect which version of GLU is available, your programs can check whether `GLU_VERSION_1_2` is defined:

```
#ifdef GLU_VERSION_1_2
#else
#endif /* GLU_VERSION_1_2 */
```

Creating a Tessellator Object

Drawing concave polygons with the OpenGL utility library is not difficult. The first thing you must do is create a tessellator object:

```
#ifdef GLU_VERSION_1_2
GLUtesselator *tess;
```

```
#else
GLUtriangulatorObj *tess;
#endif /* GLU_VERSION_1_2 */

tess = gluNewTess();
```

The GLUtriangulatorObj and GLUtesselator structures contains state information that is used by the tessellator to render the polygon. (Yes, the GLUtesselator structure is spelled wrong.)

Callback Functions

The OpenGL utility library defines several callback functions that you can use for special effects. The gluTessCallback function allows you to change these functions to do something of your own. It takes three arguments with GLU 1.1 and 1.2:

```
void gluTessCallback(GLUtriangulatorObj *tess, GLenum which, void (*fn)());
void gluTessCallback(GLUtesselator *tess, GLenum which, void (*fn)());
```

The which argument specifies the callback function to define and must be one of the arguments in Table 12.3.

Table 12.3   *Tessellator Callback Functions*

which Argument	Description
GLU_TESS_BEGIN	Specifies a function that is called to begin a GL_TRIANGLES, GL_TRIANGLE_STRIP, or GL_TRIANGLE_FAN primitive. The function must accept a single GLenum parameter that specifies the primitive to be rendered and is usually set to glBegin.
GLU_TESS_BEGIN_DATA	Like GLU_TESS_BEGIN, specifies a function [GLU 1.2] that is called to begin a GL_TRIANGLES,GL_TRIANGLE_STRIP, or GL_TRIANGLE_FAN primitive. The function must accept a Glenum parameter that specifies the primitive to be rendered and a GLvoid pointer from the call to gluTessBeginPolygon.
GLU_TESS_COMBINE	Specifies a function that is called when [GLU 1.2] vertices in the polygon are coincident; that is, they are equal. See the example for the function arguments.
GLU_TESS_COMBINE_DATA	Like GLU_TESS_COMBINE, specifies a function [GLU 1.2] that is called when vertices in the polygonare coincident. The function also receives a pointer to the user data from gluTessBeginPolygon.
GLU_TESS_EDGE_FLAG	Specifies a function that marks whether succeeding GLU_TESS_VERTEX callbacks refer to original or generated vertices. The function must accept a single GLboolean argument that is GL_TRUE for original and GL_FALSE for generated vertices.

which Argument	Description
GLU_TESS_END	Specifies a function that marks the end of a drawing primitive, usually glEnd. It takes no arguments.
GLU_TESS_ERROR	Specifies a function that is called when an error occurs. It must take a single argument of type GLenum.
GLU_TESS_VERTEX	Specifies a function that is called before every vertex is sent, usually with glVertex3dv. The function receives a copy of the third argument to gluTessVertex.
GLU_TESS_VERTEX_DATA	Like GLU_TESS_VERTEX, specifies a function [GLU 1.2] that is called before every vertex is sent. The function also receives a copy of the second argument to gluTessBeginPolygon.

Normally, you use the GLU_TESS_BEGIN, GLU_TESS_END, GLU_TESS_VERTEX, and GLU_TESS_ERROR callbacks. GLU_TESS_BEGIN, GLU_TESS_END, and GLU_TESS_VERTEX correspond to glBegin, glEnd, and glVertex3dv, respectively:

```
gluTessCallback(tess, GLU_TESS_BEGIN, glBegin);
gluTessCallback(tess, GLU_TESS_END, glEnd);
gluTessCallback(tess, GLU_TESS_VERTEX, glVertex3dv);
```

The GLU_ERROR callback accepts a single GLenum argument containing the GLU error that has occurred. A simple function to display errors sent from the tessellator is

```
gluTessCallback(tess, GLU_TESS_ERROR, tess_error_callback);
...
void
tess_error_callback(GLenum error)
    {
    MessageBeep(MB_ICONEXCLAMATION);
    MessageBox(NULL, gluErrorString(error), "GLU Error", MB_OK |
            MB_ICONEXCLAMATION);
    }
```

The GLU_COMBINE callback is needed for some types of complex polygons whose edges touch. It is only available (and needed) with GLU 1.2:

```
#ifdef GLU_VERSION_1_2
gluTessCallback(tess, GLU_TESS_COMBINE, tess_combine_callback);
#endif /* GLU_VERSION_1_2 */
...
#ifdef GLU_VERSION_1_2
void
tess_combine_callback(GLdouble *xyz,        /* I - XYZ of intersection */
                    GLvoid   *indata[4], /* I - Input vertex data */
                    GLfloat  *weights,   /* I - Input weights */
                    GLvoid   **outdata)  /* O - Output vertex  data*/
    {
```

```
    *outdata = indata[0];
    }
#endif /* GLU_VERSION_1_2 */
```

The xyz argument specifies the location of the intersection. The indata array contains the user data pointers for up to four vertices at the intersection; the weights array provides the relative weighting of each vertex, with the sum of the weights equal to 1.0.

The outdata argument must be filled with a pointer to vertex data; normally, you can just return the first indata pointer, but if you are using the GLU_TESS_VERTEX_DATA callback, you can also allocate a new vertex record that interpolates the data values in the indata array. Because only the pointer is used by the tessellation functions, this new record must not be a pointer to a local variable because the contents will be overwritten by future function calls.

Drawing Concave Polygons

For GLU 1.1, you call a sequence of gluBeginPolygon, gluTessVertex, and gluEndPolygon to render the polygon:

```
GLdouble vertices[100][3];

gluBeginPolygon(tess);
    gluTessVertex(tess, vertices[0], NULL);
    gluTessVertex(tess, vertices[1], NULL);
    ...
    gluTessVertex(tess, vertices[99], NULL);
gluEndPolygon(tess);
```

For GLU 1.2, you call gluTessBeginPolygon, gluTessBeginContour, gluTessVertex, gluEndContour, and gluEndPolygon:

```
GLdouble vertices[100][3];

gluTessBeginPolygon(tess, NULL);
    gluTessBeginContour(tess);
    gluTessVertex(tess, vertices[0], NULL);
    gluTessVertex(tess, vertices[1], NULL);
    ...
    gluTessVertex(tess, vertices[99], NULL);
    gluTessEndContour(tess);
gluEndPolygon(tess);
```

After the gluEndPolygon or gluTessEndPolygon call, the tessellator does its work and generates a series of triangles, triangle strips, and triangle fans. Because this process can take a long time, it's a good idea to put tessellated polygons into display lists to improve display performance (see Chapter 9, "3D Modeling and Object Composition").

Drawing Complex Polygons

Drawing complex polygons is a little more involved than drawing concave polygons but is not as hard as it would seem. Complex polygons can have holes and twists in them, so the `gluNextContour` function is provided with GLU 1.1 to identify the type of path you are defining. Table 12.4 lists the path types for `gluNextContour`.

Table 12.4   `gluNextContour` *Path Types*

Path Type	Description
GLU_EXTERIOR	The path lies on the exterior of the polygon.
GLU_INTERIOR	The path lies on the interior of the polygon (hole).
GLU_UNKNOWN	You don't know what the path is; the library will attempt to figure it out.
GLU_CCW	This should only be used once; it defines that counterclockwise paths are exterior paths and clockwise ones are interior.
GLU_CW	This should only be used once; it defines that counterclockwise paths are exterior paths and clockwise ones are interior.

GLU 1.2 uses the `gluTessBeginContour` and `gluTessEndContour` functions and does not need any of the path types shown in Table 12.4.

For the example shown in Figure 12.7, we define an exterior path for the outline and an interior path for the triangular hole in the middle (see Figure 12.8).

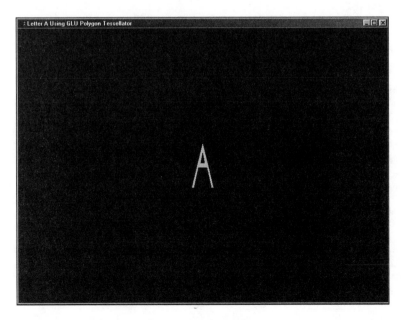

Figure 12.7   The letter A as a complex polygon.

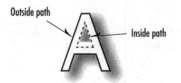

Outside path

Inside path

Figure 12.8 Polygon paths for the letter A.

To draw the letter A with GLU 1.1, we call `gluNextContour` only once before providing the interior points. The example in BOOK\CHAP12\LETTER\letter.c uses this code
to display a rotating A:

```
tess = gluNewTess();
gluBeginPolygon(tess);
    gluTessVertex(tess, outside[0], outside[0]);
    gluTessVertex(tess, outside[1], outside[1]);
    gluTessVertex(tess, outside[2], outside[2]);
    gluTessVertex(tess, outside[3], outside[3]);
    gluTessVertex(tess, outside[4], outside[4]);
    gluTessVertex(tess, outside[5], outside[5]);
    gluTessVertex(tess, outside[6], outside[6]);
gluNextContour(tess, GLU_INTERIOR);
    gluTessVertex(tess, inside[0], inside[0]);
    gluTessVertex(tess, inside[1], inside[1]);
    gluTessVertex(tess, inside[2], inside[2]);
gluEndPolygon(tess);
gluDeleteTess(tess);
```

With GLU 1.2, we call `gluTessBeginContour` and `gluTessEndContour` around the
outside and inside vertices:

```
tess = gluNewTess();
gluTessBeginPolygon(tess);
    gluTessBeginContour(tess);
    gluTessVertex(tess, outside[0], outside[0]);
    gluTessVertex(tess, outside[1], outside[1]);
    gluTessVertex(tess, outside[2], outside[2]);
    gluTessVertex(tess, outside[3], outside[3]);
    gluTessVertex(tess, outside[4], outside[4]);
    gluTessVertex(tess, outside[5], outside[5]);
    gluTessVertex(tess, outside[6], outside[6]);
    gluTessEndContour(tess);
    gluTessBeginContour(tess);
    gluTessVertex(tess, inside[0], inside[0]);
    gluTessVertex(tess, inside[1], inside[1]);
    gluTessVertex(tess, inside[2], inside[2]);
    gluTessEndContour(tess);
gluEndPolygon(tess);
gluDeleteTess(tess);
```

The order in which you specify the inner or outer loops is not important with the GLU 1.2 tessellator, but with the GLU 1.1 tessellator you must do the outer loop first.

Combining Quadrics and Polygon Tessellators

You can combine quadrics and the polygon tessellator to produce complex objects. Figure 12.9 shows how you can use them to produce an (admittedly crude) image of an F-16.

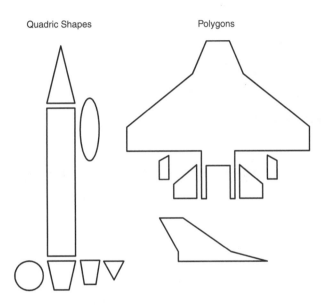

Quadric Shapes   Polygons

Figure 12.9   Objects and polygons to make an F-16.

Building an F-16 Model

The fuselage of the F-16 consists of a cone for the nose and a cylinder for the length of the body:

```
/* Nose */
glColor3f(0.8, 0.8, 0.8);
glPushMatrix();
    glTranslatef(0.0, 0.0, -2.5);
    gluCylinder(quadric, 0.0, 0.25, 1.0, 20, 2);
glPopMatrix();

/* Main fuselage */
glColor3f(0.8, 0.8, 0.8);
glPushMatrix();
    glTranslatef(0.0, 0.0, -1.5);
    gluCylinder(quadric, 0.25, 0.25, 3.5, 20, 2);
glPopMatrix();
```

We use a tapered cylinder at the end for the engine. Inside the engine is a black disk and a transparent blue cone and cylinder that simulates the jet blast of the engine:

```
/* Engine */
glPushMatrix();
    /* Cowling */
    glColor3f(0.1, 0.1, 0.1);
    glTranslatef(0.0, 0.0, 2.0);
    gluCylinder(quadric, 0.25, 0.15, 0.5, 20, 2);
    gluDisk(quadric, 0.0, 0.25, 20, 2);

    /* Exhaust */
    glPushAttrib(GL_LIGHTING_BIT);
    glColorMaterial(GL_FRONT_AND_BACK, GL_EMISSION);
    glColor3f(0.5, 0.5, 1.0);
    gluCylinder(quadric, 0.2, 0.0, 0.3, 10, 2);
    glColor4f(0.25, 0.25, 1.0, 0.75);
    gluCylinder(quadric, 0.2, 0.1, 0.4, 10, 2);
    glPopAttrib();
glPopMatrix();
```

For the canopy, we use an elongated sphere. We make the sphere transparent to simulate the glass:

```
/* Canopy */
glPushMatrix();
    glColor4f(0.5, 0.5, 1.0, 0.75);
    glTranslatef(0.0, 0.2, -1.0);
    glScalef(1.0, 1.0, 0.65 / 0.15);
    gluSphere(quadric, 0.15, 6, 12);
glPopMatrix();
```

As shown in Figure 12.9, all of the wing, tail, andfins are polygons. We draw them using the polygon tessellator:

```
/* Main wing */
glColor3f(0.8, 0.8, 0.8);
glNormal3f(0.0, 1.0, 0.0);
gluTessBeginPolygon(tess, NULL);
gluTessBeginContour(tess);

for (i = 0; i < 16; i ++)
    gluTessVertex(tess, wing[i], wing[i]);

gluTessEndContour(tess);
gluTessEndPolygon(tess);

/* Fins */
glColor3f(0.8, 0.8, 0.8);
glNormal3f(-1.0, 0.0, 0.0);
```

```
gluTessBeginPolygon(tess, NULL);
gluTessBeginContour(tess);

for (i = 0; i < 4; i ++)
    gluTessVertex(tess, left_fin[i], left_fin[i]);

gluTessEndContour(tess);
gluTessEndPolygon(tess);

glColor3f(0.8, 0.8, 0.8);
glNormal3f(1.0, 0.0, 0.0);
gluTessBeginPolygon(tess, NULL);
gluTessBeginContour(tess);

for (i = 0; i < 4; i ++)
    gluTessVertex(tess, right_fin[i], right_fin[i]);

gluTessEndContour(tess);
gluTessEndPolygon(tess);

/* Tail */
glBindTexture(GL_TEXTURE_2D, F16Texture[1]);
glColor3f(0.8, 0.8, 0.8);
glNormal3f(1.0, 0.0, 0.0);
gluTessBeginPolygon(tess, NULL);
gluTessBeginContour(tess);

for (i = 0; i < 6; i ++)
    gluTessVertex(tess, tail[i], tail[i]);

gluTessEndContour(tess);
gluTessEndPolygon(tess);
```

The rollerons (the horizontal control surfaces at the back of the F-16) are stored and drawn separately so that they can be moved depending on the position of the mouse.

Drawing the F-16 Model

Once the F-16 model has been stored in display lists (three to be exact), we just need to rotate the model for the heading, pitch, and roll. The order of these rotations is important; do it the wrong way and the model will end up upside down or flying sideways!

```
/* Setup viewing transformations for the current orientation... */
glPushMatrix();
glTranslatef(0.0, 0.0, -15.0);
glRotatef(Orientation[1], 0.0, -1.0, 0.0); /* Heading */
glRotatef(Orientation[0], 1.0, 0.0, 0.0);  /* Pitch */
glRotatef(Orientation[2], 0.0, 0.0, -1.0); /* Roll */
```

Once the rotations are set, we draw the model:

```
// Draw the main body
glCallList(F16Body);

// Draw the rollerons...
pitch = 0.1 * (MouseY - MouseStartY);
roll  = 0.1 * (MouseX - MouseStartX);

// Left rolleron
glPushMatrix();
    glTranslatef(0.0, 0.0, 2.0);
    glRotatef(roll - pitch, 1.0, 0.0, 0.0);
    glTranslatef(0.0, 0.0, -2.0);
    glCallList(F16Rolleron[0]);
glPopMatrix();

// Right rolleron
glPushMatrix();
    glTranslatef(0.0, 0.0, 2.0);
    glRotatef(roll + pitch, -1.0, 0.0, 0.0);
    glTranslatef(0.0, 0.0, -2.0);
    glCallList(F16Rolleron[1]);
glPopMatrix();
```

The rollerons tilt forward when we pitch the aircraft up and backwards when we pitch the aircraft down. Roll is controlled by rotating the rollerons in opposite directions. To rotate from the center of the rollerons, we translate before and after the rotate.

The complete code appears in BOOK\CHAP12\F16\f16.c and produces the window in Figure 12.10.

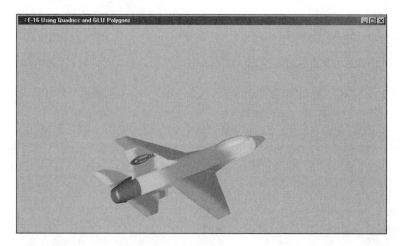

Figure 12.10　F-16 model window.

Tessellating Height Fields (Grids)

Another common tessellation problem is the rendering of height fields or grids. Height fields are used for all sorts of computer graphics displays, but the most common is perhaps the ground (terrain) that is displayed in flight simulators and games.

Drawing Height Fields with Triangle Strips

You might remember our terrain examples in Chapter 8, "Texture Mapping" and Chapter 10, "Visual Effects: Blending and Fog." All of these examples utilize a height field to display a fractal landscape that you can fly through.

To display the height field, we draw a series of triangle strips for each pair of columns in the grid. For the 9×9 grid in Figure 12.11, we draw a total of 2×(columns–1)×(rows–1), or 128 triangles.

For small grids, this method works well, but as the size of the grid increases, the number of triangles quickly gets out of hand.

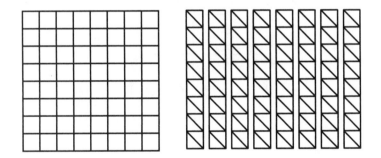

Figure 12.11   Rendering a height field using triangle strips.

Improving on the Triangle Strip Method

For medium-sized grids, you can use a modified strip algorithm to reduce the number of triangles that are drawn. To start, we make a grid using the odd numbered points; this reduces the number of points and triangles to one-fourth of the original grid.

Next, we select "important" points from the original grid and add them to the new one. For the terrain examples from Chapters 8 and 10, we select points whose change in slope is greater than 100.0:

```
/* Now scan the terrain for "interesting" postings */
for (i = TerrainCount, tp = Terrain[0] + 1; i > 0; i --, tp += 2)
    for (j = TERRAIN_COUNT - 2; j > 0; j --, tp ++)
        if (fabs(2 * tp[0].v[1] - tp[1].v[1] - tp[-1].v[1]) > 5.0)
        tp->used = 1;

for (j = 0; j < TERRAIN_COUNT; j ++)
    for (i = TerrainCount - 2, tp = Terrain[1] + j;
```

```
 i > 0;
 i --, tp += TERRAIN_COUNT)
if (fabs(2 * tp[0].v[1] - tp[TERRAIN_COUNT].v[1] -
        tp[-TERRAIN_COUNT].v[1]) > 5.0)
   tp->used = 1;
```

Finally, we scan through the new grid in "cells" of three points by three points (see Figure 12.12). For cells that have no points selected in the middle column, we can use triangle strips as before. We can also use triangle strips if only the top and bottom points are selected. In all other cases, we use a triangle fan from the middle point.

The new algorithm reduces the 9×9 grid in Figure 12.11 from 128 triangles to only 61.

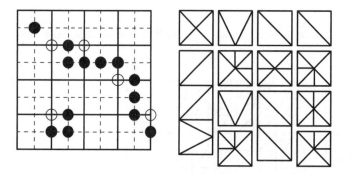

Figure 12.12   Rendering a height field using a modified triangle strip method.

Other Tessellation Algorithms

Height field tessellation is a field of computer graphics all on its own. Besides the simple algorithms described earlier, there are others based on fractal techniques and Delaunay triangulation. To learn more about these techniques, see the references in Appendix B, "Further Reading."

Improving the Terrain Viewing Program

Now that we have a way to reduce the number of triangles we need to draw, let's update the terrain programs from Chapters 8 and 10.

Rather than use a computer-generated fractal terrain, we use real terrain data for the Grand Canyon. In addition, we display the F-16 model we created earlier in this chapter, essentially making a miniature flight simulator.

The complete code for the improved terrain program appears in BOOK\CHAP12\ TERRAIN8\terrain8.c and produces the output in Figure 12.13.

Figure 12.13   Terrain viewing program using modified triangle tessellation.

Summary

In this chapter, we've covered the quadric drawing functions. OpenGL quadrics are geometric shapes that form the basic "building blocks" of many objects, both manufactured and natural. Using the quadric drawing functions is a convenient and fast way to avoid writing a lot of extra code for drawing these shapes.

You can use the OpenGL polygon tessellator to render a variety of complex polygons that OpenGL's `GL_POLYGON` primitive just can't handle. Polygon tessellation does come at a price, and you will want to put these tessellated polygons into display lists to get good performance from them.

Finally, there are many ways to tessellate height fields, including the simple triangle mesh and modified triangle mesh methods. We used the modified triangle mesh method to improve the quality of our terrain display without adversely affecting its performance.

Reference Section

gluCylinder

Purpose	Draws a quadric cylinder.
Include File	<GL/glu.h>
Syntax	void gluCylinder(GLUquadricObj *obj, GLdouble baseRadius, GLdouble topRadius, GLdouble height, GLint slices, GLint stacks);
Description	This function draws a hollow cylinder with no ends along the z-axis. If topRadius or bottomRadius is 0, a cone is drawn instead. The cylinder is projected height units along the positive z-axis. The slices argument controls the number of sides along the cylinder. The stacks argument controls the number of segments along the z-axis (across the cylinder) that are generated.
Parameters	
obj	GLUquadricObj *: The quadric state information to use for rendering.
baseRadius	GLdouble: The radius of the base (z=0) of the cylinder.
topRadius	GLdouble: The radius of the top (z=height) of the cylinder.
height	GLdouble: The height or length of the cylinder along the z-axis.
slices	GLint: The number of sides on the cylinder.
stacks	GLint: The number of segments in the cylinder along the z-axis.
Returns	None.
Example	See the example in BOOK\CHAP12\PENCIL\pencil.c.
See Also	gluDeleteQuadric, gluNewQuadric, gluQuadricCallback, gluQuadricDrawStyle, gluQuadricNormals, gluQuadricOrientation, gluQuadricTexture

gluDeleteQuadric

Purpose	Deletes a quadric state object.
Include File	<GL/glu.h>
Syntax	void gluDeleteQuadric(GLUquadricObj *obj);
Description	This function deletes a quadric state object. Once an object has been deleted, it cannot be used for drawing again.
Parameters	
obj	GLUquadricObj *: The quadric state object to delete.

Returns	None.
See Also	gluNewQuadric, gluQuadricCallback, gluQuadricDrawStyle, gluQuadricNormals, gluQuadricOrientation, gluQuadricTexture

gluDeleteTess

Purpose	Deletes a tessellator object.
Include File	<GL/glu.h>
Syntax	void gluDeleteTess(GLUtesselator *tobj);
Description	The gluDeleteTess function frees all memory associated with a tessellator object.
Parameters	
tobj	GLUtesselator *: The tessellator object to delete.
Returns	None.
Example	See the example in BOOK\CHAP12\LETTER\letter.c on the CD.
See Also	gluNewTess

gluDisk

Purpose	Draws a quadric disk.
Include File	<GL/glu.h>
Syntax	void gluDisk(GLUquadricObj *obj, GLdouble innerRadius, GLdouble outerRadius, GLint slices, GLint loops);
Description	This function draws a disk perpendicular to the z-axis. If innerRadius is 0, a solid (filled) circle is drawn instead of a washer. The slices argument controls the number of sides on the disk. The loops argument controls the number of rings generated out from the z-axis.
Parameters	
obj	GLUquadricObj *: The quadric state information to use for rendering.
innerRadius	GLdouble: The inside radius of the disk.
outerRadius	GLdouble: The outside radius of the disk.
slices	GLint: The number of sides on the cylinder.
loops	GLint: The number of rings out from the z-axis.
Returns	None.
See Also	gluDeleteQuadric, gluNewQuadric, gluQuadricCallback, gluQuadricDrawStyle, gluQuadricNormals, gluQuadricOrientation, gluQuadricTexture

gluNewQuadric

Purpose	Creates a new quadric state object.
Include File	<GL/glu.h>
Syntax	`GLUquadricObj *gluNewQuadric(void);`
Description	This function creates a new opaque quadric state object to be used for drawing. The quadric state object contains specifications that determine how subsequent images will be drawn.
Parameters	None.
Returns	`GLUquadricObj *`: NULL if no memory is available; otherwise, a valid quadric state object pointer.
Example	See the example in BOOK\CHAP12\PENCIL\pencil.c.
See Also	`gluDeleteQuadric`, `gluQuadricCallback`, `gluQuadricDrawStyle`, `gluQuadricNormals`, `gluQuadricOrientation`, `gluQuadricTexture`

gluNewTess

Purpose	Creates a tessellator object.
Include File	<GL/glu.h>
Syntax	`GLUtriangulatorObj *gluNewTess(void);`
Description	The `gluNewTess` function creates a tessellator object.
Parameters	None.
Returns	`GLUtriangulatorObj *`: The new tessellator object.
Example	See the example in CH18\LETTER.C on the CD.
See Also	`gluDeleteTess`

gluPartialDisk

Purpose	Draws a partial quadric disk.
Include File	<GL/glu.h>
Syntax	`void gluPartialDisk(GLUquadricObj *obj, GLdouble innerRadius, GLdouble outerRadius, GLint slices, GLint loops, GLdouble startAngle, GLdouble sweepAngle);`
Description	This function draws a partial disk perpendicular to the z-axis. If *innerRadius* is 0, a solid (filled) circle is drawn instead of a washer. The *slices* argument controls the number of sides on the disk. The *loops* argument controls the number of rings out from the z-axis that are generated. The *startAngle* argument specifies the

starting angle of the disk with 0° at the top of the disk and 90° at the right of the disk. The *sweepAngle* argument specifies the portion of the disk in degrees.

Parameters	
obj	GLUquadricObj *: The quadric state information to use for rendering.
innerRadius	GLdouble: The inside radius of the disk.
outerRadius	GLdouble: The outside radius of the disk.
slices	GLint: The number of sides on the cylinder.
loops	GLint: The number of rings out from the z-axis.
startAngle	GLdouble: The start angle of the partial disk.
sweepAngle	GLdouble: The angular size of the partial disk.
Returns	None.
See Also	gluDeleteQuadric, gluNewQuadric, gluQuadricCallback, gluQuadricDrawStyle, gluQuadricNormals, gluQuadricOrientation, gluQuadricTexture

gluQuadricCallback

Purpose	Defines a quadric callback function.
Include File	<GL/glu.h>
Syntax	void gluQuadricCallback(GLUquadricObj *obj, GLenum which, void (*fn)());
Description	This function defines callback functions to be used when drawing quadric shapes. At present, the only defined callback function is GLU_ERROR, which is called whenever an OpenGL or GLU error occurs.
Parameters	
obj	GLUquadricObj *: The quadric state information to use for rendering.
which	GLenum: The callback function to define. Must be GLU_ERROR.
fn	void (*)(): The callback function (receives one GLenum containing the error).
Returns	None.
See Also	gluDeleteQuadric, gluNewQuadric, gluQuadricDrawStyle, gluQuadricNormals, gluQuadricOrientation, gluQuadricTexture

gluQuadricDrawStyle

Purpose	Sets the drawing style of a quadric state object.
Include File	<GL/glu.h>
Syntax	void gluQuadricDrawStyle(GLUquadricObj *obj, GLenum drawStyle);
Description	This function selects a drawing style for all quadric shapes.
Parameters	
obj	GLUquadricObj *: The quadric state information to use for rendering.
drawStyle	GLenum: The drawing style. Valid styles are as follows:
	GLU_FILL—Quadrics are drawn filled, using polygon and strip primitives.
	GLU_LINE—Quadrics are drawn "wireframe," using line primitives.
	GLU_SILHOUETTE—Quadrics are drawn using line primitives; only the outside edges are drawn.
	GLU_POINT—Quadrics are drawn using point primitives.
Returns	None.
See Also	gluDeleteQuadric, gluNewQuadric, gluQuadricCallback, gluQuadricNormals, gluQuadricOrientation, gluQuadricTexture

gluQuadricNormals

Purpose	Sets the type of lighting normals used for quadric objects.
Include File	<GL/glu.h>
Syntax	void gluQuadricNormals(GLUquadricObj *obj, GLenum normals);
Description	This function sets the type of lighting normals that are generated when drawing shapes using the specified quadric state object.
Parameters	
obj	GLUquadricObj *: The quadric state information to use for rendering.
normals	GLenum: The type of normals to generate. Valid types are as follows:
	GLU_NONE—No lighting normals are generated.
	GLU_FLAT—Lighting normals are generated for each polygon to generate a faceted appearance.
	GLU_SMOOTH—Lighting normals are generated for each vertex to generate a smooth appearance.

Returns	None.
Example	See the example in BOOK\CHAP12\PENCIL\pencil.c.
See Also	`gluDeleteQuadric`, `gluNewQuadric`, `gluQuadricCallback`, `gluQuadricDrawStyle`, `gluQuadricOrientation`, `gluQuadricTexture`

gluQuadricOrientation

Purpose	Sets the orientation of lighting normals for quadric objects.
Include File	<GL/glu.h>
Syntax	`void gluQuadricOrientation(GLUquadricObj *obj, GLenum orientation);`
Description	This function sets the direction of lighting normals for hollow objects. The orientation parameter can be `GLU_OUTSIDE` to point lighting normals outward or `GLU_INSIDE` to point them inward.
Parameters	
obj	`GLUquadricObj *`: The quadric state information to use for rendering.
orientation	`GLenum`: The orientation of lighting normals, `GLU_OUTSIDE` or `GLU_INSIDE`. The default is `GLU_OUTSIDE`.
Returns	None.
See Also	`gluDeleteQuadric`, `gluNewQuadric`, `gluQuadricCallback`, `gluQuadricDrawStyle`, `gluQuadricNormals`, `gluQuadricTexture`

gluQuadricTexture

Purpose	Enables or disables texture coordinate generation for texture-mapping images onto quadrics.
Include File	<GL/glu.h>
Syntax	`void gluQuadricTexture(GLUquadricObj *obj, GLboolean textureCoords);`
Description	This function controls whether texture coordinates are generated for quadric shapes.
Parameters	
obj	`GLUquadricObj *`: The quadric state information to use for rendering.
textureCoords	`GLboolean`: `GL_TRUE` if texture coordinates should be generated; `GL_FALSE` otherwise.

Returns	None.
See Also	gluDeleteQuadric, gluNewQuadric, gluQuadricCallback, gluQuadricDrawStyle, gluQuadricNormals, gluQuadricOrientation

gluSphere

Purpose	Draws a quadric sphere.
Include File	<GL/glu.h>
Syntax	void gluSphere(GLUquadricObj *obj, GLdouble radius, GLint slices, GLint stacks);
Description	This function draws a hollow sphere centered at the origin. The slices argument controls the number of lines of longitude on the sphere. The stacks argument controls the number of lines of latitude on the sphere.
Parameters	
obj	GLUquadricObj *: The quadric state information to use for rendering.
radius	GLdouble: The radius of the sphere.
slices	GLint: The number of lines of longitude on the sphere.
stacks	GLint: The number of lines of latitude on the sphere.
Returns	None.
See Also	gluDeleteQuadric, gluNewQuadric, gluQuadricCallback, gluQuadricDrawStyle, gluQuadricNormals, gluQuadricOrientation, gluQuadricTexture

gluTessBeginContour

Purpose	Specifies a new contour or hole in a complex polygon.
Include File	<GL/glu.h>
Syntax	void gluTessBeginContour(GLUtesselator *tobj);
Description	This function specifies a new contour or hole in a complex polygon.
Parameters	
tobj	GLUtesselator *: The tessellator object to use for the polygon.
Returns	None.
Example	See the example in CHAP12\letter\letter.c on the CD.
See Also	gluTessBeginPolygon, gluTessEndPolygon, gluTessEndContour, gluTessVertex

gluTessBeginPolygon

Purpose	Starts tessellation of a complex polygon.
Include File	<GL/glu.h>
Syntax	void gluTessBeginPolygon(GLUtesselator *`tobj`, GLvoid *`data`);
Description	This function starts tessellation of a complex polygon.
Parameters	
tobj	GLUtesselator *: The tessellator object to use for the polygon.
data	GLvoid *: The data that is passed to GLU_TESS_*_DATA callbacks.
Returns	None.
Example	See the example in BOOK\CHAP12\LETTER\letter.c on the CD.
See Also	gluTessEndPolygon, gluTessBeginContour, gluTessEndContour, gluTessVertex

gluTessCallback

Purpose	To specify a callback function for tessellation.
Include File	<GL/glu.h>
Syntax	void gluTessCallback(GLUtesselator *`tobj`, GLenum `which`, void (*`fn`)());
Description	This function specifies a callback function for various tessellation functions. Callback functions do not replace or change the tessellator performance. Rather, they provide the means to add information to the tessellated output (such as color or texture coordinates).
Parameters	
tobj	GLUtesselator *: The tessellator object to use for the polygon.
which	GLenum: The callback function to define. Valid functions appear in Table 12.3 earlier in the chapter.
fn	void (*)(): The function to call.
Returns	None.

gluTessEndContour

Purpose	Ends a contour in a complex polygon.
Include File	<GL/glu.h>
Syntax	void gluTessEndContour(GLUtesselator *`tobj`);
Description	This function ends the current polygon contour.

Parameters

tobj GLUtesselator *: The tessellator object to use for the polygon.

Returns None.

Example See the example in BOOK\CHAP12\LETTER\letter.c on the CD.

See Also gluTessBeginPolygon, gluTessBeginContour,
gluTessEndPolygon, gluTessVertex

gluTessEndPolygon

Purpose Ends tessellation of a complex polygon and renders it.

Include File <GL/glu.h>

Syntax void gluTessEndPolygon(GLUtesselator *tobj);

Description This function ends tessellation of a complex polygon and renders the final result.

Parameters

tobj GLUtesselator *: The tessellator object to use for the polygon.

Returns None.

Example See the example in BOOK\CHAP12\LETTER\letter.c on the CD.

See Also gluTessBeginPolygon, gluTessBeginContour,
gluTessEndContour, gluTessVertex

gluTessProperty

Purpose Sets a tessellator property value.

Include File <GL/glu.h>

Syntax void gluTessProperty(GLUtesselator *tobj, GLenum which,
GLdouble value);

Description This function sets a tessellator property value.

Parameters

tobj GLUtesselator *: The tessellator object to change.

which GLenum: The property to change: GLU_TESS_BOUNDARY_ONLY,
GLU_TESS_TOLERANCE, or GLU_TESS_WINDING_RULE.

value GLdouble: The value for the property.

For GLU_TESS_BOUNDARY_ONLY, the value can be GL_TRUE or GL_FALSE. If GL_TRUE, only the boundary of the polygon is displayed (no holes).

For `GLU_TESS_TOLERANCE`, the value is the coordinate tolerance for vertices in the polygon.

For `GLU_TESS_WINDING_RULE`, the value is one of `GLU_TESS_WINDING_NONZERO`, `GLU_TESS_WINDING_POSITIVE`, `GLU_TESS_WINDING_NEGATIVE`, or `GLU_TESS_WINDING_ABS_GEQ_TWO`.

Returns	None.
Example	`gluTessProperty(tess, GLU_TESS_TOLERANCE, 0.001);`
See Also	`gluTessBeginPolygon`, `gluTessEndPolygon`, `gluTessBeginContour`, `gluTessEndContour`, `gluTessCallback`, `gluTessVertex`, `gluNewTess`, `gluDeleteTess`

gluTessVertex

Purpose	Adds a vertex to the current polygon path.
Include File	<GL/glu.h>
Syntax	`void gluTessVertex(GLUtesselator *tobj, GLdouble v[3], void *data);`
Description	This function adds a vertex to the current tessellator path. The data argument is passed through to the `GL_VERTEX` callback function.
Parameters	
tobj	`GLUtesselator *`: The tessellator object to use for the polygon.
v	`GLdouble[3]`: The 3D vertex.
data	`void *`: A data pointer to be passed to the `GL_VERTEX` callback function.
Returns	None.
Example	See the example in BOOK\CHAP12\LETTER\letter.c on the CD.
See Also	`gluTessBeginPolygon`, `gluTessEndPolygon`, `gluTessBeginContour`, `gluTessEndContour`

13

CURVES AND SURFACES: WHAT THE #%@!& ARE NURBS?

by Richard S. Wright, Jr.

What you'll learn in this chapter:

How to...	Functions You'll Use
Use maps to render Bézier curves and surfaces	`glMap/glEvalCoord`
Use evaluators to simplify surface mapping	`glMapGrid/glEvalMesh`
Create NURBS surfaces	`gluNewNurbsRenderer/gluBeginSurface/gluNurbsSurface/gluEndSurface/gluDeleteNurbsRenderer`
Create trimming curves	`gluBeginTrim/gluPwlCurve/gluEndTrim`

For most applications that use 3D graphics, you need smooth curves and surfaces. Using the techniques discussed elsewhere in this book, you can divide such a surface into many smaller quads or triangles and then calculate the normals at the various vertices, and apply lighting—producing what appears to be a smooth and flowing surface. With little more than basic algebra, you can even write code that evaluates an equation for a surface and uses something like triangle strips or quads to generate a surface with either a fine or coarse visual resolution.

Suppose, however, you want to create a curve or surface and you don't have an algebraic equation to start with. It's far from a trivial task to figure it out in reverse, starting from what you visualize as the end result and working down to a second- or third-order polynomial. Taking a rigorous mathematical approach is time-consuming and error prone, even with the aid of a computer. And forget about doing it in your head.

Recognizing this fundamental need in the art of computer-generated graphics, Pierre Bézier, an automobile designer for Renault in the 1970s, created a set of mathematical models that could represent curves and surfaces by specifying only a small set of control points. In addition to simplifying the representation of curved surfaces, the models facilitated interactive adjustments to the shape of the curve or surface.

Other types of curves and surfaces and indeed a whole new vocabulary for computer-generated surfaces soon evolved. The mathematics behind this magic show are no more complex than the matrix manipulations in Chapter 5, "Moving Around in Space: Coordinate Transformations," and an intuitive understanding of these curves is easy to grasp. As we did in Chapter 5, we take the approach that you can do a lot with these functions without a deep understanding of their mathematics.

Curves and Surfaces

A curve has a single starting point, a length, and an endpoint. It's really just a line that squiggles about in 3D space. A surface, on the other hand, has width and length and thus a surface area. We begin by showing you how to draw some smooth curves in 3D space and then extend this to surfaces. First, let's establish some common vocabulary and math fundamentals.

Parametric Representation

When you think of straight lines, you might think of this famous equation:

$$y = mx + b$$

Here, m equals the slope of the line, and b is the y intercept of the line (the place where the line crosses the y-axis). This discussion might take you back to your eighth-grade algebra class, where you also learned about the equations for parabolas, hyperbolas, exponential curves, and so on. All of these equations expressed y (or x) in terms of some function of x (or y).

Another way of expressing the equation for a curve or line is as a parametric equation. A parametric equation expresses both x and y in terms of another variable that varies across some predefined range of values that is not explicitly a part of the geometry of the curve. Sometimes in physics, for example, the x, y, and z coordinates of a particle might be in terms of some functions of time, where time is expressed in seconds. In the following, f(), g(), and h() are unique functions that vary with time (t):

$$x = f(t)$$
$$y = g(t)$$
$$z = h(t)$$

When we define a curve in OpenGL, we also define it as a parametric equation. The parametric parameter of the curve, which we call u, and its range of values is the domain of that curve. Surfaces are described using two parametric parameters: u and v. Figure 13.1 shows both a curve and a surface defined in terms of u and v domains. The important thing to realize here is that the parametric parameters (u and v) represent the extents of the equations that describe the curve; they do not reflect actual coordinate values.

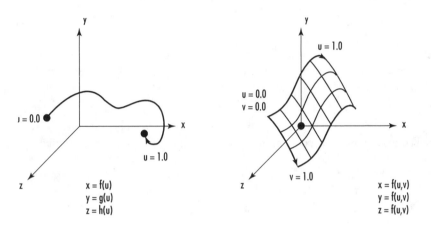

Figure 13.1   Parametric representations of curves and surfaces.

Control Points

Curves are represented by a number of control points that influence the shape of the curve. For the Bézier curves, the first and last control points are actually part of the curve. The other control points act as magnets, pulling the curve towards them. Figure 13.2 shows some examples of this concept, with varying numbers of control points.

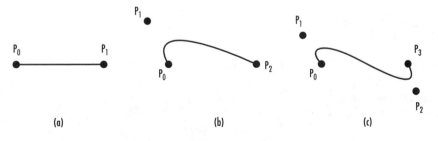

Figure 13.2   How control points affect curve shape.

The *order* of the curve is represented by the number of control points used to describe its shape. The *degree* is one less than the order of the curve. The mathematical meaning of these terms pertains to the parametric equations that exactly describe the curve, with the order being the number of coefficients and the degree being the highest exponent of the parametric parameter. If you want to read more about the mathematical basis of Bézier curves, see Appendix B, "Further Reading."

The curve in Figure 13.2(b) is called aquadratic curve (degree 2), and Figure 13.2(c) is called a cubic (degree 3). Cubic curves are the most typical. Theoretically, you could define a curve of any order, but higher-order curves start to oscillate uncontrollably and can vary wildly with the slightest change to the control points.

Continuity

If two curves placed side by side share an endpoint (called the breakpoint), they together form a piecewise curve. The continuity of these curves at this breakpoint describes how smooth the transition is between them. The four categories of continuity are none (C0), positional (C1), tangential (C2), and curvature (C3).

As you can see in Figure 13.3, no continuity is when the two curves don't meet at all. Positional continuity is achieved when the curves at least meet and share a common endpoint. Tangential continuity occurs when the two curves have the same tangent at the breakpoint. Finally, curvature continuity means the two curves' tangents also have the same rate of change at the breakpoint (thus an even smoother transition).

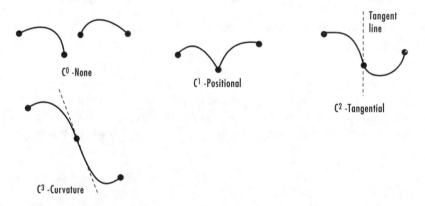

Figure 13.3 Continuity of piecewise curves.

When assembling complex surfaces or curves from many pieces, you usually strive for tangential or curvature continuity. You'll see later that some parameters for curve and surface generation can be chosen to produce the desired continuity.

Evaluators

OpenGL contains several functions that make it easy to draw Bézier curves and surfaces by specifying the control points and the range for the parametric u and v parameters. Then, by calling the appropriate evaluation function (the evaluator), OpenGL generates the points that make up the curve or surface. We start with a 2D example of a Bézier curve and then extend this to three dimensions to create a Bézier surface.

A 2D Curve

The best way to get started is with an example, explaining it line by line. Listing 13.1 shows some code from the sample program BEZIER in this chapter's subdirectory on the CD. This program specifies four control points for a Bézier curve and then renders the curve using an evaluator. The output from Listing 13.1 is shown in Figure 13.4.

Figure 13.4   Output from the BEZIER sample program.

Listing 13.1   *Code from BEZIER That Draws a Bézier Curve with Four Control Points*

```
// The number of control points for this curve
GLint nNumPoints = 4;

GLfloat ctrlPoints[4][3]= {{  -4.0f, 0.0f, 0.0f},    // Endpoint
                { -6.0f, 4.0f, 0.0f},    // Control point
                {  6.0f, -4.0f, 0.0f},    // Control point
                {  4.0f, 0.0f, 0.0f }};    // Endpoint
...
...

// This function is used to superimpose the control points over the curve
void DrawPoints(void)
    {
    int i;    // Counting variable

    // Set point size larger to make more visible
    glPointSize(5.0f);
```

continued on next page

continued from previous page

```
    // Loop through all control points for this example
    glBegin(GL_POINTS);
        for(i = 0; i < nNumPoints; i++)
            glVertex2fv(ctrlPoints[i]);
    glEnd();
    }


// Change viewing volume and viewport.  Called when window is resized
void ChangeSize(GLsizei w, GLsizei h)
    {
    // Prevent a divide by zero
    if(h == 0)
        h = 1;

    // Set viewport to window dimensions
    glViewport(0, 0, w, h);
    glMatrixMode(GL_PROJECTION);
    glLoadIdentity();

    gluOrtho2D(-10.0f, 10.0f, -10.0f, 10.0f);

    // Modelview matrix reset
    glMatrixMode(GL_MODELVIEW);
    glLoadIdentity();
    }

// Called to draw scene
void RenderScene(void)
    {
    int i;

    // Clear the window with current clearing color
    glClear(GL_COLOR_BUFFER_BIT);

    // Sets up the Bezier
    // This actually only needs to be called once and could go in
    // the setup function
    glMap1f(GL_MAP1_VERTEX_3,     // Type of data generated
    0.0f,                    // Lower u range
    100.0f,                    // Upper u range
    3,                    // Distance between points in the data
    nNumPoints,              // Number of control points
    &ctrlPoints[0][0]);         // Array of control points

    // Enable the evaluator
    glEnable(GL_MAP1_VERTEX_3);
```

```
    // Use a line strip to "connect the dots"
    glBegin(GL_LINE_STRIP);
        for(i = 0; i <= 100; i++)
            {
            // Evaluate the curve at this point
            glEvalCoord1f((GLfloat) i);
            }
    glEnd();

    // Draw the control points
    DrawPoints();

    // Show the image
    glutSwapBuffers();
    }
```

The first thing we do in Listing 13.1 is define the control points for our curve:

```
// The number of control points for this curve
GLint nNumPoints = 4;

GLfloat ctrlPoints[4][3]= {{  -4.0f, 0.0f, 0.0f},    // Endpoint
                { -6.0f, 4.0f, 0.0f},    // Control point
                {  6.0f, -4.0f, 0.0f},   // Control point
                {  4.0f, 0.0f, 0.0f }};  // Endpoint
```

We defined global variables for the number of control points and the array of control points. To experiment, you can change these by adding more control points or just modifying the position of these points.

The function DrawPoints is pretty straightforward. We call this function from our rendering code to display the control points along with the curve. This also is useful when you are experimenting with control-point placement. Our standard ChangeSize function establishes a 2D orthographic projection that spans from –10 to +10 in the x and y directions.

Finally, we get to the rendering code. The function RenderScene first calls glMap1f (after clearing the screen) to create a mapping for our curve:

```
// Called to draw scene
void RenderScene(void)
    {
    int i;

    // Clear the window with current clearing color
    glClear(GL_COLOR_BUFFER_BIT);

    // Sets up the Bezier
    // This actually only needs to be called once and could go in
```

```
// the setup function
glMap1f(GL_MAP1_VERTEX_3,    // Type of data generated
0.0f,                    // Lower u range
100.0f,                   // Upper u range
3,                       // Distance between points in the data
nNumPoints,               // Number of control points
&ctrlPoints[0][0]);        // Array of control points
...
...
```

The first parameter to glMap1f, GL_MAP1_VERTEX_3, sets up the evaluator to generate vertex coordinate triplets (x, y, and z). You can also have the evaluator generate other values, such as texture coordinates and color information. See the "Reference Section" at the end of this chapter for details.

The next two parameters specify the lower and upper bounds of the parametric u value for this curve. The lower value specifies the first point on the curve, and the upper value specifies the last point on the curve. All the values in between correspond to the other points along the curve. Here, we set the range to 0–100.

The fourth parameter to glMap1f specifies the number of floating-point values between the vertices in the array of control points. Each vertex consists of three floating-point values (for x, y, and z), so we set this value to 3. This flexibility allows the control points to be placed in an arbitrary data structure, as long as they occur at regular intervals.

The last parameter is a pointer to a buffer containing the control points used to define the curve. Here, we pass a pointer to the first element of the array. Once the mapping for the curve is created, we enable the evaluator to make use of this mapping. This is maintained through a state variable, and the following function call is all that is needed to enable the evaluator to produce points along the curve:

```
// Enable the evaluator
glEnable(GL_MAP1_VERTEX_3);
```

The function glEvalCoord1f takes a single argument: a parametric value along the curve. This function then evaluates the curve at this value and calls glVertex internally for that point. By looping through the domain of the curve and calling glEvalCoord to produce vertices, we can draw the curve with a simple line strip:

```
// Use a line strip to "connect the dots"
glBegin(GL_LINE_STRIP);
    for(i = 0; i <= 100; i++)
        {
        // Evaluate the curve at this point
        glEvalCoord1f((GLfloat) i);
        }
glEnd();
```

Finally, we want to display the control points themselves:

```
// Draw the control points
DrawPoints();
```

```
// Display the image
    glutSwapBuffers();
    }
```

Evaluating a Curve

OpenGL can make things even easier than this. We set up a grid with the function `glMapGrid`, which tells OpenGL to create an evenly spaced grid of points over the u domain (the parametric argument of the curve). Then, we call `glEvalMesh` to "connect the dots" using the primitive specified (`GL_LINE` or `GL_POINTS`). The following two function calls:

```
// Use higher level functions to map to a grid, then evaluate the
// entire thing.
```

```
// Map a grid of 100 points from 0 to 100
glMapGrid1d(100,0.0,100.0);
```

```
// Evaluate the grid, using lines
glEvalMesh1(GL_LINE,0,100);
```

completely replace this code:

```
// Use a line strip to "connect-the-dots"
glBegin(GL_LINE_STRIP);
    for(i = 0; i <= 100; i++)
        {
        // Evaluate the curve at this point
        glEvalCoord1f((GLfloat) i);
        }
glEnd();
```

As you can see, this is more compact and efficient, but its real benefit comes when evaluating surfaces rather than curves.

A 3D Surface

Creating a 3D Bézier surface is much like creating the 2D version. In addition to defining points along the u domain, we must define them along the v domain.

Listing 13.2 is from our next sample program, bez3d, and displays a wire mesh of a 3D Bézier surface. The first change from the preceding example is that we have defined three more sets of control points for the surface along the v domain. To keep this surface simple, the control points are the same except for the z value. This creates a uniform surface, as if we simply extruded a 2D Bézier along the z axis.

Listing 13.2 *bez3d Code to Create a Bézier Surface*

```
// The number of control points for this curve
GLint nNumPoints = 3;

GLfloat ctrlPoints[3][3][3]= {{{  -4.0f, 0.0f, 4.0f},          // V = 0
                     { -2.0f, 4.0f, 4.0f},
                     {  4.0f, 0.0f, 4.0f }},

                     {{  -4.0f, 0.0f, 0.0f},      // V = 1
                      { -2.0f, 4.0f, 0.0f},
                      {  4.0f, 0.0f, 0.0f }},

                       {{ -4.0f, 0.0f, -4.0f},      // V = 2
                     { -2.0f, 4.0f, -4.0f},
                     {  4.0f, 0.0f, -4.0f }}};
...
...

// Called to draw scene
void RenderScene(void)
    {
    //int i;

    // Clear the window with current clearing color
    glClear(GL_COLOR_BUFFER_BIT);

    // Save the modelview matrix stack
    glMatrixMode(GL_MODELVIEW);
    glPushMatrix();

    // Rotate the mesh around to make it easier to see
    glRotatef(45.0f, 0.0f, 1.0f, 0.0f);
    glRotatef(60.0f, 1.0f, 0.0f, 0.0f);

    // Sets up the Bezier
    // This actually only needs to be called once and could go in
    // the setup function
    glMap2f(GL_MAP2_VERTEX_3,     // Type of data generated
    0.0f,                   // Lower u range
    10.0f,                   // Upper u range
    3,                  // Distance between points in the data
    3,                  // Dimension in u direction (order)
    0.0f,                   // Lower v range
    10.0f,                   // Upper v range
    9,                  // Distance between points in the data
    3,                  // Dimension in v direction (order)
    &ctrlPoints[0][0][0]);          // Array of control points
```

```
// Enable the evaluator
glEnable(GL_MAP2_VERTEX_3);

// Use higher level functions to map to a grid, then evaluate the
// entire thing.

// Map a grid of 100 points from 0 to 100
glMapGrid2f(10,0.0f,10.0f,10,0.0f,10.0f);

// Evaluate the grid, using lines
glEvalMesh2(GL_LINE,0,10,0,10);

// Draw the control points
DrawPoints();

// Restore the modelview matrix
glPopMatrix();

// Display the image
glutSwapBuffers();

}
```

Our rendering code is different now, too. In addition to rotating the figure for better effect, we call `glMap2f` instead of `glMap1f`. This specifies control points along two domains (u and v) instead of just one (u):

```
// Sets up the Bezier
// This actually only needs to be called once and could go in
// the setup function
glMap2f(GL_MAP2_VERTEX_3,    // Type of data generated
0.0f,                 // Lower u range
10.0f,                // Upper u range
3,                // Distance between points in the data
3,                // Dimension in u direction (order)
0.0f,                 // Lower v range
10.0f,                // Upper v range
9,                // Distance between points in the data
3,                // Dimension in v direction (order)
&ctrlPoints[0][0][0]);        // Array of control points
```

We must still specify the lower and upper range for u, and the distance between points in the u domain is still 3. Now, however, we must also specify the lower and upper range in the v domain. The distance between points in the v domain is now nine values because we have a three-dimensional array of control points, with each span in the u domain being three points of three values each (3 × 3 = 9). Then, we tell `glMap2f` how many points in the v direction are specified for each u division, followed by a pointer to the control points themselves.

The two-dimensional evaluator is enabled just like the one-dimensional one, and we call `glMapGrid2f` with the number of divisions in the u and v direction:

```
// Enable the evaluator
glEnable(GL_MAP2_VERTEX_3);

// Use higher level functions to map to a grid, then evaluate the
// entire thing.

// Map a grid of 10 points from 0 to 10
glMapGrid2f(10,0.0f,10.0f,10,0.0f,10.0f);
```

After the evaluator is set up, we can call the two-dimensional (meaning u and v) version of `glEvalMesh` to evaluate our surface grid. Here, we evaluate using lines and specify the u and v domains values to range from 0 to 10:

```
// Evaluate the grid, using lines
glEvalMesh2(GL_LINE,0,10,0,10);
```

The end result is shown in Figure 13.5.

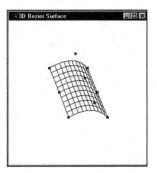

Figure 13.5 Output from the bez3d program.

Lighting and Normal Vectors

Another valuable feature of evaluators is the automatic generation of surface normals. By simply changing this code:

```
// Evaluate the grid, using lines
glEvalMesh2(GL_LINE,0,10,0,10);
```

to this:

```
// Evaluate the grid, using lines
glEvalMesh2(GL_FILL,0,10,0,10);
```

and then calling

```
glEnable(GL_AUTO_NORMAL);
```

in our initialization code, we enable easy lighting of surfaces generated by evaluators. Figure 13.6 shows the same surface as Figure 13.5, but with lighting enabled and automatic normalization turned on. The code for this program appears in bezlit in the CD subdirectory for this chapter. The program is only slightly modified from bez3d.

Figure 13.6   Output from the bezlit program.

NURBS

You can use evaluators to your heart's content to evaluate Bézier surfaces of any degree, but for more complex curves, you have to assemble your Béziers piecewise. As you add more control points, it becomes difficult to create a curve that has good continuity. A higher level of control is available through the glu library's NURBS functions. NURBS stands for non-uniform rational B-spline. Mathematicians out there might know immediately that this is just a more generalized form of curves and surfaces that can produce Bézier curves and surfaces, as well as some other kinds (mathematically speaking). They allow you to tweak the influence of the control points you specified for the evaluators to produce smoother curves and surfaces with larger numbers of control points.

From Bézier to B-Splines

A Bézier curve is defined by two points that act as endpoints and any number of other control points that influence the shape of the curve. The three Bézier curves in Figure 13.7 have three, four, and five control points specified. The curve is tangent to a line that connects the endpoints with their adjacent control points. For quadratic (three points) and cubic (four points) curves, the resulting Béziers are quite smooth, usually with a continuity of C3 (curvature). For higher numbers of control points, however, the smoothness begins to break down as the additional control points pull and tug on the curve.

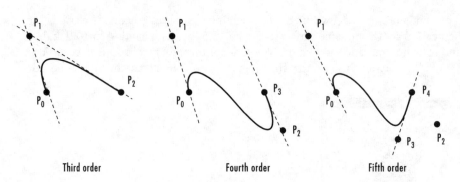

Third order   Fourth order   Fifth order

Figure 13.7 Bézier continuity as the order of the curve increases.

B-splines (bi-cubic splines), on the other hand, work much as the Bézier curves do, but the curve is broken down into segments. The shape of any given segment is influenced only by the nearest four control points, producing a piecewise assemblage of a curve with each segment exhibiting characteristics much like a fourth-order Bézier curve. A long curve with many control points is inherently smoother, with the junction between each segment exhibiting C3 continuity. It also means that the curve does not necessarily have to pass through any of the control points.

Knots

The real power of NURBS is that you can tweak the influence of the four control points for any given segment of a curve to produce the smoothness needed. This control is done via a sequence of values called knots.

Two knot values are defined for every control point. The range of values for the knots matches the u or v parametric domain and must be nondescending. The knot values determine the influence of the control points that fall within that range in u/v space. Figure 13.8 shows a curve demonstrating the influence of control points over a curve having four units in the u parametric domain. Points in the middle of the u domain have a greater pull on the curve, and only points between 0 and 3 have any effect on the shape of the curve.

The key here is that one of these influence curves exists at each control point along the u/v parametric domain. The knot sequence then defines the strength of the influence of points within this domain. If a knot value is repeated, then points near this parametric value have even greater influence. The repeating of knot values is called knot multiplicity. Higher knot multiplicity decreases the curvature of the curve or surface within that region.

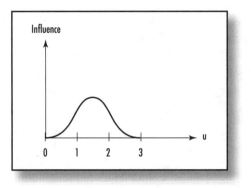

Figure 13.8   Control point influence along the u parameter.

Creating a NURBS Surface

The glu NURBS functions provide a useful high-level facility for rendering surfaces. You don't have to explicitly call the evaluators or establish the mappings or grids. To render a NURBS, you first create a NURBS object that you reference whenever you call the NURBS-related functions to modify the appearance of the surface or curve.

The function `gluNewNurbsRenderer` creates a renderer for the NURB, and `gluDeleteNurbsRenderer` destroys it. The following code fragments demonstrate these functions in use:

```
// NURBS object pointer
GLUnurbsObj *pNurb = NULL;
...
...


// Setup the NURBS object
    pNurb = gluNewNurbsRenderer();


...
// Do your NURBS things...
...
...


// Delete the NURBS object if it was created
if(pNurb)
gluDeleteNurbsRenderer(pNurb);
```

NURBS Properties

Once you have created a NURBS renderer, you can set various high-level NURBS properties for the NURB:

```
// Set sampling tolerance
gluNurbsProperty(pNurb, GLU_SAMPLING_TOLERANCE, 25.0f);

// Fill to make a solid surface (use GLU_OUTLINE_POLYGON to create a
// polygon mesh)
gluNurbsProperty(pNurb, GLU_DISPLAY_MODE, (GLfloat)GLU_FILL);
```

You typically call these functions in your setup routine, rather than repeatedly in your rendering code. In this example, the GLU_SAMPLING_TOLERANCE defines how fine the mesh that defines the surface is, and GLU_FILL tells OpenGL to fill in the mesh instead of generating a wireframe.

Define the Surface

The surface definition is passed as arrays of control points and knot sequences to the gluNurbsSurface function. As shown here, this function is also bracketed by calls to gluBeginSurface and gluEndSurface:

```
// Render the NURB
// Begin the NURB definition
gluBeginSurface(pNurb);

// Evaluate the surface
gluNurbsSurface(pNurb,          // Pointer to NURBS renderer
    8, Knots,                // No. of knots and knot array u direction
    8, Knots,                // No. of knots and knot array v direction
    4 * 3,              // Distance between control points in u dir.
    3,                  // Distance between control points in v dir.
    &ctrlPoints[0][0][0],    // Control points
    4, 4,                // u and v order of surface
    GL_MAP2_VERTEX_3);       // Type of surface

// Done with surface
gluEndSurface(pNurb);
```

You can make more calls to gluNurbsSurface to create any number of NURBS surfaces, but the properties you set for the NURBS renderer are still in effect. Often, this is desired; you rarely want two surfaces (perhaps joined) to have different fill styles (one filled and one a wire mesh).

Using the control points and knot values shown in the next code segment, we produce the NURBS surface shown in Figure 13.9. This NURBS program is found in this chapter's subdirectory on the CD:

```
// Mesh extends four units -6 to +6 along x and y axis
// Lies in Z plane
//                 u   v   (x,y,z)
GLfloat ctrlPoints[4][4][3]= {{{  -6.0f, -6.0f, 0.0f},       // u = 0,    v = 0
                      {       -6.0f, -2.0f, 0.0f},    //          v = 1
                 {   -6.0f,  2.0f, 0.0f},    //       v = 2
                 {   -6.0f,  6.0f, 0.0f}},    //        v = 3

                 {{  -2.0f, -6.0f, 0.0f},    // u = 1    v = 0
                 {   -2.0f, -2.0f, 8.0f},    //        v = 1
                 {   -2.0f,  2.0f, 8.0f},    //        v = 2
                 {   -2.0f,  6.0f, 0.0f}},    //       v = 3

                 {{   2.0f, -6.0f, 0.0f },    // u =2       v = 0
                 {    2.0f, -2.0f, 8.0f },    //       v = 1
                 {    2.0f,  2.0f, 8.0f },    //       v = 2
                 {    2.0f,  6.0f, 0.0f }}, //       v = 3

                 {{   6.0f, -6.0f, 0.0f},    // u = 3    v = 0
                 {    6.0f, -2.0f, 0.0f},    //        v = 1
                 {    6.0f,  2.0f, 0.0f},    //        v = 2
                 {    6.0f,  6.0f, 0.0f}}};    //        v =.3
// Knot sequence for the NURB
GLfloat Knots[8] = {0.0f, 0.0f, 0.0f, 0.0f, 1.0f, 1.0f, 1.0f, 1.0f};
```

Figure 13.9 Output from the NURBS program.

Trimming

Trimming means creating cutout sections from NURBS surfaces. This is often used for literally trimming sharp edges of a NURBS surface. You can also create holes in your surface just as easily. The output from the nurbt program is shown in Figure 13.10. This is the same NURBS surface used in the preceding sample (without the control points shown), with a triangular region removed. This program, too, is on the CD.

Figure 13.10 Output from the nurbt program.

Listing 13.3 is the code that was added to the NURBS sample program to produce this trimming effect. Within the `gluBeginSurface`/`gluEndSurface` delimiters, we call `gluBeginTrim`, specify a trimming curve with `gluPwlCurve`, and finish the trimming curve with `gluEndTrim`.

Listing 13.3 _Modifications to NURBS to Produce Trimming_

```
// Outside trimming points to include entire surface
GLfloat outsidePts[5][2] = /* counterclockwise */
    {{0.0f, 0.0f}, {1.0f, 0.0f}, {1.0f, 1.0f}, {0.0f, 1.0f}, {0.0f, 0.0f}};

// Inside trimming points to create triangle shaped hole in surface
GLfloat insidePts[4][2] = /* clockwise */
   {{0.25f, 0.25f}, {0.5f, 0.5f}, {0.75f, 0.25f}, { 0.25f, 0.25f}};
...
...
...

// Render the NURB
// Begin the NURB definition
gluBeginSurface(pNurb);

// Evaluate the surface
gluNurbsSurface(pNurb,          // Pointer to NURBS renderer
   8, Knots,               // No. of knots and knot array u direction
   8, Knots,               // No. of knots and knot array v direction
   4 * 3,              // Distance between control points in u dir.
   3,                  // Distance between control points in v dir.
   &ctrlPoints[0][0][0],    // Control points
   4, 4,              // u and v order of surface
   GL_MAP2_VERTEX_3);        // Type of surface
```

```
// Outer area, include entire curve
gluBeginTrim (pNurb);
gluPwlCurve (pNurb, 5, &outsidePts[0][0], 2, GLU_MAP1_TRIM_2);
gluEndTrim (pNurb);

// Inner triangular area
gluBeginTrim (pNurb);
gluPwlCurve (pNurb, 4, &insidePts[0][0], 2, GLU_MAP1_TRIM_2);
gluEndTrim (pNurb);


// Done with surface
gluEndSurface(pNurb);
```

Within the `gluBeginTrim`/`gluEndTrim` delimiters, you can specify any number of curves as long as they form a closed loop in a piecewise fashion. You can also use `gluNurbsCurve` to define a trimming region or part of a trimming region. These trimming curves must, however, be in terms of the unit parametric u and v space. This means the entire u/v domain is scaled from 0.0 to 1.0.

The `gluPwlCurve` defines a piecewise linear curve—nothing more than a list of points connected end to end. In this scenario, the inner trimming curve forms a triangle, but with many points, you could create an approximation of any curve needed.

Trimming a curve trims away surface area that is to the right of the curve's winding. Thus, a clockwise-wound trimming curve discards its interior. Typically, an outer trimming curve is specified, which encloses the entire NURBS parameter space. Then, smaller trimming regions are specified within this region with clockwise winding. Figure 13.11 illustrates this relationship.

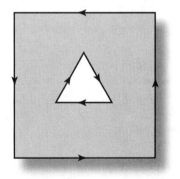

Figure 13.11   An area inside clockwise-wound curves is trimmed away.

Nurbs Curves

Just as you can have Bézier surfaces and curves, you can also have NURBS surfaces and curves. You can even use `gluNurbsCurve` to do NURBS surface trimming. By this point, we hope you have the basics down well enough to try this on your own. However, another sample, nurbc, is included on the CD if you want a starting point to play with.

Summary

This chapter could easily have been the most intimidating in the entire book. As you have seen, however, the concepts behind these curves and surfaces are not at all difficult to understand. Appendix B suggests further reading if you want in-depth mathematical information or tips on creating NURBS-based models.

The examples from this chapter give you a good starting point for experimenting with NURBS. Adjust the control points and knot sequences to create warped or rumpled surfaces. Also, try some quadratic surfaces and some with higher order than the cubic surfaces. Watch out: One pitfall to avoid as you play with these curves is trying too hard to create one complex surface out of a single NURB. You find greater power and flexibility if you compose complex surfaces out of several smaller and easy-to-handle NURBS or Bézier surfaces.

Reference Section

glEvalCoord

Purpose	Evaluates 1D and 2D maps that have been previously enabled.
Include File	<gl.h>
Variations	void glEvalCoord1d(GLdouble u);
	void glEvalCoord1f(GLfloat u);
	void glEvalCoord2d(GLdouble u, GLdouble v);
	void glEvalCoord2f(GLfloat u, GLfloat v);
	void glEvalCoord1dv(const GLdouble *u);
	void glEvalCoord1fv(const GLfloat *u);
	void glEvalCoord2dv(const GLdouble *u);
	void glEvalCoord2fv(const GLfloat *u);
Description	This function uses a previously enabled evaluator (set up with `glMap`) to produce vertex, color, normal, or texture values based on the parametric u/v values. The type of data and function calls simulated are specified by the `glMap1` and `glMap2` functions.

Parameters

u, v   These parameters specify the v and u parametric value that is to be evaluated along the curve or surface.

Returns   None.

Example   The following code from the BEZIER sample program produces equivalent calls to `glVertex3f` each time `glEvalCoord1f` is called. The exact vertex produced is from the equation for the curve at the parametric value i:

```
// Use a line strip to "connect the dots"
glBegin(GL_LINE_STRIP);
    for(i = 0; i <= 100; i++)
        {
        // Evaluate the curve at this point
        glEvalCoord1f((GLfloat) i);
        }
glEnd();
```

See Also   glEvalMesh, glEvalPoint, glMap1, glMap2, glMapGrid

glEvalMesh

Purpose   Computes a 1D or 2D grid of points or lines.

Include File   <gl.h>

Variations   void glEvalMesh1(GLenum mode, GLint i1, GLint i2);
                         void glEvalMesh2(GLenum mode, GLint i1, GLint i2, GLint j1, GLint j2);

Description   This function is used with `glMapGrid` to efficiently create a mesh of evenly spaced u and v domain values. `glEvalMesh` actually evaluates the mesh and produces the points, line segments, or filled polygons.

Parameters

mode   GLdouble: Specifies whether the mesh should be computed as points (GL_POINT), lines (GL_LINE), or filled meshes for surfaces (GL_FILL).

i1, i2   GLint: Specifies the first and last integer values for the u domain.

j1, j2   GLint: Specifies the first and last integer values for the v domain.

Returns   None.

Example   The following code from the BEZIER sample program creates a grid map from 0 to 100 with 100 partitions. The call to `glEvalMesh` then evaluates the grid and draws line segments between each point on the curve:

```
// Use higher level functions to map to a grid, then evaluate the
// entire thing.

// Map a grid of 100 points from 0 to 100
glMapGrid1d(100,0.0,100.0);

// Evaluate the grid, using lines
glEvalMesh1(GL_LINE,0,100);
```

See Also   glBegin, glEvalCoord, glEvalPoint, glMap1, glMap2, glMapGrid

glEvalPoint

Purpose	Generates and evaluates a single point in a mesh.
Include File	<gl.h>
Variations	void glEvalPoint1(GLint i); void glEvalPoint2(GLint i, GLint j);
Description	You can use this function in place of glEvalMesh to evaluate a domain at a single point. The evaluation produces a single primitive, GL_POINTS. The first variation (glEvalPoint1) is used for curves, and the second (glEvalPoint2) is for surfaces.
Parameters	
i, j	GLint: Specifies the u and v domain parametric values.
Returns	None.
Example	The following code renders the Bézier curve in the sample program BEZIER as a series of points rather than line segments. Here, we comment out the code that is no longer needed from the previous example for glEvalCoord:

```
// Use a line strip to "connect the dots"
// glBegin(GL_LINE_STRIP);
    for(i = 0; i <= 100; i++)
        {
        // Evaluate the curve at this point
        //glEvalCoord1f((GLfloat) i);
        glEvalPoint1(i);
        }
// glEnd();
```

See Also   glEvalCoord, glEvalMesh, glMap1, glMap2, glMapGrid

glGetMap

Purpose	Returns evaluator parameters.
Include File	<gl.h>
Variations	`void glGetMapdv(GLenum target, GLenum query, GLdouble *v);`
	`void glGetMapfv(GLenum target, GLenum query, GLfloat *v);`
	`void glGetMapiv(GLenum target, GLenum query, GLint *v);`
Description	This function retrieves map settings that were set by the `glMap` functions. See `glMap1` and `glMap2` in this section for explanations of the types of maps.

Parameters

target   GLenum: The name of the map; the following maps are defined: GL_MAP1_COLOR_4, GL_MAP1_INDEX, GL_MAP1_NORMAL, GL_MAP1_TEXTURE_COORD_1, GL_MAP1_TEXTURE_COORD_2, GL_MAP1_TEXTURE_COORD_3, GL_MAP1_TEXTURE_COORD_4, GL_MAP1_VERTEX_3, GL_MAP1_VERTEX_4, GL_MAP2_COLOR_4, GL_MAP2_INDEX, GL_MAP2_NORMAL, GL_MAP2_TEXTURE_COORD_1, GL_MAP2_TEXTURE_COORD_2, GL_MAP2_TEXTURE_COORD_3, GL_MAP2_TEXTURE_COORD_4, GL_MAP2_VERTEX_3, and GL_MAP2_VERTEX_4. See `glMap` in this section for an explanation of these map types.

query   GLenum: Specifies which map parameter to return in *v. May be one of the following values:
GL_COEFF: Returns an array containing the control points for the map. Coordinates are returned in row-major order. 1D maps return order control points, and 2D maps return u-order times the v-order control points.
GL_ORDER: Returns the order of the evaluator function. For 1D maps, this is a single value. For 2D maps, two values are returned (an array) that contain first the u-order and then the v-order.
GL_DOMAIN: Returns the linear parametric mapping parameters. For 1D evaluators, this is the lower and upper u value. For 2D maps, it's lower and upper u followed by lower and upper v.

*v   Pointer to storage that will contain the requested parameter. The data type of this storage should match the function used (double, float, or integer).

Returns   None.

Example   The following code shows mapping parameters being designated and later retrieved (probably in another function). In comments, we show the contents of the buffer:

```
glMap2f(GL_MAP2_VERTEX_3,      // Type of data generated
0.0f,              // Lower u range
10.0f,               // Upper u range
    3,                 // Distance between points in the data
3,                 // Dimension in u direction (order)
0.0f,              // Lower v range
    10.0f,                 // Upper v range
9,                 // Distance between points in the data
3,                 // Dimension in v direction (order)
    &ctrlPoints[0][0][0]);     // Array of control points

...
...
...


float parametricRange[4];

glGetMapfv(GL_MAP2_VERTEX_3,GL_DOMAIN,parametricRange);

/* Now parametricRange[0] = 0.0          // Lower u
    parametricRange[1] = 10.0       // Upper u
    parametricRange[2] = 0.0        // Lower v
    parametricRange[3] = 10.0       // Upper v

*/
```

See Also   glEvalCoord, glMap1, glMap2

glMap

Purpose	Defines a 1D or 2D evaluator.
Include File	<gl.h>
Variations	void glMap1d(GLenum target, GLdouble u1, GLdouble u2, GLint ustride, GLint uorder, const GLdouble *points);
	void glMap1f(GLenum target, GLfloat u1, GLfloat u2, GLint ustride, GLint uorder, const GLfloat *points);
	void glMap2d(GLenum target, GLdouble u1, GLdouble u2, GLint ustride, GLint uorder, GLdouble v1, GLdouble v2, GLint vstride, GLint vorder, const GLdouble *points);
	void glMap2f(GLenum target, GLfloat u1, GLfloat u2, GLint ustride, GLint uorder, GLfloat v1, GLfloat v2, GLint vstride, GLint vorder, const GLfloat *points);
Description	These functions define 1D or 2D evaluators. The glMap1x functions are used for 1D evaluators (curves), and the glMap2x functions are used for 2D evaluators (surfaces). Evaluators produce vertex or

other information (see the *target* parameter) evaluated along one or two dimensions of a parametric range (u and v).

Parameters

target

GLenum: Specifies what kind of values are produced by the evaluator. Valid values for 1D and 2D evaluators are as follows:

GL_MAP1_VERTEX_3 (or GL_MAP2_VERTEX_3): Control points are three floats that represent x, y, and z coordinate values. glVertex3 commands are generated internally when the map is evaluated.

GL_MAP1_VERTEX_4 (or GL_MAP2_VERTEX_4): Control points are four floats that represent x, y, z, and w coordinate values. glVertex4 commands are generated internally when the map is evaluated.

GL_MAP1_INDEX (or GL_MAP2_INDEX): The generated control points are single floats that represent a color index value. glIndex commands are generated internally when the map is evaluated. Note: The current color index is not changed as it would be if glIndex were called directly.

GL_MAP1_COLOR_4 (or GL_MAP2_COLOR_4): The generated control points are four floats that represent red, green, blue, and alpha components. glColor4 commands are generated internally when the map is evaluated. Note: The current color is not changed as it would be if glColor4f were called directly.

GL_MAP1_NORMAL (or GL_MAP2_NORMAL): The generated control points are three floats that represent the x, y, and z components of a normal vector. glNormal commands are generated internally when the map is evaluated. Note: The current normal is not changed as it would be if glNormal were called directly.

GL_MAP1_TEXTURE_COORD_1 (or GL_MAP2_TEXTURE_COORD_1): The generated control points are single floats that represent the s texture coordinate. glTexCoord1 commands are generated internally when the map is evaluated. Note: The current texture coordinates are not changed as they would be if glTexCoord were called directly.

GL_MAP1_TEXTURE_COORD_2 (or GL_MAP2_TEXTURE_COORD_2): The generated control points are two floats that represent the s and t texture coordinates. glTexCoord2 commands are generated internally when the map is evaluated. Note: The current texture coordinates are not changed as they would be if glTexCoord were called directly.

GL_MAP1_TEXTURE_COORD_3 (or GL_MAP2_TEXTURE_COORD_3): The generated control points are three floats that represent the s, t, and r texture coordinates. glTexCoord3 commands are generated internally when the map is evaluated. Note: The current texture coordinates are not changed as they would be if glTexCoord were called directly.

GL_MAP1_TEXTURE_COORD_4 (or GL_MAP2_TEXTURE_COORD_4): The generated control points are four floats that represent the s, t, r, and q texture coordinates. glTexCoord4 commands are generated internally when the map is evaluated. Note: The current texture coordinates are not changed as they would be if glTexCoord were called directly.

u1, u2   Specifies the linear mapping of the parametric u parameter.

v1, v2   Specifies the linear mapping of the parametric v parameter. This is only used for 2D maps.

ustride, vstride   Specifies the number of floats or doubles between control points in the *points data structure. The coordinates for each point occupy consecutive memory locations, but this parameter allows the points to be spaced as needed to let the data come from an arbitrary data structure.

uorder, vorder   Specifies the number of control points in the u and v direction.

points   A memory pointer that points to the control points. This can be a 2D or 3D array or any arbitrary data structure.

Returns   None.

Example   The following code is from the sample program bez3d from this chapter. It establishes a quadratic Bézier spline mapping:

```
// The number of control points for this curve
GLint nNumPoints = 3;

GLfloat ctrlPoints[3][3][3]= {{{  -4.0f, 0.0f, 4.0f},
  { -2.0f, 4.0f, 4.0f},
                    {  4.0f, 0.0f, 4.0f }},

                 {{  -4.0f, 0.0f, 0.0f},
                  { -2.0f, 4.0f, 0.0f},
                  {  4.0f, 0.0f, 0.0f }},

                 {{  -4.0f, 0.0f, -4.0f},
                  { -2.0f, 4.0f, -4.0f},
                  {  4.0f, 0.0f, -4.0f }}};

...
...



// Sets up the Bezier
// This actually only needs to be called once and could go in
// the setup function
glMap2f(GL_MAP2_VERTEX_3,    // Type of data generated
0.0f,                 // Lower u range
10.0f,                  // Upper u range
```

```
3,              // Distance between points in the data
3,              // Dimension in u direction (order)
0.0f,              // Lower v range
10.0f,              // Upper v range
9,              // Distance between points in the data
3,              // Dimension in v direction (order)
&ctrlPoints[0][0][0]);    // Array of control points
```

See Also   glBegin, glColor, glEnable, glEvalCoord, glEvalMesh,
                  glEvalPoint, glMapGrid, glNormal, glTexCoord, glVertex

glMapGrid

Purpose	Defines a 1D or 2D mapping grid.
Include File	<gl.h>

Variations	void glMapGrid1d(GLint un, GLdouble u1, GLdouble u2);
	void glMapGrid1f(GLint un, GLfloat u1, GLfloat u2);
	void glMapGrid2d(GLint un, GLdouble u1, GLdouble u2,
	GLint vn, GLdouble v1, GLdouble v2);
	void glMapGrid2f(GLint un, GLfloat u1, GLfloat u2, GLint
	vn, GLfloat v1, GLfloat v2);

Description	This function establishes a 1D or 2D mapping grid. This is used with glMap and glEvalMesh to efficiently evaluate a mapping and create a mesh of coordinates.
Parameters	
un, vn	GLint: Specifies the number of grid subdivisions in the u or v direction.
u1, u2	Specifies the lower and upper grid domain values in the u direction.
v1, v2	Specifies the lower and upper grid domain values in the v direction.
Returns	None.
Example	The following code from the bez3d sample program shows a 3D Bézier mapping being established and a mesh being created and evaluated for it:

```
// Sets up the Bezier
// This actually only needs to be called once and could go in
// the setup function
glMap2f(GL_MAP2_VERTEX_3,    // Type of data generated
0.0f,              // Lower u range
10.0f,              // Upper u range
3,              // Distance between points in the data
3,              // Dimension in u direction (order)
0.0f,              // Lower v range
10.0f,              // Upper v range
9,              // Distance between points in the data
```

```
3,                    // Dimension in v direction (order)
&ctrlPoints[0][0][0]);    // Array of control points

// Enable the evaluator
glEnable(GL_MAP2_VERTEX_3);

// Use higher level functions to map to a grid, then evaluate the
// entire thing.

// Map a grid of 10 points from 0 to 10
glMapGrid2f(10,0.0f,10.0f,10,0.0f,10.0f);

// Evaluate the grid, using lines
glEvalMesh2(GL_LINE,0,10,0,10);
```

See Also   glEvalCoord, glEvalMesh, glEvalPoint, glMap1, glMap2

gluBeginCurve

Purpose	Begins a NURBS curve definition.
Include File	<glu.h>
Syntax	void gluBeginCurve(GLUnurbsObj *nObj);
Description	This function is used with gluEndCurve to delimit a NURBS curve definition.
Parameters	
nObj	GLUnurbsObj *: Specifies the NURBS object.
Returns	None.
Example	The following code from the sample program nurbc from the CD demonstrates this function delimiting the NURBS curve definition:

```
// Render the NURB
// Begin the NURB definition
gluBeginCurve(pNurb);

// Evaluate the surface
gluNurbsCurve(pNurb,
    8, Knots,
    3,
    &ctrlPoints[0][0],
    4,
    GL_MAP1_VERTEX_3);

// Done with surface
gluEndCurve(pNurb);
```

See Also   gluEndCurve

gluBeginSurface

Purpose	Begins a NURBS surface definition.
Include File	<glu.h>
Syntax	void gluBeginSurface(GLUnurbsObj *nObj);
Description	This function is used with gluEndSurface to delimit a NURBS surface definition.

Parameters

nObj   GLUnurbsObj *: Specifies the NURBS object.

Returns	None.
Example	The following code from the sample program nurbs from this chapter demonstrates this function delimiting the NURBS surface definition:

```
// Render the NURB
// Begin the NURB definition
gluBeginSurface(pNurb);

// Evaluate the surface
gluNurbsSurface(pNurb,
    8, Knots,
    8, Knots,
    4 * 3,
    3,
    &ctrlPoints[0][0][0],
    4, 4,
    GL_MAP2_VERTEX_3);

// Done with surface
gluEndSurface(pNurb);
```

See Also   gluEndSurface

gluBeginTrim

Purpose	Begins a NURBS trimming loop definition.
Include File	<glu.h>
Syntax	void gluBeginTrim(GLUnurbsObj *nObj);
Description	You use this function with gluEndTrim to delimit a trimming curve definition. A trimming curve is a curve or set of joined curves defined with gluNurbsCurve or gluPwlCurve. The gluBeginTrim and gluEndTrim functions must reside inside the gluBeginSurface/gluEndSurface delimiters. When you use

trimming, the direction of the curve specifies which portions of the surface are trimmed. Surface area to the left of the traveling direction of the trimming curve is left untrimmed. Thus, clockwise-wound trimming curves eliminate the area inside them, and counterclockwise-wound trimming curves eliminate the area outside them.

Parameters

nObj   `GLUnurbsObj *`: Specifies the NURBS object.

Returns   None.

Example   The following code from this chapter's nurbt sample program shows two trimming curves being applied to a NURBS surface. The outer trimming curve includes the entire surface area. The inner curve is actually triangular in shape and creates a cut-away section in the surface:

```
// Render the NURB
// Begin the NURB definition
gluBeginSurface(pNurb);

// Evaluate the surface
gluNurbsSurface(pNurb,
        8, Knots,
        8, Knots,
        4 * 3,
        3,
        &ctrlPoints[0][0][0],
        4, 4,
        GL_MAP2_VERTEX_3);

// Outer area, include entire curve
gluBeginTrim (pNurb);
gluPwlCurve (pNurb, 5, &outsidePts[0][0], 2, GLU_MAP1_TRIM_2);
gluEndTrim (pNurb);

// Inner triangular area
gluBeginTrim (pNurb);
gluPwlCurve (pNurb, 4, &insidePts[0][0], 2, GLU_MAP1_TRIM_2);
gluEndTrim (pNurb);
```

See Also   `gluEndTrim`

gluDeleteNurbsRenderer

Purpose   Destroys a NURBS object.

Include File   <glu.h>

Syntax   `void gluDeleteNurbsRenderer(GLUnurbsObj *nobj);`

Description	This function deletes the NURBS object specified and frees any memory associated with it.
Parameters	
nObj	GLUnurbsObj *: Specifies the NURBS object to delete.
Returns	None.
Example	Following is from the sample program nurbs. It shows the NURBS object being deleted when the main window is destroyed. Note the pointer was initialized to NULL when the program begins and thus is not deleted unless it was successfully created:

```
// Window is being destroyed, cleanup
case WM_DESTROY:
    // Deselect the current rendering context and delete it
    wglMakeCurrent(hDC,NULL);
    wglDeleteContext(hRC);

    // Delete the NURBS object if it was created
    if(pNurb)
        gluDeleteNurbsRenderer(pNurb);

    // Tell the application to terminate after the window
    // is gone.
    PostQuitMessage(0);
    break;
```

See Also	gluNewNurbsRenderer

gluEndCurve

Purpose	Ends a NURBS curve definition.
Include File	<glu.h>
Syntax	void gluEndCurve(GLUnurbsObj *nobj);
Description	This function is used with gluBeginCurve to delimit a NURBS curve definition.
Parameters	
nObj	GLUnurbsObj *: Specifies the NURBS object.
Returns	None.
Example	See the example for gluBeginCurve.
See Also	gluBeginCurve

gluEndSurface

Purpose	Ends a NURBS surface definition.
Include File	<glu.h>
Syntax	`void gluEndSurface(GLUnurbsObj *nObj);`
Description	You use this function with `gluBeginSurface` to delimit a NURBS surface definition.
Parameters	
nObj	`GLUnurbsObj` *: Specifies the NURBS object.
Returns	None.
Example	See the example for `gluBeginSurface`.
See Also	`gluBeginSurface`

gluEndTrim

Purpose	Ends a NURBS trimming loop definition.
Include File	<glu.h>
Syntax	`void gluEndTrim(GLUnurbsObj *nobj);`
Description	Use this function with `gluBeginTrim` to mark the end of a NURBS trimming loop. See `gluBeginTrim` for more information on trimming loops.
Parameters	
nObj	`GLUnurbsObj` *: Specifies the NURBS object.
Returns	None.
Example	See the example for `gluBeginTrim`.
See Also	`gluBeginTrim`

gluGetNurbsProperty

Purpose	Retrieves a NURBS property.
Include File	<gl.h>
Syntax	`void gluGetNurbsProperty(GLUnurbsObj *nObj, GLenum property, GLfloat *value);`
Description	This function retrieves the NURBS property specified for a particular NURBS object. See `gluNurbsProperty` for an explanation of the various properties.
Parameters	
nObj	`GLUnurbsObj` *: Specifies the NURBS object.

property	`GLenum *`: The NURBS property to be retrieved. Valid properties are `GLU_SAMPLING_TOLERANCE`, `GLU_DISPLAY_MODE`, `GLU_CULLING`, `GLU_AUTO_LOAD_MATRIX`, `GLU_PARAMETRIC_TOLERANCE`, `GLU_SAMPLING_METHOD`, `GLU_U_STEP`, and `GLU_V_STEP`. See the `gluNurbsProperty` function for details on these properties.
value	`GLfloat *`: A pointer to the location into which the value of the named property is to be copied.
Returns	None.
Example	The following example shows how the NURBS property `GLU_SAMPLING_TOLERANCE` is set to 25. Later in the program (presumably in some other function), `gluGetNurbsProperty` is called to query the sampling tolerance:

```
gluNurbsProperty(pNurb, GLU_SAMPLING_TOLERANCE, 25.0f);

...
...
GLfloat fTolerance;
...

gluGetNurbsProperty(pNurb, GLU_SAMPLING_TOLERANCE, &fTolerance);
```

See Also	`gluNewNurbsRenderer`, `gluNurbsProperty`

gluLoadSamplingMatrices

Purpose	Loads NURBS sampling and culling matrices.
Include File	<gl.h>
Syntax	`void gluLoadSamplingMatrices(GLUnurbsObj *nObj, const GLfloat modelMatrix[16], const GLfloat projMatrix[16], const GLint viewport[4]);`
Description	You use this function to recompute the sampling and culling matrices for a NURBS surface. The sampling matrix is used to determine how finely the surface must be tessellated to satisfy the sampling tolerance. The culling matrix is used to determine whether the surface should be culled before rendering. Usually, this function does not need to be called, unless the `GLU_AUTO_LOAD_MATRIX` property is turned off. This might be the case when using selection and feedback modes.
Parameters	
nObj	`GLUnurbsObj *`: Specifies the NURBS object.
modelMatrix	`GLfloat[16]`: Specifies the modelview matrix.
projMatrix	`GLfloat[16]`: Specifies the projection matrix.

viewport	GLint[4]: Specifies a viewport.
Returns	None.
Example	You can use the following code to manually set up and use the sampling and culling matrices:

```
GLfloat fModelView[16],fProjection[16],fViewport[4];
...
...

pNurb = glNewNurbsRenderer(.....);
...
...

// Get the current matrix and viewport info
glGetFloatv(GL_MODELVIEW_MATRIX,fModelView);
glGetFloatv(GL_PROJECTION_MATRIX,fProjection);
glGetIntegerv(GL_VIEWPORT,fViewport);

...
...
// Load the matrices manually
gluLoadSamplingMatrices(pNurb,fModelView,fProjection,fViewport);
```

See Also	gluNewNurbsRenderer, gluNurbsProperty

gluNewNurbsRenderer

Purpose	Creates a NURBS object.
Include File	<glu.h>
Syntax	GLUnurbsObj* gluNewNurbsRenderer(void);
Description	This function creates a NURBS rendering object. This object is used to control the behavior and characteristics of NURBS curves and surfaces. The functions that allow the NURBS properties to be set all require this pointer. You must delete this object with gluDeleteNurbsRenderer when you are finished rendering your NURBS.
Returns	A pointer to a new NURBS object. This object is used when you call the rendering and control functions.
Example	This code demonstrates the creation of a NURBS object:

```
// Set up the NURBS object

// Start by creating it
pNurb = gluNewNurbsRenderer();

// Set NURBS properties
```

```
gluNurbsProperty(pNurb, GLU_SAMPLING_TOLERANCE, 25.0f);
    gluNurbsProperty(pNurb, GLU_DISPLAY_MODE, (GLfloat)GLU_FILL);

    ... other properties
...
...
```

See Also   `gluDeleteNurbsRenderer`

gluNurbsCallback

Purpose	Defines a callback for a NURBS function.
Include File	<glu.h>
Syntax	`void gluNurbsCallback(GLUnurbsObj *nObj, GLenum which,` `void(*fn)( ));`
Description	This function sets a NURBS callback function. The only supported callback is `GL_ERROR`. When an error occurs, this function is called with an argument of type `GLenum`. One of 37 NURBS errors can be specified by the defines `GLU_NURBS_ERROR1` through `GLU_NURBS_ERROR37`. A character string definition of the error can be retrieved with the function `gluErrorString`. These are listed in Table 13.1.

Parameters

nObj	`GLUnurbsObj *`: Specifies the NURBS object.
which	`GLenum`: Specifies the callback being defined. The only valid value is `GLU_ERROR`.
fn	`void *()`: Specifies the function that should be called for the callback.
Returns	None.
Example	The following is an sample error handler for NURBS errors. Some code that installs the error handler is also shown. You can see this in the NURBS sample program:

```
// NURBS callback error handler
void CALLBACK NurbsErrorHandler(GLenum nErrorCode)
    {
    char cMessage[64];

    // Extract a text message of the error
    strcpy(cMessage,"NURBS error occurred: ");
    strcat(cMessage,gluErrorString(nErrorCode));
    // Display the message to the user
    MessageBox(NULL,cMessage,NULL,MB_OK | MB_ICONEXCLAMATION);
```

```
            }

    ...
    ...
    ...

    // Set up the NURBS object
        pNurb = gluNewNurbsRenderer();

        // Install error handler to notify user of NURBS errors
        gluNurbsCallback(pNurb, GLU_ERROR, NurbsErrorHandler);

        gluNurbsProperty(pNurb, GLU_SAMPLING_TOLERANCE, 25.0f);
        ... other properties
        ...
```

See Also   `gluErrorString`

Table 13.1   *NURBS Error Codes*

Error Code	Definition
GLU_NURBS_ERROR1	Spline order unsupported.
GLU_NURBS_ERROR2	Too few knots.
GLU_NURBS_ERROR3	Valid knot range is empty.
GLU_NURBS_ERROR4	Decreasing knot sequence knot.
GLU_NURBS_ERROR5	Knot multiplicity greater than order of spline.
GLU_NURBS_ERROR6	endcurve must follow bgncurve.
GLU_NURBS_ERROR7	bgncurve must precede endcurve.
GLU_NURBS_ERROR8	Missing or extra geometric data.
GLU_NURBS_ERROR9	Can't draw pwlcurves.
GLU_NURBS_ERROR10	Missing or extra domain data.
GLU_NURBS_ERROR11	Missing or extra domain data.
GLU_NURBS_ERROR12	endtrim must precede endsurface.
GLU_NURBS_ERROR13	bgnsurface must precede endsurface.
GLU_NURBS_ERROR14	Curve of improper type passed as trim curve.
GLU_NURBS_ERROR15	bgnsurface must precede bgntrim.
GLU_NURBS_ERROR16	endtrim must follow bgntrim.
GLU_NURBS_ERROR17	bgntrim must precede endtrim.
GLU_NURBS_ERROR18	Invalid or missing trim curve.
GLU_NURBS_ERROR19	bgntrim must precede pwlcurve.

Error Code	Definition
GLU_NURBS_ERROR20	pwlcurve referenced twice.
GLU_NURBS_ERROR21	pwlcurve and nurbscurve mixed.
GLU_NURBS_ERROR22	Improper usage of trim data type.
GLU_NURBS_ERROR23	nurbscurve referenced twice.
GLU_NURBS_ERROR24	nurbscurve and pwlcurve mixed.
GLU_NURBS_ERROR25	nurbssurface referenced twice.
GLU_NURBS_ERROR26	Invalid property.
GLU_NURBS_ERROR27	endsurface must follow bgnsurface.
GLU_NURBS_ERROR28	Intersecting or misoriented trim curves.
GLU_NURBS_ERROR29	Intersecting trim curves.
GLU_NURBS_ERROR30	Unused.
GLU_NURBS_ERROR31	Unconnected trim curves.
GLU_NURBS_ERROR32	Unknown knot error.
GLU_NURBS_ERROR33	Negative vertex count encountered.
GLU_NURBS_ERROR34	Negative byte-stride encountered.
GLU_NURBS_ERROR35	Unknown type descriptor.
GLU_NURBS_ERROR36	Null control point reference.
GLU_NURBS_ERROR37	Duplicate point on pwlcurve.

gluNurbsCurve

Purpose	Defines the shape of a NURBS curve.
Include File	<glu.h>
Syntax	void gluNurbsCurve(GLUnurbsObj *nObj, GLint nknots, GLfloat *knot, GLint stride, GLfloat *ctlArray, GLint order, GLenum type);
Description	This function defines the shape of a NURBS curve. The definition of this curve must be delimited by gluBeginCurve and gluEndCurve.
Parameters	
nObj	GLUnurbsObj *: Pointer to the NURBS object (created with gluNewNurbsRenderer).
nknots	GLint: The number of knots in *knots. This is the number of control points plus order.
knot	GLfloat *: An array of knot values in nondescending order.

stride	`GLint`: Specifies the offset, as a number of single-precision floating-point values, between control points.
ctlArray	`GLfloat *`: Pointer to an array or data structure containing the control points for the NURBS surface.
order	`GLint`: The order of the NURBS surface. Order is 1 more than the degree.
type	`GLenum`: The type of surface. This can be any of the two-dimensional evaluator types: `GL_MAP2_VERTEX_3`, `GL_MAP2_VERTEX_4`, `GL_MAP2_INDEX`, `GL_MAP2_COLOR_4`, `GL_MAP2_NORMAL`, `GL_MAP2_TEXTURE_COORD_1`, `GL_MAP2_TEXTURE_COORD_2`, `GL_MAP2_TEXTURE_COORD_3`, and `GL_MAP2_TEXTURE_COORD_4`.
Returns	None.
Example	See the example for `gluBeginCurve`.
See Also	`gluBeginCurve`, `gluEndCurve`, `gluNurbsSurface`

gluNurbsProperty

Purpose	Sets a NURBS property.
Include File	<glu.h>
Syntax	`void gluNurbsProperty(GLUnurbsObj *nObj, GLenum property, GLfloat value);`
Description	This function sets the properties of the NURBS object. Valid properties are as follows:

`GLU_SAMPLING_TOLERANCE`: Sets the maximum length in pixels to use when using the `GLU_PATH_LENGTH` sampling method. The default is 50.0.

`GLU_DISPLAY_MODE`: Defines how the NURBS surface is rendered. The value parameter can be `GLU_FILL` to use filled and shaded polygons, `GLU_OUTLINE_POLYGON` to draw just the outlines of the polygons (after tessellation), and `GLU_OUTLINE_PATCH` to draw just the outlines of user-defined patches and trim curves. The default is `GLU_FILL`.

`GLU_CULLING`: The `value` parameter is interpreted as a Boolean value that indicates whether the NURBS curve should be discarded if its control points are outside the viewport.

`GLU_PARAMETRIC_TOLERANCE`: Sets the maximum pixel distance used when the sampling method is set to `GLU_PARAMETRIC_ERROR`. The default is 0.5. This property was introduced in GLU version 1.1.

`GLU_SAMPLING_METHOD`: Specifies how to tessellate the NURBS surface. This property was introduced in GLU version 1.1. The following values are valid:

GLU_PATH_LENGTH specifies that surfaces rendered with the maximum pixel length of the edges of the tessellation polygons are not greater than the value specified by GLU_SAMPLING_TOLERANCE. GLU_PARAMETRIC_ERROR specifies that the surface is rendered with the value of GLU_PARAMETRIC_TOLERANCE designating the maximum distance, in pixels, between the tessellation polygons and the surfaces they approximate.

GLU_DOMAIN_DISTANCE specifies, in parametric coordinates, how many sample points per unit length to take in the u and v dimensions. The default is GLU_PATH_LENGTH.

GLU_U_STEP: Sets the number of sample points per unit length taken along the u dimension in parametric coordinates. This value is used when GLU_SAMPLING_METHOD is set to GLU_DOMAIN_DISTANCE. The default is 100. This property was introduced in GLU version 1.1.

GLU_V_STEP: Sets the number of sample points per unit length taken along the v dimension in parametric coordinates. This value is used when GLU_SAMPLING_METHOD is set to GLU_DOMAIN_DISTANCE. The default is 100. This property was introduced in GLU version 1.1.

GLU_AUTO_LOAD_MATRIX: The value parameter is interpreted as a Boolean value. When set to GL_TRUE, it causes the NURBS code to download the projection matrix, the modelview matrix, and the viewport from the OpenGL server to compute sampling and culling matrices for each NURBS curve. Sampling and culling matrices are required to determine the tessellation of a NURBS surface into line segments or polygons and to cull a NURBS surface if it lies outside of the viewport. If this mode is set to GL_FALSE, the user needs to provide these matrices and a viewport for the NURBS renderer to use in constructing sampling and culling matrices. This can be done with the gluLoadSamplingMatrices function. The default value for this mode is GL_TRUE. Changing this mode does not affect the sampling and culling matrices until gluLoadSamplingMatrices is called.

Parameters

nObj   GLUnurbsObj *: The NURB object that is having a property modified. (This is created by calling glNewNurbsRenderer.)

property   GLenum: The property to be set or modified. This may be any of the following values: GLU_SAMPLING_TOLERANCE, GLU_DISPLAY_MODE, GLU_CULLING, GLU_AUTO_LOAD_MATRIX, GLU_PARAMETRIC_TOLERANCE, GLU_SAMPLING_METHOD, GLU_U_STEP, and GLU_V_STEP.

value   GLfloat: The value to which the indicated property is being set.

Returns   None.

Example   The following code from this chapter's nurbs program sets the NURBS display property to render the surface as a wire mesh:

```
gluNurbsProperty(pNurb, GLU_DISPLAY_MODE, GLU_OUTLINE_POLYGON);
```

See Also   gluGetNurbsProperty, gluGetString, gluLoadSamplingMatrices, gluNewNurbsRenderer

gluNurbsSurface

Purpose   Defines the shape of a NURBS surface.

Include File   <glu.h>

Syntax   void gluNurbsSurface(GLUnurbsObj *nObj, GLint uknotCount, GLfloat *uknot, GLint vknotCount, GLfloat *vknot, GLint uStride, GLint vStride, GLfloat *ctlArray, GLint uorder, GLint vorder, GLenum type);

Description   This function defines the shape of a NURBS surface. Must be delimited by gluBeginSurface and gluEndSurface. The shape of the surface is defined before any trimming takes place. You can trim a NURBS surface by using the gluBeginTrim/gluEndTrim and gluNurbsCurve or gluPwlCurve to do the trimming.

Parameters

nObj   GLUnurbsObj *: Pointer to the NURBS object (created with gluNewNurbsRenderer).

uknotCount   GLint: The number of knots in the parametric u direction.

uknot   GLfloat *: An array of knot values that represent the knots in the u direction. These values must be nondescending. The length of the array is specified in uknotCount.

vknotCount   GLint: The number of knots in the parametric v direction.

vknot   GLfloat*: An array of knot values that represent the knots in the v direction. These values must be nondescending. The length of the array is specified in vknotCount.

uStride   GLint: Specifies the offset, as a number of single-precision, floating-point values, between successive control points in the parametric u direction in ctlArray.

vStride   GLint: Specifies the offset, as a number of single-precision, floating-point values, between successive control points in the parametric v direction in ctlArray.

ctlArray   GLfloat *: Pointer to an array containing the control points for the NURBS surface. The offsets between successive control points in the parametric u and v directions are given by uStride and vStride.

uorder   GLint: The order of the NURBS surface in the parametric u direction. The order is 1 more than the degree; hence, a surface that is cubic in u has a u order of 4.

vorder	GLint: The order of the NURBS surface in the parametric v direction. The order is 1 more than the degree; hence, a surface that is cubic in v has a v order of 4.
type	GLenum: The type of surface. This can be any of the 2D evaluator types: GL_MAP2_VERTEX_3, GL_MAP2_VERTEX_4, GL_MAP2_INDEX, GL_MAP2_COLOR_4, GL_MAP2_NORMAL, GL_MAP2_TEXTURE_COORD_1, GL_MAP2_TEXTURE_COORD_2, GL_MAP2_TEXTURE_COORD_3, and GL_MAP2_TEXTURE_COORD_4.
Returns	None.
Example	See the example for gluBeginSurface.
See Also	gluBeginSurface, gluBeginTrim, gluNewNurbsRenderer, gluNurbsCurve, gluPwlCurve

gluPwlCurve

Purpose	Specifies a piecewise NURBS trimming curve.
Include File	<glu.h>
Syntax	void gluPwlCurve(GLUnurbsObj *nObj, GLint count, GLfloat *array, GLint stride, GLenum type);
Description	This function defines a piecewise linear trimming curve for a NURBS surface. The array of points are in terms of the parametric u and v coordinate space. This space is a unit square exactly 1 unit in length along both axes. Clockwise-wound trimming curves eliminate the enclosed area; counterclockwise trimming curves discard the exterior area. Typically, a trimming region is first established around the entire surface area that trims away all points not on the surface. Then, smaller trimming areas wound clockwise are placed within it to cut away sections of the curve. Trimming curves can be piecewise. This means one or more calls to gluPwlCurve or gluNurbsCurve can be called to define a trimming region as long as they share endpoints and define a close region in u/v space.
Parameters	
nObj	GLUnurbsObj *: Specifies the NURBS object being trimmed.
count	GLint: Specifies the number of points on the curve listed in *array.
array	GLfloat *: Specifies the array of boundary points for this curve.
stride	GLint: Specifies the offset between points on the curve.
type	GLenum: Specifies the type of curve. Can be GLU_MAP1_TRIM_2, used when the trimming curve is specified in terms of u and v coordinates, or GLU_MAP1_TRIM_3, used when a w (scaling) coordinate is also specified.

Returns   None.

Example   The following code from this chapter's program nurbt shows a
                     NURBS curve being trimmed with a triangular shaped region. A
                     large trimming area encloses the surface that includes all the area
                     within it. A secondary trimming area defines a triangle and discards
                     any surface area within it:

```
// Outside trimming points to include entire surface
GLfloat outsidePts[5][2] = /* counterclockwise */
        {{0.0f, 0.0f}, {1.0f, 0.0f}, {1.0f, 1.0f},
                            {0.0f, 1.0f}, {0.0f, 0.0f}};

// Inside trimming points to create triangle shaped hole in surface
GLfloat insidePts[4][2] = /* clockwise */
    {{0.25f, 0.25f}, {0.5f, 0.5f}, {0.75f, 0.25f}, { 0.25f, 0.25f}};

...
...

// Render the NURB
// Begin the NURB definition
gluBeginSurface(pNurb);

// Evaluate the surface
gluNurbsSurface(pNurb,
        8, Knots,
        8, Knots,
        4 * 3,
        3,
        &ctrlPoints[0][0][0],
        4, 4,
        GL_MAP2_VERTEX_3);

// Outer area, include entire curve
gluBeginTrim (pNurb);
gluPwlCurve (pNurb, 5, &outsidePts[0][0], 2, GLU_MAP1_TRIM_2);
gluEndTrim (pNurb);

// Inner triangular area
gluBeginTrim (pNurb);
gluPwlCurve (pNurb, 4, &insidePts[0][0], 2, GLU_MAP1_TRIM_2);
gluEndTrim (pNurb);


// Done with surface
gluEndSurface(pNurb);
```

See Also   gluBeginTrim, gluEndTrim, gluNurbsCurve

14

INTERACTIVE GRAPHICS

by Richard S. Wright, Jr.

What you'll learn in this chapter:

How to...	Functions You'll Use
Assign OpenGL selection names to primitives or groups of primitives	glInitNames/glPushName/glPopName
Use selection to determine which objects are under the mouse	glSelectBuffer/glRenderMode
Use feedback to get information about where objects are drawn	glFeedbackBuffer/gluPickMatrix

Thus far, you have learned to create some sophisticated 3D graphics using OpenGL, and many applications do no more than generate these scenes. But many graphics applications (notably, games, CAD, 3D modeling, and so on) require more interaction with the scene itself. In addition to the menu and dialog boxes, you need to provide a way for the user to interact with a graphical scene. Under Windows, this interaction usually happens with a mouse.

Selection, a powerful feature of OpenGL, allows you to take a mouse click at some position over a window and determine which of your objects are beneath it. The act of selecting a specific object on the screen is called *picking*. With Open GL's selection feature, you can specify a viewing volume and determine which objects fall within that viewing volume. A powerful utility function, gluPickMatrix, produces a matrix for you, based purely on screen coordinates and the pixel dimensions you specify; you use this matrix to create a smaller viewing volume placed beneath the mouse cursor. Then, you use selection to test this viewing volume to see which objects are contained by it.

Feedback allows you to get information from OpenGL about how your vertices are transformed and illuminated when they are drawn to the frame buffer. You can use this information to transmit rendering results over a network, send them to a plotter, or add GDI graphics (for Windows programmers) to your OpenGL scene that appear to interact with the OpenGL objects. Feedback does not serve the same purpose as selection, but the mode of operation is similar and they work productively together. You'll see this teamwork later in the select.c sample program.

Selection

Selection is actually a rendering mode, but in selection mode, no pixels are actually copied to the frame buffer. Instead, primitives that are drawn within the viewing volume (and thus would normally appear in the frame buffer) produce *hit* records in a selection buffer.

You must set up this selection buffer in advance and name your primitives or groups of primitives (your objects or models) so they can be identified in the selection buffer. You then parse the selection buffer to determine which objects intersected the viewing volume. This has marginal value unless you modify the viewing volume before entering selection mode and calling your drawing code to determine which objects are in some restricted area of your scene. In one common scenario, you specify a viewing volume that corresponds to the mouse pointer and then check which named objects the mouse is pointing to.

Naming Your Primitives

You can name every single primitive used to render your scene of objects, but this is rarely useful. More often, you name groups of primitives, thus creating names for the specific objects or pieces of objects in your scene. Object names, like display list names, are nothing more than unsigned integers.

The names list is maintained on the name stack. After you initialize the name stack, you can push names on the stack or simply replace the name currently on top of the stack. When a hit occurs during selection, all the names on the names stack are copied into the selection buffer. Thus, a single hit can return more than one name if needed.

For our first example, we keep things simple. We create a simplified (and not to scale) model of the inner planets of the solar system. When the left mouse button is down, we display a message box describing which planet was clicked. Listing 14.1 shows some of the rendering code for our sample program, PLANETS. We have created macro definitions for the Sun, Mercury, Venus, Earth, and Mars.

Listing 14.1   *Naming the Sun and Planets in the PLANETS Program*

```
#define SUN         1
#define MERCURY     2
```

```
#define VENUS         3
#define EARTH         4
#define MARS          5

...
...

// Called to draw scene
void RenderScene(void)
    {
    // Clear the window with current clearing color
    glClear(GL_COLOR_BUFFER_BIT | GL_DEPTH_BUFFER_BIT);

    // Save the matrix state and do the rotations
    glMatrixMode(GL_MODELVIEW);
    glPushMatrix();

    // Translate the whole scene out and into view
    glTranslatef(0.0f, 0.0f, -300.0f);

    // Initialize the names stack
    glInitNames();
    glPushName(0);

    // Set material color, Yellow
    // Sun
    glRGB(255, 255, 0);
    glLoadName(SUN);
    glutauxSolidSphere(15.0f, 15, 15);

    // Draw Mercury
    glRGB(128,0,0);
    glPushMatrix();
    glTranslatef(24.0f, 0.0f, 0.0f);
    glLoadName(MERCURY);
    glutauxSolidSphere(2.0f, 15, 15);
    glPopMatrix();

    // Draw Venus
    glPushMatrix();
    glRGB(128,128,255);
    glTranslatef(60.0f, 0.0f, 0.0f);
    glLoadName(VENUS);
    glutauxSolidSphere(4.0f, 15, 15);
    glPopMatrix();
...
...     Other planets
...
```

```
// Restore the matrix state
glPopMatrix();    // Modelview matrix

// Flush drawing commands and swap buffers
glutSwapBuffers();
}
```

In PLANETS, the `glInitNames` function initializes and clears the names stack, and `glPushName` pushes 0 on the stack to put at least one entry on the stack. For the Sun and each planet, we call `glLoadName` to name the object or objects about to be drawn. This name, in the form of an unsigned integer, is not pushed on the name stack but rather replaces the current name on top of the stack. Later, we discuss keeping an actual stack of names. For now, we just replace the top name of the name stack each time we draw an object (the Sun or a particular planet).

Working with Selection Mode

As mentioned, OpenGL can operate in three different rendering modes. The default mode is GL_RENDER, in which all the drawing actually occurs onscreen. To use selection, we must change the rendering mode to selection by calling the OpenGL function:

```
glRenderMode(GL_SELECTION);
```

When we actually want to draw again, we call

```
glRenderMode(GL_RENDER);
```

to place OpenGL back in rendering mode. The third rendering mode is GL_FEEDBACK, discussed later in this chapter.

The naming code in Listing 14.1 has no effect unless we first switch the rendering mode to selection mode. Most often, you use the same function to render the scene in both GL_RENDER mode and GL_SELECTION mode, as we have done here.

Listing 14.2 is the GLUT callback`code triggered by the clicking of the left mouse button. This code checks for a left button click and then forwards the mouse coordinates to `ProcessSelection`, which processes the mouse click for this example.

Listing 14.2 *Code That Responds to the Left Mouse Button Click*

```
// Process the mouse click
void MouseCallback(int button, int state, int x, int y)
    {
    if(button == GLUT_LEFT_BUTTON && state == GLUT_DOWN)
        ProcessSelection(x, y);
    }case WM_LBUTTONDOWN:
```

The Selection Buffer

The selection buffer is filled with hit records during the rendering process. A hit record is generated whenever a primitive or collection of primitives is rendered that would have been contained in the viewing volume. Under normal conditions, this is simply anything that would have appeared onscreen.

The selection buffer is an array of unsigned integers, and each hit record occupies at least four elements of the array. The first array index contains the number of names that are on the names stack when the hit occurs. For the PLANETS example (Listing 14.1), this is always 1. The next two entries contain the minimum and maximum window z coordinates of all the vertices contained by the viewing volume since the last hit record. This value, which ranges from [0,1], is scaled to the size of an unsigned integer $(2^{32}-1)$ for storage in the selection buffer. The fourth entry is the bottom of the names stack. If there is more than one name on the name stack (indicated by the first index element), then these follow the fourth element. This pattern, illustrated in Figure 14.1, is then repeated for all the hit records contained in the selection buffer. We explain why this can be useful when we discuss *picking*.

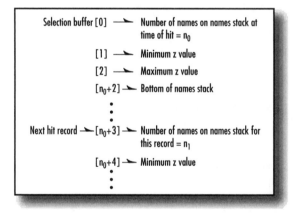

Figure 14.1 Hit record for the selection buffer.

The format of the selection buffer gives you no way of knowing how many hit records you need to parse. The selection buffer is not actually filled until you switch the rendering mode back to GL_RENDER. When you do this with the glRenderMode function, the return value of glRenderMode returns the number of hit records copied.

Listing 14.3 shows the processing function called when a mouse click occurs for the PLANETS sample program. It shows the selection buffer being allocated and specified with glSelectBuffer. This function takes two arguments: the length of the buffer and a pointer to the buffer itself.

Listing 14.3 *Function to Process the Mouse Click*

```
// Process the selection, which is triggered by a right mouse
// click at (xPos, yPos).
#define BUFFER_LENGTH 64
void ProcessSelection(int xPos, int yPos)
    {
    // Space for selection buffer
    GLuint selectBuff[BUFFER_LENGTH];

    // Hit counter and viewport storage
    GLint hits, viewport[4];

    // Set up selection buffer
    glSelectBuffer(BUFFER_LENGTH, selectBuff);

    // Get the viewport
    glGetIntegerv(GL_VIEWPORT, viewport);

    // Switch to projection and save the matrix
    glMatrixMode(GL_PROJECTION);
    glPushMatrix();

    // Change render mode
    glRenderMode(GL_SELECT);

    // Establish new clipping volume to be unit cube around
    // mouse cursor point (xPos, yPos) and extending two pixels
    // in the vertical and horizontal direction
    glLoadIdentity();
    gluPickMatrix(xPos, viewport[3] - yPos, 2,2, viewport);

    // Apply perspective matrix
    gluPerspective(45.0f, fAspect, 1.0, 425.0);

    // Draw the scene
    RenderScene();

    // Collect the hits
    hits = glRenderMode(GL_RENDER);

    // If a single hit occurred, display the info.
    if(hits == 1)
        ProcessPlanet(selectBuff[3]);

    // Restore the projection matrix
    glMatrixMode(GL_PROJECTION);
```

```
glPopMatrix();

// Go back to modelview for normal rendering
glMatrixMode(GL_MODELVIEW);
}
```

Picking

Picking occurs when you use the mouse position to create and use a modified viewing volume during selection. When you create a smaller viewing volume positioned in your scene under the mouse position, only objects that would be drawn within that viewing volume generate hit records. By examining the selection buffer, you can then see which objects, if any, were clicked by the mouse.

The `gluPickMatrix` function is a handy utility that creates a matrix describing the new viewing volume:

```
void gluPickMatrix(GLdouble x, GLdouble y, GLdouble width,
                            GLdouble height, GLint viewport[4]);
```

The *x* and *y* parameters are the center of the desired viewing volume in OpenGL window coordinates. You can plug in the mouse position here, and the viewing volume will be centered directly underneath the mouse. The *width* and *height* parameters then specify the dimensions of the viewing volume in window pixels. For clicks near an object, use a large value; for clicks right next to the object or directly on the object, use a smaller value. The *viewport* array contains the window coordinates of the currently defined viewport. This can easily be obtained by calling

```
glGetIntegerv(GL_VIEWPORT, viewport);
```

Remember, as discussed in Chapter 3, "Using OpenGL," that OpenGL window coordinates are the opposite of Microsoft's window coordinates with respect to how pixels are counted vertically. Note in Listing 14.3, we subtract the mouse y coordinate from the viewport's height. This yields the proper vertical window coordinate for OpenGL:

```
gluPickMatrix(xPos, viewport[3] - yPos, 2,2, viewport);
```

To use `gluPickMatrix`, you should first save the current projection matrix state (thus saving the current viewing volume). Then, call `glLoadIdentity` to create a unit-viewing volume. Calling `gluPickMatrix` then translates this viewing volume to the correct location. Finally, you must apply any further perspective projections you may have applied to your original scene; otherwise, you won't get a true mapping. Here's how it's done for the PLANETS example (from Listing 14.3):

```
// Switch to projection and save the matrix
glMatrixMode(GL_PROJECTION);
glPushMatrix();
```

```
// Change render mode
glRenderMode(GL_SELECT);

// Establish new clipping volume to be unit cube around
// mouse cursor point (xPos, yPos) and extending two pixels
// in the vertical and horizontal direction
glLoadIdentity();
gluPickMatrix(xPos, yPos, 2,2, viewport);

// Apply perspective matrix
gluPerspective(45.0f, fAspect, 1.0, 425.0);

// Draw the scene
RenderScene();

// Collect the hits
hits = glRenderMode(GL_RENDER);
```

In this segment, the viewing volume is saved first. Then, the selection mode is entered, the viewing volume is modified to include only the area beneath the mouse cursor, and the scene is redrawn by calling RenderScene. After the scene is rendered, we call glRenderMode again to place OpenGL back into normal rendering mode and get a count of generated hit records.

In the next segment, if a hit occurred (for this example, there is either one hit or none), we pass the entry in the selection buffer that contains the name of the object selected or our ProcessPlanet function. Finally, we restore the projection matrix (thus the old viewing volume is restored) and switch the active matrix stack back to the modelview matrix, which is usually the default:

```
// If a single hit occurred, display the info.
if(hits == 1)
    ProcessPlanet(selectBuff[3]);

// Restore the projection matrix
glMatrixMode(GL_PROJECTION);
glPopMatrix();

// Go back to modelview for normal rendering
glMatrixMode(GL_MODELVIEW);
```

The ProcessPlanet function simply displays a message box telling which planet was clicked. This code is not shown because it is fairly trivial, consisting of no more than a switch and some message-box function calls.

The output from PLANETS is shown in Figure 14.2, where you can see the result of clicking the second planet from the Sun.

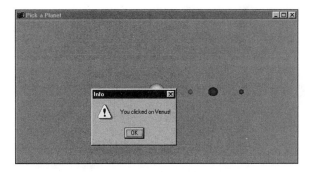

Figure 14.2   Output from PLANETS after clicking a planet.

Although we don't go into any great detail here, it is worth discussing briefly the z values from the selection buffer. In the PLANETS example, each object or model was distinct and off alone in its own space. What if you apply this same method to several objects or models that perhaps overlap? You get multiple hit records! How do you know which one the user clicked? This situation can be tricky and requires some forethought. You can use the z values to determine which object was closest to the user in viewspace, which is the most likely object that was clicked. Still, for some shapes and geometry, if you aren't careful, it can be difficult to sort out precisely what the user intended to pick.

Hierarchical Picking

For the PLANETS example, we didn't push any names on the stack, but rather just replaced the existing one whenever a new object was to be rendered. This single name residing on the name stack was the only name returned in the selection buffer. We can also get multiple names when a selection hit occurs, by placing more than one name on the name stack. This is useful, for instance, in drill-down situations when you need to know not only that a particular bolt was selected, but also that it belonged to a particular wheel, on a particular car, and so forth.

To demonstrate multiple names being returned on the names stack, we stick with the astronomy theme of our previous example. Figure 14.3 shows two planets (okay, so use a little imagination)—a large blue planet with a single moon and a smaller red planet with two moons.

Rather than just identify the planet or moon that's clicked, we want to also identify the planet that is associated with the particular moon. The code in Listing 14.4 shows our new rendering code for this scene. We push the names of the moons onto the names stack so that it contains the name of the planet as well as the name of the moon when selected.

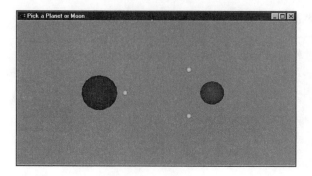

Figure 14.3   Two planets with their respective moons.

Listing 14.4   *Rendering Code for the MOONS Sample Program*

```
#define EARTH    1
#define MARS     2
#define MOON1    3
#define MOON2    4


// Called to draw scene
void RenderScene(void)
    {
    // Clear the window with current clearing color
    glClear(GL_COLOR_BUFFER_BIT | GL_DEPTH_BUFFER_BIT);

    // Save the matrix state and do the rotations
    glMatrixMode(GL_MODELVIEW);
    glPushMatrix();

    // Translate the whole scene out and into view
    glTranslatef(0.0f, 0.0f, -300.0f);

    // Initialize the names stack
    glInitNames();
    glPushName(0);

    // Draw the Earth
    glPushMatrix();
    glColor3ub(0,0,255);
    glTranslatef(-100.0f,0.0f,0.0f);
    glLoadName(EARTH);
    glutauxSolidSphere(30.0f, 15, 15);

    // Draw the Moon
```

```
glTranslatef(45.0f, 0.0f, 0.0f);
glColor3ub(220,220,220);
glPushName(MOON1);
glutauxSolidSphere(5.0f, 15, 15);
glPopName();
glPopMatrix();

// Draw Mars
glColor3ub(255,0,0);
glPushMatrix();
glTranslatef(100.0f, 0.0f, 0.0f);
glLoadName(MARS);
glutauxSolidSphere(20.0f, 15, 15);

// Draw Moon1
glTranslatef(-40.0f, 40.0f, 0.0f);
glRGB(220,220,220);
glPushName(MOON1);
glutauxSolidSphere(5.0f, 15, 15);
glPopName();

// Draw Moon2
glTranslatef(0.0f, -80.0f, 0.0f);
glPushName(MOON2);
glutauxSolidSphere(5.0f, 15, 15);
glPopName();
glPopMatrix();

// Restore the matrix state
glPopMatrix();    // Modelview matrix

// Flush drawing commands
glutSwapBuffers
}
```

Now in our `ProcessSelection` function, we still call the `ProcessPlanet` function that we wrote, but this time, we pass the entire selection buffer:

```
// If a single hit occurred, display the info.
if(hits == 1)
   ProcessPlanet(selectBuff);
```

Listing 14.5 shows the more substantial `ProcessPlanet` function for this example. In this instance, the bottom name on the names stack is always the name of the planet because it was pushed on first. If a moon is clicked, it is also on the names stack. This function displays the name of the planet selected, and if it was a moon, that information is also displayed. A sample output is shown in Figure 14.4.

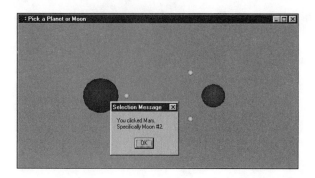

Figure 14.4 Sample output from the MOONS sample program.

Listing 14.5 *Code That Parses the Selection Buffer for the MOONS Sample Program*

```
// Parse the selection buffer to see which planet/moon was selected
void ProcessPlanet(GLuint *pSelectBuff)
    {
    int id,count;
    char cMessage[64];

    // How many names on the name stack
    count = pSelectBuff[0];

    // Bottom of the name stack
    id = pSelectBuff[3];

    // Select on earth or mars, whichever was picked
    switch(id)
        {
        case EARTH:
            strcpy(cMessage,?You clicked Earth.");

            // If there is another name on the name stack,
            // then it must be the moon that was selected
            // This is what was actually clicked on
            if(count == 2)
                strcat(cMessage,?\nSpecifically the moon.");

            break;

        case MARS:
            strcpy(cMessage,?You clicked Mars.");

            // We know the name stack is only two deep. The precise
            // moon that was selected will be here.
```

```
        if(count == 2)
            {
            if(pSelectBuff[4] == MOON1)
                strcat(cMessage,?\nSpecifically Moon #1.");
            else
                strcat(cMessage,?\nSpecifically Moon #2.");
            }

        break;

    // If nothing was clicked we shouldn't be here!
    default:
        strcpy(cMessage,?Error - Nothing was clicked on!");
        break;
    }

// Display the message about planet and moon selection
MessageBox(NULL,cMessage,?Selection Message",MB_OK);
}
```

Feedback

Feedback, like selection, is a rendering mode that does not produce output in the form of pixels on the screen. Instead, information is written to a feedback buffer about how the scene would have been rendered. This information includes transformed vertex data in window coordinates, color data resulting from lighting calculations, and texture data.

Feedback mode is entered just like selection mode, by calling `glRenderMode` with a `GL_FEEDBACK` argument. You must reset the rendering mode to `GL_RENDER` to fill the feedback buffer and return to normal rendering mode.

The Feedback Buffer

The feedback buffer is an array of floating-point values specified with the `glFeedback` function:

```
void glFeedbackBuffer(GLsizei size, GLenum type, GLfloat *buffer);
```

This function takes the size of the feedback buffer, the type and amount of drawing information wanted, and a pointer to the buffer itself.

Valid values for *type* appear in Table 14.1. The type of data specifies how much data is placed in the feedback buffer for each vertex. Color data is represented by a single value in color index mode or four values for RGBA color mode.

Table 14.1 *Feedback Buffer Types*

Type	Vertex Coordinates	Color Data	Texture Data	Total Values
GL_2D	x, y	N/A	N/A	2
GL_3D	x, y, z	N/A	N/A	3
GL_3D_COLOR	x, y, z	C	N/A	3 + C
GL_3D_COLOR_TEXTURE	x, y, z	C	4	7 + C
GL_4D_COLOR_TEXTURE	x, y, z, w	C	4	8 + C

Feedback Data

The feedback buffer contains a list of tokens followed by vertex data and possibly color and texture data. You can parse for these tokens (see Table 14.2) to determine the types of primitives that would have been rendered.

Table 14.2 *Feedback Buffer Tokens*

Token	Primitive
GL_POINT_TOKEN	Points
GL_LINE_TOKEN	Line
GL_LINE_RESET_TOKEN	Line segment when line stipple is reset
GL_POLYGON_TOKEN	Polygon
GL_BITMAP_TOKEN	Bitmap
GL_DRAW_PIXEL_TOKEN	Pixel rectangle drawn
GL_COPY_PIXEL_TOKEN	Pixel rectangle copied
GL_PASS_THROUGH_TOKEN	User-defined marker

The point, bitmap, and pixel tokens are followed by data for a single vertex and possibly color and texture data. This depends on the data type from Table 14.1 specified in the call to glFeedbackBuffer. The line tokens return two sets of vertex data, and the polygon token is immediately followed by the number of vertices that follow. The user-defined marker (GL_PASS_THROUGH_TOKEN) is followed by a single floating-point value that is user defined. Figure 14.5 shows an example of a feedback buffer's memory layout if a GL_3D type were specified.

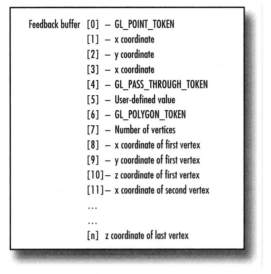

Feedback buffer [0] – GL_POINT_TOKEN
[1] – x coordinate
[2] – y coordinate
[3] – x coordinate
[4] – GL_PASS_THROUGH_TOKEN
[5] – User-defined value
[6] – GL_POLYGON_TOKEN
[7] – Number of vertices
[8] – x coordinate of first vertex
[9] – y coordinate of first vertex
[10]– z coordinate of first vertex
[11]– x coordinate of second vertex
...
...
[n] z coordinate of last vertex

Figure 14.5 A sample memory layout for a feedback buffer.

Passthrough Markers

When your rendering code is executing, the feedback buffer is filled with tokens and vertex data as each primitive is specified. Just as you can in selection mode, you can flag certain primitives by naming them. In feedback mode, you can set markers between your primitives, as well. This is done by calling glPassThrough:

```
void glPassThrough(GLfloat token );
```

This function places a GL_PASS_THROUGH_TOKEN in the feedback buffer, followed by the value you specify when calling the function. This is somewhat similar to naming primitives in selection mode. It's the only way of labeling objects in the feedback buffer.

A Feedback Example

An excellent use of feedback is to obtain window coordinate information regarding any objects that you render. You can then use this information to place controls or labels near the objects in the window or other windows around them.

To demonstrate feedback, we use selection to determine which of two objects on the screen has been clicked by the user. Then, we enter feedback mode and render the scene again to obtain the vertex information in window coordinates. Using this data, we determine the minimum and maximum x and y values for the object and use those values to draw a focus rectangle around the object. The end result is graphical selection and deselection of one or both objects.

Label the Objects for Feedback

Listing 14.6 shows the rendering code for our sample program, SELECT. Don't confuse this with a demonstration of selection mode! Even though selection mode is employed in our example to select an object on the screen, we are demonstrating the process of getting enough information about that object—using feedback—to draw a rectangle around it using normal Windows coordinates GDI commands. Notice the use of `glPassThrough` to label the objects in the feedback buffer, right after the calls to `glLoadName` to label the objects in the selection buffer. Because these functions are ignored when the render mode is `GL_RENDER`, they only have an effect when rendering for selection or feedback.

Listing 14.6 *Rendering Code for the SELECT Sample Program*

```
#define CUBE       1
#define SPHERE     2

// Render the cube and sphere
void DrawObjects(void)
    {
    // Save the matrix state and do the rotations
    glMatrixMode(GL_MODELVIEW);
    glPushMatrix();

    // Translate the whole scene out and into view
    glTranslatef(-80.0f, 0.0f, -300.0f);

    // Initialize the names stack
    glInitNames();
    glPushName(0);

    // Set material color, Yellow
    // Cube
    glColor3ub(255, 255, 0);
    glLoadName(CUBE);
    glPassThrough((GLfloat)CUBE);
    glutSolidCube(75.0f);

    // Draw Sphere
    glColor3ub(128,0,0);
    glTranslatef(130.0f, 0.0f, 0.0f);
    glLoadName(SPHERE);
    glPassThrough((GLfloat)SPHERE);

    glutSolidSphere(50.0f, 15, 15);

    // Restore the matrix state
```

```
    glPopMatrix();    // Modelview matrix
    }



// Called to draw scene
void RenderScene(void)
    {
    // Clear the window with current clearing color
    glClear(GL_COLOR_BUFFER_BIT | GL_DEPTH_BUFFER_BIT);
    // Draw the objects in the scene
    DrawObjects();

    // If something is selected, draw a bounding box around it
    if(nWho != 0)
        {
        int viewport[4];

        // Get the viewport
        glGetIntegerv(GL_VIEWPORT, viewport);

        // Remap the viewing volume to match window coordinates (approximately)
        glMatrixMode(GL_PROJECTION);
        glPushMatrix();
        glLoadIdentity();


        // Establish clipping volume (left, right, bottom, top, near, far)
        glOrtho(viewport[0], viewport[2], viewport[3], viewport[1], -1, 1);
        glMatrixMode(GL_MODELVIEW);

        glDisable(GL_LIGHTING);
        glColor3ub(255,0,0);

        glBegin(GL_LINE_LOOP);
            glVertex2i(bRect.left, bRect.top);
            glVertex2i(bRect.left, bRect.bottom);
            glVertex2i(bRect.right, bRect.bottom);
            glVertex2i(bRect.right, bRect.top);
        glEnd();
        glEnable(GL_LIGHTING);
        }

    glMatrixMode(GL_PROJECTION);
    glPopMatrix();
    glMatrixMode(GL_MODELVIEW);

    glutSwapBuffers();
    }
```

Note that for this example, the rendering code is broken into two functions: RenderScene and DrawObjects. RenderScene is our normal top-level rendering function, but we have moved the actual drawing of the objects that we may select to outside this function. The RenderScene function draws the objects, but it also draws the bounding rectangle around an object if it is selected. nWho is a variable we use in a moment to indicate which object is currently selected.

Step 1: Select the Object

Figure 14.6 shows the output from this rendering code, displaying a cube and a sphere. When the user clicks one of the objects, the function ProcessSelection is called (see Listing 14.7). This is similar to the selection code in the previous two examples (in Listings 14.3 and 14.5).

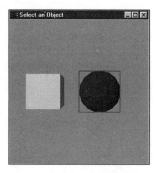

Figure 14.6   Output from the SELECT program after the sphere has been clicked.

***

Listing 14.7   *Selection Processing for the SELECT Sample Program*

```
// Process the selection, which is triggered by a right mouse
// click at (xPos, yPos).
#define BUFFER_LENGTH 64
void ProcessSelection(int xPos, int yPos)
    {
    // Space for selection buffer
    GLuint selectBuff[BUFFER_LENGTH];

    // Hit counter and viewport storage
    GLint hits, viewport[4];

    // Setup selection buffer
    glSelectBuffer(BUFFER_LENGTH, selectBuff);

    // Get the viewport
```

```
glGetIntegerv(GL_VIEWPORT, viewport);

// Switch to projection and save the matrix
glMatrixMode(GL_PROJECTION);
glPushMatrix();

// Change render mode
glRenderMode(GL_SELECT);

// Establish new clipping volume to be unit cube around
// mouse cursor point (xPos, yPos) and extending two pixels
// in the vertical and horizontal direction
glLoadIdentity();
gluPickMatrix(xPos, viewport[3] - yPos, 2,2, viewport);

// Apply perspective matrix
gluPerspective(60.0f, fAspect, 1.0, 425.0);

// Draw the scene
DrawObjects();

// Collect the hits
hits = glRenderMode(GL_RENDER);

// Restore the projection matrix
glMatrixMode(GL_PROJECTION);
glPopMatrix();

// Go back to modelview for normal rendering
glMatrixMode(GL_MODELVIEW);

// If a single hit occurred, display the info.
// If double selected, mark nothing as selected
if(hits == 1)
    {
    MakeSelection(selectBuff[3]);
    if(nWho == selectBuff[3])
        nWho = 0;
    else
        nWho = selectBuff[3];
    }

glutPostRedisplay();
}
```

Step 2: Get Feedback on the Object

Now that we have determined which object was clicked (we saved this in the nWho variable), we set up the feedback buffer and render again in feedback mode. Listing 14.8 is the code that sets up feedback mode for this example and calls DrawObjects to redraw just the cube and sphere scene. This time, however, the glPassThrough functions put markers for the objects in the feedback buffer.

Listing 14.8 *Load and Parse the Feedback Buffer*

```
// Go into feedback mode and draw a rectangle around the object
#define FEED_BUFF_SIZE    4096
void MakeSelection(int nChoice)
    {
    // Space for the feedback buffer
    GLfloat feedBackBuff[FEED_BUFF_SIZE];

    // Storage for counters, etc.
    int size,i,j,count;

    // Initial minimum and maximum values
    bRect.right = bRect.bottom = -999999.0f;
    bRect.left = bRect.top =  999999.0f;

    // Set the feedback buffer
    glFeedbackBuffer(FEED_BUFF_SIZE,GL_2D, feedBackBuff);

    // Enter feedback mode
    glRenderMode(GL_FEEDBACK);

    // Redraw the scene
    DrawObjects();

    // Leave feedback mode
    size = glRenderMode(GL_RENDER);

    // Parse the feedback buffer and get the
    // min and max X and Y window coordinates
    i = 0;
    while(i < size)
        {
        // Search for appropriate token
        if(feedBackBuff[i] == GL_PASS_THROUGH_TOKEN)
            if(feedBackBuff[i+1] == (GLfloat)nChoice)
            {
```

```
          i+= 2;
          // Loop until next token is reached
          while(i < size && feedBackBuff[i] != GL_PASS_THROUGH_TOKEN)
              {
              // Just get the polygons
              if(feedBackBuff[i] == GL_POLYGON_TOKEN)
                  {
                  // Get all the values for this polygon
                  count = (int)feedBackBuff[++i]; // How many vertices
i++;

                  for(j = 0; j < count; j++)      // Loop for each vertex
                      {
                      // Min and Max X
                      if(feedBackBuff[i] > bRect.right)
                          bRect.right = feedBackBuff[i];

                      if(feedBackBuff[i] < bRect.left)
                          bRect.left = feedBackBuff[i];
                      i++;

                      // Min and Max Y
                      if(feedBackBuff[i] > bRect.bottom)
                          bRect.bottom = feedBackBuff[i];

                      if(feedBackBuff[i] < bRect.top)
                          bRect.top = feedBackBuff[i];
                      i++;
                      }
                  }
              else
                  i++;     // Get next index and keep looking
              }
          break;
          }
      i++;
      }
  }
```

Once the feedback buffer is filled, we search it for GL_PASS_THROUGH_TOKEN. When we find one, we get the next value and determine whether it is the one we are looking for. If so, the only thing that remains is to loop through all the polygons for this object and get the minimum and maximum window x and y values. These values are stored in the bRect structure (a standard Windows RECT structure), and then used by the RenderScene function to draw a focus rectangle around the selected object.

Summary

Selection and feedback are two powerful features of OpenGL that give you the ability to facilitate the user's active interaction with the scene. Selection and picking are used to identify an object or region of a scene in OpenGL coordinates rather than just window coordinates. Feedback returns valuable information about how an object or primitive is actually drawn in the window. You can use this information to create annotations or bounding boxes in your scene.

Reference Section

glFeedbackBuffer

Purpose	Sets the feedback mode.
Include File	<gl.h>
Syntax	void glFeedbackBuffer(GLsizei *size*, GLenum *type*, GLfloat **buffer*);
Description	This function establishes the feedback buffer and the type of vertex information desired. Feedback is a rendering mode; rather than render to the frame buffer, OpenGL sends vertex data to the buffer specified here. These blocks of data can include x, y, z, and w coordinate positions (in window coordinates); color data for color index mode or RGBA color mode; and texture coordinates. The amount and type of information desired is specified by the *type* argument.
Parameters	
size	GLsizei: The maximum number of entries allocated for **buffer*. If a block of data written to the feedback would overflow the amount of space allocated, only the part of the block that will fit in the buffer is written.
type	GLenum: Specifies the kind of vertex data to be returned in the feedback buffer. Each vertex generates a block of data in the feedback buffer. For each of the following types, the block of data contains a primitive token identifier followed by the vertex data. The vertex data specifically includes the following:

GL_2D: x and y coordinate pairs.

GL_3D: x, y, and z coordinate triplets.

GL_3D_COLOR: x, y, z coordinates and color data (one value for color index, four for RGBA).

GL_3D_COLOR_TEXTURE: x, y, z coordinates, color data (one or four values), and four texture coordinates.

GL_4D_COLOR_TEXTURE: x, y, z, and w coordinates, color data (one or four values), and four texture coordinates.

buffer GLfloat*: Buffer where feedback data will be stored.

Returns None.

Example The following code from the SELECT sample program initializes the feedback buffer with glFeedbackBuffer, then switches to feedback mode, renders the scene, and fills the feedback buffer by switching back to rendering mode:

```
#define FEED_BUFF_SIZE    4096
    ...
    ...
// Space for the feedback buffer
GLfloat feedBackBuff[FEED_BUFF_SIZE];

    ...
    ...

// Set the feedback buffer
glFeedbackBuffer(FEED_BUFF_SIZE,GL_2D, feedBackBuff);

// Enter feedback mode
glRenderMode(GL_FEEDBACK);

// Redraw the scene
RenderScene();

// Leave feedback mode
size = glRenderMode(GL_RENDER);
```

See Also glPassThrough, glRenderMode, glSelectBuffer

glInitNames

Purpose Initializes the name stack.

Include File <gl.h>

Syntax void glInitNames(void);

Description The name stack is used to allow drawing primitives or groups of primitives to be named with an unsigned integer when rendered in selection mode. Each time a primitive is named, its name is pushed on the names stack with glPushName or the current name is replaced with glLoadName. This function sets the name stack to its initial condition with no names on the stack.

Returns None.

Example   The following code is from the sample program PLANETS. It initializes the names stack and places a single value on the stack:

```
// Initialize the names stack
glInitNames();
glPushName(0);
```

See Also   glInitNames, glPushName, glRenderMode, glSelectBuffer

glLoadName

Purpose	Loads a name onto the name stack.
Include File	<gl.h>
Syntax	void glLoadName(GLuint *name*);
Description	This function places the name specified on the top of the names stack. The name stack is used to name primitives or groups of primitives when rendered in selection mode. The current name on the names stack is actually replaced by the name specified with this function.

Parameters

name	GLuint: Specifies the name to be placed on the names stack. Selection names are unsigned integers.
Returns	None.
Example	The following code from the PLANETS sample program shows a name being loaded on the name stack just before an object is rendered:

```
// Set material color, Yellow
// Sun
glRGB(255, 255, 0);
glLoadName(SUN);
auxSolidSphere(15.0f);
```

See Also   glInitNames, glPushName, glRenderMode, glSelectBuffer

glPassThrough

Purpose	Places a marker in the feedback buffer.
Include File	<gl.h>
Syntax	void glPassThrough(GLfloat *token*);
Description	When OpenGL is placed in feedback mode, no pixels are drawn to the frame buffer. Instead, information about the drawing primitives is placed in a feedback buffer. This function allows you to place the token GL_PASS_THROUGH_TOKEN in the midst of the feedback buffer,

which is followed by the floating-point value specified by this function. This function is called in your rendering code and has no effect unless in feedback mode.

Parameters

token   GLfloat: A value to be placed in the feedback buffer following the GL_PASS_THROUGH_TOKEN.

Returns   None.

Example   The following code from the SELECT sample program demonstrates glPassThrough and glLoadName being used together to identify an object. This marks the object in both the selection and feedback buffers:

```
// Set material color, Yellow
// Cube
glRGB(255, 255, 0);
glLoadName(CUBE);
glPassThrough((GLfloat)CUBE);
auxSolidCube(75.0f);
```

See Also   glFeedbackBuffer, glRenderMode

glPopName

Purpose   Pops (removes) the top entry from the name stack.

Include File   <gl.h>

Syntax   void glPopName(void);

Description   The names stack is used during selection to identify drawing commands. This function removes a name from the top of the names stack. The current depth of the name stack can be retrieved by calling glGet with GL_NAME_STACK_DEPTH.

Returns   None.

Example   The following code from the MOONS sample program uses the name stack to place the name of a planet and its moon on the name stack for selection. This code in particular shows one moon's name being popped off the name stack before the name of the next moon is pushed on:

```
// Draw Mars
glRGB(255,0,0);
glPushMatrix();
glTranslatef(100.0f, 0.0f, 0.0f);
glLoadName(MARS);
```

```
auxSolidSphere(20.0f);


// Draw Moon1
glTranslatef(-40.0f, 40.0f, 0.0f);
glRGB(220,220,220);
glPushName(MOON1);
auxSolidSphere(5.0f);
glPopName();

// Draw Moon2
glTranslatef(0.0f, -80.0f, 0.0f);
glPushName(MOON2);
auxSolidSphere(5.0f);
glPopName();
glPopMatrix();
```

See Also	glInitNames, glLoadName, glRenderMode, glSelectBuffer, glPushName

glPushName

Purpose	Specifies a name that will be pushed on the name stack.
Include File	<gl.h>
Syntax	void glPushName(GLuint *name*);
Description	The names stack is used during selection to identify drawing commands. This function pushes a name on the names stack to identify any subsequent drawing commands. The names stack maximum depth can be retrieved by calling **glGet** with GL_MAX_NAME_STACK_DEPTH and the current depth by calling **glGet** with GL_NAME_STACK_DEPTH. The maximum depth of the names stack can vary with implementation, but all implementations must support at least 64 entries.
Parameters	
name	GLuint: The name to be pushed onto the names stack.
Returns	None.
Example	The following code from the MOONS sample program uses the name stack to place the name of a planet and its moon on the name stack for selection. This code in particular shows the names of the moons being pushed on the names stack after the name of the planet. This moon's name is then popped off before the next moon's name is pushed on:

```
// Draw Mars
glRGB(255,0,0);
glPushMatrix();
glTranslatef(100.0f, 0.0f, 0.0f);
glLoadName(MARS);
auxSolidSphere(20.0f);


// Draw Moon1
glTranslatef(-40.0f, 40.0f, 0.0f);
glRGB(220,220,220);
glPushName(MOON1);
auxSolidSphere(5.0f);
glPopName();

// Draw Moon2
glTranslatef(0.0f, -80.0f, 0.0f);
glPushName(MOON2);
auxSolidSphere(5.0f);
glPopName();
glPopMatrix();
```

See Also   glInitNames, glLoadName, glRenderMode, glSelectBuffer, glPopName

glRenderMode

Purpose   Sets one of three rasterization modes.

Include File <gl.h>

Syntax   GLint glRenderMode(GLenum *mode*);

Description   OpenGL operates in three modes when you call your drawing functions:

GL_RENDER: Render mode (the default). Drawing functions result in pixels in the frame buffer.

GL_SELECT: Selection mode. No changes to the frame buffer are made. Rather, hit records are written to the selection buffer that record primitives that would have been drawn within the viewing volume. The selection buffer must be allocated and specified first with a call to glSelectBuffer.

GL_FEEDBACK: Feedback mode. No changes to the frame buffer are made. Instead coordinates and attributes of vertices that would have been rendered in render mode are written to a feedback buffer. The feedback buffer must be allocated and specified first with a call to glFeedbackBuffer.

Parameters

mode   GLenum: Specifies the rasterization mode. May be any one of
                                GL_RENDER, GL_SELECT, and GL_FEEDBACK. The default value is
                                GL_RENDER.

Returns   The return value depends on the rasterization mode that was set the
                                last time this function was called:

                                GL_RENDER: Zero.

                                GL_SELECT: The number of hit records written to the selection
                                buffer.

                                GL_FEEDBACK: The number of values written to the feedback buffer.
                                Note, this is not the same as the number of vertices written.

Example   The following code shows glRenderMode being called to enter selec-
                                tion mode for the PLANETS sample program. The function is called
                                again with an argument of GL_RENDER to enter rendering mode and
                                to write the hit records into the selection buffer:

```
// Process the selection, which is triggered by a right mouse
// click at (xPos, yPos).
#define BUFFER_LENGTH 64
void ProcessSelection(int xPos, int yPos)
    {
    // Space for selection buffer
    GLuint selectBuff[BUFFER_LENGTH];

    // Hit counter and viewport storage
    GLint hits, viewport[4];

    // Set up selection buffer
    glSelectBuffer(BUFFER_LENGTH, selectBuff);


    // Get the viewport
    glGetIntegerv(GL_VIEWPORT, viewport);

    // Switch to projection and save the matrix
    glMatrixMode(GL_PROJECTION);
    glPushMatrix();

    // Change render mode
    glRenderMode(GL_SELECT);

    // Establish new clipping volume to be unit cube around
    // mouse cursor point (xPos, yPos) and extending two pixels
    // in the vertical and horizontal direction
    glLoadIdentity();
```

```
    gluPickMatrix(xPos, yPos, 2,2, viewport);

    // Apply perspective matrix

    gluPerspective(45.0f, fAspect, 1.0, 425.0);

    // Draw the scene
    RenderScene();

    // Collect the hits
    hits = glRenderMode(GL_RENDER);

    // If a single hit occurred, display the info.
    if(hits == 1)
        ProcessPlanet(selectBuff[3]);

    // Restore the projection matrix
    glMatrixMode(GL_PROJECTION);
    glPopMatrix();

    // Go back to modelview for normal rendering
    glMatrixMode(GL_MODELVIEW);
    }
```

See Also glFeedbackBuffer, glInitNames, glLoadName, glPassThrough, glPushName, glSelectBuffer

glSelectBuffer

Purpose	Sets the buffer to be used for selection values.
Include File	<gl.h>
Syntax	void glSelectBuffer(GLsizei *size*, GLuint *buffer*);
Description	When OpenGL is in selection mode (GL_SELECT), drawing commands do not produce pixels in the frame buffer. Instead, they produce hit records that are written to the selection buffer that is established by this function. Each hit record consists of the following data:

- The number of names on the names stack when the hit occurred.
- The minimum and maximum z values of all the vertices of the primitives that intersected the viewing volume. This value is scaled to range from 0.0 to 1.0.
- The contents of the name stack at the time of the hit, starting with the bottom element.

Parameters

size   GLsize: The number of values that can be written into the buffer
                            established by **buffer*.

buffer   GLuint*: A pointer to memory that will contain the selection hit
                            records.

Returns   None.

Example   The following code shows the selection buffer being created for the
                            PLANETS sample program:

```
// Process the selection, which is triggered by a right mouse
// click at (xPos, yPos).
#define BUFFER_LENGTH 64
void ProcessSelection(int xPos, int yPos)
    {
    // Space for selection buffer
    GLuint selectBuff[BUFFER_LENGTH];

    ...
    ...

    // Set up selection buffer
    glSelectBuffer(BUFFER_LENGTH, selectBuff);
```

See Also   glFeedbackBuffer, glInitNames, glLoadName, glPushName,
                            glRenderMode

gluPickMatrix

Purpose   Defines a picking region that can be used to identify user selections.

Include File   <glu.h>

Syntax   void gluPickMatrix(GLdouble *x*, GLdouble *y*, GLdouble
                            width, GLdouble *height*, GLint *viewport*[4]);

Description   This function creates a matrix that will define a smaller viewing vol-
                            ume based on screen coordinates for the purpose of selection. By
                            using the mouse coordinates with this function in selection mode,
                            you can determine which of your objects are under or near the
                            mouse cursor. The matrix created is multiplied by the current pro-
                            jection matrix. Typically, you should call glLoadIdentity before
                            calling this function and then multiply the perspective matrix that
                            you used to create the viewing volume in the first place. If you are
                            using gluPickMatrix to pick NURBS surfaces, you must turn off the
                            NURBS property GLU_AUTO_LOAD_MATRIX before using this function.

Parameters

x, y	GLdouble: The center of the picking region in window coordinates.
width, height	GLdouble: The width and height of the desired picking region in window coordinates.
viewport	GLint[4]: The current viewport. You can get the current viewport by calling glGetIntegerv with GL_VIEWPORT.

Returns   None.

Example   The following code is from the PLANETS sample program. It uses this function to create a new clipping volume that will cover an area of the window only 2 pixels by 2 pixels, centered on the mouse cursor. This is used to select the object that is directly underneath the mouse cursor:

```
// Hit counter and viewport storage
GLint hits, viewport[4];

// Set up selection buffer
glSelectBuffer(BUFFER_LENGTH, selectBuff);


// Get the viewport
glGetIntegerv(GL_VIEWPORT, viewport);

// Switch to projection and save the matrix
glMatrixMode(GL_PROJECTION);
glPushMatrix();

// Change render mode
glRenderMode(GL_SELECT);

// Establish new clipping volume to be unit cube around
// mouse cursor point (xPos, yPos) and extending two pixels
// in the vertical and horizontal direction
glLoadIdentity();
gluPickMatrix(xPos, yPos, 2,2, viewport);

// Apply perspective matrix

gluPerspective(45.0f, fAspect, 1.0, 425.0);

// Draw the scene
RenderScene();

// Collect the hits
hits = glRenderMode(GL_RENDER);

// If a single hit occurred, display the info.
```

```
if(hits == 1)
    ProcessPlanet(selectBuff[3]);

// Restore the projection matrix
glMatrixMode(GL_PROJECTION);
glPopMatrix();

// Go back to modelview for normal rendering
glMatrixMode(GL_MODELVIEW);
```

See Also   glGet, glLoadIdentity, glMultMatrix, glRenderMode,
                      gluPerspective

IMAGING WITH OPENGL

by Michael Sweet

What you'll learn in this chapter

How To...	Functions You'll Use
Do simple colorspace conversions	glMatrixMode/glEnable
Perform histogram equalization	glHistogram/glGetHistogram/glResetHistogram
Smooth and sharpen images	glConvolutionFilter1D/glConvolutionFilter2D

One of the most exciting new features in OpenGL 1.2 is the optional Imaging Subset. The Imaging Subset provides the ability to adjust the final RGB values that are put in the color buffer, keep statistics on what colors are used, and filter the output pixels using 1D or 2D convolution arrays.

At press time, most OpenGL cards (and the Mesa library) do not support the OpenGL 1.2 Imaging Subset. However, OpenGL 1.2 support should be universal within a few years.

Basics of the OpenGL Imaging Extension

The OpenGL Imaging Subset actually consists of three separate extensions[md]Color Matrix, Convolution, and Histogram[md]that work together to provide enhanced rendering capabilities to OpenGL. Unlike other OpenGL extensions that you'll learn about in Chapter 16, "Common OpenGL Extensions," these extensions don't have the traditional "ext" added to the ends of the function names. However, they are an optional part of OpenGL 1.2, so you'll have to test for them before you use them.

The Imaging Subset operations are part of the pixel transfer portion of the OpenGL rendering pipeline outlined in Chapter 2, "What Is OpenGL?" This means that they don't apply to the vector drawing primitives; however, you can draw a scene and then use the `glReadPixels` and `glDrawPixels` functions described in Chapter 7, "Raster Graphics in OpenGL," to apply the imaging operations to your scene. On systems with hardware acceleration for OpenGL imaging, you can still maintain high display rates.

Checking for the OpenGL Imaging Extension

As with all extensions, you check for the presence of the extension using the `glGetString` function. For the OpenGL imaging extension, you check for the string `"ARB_imaging"`:

```
if (strstr(glGetString(GL_EXTENSIONS), "ARB_imaging") != NULL)
```

Also, because all of the imaging functions are in OpenGL 1.2, you might need to conditionally compile your imaging code into your application:

```
#ifdef GL_VERSION_1_2
...
#endif /* GL_VERSION_1_2 */
```

The Color Matrix

One of the most useful additions in the OpenGL Imaging Subset is the color matrix. Basically, the color matrix transforms RGB color values as the modelview and projection matrices transform the XYZ values in your geometry. Like the modelview matrix, the color matrix is a 4-by-4 matrix stack; the minimum depth of the color matrix stack is two elements, so you can depend on being able to use at least one `glPushMatrix` if you need to.

To select the color matrix, use the `glMatrixMode` function:

```
glMatrixMode(GL_COLOR);
```

Color Matrix Tricks

Once you have selected the color transform matrix, you can use the `glTranslate`, `glRotate`, `glScale`, `glLoadIdentity`, `glLoadMatrix`, and `glMultMatrix` functions to change the matrix.

Brightness

You can adjust the brightness of a scene by translating the red, green, and blue values by the same amount:

```
glTranslatef(0.25, 0.25, 0.25);
```

As with your television, increasing the brightness tends to wash out colors.

Contrast

You adjust the contrast of a scene by scaling:

```
glScalef(1.25, 1.25, 1.25);
```

Scaling by numbers greater than 1.0 also brightens the image. Similarly, numbers less than 1.0 darken the image.

Color Filters

Color filters are used in real life to block certain wavelengths of light. With OpenGL imaging, we can duplicate this by scaling with the filter color:

```
GLclampf filter_red, filter_green, filter_blue;

glScalef(filter_red, filter_green, filter_blue);
```

The red, green, and blue filter values can be greater than 1.0 or less than 0.0 for special effects, but typically, you stick with the normal range.

Saturation

Saturation is the amount of colorfulness in a color. For example, hot pink and dull pink differ in the amount of magenta that is in them, which is a function of the color saturation. To adjust the color saturation with OpenGL imaging, we need to use the `glMultMatrix` operation:

```
GLclampf saturation; /* Saturation 0.0 to 1.0 */
GLfloat  matrix[16]; /* Saturation matrix */

matrix[0]  = (1.0 - saturation) * 0.3086 + saturation;
matrix[1]  = (1.0 - saturation) * 0.3086;
matrix[2]  = (1.0 - saturation) * 0.3086;
matrix[3]  = 0.0;
matrix[4]  = (1.0 - saturation) * 0.6094;
matrix[5]  = (1.0 - saturation) * 0.6094 + saturation;
matrix[6]  = (1.0 - saturation) * 0.6094;
matrix[7]  = 0.0;
matrix[8]  = (1.0 - saturation) * 0.0820;
matrix[9]  = (1.0 - saturation) * 0.0820;
matrix[10] = (1.0 - saturation) * 0.0820 + saturation;
matrix[11] = 0.0;
matrix[12] = 0.0;
matrix[13] = 0.0;
matrix[14] = 0.0;
matrix[15] = 1.0;

glMultMatrixf(matrix);
```

The matrix is initialized so that a saturation of 1.0 produces the identity matrix and a saturation of 0.0 produces a matrix that maps RGB to luminance values, using a weight of 0.3086 for red, 0.6094 for green, and 0.0820 for blue. These weights are different from the "normal" ones used for video but are more correct for the linear RGB colorspace used by OpenGL.

OpenGL generates RGB values with the assumption that the output device (your graphics card or monitor) has a linear response curve. That is, a color value of 0.5 is twice as bright as 0.25 and half as bright as 1.0.

A typical monitor does not respond in a linear fashion and must be gamma corrected to get the correct results. Gamma correction is usually accomplished using hardware lookup tables on the graphics card. Each value in the lookup table is computed using a gamma correction function like

$$f(x) = x^y$$

where x is the pixel value and y is the gamma correction factor, typically 0.45 for an RGB monitor.

You can use the pixel mapping functions described in Chapter 7 to implement gamma correction on hardware that does not support it.

If you are working with images that are already gamma corrected for the monitor, you should use RGB weights of 0.31, 0.61, and 0.08 instead of those shown in the sample code.

Color Correction

You can provide color (RGB) values that go outside of the range of 0.0 to 1.0; however, when the transformed color values are put into the color buffer, they are clamped to that range. This means that you can provide other types of color values (such as CIE XYZ) and convert the colors to RGB using the color matrix.

In addition to using a color matrix to convert from one colorspace to another, you usually have to adjust the input and output values for the devices being used. This usually only means performing gamma correction, but the OpenGL pixel transfer lookup tables support any one-to-one mapping of color values (such as from RGB to CMY).

The color matrix is set up as shown earlier. For a CIE-based color correction matrix, you probably provide one or two matrices that are multiplied with the current color matrix:

```
GLfloat lRGB_CIEXYZ[16] =
    {
    0.4124, 0.2126, 0.0193, 0.0000,
```

```
      0.3576, 0.7152, 0.1192, 0.0000,
      0.1805, 0.0722, 0.9505, 0.0000,
      0.0000, 0.0000, 0.0000, 0.0000
      };
GLfloat CIEXYZ_sRGB[16] =
      {
       3.2410, -0.9692,  0.0556, 0.0000,
      -1.5374,  1.8760, -0.2040, 0.0000,
      -0.4986,  0.0416,  1.0570, 0.0000,
       0.0000,  0.0000,  0.0000, 0.0000
      };

glMatrixMode(GL_COLOR);
glLoadIdentity();
glMultMatrixf(lRGB_CIEXYZ);
glMultMatrixf(CIEXYZ_sRGB);
```

The *lRGB_CIEXYZ* matrix converts the linear OpenGL RGB colors to the CIE XYZ colorspace, and the *CIEXYZ_sRGB* matrix converts from CIE XYZ to the sRGB colorspace, a WWW and video "standard" RGB colorspace with a gamma correction of 0.45. Other RGB transformations require similar matrices which are well documented in books on color theory. You can find out more about the **sRGB** colorspace at `http://www.srgb.com`.

Because our input colorspace is linear, no gamma correction lookup table is needed; if we did need one, we would use the `glPixelMapfv` function:

```
GLfloat gamma_in[256];

glPixelMapfv(GL_PIXEL_MAP_R_TO_R, 256, gamma_in);
glPixelMapfv(GL_PIXEL_MAP_G_TO_G, 256, gamma_in);
glPixelMapfv(GL_PIXEL_MAP_B_TO_B, 256, gamma_in);
```

The output sRGB colorspace needs a gamma correction of 0.45, so we have to use `glColorTable` to tell OpenGL that a post-color-matrix lookup table is to be used:

```
GLfloat gamma_out[256];
int     val;

for (val = 0; val < 256; val ++)
    gamma_out[val] = pow((float)val / 255.0f, 0.45f);

glColorTable(GL_POST_COLOR_MATRIX_TABLE, GL_LUMINANCE, 256, GL_LUMINANCE,
             GL_FLOAT, gamma_out);
```

You'll find more examples of using color matrices at Paul Haeberli's Graphica Obscura Web site at `http://reality.sgi.com/graphica`.

Convolution (Filtering)

Another part of the OpenGL Imaging Subset is support for convolution or filtering of images. Convolution filters allow you to perform complex image processing operations such as sharpening, blurring, and spreading on images using OpenGL.

The `glConvolutionFilter1D` and `glConvolutionFilter2D` functions specify the filter image to use:

```
GLfloat convolve_1d[width];

glConvolutionFilter1D(GL_CONVOLUTION_1D, GL_LUMINANCE, width, GL_LUMINANCE,
                      GL_FLOAT, convolve_1d);

GLfloat convolve_2d[height][width];

glConvolutionFilter2D(GL_CONVOLUTION_2D, GL_LUMINANCE, width, height,
                      GL_LUMINANCE, GL_FLOAT, convolve_2d[0]);
```

The convolution filter operates from the middle of the image, so typically, filter arrays have an odd width and height. The middle value becomes the current, or "local," RGB pixel value scaling factor, and the surrounding values are multiplied by the neighboring RGB pixel values. Depending on the filter array, the result could be a general sharpening or blurring of the image. In general, larger filter arrays, or "kernels," produce better quality output but are slower.

Sharpening Convolution Filters

A typical sharpening filter looks something like

```
-s    -s     -s
-s    1+8*s  -s
-s    -s     -s
```

This brightens the local pixel by $8*s$, where s is a value from 0.0 to 1.0. The adjacent RGB pixels subtract from this value, so identical adjacent colors produce the same, smooth appearance and changes in color produce exaggerated transitions or a general sharpening effect.

Blurring Convolution Filters

A typical blurring filter looks something like

```
s    s     s
s    1-8*s s
s    s     s
```

This darkens the local pixel by $8*s$, where s is a value from 0.0 to 1.0. The adjacent RGB pixels add to this value, so identical adjacent colors produce the same, smooth appearance and changes in color produce reduced transitions or a general blurring or softening effect.

Histogram Equalization

The final addition in the OpenGL Imaging Subset is the histogram interface. A histogram is a history of what colors are used in a scene. You can use the color histogram for a scene with the OpenGL pixel mapping facility to perform fast histogram equalization that improves the lighting and color balance of the final image in real time.

Getting Histogram Data

To track the histogram of a scene, you need to tell OpenGL where to put the histogram data:

```
glHistogram(GL_HISTOGRAM, width, GL_INTENSITY, sink);
```

The *width* parameter specifies the size of the histogram table. The *sink* parameter is a Boolean value that indicates whether OpenGL should render the scene to the screen. A GL_TRUE value causes all output to be redirected to the histogram table only.

To get the histogram data, use the glGetHistogram function:

```
GLint histogram[256];
```

```
glGetHistogram(GL_HISTOGRAM, reset, GL_INTENSITY, GL_INT, histogram);
```

The reset parameter specifies that the histogram table should be cleared after you get the values. To reset the values prior to rendering a scene, use the glResetHistogram function:

```
glResetHistogram(GL_HISTOGRAM);
```

Getting Minimum and Maximum Data

If all you need are the minimum and maximum values, you can use the glMinMax and glGetMinMax functions:

```
GLfloat minmax[2];
```

```
glMinMax(GL_HISTOGRAM, GL_INTENSITY, sink);
glGetMinMax(GL_HISTOGRAM, reset, GL_INTENSITY, GL_FLOAT, minmax);
```

The *minmax* array can be any OpenGL data type, but GLfloat works well with the pixel bias and scaling values supported by glDrawPixels.

The glResetMinMax function resets the current minimum and maximum and is usually called before rendering a scene:

```
glResetMinMax(GL_HISTOGRAM);
```

Summary

The OpenGL 1.2 Imaging Subset provides many 2D image processing acceleration functions that you can use to provide real-time image processing for your 2D and 3D applications. However, this extension is not universally available, so you must write your application so that it works both with and without OpenGL imaging.

The color matrix functions enable you to perform simple colorspace conversions and color adjustments. This is particularly important for television and movie image production.

The convolution functions enable you to specify 1D and 2D convolution filters or kernels. You can use them to provide real-time image enhancements for live video as well as special effects for 2D and 3D displays.

The histogram facility enables you to adjust the color and intensity distributions on-the-fly or dynamically adjust the black-and-white levels of an image. You can combine this facility with the color matrix functions to generate "safe" colors for television and movies that preserve the artistic intent of the rendered images.

Reference Section

glConvolutionFilter1DARB

Purpose	Specifies a one-dimensional convolution filter.
Include File	<GL/gl.h>
Syntax	void glConvolutionFilter1DARB(GLenum *target*, GLenum *internalformat*, GLsizei *width*, GLenum *format*, GLenum *type*, const GLvoid **image*);
Description	This function sets a one-dimensional convolution filter that will be used with glCopyPixels, glDrawPixels, and glReadPixels.
Parameters	
target	GLenum: The target of the filter; must be GL_CONVOLUTION_1D_ARB.
internalformat	GLenum: The internal format of the filter; typically GL_LUMINANCE8.
width	GLsizei: The width of the filter.
format	GLenum: The color format of the filter; typically GL_LUMINANCE.
type	GLenum: The data type for the filter image values; typically GL_FLOAT.
image	GLvoid *: A pointer to the filter image data.
Returns	None.
See Also	glConvolutionFilter2D, glDrawPixels, glReadPixels

glConvolutionFilter2DARB

Purpose	Specifies a two-dimensional convolution filter.
Include File	<GL/gl.h>
Syntax	void glConvolutionFilter2DARB(GLenum *target*, GLenum *internalformat*, GLsizei *width*, GLsizei *height*, GLenum *format*, GLenum *type*, const GLvoid **image*);
Description	This function sets a two-dimensional convolution filter that will be used with glCopyPixels, glDrawPixels, and glReadPixels.
Parameters	
target	GLenum: The target of the filter; must be GL_CONVOLUTION_2D_ARB.
internalformat	GLenum: The internal format of the filter; typically GL_LUMINANCE8.
width	GLsizei: The width of the filter.
height	GLsizei: The height of the filter.
format	GLenum: The color format of the filter; typically GL_LUMINANCE.
type	GLenum: The data type for the filter image values; typically GL_FLOAT.
image	GLvoid *: A pointer to the filter image data.
Returns	None.
See Also	glConvolutionFilter1D, glDrawPixels, glReadPixels

glGetHistogramARB

Purpose	Gets histogram information from the OpenGL pipeline.
Include File	<GL/gl.h>
Syntax	void glGetHistogramARB(GLenum *target*, GLboolean *reset*, GLenum *format*, GLenum *type*, GLvoid **values*);
Description	This function gets the OpenGL histogram information from the pipeline.
Parameters	
target	GLenum: The histogram buffer target; must be GL_HISTOGRAM_ARB.
reset	GLboolean: A value of GL_TRUE resets the histogram buffer values to 0.
format	GLenum: The format of the values array; typically GL_LUMINANCE or GL_RGB.
type	GLenum: The type of values in the array; typically GL_INTEGER.
values	GLvoid *: A pointer to the values array.
Returns	None.
See Also	glHistogramARB, glResetHistogramARB

glGetMinMaxARB

Purpose	Gets the minimum and maximum color values.
Include File	<GL/gl.h>
Syntax	void glGetMinmaxARB(GLenum *target*, GLboolean *reset*, GLenum *format*, GLenum *type*, GLvoid **values*);
Description	This function gets the minimum and maximum color values that have been used.
Parameters	
target	GLenum: The min/max buffer target; must be GL_MINMAX_ARB.
reset	GLboolean: A value of GL_TRUE resets the minimum and maximum buffer values.
format	GLenum: The format of the values array; typically GL_LUMINANCE or GL_RGB.
type	GLenum: The type of values in the array; typically GL_UNSIGNED_BYTE.
values	GLvoid *: A pointer to the values array.
Returns	None.
See Also	glMinMaxARB, glResetMinMaxARB

glHistogramARB

Purpose	Initializes the histogram buffer.
Include File	<GL/gl.h>
Syntax	void glHistogramARB(GLenum *target*, GLsizei *width*, GLenum *internalformat*, GLboolean *sink*);
Description	This function initializes the histogram buffer.
Parameters	
target	GLenum: The histogram buffer target; must be GL_HISTOGRAM_ARB.
width	GLsizei: The size of the histogram buffer.
internalformat	GLenum: The internal format of the values array; typically GL_LUMINANCE8 or GL_RGB8.
sink	GLboolean: If GL_TRUE, no output is produced.
Returns	None.
See Also	glGetHistogramARB

glMinMaxARB

Purpose	Initializes the min/max buffer.
Include File	<GL/gl.h>
Syntax	void glMinmaxARB(GLenum *target*, GLenum *internalformat*, GLboolean *sink*);
Description	This function initializes the min/max buffer.
Parameters	
target	GLenum: The histogram buffer target; must be GL_MINMAX_ARB.
internalformat	GLenum: The internal format of the values array; typically GL_LUMINANCE8 or GL_RGB8.
sink	GLboolean: If GL_TRUE, no output is produced.
Returns	None.
See Also	glGetMinMaxARB, glResetMinMaxARB

glResetHistogramARB

Purpose	Clears the histogram buffer.
Include File	<GL/gl.h>
Syntax	void glResetHistogramARB(GLenum *target*);
Description	This function clears the histogram buffer.
Parameters	
target	GLenum: The histogram target; must be GL_HISTOGRAM_ARB.
Returns	None.
See Also	glGetHistogramARB, glHistogramARB

glResetMinMaxARB

Purpose	Resets the min/max color values.
Include File	<GL/gl.h>
Syntax	void glResetMinMaxARB(GLenum *target*);
Description	This function resets the min/max color values.
Parameters	
target	GLenum: The min/max target; must be GL_MINMAX_ARB.
Returns	None.
See Also	glGetMinMaxARB, glMinMaxARB

16

COMMON OPENGL EXTENSIONS

by Michael Sweet

What you'll learn in this chapter:

How to...	Functions You'll Use
Check for extension availability	`glGetString`
Use special extension functions	`wglGetProcAddress`
Use the swap hint extension	`glAddSwapHintRectWIN`
Use the vertex culling extension	`glCullParameterfvEXT`
Use the multi-texture extension	`glActiveTextureARB`/ `glMultiTexCoordARB`

OpenGL extensions allow vendors to provide product-specific features within OpenGL without breaking compatibility with applications or other vendor hardware. This chapter covers the basics of detecting and using extensions in your programs.

What Extensions Are Available?

The OpenGL Architecture Review Board (ARB) manages all extensions to OpenGL. OpenGL licensees must document and submit an extension proposal to the ARB before they can use the extension in a product. You can see most of, if not all, the registered extensions on the official OpenGL Web site, `http://www.opengl.org`.

Some extensions are specific to a particular vendor. These extensions use a common suffix (such as `SGI`, `HP`, `SUN`, and `WIN`) to indicate the company that created the extension on all added functions and constants. Use vendor-specific extensions with care unless you don't care about compatibility with other OpenGL hardware.

Extensions that have been implemented by more than one vendor use the suffix EXT instead. Many extensions of this type eventually make their way into the next OpenGL specification and are generally safe to use in an application that runs on different OpenGL hardware.

Extensions that originate from the OpenGL ARB use the ARB suffix. Like EXT extensions, these are available from multiple vendors, but the design comes from the collaboration of all the ARB members and might be based on an older vendor-specific or EXT extension. This type of extension is relatively new and is used for several optional OpenGL 1.2 extensions, such as those shown in Chapter 15, "Imaging with OpenGL."

When Should I Use an Extension?

In general, only use extensions when you have to, and then, use a generalized (ARB or EXT type) extension and not a vendor-specific one.

If you have to use a vendor-specific extension, be prepared to explain why to your users. Code that relies on vendor-specific extensions will likely only run on that OpenGL hardware, so it is important that they know what hardware is required and why.

In most cases, you should be able to provide a fallback mode that allows a user to operate your software without the extension but with reduced functionality.

Checking for Extension Availability

Extensions come in two flavors—ones that extend an existing set of OpenGL functions and ones that add new OpenGL functions.

You must check for both types of extensions at runtime. To do this, we need to use the glGetString function to get the GL_EXTENSIONS string:

```
GLubyte *extensions;

extensions = glGetString(GL_EXTENSIONS);
```

Once you have the extensions string, you can use the standard C strstr functions to check for a specific extension. Each extension defines a string name that is associated with it, typically "EXT_something":

```
if (strstr(extensions, "EXT_something") != NULL)
```

If the extension is present, then strstr returns a pointer to the name in the string, and you can safely use the extension in your program.

Extensions that add new OpenGL functions are a little more complicated to support.

Accessing Extension Functions

Extension functions are not part of standard OpenGL library. Windows defines a function called `wglGetProcAddress` that you can use to dynamically look up nonstandard extension functions:

```
PROC wglGetProcAddress(LPSTR lpszProc);
```

The *lpszProc* argument provides the name of the extension function, such as `glCullParameterfvEXT`. The return value is a pointer to the function or NULL if the function isn't included with the OPENGL32.DLL file for the graphics card.

To call the extension function, you just dereference the pointer and pass in the arguments as usual:

```
PROC glCullParameterfvEXT;
...
glCullParameterfvEXT = wglGetProcAddress("glCullParameterfvEXT");
...
if (glCullParameterfvEXT)
    (*glCullParameterfvEXT)(GL_CULL_VERTEX_EYE_POSITION_EXT, vector);
```

Because extension functions are not exported by the vendor's OPENGL32.DLL file, you can use the extension function name for your pointer, improving the readability of your code.

CROSS-PLATFORM CONSIDERATION

The Windows extension mechanism is quite different from the one used on UNIX workstations. There is no facility for using different OpenGL libraries from different vendors, so all extension functions are available directly in the OpenGL library on the system, whether or not the hardware actually supports them.

This makes writing cross-platform OpenGL applications that use extensions a little more challenging and is yet another reason to be careful about which extensions you choose to use in your application.

Extension Constants

The `<GL/gl.h>` header file defines constants for each extension that is included in the library, typically named `GL_EXT_something`. By using the `#ifdef` and `#endif` preprocessor directives, you can selectively compile in the code that uses the extension:

```
#ifdef GL_EXT_something
... insert code that uses the extension ...
#endif /* GL_EXT_something */
```

However, many OpenGL extensions under Windows are not defined by the Microsoft OpenGL library header files.

To work around this, you need to define the constants yourself using the extension documentation from the OpenGL Web site (http://www.opengl.org). For the vertex culling extension, it looks like

```
#ifndef GL_CULL_VERTEX_EXT
/*
 * Define constants for vertex culling; values taken from the extension
 * specification on www.opengl.org...
 */
#   define GL_CULL_VERTEX_EXT                    0x81AA
#   define GL_CULL_VERTEX_EYE_POSITION_EXT       0x81AB
#   define GL_CULL_VERTEX_OBJECT_POSITION_EXT 0x81AC
#endif /* !GL_CULL_VERTEX_EXT */
```

Be careful to use the correct numbers for the constants, and always do a runtime check for the extension so your program functions properly on all systems.

The Swap Hint Extension

The swap hint extension is a standard Windows OpenGL extension that you can use to speed up your double-buffered display.

When you call `SwapBuffers` or `glutSwapBuffers`, Windows copies the back buffer to the front buffer, which is onscreen. This copy operation can be very fast or very slow depending on the graphics card and window size.

The main limiting factors are the copy and fill rate of the card (usually expressed in megapixels per second) and in some cases the memory bus speed. A typical OpenGL card can fill at least 100 megapixels (100 million pixels) every second.

To reduce the amount of copying that is required (and thereby speed up the display), the swap hint extension provides a function called `glAddSwapHintRectWIN` that specifies what areas of the window need to be swapped:

```
void glAddSwapHintRectWIN(GLint x, GLint y, GLsizei width, GLsizei height);
```

The *x* and *y* arguments specify the bottom-left corner of the rectangle to be swapped, and the *width* and *height* arguments specify its size. You can specify multiple rectangles to copy multiple regions of the window. The list of rectangles is cleared after every call to `SwapBuffers` or `glutSwapBuffers`.

Making a Flight Simulator

A flight simulator is a perfect candidate for optimization using the swap hint extension. Figure 16.1 shows a simple flight simulator that has an out-the-window view at the top and flight instruments in the bottom.

Figure 16.1 Flight simulator window.

The top half of the window must always be updated. The instruments at the bottom, however, only need to be updated when the airspeed, altitude, heading, or orientation change.

To use the swap hint extension, we start with the usual steps to look up the extension:

```
int  UseSwapHint;          /* Use swap hint extension? */
PROC glAddSwapHintRectWIN; /* Swap hint extension function */

if (strstr(glGetString(GL_EXTENSIONS), "WIN_swap_hint") != NULL)
    {
    UseSwapHint = 1;
    glAddSwapHintRectWIN = wglGetProcAddress("glAddSwapHintRectWIN");
    }
else
    UseSwapHint = 0;
```

Our `Redraw` function keeps track of four Boolean variables for each of the instruments, called `RedrawAirspeed`, `RedrawAltitude`, `RedrawCompass`, and `RedrawHorizon`, plus a fifth called `RedrawAll` that indicates when the entire window needs to be swapped.

The top portion of the flight simulator window displays the terrain example from Chapter 8, "Texture Mapping." To keep the aspect ratio correct, we limit the drawing to the top 5/8 of the window using `glViewport` and `glScissor`:

```
glViewport(0, 3 * Height / 8, Width, Height - 3 * Height / 8);
glScissor(0, 3 * Height / 8, Width, Height - 3 * Height / 8);
glEnable(GL_SCISSOR_TEST);
```

After the terrain is drawn, we reset the viewport to the entire window and draw the cockpit and instruments:

```
glViewport(0, 0, Width, Height);
glDisable(GL_SCISSOR_TEST);

glMatrixMode(GL_PROJECTION);
glLoadIdentity();
glOrtho(0.0f, (float)Width, 0.0f, (float)Height, -1.0, 1.0);
glMatrixMode(GL_MODELVIEW);
```

Finally, if the entire window does not need to be redrawn, we use the glAddSwapHintRectWIN function:

```
if (!RedrawAll && UseSwapHint)
    {
    /* Tell Windows just to swap the top */
    (*glAddSwapHintRectWIN)(0, 3 * Height / 8, Width,
                            Height - 3 * Height / 8);

    /* And any instruments we've changed... */
    if (RedrawAirspeed)
        (*glAddSwapHintRectWIN)(ix, iy, isize, isize);
    if (RedrawAltimeter)
        (*glAddSwapHintRectWIN)(ix + 5 * isize / 4, iy + isize / 4,
                                isize, isize);
    if (RedrawHorizon)
        (*glAddSwapHintRectWIN)(ix + 10 * isize / 4, iy + isize / 4,
                                isize, isize);
    if (RedrawCompass)
        (*glAddSwapHintRectWIN)(ix + 15 * isize / 4, iy, isize, isize);
    }
```

The final code appears on the CD-ROM in BOOK\CHAP16\FLIGHTSIM\flightsim.c.

The Vertex Culling Extension

The vertex culling extension is provided in SGI OpenGL and has been accepted as a multi-vendor extension. As with all extensions, you should only use it if you have to, and you must check for its availability before using it.

When displaying a polygon on the screen, OpenGL performs face culling on the projected vertices used by the fragments, basically so that the primitive is only displayed if it is facing the viewer.

This kind of culling can be inefficient because it requires the vertices to go through two matrices (the modelview and projection matrices), be normalized, and converted to window coordinates.

What the vertex culling extension does is allow OpenGL to do this culling earlier, specifically just after the coordinates have gone through the modelview matrix. This prevents primitives that are facing away from the viewer from being rendered, which eliminates an extra set of calculations and frees up the rasterization portion of the pipeline for those primitives that are visible.

Using the Vertex Culling Extension

The vertex culling extension adds one new function to the OpenGL library called `glCullParameterfvEXT`:

```
/* For gluPerspective() and glFrustum() projections */
GLfloat vector[4] = { 0.0, 0.0, 0.0, 1.0 };


(*glCullParameterfvSGI)(GL_CULL_VERTEX_EYE_POSITION_EXT, vector);


/* For glOrtho() and gluOrtho2D() projections */
GLfloat vector[4] = { 0.0, 0.0, 1.0, 0.0 };


glCullParameterfvEXT(GL_CULL_VERTEX_EYE_POSITION_EXT, vector);
```

As you can see, two "standard" positions are used for culling, both of which put the viewer directly in front of the scene. The `GL_CULL_VERTEX_EYE_POSITION_EXT` constant specifies that the culling should be performed on the coordinates after they have been transformed by the modelview matrix. To cull using the "raw" object coordinates, use `GL_CULL_VERTEX_OBJECT_POSITION_EXT` instead.

The vector array specifies the direction of the viewer and not the actual position. This is very much like the way OpenGL directional lighting works.

Finally, to actually use vertex culling, we need to enable it with

```
glEnable(GL_CULL_VERTEX_EXT);
```

Vertex Culling in the Terrain Examples

You can put the vertex culling extension to good use in the terrain viewing programs in Chapter 8, "Texture Mapping," Chapter 11, "Buffers: Not Just for Animation," and Chapter 12, "Beyond Lines and Triangles." To use it, we first check that the extension is available:

```
PROC glCullParameterfvEXT;

if (strstr(glGetString(GL_EXTENSIONS), "EXT_cull_vertex") != NULL)
    {
```

```
    UseCullVertex = 1;
    glCullParameterfvEXT = wglGetProcAddress("glCullParameterfvEXT");
    }
else if (strstr(glGetString(GL_EXTENSIONS), "SGI_cull_vertex") != NULL)
    {
    UseCullVertex = 1;
    glCullParameterfvEXT = wglGetProcAddress("glCullParameterfvSGI");
    }
else
    UseCullVertex = 0;
```

Then, in the Redraw function, we enable it if it's available:

```
if (UseCullVertex)
    {
    (*glCullParameter3fvEXT)(GL_CULL_VERTEX_EYE_POSITION_EXT, vector);
    glEnable(GL_CULL_VERTEX_EXT);
    }
```

The results appear in Figure 16.2. As you can see, the output is identical to that for the program in Chapter 12, but the vertex culling extension speeds up our display by almost 20 percent. Not bad for two lines of code!

You can find the whole program in BOOK\CHAP16\terrain9\terrain9.c on the CD.

Figure 16.2 Terrain program using the vertex culling extension.

The Multi-Texture Extension

The multi-texture extension was proposed by the ARB and was probably based on SGI's detail texture extension. The detail texture extension allows you to specify an additional texture image that is modulated with the main texture to show additional detail. Typically, you use the detail texture extension with a large image texture (such as satellite imagery) with a smaller detail texture image that provides some surface detail (rock, grass, and so on). The texture coordinates in the detail texture are based on the main texture coordinates multiplied by a scaling factor.

The multi-texture extension expands on this by allowing two or more textures to be modulated together. Each texture can be mipmapped and must use its own set of texture coordinates, and individual textures can be turned on and off.

Multi-texturing allows you to combine light maps (images containing spotlights or specular highlights), reflections, shadows, and detail textures with a main texture to produce real-time photorealistic images.

Checking for the Multi-Texture Extension

Your program can check for the presence of the multi-texture extension by looking for the string "ARB_multitexture" at runtime and using wglGetProcAddress to get pointers to the extension functions:

```
PROC glActiveTextureARB;
PROC glMultiTexCoord2f;

if (strstr(glGetString(GL_EXTENSIONS), "ARB_multitexture") != NULL)
    {
    glActiveTextureARB  = wglGetProcAddress("glActiveTextureARB");
    glMultiTexCoord3fARB = wglGetProcAddress("glMultiTexCoord2fARB");
    ...
    }
#endif /* GL_ARB_multitexture */
```

Using the Multi-Texture Extension

The multi-texture extension adds two new functions; the first is glActiveTextureARB:

```
void glActiveTextureARB(GLenum texture);
```

The *texture* argument is a constant named GL_TEXTUREn_ARB, where *n* is the texture number from 0 to 31. You normally use texture 0 (GL_TEXTURE0_ARB). Textures 1 through 31 are applied in turn, each acting on the texel (color) values for the given pixel. The maximum number of textures that you can use is available using the glGetInteger function:

```
max_textures = glGetInteger(GL_MAX_TEXTURE_UNITS_ARB);
```

You can count on using at least two textures (`GL_TEXTURE0_ARB` and `GL_TEXTURE1_ARB`).

The `glActiveTextureARB` function sets which texture is affected by texture functions such as `glTexImage2D` and `glBindTexture`.

The second function is actually a group of functions called `glMultiTexCoord*ARB` that set the texture coordinates for the specified texture:

```
void glMultiTexCoord1d(GLenum texture, GLdouble s);
void glMultiTexCoord1f(GLenum texture, GLfloat s);
void glMultiTexCoord1i(GLenum texture, GLint s);
void glMultiTexCoord1s(GLenum texture, GLshort s);

void glMultiTexCoord2d(GLenum texture, GLdouble s, GLdouble t);
void glMultiTexCoord2f(GLenum texture, GLfloat s, GLfloat t);
void glMultiTexCoord2i(GLenum texture, GLint s, GLint t);
void glMultiTexCoord2s(GLenum texture, GLshort s, GLshort t);

void glMultiTexCoord2dv(GLenum texture, const GLdouble *st);
void glMultiTexCoord2fv(GLenum texture, const GLfloat *st);
void glMultiTexCoord2iv(GLenum texture, const GLint *st);
void glMultiTexCoord2sv(GLenum texture, const GLshort *st);

void glMultiTexCoord3d(GLenum texture, GLdouble s, GLdouble t, GLdouble u);
void glMultiTexCoord3f(GLenum texture, GLfloat s, GLfloat t, GLfloat u);
void glMultiTexCoord3i(GLenum texture, GLint s, GLint t, GLint u);
void glMultiTexCoord3s(GLenum texture, GLshort s, GLshort t, GLshort u);

void glMultiTexCoord3dv(GLenum texture, const GLdouble *stu);
void glMultiTexCoord3fv(GLenum texture, const GLfloat *stu);
void glMultiTexCoord3iv(GLenum texture, const GLint *stu);
void glMultiTexCoord3sv(GLenum texture, const GLshort *stu);
```

When specifying texture coordinates for the main texture (`GL_TEXTURE0_ARB`), you can still use the normal `glTexCoord*` functions or generated coordinates as outlined in Chapter 8. For all other textures, however, you must use `glMultTexCoord*ARB`.

When drawing primitives, you need to enable texturing with

```
glEnable(GL_TEXTURE_2D);
```

to use the multi-texture extension features.

Summary

OpenGL extensions provide a convenient way to extend the capabilities of OpenGL without burdening the core library. You should use extensions with care, however, as many extensions are only available on particular graphics cards. Even if it runs with a reduced functionality or display rate, always make sure your application can run without the extension.

The swap hint extension optimizes what portions of a window are swapped.
The vertex culling extension provides a simple way to speed up the display of culled primitives. The multi-texture extension provides enhanced rendering quality by combining multiple textures in one pass.

Reference Section

glActiveTextureARB

Purpose	Selects a texture target.
Include File	<GL/gl.h>
Syntax	`void glActiveTextureARB(GLenum target)`
Description	This function selects a texture target for the ARB multi-texture extension.
Parameters	
target	`GLenum`: The texture target, one of `GL_TEXTUREn_ARB`.
Returns	None.
See Also	`glMultiTexCoord*ARB`, `glGetProcAddress`

glAddSwapHintRectWIN

Purpose	Specifies a rectangle that should be swapped.
Include File	<GL/gl.h>
Syntax	`void glAddSwapHintRectWIN(GLint x, GLint y, GLsizei width, GLsizei height)`
Description	This function adds a rectangle to the list of areas that should be swapped in the window on the next call to `SwapBuffers` or `glutSwapBuffers`.
Parameters	
x	`GLint`: The lower-left x coordinate in pixels.
y	`GLint`: The lower-left y coordinate in pixels.
width	`GLsizei`: The width of the rectangle in pixels.
height	`GLsizei`: The height of the rectangle in pixels.
Returns	None.

Examples	See the example in BOOK\CHAP16\FLIGHTSIM\flightsim.c on the source code CD-ROM.
See Also	`wglGetProcAddress`

glCullParameterfvSGI

Purpose	Initializes the vertex culling extension.
Include File	<GL/gl.h>
Syntax	`void glCullParameterfvSGI(GLenum param, GLfloat *value);`
Description	This function initializes the SGI vertex culling extension parameters.
Parameters	
param	GLenum: The parameter to set, typically `GL_CULL_VERTEX_EYE_POSITION_SGI`.
value	GLfloat *: The parameter value.
Returns	None.
Examples	See the example in BOOK\CHAP16\TERRAIN9\terrain9.c on the source code CD-ROM.
See Also	`wglGetProcAddress`

glMultiTexCoord*ARB

Purpose	Specifies texture coordinates for additional textures.
Include File	<GL/gl.h>

Syntax	`void glMultiTexCoord1dARB(GLenum target, GLdouble s);`
	`void glMultiTexCoord1fARB(GLenum target, GLfloat s);`
	`void glMultiTexCoord1iARB(GLenum target, GLint s);`
	`void glMultiTexCoord1sARB(GLenum target, GLshort s);`
	`void glMultiTexCoord2dARB(GLenum target, GLdouble s, GLdouble t);`
	`void glMultiTexCoord2fARB(GLenum target, GLfloat s, GLfloat t);`
	`void glMultiTexCoord2iARB(GLenum target, GLint s, GLint t);`
	`void glMultiTexCoord2sARB(GLenum target, GLshort s, GLshort t);`
	`void glMultiTexCoord2dvARB(GLenum target, GLdouble *st);`
	`void glMultiTexCoord2fvARB(GLenum target, GLfloat *st);`
	`void glMultiTexCoord2ivARB(GLenum target, GLint *st);`
	`void glMultiTexCoord2svARB(GLenum target, GLshort *st);`
	`void glMultiTexCoord3dARB(GLenum target, GLdouble s, GLdouble t, GLdouble u);`

```
void glMultiTexCoord3fARB(GLenum  target, GLfloat s,
GLfloat t,  GLfloat u);
void glMultiTexCoord3iARB(GLenum target, GLint s, GLint t,
GLint r);
void glMultiTexCoord3sARB(GLenum target, GLshort s, GLshort t,
GLshort r);
void glMultiTexCoord3dvARB(GLenum target, GLdouble *str);
void glMultiTexCoord3fvARB(GLenum target, GLfloat *str);
void glMultiTexCoord3ivARB(GLenum target, GLint *str);
void glMultiTexCoord3svARB(GLenum target, GLshort *str);
```

Description	This function sets the texture coordinates for the specified texture.
Parameters	
target	GLenum: The affected texture—GL_TEXTUREn_ARB.
s	Varies: The texture s coordinate.
t	Varies: The texture t coordinate.
r	Varies: The texture r coordinate.
st	Varies: A pointer to the texture s and t coordinates.
str	Varies: A pointer to the texture s, t, and r coordinates.
Returns	None.
See Also	glActiveTextureARB, wglGetProcAddress

wglGetProcAddress

Purpose	Gets the address of an extension function.
Include File	<GL/gl.h>
Syntax	PROC wglGetProcAddress(LPSTR lpszProc);
Description	This function retrieves the address of an extension function. If the extension function is not available in the OPENGL32.DLL file, then a NULL pointer is returned.
Parameters	
lpszProc	LPSTR: The name of the extension function.
Returns	None.
Examples	See the example in BOOK\CHAP16\FLIGHTSIM\flightsim.c on the source code CD-ROM.

PART 3

OpenGL for Windows:
OpenGL + Win32 = Wiggle

Until now, we have been using the GLUT framework for all our OpenGL example programs. GLUT takes the windowing details out of simple OpenGL programming tasks because it hides the windowing interface of each operating system to which it has been ported. GLUT however, is not a robust or complete windowing toolkit for general-purpose application development.

One of the strong attractions of OpenGL is that it is scaleable and portable to a wide variety of hardware and operating system platforms. While your OpenGL based rendering code may be portable, and in general C and C++ application code will port with little to no effort (depending on how well you plan for this in advance), GUI code is usually not very portable.

Knowing your target platform can give you a tremendous advantage when developing application programs or games. You can take advantage of OS services and features and provide your users with an application that works well and behaves as if it were in it's native environment.

Without a doubt, Microsoft Windows is the most popular operating system today for the PC. With this in mind, commercial applications or games usually find a home on Windows before anywhere else. If you're going to create top-notch applications on the Windows platform using OpenGL, then you are going to need to know more than how to use GLUT.

This last section contains three chapters that focus on using OpenGL for Microsoft Windows (95/98/NT/2000). In the first chapter, you'll discover a bit about the hardware driver model for OpenGL, how to select hardware or software rendering, and the care and feeding of OpenGL rendering contexts.

The next chapter focuses on using OpenGL to create images someplace other than on screen. This will include bitmaps, and printing your OpenGL graphics. Finally, we'll discuss some real-time techniques that are useful on the Windows platform (and some that are useful anywhere!). This final chapter is a must read for anyone interested in developing games or real-time visualization or simulation applications with OpenGL on the Windows platform.

17

THE OPENGL PIXEL FORMAT AND RENDERING CONTEXT

What you'll learn in this chapter:

How to...	Functions You'll Use

Request and select an OpenGL pixel format	`ChoosePixelFormat/`
	`DescribePixelFormat/`
	`SetPixelFormat`

Create and use OpenGL rendering contexts	`wglCreateContext/`
	`wglDeleteContext/`
	`wglMakeCurrent`

Respond to window messages	`WM_PAINT/WM_CREATE/` `WM_DESTROY/WM_SIZE`
Use double buffering in Windows	`SwapBuffers`

OpenGL is purely a graphics API, with user interaction and the screen or window handled by the host environment. To facilitate this partnership, each environment usually has some extensions that "glue" OpenGL to its own window management and user interface functions. This glue is code that associates OpenGL drawing commands to a particular window. It is also necessary to provide functions for setting buffer modes, color depths, and other drawing characteristics.

For Microsoft Windows, this glue code is embodied in a set of new functions added to the Windows API. (They are called the wiggle functions because they are prefixed with wgl rather than gl.) These gluing functions are explained in this chapter, where we dispense with using the GLUT library for our OpenGL framework.

Starting with this chapter, we build full-fledged Windows applications that can take advantage of all the operating system's features. You will see what characteristics a Windows window must have in order to support OpenGL graphics. You will learn which messages a well-behaved OpenGL window should handle and how. The concepts of this chapter are introduced gradually, as we use C to build a model OpenGL program that provides the initial framework for all future examples.

So far in this book, you've needed no prior knowledge of 3D graphics and only a rudimentary knowledge of C programming. From this point, however, we assume you have at least an entry-level knowledge of Windows programming. Otherwise, we'd have wound up writing a book twice the size of this one, and we'd have spent more time on the details of Windows programming and less on OpenGL programming. If you are new to Windows, or if you cut your teeth on one of the Application Frameworks and aren't all that familiar with Windows procedures, message routing, and so forth, you want to check out some of the recommended reading in Appendix B, "Further Reading," before going too much further in this chapter.

OpenGL Implementations on Windows

OpenGL became available for the WIN32 platform with the release of Windows NT version 3.5. It was later released as an add-on for Windows 95 and later became a shipping part of the Windows 95 operating system. OpenGL is now a native API on any WIN32 platform (Windows 95/98, Windows NT/2000), with its functions exported from opengl32.dll. You need to be aware of four flavors of OpenGL on Windows. Each has its pros and cons from both the user and the developer point of view. You should at least have a high-level understanding of how these implementations work and what their drawbacks might be.

Generic OpenGL

A generic implementation of OpenGL is simply a software implementation that does not use specific 3D hardware. The Microsoft implementation that is bundled with Windows is a generic implementation. The SGI OpenGL for Windows implementation optionally makes use of MMX instructions, but this is not considered dedicated 3D hardware, so it is still considered a generic software implementation. Mesa is not strictly a "real" OpenGL implementation (it's a work-a-like described in Chapter 3, "Using OpenGL"), but for most purposes, you can consider it to be so. Mesa can also be hooked to hardware, but this should be considered a special case of the *mini-driver* (discussed shortly).

Installable-Client Driver

The Installable-Client Driver (ICD) was the original hardware driver interface provided for Windows NT. The ICD must implement the entire OpenGL pipeline (see Chapter 2, "What Is OpenGL?") using a combination of software and the specific hardware for which it was written. An ICD is a considerable amount of work for a vendor to undertake from scratch.

The ICD drops in and works with Microsoft's OpenGL implementation. Applications linked to opengl32.dll are automatically dispatched to the ICD driver code for OpenGL calls. This mechanism is ideal because applications do not have to be recompiled to take advantage of OpenGL hardware should it become available. The ICD is actually a part of the display driver and does not affect the existing openGL32.dll system DLL. This driver model provides the vendor with the most opportunities to optimize its driver and hardware combination.

Mini-Client Driver

The Mini-Client Driver (MCD) was a compromise between a software and hardware implementation. Most early PC 3D hardware provided hardware-accelerated rasterization only. (See the pipeline description in Chapter 2.) The MCD driver model allowed applications to use Microsoft's generic implementation for features that were not available in hardware. For example, transform and lighting could come from Microsoft's OpenGL software, but the actual rendering of lit shaded triangles would be handled by the hardware.

The MCD driver implementation made it easy for hardware vendors to create OpenGL drivers for their hardware. Most of the work was done by Microsoft, and whatever features (even rasterization features) the vendors did not implement in hardware was handed back to the Microsoft generic implementation.

The MCD driver model showed great promise for bringing OpenGL to the PC mass market. Initially available for Windows NT, an SDK was provided to hardware vendors to create MCD drivers for Windows 95. After many hardware vendors had completed their MCD drivers, Microsoft decided not to license the code for public release. This gave their own proprietary 3D API a temporary advantage in the consumer marketplace.

Few vendors today use the MCD driver model for a number of reasons. One reason is that the MCD driver model cannot support AGP (Intel's Accelerated Graphics Port) texturing efficiently. Another is that SGI began providing an optimized ICD driver kit to vendors that made ICDs almost as easy to write as MCDs. (This move was a response to Microsoft's temporary withdrawal of support for OpenGL on Windows 95.) This driver kit is now jointly supported by both SGI and Microsoft.

Mini-Driver

A mini-driver is not a true Windows display driver. Instead, it is a drop-in replacement for opengl32.dll that makes calls to a hardware vendor's 3D hardware driver. Typically, these mini-drivers convert OpenGL calls to roughly equivalent calls in a vendor's proprietary 3D API. The first mini-driver was written by 3Dfx for its Voodoo graphics card. This DLL drop-in converted OpenGL calls into the Voodoo's native Glide (the 3Dfx 3D API) programming interface.

Id software first wrote a version of its popular game Quake that used OpenGL and ran with this 3dfx mini-driver. For this reason, as mini-drivers were developed for other graphics cards, they were sometimes called "Quake drivers." Many of the higher end OpenGL hardware vendors sarcastically refer to the consumer boards as *Quake accelerators*, not worthy of comparison to their hardware. Many other game hardware vendors hopped on the bandwagon and began supplying mini-drivers for their hardware, too. Although they popularized OpenGL for games, mini-drivers often had missing OpenGL functions or features. Any application that used OpenGL did not necessarily work with a mini-driver. Typically, these drivers provided only the barest functionality needed to run a popular game.

Unfortunately, the practice of creating optimized mini-drivers for a particular game still persists with some vendors. These vendors are attempting to win the benchmark game against other vendors at the expense of ISV's and consumers. Mini-drivers create compatibility problems with later versions of the game in question and often will not work at all with other games or OpenGL-based applications. Many customers are not familiar with driver installation and removal (they shouldn't have to be!), and this only exacerbates the problem.

Lately, some programmers started using the Mesa software OpenGL *work-alike* to create mini-drivers for specific 3D hardware boards. These mini-drivers are usually more complete, but you still should use them with caution. Perhaps the greatest boon to OpenGL's rapid growth is the use of Mesa-based drivers for other hardware platforms such as Linux.

Basic Windows Rendering

With the GLUT library, we had only one window, and OpenGL function calls always produced output in that window. (Where else would they go?) Your own real-world Windows applications, however, will often have more than one window. In fact, dialog boxes, controls, and even menus are actually windows at a fundamental level; it's nearly impossible to have a useful program that contains only one window. How does OpenGL know where to draw when you execute your rendering code? Before we answer this question, let's first review how we normally draw in a window without using OpenGL.

GDI Device Contexts

Normally, when you draw in a window without using OpenGL, you use the Windows GDI (Graphical Device Interface) functions. Each window has a device context that actually receives the graphics output, and each GDI function takes a device context as an argument to indicate which window you want the function to affect. You can have multiple device contexts, but only one for each window.

The sample program WinRect on the companion CD draws an ordinary window with a blue background and a red square in the center. The output from this program, shown in Figure 17.1, will look familiar to you. This is the same image produced by our second OpenGL program in Chapter 3, friendly.c. Unlike that earlier example, however, the WinRect program does not use GLUT; we wrote it entirely with the Windows API. WinRect's code is pretty generic as far as Windows programming goes. A `WinMain` gets things started and keeps the message pump going, and a `WndProc` handles messages for the main window.

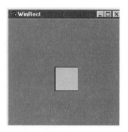

Figure 17.1   Output from WinRect.

Your familiarity with Windows programming should extend to the details of creating and displaying a window, so we cover only the code from this example that is responsible for drawing the background and square.

First, we must create a blue and a red brush for filling and painting. The handles for these brushes are declared globally:

```
// Handles to GDI brushes we will use for drawing
HBRUSH hBlueBrush,hRedBrush;
```

Then, the brushes are created in the `WinMain` function, using the RGB macro to create solid red and blue brushes:

```
// Create a blue and red brush for drawing and filling
// operations.              //     Red, green, blue
hBlueBrush = CreateSolidBrush(RGB(  0,      0,    255));
hRedBrush = CreateSolidBrush(RGB(  255,     0,      0));
```

When the window style is being specified, the background is set to use the blue brush in the window class structure:

```
wc.hbrBackground = hBlueBrush; // Use blue brush for background
```

Window size and position (previously set with glutPositionWindow and glutReshapeWindow) are set when the window is created:

```
// Create the main application window
hWnd = CreateWindow(
           lpszAppName,
           lpszAppName,
           WS_OVERLAPPEDWINDOW,
           100, 100,        // Size and dimensions of window
           250, 250,
           NULL,
           NULL,
           hInstance,
           NULL);
```

Finally, the actual painting of the window interior is handled by the WM_PAINT message handler in the WndProc function:

```
case WM_PAINT:
    {
    PAINTSTRUCT ps;
    HBRUSH hOldBrush;

    // Start painting
    BeginPaint(hWnd,&ps);

    // Select and use the red brush
    hOldBrush = SelectObject(ps.hdc,hRedBrush);

    // Draw a rectangle filled with the currently
    // selected brush
    Rectangle(ps.hdc,100,100,150,150);

    // Deselect the brush
    SelectObject(ps.hdc,hOldBrush);

    // End painting
    EndPaint(hWnd,&ps);
    }
    break;
```

The call to BeginPaint prepares the window for painting and sets the hdc member of the PAINTSTRUCT structure to the device context to be used for drawing in this window. This handle to the device context is used as the first parameter to all GDI functions, identifying which window they should operate on. This code then selects the red brush for painting operations and draws a filled rectangle at the coordinates (100,100,150,150). Then, the brush is deselected, and EndPaint cleans up the painting operation for you.

Before you jump to the conclusion that OpenGL should work in a similar way, remember that the GDI is Windows-specific. Other environments do not have device contexts, window handles, and the like. Although the ideas may be similar, they are certainly not called the same thing and might work and behave differently. OpenGL, on the other hand, was designed to be completely portable among environments and hardware platforms (and it didn't start on Windows anyway!). Adding a device context parameter to the OpenGL functions would render your OpenGL code useless in any environment other than Windows.

OpenGL does have a context identifier, however, and it is called the *rendering context*. The rendering context is similar in many respects to the GDI device context because it is the rendering context that remembers current colors, state settings, and so on, much like the device context holds onto the current brush or pen color.

Pixel Formats

The Windows concept of the device context is limited for 3D graphics because it was designed for 2D graphics applications. In Windows, you *request* a device context identifier for a given window. The nature of the device context depends on the nature of the device. If your desktop is set to 16-bit color, then the device context Windows gives you knows about and understands 16-bit color only. You cannot tell Windows, for example, that one window is to be a 16-bit color window and another is to be an 8-bit color window.

Although Windows lets you create a memory device context, you still have to give it an existing window device context to emulate. Even if you pass in NULL for the window parameter, Windows uses the device context of your desktop. You, the programmer, have no control over the intrinsic characteristics of a Windows device context.

Any window or device that will be rendering 3D graphics has far more characteristics to it than simply color depth, especially if you are using a hardware rendering device (3D graphics card). Up until now, GLUT has taken care of these details for you. When you initialized GLUT, you told it what buffers you needed (double or single color buffer, depth buffer, stencil, and alpha).

Before OpenGL can render into a window, you must first configure that window according to your rendering needs. Do you want hardware or software rendering? Will the rendering be single or double buffered? Do you need a depth buffer? How about stencil, alpha, or an accumulation buffer? Once you set these parameters for a window, they cannot be changed later. To switch from a window with only a depth and color buffer to a window with only a stencil and color buffer, you have to destroy the first window and recreate a new window with the characteristics you need.

Describing a Pixel Format

The 3D characteristics of the window are set one time, usually just after window creation. The collective name for these settings is the *pixel format*. Windows provides a structure PIXELFORMATDESCRIPTOR that describes the pixel format. This structure is defined as follows:

```
typedef struct tagPIXELFORMATDESCRIPTOR {
WORD nSize;             // Size of this structure
WORD nVersion;          // Version of structure (should be 1)
DWORD dwFlags;          // Pixel buffer properties
BYTE  iPixelType;       // Type of pixel data (RGBA or Color Index)
BYTE  cColorBits;       // Number of color bit planes in color buffer
BYTE  cRedBits;         // How many bits for red
BYTE  cRedShift;        // Shift count for red bits
BYTE  cGreenBits;       // How many bits for green
BYTE  cGreenShift;      // Shift count for green bits
BYTE  cBlueBits;        // How many bits for blue
BYTE  cBlueShift;       // Shift count for blue
BYTE  cAlphaBits;       // How many bits for destination alpha
BYTE  cAlphaShift;      // Shift count for destination alpha
BYTE  cAccumBits;       // How many bits for accumulation buffer
BYTE  cAccumRedBits;    // How many red bits for accumulation buffer
BYTE  cAccumGreenBits;  // How many green bits for accumulation buffer
BYTE  cAccumBlueBits;   // How many blue bits for accumulation buffer
BYTE  cAccumAlphaBits;  // How many alpha bits for accumulation buffer
BYTE  cDepthBits;       // How many bits for depth buffer
BYTE  cStencilBits;     // How many bits for stencil buffer
BYTE  cAuxBuffers;      // How many auxiliary buffers
BYTE  iLayerType;       // Obsolete - ignored
BYTE  bReserved;        // Number of overlay and underlay planes
DWORD dwLayerMask;      // Obsolete - ignored
DWORD dwVisibleMask;    // Transparent color of underlay plane
DWORD dwDamageMask;     // Obsolete - ignored
} PIXELFORMATDESCRIPTOR;
```

For a given OpenGL device (hardware or software), the values of these members are not arbitrary. Only a limited number of pixel formats are available for a given window. Pixel formats are said to be *exported* by the OpenGL driver or software renderer. Most of these structure members are self-explanatory, but a few require some additional explanation:

nSize	The size of the structure, set to sizeof(PIXELFORMATDESCRIPTOR);.
nVersion	Set to 1.
dwFlags	A set of bit flags that specify properties of the pixel buffer. Most of these are not mutually exclusive, but a few are used only when requesting or describing the pixel format. Table 17.1 lists the valid flags for this member.

Table 17.1 *Valid Flags to Describe the Pixel Rendering Buffer*

PFD_DRAW_TO_WINDOW	The buffer's output is displayed in a window.
PFD_DRAW_TO_BITMAP	The buffer's output is written to a Windows bitmap.
PFD_SUPPORT_GDI	The buffer supports Windows GDI drawing. Most implementations only allow this for single-buffered windows or bitmaps.
PFD_GENERIC_ACCELERATED	The buffer is accelerated by an MCD driver.
PFD_GENERIC_FORMAT	The buffer is a rendered by a software implementation. This bit is set with PFD_GENERIC_ACCELERATED for MCD drivers. Only if this bit is clear is the hardware driver an ICD.
PFD_NEED_PALETTE	The buffer is on a palette-managed device. This flag is set on Windows when running in 8-bit (256-color) mode and requires a 3-3-2 color palette.
PFD_NEED_SYSTEM_PALETTE	This flag indicates that OpenGL hardware supports rendering in 256-color mode. A 3-3-2 palette must be realized to enable hardware acceleration. Although documented, this flag can be considered obsolete. No mainstream hardware accelerator ever shipped for Windows that supported accelerated rendering in 256-color mode.
PFD_DOUBLEBUFFER	The color buffer is double buffered.
PFD_STEREO	The color buffer is stereoscopic. This is not supported by Microsoft's generic implementation. Most PC vendors that support stereo do so with custom extensions for their hardware.
PFD_SWAP_LAYER_BUFFERS	This flag is used if overlay and underlay planes are supported. If set, these planes may be swapped independently of the color buffer.
PFD_DEPTH_DONTCARE	Used only when requesting a pixel format. This flag indicates that you do not need a depth buffer. Some implementations can save memory and enhance performance by not allocating memory for the depth buffer.
PFD_DOUBLE_BUFFER_DONTCARE	Used only when requesting a pixel format. This flag indicates that you do not plan to use double buffering. Although you can force rendering to the front buffer only, this flag allows an implementation to save memory and potentially enhance performance.

continued on next page

continued from previous page

iPixelType	Specifies the type of color buffer. Only two values are valid: PFD_TYPE_RGBA and PFD_TYPE_COLORINDEX. PFD_TYPE_COLORINDEX is used to request or describe the pixel format as color index mode. This rendering mode should be considered obsolete on modern PC hardware.
cColorBits	Specifies the number of bits of color depth in the color buffer. Typical values are 8, 16, 24, and 32. 32-bit color buffers may or may not be used to store destination alpha values.
cRedBits	Specifies the number of bits in the color buffer dedicated for the red color component.
cGreenBits	Specifies the number of bits in the color buffer dedicated for the green color component.
cBlueBits	Specifies the number of bits in the color buffer dedicated for the blue color component.
cAlphaBits	Specifies the number of bits used for the alpha buffer. Destination alpha is not supported by Microsoft's generic implementation, but many hardware implementations are beginning to support this.
cAccumBits	The number of bits used for the accumulation buffer.
cDepthBits	The number of bits used for the depth buffer. Typical values are 0, 16, 24, and 32. The more bits dedicated to the depth buffer, the more accurate depth testing will be.
cStencilBits	The number of bits used for the stencil buffer.
cAuxBuffers	The number of auxiliary buffers. In implementations that support auxiliary buffers, rendering can be redirected to an auxiliary buffer from the color buffer and swapped to the screen at a later time.
iLayerType	Obsolete (ignored).
bReserved	Contains the number of overlay and underlay planes supported by the implementation. Bits 0 through 3 specify the number of overlay planes (up to 15), and bits 4 through 7 specify the number of underlay planes (also up to 15).
dwLayerMask	Obsolete (ignored).
dwVisibleMask	Specifies the transparent color of an underlay plane.
dwDamageMask	Obsolete (ignored).

Enumerating Pixel Formats

The pixel format for a window is identified by a one-based integer index number. An implementation exports a number of pixel formats from which to choose. To set a pixel format for a window, you must select one of the available formats exported by the driver. You can use the function `DescribePixelFormat` to determine the characteristics of a given pixel format. You can also use this function to find out how many pixel formats are exported by the driver. The following code shows how to enumerate all the pixel formats available for a window:

```
PIXELFORMATDESCRIPTOR pfd;          // Pixel format descriptor
int nFormatCount;                   // How many pixel formats exported
. . .

// Get the number of pixel formats
// Will need a device context
pfd.nSize = sizeof(PIXELFORMATDESCRIPTOR);
nFormatCount = DescribePixelFormat(hDC, 1, 0, NULL);

// Retrieve each pixel format
for(int i = 1; i <= nFormatCount; i++)
    {
    // Get description of pixel format
    DescribePixelFormat(hDC, i, pfd.nSize, &pfd);



. . .
. . .
}
```

The function `DescribePixelFormat` returns the maximum pixel format index. You can use an initial call to this function as shown earlier to determine how many are available. The CD includes an interesting utility program called GLView for this chapter. This program enumerates all available pixel formats available for your display driver for the given resolution and color depths. Figure 17.2 shows the output from this program when a double-buffered pixel format is selected. (A single-buffered pixel format will contain a blinking block animation.)

The MFC source code is included on the CD for GLView. This is a bit more complex than your typical sample program, and GLView is provided more as a tool for your use than as a programming example. The important code for enumerating pixel formats is presented earlier and is less than a dozen lines long.

The list box lists all the available pixel formats and displays their characteristics (driver type, color depth, and so on). A sample window in the lower-right corner displays a rotating cube using a window created with the highlighted pixel format. The `glGetString` function is used to find out the name of the vendor for the OpenGL driver, as well as other version information. Finally, a list box displays all the extensions exported by the driver. (For more information on these queries to the OpenGL driver, see Chapter 16, "Common OpenGL Extensions.")

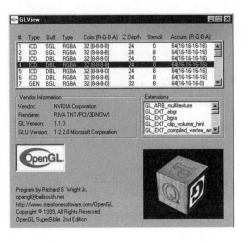

Figure 17.2 The GLView program shows all pixel formats for a given device.

If you experiment with this program, you'll discover that not all pixel formats can be used to create an OpenGL window, as shown in Figure 17.3. Even though the driver exports these pixel formats, it does not mean that you will be able to create an OpenGL-enabled window with one of them. The most important criteria is that the pixel format color depth must match the color depth of your desktop. That is, you can't create a 16-bit color pixel format for a 32-bit color desktop or vice versa.

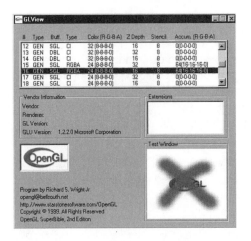

Figure 17.3 The GLView program showing an invalid pixel format.

Make special note of the fact that there are always at least 24 pixel formats enumerated, sometimes more. If you are running the Microsoft generic implementation, then you will see exactly 24 pixel formats listed (all belonging to Microsoft). If you have a hardware accelerator (either an MCD or ICD), you'll note that the accelerated pixel formats are listed first, followed by the 24 generic pixel formats belonging to Microsoft. This means that when hardware acceleration is present, you actually have two implementations of OpenGL to choose from. The first are the hardware-accelerated pixel formats belonging to the hardware accelerator. The second are the pixel formats for Microsoft's software implementation.

Knowing this can be useful. For one thing, it means that there is always a software implementation available for rendering to bitmaps or printer devices. It also means that if you so desire (for debugging purposes, perhaps), you can force software rendering, even when an application might typically select hardware acceleration.

Selecting and Setting a Pixel Format

Enumerating all the available pixel formats and examining each one to find one that meets our needs could turn out to be quite tedious. Windows provides a shortcut function that makes this process a good bit simpler. This function ChoosePixelFormat allows you to create a pixel format structure containing the desired attributes of your 3D window. The ChoosePixelFormat function then finds the closest match possible (with preference for hardware-accelerated pixel formats) and returns the most appropriate index. The pixel format is then set with a call to another new Windows function, SetPixelFormat. The following code shows the use of these two functions:

```
int nPixelFormat;
. . .

static PIXELFORMATDESCRIPTOR pfd = {
    sizeof(PIXELFORMATDESCRIPTOR),  // Size of this structure
    1,                              // Version of this structure
    PFD_DRAW_TO_WINDOW |            // Draw to window (not to bitmap)
    PFD_SUPPORT_OPENGL |            // Support OpenGL calls in window
    PFD_DOUBLEBUFFER,               // Double buffered mode
    PFD_TYPE_RGBA,                  // RGBA color mode
    32,                             // Want 32-bit color
    0,0,0,0,0,0,                    // Not used to select mode
    0,0,                            // Not used to select mode
    0,0,0,0,0,                      // Not used to select mode
    16,                             // Size of depth buffer
    0,                              // Not used to select mode
    0,                              // Not used to select mode
    0,                              // Not used to select mode
    0,                              // Not used to select mode
    0,0,0 };                        // Not used to select mode

// Choose a pixel format that best matches that described in pfd
// for the given device context
nPixelFormat = ChoosePixelFormat(hDC, &pfd);
```

```
// Set the pixel format for the device context
SetPixelFormat(hDC, nPixelFormat, &pfd);
```

Initially, the PIXELFORMATDESCRIPTOR structure is filled with the desired characteristics of the 3D-enabled window. In this case, we want a double-buffered pixel format that renders into a window. We've requested 32-bit color and a 16-bit depth buffer. If the current implementation supports 24-bit color at best, the returned pixel format will be a valid 24-bit color format. Depth buffer resolution is also subject to change. An implementation might only support a 24-bit or 32-bit depth buffer. In any case, ChoosePixelFormat always returns a valid pixel format, and if at all possible, it returns a hardware-accelerated pixel format.

Some programmers and programming needs might require more sophisticated selection of a pixel format. For most uses, however, the preceding code is sufficient to get your window primed to receive OpenGL rendering commands.

The OpenGL Rendering Context

A typical Windows application can consist of many windows. You can even set a pixel format for each one (using that windows device context) if you want! When you call OpenGL commands, how does it know which window to send its output to? In the previous chapters, we used the GLUT framework, which provided a single window that displayed our OpenGL output. Recall that with normal Windows GDI-based drawing, each window has its own device context.

To accomplish the portability of the core OpenGL functions, each environment must implement some means of specifying a current rendering window before executing any OpenGL commands. Just as the Windows GDI functions use the Windows device contexts, the OpenGL environment is embodied in what is known as the *rendering context*. Just as a device context remembers settings about drawing modes and commands for the GDI, the rendering context remembers OpenGL settings and commands.

You create an OpenGL rendering context by calling the function wglCreateContext. This function takes one parameter, the device context of a window with a valid pixel format. The data type of an OpenGL rendering context is HGLRC. The following code shows the creation of an OpenGL rendering context:

```
HGLRC hRC;    // OpenGL rendering context
HDC hDC;      // Windows device context
. . .
hRC = wglCreateContext(hDC);
```

A rendering context is initially associated with the window for which it was created. You can have more than one rendering context in your application—for instance, two windows that are using different drawing modes, perspectives, and so on. However, for OpenGL commands to know which window they are operating on, only one rendering context can be active at any one time per thread. When a rendering context is made active, it is said to be *current*.

When made current, a rendering context is also associated with a device context and thus with a particular window (or bitmap or printer context, as you'll see in the next chapter). Now, OpenGL knows which window into which to render. You can even move an OpenGL rendering context from window to window, but each window must have the same pixel format! To make a rendering context current and associate it with a particular window, you call the function `wglMakeCurrent`. This function takes two parameters, the device context of the window and the OpenGL rendering context:

```
void wglMakeCurrent(HDC hDC, HGLRC hRC);
```

Putting It All Together

We've covered a lot of ground over the last several pages. We've described each piece of the puzzle individually, but now, let's take a look at all the pieces put together. In addition to seeing all the OpenGL-related code, we should examine some of the minimum requirements for any Windows program to support OpenGL. Our sample program for this section is GLRECT. This should look somewhat familiar because it is also our first GLUT-based sample program from Chapter 3. Now, however, the program is a full-fledged Windows program written with nothing but C and the WIN32 API. Figure 17.4 shows the output of our new program, complete with bouncing square.

Figure 17.4   Output from the GLRECT program with bouncing square.

Creating the Window

The starting place for any Windows-based GUI program is the function `WinMain`. In this function, we register our window type, create our window, and start the message pump. If this is unfamiliar to you, we recommend a few good basic Windows programming books in Appendix B. Listing 17.1 shows the `WinMain` function for the first sample.

Listing 17.1 *The* WinMain *Function of the GLRECT Sample Program*

```
// Entry point of all Windows programs
int APIENTRY WinMain(      HINSTANCE      hInstance,
                           HINSTANCE      hPrevInstance,
                           LPSTR          lpCmdLine,
                           int            nCmdShow)
    {
    MSG        msg;        // Windows message structure
    WNDCLASS   wc;         // Windows class structure
    HWND       hWnd;       // Storage for window handle


    // Register window style
    wc.style        = CS_HREDRAW | CS_VREDRAW | CS_OWNDC;
    wc.lpfnWndProc  = (WNDPROC) WndProc;
    wc.cbClsExtra   = 0;
    wc.cbWndExtra   = 0;
    wc.hInstance    = hInstance;
    wc.hIcon        = NULL;
    wc.hCursor      = LoadCursor(NULL, IDC_ARROW);

    // No need for background brush for OpenGL window
    wc.hbrBackground  = NULL;

    wc.lpszMenuName   = NULL;
    wc.lpszClassName  = lpszAppName;

    // Register the window class
    if(RegisterClass(&wc) == 0)
        return FALSE;


    // Create the main application window
    hWnd = CreateWindow(
            lpszAppName,
            lpszAppName,

            // OpenGL requires WS_CLIPCHILDREN and WS_CLIPSIBLINGS
            WS_OVERLAPPEDWINDOW | WS_CLIPCHILDREN | WS_CLIPSIBLINGS,

            // Window position and size
            100, 100,
            250, 250,
            NULL,
            NULL,
            hInstance,
            NULL);
```

```
// If window was not created, quit
if(hWnd == NULL)
    return FALSE;


// Display the window
ShowWindow(hWnd,SW_SHOW);
UpdateWindow(hWnd);

// Process application messages until the application closes
while( GetMessage(&msg, NULL, 0, 0))
    {
    TranslateMessage(&msg);
    DispatchMessage(&msg);
    }

return msg.wParam;
}
```

This is pretty much your standard Windows GUI startup code. Only two things really bear mentioning here. This first is the choice of window styles set in CreateWindow. You can pretty much use whatever window styles you like, but you do need the WS_CLIPCHILDREN and WS_CLIPSIBLINGS styles set. These styles used to be required in earlier version of Windows, but later versions have dropped them as a strict requirement. The purpose of these styles is to keep the OpenGL rendering context from rendering into other windows, which can happen in GDI. However, an OpenGL rendering context must be associated with one and only one window at a time.

The second note you should make about this startup code is the use of CS_OWNDC for the window style. Why you need this innocent-looking flag requires a bit more explanation. You need a device context for both GDI rendering and for OpenGL double-buffered page flipping. In order to understand what CS_OWNDC has to do with this, we first need to take a step back and review the purpose and use of a Windows device context.

First, You Need a Device Context

Before you can draw anything in a window, you first need a Windows device context. You need it whether you're doing OpenGL, GDI, or even Direct X programming. Any drawing or painting operation in Windows (even if you are drawing on a bitmap in memory) requires a device context that identifies the specific object being drawn on. You retrieve the device context to a window with a simple function call:

```
HDC hDC = GetDC(hWnd);
```

The hDC variable is your handle to the device context of the window identified by the window handle hWnd. You use the device context for all GDI functions that draw in the window. You also need the device context for creating an OpenGL rendering context, making it current, and performing the buffer swap. You tell Windows that you don't need the device context for the window any longer with another simple function call, using the same two values:

```
ReleaseDC(hWnd ,hDC);
```

The standard Windows programming wisdom is that you retrieve a device context, use it for drawing, and then release it again as soon as possible. This advice dates back to the pre-WIN32 days when under Windows 3.1 and earlier, you had a small pool of memory allocated for system resources, such as the window device context. What happened when Windows ran out of system resources? If you were lucky, you got an error message. If you were working on something really important, the operating system could somehow tell and it would instead crash and take all your work with it.

The best way to spare your users this catastrophe was to check to make sure that the function `GetDC` succeeded. If you did get a device context, you did all your work as quickly as possible (typically within one message handler) and then released the device context so that other programs could use it. The same advice applied to other system resources such as pens, fonts, brushes, and so on.

Enter WIN32

Windows NT was a tremendous blessing for Windows programmers, in more ways than can be recounted here. Among its many benefits was that you could have all the system resources you needed until you exhausted available memory or your application crashed. (At least it wouldn't crash the OS!) It turns out that the `GetDC` function is, in computer time, quite an expensive function call to make. If you got the device context when the window was created and hung on to it until the window was destroyed, you could speed up your window painting considerably. You could hang on to brushes, fonts, and other resources that would have to be created or retrieved and potentially reinitialized each time the window was invalidated.

One popular example of the Windows NT benefit was a program that created random rectangles and put them in random locations in the window. (This was a GDI sample.) The difference between code that was written the old way and code written the new way was astonishingly obvious. Wow! WIN32 was great!

Three Steps Forward, Two Steps Back

Windows 95 brought WIN32 programming to the mainstream a couple of years later. Although Windows 95 was a 32-bit operating system, NT it was not. With Windows NT, Microsoft took a bold chance and decided that system stability was more important than being backward compatible with all the DOS and Windows 3.1 software that already existed. Windows 95 was to be the successor to Windows 3.1/DOS, and Microsoft could not afford to ignore all legacy software. (Turns out, it still didn't save *all* legacy software, but it did manage to get *most* to work).

The situation with losing system resources was considerably improved with Windows 95, but it was not eliminated entirely. The operating system could still run out of resources, but (according to Microsoft) it was unlikely. Alas, life is not so simple. Under Windows NT, when an application terminates, all allocated system resources are automatically returned to the operating system. Under Windows 95 or 98, you have a resource leak if the program crashes or the application fails to release the resources it allocated. Eventually, you will start to stress the system, and you can run out of system resources (or device contexts).

What happens when Windows doesn't have enough device contexts to go around? Well, it just takes one from someone who is being a hog with them. This means that if you call GetDC and don't call ReleaseDC, Windows 95 or Windows 98 might just appropriate your device context when it becomes stressed. The next time you call wglMakeCurrent or SwapBuffers, your device context handle might not be valid. Your application might crash or mysteriously stop rendering. Ask someone in customer support how well it goes over when you try to explain to a customer that his or her problem with your application is really Microsoft's fault!

All Is Not Lost

You actually have a way to tell Windows to create a device context just for your window's use. This feature is useful because every time you call GetDC, you have to reselect your fonts, the mapping mode, and so on. If you have your own device context, you can do this sort of initialization only once. Plus—you don't have to worry about your device context handle getting yanked out from under you. How to do this is simple: You simply specify CS_OWNDC as one of your class styles when you register the window. A common error is to use CS_OWNDC as a window style when you call Create. There are window styles and there are class styles, but you can't mix and match.

Code to register your window style generally looks something like this:

```
WNDCLASS wc; // Windows class structure
...

...
// Register window style
wc.style = CS_HREDRAW | CS_VREDRAW | CS_OWNDC;
wc.lpfnWndProc = (WNDPROC) WndProc;
...
...
wc.lpszClassName = lpszAppName;
// Register the window class
if(RegisterClass(&wc) == 0)
return FALSE;
```

You then specify the class name when you create the window:

```
hWnd = CreateWindow( wc.lpszClassName, szWindowName, ...
```

Graphics programmers should always use CS_OWNDC in the window class registration. This ensures that you have the most robust code possible on the Windows platform. Another consideration is that many OpenGL hardware drivers have bugs because they expect the CS_OWNDC to be specified. They might have been originally written for NT, so the drivers do not account for the possibility that the device context might become invalid. The driver might also trip up if the device context does not retain its configuration (as is the case in the GetDC/ReleaseDC scenario).

Regardless of the specifics, some drivers are not very stable unless you specify the CS_OWNDC flag. Many if not most vendors are addressing this well-known issue as their drivers mature. Still, the other reasons outlined here provide plenty of incentive to make what is basically a minor code adjustment.

Using the OpenGL Rendering Context

The real meat of our GLRECT sample program is in the window procedure, WndProc. The window procedure receives window messages from the operating system and responds appropriately. This model of programming, called *message-based* programming, is the foundation of the modern Windows GUI.

When a window is created, it first receives a WM_CREATE message from the operating system. This is the ideal location to create and set up our OpenGL rendering context. A window also receives a WM_DESTROY message when it is being destroyed. Naturally, this is the ideal place to put cleanup code. Listing 17.2 shows the function SetDCPixelFormat, which we use to select and set the pixel format, along with the window procedure for our application. This function contains the same basic functionality that we have been using with the GLUT framework.

___

Listing 17.2 *Setting the Pixel Format and Handling the Creation and Deletion of the OpenGL Rendering Context*

```
// Select the pixel format for a given device context
void SetDCPixelFormat(HDC hDC)
    {
    int nPixelFormat;

    static PIXELFORMATDESCRIPTOR pfd = {
        sizeof(PIXELFORMATDESCRIPTOR), // Size of this structure
        1,                             // Version of this structure
        PFD_DRAW_TO_WINDOW |           // Draw to window (not to bitmap)
        PFD_SUPPORT_OPENGL |           // Support OpenGL calls in window
        PFD_DOUBLEBUFFER,              // Double-buffered mode
        PFD_TYPE_RGBA,                 // RGBA color mode
        32,                            // Want 32-bit color
        0,0,0,0,0,0,                   // Not used to select mode
        0,0,                           // Not used to select mode
```

```
        0,0,0,0,0,                        // Not used to select mode
        16,                               // Size of depth buffer
        0,                                // Not used to select mode
        0,                                // Not used to select mode
        0,                                // Not used to select mode
        0,                                // Not used to select mode
        0,0,0 };                          // Not used to select mode

    // Choose a pixel format that best matches that described in pfd
    nPixelFormat = ChoosePixelFormat(hDC, &pfd);

    // Set the pixel format for the device context
    SetPixelFormat(hDC, nPixelFormat, &pfd);
    }

// Window procedure, handles all messages for this program
LRESULT CALLBACK WndProc(HWND      hWnd,
            UINT      message,
            WPARAM    wParam,
            LPARAM    lParam)
    {
    static HGLRC hRC = NULL;      // Permanent rendering context
    static HDC hDC = NULL;        // Private GDI device context

    switch (message)
        {
        // Window creation, set up for OpenGL
        case WM_CREATE:
            // Store the device context
            hDC = GetDC(hWnd);

            // Select the pixel format
            SetDCPixelFormat(hDC);

            // Create the rendering context and make it current
            hRC = wglCreateContext(hDC);
            wglMakeCurrent(hDC, hRC);

            // Create a timer that fires 30 times a second
            SetTimer(hWnd,33,1,NULL);
            break;

        // Window is being destroyed, clean up
        case WM_DESTROY:
            // Kill the timer that we created
            KillTimer(hWnd,101);
```

continued on next page

continued from previous page

```
        // Deselect the current rendering context and delete it
        wglMakeCurrent(hDC,NULL);
        wglDeleteContext(hRC);

        // Tell the application to terminate after the window
        // is gone.
        PostQuitMessage(0);
        break;

    // Window is resized.
    case WM_SIZE:
        // Call our function which modifies the clipping
        // volume and viewport
        ChangeSize(LOWORD(lParam), HIWORD(lParam));
        break;

    // Timer moves and bounces the rectangle, simply calls
    // our previous OnIdle function, then invalidates the
    // window so it will be redrawn.
    case WM_TIMER:
        {
        IdleFunction();

        InvalidateRect(hWnd,NULL,FALSE);
        }
        break;

    // The painting function. This message is sent by Windows
    // whenever the screen needs updating.
    case WM_PAINT:
        {
        // Call OpenGL drawing code
        RenderScene();

        // Call function to swap the buffers
        SwapBuffers(hDC);

        // Validate the newly painted client area
        ValidateRect(hWnd,NULL);
        }
        break;

.  . .
```

```
default:   // Passes it on if unprocessed
    return (DefWindowProc(hWnd, message, wParam, lParam));

}

return (0L);
}
```

Initializing the Rendering Context

The first thing we do when the window is being created is retrieve the device context (remember, we hang on to this) and set the pixel format:

```
// Store the device context
hDC = GetDC(hWnd);

// Select the pixel format
SetDCPixelFormat(hDC);
```

Then, we create the OpenGL rendering context and make it current:

```
// Create the rendering context and make it current
hRC = wglCreateContext(hDC);
wglMakeCurrent(hDC, hRC);
```

The last task we handle while processing the WM_CREATE message is creating a Windows timer for the window. We use this shortly to effect our animation loop:

```
// Create a timer that fires 30 times a second
SetTimer(hWnd,33,1,NULL);
break;
```

At this point, the OpenGL rendering context has been created and associated with a window with a valid pixel format. From this point forward, all OpenGL rendering commands will be routed to this context and window.

Shutting Down the Rendering Context

When the window procedure receives the WM_DESTROY message, the OpenGL rendering context must be deleted. Before you delete the rendering context with the wglDeleteContext function, you must first call wglMakeCurrent again, but this time with NULL as the parameter for the OpenGL rendering context:

```
// Deselect the current rendering context and delete it
wglMakeCurrent(hDC,NULL);
wglDeleteContext(hRC);
```

Before deleting the rendering context, you should delete any display lists, texture objects, or other OpenGL allocated memory.

Other Windows Messages

Creating and destroying the OpenGL rendering context is all that is required to enable OpenGL to render into a window. However, to make your application well behaved, you need to follow some conventions with respect to message handling. For example, you need to set the viewport when the window changes size, by handling the WM_SIZE message:

```
// Window is resized.
case WM_SIZE:
    // Call our function which modifies the clipping
    // volume and viewport
    ChangeSize(LOWORD(lParam), HIWORD(lParam));
    break;
```

The processing that happens in response to the WM_SIZE message is the same as in the function you handed off to the glutReshapeFunc in GLUT-based programs. The window procedure also receives two parameters, lParam and wParam. The low word of lParam is the new width of the window, and the high word is the height.

In this example, we use the WM_TIMER message handler to do our idle processing. The process is not really idle, but the previous call to SetTimer causes the WM_TIMER message to be received on a fairly regular basis (*fairly* because the exact interval is not guaranteed). This is not always the best way to handle animation, and we discuss some alternatives in Chapter 19, "Real-Time Programming with OpenGL."

Other Windows messages handle things such as keyboard activity (WM_CHAR, WM_KEY-DOWN), mouse movements (WM_MOUSEMOVE), and palette management. (We discuss these messages shortly.)

The WM_PAINT *Message*

The WM_PAINT message bears a closer examination. This message is sent to a window whenever Windows needs to draw or redraw its contents. To tell Windows to redraw a window anyway, you *invalidate* the window with one function call in the WM_TIMER message handler:

```
    IdleFunction();
InvalidateRect(hWnd,NULL,FALSE);
```

Here, IdleFunction updates the position of the square, and InvalidateRect tells Windows to redraw the window (now that the square has moved).

Most Windows programming books will show you a WM_PAINT message handler with the well-known BeginPaint/EndPaint function pairing. BeginPaint retrieves the device context so it can be used for GDI drawing, and EndPaint releases the context and validates the window. In our previous discussion of why you need the CS_OWNDC class style, we pointed out that using this function pairing is generally a bad idea for high-performance graphics applications. The following code shows roughly the equivalent functionality, without quite so much overhead:

```
// The painting function. This message is sent by Windows
// whenever the screen needs updating.
case WM_PAINT:
    {
    // Call OpenGL drawing code
    RenderScene();

    // Call function to swap the buffers
    SwapBuffers(hDC);

    // Validate the newly painted client area
    ValidateRect(hWnd,NULL);
    }
    break;
```

Because we have a device context (hDC), there is no need to continually get and release it. The SwapBuffers function has been mentioned previously but not fully explained. This function takes the device context as an argument and performs the buffer swap for double-buffered rendering. This is why we need the device context readily available when rendering.

Notice that we must manually validate the window with the call to ValidateRect after rendering. Without the BeginPaint/EndPaint functionality in place, there is no way to tell Windows that you have finished drawing the window contents. One alternative to using the WM_TIMER to invalidate the window (thus forcing a redraw) is to simply not validate the window. If the window procedure returns from a WM_PAINT message and the window is not validated, then another WM_PAINT message is generated by the operating system. This chain reaction causes an endless stream of repaint messages. One problem with this approach to animation is that it can leave little opportunity for other window messages to be processed. Although rendering might be occurring very quickly, it might be difficult or impossible for the user to do things such as resize the window or use the menu.

Windows Palettes

In Chapter 6, "Color, Lighting, and Materials," we discussed the various color modes available on the modern PC running Windows. Hardware-accelerated 3D graphics cards for the PC support 16-bit or higher color resolutions. If you drop down to 8-bit color (256 colors), you most likely are running Microsoft's generic software implementation. Although this graphics mode is becoming less common, it is still possible that your application could find itself running in such an environment. Not all 3D applications require hardware acceleration, and many users might not even care about hardware versus software rendering.

Color Matching

What happens when you try to draw a pixel of a particular color using the RGB values in glColor? If the PC graphics card is in 24-bit color mode, each pixel is displayed precisely in the color specified by the 24-bit value (three 8-bit intensities). In the 15- and 16-bit color modes, Windows passes the 24-bit color value to the display driver, which reduces the color to a 15- or 16-bit color value before displaying it. Internal color calculations due to lighting and texturing are usually (depending on the implementation) done at full precision. Reducing a color's precision from 24-bit to 16-bit will result in some loss of visual fidelity but can be acceptable for many applications.

On a Windows display with only 8 bits of color resolution (256 colors), Windows creates a palette of colors for the display device. A palette is a list of color values specified at full color. When an application needs to specify one of these colors, it does so by index rather than by specifying the exact color. In practice, the color entries in a palette can be arbitrary and are often chosen to match a particular application's needs.

When Windows is running in a color mode that supports 256 colors, it would make sense if those colors were evenly distributed across RGB color space. (See the color cube example in Chapter 6.) Then, all applications would have a relatively wide choice of colors, and when a color was selected, the nearest available color would be used. This is exactly the type of palette that OpenGL requires when running in a paletted color mode. Unfortunately, this arrangement is not always practical for other applications.

Because the 256 colors in the palette for the device can be selected from more than 16 million different colors, an application can substantially improve the quality of its graphics by carefully selecting those colors—and many do. For example, to produce a seascape, additional shades of blue might be needed. CAD and modeling applications can modify the palette to produce smooth shading of a surface of a particular single color. For example, the scene might require as many as 200 shades of gray to accurately render the image of a pipe's cross section. Thus, applications for the PC typically change the palette to meet their needs, resulting in near-photographic quality for many images and scenes. For 256-color bitmaps, the Windows .BMP format even has an array that's 256 entries long, containing 24-bit RGB values specifying the palette for the stored image.

An application can create a palette with the Windows CreatePalette function, identifying the palette by a handle of type HPALETTE. This function takes a logical palette structure (LOGPALETTE) that contains 256 entries, each specifying 8-bit values for red, green, and blue components. Before we examine palette creation, let's take a look at how multitasked applications can share the single system palette in 8-bit color mode.

Palette Arbitration

Windows multitasking allows many applications to be onscreen at once. If the hardware supports only 256 colors onscreen at once, then all applications must share the same system palette. If one application changes the system palette, images in the other windows might have scrambled colors, producing some undesired psychedelic effects. To arbitrate palette usage among applications, Windows sends a set of messages. Applications are notified when another application has changed the system palette, and they are notified when their window has received focus and palette modification is allowed.

When an application receives keyboard or mouse input focus, Windows sends a WM_QUERYNEWPALETTE message to the main window of the application. This message asks the application whether it wants to realize a new palette. *Realizing* a palette means the application copies the palette entries from its private palette to the system palette. To do this, the application must first select the palette into the device context for the window being updated and then call RealizePalette.

Another message sent by Windows for palette realization is WM_PALETTECHANGED. This message is sent to windows that can realize their palette but might not have the current focus. When this message is sent, you must also check the value of wParam. If wParam contains the handle to the current window receiving the message, then WM_QUERYNEWPALETTE has already been processed, and the palette does not need to be realized again. Listing 17.3 shows the message handler for these two messages.

Listing 17.3 *Message Handlers for Windows Palette Management*

```
// Windows is telling the application that it may modify
// the system palette. This message in essence asks the
// application for a new palette.
case WM_QUERYNEWPALETTE:
    // If the palette was created.
    if(hPalette)
        {
        int nRet;

        // Selects the palette into the current device context
        SelectPalette(hDC, hPalette, FALSE);

        // Map entries from the currently selected palette to
        // the system palette. The return value is the number
        // of palette entries modified.
        nRet = RealizePalette(hDC);

        // Repaint, forces remap of palette in current window
        InvalidateRect(hWnd,NULL,FALSE);

        return nRet;
        }
    break;
```

continued on next page

continued from previous page

```
// This window may set the palette, even though it is not the
// currently active window.
case WM_PALETTECHANGED:
    // Don't do anything if the palette does not exist or if
    // this is the window that changed the palette.
    if((hPalette != NULL) && ((HWND)wParam != hWnd))
        {
        // Select the palette into the device context
        SelectPalette(hDC,hPalette,FALSE);

        // Map entries to system palette
        RealizePalette(hDC);

        // Remap the current colors to the newly realized palette
        UpdateColors(hDC);
        return 0;
        }
    break;
```

A Windows palette is identified by a handle of type HPALETTE. The hPalette variable shown in Listing 17.3 is this type. Note that the value of hPalette is checked against NULL before either of these palette-realization messages is processed in order to check for a potential error. If the application is not running in 8-bit color mode, then these messages are not posted to your application.

Creating a Palette for OpenGL

Unfortunately, palette considerations are a necessary evil if your application is to run on the 8-bit hardware that's still widely in use. What do you do if your code is executing on a machine that only supports 256 colors?

For an application such as image reproduction, we recommend selecting a range of colors that closely match the original colors. The topic of selecting the best reduced palette for a given full color image has been the subject of much study over the years and is well beyond the scope of this book. For OpenGL rendering under most circumstances, you want the widest possible range of colors for general-purpose use. The trick is to select the palette colors so that they're evenly distributed throughout the color cube. Then, whenever a color is specified that is not already in the palette, Windows will select the nearest color in the color cube. As mentioned earlier, this arrangement is not ideal for some applications, but for OpenGL rendered scenes, it is the best we can do. Unless the scene has substantial texture mapping with a wide variety of colors, the results are usually acceptable.

The sample program GLPalette, shown in Figure 17.5, demonstrates the results. This program creates a spinning cube textured on each side with a familiar face. Run this program on your PC in both full color (16 bit or higher) and 256-color mode. The effect can't be accurately reproduced as a grayscale image in this book, but you will be able to see that even in 8-bit color mode, OpenGL is able to reproduce the image quite well, despite the limited range of colors available.

Figure 17.5   The Mona Lisa cube, quite recognizable even in 8-bit color mode.

Do You Need a Palette?

To determine whether your application needs a palette, you examine the PIXELFORMATDESCRIPTOR returned by a call to DescribePixelFormat. Test the dwFlags member of the PIXELFORMATDESCRIPTOR structure, and if the bit value PFD_NEED_PALETTE is set, you need to create a palette for your application:

```
DescribePixelFormat(hDC, nPixelFormat, sizeof(PIXELFORMATDESCRIPTOR),
&pfd);

// Does this pixel format require a palette?
if(!(pfd.dwFlags & PFD_NEED_PALETTE))
    return NULL;    // Does not need a palette
    // Palette creation code
    ...
    ...
```

The Palette's Structure

To create a palette, you must first allocate memory for a Windows LOG-PALETTE structure. This structure is filled with the information that describes the palette and then is passed to the WIN32 function CreatePalette. The LOGPALETTE structure is defined as follows:

```
typedef struct tagLOGPALETTE { // lgpl
    WORD         palVersion;
    WORD         palNumEntries;
    PALETTEENTRY palPalEntry[1];
} LOGPALETTE;
```

The first two members are the palette header and contain the palette version (always set to `0x300`) and the number of color entries (256 for 8-bit modes). Each entry is then defined as a `PALETTEENTRY` structure that contains the RGB components of the color entry. Additional entries are located at the end of the structure in memory.

The following code allocates space for the logical palette:

```
LOGPALETTE *pPal;          // Pointer to memory for logical palette
   ...
   ...
// Allocate space for a logical palette structure plus all the palette
// entries
pPal = (LOGPALETTE*)malloc(sizeof(LOGPALETTE) + nColors*sizeof(PALETTEENTRY));
```

Here, nColors specifies the number of colors to place in the palette, which for our purposes is always 256.

Each entry in the palette then is a `PALETTEENTRY` structure, which is defined as follows:

```
typedef struct tagPALETTEENTRY { // pe
    BYTE peRed;
    BYTE peGreen;
    BYTE peBlue;
    BYTE peFlags;
} PALETTEENTRY;
```

The *peRed*, *peGreen*, and *peBlue* members specify an 8-bit value that represents the relative intensities of each color component. In this way, each of the 256 palette entries contains a 24-color definition. The *peFlags* member describes advanced use of the palette entries. For OpenGL purposes, you can just set it to NULL.

The 3-3-2 Palette

Now comes the tricky part: Not only must our 256 palette entries be spread evenly throughout the RGB color cube, but also they must be in a certain order. It is this order that enables OpenGL to find the color it needs or the closest available color in the palette. In 8-bit color mode, you have 3 bits each for red and green color components and 2 bits for the blue component. This is commonly referred to as a 3-3-2 palette. So our RGB color cube measures 8×8×3 along the red, green, and blue axes, respectively.

To find the color needed in the palette, an 8-8-8 color reference (the 24-bit color mode setup) is scaled to a 3-3-2 color value. This 8-bit value is then the index into our palette array. The red intensities of 0 to 7 in the 3-3-2 palette must correspond to the intensities 0 to 255 in the 8-8-8 palette. Figure 17.6 illustrates how the red, green, and blue components are combined to make the palette index.

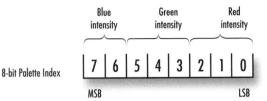

Figure 17.6 3-3-2 palette packing.

When we build the palette, we loop through all values from 0 to 255. We then decompose the index into the red, green, and blue intensities represented by these values (in terms of the 3-3-2 palette). Each component is multiplied by 255 and divided by the maximum value represented, which has the effect of smoothly stepping the intensities from 0 to 7 for red and green and from 0 to 3 for the blue. Table 17.2 shows some sample palette entries, to demonstrate component calculation.

Table 17.2 A Few Sample Palette Entries for a 3-3-2 Palette

Palette Entry	Binary (B G R)	Blue Component	Green Component	Red Component
0	00 000 000	0	0	0
1	00 000 001	0	0	1*255/7
2	00 000 010	0	0	2*255/7
3	00 000 011	0	0	3*255/7
9	00 001 001	0	1*255/7	1*255/7
10	00 001 010	0	1*255/7	2*255/7
137	10 001 001	2*255/3	1*255/7	1*255/7
138	10 001 010	2*255/7	1*255/7	2*255/3
255	11 111 111	3*255/3	7*255/7	7*255/7

Building the Palette

The 3-3-2 palette is actually specified by the `PIXELFORMATDESCRIPTOR` returned by `DescribePixelFormat`. The members `cRedBits`, `cGreenBits`, and `cBlueBits` specify 3, 3, and 2, respectively, for the number of bits that can represent each component. Furthermore, the `cRedShift`, `cGreenShift`, and `cBlueShift` values specify how much to shift the respective component value to the left (in this case, 0, 3, and 6 for red, green, and blue shifts). These sets of values compose the palette index (see Figure 17.6).

The code in Listing 17.4 creates a palette if needed and returns its handle. This function makes use of the component bit counts and shift information in the PIXELFORMATDESCRIPTOR to accommodate any subsequent palette requirements, such as a 2-2-2 palette.

Listing 17.4   *Function to Create a Palette for OpenGL*

```
// If necessary, creates a 3-3-2 palette for the device context listed.
HPALETTE GetOpenGLPalette(HDC hDC)
    {
    HPALETTE hRetPal = NULL;      // Handle to palette to be created
    PIXELFORMATDESCRIPTOR pfd;    // Pixel format descriptor
    LOGPALETTE *pPal;             // Pointer to memory for logical palette
    int nPixelFormat;             // Pixel format index
    int nColors;                  // Number of entries in palette
    int i;                        // Counting variable
    BYTE RedRange,GreenRange,BlueRange;
                                  // Range for each color entry (7,7,and 3)

    // Get the pixel format index and retrieve the pixel format description
    nPixelFormat = GetPixelFormat(hDC);
    DescribePixelFormat(hDC, nPixelFormat,
                                sizeof(PIXELFORMATDESCRIPTOR), &pfd);

    // Does this pixel format require a palette?  If not, do not create a
    // palette and just return NULL
    if(!(pfd.dwFlags & PFD_NEED_PALETTE))
        return NULL;

    // Number of entries in palette. 8 bits yields 256 entries
    nColors = 1 << pfd.cColorBits;

// Allocate space for a logical palette structure plus all the palette
// entries
    pPal = (LOGPALETTE*)malloc(sizeof(LOGPALETTE) +
                            nColors*sizeof(PALETTEENTRY));

    // Fill in palette header
    pPal->palVersion = 0x300;       // Windows 3.0
    pPal->palNumEntries = nColors;  // table size

    // Build mask of all 1s. This creates a number represented by having
    // the low order x bits set, where x = pfd.cRedBits, pfd.cGreenBits, and
    // pfd.cBlueBits.
    RedRange = (1 << pfd.cRedBits) -1;        // 7 for 3-3-2 palettes
```

```
GreenRange = (1 << pfd.cGreenBits) - 1;    // 7 for 3-3-2 palettes
BlueRange = (1 << pfd.cBlueBits) -1;       // 3 for 3-3-2 palettes

// Loop through all the palette entries
for(i = 0; i < nColors; i++)
    {
    // Fill in the 8-bit equivalents for each component
    pPal->palPalEntry[i].peRed = (i >> pfd.cRedShift) & RedRange;
    pPal->palPalEntry[i].peRed = (unsigned char)(
        (double) pPal->palPalEntry[i].peRed * 255.0 / RedRange);

    pPal->palPalEntry[i].peGreen = (i >> pfd.cGreenShift) & GreenRange;
    pPal->palPalEntry[i].peGreen = (unsigned char)(
        (double)pPal->palPalEntry[i].peGreen * 255.0 /GreenRange);

    pPal->palPalEntry[i].peBlue = (i >> pfd.cBlueShift) & BlueRange;
    pPal->palPalEntry[i].peBlue = (unsigned char)(
        (double)pPal->palPalEntry[i].peBlue * 255.0 / BlueRange);

    pPal->palPalEntry[i].peFlags = (unsigned char) NULL;
    }

// Create the palette
hRetPal = CreatePalette(pPal);

// Go ahead and select and realize the palette for this device context
SelectPalette(hDC,hRetPal,FALSE);
RealizePalette(hDC);

// Free the memory used for the logical palette structure
free(pPal);

// Return the handle to the new palette
return hRetPal;
}
```

Palette Creation and Disposal

The Windows palette should be created and realized before the OpenGL rendering context is created or made current. The function in Listing 17.4 requires only the device context once the pixel format has been set. It then returns a handle to a palette if one is needed. Listing 17.5 shows the sequence of operations when the window is created and destroyed. This is similar to code presented previously for the creation and destruction of the rendering context, but now it also takes into account the possible existence of a palette.

Listing 17.5   *A Palette is Created and Destroyed*

```
// Window creation, set up for OpenGL
case WM_CREATE:
    // Store the device context
    hDC = GetDC(hWnd);

    // Select the pixel format
    SetDCPixelFormat(hDC);

    // Create the palette if needed
    hPalette = GetOpenGLPalette(hDC);

    // Create the rendering context and make it current
    hRC = wglCreateContext(hDC);
    wglMakeCurrent(hDC, hRC);
    break;


// Window is being destroyed, clean up
case WM_DESTROY:
    // Deselect the current rendering context and delete it
    wglMakeCurrent(hDC,NULL);
    wglDeleteContext(hRC);

    // If a palette was created, destroy it here
    if(hPalette != NULL)
        DeleteObject(hPalette);

    // Tell the application to terminate after the window
    // is gone.
    PostQuitMessage(0);
    break;
```

Some Restrictions Apply

Not all of your 256 palette entries will actually be mapped to the system palette. Windows reserves 20 entries for static system colors that include the standard 16 VGA/EGA colors. This protects the standard Windows components (title bars, buttons, and so on) from alteration whenever an application changes the system palette. When your application realizes its palette, these 20 colors will not be overwritten. Fortunately, some of these colors already exist or are closely matched in the 3-3-2 palette. Those that don't are closely enough matched that you shouldn't be able to tell the difference for most purposes.

OpenGL and Windows Fonts

One of the nicer features of Windows is its support for TrueType fonts. These fonts have been native to Windows since before Windows became a 32-bit operating system. TrueType fonts enhance text appearance because they are device independent and can be easily scaled while still keeping a smooth shape. TrueType fonts are vector fonts, not bitmap fonts. What this means is that the character definitions consist of a series of point and curve definitions. When a character is scaled, the overall shape and appearance remain smooth. (This is similar to the Bezier and NURBS curve definitions in Chapter 13, "Curves and Surfaces: What the #%@!& Are NURBS?")

Textual output is a part of nearly any Windows application, and 3D applications are no exception. Microsoft provided support for TrueType fonts in OpenGL with two new wiggle functions. You can use the first, `wglUseFontOutlines`, to create 3D fonts models that can be used to create 3D text effects. The second, `wglUseFontBitmaps`, creates a series of font character bitmaps that can be used for 2D text output in a double-buffered OpenGL window.

3D Fonts and Text

The `wglUseFontOutlines` function takes a handle to a device context. It uses the TrueType font currently selected into that device context to create a set of display lists for that font. Each display list renders just one character from the font. Listing 17.6 shows the `SetupRC` function from the sample program Text3d, where you can see the entire process of creating a font, selecting it into the device context, creating the display lists, and finally, deleting the (Windows) font.

Listing 17.6 *Creating a Set of 3D Characters*

```
void SetupRC(HDC hDC)
    {
    // Set up the font characteristics
    HFONT hFont;
    GLYPHMETRICSFLOAT agmf[128]; // Throw away
    LOGFONT logfont;

    logfont.lfHeight = -10;
    logfont.lfWidth = 0;
    logfont.lfEscapement = 0;
    logfont.lfOrientation = 0;
    logfont.lfWeight = FW_BOLD;
    logfont.lfItalic = FALSE;
    logfont.lfUnderline = FALSE;
    logfont.lfStrikeOut = FALSE;
```

continued on next page

continued from previous page

```
logfont.lfCharSet = ANSI_CHARSET;
logfont.lfOutPrecision = OUT_DEFAULT_PRECIS;
logfont.lfClipPrecision = CLIP_DEFAULT_PRECIS;
logfont.lfQuality = DEFAULT_QUALITY;
logfont.lfPitchAndFamily = DEFAULT_PITCH;
strcpy(logfont.lfFaceName,"Arial");

// Create the font and display list
hFont = CreateFontIndirect(&logfont);
SelectObject (hDC, hFont);


// Create display lists for glyphs 0 through 128 with 0.1 extrusion
// and default deviation. The display list numbering starts at 1000
// (it could be any number).
nFontList = glGenLists(128);
wglUseFontOutlines(hDC, 0, 128, nFontList, 0.0f, 0.5f,
            WGL_FONT_POLYGONS, agmf);

DeleteObject(hFont);

 . . .
 . . .
}
```

The function call to wglUseFontOutlines is the key function call to create your 3D character set:

```
wglUseFontOutlines(hDC, 0, 128, nFontList, 0.0f, 0.5f,
            WGL_FONT_POLYGONS, agmf);
```

The first parameter is the handle to the device context where the desired font has been selected. The next two parameters specify the range of characters (called *glyphs*) in the font to use. In this case, we use the first through 127th character. (The indexes are zero based.) Our third parameter, nFontList, is the beginning of the range of display lists we created previously. It is important to allocate your display list space before using either of the wgl font functions. The next parameter is the *chordal deviation*. Think of it as specifying how smooth you want the font to appear, with 0.0 being the most smooth.

The 0.5f is the *extrusion* of the character set. The 3D characters are defined to lay in the xy plane. The extrusion determines how far along the z-axis the characters extend. WGL_FONT_POLYGONS tells OpenGL to create the characters out of triangles and quads so that they are solid. When this is specified, normals are also supplied for each letter. Only one other value is valid for this parameter, WGL_FONT_LINES. This produces a wireframe version of the character set and does not generate normals.

The last argument is an array of type GLYPHMETRICSFLOAT, which is defined as follows:

```
typedef struct _GLYPHMETRICSFLOAT {
    FLOAT       gmfBlackBoxX;      // Extent of character cell in x direction
    FLOAT       gmfBlackBoxY;      // Extend of character cell in y direction
    POINTFLOAT  gmfptGlyphOrigin;  // Origin of character cell
    FLOAT       gmfCellIncX;   // Horizontal distance to origin of next cell
    FLOAT       gmfCellIncY;   // Vertical distance to origin of next cell
}; GLYPHMETRICSFLOAT
```

This array is filled in by Windows according to the selected font's characteristics. These values can be useful when you want to determine the size of a string rendered with 3D characters.

Rendering 3D Text

When the display list for each character is called, it renders the character and advances the current position to the right by the width of the character cell. This is like calling glTranslate after each character, with the translation in the positive x direction. We can use the glCallLists function covered in Chapter 9, "3D Modeling and Object Composition," in conjunction with glListBase to treat a character array (a string) as an array of offsets from the first display list in the font. A simple text output method is shown in Listing 17.7. The output from the Text3d program appears in Figure 17.7.

Listing 17.7 *Rendering a 3D Text String*

```
void RenderScene(void)
    {
    glClear(GL_COLOR_BUFFER_BIT | GL_DEPTH_BUFFER_BIT);

    // Blue 3D text
    glColor3ub(0, 0, 255);

    glPushMatrix();
    glListBase(nFontList);
    glCallLists (6, GL_UNSIGNED_BYTE, "OpenGL");
    glPopMatrix();
    }
```

Figure 17.7   3D text in OpenGL.

2D Fonts and Text

The function `wglUseFontBitmaps` is similar to its 3D counterpart. This function does not extrude the bitmaps into 3D, however, but instead creates a set of bitmap images of the glyphs in the font. Output to the screen is done using the bitmap functions discussed in Chapter 7, "Raster Graphics in OpenGL." Although the invention of `wglUseFontBitmaps` was intended to make 2D text with TrueType fonts easier, it has become a thorn in the Windows-OpenGL implementations. The raster output functions discussed in Chapter 7 are difficult to optimize. Although using this method for 2D text output might seem intuitively to be the simplest route, it is the worst possible method in terms of rendering performance.

Using texture mapping for 2D text output is magnitudes faster, and for this reason, we are not even going to demonstrate the use of `wglUseFontbitmaps`. Consider it a legacy API, much as we do many old Windows functions left over from the days of 16-bit operating systems. Don't distress! We show you a very fast, high-quality method of generating 2D text using TrueType fonts in Chapter 19 when we discuss real-time rendering techniques.

Full-Screen Rendering

With OpenGL becoming popular among PC game developers, a common question is "How do I do full-screen rendering with OpenGL"? The truth is, if you've read this chapter you already know how to do full-screen rendering with OpenGL—it's just like rendering into any other window! The real question is: "How do I create a window that takes up the entire screen and has no borders?" Once you do this, rendering into this window is no different than rendering into any other window in any other sample in this book.

Even though this isn't strictly an OpenGL issue, it is of enough interest to a wide number of our readers, and therefore we give this topic some coverage here.

Creating a Frameless Window

Our first task is to create a window that has no border or caption. This is quite simple. Below, we show the window creation code from the GLRECT sample program. We've made one small change by making the window style WS_POPUP instead of WS_OVERLAPPEDWINDOW. The result of this change is shown in Figure 17.8.

```
// Create the main application window
hWnd = CreateWindow(lpszAppName,
                    lpszAppName,

                    // OpenGL requires WS_CLIPCHILDREN and WS_CLIPSIBLINGS
                    WS_POPUP | WS_CLIPCHILDREN | WS_CLIPSIBLINGS,

                    // Window position and size
                    100, 100,
                    250, 250,
                    NULL,
                    NULL,
                    hInstance,
                    NULL);
```

Figure 17.8   A window with no caption or border.

As you can see, without the proper style settings, the window has neither a caption nor a border of any kind. Don't forget to take into account that now the window no longer has a close button on it. The user will have to press Alt-F4 to close the window and exit the program. Most user-friendly programs will watch for a keystroke such as the ESC key or 'Q' to terminate the program.

Creating a Full-Screen Window

Creating a window the size of the screen is almost as trivial as creating a window with no caption or border. The parameters of the `CreateWindow` function allow you to specify where onscreen the upper left corner of the window will be positioned and the width and height of the window. To create a full screen window, the upper left corner will always be (0,0). The only trick would be determining what size the desktop is so you know how wide and high to make the window. This is easily determined using the Windows function `GetDeviceCaps`.

Listing 17.8 is the new `WinMain` function from GLRECT, which is now our new sample FSCREEN. In order to use `GetDeviceCaps`, we need a device context handle. Because we are in the process of creating the main window, we need to use the device context from the desktop window.

Listing 17.8   *Creating a Full-Screen Window*

```
// Entry point of all Windows programs
int APIENTRY WinMain( HINSTANCE      hInstance,
                      HINSTANCE      hPrevInstance,
                      LPSTR          lpCmdLine,
                      int            nCmdShow)
    {
    MSG           msg;          // Windows message structure
    WNDCLASS      wc;           // Windows class structure
    HWND          hWnd;         // Storeage for window handle
    HWND          hDesktopWnd;  // Storeage for desktop window handle
    HDC           hDesktopDC;   // Storeage for desktop window device context
    int           nScreenX, nScreenY; // Screen Dimensions

    // Register Window style
    wc.style                = CS_HREDRAW | CS_VREDRAW | CS_OWNDC;
    wc.lpfnWndProc          = (WNDPROC) WndProc;
    wc.cbClsExtra           = 0;
    wc.cbWndExtra           = 0;
    wc.hInstance            = hInstance;
    wc.hIcon                = NULL;
    wc.hCursor              = LoadCursor(NULL, IDC_ARROW);

    // No need for background brush for OpenGL window
    wc.hbrBackground    = NULL;
    wc.lpszMenuName     = NULL;
    wc.lpszClassName    = lpszAppName;

    // Register the window class
    if(RegisterClass(&wc) == 0)
        return FALSE;
```

```
// Get the Window handle and Device context to the desktop
hDesktopWnd = GetDesktopWindow();
hDesktopDC = GetDC(hDesktopWnd);

// Get the screen size
nScreenX = GetDeviceCaps(hDesktopDC, HORZRES);
nScreenY = GetDeviceCaps(hDesktopDC, VERTRES);

// Release the desktop device context
ReleaseDC(hDesktopWnd, hDesktopDC);

// Create the main application window
hWnd = CreateWindow(lpszAppName,
                    lpszAppName,

                    // OpenGL requires WS_CLIPCHILDREN and WS_CLIPSIBLINGS
                    WS_POPUP | WS_CLIPCHILDREN | WS_CLIPSIBLINGS,

                    // Window position and size
                    0, 0,
                    nScreenX, nScreenY,
                    NULL,
                    NULL,
                    hInstance,
                    NULL);


// If window was not created, quit
if(hWnd == NULL)
    return FALSE;

// Display the window
ShowWindow(hWnd,SW_SHOW);
UpdateWindow(hWnd);

// Process application messages until the application closes
while( GetMessage(&msg, NULL, 0, 0))
    {
    TranslateMessage(&msg);
    DispatchMessage(&msg);
    }

return msg.wParam;
}
```

The key code here is the lines that get the desktop window handle and device context. The device context can then be used to get the screens horizontal and vertical resolution.

```
hDesktopWnd = GetDesktopWindow();
hDesktopDC = GetDC(hDesktopWnd);

// Get the screen size
nScreenX = GetDeviceCaps(hDesktopDC, HORZRES);
nScreenY = GetDeviceCaps(hDesktopDC, VERTRES);

// Release the desktop device context
ReleaseDC(hDesktopWnd, hDesktopDC);
```

If your system has multiple monitors, you should note that the values returned here would be for the primary display device. You might also be tempted to force the window to be a topmost window (using the WS_EX_TOPMOST window style). However, this makes it possible for your window to lose focus, but remain on top of other active windows. This may confuse the user when the program stops responding to keyboard strokes.

You may also want to take a look at the WIN32 function ChangeDisplaySettings in your Windows SDK documentation. This function allows you to dynamically change the desktop size at runtime and restore it when your application terminates. This may be desirable if you want to have a full screen window, but at a lower or higher display resolution than the default.

Multithreaded Rendering

A powerful feature of the WIN32 API is *multithreading*. The topic of threading is beyond the scope of a book on computer graphics. If you are unfamiliar with using threads on the Windows platform, we suggest some of the Windows programming books listed in Appendix B. Basically, a thread is the unit of execution for an application. Most programs execute instructions sequentially from the start of the program until the program terminates. A thread of execution is the path through the machine code that the CPU traverses as it fetches and executes instructions. By creating multiple threads using the WIN32 API, you can create multiple paths through your source code that are followed simultaneously.

Think of multithreading as being able to call two functions at the same time, which then are executed simultaneously. Of course, the CPU cannot actually execute two code paths simultaneously but switches between threads during normal program flow much the same way a multitasking operating system switches between tasks.

A program carefully designed for multithreaded execution can outperform a single-threaded application in many circumstances. On a single processor machine, one thread can service I/O requests, for example, while another handles the GUI. On a multiprocessor machine employing SMP (Symmetric Multi-Processing), your program can actually be executed by more than one CPU simultaneously. Note however that SMP processing is not supported by older versions of Windows (95/98).

Multithreading requires careful planning and usually causes applications to run more slowly or inefficiently when used improperly on a single CPU system. In addition, if a program is not thoroughly tested, it might never fail on a single CPU machine but have new bugs manifest on a machine with multiple processors.

Some OpenGL implementations take advantage of a multiprocessor system. If, for example, the transformation and lighting units of the OpenGL pipeline are not hardware accelerated, a driver can create another thread so that these calculations are performed by one CPU while another CPU feeds the transformed data to the rasterizer.

You might think that using two threads to do your OpenGL rendering would speed up your rendering as well. You could perhaps have one thread draw the background objects in a scene while another thread draws the more dynamic elements. This is almost always a bad idea. Although you can create two OpenGL rendering contexts for two different threads, most drivers fail if you try to render with both of them in the same window. Technically, this multithreading should be possible, and the Microsoft generic implementation will succeed if you try it. In the real world, you are creating a nightmare for your support staff. The extra work you place on the driver with two contexts trying to share the same frame buffer will most likely outweigh any performance benefit you hope to gain from using multiple threads.

There are at least two ways that multithreading can benefit your OpenGL rendering on a multiprocessor system or even on a single processor system. In the first scenario, you have two different windows, each with its own rendering context and thread of execution. This case could still stress some drivers (some of the low-end game boards are stressed just by two applications using OpenGL simultaneously!), but many professional OpenGL implementations can handle it quite well.

The second example is if you are writing a game or a real-time simulation. You can have a worker thread perform physics calculations or artificial intelligence or handle player interaction while another thread does the OpenGL rendering. This requires careful sharing of data between threads but can provide a substantial performance boost on a dual processor machine, and even a single processor machine can improve the responsiveness of your program. Although we've made the disclaimer that multithreaded programming is outside the scope of this book, we present for your use a sample implementation in Chapter 19. Creating a separate rendering thread is the technique we demonstrate for sustained real-time rendering.

Summary

This chapter introduced you to using OpenGL on the WIN32 platform (Windows). We talked about the different driver models and implementations available for Windows and what to watch. You've seen how to enumerate and select a pixel format to get the kind of hardware-accelerated or software rendering support you want. We've seen the basic framework for a WIN32 program that replaces the GLUT framework so you can write true native WIN32 application code.

We've also shown you how to create a 3-3-2 palette to enable OpenGL rendering with only 256 available colors for output, and we've shown you how to create a full-screen window for games or simulation type applications. Finally, we discussed some of the Windows-specific features of OpenGL on Windows, such as support for TrueType fonts and multiple rendering threads.

Reference Section

ChoosePixelFormat

Purpose	Selects the pixel format that is closest to that specified by the PIXELFORMATDESCRIPTOR and that can be supported by the given device context.
Include File	<wingdi.h>
Syntax	`int ChoosePixelFormat(HDC hDC, CONST PIXELFORMATDESCRIPTOR *ppfd);`
Description	This function is used to determine the best available pixel format for a given device context based on the desired characteristics described in the PIXELFORMATDESCRIPTOR structure. This returned format index is then used in the SetPixelFormat function.
Parameters	
hDC	HDC: The device context for which this function seeks a best-match pixel format.
ppfd	PIXELFORMATDESCRIPTOR*: Pointer to a structure that describes the ideal pixel format that is being sought. The entire contents of this structure are not pertinent to this function's use. For a complete description of the PIXELFORMATDESCRIPTOR structure, see the DescribePixelFormat function. Here are the relevant members for this function:

nSize	WORD: The size of the structure, usually set to `sizeof(PIXELFORMATDESCRIPTOR)`.
nVersion	WORD: The version number of this structure, set to 1.
dwFlag	DWORD: A set of flags that specify properties of the pixel buffer.
iPixelType	BYTE: The color mode (RGBA or color index) type.
cColorBits	BYTE: The depth of the color buffer.

cAlphaBits	BYTE: The depth of the alpha buffer.
cAccumBits	BYTE: The depth of the accumulation buffer.
cDepthBits	BYTE: The depth of the depth buffer.
cStencilBits	BYTE: The depth of the stencil buffer.
cAuxBuffers	BYTE: The number of auxiliary buffers (not supported by Microsoft).
iLayerType	BYTE: The layer type (not supported by Microsoft).

Returns   The index of the nearest matching pixel format for the logical format specified or zero if no suitable pixel format can be found.

Example   This code from the GLRECT example in this chapter demonstrates a pixel format being selected:

```
int nPixelFormat;

static PIXELFORMATDESCRIPTOR pfd = {
    sizeof(PIXELFORMATDESCRIPTOR),     // Size of this structure
    1,                                 // Version of this structure
    PFD_DRAW_TO_WINDOW |               // Draw to window (not to bitmap)
    PFD_SUPPORT_OPENGL |               // Support OpenGL calls in window
    PFD_DOUBLEBUFFER,                  // Double-buffered mode
    PFD_TYPE_RGBA,                     // RGBA color mode
    32,                                // Want 32-bit color
    0,0,0,0,0,0,                       // Not used to select mode
    0,0,                               // Not used to select mode
    0,0,0,0,0,                         // Not used to select mode
    16,                                // Size of depth buffer
    0,                                 // Not used to select mode
    0,                                 // Not used to select mode
    0,                                 // Not used to select mode
    0,                                 // Not used to select mode
    0,0,0 };                           // Not used to select mode

// Choose a pixel format that best matches that described in pfd
nPixelFormat = ChoosePixelFormat(hDC, &pfd);

// Set the pixel format for the device context
SetPixelFormat(hDC, nPixelFormat, &pfd);
```

See Also   DescribePixelFormat, SetPixelFormat

DescribePixelFormat

Purpose	Obtains detailed information about a pixel format.
Include File	<wingdi.h>
Syntax	int DescribePixelFormat(HDC *hDC*, int *iPixelFormat*, UINT *nBytes*, LPPIXELFORMATDESCRIPTOR *ppfd*);
Description	This function fills the PIXELFORMATDESCRIPTOR structure with information about the pixel format specified for the given device context. It also returns the maximum available pixel format for the device context. If ppfd is NULL, the function still returns the maximum valid pixel format for the device context. Some fields of the PIXELFORMATDESCRIPTOR are not supported by the Microsoft generic implementation of OpenGL, but these values might be supported by individual hardware manufacturers.

Parameters

hDC	HDC: The device context containing the pixel format of interest.
iPixelFormat	int: The pixel format of interest for the specified device context.
nBytes	UINT: The size of the structure pointed to by ppfd. If this value is zero, no data will be copied to the buffer. This should be set to sizeof(PIXELFORMATDESCRIPTOR).
ppfd	LPPIXELFORMATDESCRIPTOR: A pointer to the PIXELFORMATDESCRIPTOR that on return will contain the detailed information about the pixel format of interest. The PIXELFORMATDESCRIPTOR structure is defined as follows:

```
typedef struct tagPIXELFORMATDESCRIPTOR {
    WORD nSize;
    WORD nVersion;
    DWORD dwFlags;
    BYTE iPixelType;
    BYTE cColorBits;
    BYTE cRedBits;
    BYTE cRedShift;
    BYTE cGreenBits;
    BYTE cGreenShift;
    BYTE cBlueBits;
    BYTE cBlueShift;
    BYTE cAlphaBits;
    BYTE cAlphaShift;
    BYTE cAccumBits;
    BYTE cAccumRedBits;
    BYTE cAccumGreenBits;
    BYTE cAccumBlueBits;
    BYTE cAccumAlphaBits;
```

```
    BYTE cDepthBits;
    BYTE cStencilBits;
    BYTE cAuxBuffers;
    BYTE iLayerType;
    BYTE bReserved;
    DWORD dwLayerMask;
    DWORD dwVisibleMask;
    DWORD dwDamageMask;
}   PIXELFORMATDESCRIPTOR;
```

nSize contains the size of the structure. It should always be set to sizeof(PIXELFORMATDESCRIPTOR).

nVersion holds the version number of this structure. It should always be set to 1.

dwFlags contains a set of bit flags (see Table 17.1) that describe properties of the pixel format. Except as noted, these flags are not mutually exclusive.

iPixelType specifies the type of pixel data. More specifically, it specifies the color selection mode. Valid values are GL_TYPE_RGBA for RGBA color mode or GL_TYPE_COLORINDEX for color index mode.

cColorBits specifies the number of color bit planes used by the color buffer, excluding the alpha bit planes in RGBA color mode. In color index mode, it specifies the size of the color buffer.

cRedBits specifies the number of red bit planes in each RGBA color buffer.

cRedShift specifies the shift count for red bit planes in each RGBA color buffer.

cGreenBits specifies the number of green bit planes in each RGBA color buffer.

cGreenShift specifies the shift count for green bit planes in each RGBA color buffer.

cBlueBits specifies the number of blue bit planes in each RGBA color buffer.

cBlueShift specifies the shift count for blue bit planes in each RGBA color buffer.

cAlphaBits specifies the number of alpha bit planes in each RGBA color buffer. This is not supported by the Microsoft implementation.

cAlphaShift specifies the shift count for alpha bit planes in each RGBA color buffer. This is not supported by the Microsoft implementation.

cAccumBits is the total number of bit planes in the accumulation buffer. See Chapter 15, "Imaging with OpenGL."

cAccumRedBits is the total number of red bit planes in the accumulation buffer.

cAccumGreenBits is the total number of green bit planes in the accumulation buffer.

cAccumBlueBits is the total number of blue bit planes in the accumulation buffer.

cAccumAlphaBits is the total number of alpha bit planes in the accumulation buffer.

cDepthBits specifies the depth of the depth buffer.

cStencilBits specifies the depth of the stencil buffer.

cAuxBuffers specifies the number of auxiliary buffers. This is not supported by the Microsoft implementation.

iLayerType is obsolete. Do not use.

bReserved contains the number of overlay and underlay planes supported by the implementation. Bits 0 through 3 specify the number of overlay planes (up to 15), and bits 4 through 7 specify the number of underlay planes (also up to 15).

dwLayerMask is obsolete. Do not use.

dwVisibleMask is used in conjunction with the dwLayerMask to determine if one layer overlays another. Layers are not supported by the current Microsoft implementation.

dwDamageMask is obsolete. Do not use.

Returns

The maximum pixel format supported by the specified device context or zero on failure.

Example

This example is from the GLRECT sample program on the CD. It queries the pixel format to see if the device context needs a color palette defined:

```
PIXELFORMATDESCRIPTOR pfd;    // Pixel format descriptor
    int nPixelFormat;         // Pixel format index

    . . .
    . . .


    // Get the pixel format index and retrieve the
    // pixel format description
    nPixelFormat = GetPixelFormat(hDC);
    DescribePixelFormat(hDC, nPixelFormat,
            sizeof(PIXELFORMATDESCRIPTOR), &pfd);
```

```
// Does this pixel format require a palette? If not, do not create a
// palette and just return NULL
if(!(pfd.dwFlags & PFD_NEED_PALETTE))
    return NULL;

// Go on to create the palette
...
...
```

See Also   `ChoosePixelFormat, GetPixelFormat, SetPixelFormat`

GetPixelFormat

Purpose	Retrieves the index of the pixel format currently selected for the given device context.
Include File	<wingdi.h>
Syntax	`int GetPixelFormat(HDC hDC);`
Description	This function retrieves the selected pixel format for the device context specified. The pixel format index is a 1-based positive value.
Parameters	
hDC	HDC: The device context of interest.
Returns	The index of the currently selected pixel format for the given device or zero on failure.
Example	See the example given for `DescribePixelFormat`.
See Also	`DescribePixelFormat, ChoosePixelFormat, SetPixelFormat`

SetPixelFormat

Purpose	Sets a device context's pixel format.
Include File	<wingdi.h>
Syntax	`BOOL SetPixelFormat(HDC hDC, int nPixelFormat, CONST PIXELFORMATDESCRIPTOR * ppfd);`
Description	This function actually sets the pixel format for a device context. Once the pixel format has been selected for a given device, it cannot be changed. This function must be called before creating an OpenGL rendering context for the device.
Parameters	
hDC	HDC: The device context whose pixel format is to be set.
nPixelFormat	int: Index of the pixel format to be set.

ppfd	LPPIXELFORMATDESCRIPTOR: A pointer to a PIXELFORMATDE- SCRIPTOR that contains the logical pixel format descriptor. This structure is used internally to record the logical pixel format specification. Its value does not influence the operation of this function.
Returns	TRUE if the specified pixel format was set for the given device context. FALSE if an error occurs.
Example	See the example given for ChoosePixelFormat.
See Also	DescribePixelFormat, GetPixelFormat, ChoosePixelFormat

SwapBuffers

Purpose	Quickly copies the contents of the back buffer of a window to the front buffer (foreground).
Include File	<wingdi.h>
Syntax	BOOL SwapBuffers(HDC *hDC*);
Description	When a double-buffered pixel format is chosen, a window has a front (displayed) and back (hidden) image buffer. Drawing commands are sent to the back buffer. This function is used to copy the contents of the hidden back buffer to the displayed front buffer, to support smooth drawing or animation. Note that the buffers are not really swapped. After this command is executed, the contents of the back buffer are undefined.
Parameters	
hDC	HDC: Specifies the device context of the window containing the offscreen and onscreen buffers.
Returns	TRUE if the buffers were swapped.
Example	The following sample shows the typical code for a WM_PAINT mes- sage. This is where the rendering code is called, and if in double-buffered mode, the back buffer is brought forward. You can see this code in the GLRECT sample program from this chapter:

```
// The painting function. This message is sent by Windows
// whenever the screen needs updating.
case WM_PAINT:
    {
    // Call OpenGL drawing code
    RenderScene();

    // Call function to swap the buffers
    SwapBuffers(hDC);
```

```
// Validate the newly painted client area
ValidateRect(hWnd,NULL);
}
break;
```

See Also   `glDrawBuffer`

wglCreateContext

Purpose	Creates a rendering context suitable for drawing on the specified device context.
Include File	<wingdi.h>
Syntax	`HGLRC wglCreateContext(HDC hDC);`
Description	Creates an OpenGL rendering context suitable for the given Windows device context. The pixel format for the device context should be set before the creation of the rendering context. When an application is finished with the rendering context, it should call `wglDeleteContext`.
Parameters	
hDC	`HDC`: The device context that will be drawn on by the new rendering context.
Returns	The handle to the new rendering context or `NULL` if an error occurs.
Example	The following code shows the beginning of a `WM_CREATE` message handler. Here, the device context is retrieved for the current window, a pixel format is selected, and then the rendering context is created and made current:

```
case WM_CREATE:
    // Store the device context
    hDC = GetDC(hWnd);

    // Select the pixel format
    SetDCPixelFormat(hDC);

    // Create the rendering context and make it current
    hRC = wglCreateContext(hDC);
    wglMakeCurrent(hDC, hRC);
    ...
    ...
```

See Also   `wglCreateLayerContext`, `wglDeleteContext`, `wglGetCurrentContext`, `wglMakeCurrent`

wglCreateLayerContext

Purpose	Creates a new OpenGL rendering context suitable for drawing on the specified layer plane.
Include File	<wingdi.h>
Syntax	`HGLRC wglCreateLayerContext(HDC hDC, int iLayerPlane);`
Description	Creates an OpenGL rendering context suitable for the given layer plane. When overlay and underlay planes are supported (only by some hardware implementations), you need a separate OpenGL rendering context for each one. The layer plane with index 0 is the main plane (what you normally render to). Positive indexes are overlay planes, and negative values are underlay planes.
Parameters	
hDC	`HDC`: The device context that will be drawn on by the new overlay or underlay rendering context.
iLayerPlane	`int`: The index of the layer plane for which to create the context.
Returns	The handle to the new rendering context or `NULL` if an error occurs.
Example	The following code creates a new rendering context for an overlay plane:

```
HGLRC hOverlay;
    . . .
    . . .
hOverlay = wglCreateLayerContext(hDC, 1);
    . . .
```

See Also	`wglCreateContext`, `wglDeleteContext`, `wglGetCurrentContext`, `wglMakeCurrent`

wglCopyContext

Purpose	Copies selected groups of rendering states from one OpenGL context to another.
Include File	<wingdi.h>
Syntax	`BOOL wglCopyContext(HGLRC hSource, HGLRC hDest, UINT mask);`
Description	This function can be used to synchronize the rendering state of two OpenGL rendering contexts. Any valid state flags that can be specified with `glPushAttrib` can be copied with this function. You can use `GL_ALL_ATTRIB_BITS` to copy all attributes.

Parameters

hSource	HGLRC: The source rendering context from which to copy state information.
hDest	HGLRC: The destination rendering context to which to copy state information.
mask	UINT: The handle of the rendering context to be deleted.
Returns	TRUE if the rendering context state information is copied.
Example	This example shows lighting state flags being copied from one rendering context to another:

```
wglCopyContext(hWindowContext, hPrinterContext, GL_LIGHTING_BIT);
```

See Also	glPushAttrib, wglCreateContext, wglGetCurrentContext, wglMakeCurrent

wglDeleteContext

Purpose	Deletes a rendering context after it is no longer needed by the application.
Include File	<wingdi.h>
Syntax	BOOL wglDeleteContext(HGLRC *hglrc*);
Description	Deletes an OpenGL rendering context. This frees any memory and resources held by the context.
Parameters	
hglrc	HGLRC: The handle of the rendering context to be deleted.
Returns	TRUE if the rendering context is deleted; FALSE if an error occurs. It is an error for one thread to delete a rendering context that is the current context of another thread.
Example	This example shows the message handler for the destruction of a window. Assuming the rendering context was created when the window was created, this is where you would delete the rendering context. Before you can delete the context, it must be made noncurrent:

```
// Window is being destroyed, clean up
case WM_DESTROY:

    // Deselect the current rendering context and delete it
    wglMakeCurrent(hDC,NULL);
    wglDeleteContext(hRC);
```

```
// Tell the application to terminate after the window
// is gone.
PostQuitMessage(0);
break;
```

See Also	wglCreateContext, wglGetCurrentContext, wglMakeCurrent

wglDescribeLayerPlane

Purpose	Retrieves information about overlay and underlay planes of a given pixel format.
Include File	<wingdi.h>
Syntax	BOOL wglDescribeLayerPlane(HDC *hdc*, int *iPixelFormat*, int *iLayerPlane*, UINT *nBytes*, LPLAYERPLANEDESCRIPTOR *PLPD*);
Description	This function serves a purpose similar to DescribePixelFormat but retrieves information about overlay and underlay planes. Layered planes are numbered with negative and positive integers. Plane 0 is the main plane, and negative plane numbers are underlays. Positive numbers greater than 0 are overlay planes.

Parameters

hdc	HDC: The handle of device context whose layer planes are to be described.
iPixelFormat	int: The pixel format of the desired layer plane.
iLayerPlane	int: The overlay or underlay plane identifier. Negative values are underlays, positive values are overlays, and 0 is the main plane.
nBytes	UINT: The size in bytes of the LAYERPLANEDESCRIPTOR.
plpd	LPLAYERPLANEDESCRIPTOR: Pointer to a LAYERPLANEDESCRIPTOR structure.
Returns	Returns TRUE if successful and fills in the data members of the LAYERPLANEDESCRIPTOR structure. This structure is defined as follows:

```
typedef struct tagLAYERPLANEDESCRIPTOR {
    WORD nSize;
    WORD nVersion;
    DWORD dwFlags;
    BYTE iPixelType;
    BYTE cColorBits;
    BYTE cRedBits;
    BYTE cRedShift;
    BYTE cGreenBits;
    BYTE cGreenShift;
```

```
        BYTE cBlueBits;
        BYTE cBlueShift;
        BYTE cAlphaBits;
        BYTE cAlphaShift;
        BYTE cAccumBits;
        BYTE cAccumRedBits;
        BYTE cAccumGreenBits;
        BYTE cAccumBlueBits;
        BYTE cAccumAlphaBits;
        BYTE cDepthBits;
        BYTE cStencilBits;
        BYTE cAuxBuffers;
        BYTE iLayerType;
        BYTE bReserved;
        COLOREF crTransparent;
}       LAYERPLANEDESCRIPTOR;
```

nSize contains the size of the structure. It should always be set to `sizeof(LAYERPLANEDESCRIPTOR)`.

nVersion holds the version number of this structure. It should always be set to 1.

dwFlags contains a set of bit flags that describe properties of the pixel format. Except as noted, these flags are not mutually exclusive.

LPD_SUPPORT_OPENGL supports OpenGL rendering.

LPD_SUPPORT_GDI supports GDI drawing.

LPD_DOUBLEBUFFER indicates the layer plane is double-buffered.

LPD_STEREO indicates the layer plane is stereoscopic.

LPD_SWAP_EXCHANGE means that in double-buffering, the front and back buffers contents are swapped.

LPD_SWAP_COPY means that in double-buffering, the back buffer is copied to the front buffer. The back buffer is unaffected.

LPD_TRANSPARENT indicates the crTransparent member of this structure contains a color value that should be considered the transparent color.

LPD_SHARE_DEPTH indicates the layer plane shares the depth buffer with the main plane.

LPD_SHARE_STENCIL indicates the layer plane shares the stencil buffer with the main plane.

LPD_SHARE_ACCUM indicates the layer plane shares the accumulation buffer with the main plane.

iPixelType specifies the type of pixel data. More specifically, it specifies the color selection mode. Valid values are `LPD_TYPE_RGBA` for RGBA color mode or `LPD_TYPE_COLORINDEX` for color index mode.

`cColorBits` specifies the number of color bit planes used by the color buffer, excluding the alpha bit planes in RGBA color mode. In color index mode, it specifies the size of the color buffer.

`cRedBits` specifies the number of red bit planes in each RGBA color buffer.

`cRedShift` specifies the shift count for red bit planes in each RGBA color buffer.

`cGreenBits` specifies the number of green bit planes in each RGBA color buffer.

`cGreenShift` specifies the shift count for green bit planes in each RGBA color buffer.

`cBlueBits` specifies the number of blue bit planes in each RGBA color buffer.

`cBlueShift` specifies the shift count for blue bit planes in each RGBA color buffer.

`cAlphaBits` specifies the number of alpha bit planes in each RGBA color buffer. This is not supported by the Microsoft implementation.

`cAlphaShift` specifies the shift count for alpha bit planes in each RGBA color buffer. This is not supported by the Microsoft implementation.

`cAccumBits` is the total number of bit planes in the accumulation buffer. See Chapter 15.

`cAccumRedBits` is the total number of red bit planes in the accumulation buffer.

`cAccumGreenBits` is the total number of green bit planes in the accumulation buffer.

`cAccumBlueBits` is the total number of blue bit planes in the accumulation buffer.

`cAccumAlphaBits` is the total number of alpha bit planes in the accumulation buffer.

`cDepthBits` specifies the depth of the depth buffer.

`cStencilBits` specifies the depth of the stencil buffer.

`cAuxBuffers` specifies the number of auxiliary buffers. This is not supported by the Microsoft implementation.

`iLayerType` is the layer plane number. Positive values are overlays, and negative numbers are underlays.

bReserved is not used. Must be zero.

crTransparent indicates that when the LPD_TRANSPARENT flag is set, this is the transparent color value. Typically, this is set to black. The color is specified as a Windows COLORREF value. You can use the Windows RGB macro to construct this value.

Example

The following code shows a typical query operation to determine the characteristics of the first overlay plane:

```
LAYERPLANEDESCRIPTOR desc;
. . .
wglDescribeLayerPlane(hDC, nPixelFormat, 1,
        sizeof(LAYERPLANEDESCRIPTOR), &desc);
```

See Also

DescribePixelFormat, wglCreateLayerContext

wglGetCurrentContext

Purpose

Retrieves a handle to the current thread's OpenGL rendering context.

Include File

<wingdi.h>

Syntax

HGLRC wglGetCurrentContext(void);

Description

Each thread of an application can have its own current OpenGL rendering context. You can use this function to determine which rendering context is currently active for the calling thread.

Example

The following code demonstrates testing to see if an OpenGL rendering context is current:

```
HGLRC hRC;
. . .
hRC = wglGetCurrentContext();
if(hRC)
    {
    // Do some rendering...
    }
else
    {
    // Display error message
    }
```

Returns

If the calling thread has a current rendering context, this function returns its handle. If not, the function returns NULL.

See Also

wglCreateContext, wglDeleteContext, wglMakeCurrent, wglGetCurrentDC

wglGetCurrentDC

Purpose	Gets the Windows device context associated with the current OpenGL rendering context.
Include File	<wingdi.h>
Syntax	`HDC wglGetCurrentDC(void);`
Description	This function is used to acquire the Windows device context of the window that is associated with the current OpenGL rendering context. Typically used to obtain a Windows device context to combine OpenGL and GDI drawing functions in a single window.
Returns	If the current thread has a current OpenGL rendering context, this function returns the handle to the Windows device context associated with it. Otherwise, the return value is `NULL`.
Example	The code fragment below shows one possible use of this function. At any time, you can get a handle to the device context that the current rendering context is bound to. Using this device context, you can create and select a font, which can then be used to create a set of font bitmap display lists for the current OpenGL context.

```
HDC hDC;
hDC = wglGetCurrentDC();
// Create and select a font
. . .
wglUseFontBitmaps(hDC, . . .
```

See Also	wglGetCurrentContext

wglMakeCurrent

Purpose	Makes a given OpenGL rendering context current for the calling thread and associates it with the specified device context.
Include File	<wingdi.h>
Syntax	`BOOL wglMakeCurrent(HDC hdc, HGLRC hglrc);`
Description	This function makes the specified rendering context the current rendering context for the calling thread. This rendering context is associated with the given Windows device context. The device context need not be the same as that used in the call to `wglCreateContext`, as long as the pixel format is the same for both and they both exist on the same physical device (not one on the screen and one on a printer). Any outstanding OpenGL commands for the previous rendering context are flushed before the new rendering context is made current. You can also use this function to make no rendering context active, by calling it with `NULL` for the `hglrc` parameter.

Parameters

hdc	HDC: The device context that will be used for all OpenGL drawing operations performed by the calling thread.
hglrc	HGLRC: The rendering context to make current for the calling thread.
Returns	TRUE on success or FALSE if an error occurs. If an error occurs, no rendering context will remain current for the calling thread.
Example	See the example for wglCreateContext.
See Also	wglCreateContext, wglDeleteContext, wglGetCurrentContext, wglGetCurrentDC

wglShareLists

Purpose	Allows multiple rendering contexts to share display lists.
Include File	<wingdi.h>
Syntax	BOOL wglShareLists(HGLRC *hRC1*, HGLRC *hRC2*);
Description	A display list is a list of "precompiled" OpenGL commands and functions (see Chapter 9). Memory is allocated for the storage of display lists within each rendering context. As display lists are created within that rendering context, it has access to its own display list memory. This function allows multiple rendering contexts to share this memory. This is particularly useful when large display lists are used by multiple rendering contexts or threads to save memory. Any number of rendering contexts can share the same memory for display lists. This memory is not freed until the last rendering context using that space is deleted. When using a shared display list space between threads, you should synchronize display list creation and usage.

Parameters

hRC1	HGLRC: Specifies the rendering context with which to share display list memory.
hRC2	HGLRC: Specifies the rendering context that will share the display list memory with hRC1. No display lists for hRC2 should be created until after its display list memory is shared.
Returns	TRUE if the display list space is shared; FALSE if they are not.
Example	The code below shows two different rendering contexts being set up to share display lists.

```
HGLRD hRC1, hRC2;
. . .
// Create rendering contexts
. . .
// Share All future display lists
wglShareLists(hRC1, hRC2);
```

See Also   glIsList, glNewList, glCallList, glCallLists, glListBase,
                                        glDeleteLists, glEndList, glGenLists

wglSwapLayerBuffers

Purpose	Swaps the front and back buffers in the overlay, underlay, and main planes belonging to the specified device context.
Include File	<wingdi.h>
Syntax	BOOL wglSwapLayerBuffers(HDC *hDC*, UINT *fuPlanes*);
Description	When a double-buffered pixel format is chosen, a window has a front (displayed) and back (hidden) image buffer. Drawing commands are sent to the back buffer. This function is used to copy the contents of the hidden back buffer to the displayed front buffer, to support smooth drawing or animation. Note that the buffers are not really swapped. After this command is executed, the contents of the back buffer are undefined.

Parameters

hDC	HDC: Specifies the device context of the window containing the offscreen and onscreen buffers.
fuPlanes	UINT: Specifies the device context of the window containing the offscreen and onscreen buffers.
Returns	True if the buffers were swapped.
Example	The following sample shows the typical code for a WM_PAINT message. This is where the rendering code is called, and if in double-buffered mode, the back buffer is brought forward. You can see this code in the GLRECT sample program from this chapter:

```
// The painting function. This message is sent by Windows
// whenever the screen needs updating.
case WM_PAINT:
    {
    // Call OpenGL drawing code
    RenderScene();

    // Call function to swap the buffers
    SwapBuffers(hDC);
```

```
        // Validate the newly painted client area
        ValidateRect(hWnd,NULL);
        }
        break;
```

See Also   glSwapBuffers

wglUseFontBitmaps

Purpose   Creates a set of OpenGL display list bitmaps for the currently
                     selected GDI font.

Include File   <wingdi.h>

Syntax   BOOL wglUseFontBitmaps(HDC *hDC*, DWORD *dwFirst*, DWORD
                     dwCount, DWORD *dwListBase*);

Description   This function takes the font currently selected in the device con-
                     text specified by hDC and creates a bitmap display list for each
                     character, starting at dwFirst and running for dwCount charac-
                     ters. The display lists are created in the currently selected ren-
                     dering context and are identified by numbers starting at
                     dwListBase. Typically, this is used to draw text into an OpenGL
                     double-buffered scene because the Windows GDI will not allow
                     operations to the back buffer of a double-buffered window. This
                     function is also used to label OpenGL objects onscreen.

Parameters

hDC   HDC: The Windows GDI device context from which the font def-
                     inition is to be derived. You can change the font used by creat-
                     ing and selecting the desired font into the device context.

dwFirst   DWORD: The ASCII value of the first character in the font to use
                     for building the display lists.

dwCount   DWORD: The consecutive number of characters in the font to use
                     succeeding the character specified by dwFirst.

dwListBase   DWORD: The display list base value to use for the first display list
                     character.

Returns   TRUE if the display lists could be created; FALSE otherwise.

Example   The following code shows how to create a set of display lists for
                     the ASCII character set. It is then used to display the text
                     "OpenGL" at the current raster position:

```
    // Create the font outlines based on the font for this device
    // context
    //
    wglUseFontBitmaps(hDC,    // Device context
```

```
    0,      // First character
    255,      // Last character
    nListBase);    // Display list base number


        ...
        ...



        // Draw the string
        glListBase(nListBase);
        glPushMatrix();
        glCallLists (3, GL_UNSIGNED_BYTE, "OpenGL");
        glPopMatrix();
```

See Also   wglUseFontOutlines, glIsList, glNewList, glCallList, glCallLists, glListBase, glDeleteLists, glEndList, glGenLists

wglUseFontOutlines

Purpose   Creates a set of OpenGL 3D display lists for the currently selected GDI font.

Include File   <wingdi.h>

Syntax   BOOL wglUseFontOutlines(HDC *hDC*, DWORD *first*, DWORD count, DWORD *listBase*, FLOAT *deviation*, FLOAT *extrusion*, int *format*, LPGLYPHMETRICSFLOAT *lpgmf*);

Description   This function takes the TrueType font currently selected into the GDI device context *hDC* and creates a 3D outline for *count* characters starting at *first*. The display lists are numbered starting at the value *listBase*. The outline can be composed of line segments or polygons as specified by the *format* parameter. The character cell used for the font extends 1.0 unit length along the x- and y-axes. The parameter *extrusion* supplies the length along the negative z-axis on which the character is extruded. The deviation is an amount 0 or greater that determines the chordal deviation from the original font outline. This function will only work with TrueType fonts. Additional character data is supplied in the *lpgmf* array of *GLYPHMETRICSFLOAT* structures.

Parameters

hDC   HDC: Device context of the font.

first   DWORD: First character in the font to be turned into a display list.

count	DWORD: Number of characters in the font to be turned into display lists.
listBase	DWORD: The display list base value to use for the first display list character.
deviation	FLOAT: The maximum chordal deviation from the true outlines.
extrusion	FLOAT: Extrusion value in the negative z direction.
format	int: Specifies whether the characters should be composed of line segments or polygons in the display lists. May be one of the following values:

	WGL_FONT_LINES	Use line segments to compose character.
	WGL_FONT_POLYGONS	Use polygons to compose character.

lpgmf	LPGLYPHMETRICSFLOAT: Address of an array to receive glyphs metric data. Each array element is filled with data pertaining to its character's display list. Each is defined as follows:

```
typedef struct _GLYPHMETRICSFLOAT { // gmf
   FLOAT    gmfBlackBoxX;
   FLOAT    gmfBlackBoxY;
   POINTFLOAT gmfptGlyphOrigin;
   FLOAT    gmfCellIncX;
   FLOAT    gmfCellIncY;
} GLYPHMETRICSFLOAT;
```

Members

gmfBlackBoxX	Width of the smallest rectangle that completely encloses the character.
gmfBlackBoxY	Height of the smallest rectangle that completely encloses the character.
gmfptGlyphOrigin	The x and y coordinates of the upper-left corner of the rectangle that completely encloses the character. The POINTFLOAT structure is defined as

```
typedef struct _POINTFLOAT { // ptf
   FLOAT   x;        // The horizontal coordinate of a point
   FLOAT   y;        // The vertical coordinate of a point
} POINTFLOAT;
```

gmfCellIncX	The horizontal distance from the origin of the current character cell to the origin of the next character cell.
gmfCellIncY	The vertical distance from the origin of the current character cell to the origin of the next character cell.
Returns	TRUE if the display lists could be created; FALSE otherwise.

Example The following code shows a set of 128 display lists being generated for the first 128 glyphs in the current font:

```
hDC = (HDC)pData;
hFont = CreateFontIndirect(&logfont);
SelectObject (hDC, hFont);


// Create display lists for glyphs 0 through 128 with 0.1
// extrusion and default deviation. The display list numbering
// starts at nListBase (it could be any number).
wglUseFontOutlines(hDC, 0, 128, nListBase, 0.0f, 0.3f, WGL_FONT_POLYGONS,
➥agmf);

DeleteObject(hFont);
```

See Also wglUseFontBitmaps, glIsList, glNewList, glCallList, glCallLists, glListBase, glDeleteLists, glEndList, glGenLists

NON-WINDOWED RENDERING

by Michael Sweet

Besides rendering to the screen, OpenGL supports offscreen rendering, which allows you to generate images for photorealistic reflections or high-quality printed output. You can also save these images to files for inclusion in other documents.

The Basics of Offscreen Rendering

Windows defines several types of *device contexts*. In addition to the display device context that we've been using with all of the sample programs in this book so far, Windows has printer, memory, enhanced metafile, and information device contexts. You use the printer device context when printing images and graphics to a physical printer.

You use memory device contexts to render to device-independent bitmaps (DIBs.). You use memory device contexts to render high-resolution image files and generate image data for printing.

Enhanced metafile device contexts basically record drawing commands to a file that can be printed or imported into another application. You can use these device contexts under Windows NT to print your OpenGL scene or just to save your OpenGL scene to a file.

Information device contexts are only used to retrieve device capabilities. You can't draw using one of these contexts, but you can find out what Windows is using for the default brush color and so on. Because information device contexts are not associated with any hardware device, they are smaller and faster than the other types of contexts.

Limitations of Offscreen Rendering

Although many graphics cards support accelerated OpenGL rendering, few support acceleration to offscreen buffers. This means that your offscreen rendering will likely be considerably slower than the onscreen display.

Currently, none of the available printer drivers support OpenGL rendering, so if you need to print your OpenGL display, you have to use an offscreen buffer or enhanced metafile. (The latter is only available under Windows NT.)

Finally, offscreen buffers cannot share display lists or texture objects with their onscreen cousins.

Creating an Offscreen Buffer for Rendering

Creating an offscreen buffer under Windows is a four-step process. The first step is to create a device context using the `CreateCompatibleDC` function:

```
HDC CreateCompatibleDC(HDC dc);
```

The *dc* argument is normally NULL.

Once we create the device context, we need to create and select a bitmap using the `CreateDIBSection` and `SelectObject` functions. Because we're interested in producing 24-bit RGB images, the `BITMAPINFO` structure is initialized accordingly:

```
HDC       dc;
HBITMAP   bitmap;
BITMAPINFO info;
GLubyte   *bits;

dc = CreateCompatibleDC(NULL);

memset(&info, 0, sizeof(info));
info.bmiHeader.biSize       = sizeof(BITMAPINFOHEADER);
info.bmiHeader.biWidth      = Width;
info.bmiHeader.biHeight     = Height;
info.bmiHeader.biPlanes     = 1;
info.bmiHeader.biBitCount   = 24;      /* 24-bit */
info.bmiHeader.biCompression = BI_RGB; /* RGB */

bitmap = CreateDIBSection(dc, &info, DIB_RGB_COLORS, &bits, NULL, 0);

SelectObject(dc, bitmap);
```

We use a DIB section instead of a regular bitmap for a couple reasons. First, DIB sections give you direct access to the image being drawn; this eliminates an extra "copy" buffer and makes saving or using the rendered image that much easier.

The second, and most important, reason is that OpenGL only works with DIB sections. Regular bitmaps can only be drawn using GDI (Windows) graphics functions.

The third step is to select a pixel format using the `ChoosePixelFormat` and `SelectPixelFormat` functions:

```
PIXELFORMATDESCRIPTOR pfd; /* Pixel format description structure */
int                   pf;  /* Pixel format */

memset(&pfd, 0, sizeof(pfd));
pfd.nSize      = sizeof(pfd);
pfd.nVersion   = 1;
pfd.dwFlags    = PFD_DRAW_TO_BITMAP | PFD_SUPPORT_OPENGL;
pfd.iPixelType = PFD_TYPE_RGBA;
pfd.cColorBits = 24;
pfd.cRedBits   = 8;
pfd.cGreenBits = 8;
pfd.cBlueBits  = 8;
pfd.cDepthBits = 16;

pf = ChoosePixelFormat(dc, &pfd);
SetPixelFormat(dc, pf, &pfd);
```

For regular OpenGL windows, we use a pixel format with the `PFD_DRAW_TO_WINDOW` flag set. For bitmaps, we use the `PFD_DRAW_TO_BITMAP` flag instead to indicate that we want to draw to an offscreen bitmap or DIB section. The other fields match up with our bitmap, specifically with 24 bits per pixel with 8 bits of red, green, and blue.

The final step is to create and bind an OpenGL rendering context for the bitmap using the `wglCreateContext` and `wglMakeCurrent` functions:

```
HGLRC rc;

rc = wglCreateContext(dc);
wglMakeCurrent(dc, rc);
```

Destroying an Offscreen Buffer

Unlike most other operating systems, Windows usually does not automatically destroy resources when your program is finished.

You use the `DeleteObject`, `DeleteDC`, and `wglDeleteContext` functions to delete the offscreen buffer:

```
wglDeleteContext(rc);
DeleteObject(dc, bitmap);
DeleteDC(dc);
```

IT'S GOOD PRACTICE TO DESTROY BUFFERS!
Although Windows NT does keep track of the resources your program uses, certain shared resources can stay resident for a long time, degrading system performance. It is important to destroy all offscreen buffers when you are done with them to prevent this from happening. Also, destroying offscreen buffers is a necessity under Windows 95 and 98 because they do not perform any cleanup of unused resources.

Sharing Display Lists

Many OpenGL program utilize display lists and texture objects to speed up their displays. These *cannot* be shared with contexts that are used with a window because the pixel formats are different.

Remember to build new copies of all display lists and texture objects or draw your scene without them when rendering to an offscreen buffer.

Saving to a .BMP File

In Chapter 7, "Raster Graphics in OpenGL," we explored loading and saving .BMP files in our OpenGL programs. When saving the .BMP, we read RGB information from the screen using the `glReadPixels` function, which has a few problems. The first is that the onscreen color buffer may only have 8 or 16 bits of color precision, which limits the accuracy of the colors that are stored in the file; ideally, we want to have the full 24 bits that are available from Windows.

The second problem is that windows covering our display might end up in our saved image. This depends entirely on the graphics card and driver software, but it would be nice not to have to worry about that!

Enter our offscreen buffer. By rendering to an offscreen buffer, we eliminate both of these problems.

Figure 18.1 shows the output of our terrain viewing program; this version is different from the ones in previous chapters in that it does not display the terrain on the screen but instead renders it to a .BMP file. You'll find the code in BOOK\CHAP18\ TERRAIN10\terrain10.c on the CD.

Figure 18.1   Terrain viewing program .BMP output image.

Rendering to the Offscreen Buffer

The main function creates a memory device context and bitmap to hold the scene:

```
/* Create the device context... */
dc = CreateCompatibleDC(NULL);

/* Create and bind the bitmap */
memset(&info, 0, sizeof(info));
info.bmiHeader.biSize        = sizeof(BITMAPINFOHEADER);
info.bmiHeader.biWidth       = Width;
info.bmiHeader.biHeight      = Height;
info.bmiHeader.biPlanes      = 1;
info.bmiHeader.biBitCount    = 24;
info.bmiHeader.biCompression = BI_RGB;

bitmap = CreateDIBSection(dc, &info, DIB_RGB_COLORS, &bits, NULL, 0);

SelectObject(dc, bitmap);

/* Set the pixel format... */
memset(&pfd, 0, sizeof(pfd));
pfd.nSize     = sizeof(pfd);
pfd.nVersion  = 1;
pfd.dwFlags   = PFD_DRAW_TO_BITMAP | PFD_SUPPORT_OPENGL;
```

```
pfd.iPixelType = PFD_TYPE_RGBA;
pfd.cColorBits = 24;
pfd.cRedBits   = 8;
pfd.cGreenBits = 8;
pfd.cBlueBits  = 8;
pfd.cDepthBits = 16;

pf = ChoosePixelFormat(dc, &pfd);
SetPixelFormat(dc, pf, &pfd);

/* Create and bind the rendering context */
rc = wglCreateContext(dc);
wglMakeCurrent(dc, rc);
```

Second, it creates all of the display lists and texture objects and loads the terrain:

```
/* Load textures and objects... */
puts("Loading objects and textures...");

BuildF16();
BuildTree();

LandTexture = TextureLoad("land.bmp", GL_FALSE, GL_LINEAR_MIPMAP_LINEAR,
                          GL_LINEAR, GL_REPEAT);
SkyTexture  = TextureLoad("sky.bmp", GL_FALSE, GL_LINEAR, GL_LINEAR,
                          GL_CLAMP);
TreeTexture = TextureLoad("tree.bmp", GL_TRUE, GL_LINEAR, GL_LINEAR,
                          GL_CLAMP);

LoadTerrain(36, -112);
```

Then, it calls the `Redraw` function to draw the terrain:

```
Redraw();
```

Finally, it calls the `SaveDIBitmap` function presented in Chapter 7 to save the bitmap to a file:

```
SaveDIBitmap("terrain.bmp", &info, bits);
```

Finally, it deletes all of the memory device storage and exits:

```
/* Free everything... */
wglDeleteContext(rc);
DeleteObject(bitmap);
DeleteDC(dc);
```

Printing Images

To print your OpenGL scenes, you use the same DIB section code in the previous section, but this time, you send the DIB to a printer device instead of a .BMP file.

Ideally, you want to create a DIB that matches the size of the printer's page and resolution. However, for a letter-size page, a typical inkjet printer at 720 DPI requires a 130MB buffer!

Another thing to keep in mind is that most printers only provide two or four intensities of each color and must "dither" the output to get the right color shades. This effectively reduces the usable resolution to about one fourth of the full resolution with the current printers.

Because of this, we can use a smaller DIB; in our next example, we make it one fourth the resolution of the printer. For our 720 DPI inkjet printer, this means that the bitmap is slightly less than 8MB in size, a significant improvement.

Printing from the Terrain Viewing Program

The example in BOOK\CHAP18\TERRAIN11\terrain11.c prints the terrain scene to a printer. The first thing we need to do is select a printer and its options. The easiest way to do that is to use the standard Windows print dialog, PrintDlg:

```
PRINTDLG pd;        /* Print dialog information */
HDC      printer;   /* Printer device context */

/* Show the printer dialog... */
memset(&pd, 0, sizeof(pd));
pd.lStructSize = sizeof(pd);
pd.hwndOwner   = NULL;
pd.Flags       = PD_RETURNDC | PD_NOPAGENUMS | PD_NOSELECTION;
pd.hInstance   = NULL;
if (!PrintDlg(&pd))
    {
    puts("Printing cancelled!");
    return (0);
    }

/* Set the bitmap size to 1/16 the actual (1/4 the resolution) */
Width  = GetDeviceCaps(pd.hDC, HORZRES) / 4;
Height = GetDeviceCaps(pd.hDC, VERTRES) / 4;

printer = pd.hDC;
```

The PrintDlg function accepts a single pointer to a PRINTDLG structure. In it, we specify that we don't want the user to be able to select ranges of pages (PD_NOPAGENUMS) or the "print selection" option (PD_NOSELECTION), but we do want to get a printer device context when the user clicks the OK button (PD_RETURNDC).

Once we know that the user wants to print something, we create the offscreen buffer for OpenGL as before and set up the display lists and textures we need.

Before we render the scene, we tell the printer driver about the file we are going to print using the `SetMapMode`, `StartDoc`, and `StartPage` functions:

```
/* Start the document... */
SetMapMode(printer, MM_TEXT);
memset(&doc, 0, sizeof(doc));
doc.cbSize       = sizeof(DOCINFO);
doc.lpszDocName = "Off-Screen Terrain";
doc.lpszOutput  = NULL;

StartDoc(printer, &doc);
StartPage(printer);
```

The `SetMapMode` function tells the printer driver that we will be using physical (pixel) coordinates for our drawing commands instead of logical (Windows units) coordinates.

The `StartDoc` function starts a new document file for printing, and the `StartPage` function starts the first (and only) page that will contain the scene.

Once we render the scene, we need to copy it to the printer using the `StretchBlt` function:

```
StretchBlt(printer, 0, 0, Width * 4, Height * 4, dc, 0, 0, Width, Height,
           SRCCOPY);
```

We use `StretchBlt` because the DIB section is 1/16 the size of the printer's bitmap.

Finally, we tell the printer driver that we are done using the `EndPage` and `EndDoc` functions and delete the printer device context with `DeleteDC`:

```
EndPage(printer);
EndDoc(printer);
DeleteDC(printer);
```

Metafiles

Metafiles are basically recordings of all the graphics operations performed on a device context. Although only Windows NT supports direct printing of metafiles, many applications can import these metafiles into a document and print them, so their use is not limited to Windows NT.

Metafiles store primitives such as lines and triangles in vector format, making them ideal for printing or publishing; the scaled metafile automatically supports the full device resolution. As a result, metafiles can be considerably smaller than their high-resolution .BMP file counterparts.

Creating an Enhanced Metafile Device Context

The `CreateEnhMetaFile` function is used to create a metafile:

```
HDC CreateEnhMetaFile(HDC hdcRef, LPCTSTR lpFilename, CONST RECT *lpRect,
                LPCTSTR lpDescription);
```

The *hdcRef* parameter can be `NULL` to use the system default resolution and so on. It is used to record the original resolution and units of the metafile.

The *lpFilename* parameter is the file that you want to create, such as `filename.emf`.

The *lpRect* parameter specifies the bounding rectangle of the scene you're about to render. The units are 1/100 of a millimeter. You use this argument *instead* of a call to `glViewport`.

The *lpDescription* parameter is a title for the metafile, such as `Metafile Terrain`.

The return value is a device context that you can use for rendering the metafile as before.

Once you are done rendering, you just call `DeleteEnhMetaFile` to close the file and delete the device context:

```
void DeleteEnhMetaFile(HDC dc);
```

Metafiles and OpenGL Viewports

Rendering to a metafile is different from rendering to an offscreen buffer. When rendering to a metafile, you do not need to call the `glViewport` function. Instead, the bounding rectangle you specify when calling `CreateEnhMetaFile` is used automatically.

Keep in mind that you still need to take into account the aspect ratio of the bounding rectangle. Otherwise, the metafile will appear distorted.

Generating a Metafile from the Terrain Viewing Program

The file BOOK\CHAP18\TERRAIN12\terrain12.c contains an adaptation of the previous two examples that generates a metafile instead of a .BMP file or printing an image.

Summary

OpenGL under Windows supports offscreen rendering, which allows you to generate and print images at higher resolutions and with better color fidelity than may be possible on the screen.

Offscreen rendering is typically slower than onscreen rendering because many graphics boards cannot render to host memory. Also, display lists and texture objects cannot be shared between offscreen and onscreen device contexts, so rendering to an offscreen buffer typically requires additional setup time or the use of slower OpenGL techniques.

DIB sections provide the basis for rendering RGB image data and are supported on all versions of Windows NT and 9x. Metafiles provide resolution-independent output, which is generally smaller than a high-resolution RGB image. Metafiles can be printed directly under Windows NT or imported into many applications under all versions of Windows NT and 9x.

REAL-TIME PROGRAMMING WITH OPENGL

by Richard S. Wright, Jr.

What you'll learn in this chapter:

- How to measure your rendering performance
- How to improve your rendering performance
- How to improve your program's responsiveness
- How to use the keyboard and joystick to move a camera in a scene
- How to create a basic scene graph
- Eliminate geometry that falls outside the viewing volume

OpenGL was designed from the start for real-time 3D interactive computer graphics. High-quality ray tracers and rendering engines can produce exceptionally good 3D animated sequences for film, TV, commercial, or educational uses (to name but a few). This type of computer graphics has its uses, and the quality of the images from these specialized programs and hardware is often unsurpassed.

An animated playback, however, is not considered real time because the graphics aren't really being generated; they are just playing back from a previous recording. We touched on this briefly in Chapter 1, "3D Graphics Fundamentals," where we introduced some of the concepts of real-time interactive graphics and their uses. In this, our final chapter, we are going to discuss some of the techniques for creating high-performance interactive 3D renderings.

It's not enough to just know the API for doing 3D graphics. Just as knowing the C language does not necessarily make you a good programmer, it is only the beginning. We hope that this book has helped you get to this point with knowing how to use OpenGL as a rendering API. Typically, you follow up a school course on C programming (or any language) with a class on algorithms or data structure techniques. The purpose of this chapter is to get you started along this road. For C programming, you learned not to use the *bubble sort*, for database programming, you learned the rules of *data normalization*, and for real-time 3D, you'll learn about *frustum culling*. Let the fun begin!

How Fast Is Fast?

In Chapter 1, we had a pretty simplistic definition of what real time means. Real time simply means that a program (or process) is interactive, usually with an immediate response: You press a button, and a light comes on. Okay, but this begs the question of *how* immediate is that response? Does the light come on in one second…that's pretty quick, isn't it? What about a minute…probably not.

When it comes to computer graphics, real time can mean many things to many people. An artist working with a high-end animation program might consider a 10-second delay before seeing a preview of his work to be real time. A business analyst working with a graphics package might consider a 3D bar graph that can be moved around with the mouse to be a real-time response.

A game programmer, on the other hand, needs the graphics on the screen to react as fast or faster than the player can tap on keys or move his joystick. Military simulations (such as a flight simulator) often push the limits of real-time graphics. These graphics need to be so smooth and quick to respond that to the human eye, they are indistinguishable from real-life motion!

Performance Metrics

Before we can discuss ways of improving performance, we need a way to measure performance. The performance of a given application is usually measured in terms of *frames per second* (fps). This is the number of times a screen (or animation frame) can be updated in a second. For our artist friend who got his image after 10 seconds, this is 1/10 (or 0.1) frames per second. An animated effect can be achieved at nearly any frame rate (as long as you're willing to wait!). At low frame rates (2 or 3 fps), your eye can see the image "pop" from one state to the next. To achieve something that starts to look like a smooth motion, you need a higher frame rate.

Typically, applications start to feel interactive to a user and have a relatively smooth motion at around 15 fps or better. This is pretty much the bare minimum for 3D computer games to be playable. The smooth motion of a film-based motion picture is achieved at 24 frames per second. A 24 fps computer animation starts to look pretty smooth and might still appear jerky from frame to frame. The reason the movie or television image is so smooth at such a low frame rate is because each image is actually a combination of the images preceding and following it. Motion blur and your eye's persistence of vision blend the frames together, providing a higher quality illusion.

The typical computer graphics animation consists of a series of distinct images that must be swapped very rapidly to achieve the same fidelity. Applying motion blur can actually improve the animation quality, even if the frame rate is lowered. Unfortunately, motion blur requires multiple images to be rendered anyway and blended together. At least on current (affordable) hardware, it is still less expensive computationally to just generate more frames and show them to the user. The minimum threshold for really smooth computer animation is about 30 fps. Even this rate isn't enough for some situations. If you are looking out over a large area, objects far in the background appear to hop from frame to frame, and closer objects appear to move more smoothly. The magic number for real-time computer animation to appear completely smooth (on a computer screen or projector) is about 60 fps. Most military applications or commercial flight or driving simulators require at least a sustained 60 fps for visual simulations.

Measuring Performance

Calculating the frames per second for your animation or rendering code is about as simple as math gets for 3D graphics. You measure the time and count the number of frames (or `SwapBuffers` calls) for a while. Then, you divide the time in seconds by the number of frames:

Time in seconds / number of frames = fps

It's that simple.

To get an accurate value, however, you need to be able to measure time accurately. Most operating systems have support for time-keeping functions. Some have a resolution of up to one hundredth of a second. This is probably all that is necessary for coarse-grained frame rate measurements. We use a much higher resolution timer available to all versions of Windows running on a Pentium class machine or better.

You might be aware of the PC `clock` function, which increments its return value 18.2 times every second. If we measure a large number of frames and divide by the time kept by this function, we come very close to a true measurement. If we want to measure a small number of frames (perhaps even only one), however, the results might be inaccurate. Consider that if your goal is to get 60 frames per second, a clock with a resolution of 18 times a second can give you a one second frame rate that is off by as much as 300 percent!

Windows has two functions that provide you with a high-performance timer, `QueryPerformanceFrequency` and `QueryPerformanceCounter`. The first retrieves the frequency and availability of a high-performance counter. The SDK documentation is careful to point out that such a counter might not exist. It turns out the hardware for this counter is just the Intel Pentium processor (or compatible, such as the AMD processors). If you're trying to do real-time rendering on an older machine, you can always use the `clock` function instead—good luck.

Both functions use a pointer to a 64-bit integer defined under Windows as a `LARGE_INTEGER`. This is actually a union that can be accessed as a true 64-bit integer or by high and low order 32 bits. We simply subtract the beginning from the ending count and divide by the frequency. This gives the elapsed time in seconds to an exceptionally high resolution (more than a millionth of a second). We demonstrate this in our first sample program.

Windows Animation Techniques

There are a number of ways to achieve an animation effect under the Windows programming model. The basic goal is to refresh the display repeatedly with a different image each time. Using the normal Windows event model, you do all your drawing (or rendering) in the WM_PAINT message handler. Whenever the window needs to be refreshed, the next frame is generated. To achieve a rapid succession of frames, you simply need to generate a series of WM_PAINT messages. This works, as you'll see, but it might not always be the best method depending on what your real-time needs are.

Using Timers for Animation

Windows timers are an easy-to-program method of generating an animation sequence. You create a timer by telling Windows how often you want a WM_TIMER message posted to your window. By responding to this message, you have the ability to perform some task at fairly regular intervals. Our first sample program for this chapter, timer, uses this method to create an animated rotating globe. The following code (from the window procedure) show the basic framework for doing this:

```
case WM_CREATE:
. . .

    // Create a timer that fires 30 times a second
    SetTimer(hWnd,101,33,NULL);
    . . .
break;

// Timer moves and bounces the rectangle, simply calls
// our previous OnIdle function, then invalidates the
// window so it will be redrawn.
case WM_TIMER:
    InvalidateRect(hWnd,NULL,FALSE);
    break;

case WM_PAINT:
```

```
    // Rendering code . . .
    break;

// Window is being destroyed, cleanup
case WM_DESTROY:
    // Kill the timer that we created
    KillTimer(hWnd,101);
```

The call to `SetTimer` is generally made in the `WM_CREATE` message handler. This function takes four arguments:

```
UINT SetTimer(HWND hWnd, UINT nIDEvent, UINT uElapse, TIMERPROC lpTimerFunc);
```

The first argument is the window handle for which you are setting up a timer. The second, `nIDEvent`, is the event ID of the timer. You can actually set up multiple timers. When handling the `WM_TIMER` message, the `wParam` message parameter contains the timer ID. If we create only one timer, we don't need to worry about this. The `uElapse` parameter is the time in milliseconds between each timer notification. Unlike the GLUT-based timers we previously used for animation, the Windows timer is repetitive and does not need to be reset on each timer call. If desired, you can also set up a callback function with the `lpTimerFunc` parameter.

To handle the timer events, you set up a case to handle the `WM_TIMER` message, which simply invalidates the application window. Because you are doing all your rendering in the `WM_PAINT` message handler, you get the opportunity to continually update your image, thus producing an animation.

Finally, you need to delete your timer in the `WM_DESTROY` message handler. The function `KillTimer` does this for you, taking only the window handle and the timer ID. There are a limited number of timers available under Windows 95 and 98, but Windows NT and 2000 pose no limit. Because timers are a system resource, you should remember to delete them when you no longer need them.

Windows timers sound like the perfect solution to creating a regular stream of timed events (such as alternating frames in a computer animation). By spacing out your animation frames, you can ensure that some time is devoted between frames to handling other Windows messages or other application processing. Timers work great with hardware acceleration when you want a fixed frame rate that should not be exceeded. For some applications, you might not want your animation to suddenly become too fast because the application is running on a faster machine. (We discuss this topic a bit more later.)

However, in the case where you do want as many frames per second generated as possible, Windows timers fall far short of the mark. Remember that Windows timers are message based (even if you use the callback function), and thus if the operating system is busy with other tasks, your window might not get a `WM_TIMER` message when you might expect. In fact, timer messages are not high on the priority list of messages to be handled by Windows. Furthermore, the interval you specify is in thousandths of a second, but the best resolution you actually get from Windows is about 40 milliseconds (recall our discussion about the resolution of normal Windows timing), which is about 25 frames per second.

A Simple Benchmark

This is a good time to make use of the performance counter functions (discussed earlier) available on modern PC hardware to measure our frame rate. In our sample program TIMER, we set up a Windows timer with a refresh frequency of 33 milliseconds. This should give us about 30 fps (assuming the rendering hardware is fast enough). In Listing 19.1, we show a substantial portion of the window procedure for this program. Here, you can see the WM_TIMER animation code, along with the actual WM_PAINT message and the code for calculating the frame rate.

Listing 19.1   *Code From TIMER Program Demonstrating fps Calculation*

```
// Window procedure, handles all messages for this program
LRESULT CALLBACK WndProc(    HWND      hWnd,
                             UINT      message,
                             WPARAM    wParam,
                             LPARAM    lParam)
    {
static LARGE_INTEGER timerFrequency;    // Storage for timer frequency
static LARGE_INTEGER startTime;    // Start time when frame count is zero
static int nFrames = 0;          // Storage for frame count

switch (message)
        {
        // Window creation, setup for OpenGL
        case WM_CREATE:
        . . .
        . . .
        QueryPerformanceFrequency(&timerFrequency);
        QueryPerformanceCounter(&startTime);

        // Create a timer that fires 30 times a second
        SetTimer(hWnd,101,33,NULL);
        break;

        // Timer moves and bounces the rectangle, simply calls
        // our previous OnIdle function, then invalidates the
        // window so it will be redrawn.
        case WM_TIMER:
            InvalidateRect(hWnd,NULL,FALSE);
            break;
```

```
case WM_PAINT:
    {
    // Call OpenGL drawing code
    RenderScene();

    // Call function to swap the buffers
    SwapBuffers(hDC);

    nFrames++;
    if(nFrames > 100)
        {
        char cOutBuffer[32];
        LARGE_INTEGER currentTime;
        float fps;

        // Get the current time
        QueryPerformanceCounter(&currentTime);

        fps = (float)nFrames/((float)(currentTime.QuadPart -
                                startTime.QuadPart)/
                        (float)timerFrequency.QuadPart);

        // Display the fps
        sprintf(cOutBuffer,"%0.1f",fps);
        SetWindowText(hWnd, cOutBuffer);
        nFrames = 0;

        // Resets the timer
        QueryPerformanceCounter(&startTime);
        }

    // Validate the newly painted client area
    ValidateRect(hWnd,NULL);
    }
    break;. . .
```

First, the three lines

```
static LARGE_INTEGER timerFrequency;    // Storage for timer frequency
static LARGE_INTEGER startTime;    // Start time when frame count is zero
static int nFrames = 0;        // Storage for frame count
```

declare storage for the frame counter, nFrames, and the timer frequency and the start time for our timings. We initialize the timing values in the WM_CREATE message handler:

```
QueryPerformanceFrequency(&timerFrequency);
QueryPerformanceCounter(&startTime);
```

Note that in the WM_PAINT message handler, we do not calculate the frame rate every frame (although we could, with these functions) but instead wait until we have measured the time for 100 frames:

```
case WM_PAINT:
    {
    . . .
    nFrames++;
    if(nFrames > 100)
        {
```

Measuring frame rate performance over a range of frames typically produces more accurate results. One thing to avoid is trying to measure the amount of time it takes to execute a group of OpenGL function calls. OpenGL function calls are frequently cached until some internal execute buffer is full or the driver determines that the batch of hardware commands should be sent to the hardware. Many OpenGL commands then return immediately because they have no real rendering effect until the pipeline is flushed. (See Chapters 1 and 3, "Using OpenGL," for a discussion of the OpenGL pipeline and the glFlush function.) Measuring the frame as a whole (take the reading after the SwapBuffers call) is the best way to measure your overall rendering efficiency.

The details of calculating the frame rate are pretty self-explanatory. Note, however, that we are putting the frame rate in the window caption:

```
SetWindowText(hWnd, cOutBuffer);
nFrames = 0;
```

Writing text to the OpenGL Window with GDI is not allowed in double-buffered OpenGL windows. (Your text vanishes on the SwapBuffers call.) This is also a convenient spot because it does not have to be refreshed each frame. Any work you do between frames is going to adversely affect your frame rate. Because we are only calculating this value every one hundred frames anyway, there is no point wasting CPU time refreshing this text.

The output for the timer program is shown in Figure 19.1. Note that the frame rate is not as high as we had hoped (30 fps). In an environment without hardware rendering, it is unlikely that even 25 frames per second would be reached, but with hardware assistance, this animation is limited to a maximum of 25 frames per second. You might actually desire this limit for some applications, in which case you need look no further for your means of generating an animated or interactive 3D scene.

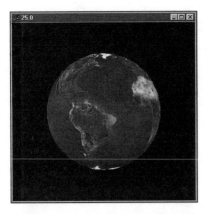

Figure 19.1   Output from the TIMER program; it falls short of 30 fps.

Short-Circuiting the WM_PAINT **Mechanism**

A maximum of 25 frames per second might be sufficient for some applications, but if you run this program, you can see that the animation is still not perfectly smooth (assuming you even get 25 fps). For most true real-time applications (games and simulation), you need much better frame rates. One way of doing this is to dispense with the Windows timer approach and short circuit the WM_PAINT mechanism. You'll notice in Listing 19.1 that at the end of the WM_PAINT message handler, the window is validated. In the course of normal Windows graphics programming, this is how we tell Windows that we are done refreshing the window:

```
// Validate the newly painted client area
ValidateRect(hWnd,NULL);
```

When we received the WM_TIMER message previously, we even invalidated the window so that Windows would know to send a new WM_PAINT message to our application:

```
InvalidateRect(hWnd,NULL,FALSE);
```

We can short-circuit this whole mechanism by never validating the window at the end of the WM_PAINT message handler. This move causes Windows (the operating system) to think that the window is always in need of being refreshed and triggers a never-ending stream of WM_PAINT messages being posted to your application. Listing 19.2 shows our now slightly modified WM_PAINT message handler. This code appears in the sample program NOVALIDATE.

Listing 19.2 *A Painting Message Handler That Is Continuously Called by Windows*

```
// The painting function. This message sent by Windows
// whenever the screen needs updating.
case WM_PAINT:
    {
    // Call OpenGL drawing code
    RenderScene();

    // Call function to swap the buffers
    SwapBuffers(hDC);

    nFrames++;
    if(nFrames > 100)
        {
        char cOutBuffer[32];
        LARGE_INTEGER currentTime;
        float fps;

        // Get the current time
        QueryPerformanceCounter(&currentTime);

        fps = (float)nFrames/((float)(currentTime.QuadPart -
            startTime.QuadPart)/
            (float)timerFrequency.QuadPart);

        // Display the fps
        sprintf(cOutBuffer,"%0.1f",fps);
        SetWindowText(hWnd, cOutBuffer);
        nFrames = 0;

        // Resets the timer
        QueryPerformanceCounter(&startTime);
        }
    }
    break;
```

You can see in Figure 19.2 that the frame rate of the animation has increased tremendously (this is with hardware acceleration). Here, the globe is spinning very fast at more than 360 fps. In our animation, we are updating the angle of rotation by one degree each time we rerender the scene. The net effect here is that the globe makes a complete revolution every second. The faster the frame rate, the faster the animation.

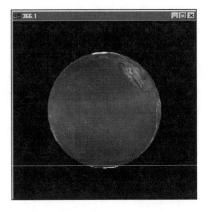

Figure 19.2   Dramatically increased frame rate resulting from a continuously updating window.

A good question might be coming to your mind now. What if you want the globe to spin at a fixed rate, say one revolution every five seconds? Increasing frame rate was supposed to make things smoother, not just speed up our animations! Hold this thought in the back of your mind. For now, speeding up the animation is the easiest way to see the difference in graphics performance. We will approach this topic soon, but under a different context.

Short-circuiting the WM_PAINT mechanism is the fastest way to do your animations while still maintaining the message-based Windows programming paradigm. Using this method, your program can still respond to other critical Windows messages, such as keystrokes, mouse movements, and so on. Under general circumstances when you want as many frames rendered as possible per second, this is a good method to choose.

Event Loop Insertion

You can still go one step further to get the maximum frame rate possible using the message-based Windows programming model. Although the WM_PAINT method is usually fast enough, the WM_PAINT message is not the highest priority window message. Window manipulation or system messages often take priority and can slow down your rendering. Although not common for a general-purpose animation, you might have a need to render as many frames as possible, as fast as possible. Probably the most common application with this need is the graphics demonstration or benchmarking program. These programs are not interactive, so they do not need or want to be slowed down by other system or window events. Typically, the goal is to see on what graphics card or environment the program finishes its run on the quickest.

To do this, we short-circuit not only the WM_PAINT mechanism, but also the entire message-handling loop for the application. The following code shows the typical message loop in WinMain:

```
// Process application messages until the application closes
while( GetMessage(&msg, NULL, 0, 0))
    {
    TranslateMessage(&msg);
    DispatchMessage(&msg);
    }
```

This is Windows 101. The messages received from the operating system are dispatched here to the individual window procedures for each window in your application. This loop stalls when there are no messages in your applications message queue. We can replace GetMessage with PeekMessage and the loop will run continuously until a WM_QUIT message is posted to the application. This loop then runs continuously as long as the application is active—no waiting around for window messages or for windows to be invalidated. Listing 19.3 shows how we might insert our rendering code and frame rate calculations into this loop. The sample program EVENTLOOP demonstrates this.

Listing 19.3   *A Message Loop Modified to Do Repetitive Rendering*

```
// Process application messages until the application closes
while(1)
    {
    // If there is a message, process it
    if(PeekMessage(&msg, NULL, 0, 0, PM_REMOVE))
        {
        TranslateMessage(&msg);
        DispatchMessage(&msg);

        // Break when program terminates
        if(msg.message == WM_QUIT)
            break;
        }

    if(hRC)
        {
        // Call OpenGL drawing code
        RenderScene();

        // Call function to swap the buffers
        SwapBuffers(hDC);

        nFrames++;
        if(nFrames > 100)
```

```
        {
        char cOutBuffer[32];
        LARGE_INTEGER currentTime;
        float fps;

        // Get the current Time
        QueryPerformanceCounter(&currentTime);

        fps = (float)nFrames/((float)(currentTime.QuadPart -
            startTime.QuadPart)/
            (float)timerFrequency.QuadPart);

        // Display the fps
        sprintf(cOutBuffer,"%0.1f",fps);
        SetWindowText(hWnd, cOutBuffer);
        nFrames = 0;

        // Resets the timer
        QueryPerformanceCounter(&startTime);
        }
    }
}
```

We leave the details of using PeekMessage or GetMessage to a book on Windows programming (and we hope they leave the OpenGL to us!). What is important to us is that we check the value of hRC before we do any rendering. This variable is set to NULL when it is declared:

```
static HGLRC hRC = NULL;           // Permanent Rendering context
```

The rendering context is created as normal in the WM_CREATE message handler but set to NULL again when the window is destroyed:

```
// Window is being destroyed, cleanup
case WM_DESTROY:

// Deselect the current rendering context and delete it
wglMakeCurrent(hDC,NULL);
wglDeleteContext(hRC);
hRC = NULL;
. . .
```

You must follow this convention because the message loop starts long before the window is actually created and continues for a while after the window is destroyed. (There are a lot of window messages that fly around!) If you do not, you run the risk of trying to render to a nonexistent OpenGL rendering context, and your program will usually crash.

The biggest disadvantage to this method is that one frame must be rendered between every single window message to be processed. This can hinder keystrokes, mouse movements, window manipulation, and even program termination from occurring until all the intermediate OpenGL rendered frames are processed and displayed. The only advantage is that you might get slightly better performance than you do from any other message-based method.

Using a Rendering Thread

The last alternative for generating repeated frames of animation under Windows is to abandon the message-based paradigm altogether and create your own rendering thread. This method is a bit more complex and might not necessarily give you the highest possible overall frame rate, but there are many compelling advantages to using this approach.

The problem with message-based programming is that your code must wait until the operating system tells it to execute. Although all our previous examples have been able to demonstrate a high frame rate, their animation or the processing of each frame is limited by either Windows or by other portions of the program. Even the event loop insertion method can be hampered by a message handler that takes a great deal of CPU time before returning. Run any of the previous examples and move the window around onscreen. You'll notice that the rotating globe slows down or stops completely when you do. In all of these examples, every message the window receives is an interruption in the flow of continually generating rendered frames. Another thing you might notice is that with the exception of the timer-based animation, the frame rate might bounce around wildly, perhaps by as much as +/– 10 frames per second of their mean. The animation is influenced strongly (and irregularly) by window messages, idle processing, and other applications running in the background. The large number of frames per second just amplifies this effect. With a more complex animation or scene, you get a lower frame rate, and the bounce might be considerably less noticeable.

For many 3D games, or simulations (flight, combat, and so on), the raw frame rate is not as important as a consistent frame rate. (We dwell on this topic a bit more in the next section.) To get a consistent frame rate, you need an animation loop that cannot be interrupted by random acts of window maintenance. You might intuitively fashion a rendering loop to be something like the following:

```
while(GameRunning)
    {
    RenderAFrame();
    }
```

The overall speed and consistency of your frame rate is still influenced by the overall CPU load on the system. (Remember, Windows is a preemptive OS nowadays,) This is always the case, but your loop does not get stopped several times a second so that some message handler can determine whether it needs to respond to a key press.

Normally, you couldn't put this kind of a loop in your Windows program because it never checks for keystrokes, window closing or resizing, or even program termination! Fortunately, Win32 has a feature called *threads*, which allows you to create a new unit of execution. Your threads are started just like a normal function call, but the operating system switches CPU time between your thread and the main program (called the main process thread). Your process and its threads in turn share CPU time with all other processes and threads running in the operating system. If you are unfamiliar with threads or thread-based programming, this is a good time to get one of the Windows programming books mentioned in Appendix B, "Further Reading." The code fragments and listings that follow are from the rthread sample program for this chapter.

Creating an OpenGL Rendering Thread

You create an OpenGL rendering thread the same way you do any other worker thread (as opposed to a GUI thread) in your application. You need to declare a thread handler somewhere so you can access the thread if needed (to terminate the thread prematurely or to determine whether the thread has terminated on its own, for example):

```
static HANDLE hThreadHandle = NULL;
```

This variable is assigned the return value from the _beginthread function call:

```
// Create the rendering thread
hThreadHandle = (HANDLE) _beginthread(RenderingThreadEntryPoint,0,NULL);
```

This function creates a thread of execution starting with the user-defined function RenderingThreadEntryPoint. This is your rendering loop function. Do not use the Win32 API function CreateThread unless you absolutely will not be using any functions from the C runtime library. Our entire rendering loop from the rthread sample program appears in Listing 19.4.

Listing 19.4   *The Thread-Based Rendering Loop for rthread*

```
///////////////////////////////////////////////////////////////////////
// Rendering Thread Entry Point
void RenderingThreadEntryPoint(void *pVoid)
    {
    // Set up the rendering context
    SetupRC();

    // Main loop for rendering
    while(1)
        {
        // Check rendering state info, terminate if flagged
```

continued on next page

continued from previous page

```
        if(CheckStates())
            break;

        RenderScene();

        // Swap buffers
        SwapBuffers(hDC);
        }

    // Do any necessary cleanup and terminate
    gluDeleteQuadric(pSphere);

    // Finally, shut down OpenGL Rendering context
    wglMakeCurrent(hDC, NULL);
    wglDeleteContext(hRC);

    _endthread();     // Terminate the thread nicely
    }
```

We discuss the `CheckStates` function call in the next section on thread communication. First, you should note some important things about this thread-based rendering loop. The first is that the `SetupRC` function is called here rather than in the main process thread when the window is created. In fact, we modified the `SetupRC` function so that the pixel format for the window is actually set here, along with the creation of the rendering context. (We don't show this code because it should be second nature by now.) Recall that in Chapter 17, "The OpenGL Pixel Format and Rendering Context," we discussed that only one rendering context could be current per thread. Although theoretically possible to create a context in one thread and pass it to another thread, this rarely works as designed, in our experience. For best compatibility, it is best to do all initialization, rendering, and cleanup in the same thread.

The rendering loop simply runs oblivious to all else, rendering and swapping buffers, until signaled to terminate by the return value of `CheckStates`. Although the execution of this loop will depend and could vary based on CPU load and accelerator performance, there should be little to no intermittent disruptions due to message-handling calls. The work of the message handlers is still being done by the main process thread, but now the transition of CPU time between rendering and any GUI activity is more smoothly arbitrated by the operating system.

Figure 19.3 shows the output of the rthread program. This looks much like the previous animation samples. What can't be captured in a screen shot is that the frame rate is holding more consistent. You can move the window around and the globe slows but continues spinning at all times. The same can be seen when resizing the window.

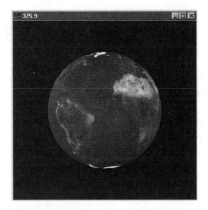

Figure 19.3   Output from the rthread example using a dedicated rendering thread.

Communicating with the Rendering Thread

If the rendering thread is running away and unconcerned with any GUI activity, how then does it know when to reset the viewport or even when it should stop running? The GUI thread tells it! Many methods and functions support communication and data sharing between threads on the Win32 platform. The most efficient is the *critical section*. Two threads running at the same time often run the danger of trying to access the same memory location or system resource at the same time. This can end in disaster for your code, and the problem is only made worse when you have multiple CPUs; two threads could actually physically be writing and reading from the same memory location at the same time.

To keep this sort of misadventure from occurring, you must synchronize access to all variables that will be modified or read by more than one thread. This is precisely what critical sections were designed to do. For the rthread example (actually, for all future examples), we defined a structure that will contain status flags about changes or events that may be of interest across threads. You could easily extend this to contain any number of flags or other types of data. We then synchronize access to this structure across threads using a critical section:

```
// Shared rendering state information
struct RENDER_STATE
    {
    unsigned int uiFrames;          // Running frame count
    BOOL bResize;              // Flag that window was resized
    BOOL bTerminate;           // Flag to terminate rendering loop
    BOOL bFatalError;          // Fatal error has occurred in render thread
    BOOL bModifyFlag;          // Flag set whenever something changes
    };
```

Using a critical section is fairly easy. You start by declaring a structure of type
CRITICAL_SECTION (you also need a copy of the structure that is going to be shared!):

```
CRITICAL_SECTION        csThreadSafe;      // Critical section
struct RENDER_STATE      rsRenderData;      // Communication between threads
```

Then, someplace in your initialization code (before the thread is created), you initialize the critical section structure and initialize your shared data structure with its
default values. A good place to do this is in your WM_CREATE message handler, just
before the call to create the rendering thread:

```
case WM_CREATE:
. . .
// Initialize the critical section
        InitializeCriticalSection(&csThreadSafe);

        // Initialize interthread communication
        rsRenderData.uiFrames = 0;
        rsRenderData.bResize = FALSE;
        rsRenderData.bTerminate = FALSE;
        rsRenderData.bFatalError = FALSE;
        rsRenderData.bModifyFlag = TRUE;


        . . .
        // Create the rendering thread
        hThreadHandle = (HANDLE) _beginthread(RenderingThreadEntryPoint,0,NULL);
        . . .
```

Note that you need to delete the critical section with a call to DeleteCriticalSection
when your program terminates. Now within your GUI code, you update the values of
this data structure to let the rendering thread know what is going on. Take, for example, when the window is moved or its size is changed:

```
case WM_MOVE:
case WM_SIZE:
EnterCriticalSection(&csThreadSafe);
    rsRenderData.bResize = TRUE;
    rsRenderData.bModifyFlag = TRUE;
    LeaveCriticalSection(&csThreadSafe);
    break;
```

The function call to EnterCriticalSection takes as an argument a pointer to our
CRITICAL_SECTION structure, as does the call to LeaveCriticalSection. The entering
and leaving of a critical section is what synchronizes thread access to our variables. If
the GUI thread enters the critical section, the rendering thread is blocked from entering the same critical section until the GUI thread leaves the critical section. If you
place all shared components between these two function calls, it becomes impossible
for both threads to access the data within them simultaneously. If one thread has

control of a critical section, and another thread calls EnterCriticalSection, it is said to be *blocked*. The thread will essentially be stopped from executing until the first thread releases the critical section.

You must be careful to place as little code as possible within protected critical sections, or you could end up with the same types of rendering interruptions that we had with the message-based rendering paradigm. Let's look at how our rendering thread accesses the data in this structure. Listing 19.5 shows the CheckStates function that is called for every frame of the rendering loop shown in Listing 19.4. Note that every time we made any changes to any flags in the rsRenderData structure, we set the bModifyFlag member to TRUE. By checking this flag first, we can avoid redundantly checking every flag in the structure if nothing has changed.

Listing 19.5 *The* CheckStates *Function from the rthread Sample Program*

```
/////////////////////////////////////////////////////////////////////////////
// Check rendering states and make appropriate adjustments. Returns true on
// termination flag.
BOOL CheckStates()
    {
    BOOL bRet = FALSE;

    // Is it time to leave or anything else
    EnterCriticalSection(&csThreadSafe);

    if(rsRenderData.bModifyFlag)
        {
        // Flag set to terminate
        if(rsRenderData.bTerminate)
            bRet = TRUE;

        // Window resized
        if(rsRenderData.bResize)
            ResetViewport();

        // Reset the modify flag and exit
        rsRenderData.bModifyFlag = FALSE;
        }

    // Increment frame count
    rsRenderData.uiFrames++;

    LeaveCriticalSection(&csThreadSafe);
    return bRet;
    }
```

The frame count is also maintained in this structure in the `uiFrames` data member. The main GUI thread uses a timer to update the frame rate. Every five seconds, a `WM_TIMER` message is sent to the main window, which reads this value and determines the running frame rate. The `bTerminate` flag is set by the GUI and returned by this function. As shown in Listing 19.4, this tells the rendering loop that it should terminate.

Terminating the Rendering Thread

If you use threads in your program, you can't just terminate the main program. Actually, you can, but it's a bad idea to kill a thread indiscriminately as it can have messy consequences (resource leaks, lost files, and so on). The proper way to handle this is to let your threads terminate themselves and then exit the main program after any worker threads have finished and exited themselves. The main application thread tells the rendering thread to terminate by setting the `bTerminate` flag of our `RENDER_STATE` structure. This is done in the `WM_DESTROY` message handler before the device context is deleted. If we don't wait for the thread to terminate, then it is likely that the rendering loop will try to render to a now invalid device context. Listing 19.6 shows the complete `WM_DESTROY` message handler for our main application window in rthread.

Listing 19.6   *The Main Program Signals the Rendering Thread to Terminate and Then Waits*

```
// Tell the application to terminate after the window
// is gone.
case WM_DESTROY:
    {
    // Tell the rendering loop to terminate itself
    EnterCriticalSection(&csThreadSafe);
    rsRenderData.bTerminate = TRUE;
    rsRenderData.bModifyFlag = TRUE;
    LeaveCriticalSection(&csThreadSafe);

    // Need to wait for rendering thread to terminate so it can clean
    // up. Wait for the thread handle to become signaled. Give it five
    // seconds, then terminate anyway if it hasn't yet (it's probably
    // stuck if it hasn't terminated by now)
    WaitForSingleObject(hThreadHandle, 5000);

    DeleteCriticalSection(&csThreadSafe);

    ReleaseDC(hWnd, hDC);
    PostQuitMessage(0);
    }
    break;
```

After setting the termination flag, the main thread needs to wait for the rendering thread to terminate. Recall that for each frame, the rendering thread checks the state of this flag. Using the handle to the thread returned by `_beginthread`, we can use the Windows API function `WaitForSingleObject` to wait for the threads handle to become *signaled*:

```
WaitForSingleObject(hThreadHandle, 5000);
```

For our purposes, this just means that our thread has terminated. Because we do our entire OpenGL cleanup in the thread before it returns, we can now safely do our main application's window cleanup and finally end the program.

Putting the "Real" in Real-Time

Until this point, we have had a fairly loose definition of what real time means when applied to computer graphics. From the graphics API's standpoint, we can say that graphics are generated in real time in response to graphics API calls. This is typically made possible by the presence of 3D rendering hardware, although this hasn't been strictly required. However, except for the most casual of users of real-time 3D applications, this is often not an adequate working definition.

Previously, we have demonstrated the various means by which you can achieve a rapid succession of frames on the Windows platform. One side effect you've seen from our crude examples is that the faster the frame rate, the faster the animation ran. The animation sequence was keyed to the change of frames, not to the passage of time. For example, the spinning globe was rotated by one more degree every time a new frame was rendered. In "real" real-time graphics, a faster frame rate should yield a smoother animation, not a faster animation.

In most real-time 3D applications, the graphics are approximating real-world effects, only in a virtual environment or setting. Certainly, you can't *really* be on Ceti-Alpha Prime, running for you life from a large Grue. However, if you can run at a rate of 1 meter per second on Ceti-Alpha Prime, then you should only travel one meter across the virtual terrain every second. Upgrading your graphics card to the latest wiz-bang GPU (Graphics Processing Unit—a fancy name for OpenGL implementations with hardware supported transform and lighting) on the market should not enable you to suddenly run two meters per second! Instead, you should see a much high quality and thus believable virtual experience as a result of the higher frame rates, smoother animation, and possibly more detailed and complex visual environments.

Time-Based Key Framing

The sample program rtime demonstrates a globe that rotates at a fixed speed regardless of frame rate. (Yes, this is the last globe example!) It does this by rotating the globe one entire revolution every 10 seconds. The amount of rotation the globe receives is a function of the amount of time that has passed since the animation started:

Angle = (time in seconds * 360.0)/10.0

This produces one complete 360-degree revolution every 10 seconds. With a little ingenuity, we can rewrite this as

Angle = time in seconds * 36.0

We save ourselves an extra mathematical operation. Listing 19.7 shows our modifications to the rthread example to accomplish this.

Listing 19.7   *Animating the Globe Based on Elapsed Time Instead of Frame Rate*

```
static LARGE_INTEGER globeTime;    // Start time of the animation

// Called by GLUT library to draw scene
void RenderScene(void)
    {
    LARGE_INTEGER currentTime;     // The current time
    double fSeconds;               // Elapsed time in seconds
    float fAngle, fRot;

    // Get the current time, subtract the beginning time, get the seconds
    QueryPerformanceCounter(&currentTime);
    fSeconds = (double)(currentTime.QuadPart - globeTime.QuadPart)/
               (double)timerFrequency.QuadPart;

    // The Angle is a function of time - one revolution every 5 seconds
    fAngle = (float)(fSeconds * 36.0);
    fRot = fmod(fAngle, 360.0f); // Keep it always within 0-360 range

    // Clear the window with current clearing color
    glClear(GL_COLOR_BUFFER_BIT);

    glPushMatrix();
    glRotatef(fRot, 0.0f, 0.0f, 1.0f);
    gluSphere(pSphere, 20.0f, 15, 15);
    glPopMatrix();
    }

/////////////////////////////////////////////////////////////////////////
// Rendering Thread Entry Point
void RenderingThreadEntryPoint(void *pVoid)
    {
```

```
// Set up the rendering context
SetupRC();

// Get start time of animation
QueryPerformanceCounter(&globeTime);

// Main loop for rendering
. . .
```

Now, the globe rotates at a fixed rate, regardless of what hardware it is run on. If you run it on a slow computer with only a software implementation, you might get around 10 fps, and you'll see a choppy animation as the globe completes its rotation. Even on a faster machine that can render over 300 fps, you just see a silky smooth animation of a globe slowly spinning in space.

Practical Limitations

Ultra high frame rates make for good benchmark numbers that the marketing people can toss around. However, you should know two things before beginning your quest for the ultimate frame rate. The first is that the human eye cannot really tell the difference after about 60 fps. It's hard enough to tell the difference between 48 and 51 fps, but above 60, you pretty much can't tell the difference, unless your animations are keyed on frame rate (in which case the activity will be much faster—and you certainly can tell).

The other is that the computer monitor's refresh rate pretty much limits the number of frames that are actually exposed to your eye. If your monitor refresh rate is set to 60, and your application is generating more than 100 fps, then some frames are being generated, displayed, and blown away by the next frame before the monitor even has a chance to refresh what is shown. Our spinning globe was running at more than 300 fps on some hardware that is actually two generations behind what is currently on the market. What do we do with all this power?

What you need to realize is that the globe was pretty lame in terms of what constitutes a complex real-time 3D scene. The more objects you put into your scene, with the more textures, special effects, and so on, the slower the rendering will become. Performance-tuning your rendering code becomes a lot more complex when your virtual environments start getting more realistic. Games and simulations can add more polygons for more detailed models, more special effects, higher resolution textures, and so on. We are still a long way from being able to reproduce the real world with 3D graphics in real time.

In addition to stressing your 3D hardware, ultra high frame rates waste a lot of CPU time. If you restrict yourself to 30 or 60 frames per second, you can use a lot of that CPU time to do other things, such as opponent AI (artificial intelligence), physics modeling and calculations, and so on. If you find yourself in the situation where you are getting more than enough frames per second, but you need to devote more time to threads doing other work, you can always put your rendering thread to sleep. The Windows API function Sleep takes one argument, the number of milliseconds to suspend the current thread:

```
SwapBuffers(hDC);     // Swap buffers
Sleep(10);            // Sleep for 10 milliseconds
```

As shown here, always do this (if you do it at all) after the buffer swap. There is typically a stall in the hardware before it can accept new rendering commands just after a buffer swap (because a flush is also invoked). This way, you are doing something else more useful while the driver is doing other work. You can also call Sleep with a zero argument. This tells Windows that you want to surrender your thread's time slice now, but not that it should wait any extra time before reassigning your thread CPU time. Balancing the amount of time to suspend your rendering thread against other considerations such as varying hardware abilities or the time needed for other calculations can be tricky. For this reason, few consumer applications (games!) employ this technique. This might be more appropriate for a more complex simulation application that tends to run on a much more restricted range of hardware.

Real-Time Response

Real-time graphics often involve not just real-time graphics animation, but real-time interaction with a user. Keystrokes or joystick movements should correspond immediately to some visual feedback or response. Although we have covered what it takes to get graphics onscreen as quickly as possible, we should also point out a few hints for getting input from the user as quickly as possible.

Just as message-based screen refresh methods prove inadequate for generating consistent real-time frame rates, so too does it prove inadequate for getting user input. Whenever you press a key on the keyboard, a WM_CHAR message is generated and sent to your application window. If you tap a key very rapidly, you get a whole stream of messages. However, if you hold down the key, there is a short delay, followed by the stream of keyboard messages. This can be a real problem if you are using keystrokes for player movement, such as in a game. Although your game engine might be rendering between 30 and 60 frames per second, the best you're going to get out of the keyboard is about 10 keystrokes per second (even when holding down the key). If you're moving the player's camera with keystrokes, then you are going to reduce a 30 fps graphics experience to an effective 10 fps experience. The same can be said for joystick or mouse messages.

Never use Windows messages for real-time user or player input. Although we can excuse timer-based animations for some applications, in a true real-time environment, the long delay before keystrokes or other types in input are translated into graphical responses will prove quite distracting. Windows provides two functions for getting at keyboard and joystick information faster than the old message-based methods. We use them to manipulate the camera location in our next set of sample programs, tank.

The tank samples are our test framework for the rest of the chapter. In tank, we use the keyboard or joystick to move ourselves around in a virtual world. This environment might be similar to a first-person shooter type game, but we are just going to wander around a wide open area with "stuff" littered about. To keep this example even more simple, we use a closed-in area (200×200) from which we cannot wander. The terrain is also flat, so our camera movements are restricted to moving around on a flat surface. The first version of tank, tanksimple, contains no scenery, save for a ball to mark the center of the coordinate system, and is drawn in wireframe mode. This design keeps the program responsive and still demonstrates the real-time response of the keyboard and joystick even with a software implementation of OpenGL.

Reading the Keyboard

Windows provides a function to asynchronously read the state of the keyboard. This allows you to ask whether a certain key is pressed, without waiting on any keyboard messages to be processed. If you have a certain set of keys set aside for player movement, you can test these keys every pass through the rendering loop. This means not a single frame is rendered without the opportunity for a key press to affect the camera position (or fire a weapon). The function is `GetAsyncKeyState`:

```
SHORT GetAsyncKeyState(int vKey);
```

You identify the virtual key (using standard Windows Virtual Key Codes) you want to test in the `vKey` parameter, and the return value tells you whether the key has been pressed since the last call and whether the key is currently up or down. If the most significant bit is set, the key is currently down. If the least significant bit is set, the key has been pressed since the last call to `GetAsyncKeyState`, but it is up. For our purposes of real-time camera movement, it is enough to test for zero. (If it is down now or was down since the last time we checked, we still count it as down.)

Reading a Joystick

Reading a joystick asynchronously is only slightly more complex. You have a function, `joyGetPos`, and a structure, `JOYINFO`. The function is defined as

```
MMRESULT joyGetPos(uJoyID, LPJOYINFO pji);
```

The first parameter, `uJoyID`, identifies which joystick you want to poll. Two values are valid: `JOYSTICKID1` and `JOYSTICKID2`. The second parameter is a pointer to a structure that will contain information about the joystick state on return. The return value should be tested against `JOYERR_NOERROR` to be sure the joystick is attached and working properly.

The `JOYINFO` structure is defined as follows:

```
typedef struct {
    UINT wXpos;
    UINT wYpos;
```

```
    UINT wZpos;
    UINT wButtons;
} JOYINFO;
```

The *wXPos*, *wYpos*, and *wZpos* values return the current x, y, and z coordinate values of the joystick. These values range from 0 to 65,536, with 32,768 being in the center position. The *wButton* parameter is set to one of four values (JOY_BUTTON1, JOY_BUTTON2, JOY_BUTTON3, or JOY_BUTTON4) if any of the four joystick buttons are pressed.

Moving the Camera

In our sample program tanksimple, we test for keyboard or joystick activity right in the rendering loop and update our viewing transformation based on the new position of our "camera." We define a simple structure to contain our camera's position and orientation:

```
struct CAMERA
    {
    float position[3];    // Camera XYZ location
    float orientation[3];    // Camera XYZ orientation
    } cameraData;
```

This is initialized in our SetupRC function:

```
// Camera initial position and orientation
// Initially at origin, slightly above the ground
cameraData.position[0] = 0.0f;
cameraData.position[1] = -0.2f;
cameraData.position[2] = -3.0f;

// Looking down negative z axis (north). Positive x is to the right
cameraData.orientation[0] = 0.0f;
cameraData.orientation[1] = 0.0f;
cameraData.orientation[2] = 0.0f;
```

Next, we update our RenderingThreadEntryPoint function, where the rendering loop is located. Here, we call a new function, UpdatePosition, passing it a pointer to the camera structure. The camera location is updated based on keyboard and joystick activity. On return, this information is then used to set the initial viewing transform:

```
// Main loop for rendering
while(1)
    {
    // Check rendering state info, terminate if flagged
    if(CheckStates())
        break;

    // Get the new camera position and update the viewing transformation
    // accordingly
```

```
    UpdatePosition(&cameraData);      // Based on joystick/keyboard

    // Position lights, and camera location
    glMatrixMode(GL_MODELVIEW);
    glLoadIdentity();      // Z-X-Y (Boom specific)

    glRotatef(cameraData.orientation[2], 0.0f, 0.0f, 1.0f);
    glRotatef(cameraData.orientation[0], 1.0f, 0.0f, 0.0f);
    glRotatef(cameraData.orientation[1], 0.0f, 1.0f, 0.0f);
    glTranslatef(-cameraData.position[0],cameraData.position[1],
                                     cameraData.position[2]);


    RenderScene();

    // Swap buffers
    SwapBuffers(hDC);
    }
```

The UpdatePosition function appears in Listing 19.8. This function moves the viewpoint based on keyboard and joystick movements but applies the time-based key framing concept. The distance traveled by a keystroke depends on the time the key is held down, not the number of keystroke tests. The same principle is used for joystick movement. Because the function is called repeatedly, if the keys are not pressed, then the net change turns out to be zero. Although a bit more complex, this method of managing camera movement (or any type of movement or animation) is what real real-time programming is all about.

Listing 19.8   *Moving the Camera Position Based on Time and User Interaction*

```
////////////////////////////////////////////////////////////////////////////
// Update the position of the camera. This function can vary widely depending
// on how motion is achieved. For a flight sim, motion will always be along the
// viewer's z axis. For a first person walking around, motion will always be in
// the xy plane. Even if the camera tilts down (to look at the ground) or up
// (to look at the sky), the player still only moves along the xy plane.
// This function must be called continuously, or the timed motion will not
// work. If this function is called only when a key press is made, then the
// time between calls will be huge and the camera will "rocket" to the new
// location with each key press
void UpdatePosition(struct CAMERA *pCamera)
    {
    float fLinearVelocity = 0.0f;
    float fAngularVelocityY = 0.0f;
    float fAngularVelocityX = 0.0f;
    float fAngularVelocityZ = 0.0f;
```

continued on next page

continued from previous page

```
float fTime,fAngle,fXDelta,fZDelta;
JOYINFO ji;
LARGE_INTEGER currentTime;

// Check joystick if present
if(joyGetPos(JOYSTICKID1, &ji) == JOYERR_NOERROR)
    {
    // Button 1 moves forward, button 2 moves backwards
    if(ji.wButtons & JOY_BUTTON1)
        fLinearVelocity = 0.8f;

    if(ji.wButtons & JOY_BUTTON2)
        fLinearVelocity = -0.8f;

    // Check for spin left/right (y axis rotation)
    // Move quicker if joystick is moved hard
    if(ji.wXpos < 20000)
        fAngularVelocityY = -15.0f;
    if(ji.wXpos < 3000)
        fAngularVelocityY = -22.0f;

    if(ji.wXpos > 45536)
        fAngularVelocityY = 15.0f;
    if(ji.wXpos > 62536)
        fAngularVelocityY = 22.0f;

    // Check for looking up and down
    if(ji.wYpos < 20000)
        fAngularVelocityX = 14.0f;
    if(ji.wYpos < 3000)
        fAngularVelocityX = 21.0f;

    if(ji.wYpos > 45536)
        fAngularVelocityX = -14.0f;
    if(ji.wYpos > 63536)
        fAngularVelocityX = - 21.0f;
    }


// Keyboard input
// Check for forward or backwards motion
if(GetAsyncKeyState(VK_UP))
    fLinearVelocity = 0.8f;
```

```
if(GetAsyncKeyState(VK_DOWN))
    fLinearVelocity = -0.8f;

// Check for spin left/right (y axis rotation)
if(GetAsyncKeyState(VK_LEFT))
    fAngularVelocityY = -14.0f;

if(GetAsyncKeyState(VK_RIGHT))
    fAngularVelocityY = 14.0f;

// Check for looking up and down
if(GetAsyncKeyState(0x41))          // A key
    fAngularVelocityX = 14.0f;

if(GetAsyncKeyState(0x5a))          // Z key
    fAngularVelocityX = -14.0f;


// Adjust position and orientation. Get the time since the last
// check. If the velocity = 0 (no keypress or mouse movement)
// then the motion will be nil...
// D = vt
QueryPerformanceCounter(&currentTime);
fTime = (float)(currentTime.QuadPart - lastTime.QuadPart)/
            (float)timerFrequency.QuadPart;
lastTime = currentTime;

// Update rotation angles (clamp the x rotation)
fAngle = fTime * fAngularVelocityX;
fAngle += pCamera->orientation[0];

if((fAngle < 90.0f) && (fAngle > -90.0f))
    pCamera->orientation[0] = fAngle;

pCamera->orientation[1] += fTime * fAngularVelocityY;

// Update linear position
fTime = fTime * fLinearVelocity;
fXDelta = fTime * (float)(sin(DEGTORAD(pCamera->orientation[1])));
fXDelta += pCamera->position[0];
fZDelta = fTime * (float)(cos(DEGTORAD(pCamera->orientation[1])));
fZDelta += pCamera->position[2];


pCamera->position[0] = fXDelta;
```

continued on next page

continued from previous page

```
pCamera->position[2] = fZDelta;

// Halt the camera at the boundaries of the virtual world.
// The maximum range for the person is +/- 95 from the center
// The boundaries of the world are +/- 100 in all directions
if(pCamera->position[0] > 95.0f)
    pCamera->position[0] = 95.0f;

if(pCamera->position[0] < -95.0f)
    pCamera->position[0] = -95.0f;

if(pCamera->position[2] > 95.0f)
    pCamera->position[2] = 95.0f;

if(pCamera->position[2] < -95.0f)
    pCamera->position[2] = -95.0f;
}
```

Make special note that this function is written specifically for our tank simulator. Movement is restricted to the xz plane, for example. The bounds of movement are arbitrarily set to +/– 95 coordinate units. (These can be anything you want them to be—yards, feet, miles, and so on—as long as you stick to one convention.) You might add collision detection to this function in the future to prevent the tank from moving through objects in the scene. It's the *flavor* of this function that is important for you to grasp. Figure 19.4 shows the tanksimple program.

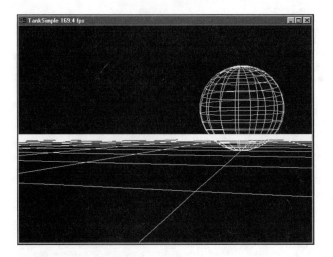

Figure 19.4   Output from the tanksimple program.

Scene Graph Basics

So far, all of our examples have been rather simplistic. To demonstrate frame rate, we spin a textured sphere faster and faster. To demonstrate camera movement with keyboard and joystick, we create another big ball, but this time put a floor under it and let the viewpoint wander around. Simply *programming* or *hard-coding* your 3D scene will not get you very far when your 3D environments start getting more complex. Image that your scene consists of hundreds or thousands of objects, all of which might be behaving independently or in special relationships to one another. Managing a complex scene can get hairy quickly.

The code you create to manage scene complexity is called your *scene graph*. Typically, you have multiple objects in a scene, each of which maintaining a relationship with other objects. For example, you might have spokes that belong to a rim, which belongs to a tire, which in turn belongs to car. Representing such a hierarchical relationship typically requires a data structure called a tree, or more generally a graph. This topic has generated no small amount of study, industry standard wars, and flame mail. Representing hierarchical relationships is also well beyond the scope of this book, but it is still of interest to us because we are studying real-time computer graphics.

We now enhance our tank-based program considerably. We add a lot more objects (models) to the scene. We also throw in some lights and texturing to give the environment a little life. To manage all these objects in our scene, we construct the simplest scene graph that you can possibly construct. It consists not of a graph data structure, but of a simple linear array of objects in the scene and information about where they are located. This simple approach will give you a good idea of the goals of a more sophisticated scene graph. As you further your studies of computer graphics with OpenGL, you'll encounter a wealth of free, open source, or public domain scene graph libraries on the Web (most are in C++). We hope that after the next two examples, you'll appreciate the work that went into these libraries.

Cluttering Up the Landscape

The next variation on the tank theme is tanksg. In this program, we add a light, a texture to the ground, and three kinds of textured objects: spheres, pyramids, and columns. We create a simple model structure that will contain an identifier for the object type and the position of the object:

```
struct MODEL {
    float position[3];
    int nObjectType;
    } *pModelList;
```

We define a value for the number of each type of model to place in our world and allocate an array to contain all the models:

```
#define MODEL_COUNT    100
. . .
// Populate the world
pModelList = (struct MODEL *)malloc(sizeof(struct MODEL) * 3 * MODEL_COUNT);
```

This means there are 100 of each of three kinds of models. That's 300 individual objects lying around on our terrain! To initialize the scene graph (actually, we could say *scene list*), we place each model at a completely random location:

```
// Populate spheres
for(nIndex = 0; nIndex < MODEL_COUNT; nIndex++)
    {
    pModelList[nIndex].nObjectType = TO_SPHERE;
    pModelList[nIndex].position[0] = RandomPos();
    pModelList[nIndex].position[1] = 0.25;
    pModelList[nIndex].position[2] = RandomPos();
    }
```

```
. . .
// Do the same for columns and pyramids
```

Our render scene function has changed substantially as well. Listing 19.9 shows the entire function. We render the ground as one large quad and we under-sample the ground texture to give it a mottled look. Then, we traverse a list of objects in our scene list (you traverse a tree for a more substantial scene graph), do whatever translation is necessary, select the appropriate texture object, and then draw the correct model. The output to tangsg is shown in Figure 19.5.

Listing 19.9   *The New Rendering Function That Traverses the List of Models*

```
//////////////////////////////////////////////////////////////////////////
// Called by rendering thread to draw scene
void RenderScene(void)
    {
    int nModel;

    // Clear the window with current clearing color
    glClear(GL_COLOR_BUFFER_BIT | GL_DEPTH_BUFFER_BIT);

    // Draw the ground
    // One big quad with a tiled texture
        glTexEnvi(GL_TEXTURE_ENV,GL_TEXTURE_ENV_MODE, GL_DECAL);
    glBindTexture(GL_TEXTURE_2D, tobjects[TO_EARTH]);
    glBegin(GL_QUADS);
```

```
    glNormal3i(0, 1, 0);
    glTexCoord2f(10.0f, 10.0f);
    glVertex3i(100, 0, -100);
    glTexCoord2f(10.0f, 0.0f);
    glVertex3i(-100,0,-100);
    glTexCoord2f(0.0f, 0.0f);
    glVertex3i(-100,0,100);
    glTexCoord2f(0.0f, 10.0f);
    glVertex3i(100, 0, 100);
glEnd();

// All other geometry is lit, modulated
glTexEnvi(GL_TEXTURE_ENV,GL_TEXTURE_ENV_MODE, GL_MODULATE);

for(nModel = 0; nModel < (MODEL_COUNT * 3); nModel++)
    {
    glPushMatrix();
    glTranslatef(pModelList[nModel].position[0],
        pModelList[nModel].position[1],    pModelList[nModel].position[2]);

    switch(pModelList[nModel].nObjectType)
        {
        case TO_SPHERE:
            glRotatef(90.0f, 1.0f, 0.0f, 0.0f);
            glBindTexture(GL_TEXTURE_2D, tobjects[TO_SPHERE]);
            gluSphere(pQuad, 0.25f, 20, 20);
            break;

        case TO_COLUMN:
            glRotatef(-90.0f, 1.0f, 0.0f, 0.0f);
            glBindTexture(GL_TEXTURE_2D, tobjects[TO_COLUMN]);
            gluCylinder(pQuad, 0.1f, 0.1f, 0.75, 15, 15);
            break;

        case TO_PYRAMID:
            glBindTexture(GL_TEXTURE_2D, tobjects[TO_PYRAMID]);
            DrawPyramid();
            break;

        }
    glPopMatrix();
    }
}
```

Figure 19.5   Output from the simple scene graph based tanksg.

What's Wrong With This Picture?

If you look carefully, you might be wondering whether Figure 19.5 was taken on the same hardware that was producing more than 300 fps on the spinning globe. Indeed it was, but now there are four textures instead of one and 300 times more objects in the scene. The overhead due to the extra textures is actually marginal. By using texture objects, we greatly speed up texture access. Also, because all the models of like textures are grouped together, we have few true texture state changes. Most drivers realize you are switching to the same texture, and the overhead for a redundant texture switch is little to nothing more than the extra function call. (You can still tune this out with a little extra work.)

The biggest problem with tanksg is all the extra geometry in the scene. We are sending OpenGL 100 spheres, 100 columns, and 100 pyramids to render each and every frame. You might notice that you don't see all 300 of these objects in the scene at once. Most of the objects are either behind your viewpoint or too far to the left or right to be seen. These models are outside the frustum (see Chapter 5, "Moving Around in Space: Coordinate Transformations"). If they aren't being drawn anyway, why are they slowing down OpenGL?

Model Culling

The reason OpenGL is choked by all the models that aren't shown is because OpenGL doesn't know what a model is. Remember that OpenGL is a low-level API and all that OpenGL understands are polygons. If a model that is positioned outside your viewing volume (the frustum) consists of 500 polygons, OpenGL tests each and every one of those polygons to see whether they should be drawn or clipped (partially drawn). If you could somehow determine which models can't be seen anyway and avoid sending them to OpenGL, you'd save a tremendous amount of processing time and thus dramatically improve your performance. This process is called model or frustum culling.

All commercial scene graph libraries (and most free ones too) have some kind of built-in support for culling objects from the scene that fall outside the view frustum. Again, we are tip-toeing into an area of computer science that has been the topic of many a paper. For our example, we are going to take a simplified approach. You'll see that even a simplified scene-management system coupled with a rudimentary scene-culling routine can produce very powerful results.

Just Plane Math

When we covered one of the methods of generating shadows in Chapter 6, "Color, Lighting, and Materials," we gave you an overview of what the math did (squishing the image into a plane) and then told you to trust us on the math. This time, the math is worse, and the explanation is not so trivial. However, we can take a few shortcuts and use a less-than-rigorous approach that will still yield significant results.

Figure 19.6 shows a frustum volume. There is one object inside the frustum and another object outside the frustum. The trick is, given the dimensions of the frustum (taken from the parameters given to `gluPerspective`) and the location and size of an object, finding out whether the object is inside or outside the frustum. Recall that a frustum is wider at the back than at the front. For a rigorous approach, you can take the corners of the frustum and construct six plane equations to describe each face. Then, you determine the distance from the center of your model to each of the planes. If the distance is greater than the size of a bounding sphere, then the model is outside the frustum. Many methods have been devised to improve on this, such as testing axis-aligned bounding boxes (a slight improvement over the bounding sphere approximation).

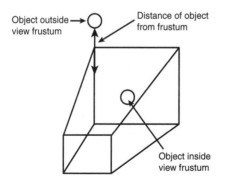

Figure 19.6 Objects inside and outside the viewing frustum.

Shortcuts Rule!

Any programmer worth her salt knows that shortcuts are what get projects done on time, beat performance goals, and generally pay the bills on a regular basis. The previously described method of frustum culling is a good approach (arguably, the best) but requires a lot of work, and fully explaining it is a bit beyond the aim of this book. A little ingenuity will show you that any means you can use to eliminate objects from the pipeline is better than just throwing your entire scene at OpenGL every frame.

We can make a couple of observations about our tank scenario, which we incorporate into our tankculled sample program. The first is that all objects are lying in the plane of our sight. There are no objects above or below us, nor will there ever be. Thus, we have eliminated two tests immediately (the top and bottom planes of the frustum). As you can see, even for a rigorous approach, we can find ways to shave tests and calculations.

Note we used the following call to `gluPerspective` to set up our viewing volume:

```
gluPerspective(35.0f, fAspect, 0.5f, 50.0f);
```

This puts the back of the frustum 50 units away. If we approximate the frustum with a sphere of sufficient radius to encompass the frustum and place it in the center of our viewing volume, we can devise a simple test. It is extremely simple to determine whether a point (or model) is inside a sphere. If the distance between the two centers is greater than the radius of the sphere (minus the radius of the models bounding sphere), we know we can drop the geometry. Figure 19.7 shows the frustum and our spherical approximation.

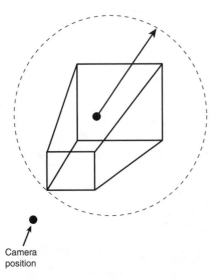

Camera
position

Figure 19.7 Using a spherical approximation for the view frustum.

The following code shows some changes we make to our rendering code to calculate the center of our frustum based on our camera's position and orientation. We then find the distance between this point and any models considered for rendering. If the distance is less than the radius of our test sphere, then we render it; if not, we drop it:

```
// Translate the frustum center by the camera translation
fCenterX = cameraData.position[0];
fCenterZ = -cameraData.position[2];

// Extend the point outward
fCenterX += sin(DEGTORAD(cameraData.orientation[1]))*25.0;
fCenterZ -= cos(DEGTORAD(cameraData.orientation[1]))*25.0;

for(nModel = 0; nModel < (MODEL_COUNT * 3); nModel++)
    {
    // If the model center is outside the sphere/frustum eliminate it
    if( ((fCenterX - pModelList[nModel].position[0])*
        (fCenterX - pModelList[nModel].position[0])
        + (fCenterZ - pModelList[nModel].position[2])*
        (fCenterZ - pModelList[nModel].position[2]))
        > (30.0 * 30.0))
        {
        nCulled ++;
        continue;
        }
```

Note that instead of taking the square root of the difference between the points and comparing to 30, we compare them to 30 squared. This saves an expensive call to the sqrt function. Figure 19.8 shows our new and improved (culled) tank program, with a substantially better frame rate. Motion with this version will be smooth and regular throughout the virtual world.

Figure 19.8   The new and improved culled tank scene.

Other Real-Time Techniques

The art of performance tuning is something that you will practice and pursue throughout your professional career. You can tune for one specific 3D graphics hardware platform through trial and error if necessary, but getting the best performance on a wide range of host environments takes some practice. We do have few tips and general guidelines to help you along the way.

Direct X

That's right; use Direct X! If you don't use Direct X, at least use some other similar technology for Windows. Direct X is a family of APIs that enable high-performance multimedia applications to run better on PCs. Although it does suffer from an inferior 3D graphics API (sic), it does have other useful features. *DirectSound* can make sound effects instantaneous and can take advantage of 3D sound hardware if present. *DirectInput* can give you even faster polling times for the keyboard, mouse, and joystick. *DirectInput* has a rich API for dealing with joysticks, especially over the `getJoyPos` function that we used, and can even support force feedback devices.

Furthermore, the *DirectPlay* interface gives you a ready-to-use network infrastructure for networked games. Although you cannot use *DirectDraw* for blitting with OpenGL, you can still use it to arbitrarily set the display mode resolution and color depth before creating your OpenGL window.

General OpenGL Performance Tips

Some OpenGL performance tips can help you get the fastest rendering. Use texture objects for texture management, and use the texture object prioritization mechanism to keep large, frequently used textures loaded on the graphics card. Use display lists over vertex arrays when you have lit geometry, but do not put texture loads in a display list. (Use texture objects!) Do not use the OpenGL rasterization functions when possible because they are very slow on PC hardware. If you want to create text output onscreen, resist the urge to use `wglUseFontBitmaps`. Instead, create a series of texture-mapped quads, using a different letter for each texture. Then, you can assemble them to create whatever text output you need. If you really need high-quality text output, use the Windows GDI to render a string into a bitmap, and then use that bitmap as the source for an OpenGL texture.

One of the most often overlooked optimization techniques is state sorting. Most drivers incur an enormous penalty for state changes such as turning lighting on and off. It's better to trade off some extra transformation work for rendering all textured lit objects at once, then all textured unlit objects, then all untextured unlit objects, and so on. Even though texture objects are fast, it is still wise to sort their usage as well to prevent thrashing textures in and out of local texture memory.

Finally, reduce geometry whenever possible. Cull objects that won't be seen because they are not in the viewing volume or because they are hidden behind some object. An example of this is rendering the contents of a house when the viewpoint is outside the house (unless you're looking in the window). Another effective technique similar to texture mipmapping is geometric LOD (level of detail). Use lower resolution models with less geometry for objects that are far away and higher resolution models when they are close and the detail makes more of a visual difference.

Summary

In this chapter, we give you a glimpse into applying OpenGL in a real-time environment. You saw how on the WIN32 platform to create your rendering loops to get the maximum frame rate for a given application. We showed you how to create a rendering thread to achieve the best consistent overall frame rates and how to communicate GUI and application data to that thread. Finally, we demonstrated that culling unneeded geometry from the OpenGL pipeline is perhaps one of the most valuable optimization techniques you can apply.

We have only scratched the surface of this exciting discipline. Now, equipped with a knowledge of the OpenGL API and the fundamentals of how to achieve your desired graphical effects, you are ready to begin learning more of the discipline of computer graphics. Entire books will dwell on the topic of this chapter alone, and you will never run out of new and exciting techniques to apply to your work. We even included some of our favorite graphics books in Appendix B, "Further Reading," if you want a good place to start!

PART 4

Appendixes

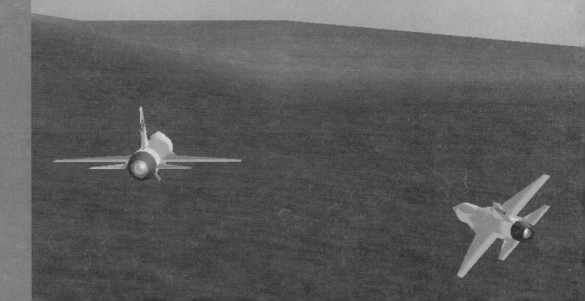

A
SUMMARY OF OPENGL UPDATES

The first edition of this book provided coverage of OpenGL 1.0. There have been two major revisions since the original July 1992 release of version 1.0. At the time the first edition of this book was published, OpenGL 1.1 was just being released and rapidly becoming popular. There is usually some lag between the time a new OpenGL spec is approved and the time hardware and operating system vendors begin releasing implementations. This was true of OpenGL 1.1 and turns out to also be true of OpenGL 1.2. While this book is being written, at least one software implementation of OpenGL 1.2 is available (MESA). Hardware vendors are releasing OpenGL 1.2 functionality in their 1.1 drivers by means of the OpenGL extension mechanism. By the time this book is available in stores, hardware implementations for the PC should be gaining some ground. Here, we list the highlights of each new OpenGL release since 1.0 and the chapter that covers the material.

Version 1.1 (December 1995)

Vertex array functions	Chapter 9, "3D Modeling and Object Composition"
Polygon offset	Chapter 11, "Buffers: Not Just for Animation"
Internal texture image formats	Chapter 8, "Texture Mapping"
Texture replace environment	Chapter 8
Texture proxies	Chapter 8
Copy texture and subtexture	Chapter 8
Texture objects	Chapter 8

Version 1.2 (March 1998)

Three-dimensional texturing	Chapter 8
BGRA pixel formats	Chapter 8
Packed pixel formats	Chapter 8
Normal rescaling	Chapter 6, "Color, Lighting, and Materials"
Separate specular color	Chapter 8
Texture coordinate edge clamping	Chapter 8
Texture level of detail control	Chapter 8
Vertex array draw element range	Chapter 9
Imaging subset	Chapter 15, "Imaging with OpenGL"

B

FURTHER READING

Real-time 3D graphics and OpenGL are popular topics, and there is more information and techniques in practice than can ever be published in a single book. You might find the following resources helpful as you further your knowledge and experience.

Windows Programming Books

Windows 95 Win32 Programming API Bible. Richard J. Simon. Waite Group Press, 1996.

Programming Windows, Fifth Edition. Charles Petzold. Microsoft Press, 1998.

OpenGL Books

OpenGL Programming Guide, 2nd Edition: The Official Guide to Learning OpenGL, Version 1.1. OpenGL Architecture Board, Mason Woo, Jackie Neider, and Tom Davis. Addison-Wesley, 1997.

OpenGL Programming for the X Window System. Mark J. Kilgard. Addison-Wesley, 1996.

Interactive Computer Graphics: A Top-Down Approach with OpenGL, Second Edition. Edward Angel, Addison-Wesley, 1999.

3D Graphics Books

3D Computer Graphics. Alan Watt. Addison-Wesley, 1993.

Advanced Animation and Rendering Techniques: Theory and Practice. Alan Watt and Mark Watt (contributor). Addison-Wesley, 1992.

Introduction to Computer Graphics. James D. Foley, Andries van Dam, Steven K. Feiner, John F. Hughes, and Richard L. Phillips. Addison-Wesley, 1993.

Open Geometry: OpenGL + Advanced Geometry. Georg Glaeser and Hellmuth Stachel. Springer-Verlag, 1999.

The Web

`http://www.opengl.org`	The Official OpenGL Web site
`http://www.starstonesoftware.com/OpenGL`	OpenGL SuperBible's Authors' Web site
`http://www.mesa3d.org`	The Mesa Web site
`http://reality.sgi.com/opengl/glut3/glut3.html`	The GLUT Home Page

C

THE OPENGL STATE MACHINE

The rendering state is one of the things that make OpenGL so fast and efficient at drawing 3D graphics. This state is grouped logically into different categories such as color, lighting, texturing, and so forth. Each rendering context (HRC) that you create has its own rendering state specific to a window or offscreen bitmap.

This appendix does not contain any complete sample programs. Rather, you will find these state functions used in examples in most of the chapters in the book.

Basic OpenGL State Functions

OpenGL's two functions that enable and disable rendering features are called, appropriately enough, glEnable and glDisable. You pass these functions a single enumerated constant, such as GL_DEPTH_TEST, as follows:

```
glEnable(GL_DEPTH_TEST);    /* Enable depth buffer testing */
glDisable(GL_DEPTH_TEST);   /* Disable depth buffer testing */
```

You can retrieve the current state using glIsEnabled, glIsDisabled, and glGetBooleanv, as in the following:

```
GLboolean state;

/*
 * GL_TRUE if depth testing is enabled...
 */
state = glIsEnabled(GL_DEPTH_TEST);

/*
 * GL_TRUE if depth testing is disabled...
 */
```

```
state = glIsDisabled(GL_DEPTH_TEST);

/*
 * Returns Boolean state value; GL_TRUE if depth testing is enabled...
 */
glGetBooleanv(GL_DEPTH_TEST, &state);
```

Most OpenGL state variables are Boolean values, on or off. Some, like the current viewport, are an array of integers or an array of floating-point numbers for the current RGBA color. To address these types of state values, OpenGL adds `glGetDoublev`, `glGetFloatv`, and `glGetInteger`:

```
GLint      istate[4];
GLfloat    fstate[4];
GLdouble   dstate[3];

glGetIntegerv(GL_VIEWPORT, istate);
glGetFloatv(GL_CURRENT_COLOR, fstate);
glGetDoublev(GL_CURRENT_NORMAL, dstate);
```

You'll learn more about the various state variables later in this appendix.

Saving and Restoring States

Just as OpenGL maintains a stack of projection, modelview, and texture matrices, it has a stack for the current rendering state. Unlike the matrix stack, the state stack gives you much more control over exactly what you save (push) or restore (pop) from the stack (see Figure C.1).

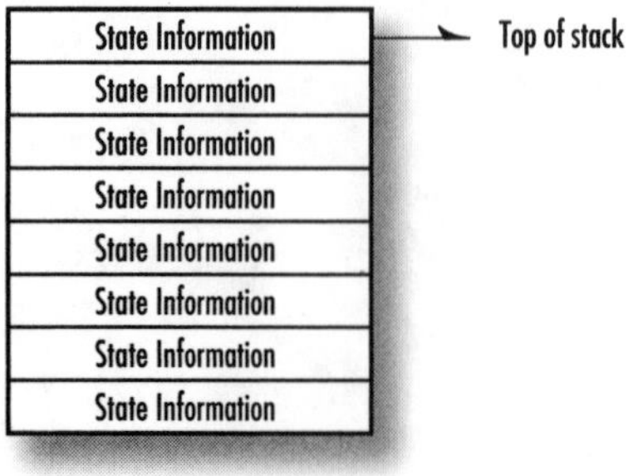

Figure C.1 The OpenGL attribute stack.

The OpenGL functions to save and restore rendering state attributes are `glPushAttrib` and `glPopAttrib`. The `glPushAttrib` function works a lot like `glPushMatrix`, except that you can select the state values to put on the stack. To save all of the current rendering state, you call

```
glPushAttrib(GL_ALL_ATTRIB_BITS);
```

Usually, however, you're only interested in saving a specific set of information, such as the current color, line width, and so forth. OpenGL defines many constants for specific types of information (see Table C.1):

```
glPushAttrib(GL_CURRENT_BIT);    /* Save current drawing color, etc */
glPushAttrib(GL_LIGHTING_BIT);   /* Save current lighting settings */
glPushAttrib(GL_TEXTURING_BIT);  /* Save current texturing settings */
```

Once you have done your rendering, you restore those state bits with `glPopAttrib`. This function accepts no arguments and restores only what was saved with the last `glPushAttrib`.

Table C.1 `glPushAttrib` *Attribute Bits*

Attribute Bit	Description
GL_ACCUM_BUFFER_BIT	Accumulation buffer clear value.
GL_COLOR_BUFFER_BIT	Alpha test state, function, and values. Blending state, function, and values. GL_DITHER state. Current drawing buffers. Current logical operation state and function. Current RGBA/index clear color and write masks.
GL_CURRENT_BIT	Current RGBA color or color index. Current lighting normal and texture coordinate. Current raster position, GL_CURRENT_RASTER_POSITION_VALID, and GL_EDGE_FLAG.
GL_DEPTH_BUFFER_BIT	GL_DEPTH_TEST state, depth buffer function, depth buffer clear value, and GL_DEPTH_WRITEMASK state.
GL_ENABLE_BIT	GL_ALPHA_TEST, GL_AUTO_NORMAL, and GL_BLEND state. User-defined clipping plane state. GL_COLOR_MATERIAL, GL_CULL_FACE, GL_DEPTH_TEST, GL_DITHER, GL_FOG, GL_LIGHT, GL_LIGHTING, GL_LINE_SMOOTH, GL_LINE_STIPPLE, GL_LOGIC_OP, GL_MAP1_x, GL_MAP2_x, GL_NORMALIZE, GL_POINT_SMOOTH, GL_POLYGON_SMOOTH, GL_POLYGON_STIPPLE, GL_SCISSOR_TEST, GL_STENCIL_TEST, GL_TEXTURE_1D, GL_TEXTURE_2D, and GL_TEXTURE_GEN_x states.
GL_EVAL_BIT	GL_MAP1_x and GL_MAP2_x state, 1D and 2D grid endpoints and divisions, GL_AUTO_NORMAL state.
GL_FOG_BIT	GL_FOG state, fog color, fog density, linear fog start, linear fog end, fog index, GL_FOG_MODE value.
GL_HINT_BIT	GL_PERSPECTIVE_CORRECTION_HINT, GL_POINT_SMOOTH_HINT, GL_LINE_SMOOTH_HINT, GL_POLYGON_SMOOTH_HINT, and GL_FG_HINT state.

continued on next page

continued from previous page

Attribute Bit	Description
GL_LIGHTING_BIT	GL_COLOR_MATERIAL state. GL_COLOR_MATERIAL_FACE value. Color material parameters that are tracking the ambient scene color. GL_LIGHT_MODEL_LOCAL_VIEWER and GL_LIGHT_MODEL_TWO_SIDE values. GL_LIGHTING and GL_LIGHTx states. All light parameters. GL_SHADE_MODEL value.
GL_LINE_BIT	GL_LINE_SMOOTH and GL_LINE_STIPPLE states. Line stipple pattern and repeat counter. Line width.
GL_LIST_BIT	GL_LIST_BASE value.
GL_PIXEL_MODE_BIT	GL_RED_BIAS, GL_RED_SCALE, GL_GREEN_BIAS, GL_GREEN_SCALE, GL_BLUE_BIAS, GL_BLUE_SCALE, GL_ALPHA_BIAS, GL_ALPHA_SCALE, GL_DEPTH_BIAS, GL_DEPTH_SCALE, GL_INDEX_OFFSET, GL_INDEX_SHIFT, GL_MAP_COLOR, GL_MAP_DEPTH, GL_ZOOM_X, GL_ZOOM_Y, and GL_READ_BUFFER settings.
GL_POINT_BIT	GL_POINT_SMOOTH state, point size.
GL_POLYGON_BIT	GL_CULL_FACE, GL_CULL_FACE_MODE, GL_FRONT_FACE, GL_POLYGON_MODE, GL_POLYGON_SMOOTH, GL_POLYGON_STIPPLE.
GL_POLYGON_STIPPLE_BIT	Polygon stipple image.
GL_SCISSOR_BIT	GL_SCISSOR_TEST state, scissor box.
GL_STENCIL_BUFFER_BIT	GL_STENCIL_TEST state. Stencil function and reference value. Stencil value mask. Stencil fail, pass, and depth buffer pass action. Stencil buffer clear value and writemask.
GL_TEXTURE_BIT	Enable bits for all texture coordinates. Border color for each texture image. Minification filter and magnification filter. Texture coordinates and wrap modes. Color and mode for each texture environment. GL_TEXTURE_GEN_x, GL_TEXTURE_GEN_MODE settings. glTexGen plane equations.
GL_TRANSFORM_BIT	Coefficients of the six clipping planes, enable bits for the clipping planes, GL_MATRIX_MODE setting, GL_NORMALIZE state.
GL_VIEWPORT_BIT	Depth range, viewport origin, andextent.

Drawing States

OpenGL has a large number of states associated with drawing actions for the basic glBegin/glEnd primitives. Most are saved with a call to glPushAttrib(GL_CURRENT_BIT ¦ GL_LINE_BIT). See Table C.2.

Table C.2   *Drawing State Variables*

State Variable	Description
GL_ALPHA_TEST	Do alpha value testing.
GL_BLEND	Perform pixel blending operations.
GL_CLIP_PLANEx	Clip drawing operations outside the specified clipping plane.
GL_CULL_FACE	Cull back- or front-facing polygons.
GL_DITHER	Dither color values.
GL_LINE_SMOOTH	Anti-alias lines.
GL_LINE_STIPPLE	Apply a bit pattern to lines.
GL_LOGIC_OP	Do logical operations on pixels when drawing.
GL_POINT_SMOOTH	Anti-alias points.
GL_POLYGON_SMOOTH	Anti-alias polygons.
GL_POLYGON_STIPPLE	Apply a bit pattern to polygons.
GL_SCISSOR_TEST	Clip drawing outside the glScissor region.

Depth Buffer States

The most common mistake made by beginning OpenGL programmers is to forget to enable depth testing with glEnable(GL_DEPTH_TEST). Without depth testing, hidden surface removal is not performed using the depth buffer. Calling glPushAttrib with GL_DEPTH_BUFFER_BIT takes care of saving the GL_DEPTH_TEST state.

Stencil Buffer States

The stencil buffer supports many special effects, including shadows. Like the depth buffer, however, the stencil buffer is easy to control. Save stencil buffer state information with glPushAttrib(GL_STENCIL_BUFFER_BIT), which saves the current GL_STENCIL_TEST value.

Lighting States

Of all the OpenGL features, lighting has the most OpenGL state information. The state information for lighting includes the current lighting environment (model) settings for color and lighting mode; material definitions; the color, position, and direction of light; and other parameters. Moreover, OpenGL adds even more state information with automatic lighting normal generation.

Table C.3 lists all the available variables. At the minimum, you need to call glEnable(GL_LIGHTING) and glEnable(GL_LIGHT0). To save the current lighting state, call glPushAttrib(GL_LIGHTING_BIT | GL_EVAL_BIT).

Table C.3 *Lighting State Variables*

State Variable	Description
GL_AUTO_NORMAL	Automatically generate lighting normals from glMap parameters.
GL_COLOR_MATERIAL	Assign material colors from the current drawing color.
GL_LIGHTING	Enable lighting calculations.
GL_LIGHT*x*	Enable light *x*.
GL_MAP1_NORMAL	Enable mapping of lighting normals from 1D coordinates.
GL_MAP2_NORMAL	Enable mapping of lighting normals from 2D coordinates.
GL_NORMALIZE	Normalize all lighting normals prior to doing calculations.

Texturing States

In terms of complexity, texturing in OpenGL is second only to lighting. Table C.4 lists the available variables.

To save the current texturing parameters, call **glEnable** with **GL_TEXTURE_BIT** and **GL_EVAL_BIT**. When you're enabling texturing, make sure to enable only one of the texturing modes—either **GL_TEXTURE_1D** or **GL_TEXTURE_2D**. The OpenGL spec states that 2D texturing overrides 1D texturing, but some implementations do not comply with this.

Table C.4 *Texturing State Variables*

State Variable	Description
GL_MAP1_TEXTURE_COORD_1	The s texture coordinate will be generated by calls to glEvalPoint1, glEvalMesh1, and glEvalCoord1.
GL_MAP1_TEXTURE_COORD_2	The s and t texture coordinates will be generated by calls to glEvalPoint1, glEvalMesh1, and glEvalCoord1.
GL_MAP1_TEXTURE_COORD_3	The s, t, and r texture coordinates will be generated by calls to glEvalPoint1, glEvalMesh1, and glEvalCoord1.
GL_MAP1_TEXTURE_COORD_4	The s, t, r, and q texture coordinates will be generated by calls to glEvalPoint1, glEvalMesh1, and glEvalCoord1.
GL_MAP2_TEXTURE_COORD_1	The s texture coordinate will be generated by calls to glEvalPoint2, glEvalMesh2, and glEvalCoord2.
GL_MAP2_TEXTURE_COORD_2	The s and t texture coordinates will be generated by calls to glEvalPoint2, glEvalMesh2, and glEvalCoord2.
GL_MAP2_TEXTURE_COORD_3	The s, t, and r texture coordinates will be generated by calls to glEvalPoint2, glEvalMesh2, and glEvalCoord2.

State Variable	Description
GL_MAP2_TEXTURE_COORD_4	The s, t, r, and q texture coordinates will be generated by calls to glEvalPoint2, glEvalMesh2, and glEvalCoord2.
GL_TEXTURE_1D	Enable 1D texturing unless 2D texturing is enabled.
GL_TEXTURE_2D	Enable 2D texturing.
GL_TEXTURE_GEN_Q	Automatically generate the q texture coordinate from calls to glVertex.
GL_TEXTURE_GEN_R	Automatically generate the r texture coordinate from calls to glVertex.
GL_TEXTURE_GEN_S	Automatically generate the s texture coordinate from calls to glVertex.
GL_TEXTURE_GEN_T	Automatically generate the t texture coordinate from calls to glVertex.

Pixel States

Pixel transfer, storage, and mapping modes are probably the least understood and least optimized OpenGL features. Save them with a call to glPushAttrib(GL_PIXEL_BIT). There are no glEnable states for these modes.

Reference Section

glDisable, glEnable

Purpose	Disables or enables an OpenGL feature.
Include File	<GL/gl.h>
Syntax	void glDisable(GLenum feature); glEnable
Description	glDisable disables an OpenGL drawing feature, and glEnable enables an OpenGL drawing feature.
Parameters	
feature	GLenum: The feature to disable or enable from Table C.5.
Returns	None.
See Also	glIsEnabled, glPopAttrib, glPushAttrib

Table C.5   *Features Enabled/Disabled by* `glEnable/glDisable`

Feature	Description
GL_AUTO_NORMAL	Automatically generate lighting normals from `glMap` parameters.
GL_COLOR_MATERIAL	Assign material colors from the current drawing color.
GL_LIGHTING	Enable lighting calculations.
GL_LIGHTx	Enable light *x*.
GL_MAP1_NORMAL	Enable mapping of lighting normals from 1D coordinates.
GL_MAP2_NORMAL	Enable mapping of lighting normals from 2D coordinates.
GL_NORMALIZE	Normalize all lighting normals prior to doing calculations.
GL_MAP1_TEXTURE_COORD_1	The s texture coordinate will be generated by calls to `glEvalPoint1`, `glEvalMesh1`, and `glEvalCoord1`.
GL_MAP1_TEXTURE_COORD_2	The s and t texture coordinates will be generated by calls to `glEvalPoint1`, `glEvalMesh1`, and `glEvalCoord1`.
GL_MAP1_TEXTURE_COORD_3	The s, t, and r texture coordinates will be generated by calls to `glEvalPoint1`, `glEvalMesh1`, and `glEvalCoord1`.
GL_MAP1_TEXTURE_COORD_4	The s, t, r, and q texture coordinates will be generated by calls to `glEvalPoint1`, `glEvalMesh1`, and `glEvalCoord1`.
GL_MAP2_TEXTURE_COORD_1	The s texture coordinate will be generated by calls to `glEvalPoint2`, `glEvalMesh2`, and `glEvalCoord2`.
GL_MAP2_TEXTURE_COORD_2	The s and t texture coordinates will be generated by calls to `glEvalPoint2`, `glEvalMesh2`, and `glEvalCoord2`.
GL_MAP2_TEXTURE_COORD_3	The s, t, and r texture coordinates will be generated by calls to `glEvalPoint2`, `glEvalMesh2`, and `glEvalCoord2`.
GL_MAP2_TEXTURE_COORD_4	The s, t, r, and q texture coordinates will be generated by calls to `glEvalPoint2`, `glEvalMesh2`, and `glEvalCoord2`.
GL_TEXTURE_1D	Enable 1D texturing unless 2D texturing is enabled.
GL_TEXTURE_2D	Enable 2D texturing.
GL_TEXTURE_GEN_Q	Automatically generate the q texture coordinate from calls to `glVertex`.
GL_TEXTURE_GEN_R	Automatically generate the r texture coordinate from calls to `glVertex`.
GL_TEXTURE_GEN_S	Automatically generate the s texture coordinate from calls to `glVertex`.
GL_TEXTURE_GEN_T	Automatically generate the t texture coordinate from calls to `glVertex`.
GL_STENCIL_TEST	Enable stencil buffer comparisons.
GL_DEPTH_TEST	Enable depth buffer comparisons.

Feature	Description
GL_ALPHA_TEST	Do alpha value testing.
GL_BLEND	Perform pixel blending operations.
GL_CLIP_PLANEx	Clip drawing operations outside the specified clipping plane.
GL_CULL_FACE	Cull back- or front-facing polygons.
GL_DITHER	Dither color values.
GL_LINE_SMOOTH	Anti-alias lines.
GL_LINE_STIPPLE	Apply a bit pattern to lines.
GL_LOGIC_OP	Do logical operations on pixels when drawing.
GL_POINT_SMOOTH	Anti-alias points.
GL_POLYGON_SMOOTH	Anti-alias polygons.
GL_POLYGON_STIPPLE	Apply a bit pattern to polygons.
GL_SCISSOR_TEST	Clip drawing outside the glScissor region.

glIsEnabled

Purpose	Tests whether an OpenGL feature is enabled.
Include File	<GL/gl.h>
Syntax	GLboolean glIsEnabled(GLenum *feature*);
Description	This function returns GL_TRUE if the specified feature has been enabled and GL_FALSE otherwise.
Parameters	
feature	GLenum: The feature to test (see glEnable).
Returns	GLboolean: GL_TRUE if the feature is enabled; GL_FALSE otherwise.
See Also	glDisable, glEnable, glPopAttrib, glPushAttrib

glPopAttrib

Purpose	Restores state information saved with glPushAttib.
Include File	<GL/gl.h>
Syntax	void glPopAttrib(void);
Description	glPopAttrib restores previously saved state information from a call to glPushAttrib. If the attribute stack is empty, the current OpenGL error state is set, and the call is ignored.
Parameters	None.
Returns	None.
See Also	glDisable, glEnable, glIsEnabled, glPushAttrib

glPushAttrib

Purpose	Saves OpenGL state information.
Include File	<GL/gl.h>
Syntax	void glPushAttrib(GLuint *bits*);
Description	This function saves OpenGL state information specified by *bits*. If the attribute stack is full, the current OpenGL error state is set, and the top of the stack is overwritten.
Parameters	
bits	GLuint: The state information to save (see Table C.1).
Returns	None.
See Also	glDisable, glEnable, glIsEnabled, glPopAttrib

GLOSSARY

Alpha   A fourth color value added to provide a degree of transparency to the color of an object. An alpha value of 0.0 means complete transparency: 1.0 denotes no transparency (opaque).

Ambient light   Light in a scene that doesn't come from any specific point source or direction. Ambient light illuminates all surfaces evenly and on all sides.

Anti-aliasing   A rendering method used to smooth lines and curves and polygon edges. This technique averages the color of pixels adjacent to the line. It has the visual effect of softening the transition from the pixels on the line and those adjacent to the line, thus providing a smoother appearance.

ARB   The Architecture Review Board. The OpenGL ARB meets quarterly and consists of 3D graphics hardware vendors. The ARB maintains the OpenGL Specification document and promotes the OpenGL standard.

Aspect ratio   The ratio of the width of a window to the height of the window. Specifically, the width of the window in pixels divided by the height of the window in pixels.

AUX library   A window system independent utility library. Limited but useful for quick and portable OpenGL demonstration programs. Now largely replaced by the GLUT library.

Bézier curve   A curve whose shape is defined by control points near the curve rather than by the precise set of points that define the curve itself.

Bitplane   An array of bits mapped directly to screen pixels.

Buffer   An area of memory used to store image information. This can be color, depth, or blending information. The red, green, blue, and alpha buffers are often collectively referred to as the *color buffers*.

Cartesian   A coordinate system based on three directional axes placed at a 90° orientation to one another. These coordinates are labeled x, y, and z.

Clipping   The elimination of a portion of a single primitive or group of primitives. The points that would be rendered outside the clipping region or volume are not drawn. The *clipping volume* is generally specified by the projection matrix.

Color index mode   A color mode in which colors in a scene are selected from a fixed number of colors available in a palette. These entries are referenced by an index into the palette. This mode is rarely used and even more rarely hardware accelerated.

Convex   Refers to the shape of a polygon. A convex polygon has no indentations, and no straight line can be drawn through the polygon that intersects it more than twice (once entering, once leaving).

Culling   The elimination of graphics primitives that would not be seen if rendered. Backface culling eliminates the front or back face of a primitive so that the face isn't drawn. Frustum culling eliminates whole objects that would fall outside the viewing frustum.

Display list   A compiled list of OpenGL functions and commands. When called, a display list executes faster than a manually called list of single commands.

Dithering   A method used to simulate a wider range of color depth by placing different-colored pixels together in patterns that give the illusion of shading between the two colors.

Double buffered   A drawing technique used by OpenGL. The image to be displayed is assembled in memory and then placed on the screen in a single update operation, as opposed to building the image primitive-by-primitive on the screen. Double buffering is a much faster and smoother update operation and can produce animations.

Extruded   The process of taking a 2D image or shape and adding a third dimension uniformly across the surface. This can transform 2D fonts into 3D lettering.

Eye coordinates   The coordinate system based on the position of the viewer. The viewer's position is placed along the positive z-axis, looking down the negative z-axis.

Frustum   A pyramid-shaped viewing volume that creates a perspective view. (Near objects are large; far objects are small.)

GLUT library   The OpenGL utility library. A window system independent utility library useful for creating sample programs and simple 3D rendering programs that are independent of the operating system and windowing system. Typically used to provide portability between Windows, X-Window, Linux, and so on.

Immediate mode   A graphics rendering mode in which commands and functions have an immediate effect on the state of the rendering engine.

Literal   A value, not a variable name. A specific string or numeric constant embedded directly in source code.

Matrix   A 2D array of numbers. Matrices can be operated on mathematically and are used to perform coordinate transformations.

Modelview matrix   The OpenGL matrix that transforms primitives to eye coordinates from object coordinates.

Normal   A directional vector that points perpendicularly to a plane or surface. When used, normals must be specified for each vertex in a primitive.

Normalize   Refers to the reduction of a normal to a unit normal. A *unit normal* is a vector that has a length of exactly 1.0.

NURBS   An acronym for non-uniform rational b-spline. This is a method of specifying parametric curves and surfaces.

Open Inventor   A C++ class library and toolkit for building interactive 3D applications. Open Inventor is built on OpenGL.

Orthographic   A drawing mode in which no perspective or foreshortening takes place. Also called *parallel projection*. The lengths and dimensions of all primitives are undistorted regardless of orientation or distance from the viewer.

Palette   A set of colors available for drawing operations. For 8-bit Windows color modes, the palette contains 256 color entries, and all pixels in the scene can only be colored from this set.

Parametric curve   A curve whose shape is determined by one (for a curve) or two (for a surface) parameters. These parameters are used in separate equations that yield the individual x, y, and z values of the points along the curve.

Perspective   A drawing mode in which objects farther from the viewer appear smaller than nearby objects.

Pixel   Condensed from the words *picture element*. This is the smallest visual division available on the computer screen. Pixels are arranged in rows and columns and are individually set to the appropriate color to render any given image.

Polygon   A 2D shape drawn with any number of sides (must be at least three sides).

Primitive   A 2D polygonal shape defined by OpenGL. All objects and scenes are composed of various combinations of primitives.

Projection   The transformation of lines, points, and polygons from eye coordinates to clipping coordinates on the screen.

Quadrilateral   A polygon with exactly four sides.

Rasterize   The process of converting projected primitives and bitmaps into pixel fragments in the frame buffer.

Render   The conversion of primitives in object coordinates to an image in the frame buffer. The *rendering pipeline* is the process by which OpenGL commands and statements become pixels on the screen.

Spline   A general term used to describe any curve created by placing control points near the curve, which have a pulling effect on the curve's shape. This is similar to the reaction of a piece of flexible material when pressure is applied at various points along its length.

Stipple   A binary bit pattern used to mask out pixel generation in the frame buffer. This is similar to a monochrome bitmap, but one-dimensional patterns are used for lines and two-dimensional patterns are used for polygons.

Tessellation   The process of breaking down a complex polygon or analytic surface into a mesh of convex polygons. This can also be applied to separate a complex curve into a series of less complex lines.

Texel   Similar to pixel (picture element), a texel is a texture element. A texel represents a color from a texture that is applied to a pixel fragment in the frame buffer.

Texture   An image pattern of colors applied to the surface of a primitive.

Texture mapping   The process of applying a texture image to a surface. The surface does not have to be planar (flat). Texture mapping is often used to wrap an image around a curved object or to produce patterned surfaces such as wood or marble.

Transformation   The manipulation of a coordinate system. This can include rotation, translation, scaling (both uniform and nonuniform), and perspective division.

Translucence   A degree of transparency of an object. In OpenGL, this is represented by an alpha value ranging from 1.0 (opaque) to 0.0 (transparent).

Vertex   A single point in space. Except when used for point and line primitives, it also defines the point at which two edges of a polygon meet.

Viewing volume   The area in 3D space that can be viewed in the window. Objects and points outside the viewing volume are clipped (cannot be seen).

Viewport   The area within a window that is used to display an OpenGL image. Usually, this encompasses the entire client area. Stretched viewports can produce enlarged or shrunken output within the physical window.

Wireframe   The representation of a solid object by a mesh of lines rather than solid shaded polygons. Wireframe models are usually rendered faster and can be used to view both the front and back of an object at the same time.

INDEX

F

Waite Group
P R E S S

The mission of Waite Group Press is to provide professional programmers with the books and information products they need to build valuable and creative technology solutions. The hallmarks of Waite Group Press are quality, accuracy, focus, and innovation.

At Waite Group Press, we believe in

- Publishing on topics of keen interest to professional programmers
- Seeing the world from the programmer's perspective and offering books and information products that meet that interest and need
- An unfailing dedication to quality, accuracy, and utility
- Innovation—the vision to see beyond the obvious
- Investing in our authors
- Giving back to the community

Why Waite?

In a recent study conducted by RDI Marketing Services of Cincinnati, Ohio, Waite Group Press garnered a very high name recognition score among professional programmers and system administrators. More than 44% of those surveyed were familiar with Waite Group Press. Those recognizing Waite Group Press reported a high degree of satisfaction with the usability, author selection, and overall quality of Waite Group Press products.

Why now?

Waite Group Press has always been on the forefront of change in technology. The start of the 21st century represents a phenomenal time of growth for programmers working with new technologies such as Linux, Java, and the Internet. Waite Group Press is poised to contribute by providing the foundational information necessary to fuel the minds who drive innovation and by publishing content designed to highlight and promote new technologies.

Crusader Series

Most Waite Group Press books are designed to inform and enlighten readers by addressing specific programming technologies. Following in the tradition of Robert Lafore's classic *Object-Oriented Programming in C++*, each book offers a combination of intelligence and insight unique to the character and experience of the author. All titles are carefully designed to offer a long useful life and present only information relevant to the professional programmer implementing that technology.

Primer Plus Series

The Primer Plus series offers straightforward tutorial presentations designed to introduce topics of interest to programmers. The Primer Plus books serve as "101" courses and move quickly from a beginning to intermediate-level coverage of the subject at hand. Programmers can turn to a Primer Plus title when learning a new programming language or any other technology they need to acquire. The Primer Plus series includes *C Primer Plus*, *C++ Primer Plus*, and *Unix Primer Plus*.

SuperBible Series

The SuperBible series provides definitive API references, designed to give programmers a quick, well-organized way to identify the appropriate syntax and application for the programming APIs governing a particular development platform or tool. Successful SuperBibles have included *Windows NT Win32 API SuperBible* and *OpenGL SuperBible*.

Waite Group Press in 2000

In 2000, look for the following titles from Waite Group Press:

Java Programming on Linux

OpenGL SuperBible, 2E

KDE 2.0 Development

Linux Socket Programming

Developing Portable Open Source Software

Linux Kernel Programming

And others

Other Waite Group Titles

Visual Basic
Source Code
Library
Brian Shea, et al.
0-672-31387-1
$34.99 USA/
$50.95 CAN

Visual Basic 6
How-To
Eric Brierley,
Anthony Prince, &
David Rinaldi
1-57169-153-7
$39.99 US/
$57.95 CAN

Visual Basic 6
Client/Server
How-To
Noel Jerke,
George Szabo,
David Jung, &
Don Kiely
1-57169-154-5
$49.99 US/
$71.95 CAN

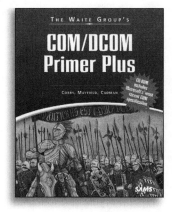

DOM/DCOM
Primer Plus
Corry, Mayfield,
Cadman
0-672-31492-4
$39.99 US/
$57.95 CAN

All prices are subject to change.

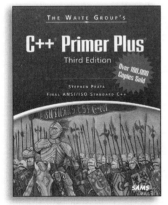

C++ How-To
Kalev, Tobler, &
Walter, Et Al.
1-57169-159-6
$39.99 US/
$57.95 CAN

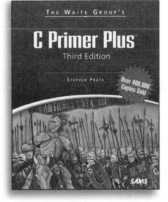

C Primer Plus
Stephen Prata
1-57169-161-8
$29.99 US/
$42.95 CAN

C++ Primer Plus
Stephen Prata
1-57169-162-6
$35.00 US/
$49.95 CAN

Java 1.2 How-To
Steve Potts
1-57169-157-X
$39.99 US/
$57.95 CAN

Waite Group Press
A Division of Macmillan USA, Inc.
201 West 103rd St., Indianapolis, Indiana, 46290 USA

GNU GENERAL PUBLIC LICENSE

Version 2, June 1991
Copyright (C) 1989, 1991 Free Software Foundation, Inc.
675 Mass Ave, Cambridge, MA 02139, USA

Preamble

The licenses for most software are designed to take away your freedom to share and change it. By contrast, the GNU General Public License is intended to guarantee your freedom to share and change free software—to make sure the software is free for all its users. This General Public License applies to most of the Free Software Foundation's software and to any other program whose authors commit to using it. (Some other Free Software Foundation software is covered by the GNU Library General Public License instead.) You can apply it to your programs, too.

When we speak of free software, we are referring to freedom, not price. Our General Public Licenses are designed to make sure that you have the freedom to distribute copies of free software (and charge for this service if you wish), that you receive source code or can get it if you want it, that you can change the software or use pieces of it in new free programs; and that you know you can do these things.

To protect your rights, we need to make restrictions that forbid anyone to deny you these rights or to ask you to surrender the rights. These restrictions translate to certain responsibilities for you if you distribute copies of the software, or if you modify it. For example, if you distribute copies of such a program, whether gratis or for a fee, you must give the recipients all the rights that you have. You must make sure that they, too, receive or can get the source code. And you must show them these terms so they know their rights.

We protect your rights with two steps: (1) copyright the software, and (2) offer you this license which gives you legal permission to copy, distribute, and/or modify the software. Also, for each author's protection and ours, we want to make certain that everyone understands that there is no warranty for this free software. If the software is modified by someone else and passed on, we want its recipients to know that what they have is not the original, so that any problems introduced by others will not reflect on the original authors' reputations. Finally, any free program is threatened constantly by software patents. We wish to avoid the danger that redistributors of a free program will individually obtain patent licenses, in effect making the program proprietary. To prevent this, we have made it clear that any patent must be licensed for everyone's free use or not licensed at all.

The precise terms and conditions for copying, distribution and modification follow.

GNU GENERAL PUBLIC LICENSE: TERMS AND CONDITIONS FOR COPYING, DISTRIBUTION, AND MODIFICATION

0. This License applies to any program or other work which contains a notice placed by the copyright holder saying it may be distributed under the terms of this General Public License. The "Program" below refers to any such program or work, and a "work based on the Program" means either the Program or any derivative work under copyright law: That is to say, a work containing the Program or a portion of it, either verbatim or with modifications and/or translated into another language. (Hereinafter, translation is included without limitation in the term "modification".) Each licensee is addressed as "you". Activities other than copying, distribution, and modification are not covered by this License; they are outside its scope. The act of running the Program is not restricted, and the output from the Program is covered only if its contents constitute a work based on the Program (independent of having been made by running the Program). Whether that is true depends on what the Program does.

1. You may copy and distribute verbatim copies of the Program's source code as you receive it, in any medium, provided that you conspicuously and appropriately publish on each copy an appropriate copyright notice and disclaimer of warranty; keep intact all the notices that refer to this License and to the absence of any warranty; and give any other recipients of the Program a copy of this License along with the Program.

You may charge a fee for the physical act of transferring a copy, and you may at your option offer warranty protection in exchange for a fee.

2. You may modify your copy or copies of the Program or any portion of it, thus forming a work based on the Program, and copy and distribute such modifications or work under the terms of Section 1 above, provided that you also meet all of these conditions:

a) You must cause the modified files to carry prominent notices stating that you changed the files and the date of any change.

b) You must cause any work that you distribute or publish, that in whole or in part contains or is derived from the Program or any part thereof, to be licensed as a whole at no charge to all third parties under the terms of this License.

c) If the modified program normally reads commands interactively when run, you must cause it, when started running for such interactive use in the most ordinary way, to print or display an announcement including an appropriate copyright notice and a notice that there is no warranty (or else, saying that you provide a warranty) and that users may redistribute the program under these conditions, and telling the user how to view a copy of this License. (Exception: if the Program itself is interactive but does not normally print such an announcement, your work based on the Program is not required to print an announcement.)

These requirements apply to the modified work as a whole. If identifiable sections of that work are not derived from the Program and can be reasonably considered independent and separate works in themselves, then this License, and its terms, do not apply to those sections when you distribute them as separate works. But when you distribute the same sections as part of a whole which is a work based on the Program, the distribution of the whole must be on the terms of this License, whose permissions for other licensees extend to the entire whole, and thus to each and every part regardless of who wrote it. Thus, it is not the intent of this section to claim rights or contest your rights to work written entirely by you; rather, the intent is to exercise the right to control the distribution of derivative or collective works based on the Program.
In addition, mere aggregation of another work not based on the Program with the Program (or with a work based on the Program) on a volume of a storage or distribution medium does not bring the other work under the scope of this License.

3. You may copy and distribute the Program (or a work based on it, under Section 2) in object code or executable form under the terms of Sections 1 and 2 above provided that you also do one of the following:

a) Accompany it with the complete corresponding machine-readable source code, which must be distributed under the terms of Sections 1 and 2 above on a medium customarily used for software interchange; or,

b) Accompany it with a written offer, valid for at least three years, to give any third party, for a charge no more than your cost of physically performing source distribution, a complete machine-readable copy of the corresponding source code, to be distributed under the terms of Sections 1 and 2 above on a medium customarily used for software interchange; or,

c) Accompany it with the information you received as to the offer to distribute corresponding source code. (This alternative is allowed only for noncommercial distribution and only if you received the program in object code or executable form with such an offer, in accord with Subsection b above.)

The source code for a work means the preferred form of the work for making modifications to it. For an executable work, complete source code means all the source code for all modules it contains, plus any associated interface definition files, plus the scripts used to control compilation and installation of the executable. However, as a special exception, the source code distributed need not include anything that is normally distributed (in either source or binary form) with the major components (compiler, kernel, and so on) of the operating system on which the executable runs, unless that component itself accompanies the executable. If distribution of executable or object code is made by offering access to copy from a designated place, then offering equivalent access to copy the source code from the same place counts as distribution of the source code, even though third parties are not compelled to copy the source along with the object code.

4. You may not copy, modify, sublicense, or distribute the Program except as expressly provided under this License. Any attempt otherwise to copy, modify, sublicense or distribute the Program is void, and will automatically terminate your rights under this License. However, parties who have received copies, or rights, from you under this License will not have their licenses terminated so long as such parties remain in full compliance.

5. You are not required to accept this License, since you have not signed it. However, nothing else grants you permission to modify or distribute the Program or its derivative works. These actions are prohibited by law if you do not accept this License. Therefore, by modifying or distributing the Program (or any work based on the Program), you indicate your acceptance of this License to do so, and all its terms and conditions for copying, distributing or modifying the Program or works based on it.

6. Each time you redistribute the Program (or any work based on the Program), the recipient automatically receives a license from the original licensor to copy, distribute or modify the Program subject to these terms and conditions. You may not impose any further restrictions on the recipients' exercise of the rights granted herein. You are not responsible for enforcing compliance by third parties to this License.

7. If, as a consequence of a court judgment or allegation of patent infringement or for any other reason (not limited to patent issues), conditions are imposed on you (whether by court order, agreement or otherwise) that contradict the conditions of this License, they do not excuse you from the conditions of this License. If you cannot distribute so as to satisfy simultaneously your obligations under this License and any other pertinent obligations, then as a consequence you may not distribute the Program at all. For example, if a patent license would not permit royalty-free redistribution of the Program by all those who receive copies directly or indirectly through you, then the only way you could satisfy both it and this License would be to refrain entirely from distribution of the Program.

If any portion of this section is held invalid or unenforceable under any particular circumstance, the balance of the section is intended to apply and the section as a whole is intended to apply in other circumstances.

It is not the purpose of this section to induce you to infringe any patents or other property right claims or to contest validity of any such claims; this section has the sole purpose of protecting the integrity of the free software distribution system, which is implemented by public license practices. Many people have made generous contributions to the wide range of software distributed through that system in reliance on consistent application of that system; it is up to the author/donor to decide if he or she is willing to distribute software through any other system and a licensee cannot impose that choice.

This section is intended to make thoroughly clear what is believed to be a consequence of the rest of this License.

8. If the distribution and/or use of the Program is restricted in certain countries either by patents or by copyrighted interfaces, the original copyright holder who places the Program under this License may add an explicit geographical distribution limitation excluding those countries, so that distribution is permitted only in or among countries not thus excluded. In such case, this License incorporates the limitation as if written in the body of this License.

9. The Free Software Foundation may publish revised and/or new versions of the General Public License from time to time. Such new versions will be similar in spirit to the present version, but may differ in detail to address new problems or concerns. Each version is given a distinguishing version number. If the Program specifies a version number of this License which applies to it and "any later version", you have the option of following the terms and conditions either of that version or of any later version published by the Free Software Foundation. If the Program does not specify a version number of this License, you may choose any version ever published by the Free Software Foundation.

10. If you wish to incorporate parts of the Program into other free programs whose distribution conditions are different, write to the author to ask for permission. For software which is copyrighted by the Free Software Foundation, write to the Free Software Foundation; we sometimes make exceptions for this. Our decision will be guided by the two goals of preserving the free status of all derivatives of our free software and of promoting the sharing and reuse of software generally.

NO WARRANTY

11. BECAUSE THE PROGRAM IS LICENSED FREE OF CHARGE, THERE IS NO WARRANTY FOR THE PROGRAM, TO THE EXTENT PERMITTED BY APPLICABLE LAW. EXCEPT WHEN OTHERWISE STATED IN WRITING THE COPYRIGHT HOLDERS AND/OR OTHER PARTIES PROVIDE THE PROGRAM "AS IS" WITHOUT WARRANTY OF ANY KIND, EITHER EXPRESSED OR IMPLIED, INCLUDING, BUT NOT LIMITED TO, THE IMPLIED WARRANTIES OF MERCHANTABILITY AND FITNESS FOR A PARTICULAR PURPOSE. THE ENTIRE RISK AS TO THE QUALITY AND PERFORMANCE OF THE PROGRAM IS WITH YOU. SHOULD THE PROGRAM PROVE DEFECTIVE, YOU ASSUME THE COST OF ALL NECESSARY SERVICING, REPAIR OR CORRECTION.

12. IN NO EVENT UNLESS REQUIRED BY APPLICABLE LAW OR AGREED TO IN WRITING WILL ANY COPYRIGHT HOLDER, OR ANY OTHER PARTY WHO MAY MODIFY AND/OR REDISTRIBUTE THE PROGRAM AS PERMITTED ABOVE, BE LIABLE TO YOU FOR DAMAGES, INCLUDING ANY GENERAL, SPECIAL, INCIDENTAL OR CONSEQUENTIAL DAMAGES ARISING OUT OF THE USE OR INABILITY TO USE THE PROGRAM (INCLUDING BUT NOT LIMITED TO LOSS

OF DATA OR DATA BEING RENDERED INACCURATE OR LOSSES SUSTAINED BY YOU OR THIRD PARTIES OR A FAILURE OF THE PROGRAM TO OPERATE WITH ANY OTHER PROGRAMS), EVEN IF SUCH HOLDER OR OTHER PARTY HAS BEEN ADVISED OF THE POSSIBILITY OF SUCH DAMAGES.

END OF TERMS AND CONDITIONS

Appendix: How to Apply These Terms to Your New Programs

If you develop a new program, and you want it to be of the greatest possible use to the public, the best way to achieve this is to make it free software which everyone can redistribute and change under these terms. To do so, attach the following notices to the program. It is safest to attach them to the start of each source file to most effectively convey the exclusion of warranty; and each file should have at least the "copyright" line and a pointer to where the full notice is found.

<one line to give the program's name and a brief idea of what it does.>

Copyright (C) 19yy <name of author>

This program is free software; you can redistribute it and/or modify it under the terms of the GNU General Public License as published by the Free Software Foundation; either version 2 of the License, or (at your option) any later version.

This program is distributed in the hope that it will be useful, but WITHOUT ANY WARRANTY; without even the implied warranty of MERCHANTABILITY or FITNESS FOR A PARTICULAR PURPOSE. See the GNU General Public License for more details.

You should have received a copy of the GNU General Public License along with this program; if not, write to the Free Software Foundation, Inc., 675 Mass Ave, Cambridge, MA 02139, USA. Also add information on how to contact you by electronic and paper mail.

If the program is interactive, make it output a short notice like this when it starts in an interactive mode:

Gnomovision version 69, Copyright (C) 19yy name of author

Gnomovision comes with ABSOLUTELY NO WARRANTY; for details type 'show w'.

This is free software, and you are welcome to redistribute it under certain conditions; type 'show c' for details.

The hypothetical commands 'show w' and 'show c' should show the appropriate parts of the General Public License. Of course, the commands you use may be called something other than 'show w' and 'show c'; they could even be mouse-clicks or menu items—whatever suits your program. You should also get your employer (if you work as a programmer) or your school, if any, to sign a "copyright disclaimer" for the program, if necessary. Here is a sample; alter the names:

Yoyodyne, Inc., hereby disclaims all copyright interest in the program 'Gnomovision' (which makes passes at compilers) written by James Hacker.

<signature of Ty Coon>, 1 April 1989

Ty Coon, President of Vice

This General Public License does not permit incorporating your program into proprietary programs. If your program is a subroutine library, you may consider it more useful to permit linking proprietary applications with the library. If this is what you want to do, use the GNU Library General Public License instead of this License.